CookingLight®

ANNUAL RECIPES 2019

Oxmoor
House®

A YEAR AT

COOKING LIGHT®

2018 WAS A YEAR FOR DIGGING OUR STAKE A
little deeper into the ground, so to speak. We focused
on our commitment to healthy eating—and our
always-present goal of empowering readers to cook
more at home for good health—with several themed
issues that highlighted some of our key values, such
as more plant-based meals, a focus on gut health, and
enjoying more seafood.

We also doubled down on ways to help readers
who want to eat better but struggle to find time to
cook. We placed greater focus on weeknight-friendly
recipes in Dinner Tonight and created a special
feature section in September devoted to Big-Batch
Cooking (page 244)—weekend warrior–style recipes
and meal-prep tips for breakfast, lunch, snack,
and dinner. And for chilly nights when only hearty
comfort food will do, we offered up Dutch Oven

Dinners (page 268) with additional slow cooker
instructions for added convenience, plus Super
Simple Soups (page 317) with both slow cooker and
Instant Pot directions so dinner can come together in
whatever way works best for you.

In this collection, you'll find recipes for health,
recipes for celebrations, and recipes that simply—and
importantly—deliver a delicious dinner on a busy
night. We are proud of the work we've done this past
year and hope you love it as much as we do.

Pork and Charred Pineapple Sliders, Page 174

These party-perfect sliders deliver a knockout
balance of sweet and savory flavors. Charred
pineapple rings make a smoky next-level
topper; leftover pineapple juice makes the
fast-fix slaw sing with a sweet and tangy zip.

HERE ARE SOME HIGHLIGHTS FROM 2018:

WE KICKED OFF THE YEAR WITH MEALS THAT HEAL, a special feature package devoted to our belief that food has the power to impact your health. In Good Mood Food (page 19), we shared recipes to brighten up the dull days of winter and put a little spring in your step. We created our second-annual *Cooking Light* 3-Day Detox (page 29) to help you reset after all the holiday feasting, and provided recipes built around ingredients shown to boost your health in The Spices of Life (page 21) and Food Rx (page 26).

MAY MARKED OUR SECOND-ANNUAL EAT-MORE-VEGETABLES ISSUE, a volume full of recipes to inspire you to pack more produce into your meals. From meat-free mains to vegetable-heavy entrées that use meat as an accent, we celebrated spring's most beautiful offerings of peas, carrots, beets, asparagus, artichokes, tender greens, and more.

IN JUNE, WE DEVOTED NEARLY THE ENTIRE ISSUE TO THE NEXT FRONTIER IN NUTRITION SCIENCE: GUT HEALTH. We shared probiotic-rich recipes incorporating tasty ingredients like yogurt, kimchi, sauerkraut, and miso, as well as a fiber-rich meal plan packed with prebiotics (food for probiotics)—to distill the complicated, emerging field of gut health into easy, tasty recipes that translate the science into what matters most for home cooks: delicious, easy-to-make recipes.

OUR ANNUAL ODE TO SUMMER PRODUCE ARRIVED IN JULY, with New Summer Essentials (page 157), in which we took the season's most iconic recipes and gave them a fresh new twist. Traditional red gazpacho went white, with an alluring combination of green grapes, cucumbers, and almonds (White Gazpacho with Lobster, page 157), the standard backyard burger picked up some Vietnamese flair (Banh Mi Burgers, page 162), and a classic pie inspired a fun frosty treat (Key Lime Ice Pops, page 166).

AUGUST BROUGHT OUR FIRST-EVER SEAFOOD ISSUE, full of recipes, techniques, and shopping tips—because we should all be eating more seafood for our health. We tackled the "fab four," the most popular options (salmon, shrimp, tilapia, and tuna) with 12 weeknight-friendly recipes to help you get seafood on the table more often. How to Cook Fish (Like a Pro) (page 192) detailed savvy techniques for next-level fish dishes, complete with step-by-step photos. And Share a Fresh Summer Feast (page 189) showed how to make fish the center of a casual party with friends.

Crispy Fish with Scallions and Peppers, Page 188

For a fresh spin on a food court favorite, tilapia is pan-fried (think crispy breaded chicken, but in less time) before being tossed in a tangy, sticky-sweet sauce. Sautéed scallions take on a star role here, upgrading the dish with a generous dose of aromatics to play off the umami-rich sauce.

OUR NOVEMBER DOUBLE ISSUE WAS PACKED WITH CELEBRATORY DISHES. We went all in on the best part of the Turkey Day feast with The Ultimate Guide to Thanksgiving Sides (page 290), with 32 recipes to fill your holiday table with abundance and joy. Not to be outdone, Pies of Many Sizes (page 328) presented glorious sweets for the dessert buffet, and How to Roast Everything (page 309) shared the best way to roast your turkey, along with several other groundbreaking recipes. To give your palate a taste trip, we also included Moroccan Vegetable Cooking (page 320) and Beautifully Bitter (page 324).

FINALLY, DECEMBER'S FOCUS ON HOLIDAY CHEER RANG TRUE with Thumbprints and Snowballs and Shortbread, Oh My! (page 356), a collection of our most festive holiday cookies. And The Amazing, No-Fail, One-Hour Dinner Party (page 350) and Make-Ahead Appetizers (page 354) gave easy ways to entertain friends and family at the most joyful time of the year.

After each issue comes out, we look forward to the feedback you, our valued readers, provide in the form of emails, letters, and social media comments—and we take all your insights to heart. Thank you for your dedication to *Cooking Light*.

The Editors of *Cooking Light*

OUR FAVORITE RECIPES

Not all recipes are created equal.

At *Cooking Light*, only those that have received a passing grade from our Test Kitchen staff and food editors—a group with very high standards—make it onto the pages of the magazine. Each recipe is tested vigorously, often two or three times, to make sure it's healthy, reliable, and tastes the best it possibly can. So, here we've gathered together this past year's most unforgettable recipes. They're the ones we hear about most from readers and the ones we make regularly for our friends and families.

Strawberry, Basil, and Balsamic "Slablova," Page 89
Spreading the meringue on a sheet pan makes this pavlova fit for a crowd. A "slablova," as this kind of dish has been called on Food 52, is an impressive yet simple dessert, dressed with bright, ripe strawberries; tangy balsamic; and peppery basil.

Spicy Scallops with Watermelon Salsa,
Page 144

Buttery-sweet scallops are our go-to for an elegant and effortless dinner. Coated with a mild blend of spices and seared to perfection, they're even better topped with a sweet and juicy spoonful of this fast-fix watermelon salsa.

Milk Chocolate Yogurt with Granola and Blueberries, Page 191
A double dose of chocolate—cocoa powder and melted milk chocolate—makes these parfaits taste ultra decadent. Toasted sesame seeds lend rich, nutty flavor plus satisfying crunch. This recipe packs a one-two punch of protein and fiber, so feel free to start your day with an indulgence.

Sesame Salmon with Kimchi-Miso Butter, Page 133

We love the funky, vinegary crunch of kimchi, but it's even better blended with creamy butter and savory miso. The real magic happens when it melts together over the hot-from-the-oven salmon, soaking it in the perfect balance of creamy and tangy flavors.

Broccoli-and-Kraut Slaw, Page 133

Gut health is a big deal to us, and this speedy side delivers in a major way. Crunchy broccoli and cabbage contribute valuable prebiotic insoluble fiber, while fermented sauerkraut comes to the party with a tasty probiotic punch. Oh, and it tastes amazing, too.

Pasta with Miso Cream Sauce, Page 115

White miso makes all the difference in this easy pasta dish, bringing meaty, umami flavor to the veggie-forward mix. The miso blends into the creamy sauce dispersing its flavor throughout the dish. Use vegetable stock in place of chicken to make this vegetarian, if you prefer.

Oatmeal-Raisin Skillet Cookie with Miso-Caramel Sauce, Page 113

A chewy-crisp cookie baked in a cast-iron skillet and topped with miso-salted caramel is a dazzling dessert fit for company, but simple enough to pull off any night of the week. We've given the cookie an oatmeal-raisin flavor profile, but use any kind of dried fruit in place of the raisins, if you prefer.

Salmon and Lentil Bowl with Kefir Dressing, Page 145
Supermarket shortcuts are a marvelous way to cut yourself some slack and get an amazing meal on the table at the same time. Precooked salmon and lentils are the timesaving heroes here—just whisk up the dressing, assemble the bowls, and enjoy.

Banh Mi Burgers, Page 162

We took everything we love about our favorite Vietnamese sandwich—tart pickles, fresh cilantro and chiles, spicy mayo—to transform basic burgers into the star of your next barbecue. Garlic and ginger give the beefy patties an extra punch of exotic flavor.

Slow Cooker Chicken Mole Tacos, Page 41
Our simplified version of Mexican mole turns what would usually be a weekend project into a delicious weeknight reality. After just 10 minutes of prep, meaty chicken thighs slowly simmer to perfection in a rich, heady sauce.

Creamed Corn, Page 172

This highly-heralded summer side often owes its smooth texture to copious amounts of cream and butter; here we've pureed sweet corn to create a velvety smooth, indulgent-tasting dish with just a tablespoon of butter and a dash of cream. Use the freshest corn you can find for the best-tasting results.

CONTENTS

©2018 Time Inc. Books, a division of Meredith Corporation

Published by Oxmoor House,
an imprint of Time Inc. Books
225 Liberty Street, New York, NY 10281

Be sure to check with your health-care provider before making any changes in your diet.

Cooking Light® Annual Recipes 2019
Senior Editor: Rachel Quinlivan West, R.D.
Project Editor: Melissa Brown
Designer: Matt Ryan
Associate Manager for Project Management
    and Production: Anna Muñiz
Assistant Production Manager: Diane Rose Keener
Copy Editor: Jacqueline Giovanelli
Proofreader: Adrienne Davis
Indexer: Mary Ann Laurens

We welcome your comments and suggestions about
    Time Inc. Books.

Time Inc. Books
Attention: Book Editors
P.O. Box 62310
Tampa, Florida 33662-2310
(800) 765-6400

Cooking Light®
Editor in Chief: Hunter Lewis
Digital Content Director, Food and Travel: Stacey Rivera
Creative Director: Rachel Lasserre
Executive Editor: Ann Taylor Pittman
Managing Editor: Caitlin Murphree Miller
Editorial Assistant: Grace Guffin
Business Manager: Alice E. Summerville
Food & Nutrition Director: Brierley Horton
Senior Food Editor: Tim Cebula
Food Editor: Josh Miller
Assistant Nutrition Editor: Jamie Vespa, MS, RD
Photo Director: Tori Katherman
Photo Editor: Dan Bailey
Production Director: Liz Rhoades
Associate Production Manager: Brianne Twilley
Copy Director: Jessica Campbell-Salley
Copy Editor: Erin Clyburn
Associate Copy Editor: Winn Duvall
Contributors: Jessica Atkinson; Kevin Brainard;
    Cybele Grandjean; Elizabeth Laseter, Robert Perino;
    Susan Porch; Robin Rosenthal; Tania Roulston; Antara
    Sinha; Jennifer Skarda; Brennan Smith; Sheri Wilson
Fellows: Katie Akin, Arielle Weg

COOKINGLIGHT.COM
Digital Content Manager: Ashley Kappel
Digital Production Director: Jim Sheetz
Digital Editor: Christopher Michel
Associate Editor, Digital: Jaime Milan
Assistant Editor, Digital: Zee Krstic
Social Media Editor: Kaylee Hammonds
Community and Content Manager, Cooking Light Diet:
    Matthew A. Moore

ISBN-13: 978-0-8487-5792-2

Printed in the United States of America
10 9 8 7 6 5 4 3 2 1
First Printing 2018

Cover: *Pot Roast Tacos with Chimichurri (page 246)*
Back Cover (top to bottom, left to right): *Creamy Potato Salad (page 180), The Ultimate Vegetarian Club (page 284), Seared Chicken with Shallots and Grapes (page 277), Striped Yogurt-and-Sorbet Sandwiches (page 164), Lemon Chicken with Artichokes and Kale (page 52)*

GOOD MOOD FOOD

Brighten up dark days and light up your palate with these zingy, happy recipes packed full of feel-good ingredients.

Gluten Free • Vegetarian

Beet, Carrot, and Pistachio Salad

Hands-on: 15 min. **Total:** 1 hr. 25 min.
Bring a bit of sunshine to your plate with this golden beet and purple carrot salad. Fresh dill has a grassiness that will transport you to warmer days; it also contrasts beautifully with the earthy sweetness of the beets.

2 lb. golden beets, trimmed (about 4 medium)
½ cup thinly vertically sliced red onion
2 purple carrots, thinly diagonally sliced
¼ cup chopped roasted unsalted pistachios, divided
2 Tbsp. very coarsely chopped fresh dill, divided
3 Tbsp. fresh orange juice
2 Tbsp. olive oil
1 Tbsp. white wine vinegar
½ tsp. black pepper
¼ tsp. kosher salt

1. Preheat oven to 400°F.
2. Wrap beets in foil; bake at 400°F for 1 hour or until tender. Cool beets slightly; peel and cut into wedges.

3. Combine beets, onion, carrots, 2 tablespoons pistachios, and 1½ tablespoons dill in a medium bowl. Combine orange juice, oil, vinegar, pepper, and salt in a small bowl, stirring with a whisk until smooth. Add juice mixture to beet mixture; toss gently to coat. Arrange beet mixture on a platter. Sprinkle with remaining 2 tablespoons pistachios and remaining 1½ teaspoons dill. Serves 6 (serving size: about 1 cup)

CALORIES 151; **FAT** 7g (sat 1g, unsat 6g); **PROTEIN** 4g; **CARB** 20g; **FIBER** 6g; **SUGARS** 13g (added sugars 0g); **SODIUM** 213mg; **CALC** 4% DV; **POTASSIUM** 18% DV

Fast

Tuna, Avocado, and Pickled Onion Sandwich

Hands-on: 10 min. **Total:** 15 min.
Aside from being delicious, this open-faced whole-grain sandwich is all about healthy fats, with omega-3 fatty acids in the tuna and monounsaturated fat in the avocado. The first boosts brain function, and both offer heart-health benefits.

¾ cup thinly sliced red onion
⅔ cup apple cider vinegar
¼ cup water
1 tsp. sugar
2 ripe peeled avocados, sliced
4 (1½-oz.) whole-wheat sourdough bread slices, toasted
½ tsp. kosher salt, divided
½ tsp. black pepper, divided
1 (4-oz.) can albacore tuna in water, drained
½ cup fresh flat-leaf parsley leaves
2 Tbsp. chopped roasted unsalted almonds
2 Tbsp. chopped pitted Castelvetrano olives

1. Bring onion, vinegar, ¼ cup water, and sugar to a boil in a small saucepan over medium-high. Remove pan from heat; let stand 5 minutes. Drain.
2. Divide the avocado slices evenly among bread slices; mash with a fork. Sprinkle with ¼ teaspoon salt and ¼ teaspoon pepper. Top evenly with tuna, onions, parsley, almonds, and olives. Sprinkle with remaining ¼ teaspoon salt and remaining ¼ teaspoon pepper. Serves 4 (serving size: 1 sandwich)

CALORIES 304; **FAT** 16g (sat 2g, unsat 12g); **PROTEIN** 16g; **CARB** 28g; **FIBER** 8g; **SUGARS** 3g (added sugars 0g); **SODIUM** 570mg; **CALC** 13% DV; **POTASSIUM** 17% DV

Citrus-Pickled Shrimp with Fennel and Potatoes

Hands-on: 30 min. **Total:** 8 hr. 30 min. This heaped platter wouldn't be out of place at a summer picnic, but it's so satisfying on winter nights, too. The shrimp picks up plenty of acid and heat with a gentle pickle of citrus, crushed red pepper, and garlic.

1¼ lb. large raw shrimp, peeled and deveined (tails on)
¾ cup white wine vinegar
½ cup fresh lemon juice
2 Tbsp. olive oil
1 tsp. kosher salt
1 tsp. sugar
2 cups thinly vertically sliced yellow onion
1 tsp. celery seeds
1 tsp. crushed red pepper
4 garlic cloves, smashed
2 large or 4 small bay leaves
1 lemon, halved lengthwise and thinly sliced
1 orange, halved lengthwise and thinly sliced
1 medium fennel bulb, cored and sliced, fronds reserved
1 lb. small red potatoes
2 celery stalks, thinly diagonally sliced
2 Tbsp. celery leaves

1. Bring a large saucepan filled with water to a boil over medium-high. Add shrimp; cook 2 minutes or just until pink. Drain; plunge shrimp into a bowl of ice water. Let stand 5 minutes; drain.
2. Combine vinegar, lemon juice, olive oil, salt, and sugar in a large bowl, stirring until sugar dissolves. Add shrimp, onion, and next 7 ingredients (through fennel bulb); toss to coat. Divide shrimp mixture between 2 (1-quart) containers. Cover and refrigerate 8 hours or overnight.
3. Bring a large saucepan filled with water to a boil over medium-high. Add potatoes; cook 15 minutes or until tender. Drain. Let stand 15 minutes; cut in half.
4. Pour both containers of shrimp mixture through a fine-mesh sieve over a bowl; reserve ⅓ cup pickling liquid. Remove garlic and bay leaves; discard. Chop reserved fennel fronds to equal 2 tablespoons. Combine potatoes, shrimp mixture, reserved ⅓ cup pickling liquid, fennel fronds, celery, and celery leaves in a large bowl; toss. Arrange shrimp mixture on a platter. Serves 6 (serving size: about 1⅓ cups)

CALORIES 210; FAT 3g (sat 0g, unsat 2g); PROTEIN 19g; CARB 28g; FIBER 4g; SUGARS 7g (added sugars 0g); SODIUM 321mg; CALC 12% DV; POTASSIUM 25% DV

CAN FOOD TRULY HELP YOUR MOOD?

Absolutely. Turns out more than 90% of the feel-good hormone serotonin is produced in your gastrointestinal tract. So fueling the nerve cells and "good" bacteria that line your gut doesn't just play a role in your physical health but also your mental health. Plus, research suggests that people with so-called healthy diets are less likely to be depressed. In a review published in *The American Journal of Clinical Nutrition*, scientists found that people who ate a lot of fruits, veggies, fish, and whole grains significantly cut their odds of depression. And other research shows that people who eat a Mediterranean diet have a lower risk of developing depression versus folks who eat a typical "Western" diet. So go on: Get ahead of the winter blues and load up on healthy food. What's good for the body is good for the mind.

Grapefruit, Apple, and Pomegranate Salad

Hands-on: 25 min. **Total:** 25 min. This quick fruit salad gives you 133% of your daily recommended intake of vitamin C. It's also superfun to eat: The pearls of grapefruit pulp and delicate flakes of sea salt pop on the tongue. A drizzle of honey will tame the pucker from the fruit and the serrano's heat. Use the chile sparingly; a little goes a very long way here.

3 cups pink or red grapefruit sections (about 3 large)
2 cups julienne-cut Granny Smith apple
⅓ cup pomegranate arils
¼ cup chopped fresh mint
1 Tbsp. seeded minced serrano chile
2 Tbsp. fresh lime juice
1 Tbsp. honey
⅛ tsp. flaked sea salt (such as Maldon)

1. Arrange grapefruit and apple on a platter; sprinkle with pomegranate, mint, and minced chile. Combine juice and honey in a small bowl; drizzle over salad. Sprinkle with salt. Serves 4 (serving size: about ¾ cup)

CALORIES 121; FAT 0g; PROTEIN 2g; CARB 30g; FIBER 4g; SUGARS 22g (added sugars 4g); SODIUM 74mg; CALC 3% DV; POTASSIUM 10% DV

Thai Green Chicken Soup

Hands-on: 30 min. **Total:** 30 min.
Chicken soup soothes the soul (not a
scientific fact, but it may as well be).

- 2 (1-in.) pieces peeled fresh ginger,
  divided
- 1 Tbsp. canola oil
- 2 tsp. minced garlic
- 2 Tbsp. green curry paste
- 1 lb. skinless, boneless chicken
  breasts, cut into bite-sized pieces
- 2 cups unsalted chicken stock
- ¼ cup water
- 2 Tbsp. fresh lime juice
- 1 (13.5-oz.) can light coconut milk
- ¼ cup fresh cilantro stems
- 1 cup fresh snow peas, diagonally
  sliced
- 3 oz. uncooked brown rice
  vermicelli noodles
- ½ cup fresh cilantro sprigs
- Lime wedges

1. Mince 1 piece of ginger to equal
about 1 tablespoon. Heat oil in a
Dutch oven over medium-high.
Add minced ginger and garlic;
sauté 1 minute. Stir in curry paste;
cook 1 minute. Add chicken; cook
3 minutes, stirring occasionally.
Add remaining piece of ginger,
stock, ½ cup water, juice, coconut
milk, and cilantro stems; bring to a
simmer, and cook 10 minutes.
2. Discard ginger piece. Stir in peas
and noodles; cook 3 minutes or
until noodles are tender. Top with
cilantro sprigs; serve with lime
wedges. Serves 4 (serving size:
about 1½ cups)

CALORIES 336; **FAT** 12g (sat 5g, unsat 5g);
PROTEIN 30g; **CARB** 27g; **FIBER** 4g; **SUGARS** 4g
(added sugars 0g); **SODIUM** 529mg; **CALC** 2%
DV; **POTASSIUM** 13% DV

THE SPICES OF LIFE

Your spice pantry is your kitchen's
medicine cabinet—brimming with
seasonings that fight inflammation and
chronic disease. Not only a prescription
for good health, spices also add
fragrance and flavor to beefy chili,
soothing cauliflower soup, crispy pizza,
crunchy celery salad, and more.

SUGAR-PUSHING MARY POPPINS had it all wrong. Can't fault her
entirely—a spoonful of cumin doesn't have the same appeal. But the point of
the cumin isn't to help the medicine go down: The cumin is the medicine.

Cultures around the world have used culinary spices medicinally for
millennia. Researchers today seek to determine spices' full potential as health
boosters, as ongoing medical studies explore their effectiveness in battling
everything from headaches and indigestion to chronic diseases like cancer
and Alzheimer's.

Here we focus on six spices—Aleppo pepper, celery seed, cardamom,
cumin, cinnamon, and turmeric—and consult with Lipi Roy, MD, MPH,
clinical assistant professor at New York University's School of Medicine,
founder of the blog Spices for Life MD, and former instructor at Harvard
Medical School, to learn the healthful properties of each. Our recipes serve
as delectable delivery devices, and spice guru Lior Lev Sercarz, author of
The Spice Companion (see p. 23), suggests other easy ways to work these spices
into your weekly meals. So never mind the sugar—this medicine is quite
delicious as is.

HOW TO SOURCE AND STORE SPICES

Because spices lose aroma and flavor over time, Sercarz advises buying small
quantities—only what you'll use within a few months. Replace spices after a
year. Shop for spices with vibrant color. If they look faded, they may have been
on the store shelf for a long time. Similarly, whole spices with a lot of powder at
the bottom of the jar may indicate advanced age. Keep spices in sealed,
airtight containers away from sunlight, heat, and humidity—not near a window
or oven or in the refrigerator or freezer. Sercarz recommends finding a dry, cool
space for them on the kitchen counter, not tucked away in a cabinet, so you'll
be aware of your inventory and more likely to use them while they're fresh.

Fast

Cumin Lamb Stir-Fry

Hands-on: 25 min. **Total:** 25 min.

2 (8.8-oz.) pkg. precooked jasmine rice (such as Uncle Ben's)
1½ Tbsp. cumin seeds
2 tsp. Szechuan peppercorns or black peppercorns
4 tsp. canola oil, divided
1 lb. boneless lamb shoulder, cut into 3-in. strips
1½ cups very thinly sliced yellow onion
1 small julienne-cut red bell pepper
6 garlic cloves, thinly sliced
¼ tsp. crushed red pepper
2 Tbsp. lower-sodium soy sauce
2 Tbsp. sherry vinegar
½ tsp. kosher salt
¼ tsp. sugar
1 cup (½-in.) sliced scallions
1 tsp. crushed Aleppo pepper (optional)

1. Heat rice according to package directions. Set aside; keep warm.
2. Heat cumin and peppercorns in a large skillet over high. Cook 1 minute or until fragrant and toasted, stirring frequently. Cool slightly; crush with a mortar and pestle, or grind coarsely in an electric spice grinder.
3. Heat 2 teaspoons oil in pan over medium-high. Add half of lamb; stir-fry 3 minutes or until browned. Sprinkle with 1 teaspoon spice mixture. Transfer to a plate. Repeat procedure with remaining oil and lamb and 1 teaspoon spice mixture.
4. Add onion, bell pepper, and garlic to pan; stir-fry 4 minutes or until lightly charred. Add crushed red pepper and remaining spice mixture; stir-fry 1 minute. Add cooked lamb and any juices from plate, soy sauce, vinegar, salt, and sugar. Cook, tossing constantly, until liquid coats meat and vegetables. Remove from heat. Add scallions; toss to wilt. Serve stir-fry over rice. Sprinkle with Aleppo pepper, if desired. Serves 4 (serving size: ¾ cup rice and 1 cup meat and vegetables)

CALORIES 418; FAT 14g (sat 5g, unsat 8g); PROTEIN 25g; CARB 50g; FIBER 6g; SUGARS 5g (added sugars 0g); SODIUM 636mg; CALC 8% DV; POTASSIUM 17% DV

Make Ahead

Cinnamon-Laced Chili

Hands-on: 25 min. **Total:** 1 hr. 10 min. This take on Cincinnati chili forgoes the traditional spaghetti accompaniment, though you can serve it over hot cooked noodles if you like. While many cooks think of cinnamon only as a spice for baked goods and sweets, it's fantastic in savory dishes—particularly roasted, braised, and stewed meats like beef, pork, and chicken.

2 Tbsp. canola oil
1½ lb. beef chuck, cubed
2 cups chopped yellow onion
1¼ cups seeded and chopped poblano chile
8 garlic cloves, chopped
2 Tbsp. chopped fresh oregano
1 Tbsp. unsalted tomato paste
1¼ tsp. ground cumin
2¼ cups unsalted chicken stock
2 Tbsp. paprika
2 Tbsp. red wine vinegar
1½ Tbsp. light brown sugar
1 Tbsp. reduced-sodium Worcestershire sauce
1 tsp. kosher salt
3 cinnamon sticks
1 (15.5-oz.) can unsalted black beans, rinsed and drained
2 oz. sharp cheddar cheese, shredded
1 Tbsp. sliced fresh chives

1. Heat oil in a large Dutch oven over high. Add beef, and cook 8 minutes or until browned on all sides, turning occasionally. Place on a plate.
2. Add onion, poblano, and garlic to Dutch oven, and cook 5 minutes, stirring frequently. Add oregano, tomato paste, and cumin, and cook, stirring constantly, 1 minute and 30 seconds. Stir in stock, paprika, vinegar, brown sugar, Worcestershire, salt, and cinnamon sticks; bring to a boil. Reduce heat to medium. Add browned beef, cover, and simmer 45 minutes or until beef is tender, stirring occasionally.
3. Remove cinnamon sticks; discard. Stir in beans; serve. Sprinkle each serving with shredded cheese and chives. Serves 6 (serving size: 1 cup)

CALORIES 370; FAT 14g (sat 5g, unsat 8g); PROTEIN 35g; CARB 29g; FIBER 8g; SUGARS 5g (added sugars 2g); SODIUM 564mg; CALC 16% DV; POTASSIUM 22% DV

HOW TO USE HEALTHY SPICES

LIOR LEV SERCARZ, CHEF AND OWNER OF LA BOÎTE IN NEW YORK CITY, HAS ESTABLISHED HIMSELF AS ONE OF THE WORLD'S FOREMOST SPICE SPECIALISTS. DRAWING FROM THE WISDOM IN HIS ESSENTIAL SEASONINGS GUIDE, *THE SPICE COMPANION*, HERE ARE LOADS OF WAYS TO WORK THESE HEALTH-BOOSTING SPICES INTO YOUR COOKING.

ALEPPO PEPPER
The Taste: Syrian dried chile flakes with mild to moderate heat and subtle fruity notes.
Try It: Sprinkle on grilled fish; stir into guacamole; toss with pasta dishes; mix into brownie batter or chocolate chip cookie dough.

GREEN CARDAMOM
The Taste: Strong and complex, slightly sweet and floral, with pepper and citrus notes.
Try It: Stir into iced tea or chicken soup; cook with rice pilaf; mix into applesauce; blend into vanilla or chocolate puddings.

CINNAMON
The Taste: Warm and lightly astringent, with strong, clovelike fragrance.
Try It: Season roast lamb; stir into tomato sauce; mix with chicken tagine or other North African meat dishes; rub onto winter squash before roasting.

CELERY SEED
The Taste: Like the herby essence of celery, with a touch of natural sodium so you don't need as much added salt.
Try It: Mix into potato salad; simmer with beef-barley soup; sprinkle on poached white fish; stir into pickling brines.

CUMIN
The Taste: Earthy with pleasant mustiness, nutty, and slightly peppery.
Try It: Stir into yogurt dressing for roasted veggies or raw salads; simmer with lentil stew; season roasted cauliflower; flavor-braised or roasted chicken.

TURMERIC
The Taste: Bright scent, floral notes, sweet, slightly bitter.
Try It: Blend into fruit smoothies; add to stock to simmer potatoes; stir into citrus salad dressing; add to batter for blondies.

Make Ahead

Creamy Turmeric Cauliflower Soup

Hands-on: 30 min. **Total:** 45 min.

¼ cup raw hulled pumpkin seeds (pepitas)
1 tsp. ground cumin
2 Tbsp. olive oil, divided
2 cups vertically sliced yellow onion
1 Tbsp. chopped fresh thyme
6 garlic cloves, chopped
1 Tbsp. ground turmeric
1 Tbsp. all-purpose flour
2½ cups unsalted chicken stock, divided
½ tsp. kosher salt
1 small head cauliflower, cut into florets
2 tsp. rice vinegar
2 tsp. light brown sugar
½ tsp. black pepper
¼ cup light sour cream
2 Tbsp. chopped fresh chives

1. Combine pumpkin seeds, cumin, and 1½ teaspoons oil in a bowl; toss to coat. Heat a large nonstick skillet over medium-high. Add pumpkin seed mixture to skillet, and toast, stirring often, until lightly browned, 2 to 3 minutes. Set aside.
2. Heat remaining 1½ tablespoons oil in a large saucepan over medium-high. Add onion, thyme, and garlic. Cook, stirring occasionally, until softened, 5 to 6 minutes. Add turmeric, and cook, stirring constantly, 1 minute. Remove from heat.
3. Whisk together flour and ½ cup stock in a small bowl until smooth. Add flour mixture, salt, cauliflower florets, and remaining 2 cups stock to onion mixture in saucepan. Increase heat to high, and bring to a boil, stirring occasionally. Reduce heat to medium-low, and simmer, covered, until cauliflower is very tender, about 15 minutes.
4. In batches, place soup in a blender. Remove center piece of blender lid (to allow steam to escape); secure lid on blender. Place a clean towel over opening in lid. Process on high until smooth. Return soup to pot. Stir in vinegar, brown sugar, and pepper.
5. Serve in bowls; top evenly with pumpkin seeds, sour cream, and chives. Serves 6 (serving size: ¾ cup soup, 2 tsp. pumpkin seeds, 2 tsp. sour cream, and 1 tsp. chives)

CALORIES 149; **FAT** 8g (sat 2g, unsat 4g); **PROTEIN** 6g; **CARB** 14g; **FIBER** 3g; **SUGARS** 6g (added sugars 1g); **SODIUM** 279mg; **CALC** 6% DV; **POTASSIUM** 10% DV

TURMERIC

Turmeric has been investigated and is remarkably safe. Studies have shown that turmeric has anti-inflammatory, antioxidant, and anti-cancer properties. —LR

Staff Favorite • Fast
Gluten Free • Vegetarian

Celery Salad with Celery Seed Vinaigrette

Hands-on: 20 min. **Total:** 20 min.
We love that this salad comes together with kitchen staples you're likely to have on hand.

3 cups diagonally sliced peeled celery (about 5 large stalks)
3 cups shaved carrots (about 3 large)
1 (6-oz.) pkg. large cremini mushrooms, very thinly sliced
¼ cup packed celery leaves
¼ cup packed fresh flat-leaf parsley leaves
2 Tbsp. extra-virgin olive oil
1 tsp. grated lemon rind
2 Tbsp. fresh lemon juice
1 Tbsp. minced shallot
2 tsp. chopped fresh thyme
2 tsp. celery seeds
2 tsp. honey
⅜ tsp. kosher salt
¼ tsp. black pepper
1 oz. Parmigiano-Reggiano cheese, finely grated (about ⅔ cup), divided

1. Combine celery, carrots, mushrooms, celery leaves, and parsley leaves in a bowl.
2. Whisk together oil, rind, juice, shallot, thyme, celery seeds, honey, salt, and pepper in a medium bowl.

Add dressing and half of the cheese to vegetables, and toss to coat. Top each serving with the remaining cheese. Serves 6 (serving size: 1 cup)

CALORIES 97; FAT 6g (sat 1g, unsat 5g); PROTEIN 3g; CARB 8g; FIBER 2g; SUGARS 4g (added sugars 1g); SODIUM 252mg; CALC 8% DV; POTASSIUM 10% DV

Fast • Vegetarian

Pizza with Olives, Aleppo Pepper, and Fresh Mozzarella

Hands-on: 10 min. **Total:** 25 min.
Less assertive and more nuanced than red pepper flakes, Aleppo pepper makes a terrific pizza seasoning—a little spicy and a little fruity to complement the tangy sauce and rich cheese. Find it at spice stores, gourmet grocers, or Middle Eastern markets. A sprinkle of briny kalamata olives adds a touch of umami.

1 (28-oz.) can unsalted whole peeled tomatoes
⅜ tsp. kosher salt
½ cup thinly sliced fresh basil, divided
2 Tbsp. extra-virgin olive oil, divided
1 Tbsp. crushed Aleppo pepper, divided
1 Tbsp. plain yellow cornmeal
12 oz. fresh or frozen thawed prepared whole-wheat pizza dough
4 oz. small fresh mozzarella cheese balls (bocconcini)
1 oz. coarsely chopped pitted kalamata olives

1. Place a pizza stone or baking sheet on center rack in oven; preheat oven to 450°F. (Leave stone in the oven to preheat.)
2. Pour tomatoes into a colander set over a large bowl; squeeze and break into chunks. Reserve liquid for another use. Stir together tomato chunks, salt, ¼ cup basil, 1½ tablespoons olive oil, and 1½ teaspoons Aleppo pepper in a bowl.
3. Sprinkle cornmeal on a piece of parchment paper. Roll pizza dough on cornmeal into a 14- x 8-inch rectangle or a 12-inch circle. Spread tomato mixture over dough, leaving a ½-inch border. Top with cheese balls and olives. Leaving pizza on parchment paper, place onto hot pizza stone. Bake at 450°F for 10 minutes or until crust is done and cheese is bubbly. Brush edges of crust with remaining 1½ teaspoons oil.
4. Sprinkle with remaining basil and remaining Aleppo pepper. Cut into 8 slices. Serves 4 (serving size: 2 slices)

CALORIES 374; FAT 22g (sat 5g, unsat 17g); PROTEIN 12g; CARB 43g; FIBER 5g; SUGARS 3g (added sugars 0g); SODIUM 688mg; CALC 15% DV; POTASSIUM 8% DV

Red Wine–Poached Pears with Cardamom and Vanilla Mascarpone

Hands-on: 10 min. **Total:** 8 hr. 55 min. Perfumy cardamom heightens the sweetness of poached winter fruit. We use whole pods here to infuse the poaching liquid with the taste of cardamom. Red wine flavors the liquid, rather than serving entirely as the base, so its bitter tannins are much more subtle.

2 cups water
6 Tbsp. sugar
¼ cup cardamom pods
3 Tbsp. dry red wine (such as Burgundy)
2 whole star anise (optional)
3 firm pears (such as Bosc), peeled (about 1¼ lb.)
¼ cup mascarpone cheese
2 tsp. whole milk
1 tsp. vanilla bean paste or ¼ tsp. vanilla extract

1. Stir together 2 cups water, sugar, cardamom, wine, and star anise, if using, in a saucepan over high; bring to a boil. Add pears; reduce heat to medium. Cut a circle of parchment paper slightly larger than circumference of pan; press paper onto the surface of pears to keep them submerged. Simmer pears 20 minutes or until just tender. Remove from heat; cool completely. Chill pears in liquid in pan 8 hours.

2. Remove pears from liquid with a slotted spoon. Halve pears vertically. Gently remove seeds and core with a spoon. Chill until serving.

3. Place pan with poaching liquid over high, and cook, stirring occasionally, until syrupy and reduced to about ½ cup, about 25 minutes. Pour through a fine wire-mesh strainer into a bowl; discard solids.

4. Whisk together mascarpone, milk, and vanilla in a bowl until smooth. Place pears on plates. Drizzle each serving with poaching liquid syrup; top each with about vanilla mascarpone. Serves 6 (serving size: ½ pear, 1½ Tbsp. poaching syrup, and 1 Tbsp. mascarpone)

CALORIES 222; FAT 9g (sat 5g, unsat 4g); PROTEIN 2g; CARB 33g; FIBER 4g; SUGARS 24g (added sugars 16g); SODIUM 13mg; CALC 5% DV; POTASSIUM 5% DV

TOAST AND BLOOM SPICES FOR MAXIMUM FLAVOR

TOASTING
Spices contain essential oils, the source of their core aroma and taste. Toasting whole or ground spices in a dry pan before blending them into a dish draws out these oils and amps up their fragrance and flavor. Pay close attention as they heat, and toss or stir them often to make sure they don't scorch. We toast cumin seeds and peppercorns for our Cumin Lamb Stir-Fry (p. 22).

BLOOMING
This means heating spices in oil before mixing them in with the recipe. It's a fundamental technique in Indian cooking and a smart method to boost spice flavor in any cuisine. We put it to use in our Creamy Turmeric Cauliflower Soup (p. 23).

Job's Tears Salad with Bacon Dressing

Hands-on: 14 min. **Total:** 1 hour, 4 min. Job's tears are a gluten-free ancient whole grain. The large grains have a versatile corn-rice flavor. Find it at health-food stores and Asian markets. The warm vinaigrette will tenderize the thinly shaved vegetables while the salad stands before serving.

1 cup uncooked Job's tears grains
2 bacon slices, finely chopped
2 Tbsp. cider vinegar
1 Tbsp. olive oil
2 tsp. honey
½ tsp. kosher salt
½ tsp. black pepper
¼ tsp. dry mustard
1½ cups thinly shaved peeled golden beets
1 cup thinly shaved Brussels sprouts
½ cup shaved sweet apple (such as Honeycrisp)
¼ cup shaved red onion

1. Place Job's tears in a medium saucepan; add cold water to cover by 2 inches. Place pan over medium-high; bring to a boil. Reduce heat to medium-low; simmer 45 minutes or until chewy-tender. Drain well; place in a large bowl.

2. Cook bacon in a skillet over medium until crisp. Stir in vinegar, oil, honey, salt, pepper, and mustard until blended. Stir bacon mixture into cooked Job's tears. Fold in remaining ingredients. Let stand 5 minutes before serving. Serves 6 (serving size: about ¾ cup)

CALORIES 213; FAT 6g (sat 2g, unsat 4g); PROTEIN 6g; CARB 35g; FIBER 7g; SUGARS 6g (added sugars 2g); SODIUM 256mg; CALC 2% DV; POTASSIUM 9% DV

FOOD RX

Sometimes, easing what ails you is as simple as enjoying a home-cooked meal. We've chosen some of the best ingredients to ease inflammation, help you sleep, and boost your brain, gut, and immunity—and created recipes that show you just how easy it is to get these foods into your diet.

▶ BOOST IMMUNITY

BEEF A 3½-ounce serving of beef provides 50% of your daily zinc needs; the mineral helps white blood cells grow and function—and white blood cells attack harmful foreign invaders in your body.

GARLIC Zinc isn't very accessible to your body, which is why garlic is key: It contains sulfur, which helps your body better absorb zinc from food.

MUSHROOMS Mushrooms are one of the only natural food sources that, when exposed to sunlight, make vitamin D, which is critical in your body's immune response. Vitamin D helps your body create substances that interfere with the functioning of harmful bacteria.

GREEN TEA Though not part of the soup recipe, it's a fitting accompaniment for this spicy soup and a warming drink for a cold winter night. Plus, an active ingredient in green tea has been shown to help support your T-cells, a type of white blood cell.

Staff Favorite

Spicy Beef Noodle Soup

Hands-on: 35 min. **Total** 1 hr. 50 min.
This sinus-clearing, immunity-boosting bowl of soup is inspired by Szechuan beef noodle soup. Because some of the ingredients to make the traditional version require a trip to an Asian market, we approximated the flavors with easier-to-find items.

2 Tbsp. canola oil, divided
2 lb. boneless chuck roast, trimmed and cut into 1-in. pieces
1½ cups chopped white onion
⅓ cup minced garlic (15 cloves)
1 Tbsp. finely chopped peeled fresh ginger
3 plum tomatoes, chopped
¼ cup sambal oelek (ground fresh chile paste)
3 Tbsp. white miso
1½ tsp. ground coriander
1½ tsp. coarsely ground black pepper
8 cups unsalted beef stock
2 Tbsp. lower-sodium soy sauce
1½ Tbsp. light brown sugar
8 oz. presliced vitamin D–enhanced mushrooms (such as Monterey Mushrooms)
1 (8-oz.) pkg. pad Thai brown rice noodles
4 (4-oz.) baby bok choy, quartered lengthwise
½ cup sliced green onions
¼ cup cilantro sprigs

1. Heat 1 teaspoon oil in a Dutch oven over medium-high. Add half of beef; cook, turning occasionally, until browned on all sides, about 6 minutes. Transfer cooked beef to a plate. Repeat procedure with 1 teaspoon oil and remaining beef.
2. Heat remaining 4 teaspoons oil in Dutch oven over medium-high. Add onion, garlic, and ginger; cook, stirring often, until onion is almost tender, about 6 minutes. Stir in tomatoes, sambal oelek, miso, coriander, and pepper; cook, stirring constantly, 1 minute. Add stock, soy sauce, brown sugar, and browned beef. Bring to a boil; partially cover, and reduce heat to medium-low to maintain a simmer. Cook until beef is almost tender, about 45 minutes. Add mushrooms; cover and cook until beef is tender, about 30 minutes.
3. Cook noodles according to package directions; drain and rinse with cold water. Drain well.
4. Add bok choy to soup; cover and cook until crisp-tender, about 4 minutes. Arrange about ½ cup noodles and 2 bok choy quarters in each of 8 bowls. Ladle about 1½ cups soup into each bowl; sprinkle each serving with 1 tablespoon green onions. Top with cilantro sprigs. Serves 8 (serving size: about 2 cups)

CALORIES 459; **FAT** 20g (sat 7g, unsat 11g); **PROTEIN** 31g; **CARB** 39g; **FIBER** 5g; **SUGARS** 8g (added sugars 3g); **SODIUM** 736mg; **CALC** 4% DV; **POTASSIUM** 10% DV

JASMINE RICE Eating high glycemic index foods (such as jasmine rice) four hours before bedtime shortened the time it took to fall asleep compared to consuming low GI foods (such as barley or bulgur), says a study published in the *American Journal of Clinical Nutrition*.

MILK If you're having difficulty falling asleep, mild exercise during the day in addition to eating calcium-rich dairy products may help you snooze faster, according to a 2014 study.

PUMPKIN SEEDS Tryptophan, the amino acid that is more notoriously associated with turkey, is jam-packed into pumpkin seeds. Your body uses tryptophan to synthesize the hormone melatonin that helps regulate sleep.

Staff Favorite • Gluten Free
Vegetarian

Easy Jasmine Rice Pudding

Hands-on: 35 min. **Total:** 45 min.
If you have trouble finding goji berries or pepitas, sub tart cherries or pomegranates and walnuts; walnuts also contain tryptophan.

3½ cups 2% reduced-fat milk
⅔ cup water
⅓ cup honey
¼ tsp. kosher salt
¾ cup uncooked jasmine rice
1½ tsp. vanilla extract
6 Tbsp. chopped dried goji berries
6 Tbsp. toasted unsalted pepitas (shelled pumpkin seeds)

1. Bring milk, water, honey, and salt to a simmer in a medium saucepan over medium-high. Stir in rice, and reduce heat to medium-low. Cook, uncovered, stirring often, until rice is tender and mixture is thickened, about 30 minutes.

2. Remove from heat, and stir in vanilla. Divide mixture evenly among 6 bowls; top each with 1 tablespoon goji berries and 1 tablespoon pepitas. Serve warm. Serves 6 (serving size: about ⅔ cup)

CALORIES 276; FAT 7g (sat 2g, unsat 4g); PROTEIN 9g; CARB 46g; FIBER 2g; SUGARS 25g (added sugars 15g); SODIUM 245mg; CALC 20% DV; POTASSIUM 8% DV

SALMON Diets high in omega-3 fats (salmon is chock-full of them) are associated with a reduced risk of cognitive decline, Alzheimer's disease, and dementia.

KALE Dark leafy greens like kale are full of vitamin E, which has been associated with better neurological performance in mice (in a study, they navigated a maze faster), possibly because it protects brain cells from oxidation.

WALNUTS These nuts are packed with polyunsaturated fats, which can help with signaling between brain cells and help the brain grow and repair neurons.

EXTRA-VIRGIN OLIVE OIL Its antioxidants may help with learning and memory.

TURMERIC Curcumin, the compound that gives turmeric its color, has been shown to help with memory. It also may help protect your brain from the buildup of amyloid plaques, which are associated with Alzheimer's disease.

Fast • Gluten Free

Salmon with Kale, Walnut, and White Bean Salad

Hands-on: 15 min. **Total:** 15 min.
Our cooking method in step 1 gives you perfectly moist salmon with supercrisp skin.

4 (6-oz.) skin-on sustainable salmon fillets
1 tsp. kosher salt, divided
½ tsp. freshly ground black pepper, divided
3 Tbsp. extra-virgin olive oil
2 Tbsp. red wine vinegar
1 tsp. ground turmeric
1 tsp. Dijon mustard
1 tsp. honey
6 oz. baby kale (about 6 cups)
1 (15-oz.) can unsalted cannellini beans, drained and rinsed
¼ cup chopped walnuts, toasted

1. Pat fillets dry with paper towels; sprinkle flesh side with ½ teaspoon salt and ¼ teaspoon pepper. Heat 1 tablespoon oil in a large nonstick skillet over medium-high. Cook fillets, skin side down, 3 minutes. Reduce heat to medium; cook 2 minutes. Turn fillets; cook to desired degree of doneness, 1 to 2 minutes.

2. Whisk together the vinegar, turmeric, mustard, honey, remaining 2 tablespoons oil, remaining ½ teaspoon salt, and remaining ¼ teaspoon pepper in a large bowl. Add kale and beans; toss.

3. Divide salad evenly among 4 plates; top each with 1 salmon fillet and 1 tablespoon walnuts. Serves 4

CALORIES 479; FAT 25g (sat 4g, unsat 18g); PROTEIN 43g; CARB 18g; FIBER 5g; SUGARS 3g (added sugars 1g); SODIUM 677mg; CALC 13% DV; POTASSIUM 23% DV

▼ BETTER GUT HEALTH

SAUERKRAUT Fermented sauerkraut is abundant in lactic acid bacteria—the good kind that help with digestion. Opt for the refrigerated stuff; shelf-stable versions are heated, which kills bacteria.

KEFIR Kefir is also replete with lactic acid bacteria, which helps in digestion, fights off harmful bacteria, and is possibly effective in treating irritable bowel syndrome, ulcerative colitis, and other tummy troubles.

ONION AND GARLIC Both alliums are prebiotics, meaning they provide food for the nearly 1,000 species of healthy bacteria—probiotics—to thrive in your gut.

BROCCOLI Full of fiber, broccoli boasts plenty of prebiotic fodder for probiotics in your intestines to flourish—meaning a happier and healthier gut.

Fast • Gluten Free
Make Ahead • Vegetarian

Savory Broccoli-and-Sauerkraut Salad

Hands-on: 10 min. **Total:** 20 min.
This crunchy, make-ahead salad is a far cry from the supersweet broccoli salad you might be used to; it's more savory than sweet, with a delicious floral lift from lemon rind.

⅓ cup thinly vertically sliced red onion
¾ cup plain whole-milk kefir
2 Tbsp. canola mayonnaise
1 Tbsp. extra-virgin olive oil
2 tsp. grated lemon rind
¼ tsp. black pepper
⅛ tsp. kosher salt

1 garlic clove, finely grated
1 lb. broccoli with stalks
½ cup drained refrigerated red sauerkraut (such as Wildbrine)
⅓ cup unsalted roasted almonds, coarsely chopped

1. Soak onion slices in cold water 10 minutes; drain well.
2. While onion soaks, whisk together kefir, mayonnaise, olive oil, lemon rind, pepper, salt, and garlic in a large bowl.
3. Coarsely chop broccoli florets. Peel stalks; cut stalks into half-moons. Add broccoli, onion, and sauerkraut to kefir mixture; toss to coat. Sprinkle with almonds. Serves 6 (serving size: about 1 cup)

CALORIES 131; **FAT** 9g (sat 1g, unsat 7g); **PROTEIN** 5g; **CARB** 10g; **FIBER** 3g; **SUGARS** (added sugars 0g); **SODIUM** 240mg; **CALC** 10% DV; **POTASSIUM** 9% DV

▶ EASE INFLAMMATION

AVOCADO This fruit may help negate the effects of eating inflammatory foods, per a study in *Food & Function*. People who ate a hamburger with avocado didn't show the same inflammatory response as those who ate it without.

TART CHERRY JUICE In a study of runners, participants who drank antioxidant-rich tart cherry juice the days leading up to and after a marathon saw reduced inflammation and recovered their strength faster than those who did not.

SPINACH Dark leafy greens such as spinach are high in vitamin K, which may help tamp down inflammation.

BERRIES Packed with phenolic compounds, berries can trigger your body's anti-inflammatory response.

CHIA SEEDS These fiber-rich seeds have been associated with a drop in inflammatory markers.

Fast • Gluten Free
Vegetarian

Avo-Berry Smoothie Bowls

Hands-on: 5 min. **Total:** 5 min.
This breakfast bowl gives you more than half your daily fiber—enough to help keep you full until lunchtime. Keep the berries frozen for great texture.

1 cup unsweetened tart cherry juice (such as R.W. Knudsen Family), chilled
1 cup packed baby spinach
¾ cup plain 2% reduced-fat Greek yogurt
1 ripe avocado, halved, pitted, and peeled
2 cups unsweetened frozen mixed berries, divided
2 Tbsp. chia seeds

1. Process juice, spinach, yogurt, avocado, and ¾ cup berries in a blender until smooth, about 30 seconds. Divide mixture between 2 bowls; top servings evenly with chia seeds and remaining 1¼ cups berries. Serves 2 (serving size: 1¼ cups smoothie, 1 Tbsp. chia seeds, and about ⅔ cup berries)

CALORIES 361; **FAT** 17g (sat 3g, unsat 12g); **PROTEIN** 14g; **CARB** 48g; **FIBER** 13g; **SUGARS** 27g (added sugars 0g); **SODIUM** 71mg; **CALC** 22% DV; **POTASSIUM** 20% DV

THE COOKING LIGHT 3-DAY DETOX

Hit reset and kick-start your healthiest New Year yet with this clean meal plan featuring whole grains, tons of produce, and no added sugar.

THE HUSTLE OF THE HOLIDAYS is behind you, and the New Year thrills with the promise of a fresh start. Whether you overindulged during the holidays or not, you may be entering the New Year with the goal to lose weight, exercise more, or simply restore healthy habits that fell by the wayside amid the holiday feasts and cookie exchanges.

Rather than getting bogged down in a lofty list of health resolutions, an overly restricted diet, a nutrient-deplete cleanse, or an exercise regimen you can't commit to, reconnect with the basics. Try consuming more fruits, vegetables, and whole grains; less added sugar, meat, and refined grains; minimal alcohol; and plenty of water. Our detox lays the groundwork in an easy-to-follow meal plan that delivers on both taste and nutrition. Each day supplies 5½ cups of fruits and vegetables (experts recommend 4 to 5 cups per day for adults) and 100% of your daily fiber needs (a well-known natural slimming aid) to help you feel full for under 1,500 calories, an amount that most people will lose weight on. You'll also notice a heavy emphasis on plant-based meals, which research shows are correlated with improved diet quality compared to traditional, calorie-restricted diet approaches. Other studies also suggest that a more plant-based diet can help thwart weight gain.

Think of this detox as your reset as you enter the New Year—a way to tune up your diet by building a foundation you can sustain. Ready to get started?

PLAN AHEAD

Gluten Free • Make Ahead Vegetarian

Parslied Brown Rice Pilaf

Hands-on: 10 min. **Total:** 40 min. Fresh parsley is pleasantly verdant and pairs wonderfully with zippy lemon zest and nutty brown rice. We opt for brown rice because, compared to white, it is higher in fiber, protein, B vitamins, iron, and magnesium. Plus, new research shows that eating whole grains like brown rice daily reduces colorectal cancer risk, and the more you eat, the lower your risk. Leftovers will keep for three to five days.

½ cup uncooked brown rice
2 tsp. olive oil
⅓ cup chopped yellow onion
¼ cup chopped baby carrot
2 tsp. minced garlic
2 Tbsp. chopped fresh flat-leaf parsley
2 tsp. grated lemon rind
¼ tsp. kosher salt
¼ tsp. black pepper

1. Cook rice according to package directions, omitting salt and fat.
2. While rice cooks, heat oil in a large nonstick skillet over medium. Add onion and carrot; cook, stirring occasionally, until tender, about 5 minutes. Add garlic; cook until fragrant, about 1 minute. Remove from heat; stir in parsley, rind, salt, and pepper.
3. Place cooked rice in a large bowl, and fluff with a fork. Add onion mixture, and stir to combine. Serves 4 (serving size: ½ cup)

CALORIES 117; **FAT** 3g (sat 0g, unsat 2g); **PROTEIN** 2g; **CARB** 20g; **FIBER** 2g; **SUGARS** 1g (added sugars 0g); **SODIUM** 249mg; **CALC** 2% DV; **POTASSIUM** 4% DV

SHOPPING LIST

STAPLES YOU'LL LIKELY HAVE ON HAND

☐ Chili powder

☐ Cooking spray

☐ Crushed red pepper

☐ Curry powder

☐ Dijon mustard

☐ Ground coriander

☐ Ground cumin

☐ Ground ginger

☐ Large eggs

☐ Olive oil

☐ Kosher salt and pepper

☐ Sherry vinegar

☐ White wine vinegar

PRODUCE

☐ Apple (1)

☐ Avocado (1)

☐ Baby carrots (1 [1-lb.] bag)

☐ Baby spinach (1 [5-oz.] pkg.)

☐ Banana (1)

☐ Cherry tomatoes (1 pint)

☐ Fresh cilantro (1 bunch)

☐ Fresh flat-leaf parsley (1 bunch)

☐ Garlic (1 head)

☐ Lacinato kale (2 bunches)

☐ Lemons (2)

☐ Lime (1)

☐ Navel or blood oranges (3)

☐ Red bell peppers (2)

☐ Sweet potato (10 to 12 oz.)

☐ Thyme sprigs (1 pkg.)

☐ Yellow onions (2)

DAIRY CASE

☐ Plain 2% reduced-fat Greek yogurt (1 [17.6-oz.] container)

☐ Unsweetened refrigerated coconut milk (such as Silk) (1 [1.89-liter] container)

MEAT AND SEAFOOD

☐ Boneless, skinless chicken breasts (2 [4-oz.] pieces)

☐ Peeled and deveined raw large shrimp (6 oz.)

DRY GOODS

☐ Cooked quinoa (1½ cups)

☐ Dried brown rice (½ cup)

☐ Dried green lentils (1 cup)

☐ Peanut butter (1 [1.15-oz.] creamy natural packet)

☐ Reduced-sodium vegetable broth (1 qt.)

☐ Unsalted black beans (1 [15-oz.] can)

☐ Unsalted chickpeas (2 [15-oz.] cans)

☐ Walnuts (⅔ cup)

FROZEN

☐ Mango (12 oz.)

TOTAL COST: $66.92
(Total cost includes three days of breakfast, lunch, dinner, and two daily snacks.)

Fast • Gluten Free
Make Ahead • Vegetarian

Green Goddess Avocado Sauce

Hands-on: 5 min. **Total:** 5 min.
Avocados are nutrition heavy-hitters, boasting nearly 20 vitamins, minerals, and phytonutrients. The fruit is also rich in fiber, heart-healthy unsaturated fats, and plant sterols, which can help lower cholesterol. When blended into a bright, herbaceous sauce, they breathe life into humble rice dishes and make salads sing. Enjoy as either a dressing or dip.

½ ripe avocado
½ cup fresh flat-leaf parsley leaves
½ cup fresh cilantro leaves
¼ cup water
2 Tbsp. olive oil
2 Tbsp. coarsely chopped walnuts
2 Tbsp. fresh lemon juice
1 tsp. ground coriander
½ tsp. white wine vinegar
½ tsp. kosher salt
¼ tsp. freshly ground black pepper

1. Place all ingredients in a food processor; process until smooth. Chill until ready to use. Serves 6 (serving size: about 2 Tbsp.)

CALORIES 89; **FAT** 9g (sat 1g, unsat 7g); **PROTEIN** 1g; **CARB** 3g; **FIBER** 2g; **SUGARS** 0g (added sugars 0g); **SODIUM** 165mg; **CALC** 1% DV; **POTASSIUM** 4% DV

DAY 1

TOTAL CALORIES: **1,499**
TOTAL FIBER: **26g**

Fast • Gluten Free
Make Ahead

Citrus Sunrise Smoothie

Hands-on: 5 min. **Total:** 5 min.
This recipe calls for frozen fruit, letting you reap the nutritional benefits of out-of-season fruit like mango. Just one serving of this smoothie offers 100% of daily vitamin C and over 25% of daily calcium needs in a low-calorie package.

½ cup unsweetened refrigerated
  coconut milk (such as Silk)
¼ cup fresh orange juice
1 small banana, frozen
½ cup frozen mango
½ cup plain 2% reduced-fat Greek
  yogurt
2 tsp. chopped walnuts

1. Place coconut milk and orange juice in a blender. Add banana, mango, and yogurt; process until smooth. Pour into a glass; top with walnuts. Serves 1 (serving size: about 2 cups)

CALORIES 307; **FAT** 8g (sat 4g, unsat 3g);
PROTEIN 14g; **CARB** 48g; **FIBER** 4g;
SUGARS 33g (added sugars 0g); **SODIUM** 59mg;
CALC 36% DV; **POTASSIUM** 18% DV

Staff Favorite • Gluten Free
Make Ahead

Lemon Chicken Citrus Bowl

Hands-on: 15 min. **Total:** 1 hr. 15 min.
Because there's no center stage in a bowl, a smaller portion of meat travels far, putting more emphasis on the vegetables, whole grains, and fruit.

2 (4-oz.) boneless, skinless chicken
  breasts
1 Tbsp. fresh lemon juice
2 tsp. Dijon mustard
1 garlic clove, minced
⅛ tsp. kosher salt
⅛ tsp. black pepper
2 tsp. olive oil
2 cups coarsely chopped lacinato kale
¼ cup Parslied Brown Rice Pilaf
  (p. 29)
2 tsp. fresh orange juice
2 Tbsp. Green Goddess Avocado
  Sauce (p. 30)
¼ cup navel or blood orange slices

1. Combine chicken, lemon juice, mustard, garlic, salt, and pepper in a large ziplock plastic bag; seal. Chill 1 hour, or let stand at room temperature 30 minutes.
2. Heat oil in a large nonstick skillet over medium-high. Add chicken, and cook until a thermometer inserted in thickest portion registers 165°F, about 4 minutes per side; transfer to a cutting board.
3. Reduce heat to medium. Add kale to pan, and cook, stirring occasionally, until softened, about 3 minutes. Stir in pilaf and orange juice; cook, stirring often, until heated through, about 1 minute.
4. Place kale mixture in a bowl. Slice 1 chicken breast into strips (reserve remaining chicken for Day 2 Lunch); place on kale mixture. Top with Green Goddess Avocado Sauce and orange slices. Serves 1 (serving size: 1 bowl)

CALORIES 428; **FAT** 20g (sat 3g, unsat 15g);
PROTEIN 30g; **CARB** 34g; **FIBER** 6g; **SUGARS** 8g
(added sugars 0g); **SODIUM** 662mg; **CALC** 11%
DV; **POTASSIUM** 26% DV

Fast • Gluten Free
Make Ahead • Vegetarian

Chickpea and Kale Curry

Hands-on: 10 min. **Total:** 25 min.
This meatless main offers plenty of protein thanks to quinoa and chickpeas, and it boasts 40% of your daily fiber goal. Bonus: This recipe is a twofer; it makes enough for dinner tonight and a second full serving to freeze for another day.

2 tsp. olive oil
½ cup chopped red bell pepper
⅓ cup chopped yellow onion
3 cups chopped lacinato kale
2 tsp. minced garlic
1 tsp. curry powder
½ tsp. ground ginger
½ tsp. kosher salt
¼ tsp. black pepper
1 Tbsp. creamy natural peanut
  butter
1½ cups unsweetened refrigerated
  coconut milk (such as Silk)
1 cup canned unsalted chickpeas,
  rinsed and drained
1 Tbsp. fresh lime juice
1 cup cooked quinoa
2 Tbsp. cilantro sprigs

1. Heat oil in a large nonstick skillet over medium. Add bell pepper and

continued

onion; cook, stirring occasionally, until softened, about 5 minutes. Add kale and garlic; cook, stirring often, until kale is softened, about 2 minutes. Stir in curry powder, ginger, salt, and pepper. Add peanut butter; cook, stirring constantly, 30 seconds. Stir in coconut milk and chickpeas, and cook, stirring occasionally, until sauce starts to thicken slightly, 12 to 14 minutes. Remove from heat; stir in lime juice. **2.** Place ½ cup cooked quinoa in a bowl. Top with 1 cup curry mixture and cilantro sprigs. Refrigerate or freeze remaining quinoa and curry for later use. Serves 2 (serving size: ½ cup quinoa and 1 cup curry mixture)

CALORIES 409; FAT 15g (sat 5g, unsat 9g); PROTEIN 15g; CARB 53g; FIBER 11g; SUGARS 6g (added sugars 0g); SODIUM 595mg; CALC 48% DV; POTASSIUM 20% DV

DAY 2 MENU

BREAKFAST
Quinoa Breakfast Bowl with 6-Minute Egg

A.M. SNACK
½ cup plain 2% reduced-fat Greek yogurt, ⅛ cup thawed frozen mango, and 1 Tbsp. walnuts (174 calories)

LUNCH
Chickpea Spinach Salad

P.M. SNACK
½ cup baby carrots, ½ cup cherry tomatoes, and 2 Tbsp. Green Goddess Avocado Sauce (133 calories; p. 30)

DINNER
Slow Cooker Creamy Lentil Soup

DAY 2

TOTAL CALORIES: **1,464**
TOTAL FIBER: **43g**

Fast • Gluten Free
Vegetarian

Quinoa Breakfast Bowl with 6-Minute Egg

Hands-on: 5 min. **Total:** 15 min.
New research shows that eating eggs with raw vegetables like tomatoes increases your absorption of carotenoids—antioxidants that may ward off heart disease.

1 large egg, at room temperature
1½ tsp. olive oil, divided
½ tsp. minced garlic
1 cup lacinato kale, roughly chopped
½ cup cooked quinoa
⅓ cup halved cherry tomatoes
¼ ripe avocado
¼ tsp. kosher salt
⅛ tsp. freshly ground black pepper

1. Bring 3 inches of water to a boil in a medium saucepan. Add egg; boil 6 minutes. Plunge egg into ice water; let stand 1 minute. Drain and peel.
2. Heat 1 teaspoon oil in a small skillet over medium. Add garlic; cook 30 seconds. Add kale; cook, stirring often, until softened, 2 to 3 minutes.
3. Combine quinoa, kale, tomatoes, and avocado in a bowl. Drizzle with remaining ½ teaspoon oil; season with salt and pepper. Place egg on top; slice egg in half. Serves 1 (serving size: 2 cups)

CALORIES 366; FAT 21g (sat 4g, unsat 16g); PROTEIN 14g; CARB 33g; FIBER 8g; SUGARS 3g (added sugars 0g); SODIUM 592mg; CALC 17% DV; POTASSIUM 17% DV

Fast • Gluten Free

Chickpea Spinach Salad

Hands-on: 10 min. **Total:** 10 min.
This 10-minute salad is a nutritional powerhouse, brimming with antioxidants from the oranges, heart-healthy fats from the walnuts and avocado, and folate and vitamin A from the spinach. We skip the croutons and add toasted walnuts for a healthier crunch.

2½ cups fresh baby spinach
⅓ cup canned unsalted chickpeas, rinsed and drained
2 Tbsp. Green Goddess Avocado Sauce (p. 30)
¼ cup navel or blood orange segments
1 (4-oz.) lemon chicken breast (from Day 1 Lunch, p. 31), sliced
1 Tbsp. chopped toasted walnuts

1. Combine spinach, chickpeas, and sauce in a large bowl; toss gently to coat. Arrange spinach mixture on a plate; top with orange segments, chicken, and walnuts. Serves 1 (serving size: about 3½ cups)

CALORIES 479; FAT 22g (sat 3g, unsat 17g); PROTEIN 37g; CARB 34g; FIBER 11g; SUGARS 10g (added sugars 0g); SODIUM 530mg; CALC 24% DV; POTASSIUM 25% DV

Gluten Free · Make Ahead
Vegetarian

Slow Cooker Creamy Lentil Soup

Hands-on: 15 min. **Total:** 7 hr. 45 min.
Chickpeas are the secret ingredient to supreme creaminess. They become silky smooth when blended and sneak in an extra 3g of fiber per serving. Bonus: Leftovers freeze beautifully.

Cooking spray
4 cups reduced-sodium vegetable broth
1 cup uncooked green lentils
1 cup chopped yellow onion
¾ cup chopped baby carrots
2 tsp. ground cumin
1 tsp. kosher salt
½ tsp. freshly ground black pepper
5 thyme sprigs
4 garlic cloves, minced
1 (15-oz.) can unsalted chickpeas, rinsed and drained
¾ cup water
2 Tbsp. olive oil
1 Tbsp. fresh lemon juice
2 cups thinly sliced lacinato kale
½ tsp. sherry or red wine vinegar

1. Coat a 5- to 6-quart slow cooker with cooking spray. Place broth and next 8 ingredients (through garlic) in slow cooker; stir well. Cover and cook on low 7 hours.
2. Process chickpeas, ¾ cup water, oil, and lemon juice in a blender until smooth. Add chickpea mixture and kale to slow cooker; stir well. Cover and cook on low 30 minutes. Stir in vinegar. Serves 5 (serving size: about 1½ cups)

CALORIES 312; **FAT** 7g (sat 1g, unsat 5g);
PROTEIN 15g; **CARB** 47g; **FIBER** 12g; **SUGARS** 5g
(added sugars 0g); **SODIUM** 547mg; **CALC** 12%
DV; **POTASSIUM** 16% DV

DAY 3 MENU

BREAKFAST
Southwestern Sweet Potato and Egg Hash

A.M. SNACK
½ cup navel or blood orange wedges with 10 walnut halves (173 calories)

LUNCH
1½ cups leftover Slow Cooker Creamy Lentil Soup

P.M. SNACK
½ cup baby carrots, ½ cup bell pepper slices, and 2 Tbsp. Green Goddess Avocado Sauce (142 calories; p. 30)

DINNER
Pan-Seared Shrimp with Walnut and Herb Gremolata

DAY 3

TOTAL CALORIES: **1,425**
TOTAL FIBER: **37g**

Fast · Gluten Free
Make Ahead · Vegetarian

Southwestern Sweet Potato and Egg Hash

Hands-on: 15 min. **Total:** 30 min.
Hashes are a great way to incorporate vegetables into the first meal of the day. Give the potatoes a head start by microwaving them until just shy of tender, and then finish them off in the skillet for that coveted crispy texture. Use the leftover black beans to boost protein and fiber in salads, soups, or grain bowls.

¾ cup (½-in.) diced peeled sweet potato
2 tsp. water
1½ tsp. olive oil, divided
⅔ cup chopped red bell pepper
¼ tsp. chili powder
⅛ tsp. kosher salt
⅛ tsp. ground cumin
¼ cup unsalted canned black beans, rinsed and drained
1 large egg
2 Tbsp. Green Goddess Avocado Sauce (p. 30)
1 Tbsp. chopped fresh cilantro

1. Place potatoes and 2 teaspoons water in a microwave-safe dish; cover with plastic wrap. Microwave at high until tender, about 4 minutes. Place potatoes on a paper towel–lined plate. Let stand 5 minutes.
2. Heat 1 teaspoon oil in a cast-iron skillet over medium-high. Add potatoes, bell pepper, chili powder, salt, and cumin; cook until potatoes are crisp, 6 to 8 minutes. Stir in black beans; transfer to a plate.
3. Reduce heat to medium. Add remaining ½ teaspoon oil to pan. Crack egg into pan; cook until white is set, 3 to 4 minutes. Place egg on potato mixture. Top with Green Goddess Avocado Sauce and cilantro. Serves 1 (serving size: about 2 cups)

CALORIES 397; **FAT** 21g (sat 4g, unsat 16g);
PROTEIN 13g; **CARB** 38g; **FIBER** 10g;
SUGARS 9g (added sugars 0g); **SODIUM** 563mg;
CALC 11% DV; **POTASSIUM** 25% DV

continued

Pan-Seared Shrimp with Walnut and Herb Gremolata

Hands-on: 10 min. **Total:** 15 min.
Fresh herbs and lemon make a bright, tasty topper for succulent shrimp. Fish and shellfish are excellent sources of protein for fewer calories than most meats. Paired with spinach and rice pilaf, this weeknight-friendly main comes together in just 15 minutes.

1 Tbsp. chopped fresh flat-leaf
   parsley
2 tsp. chopped fresh cilantro
1½ tsp. minced garlic, divided
1 tsp. chopped walnuts
⅛ tsp. grated lemon rind
1 tsp. fresh lemon juice
⅛ tsp. kosher salt
⅛ tsp. crushed red pepper
1 Tbsp. olive oil, divided
6 oz. raw large shrimp, peeled and
   deveined
2 cups fresh baby spinach
½ cup Parslied Brown Rice Pilaf
   (p. 29)

1. Combine parsley, cilantro, ½ teaspoon garlic, walnuts, rind, juice, salt, red pepper, and 2 teaspoons oil in a small bowl; stir to combine. Set aside.
2. Heat remaining 1 teaspoon oil in a large skillet over medium-high. Add shrimp; cook until done, about 3 minutes. Remove shrimp from pan; reduce heat to medium.
3. Add remaining 1 teaspoon garlic to pan; cook until fragrant, about 30 seconds. Add spinach, and cook, stirring constantly, until wilted, 1 to 2 minutes. Transfer to a plate. Add Parslied Brown Rice Pilaf to pan;

cook, stirring constantly, until pilaf is heated through, about 1 minute. Add to plate with spinach. Top with shrimp and gremolata. Serves 1 (serving size: ½ cup rice, ½ cup spinach, 6 oz. shrimp, and about 2 Tbsp. gremolata)

CALORIES 401; **FAT** 20g (sat 3g, unsat 16g); **PROTEIN** 27g; **CARB** 26g; **FIBER** 3g; **SUGARS** 1g (added sugars 0g); **SODIUM** 781mg; **CALC** 17% DV; **POTASSIUM** 11% DV

THE RECIPE MAKEOVER

LIGHTEN UP PASTA BOLOGNESE

Boost the veg, replace the meat, and drop more than 500 calories with our lean version.
When it comes to meat-sauced pasta, Bolognese is the heavyweight champion, clocking in at over 800 calories with almost 1,800mg sodium. The traditional dish has a rich cast of characters—up to three kinds of meat, plus cream, cheese, and pasta—and packs half a day's worth of sat fat into just one serving. Here, tempeh and two types of mushrooms mimic the texture of ground meat while adding plenty of savory depth. By upping the veggies and nixing the cream, we leave plenty of room for the good stuff: Parmigiano-Reggiano cheese. Simmering the cheese rind with the sauce infuses even more full-bodied flavor and salty tang. Our makeover delivers classic satisfaction for less than half the calories and 1,300mg less sodium than the standard.

Vegetarian Bolognese

Hands-on: 40 min. **Total:** 2 hr.

2 tsp. fennel seeds
1 tsp. crushed red pepper
2 bay leaves
1 oz. dried porcini mushrooms
1½ cups warm water
3 cups fresh shiitake mushrooms
1 cup chopped onion
1 cup chopped carrots
½ cup chopped celery
2 Tbsp. extra-virgin olive oil
1 (8-oz.) pkg. tempeh, crumbled
1¼ tsp. kosher salt
½ tsp. black pepper
5 garlic cloves, minced
1 (28-oz.) can whole peeled
   tomatoes
1 cup whole milk
½ cup dry red wine
1 (2-in.) Parmigiano-Reggiano
   cheese rind
2 Tbsp. chopped fresh oregano
2 Tbsp. chopped fresh basil
1 tsp. granulated sugar
2 oz. Parmigiano-Reggiano cheese,
   grated (about ½ cup)
1½ lb. uncooked whole-wheat
   spaghetti
1 Tbsp. unsalted butter
Fresh basil leaves (optional)

1. Toast fennel seeds, red pepper, and bay leaves in a skillet over medium for 2 minutes, stirring often, until fragrant. Cool 10 minutes. Transfer to a spice mill (or mortar and pestle); finely grind. Set aside.
2. Place porcini mushrooms and 1½ cups warm water in a bowl; let stand 15 minutes. Drain, reserving ½ cup soaking liquid. Finely chop mushrooms; set aside.
3. Pulse shiitake mushrooms, onion, carrots, and celery in a food processor until finely chopped, 10 to 12 times.

4. Heat oil in a large Dutch oven over medium. Add tempeh; cook 5 minutes or until golden. Add shiitake mixture, salt, and pepper; cook 10 minutes or until softened. Add garlic, ground spices, and chopped porcinis; cook 5 minutes or until mixed well.

5. Pulse tomatoes in a food processor until finely chopped, 8 to 10 times.

6. Stir chopped tomatoes, milk, wine, cheese rind, oregano, basil, sugar, and reserved ½ cup porcini soaking liquid into tempeh mixture in Dutch oven. Reduce heat to medium-low, and simmer, partially covered, stirring occasionally, about 1 hour. Remove cheese rind; stir in grated cheese.

7. Cook spaghetti per package directions. Toss with butter to coat; serve with Bolognese; garnish with fresh basil, if desired. Serves 12 (serving size: about ⅔ cup pasta and ⅔ cup Bolognese)

CALORIES 353; **FAT** 10g (sat 3g, unsat 6g); **PROTEIN** 16g; **CARB** 53g; **FIBER** 7g; **SUGARS** 6g (added sugars 0g); **SODIUM** 475mg; **CALC** 14% DV; **POTASSIUM** 14% DV

THE PICKY EATER GURU

STUFFED PEPPERS WITH HALF THE CLEANUP

BY GINA HOMOLKA

Your whole family will love this dish—and it comes together in one pot!

I love my Instant Pot®, a multiuse countertop cooker (pressure cooker, slow cooker, and steamer in one) that may be the world's first viral kitchen appliance. I use it so much that it has earned itself a permanent space on my kitchen counter because, hey, what's not to love about dinner cooked in half the time?

Here's another fun fact: As much as I love cooking, I do not enjoy washing the dishes. My husband, Tommy, is the official dishwasher in our house, but since I'm cooking all day long developing and testing new recipes, I dirty a lot of dishes! So when it comes to preparing weeknight dinners, I really love a meal that uses only one pot.

These stuffed peppers are perfect in the pressure cooker—they only take about 15 minutes to cook (that's about a third of the time they take in the oven), and they always come out super tender and packed with flavor. I always keep homemade marinara sauce on hand in my freezer, so this dish is that much easier to whip up whenever the mood strikes. But a good-quality jarred sauce is a helpful alternative.

Instant Pot Turkey-Stuffed Peppers

Hands-on: 31 min. **Total:** 48 min. Don't have an Instant Pot? No worries! Make this recipe in your Dutch oven instead. Preheat the oven to 350°F, make the peppers as instructed, then place in your Dutch oven with ½ to 1 cup water (depending on the pot size). Cover and bake until cooked through, about 45 to 50 minutes. If you like your cheese browned, remove the lid after cooking and turn on the broiler for a few minutes.

4 large multicolored bell peppers, tops cut off and chopped, peppers hollowed and seeded
1 lb. 93% lean ground turkey
¾ cup cooked brown rice [I love Trader Joe's frozen brown rice.]
⅓ cup seasoned breadcrumbs
¾ cup reduced-sodium marinara sauce, divided
¼ cup minced fresh onion
1 oz. grated Parmesan cheese (about ¼ cup)
3 Tbsp. chopped fresh parsley
2 tsp. tomato paste
¼ tsp. kosher salt
Black pepper to taste
1 large egg, beaten
1 garlic clove, minced
½ cup water
1 oz. shredded mozzarella cheese (about ¼ cup)

1. Combine chopped pepper tops with ground turkey, cooked brown rice, breadcrumbs, ¼ cup marinara sauce, onion, Parmesan cheese, parsley, tomato paste, salt, black pepper, egg, and garlic. Mix thoroughly.

2. Stuff about 1 cup ground turkey mixture into each pepper. Pour ½ cup water into bottom of Instant Pot. Place a rack in the pot; stand stuffed peppers upright on the rack. Cover each pepper top with 2 tablespoons marinara sauce. Cover and cook on high pressure 15 minutes; natural release. Open the lid, top with mozzarella cheese, and cover until cheese melts, about 2 minutes. Serves 4 (serving size: 1 stuffed pepper)

CALORIES 399; **FAT** 16g (sat 5g, unsat 10g); **PROTEIN** 35g; **CARB** 31g; **FIBER** 6g; **SUGARS** 10g (added sugars 0g); **SODIUM** 648mg; **CALC** 25% DV; **POTASSIUM** 14% DV

THE ONLY POT STICKER PRIMER YOU'LL NEED

BY ANDREA NGUYEN

The secret to tender, crispy pot stickers is as straightforward as three words: fry, steam, fry.

When I noticed my assistant adding pot stickers to a skillet half-filled with smoking oil, I realized I had a problem. A cooking school student, he assured me he knew how to pan-fry Asian dumplings, so I let him do it while I taught the class. That was my mistake, because shallow-frying isn't how pot stickers are cooked. The little morsels were getting overly browned, too.

I rushed over, and, turning a near disaster into a teaching moment, I told the story of how pot stickers supposedly came about: A Chinese chef forgot about a batch of boiling dumplings, and by the time he remembered, the water had evaporated and the dumplings were stuck to the pan. He pried them off and served them anyway. Guests adored the wonderment of contrasts—succulent filling, tender-chewy skins, and crispy bottoms.

Over time, the dumpling mistake became known as pot stickers, and a refined cooking technique emerged. Brown the bottoms in oil, then add water, and cover the skillet to cook things through. After the water disappears, refry the bottoms. In a dramatic summary, I blurted out, "Fry, steam, fry!" People got it. Those words are now my pot sticker mantra.

I've prepared and eaten many pot stickers over the years. Making them well requires practice, but if you keep certain things in mind, you'll master them faster. For juicy pot stickers, make a moist filling; ground chicken thigh is naturally high in moisture (ask your butcher to grind chicken thighs). For ground pork or beef, add a touch of water or broth. Vegetable fillings are often precooked with a little sauce bound by cornstarch.

You don't need pretty pot stickers for them to be tasty. Just get the darn things closed! When folding, the thumbs and index fingers do most of the work. Hold the wrapper in your hand to manipulate the wrapper and tell it who's boss. Press out air bubbles, and firmly pinch to seal the rim, or there may be leaks during cooking. You can choose from three basic shapes. Half-Moons (below, top) are great for boiling, but they won't sit up in a skillet. Pea Pod One (below, center) starts from a Half-Moon then makes three or four pleats at the top to help the dumpling sit upright. Lastly, there's

Pea Pod Two (below, bottom)—again, start from a Half-Moon, but then make two tiny center pleats. Set the dumpling down and press to make sure it sits well. Put shaped dumplings on a floured, parchment paper–lined baking sheet to prevent sticky bottoms; cover loosely with plastic wrap or a dish towel to avoid dried-out tops.

Ensure your ta-da moment by pan-frying in a nonstick or well-seasoned carbon steel or cast-iron skillet. When eyeballing the water addition, hedge by adding less; you can always add more. If the dumplings stick at the end, drizzle water into the problem spots, cook on medium heat to loosen (shake the pan or use a turner), then let them refry. Eat pot stickers as finger food, or do it elegantly with spoon and chopsticks. The spoon catches any hot juices that can go back into the dumpling.

Usher in the Year of the Dog on February 16 with pot stickers, a harbinger of wealth according to the Chinese. Heck, make them anytime. Just remember: fry, steam, fry!

Gingery Chicken Pot Stickers

Hands-on: 45 min. **Total:** 1 hr. 15 min.

FILLING
12 oz. ground chicken thigh meat
⅓ cup finely chopped scallions, white and light green parts only (about 3 medium scallions)
1 Tbsp. minced peeled fresh ginger
1 Tbsp. dry sherry
1 Tbsp. lower-sodium soy sauce
1 Tbsp. toasted sesame oil
1 Tbsp. canola oil
⅛ tsp. ground white or black pepper

SAUCE
3 Tbsp. unseasoned rice vinegar
2½ Tbsp. regular soy sauce
1 Tbsp. chile oil or toasted sesame oil
1 tsp. minced fresh ginger

ADDITIONAL INGREDIENTS
Flour, as needed
30 pot sticker or gyoza wrappers
1½ Tbsp. canola oil

1. To prepare filling, combine all filling ingredients in a bowl. Use a fork or spatula to stir and fold the ingredients into a cohesive, thick mixture with no large chunks of meat. Cover and set aside at room temperature for 30 minutes.
2. Meanwhile, combine all sauce ingredients in a small bowl and set at the table.
3. Line a baking sheet with parchment paper, and generously dust with flour. Lay 4 to 6 wrappers on your work surface. Brush the edges of the wrappers with water. For each dumpling, hold a wrapper in a slightly cupped hand. Use a dinner knife or teaspoon to scoop up about 1½ to 2 teaspoons of the filling (the amount depends on the wrapper size). Place the filling slightly off-center toward the upper half of the wrapper. Shape it into a flat mound, and keep a knuckle's length (¾ inch) of wrapper clear on all sides.
4. Create your favorite shape. Otherwise, bring up the wrapper edge closest to you to close, then press to seal well and create a half-moon. To help the dumpling sit up during pan-frying, make a series of large pleats at the rim from one end to the other, firmly pressing into place. (Or, form 2 small pleats near the center, pressing firmly to hold.)
5. Place the dumpling on the prepared baking sheet. Repeat, spacing the dumplings ½ inch apart. Cover finished ones with a dry dish towel to prevent drying.
6. To cook, use a medium or large skillet (nonstick, carbon steel, or cast iron); if both sizes are handy, cook 2 batches at once. Heat over medium-high. Add 1½ tablespoons oil to film the bottom. Add the dumplings 1 at a time, placing sealed edges up in a winding circle pattern or several straight rows. Let them touch. Crowd them. Fry until golden or light brown (lift one to check), 1 to 2 minutes.
7. Holding a lid close to the skillet as a shield, use a kettle or measuring cup to add water to a depth of about ¼ inch. Cover and reduce the heat to medium. Let cook until the water is mostly gone, 4 to 6 minutes. After about 3 minutes, slide the lid ajar to allow steam to escape.
8. When you hear a gentle frying sound (most of the water is gone), uncover. Fry the dumplings for 1 to 2 minutes to crisp the bottoms. Remove from heat. When the sizzling stops, use a spatula to transfer the dumplings to a plate, with crisp bottoms up. Eat with the dipping sauce. Serves 6 (serving size: 5 pot stickers and about 1 Tbsp. sauce)

CALORIES 289; **FAT** 14g (sat 2g, unsat 10g); **PROTEIN** 16g; **CARB** 25g; **FIBER** 1g; **SUGARS** 0g (added sugars 0g); **SODIUM** 632mg; **CALC** 4% DV; **POTASSIUM** 2% DV

> ## "You don't need pretty pot stickers for them to be tasty. Just get the darn things closed!"
>
> —Andrea Nguyen

Ease into your post-holiday routine and start your year off right with these satisfying meals. Enjoy cold-weather comforts like tomato soup or bold, bright mains like crispy shrimp.

WEEKNIGHT MAINS

Fast

Kale, Tomato, and Pancetta Pasta

Hands-on: 25 min. **Total:** 25 min.
Tomatoes need a little extra love during winter. To coax out more flavor, we melt some in pancetta drippings for a saucy base and sauté the rest until lightly blistered.

8 oz. uncooked whole-wheat orecchiette pasta
3 cups cherry tomatoes, divided
3 oz. prediced pancetta (such as Boar's Head)
4 cups chopped stemmed lacinato kale
2 garlic cloves, minced
1 tsp. chopped fresh rosemary
½ tsp. freshly ground black pepper
¼ tsp. kosher salt
1 oz. Parmesan cheese, grated (about ¼ cup)
2 Tbsp. pine nuts, toasted

1. Cook pasta according to package directions, omitting salt and fat. Drain in a colander over a bowl; reserve 1½ cups cooking liquid.
2. Chop 1 cup tomatoes. Halve remaining 2 cups tomatoes. Cook pancetta in a large nonstick skillet over medium until crisp, about 8 minutes. Remove pancetta from pan with a slotted spoon. Add chopped tomatoes to drippings in pan; cook, stirring occasionally, until softened, about 2 minutes. Add halved tomatoes, kale, garlic, rosemary, pepper, and salt; cook 2 minutes. Add 1 cup reserved cooking liquid; cover and cook until kale is wilted, about 2 minutes. Stir in pasta and pancetta. Add remaining ½ cup cooking liquid, 2 tablespoons at a time, as needed to thin sauce. Top with cheese and pine nuts. Serve immediately. Serves 4 (serving size: about 1½ cups)

CALORIES 380; **FAT** 15g (sat 5g, unsat 9g); **PROTEIN** 16g; **CARB** 50g; **FIBER** 7g; **SUGARS** 5g (added sugars 0g); **SODIUM** 575mg; **CALC** 12% DV; **POTASSIUM** 18% DV

Make Ahead

Chicken with Broccolini and Farro-Beet Salad

Hands-on: 45 min. **Total:** 45 min.
This recipe gives you a full meal for four people—a plate that's heavy on veggies and provides nearly 30% of your daily fiber and over 80% of your protein. Precooked farro is convenient. If you have time, cook your own.

⅔ cup water
⅔ cup plus 1½ tsp. cider vinegar, divided
1 cup vertically sliced red onion
4 small red beets, trimmed (11 oz.)
¾ tsp. garlic powder
½ tsp. paprika
½ tsp. ground cumin
1¼ tsp. kosher salt, divided
4 (6-oz.) skinless, boneless chicken breasts
6 Tbsp. extra-virgin olive oil, divided
12 oz. Broccolini, trimmed
1 garlic clove
½ cup fresh flat-leaf parsley leaves
1 (8.5-oz.) pkg. precooked farro (such as Simply Balanced)
2 navel oranges, peeled and sliced
Chopped fresh dill (optional)

1. Bring ⅔ cup water and ⅔ cup vinegar to a boil in a saucepan. Add onion; boil 1 minute. Remove from heat; let stand 15 minutes. Drain.
2. While onion stands, pierce beets a few times with a knife; wrap in a large piece of microwave-safe parchment paper. Microwave at high until tender, about 8 minutes. Cool slightly; rub off skins with a paper towel. Cut beets into wedges.
3. While beets cook, heat a large skillet over medium-high. Combine garlic powder, paprika, cumin, and ¼ teaspoon salt; rub over chicken. Add 1 tablespoon oil to pan; swirl. Add chicken; cook until done, 6 minutes per side. Let stand 5 minutes. Cut into slices.
4. Bring a medium saucepan of water to a boil. Add Broccolini, and cook until just crisp-tender, about 2 minutes; drain. Rinse with cold water; drain.
5. Place garlic in a mini food processor; pulse until finely chopped. Add parsley; pulse until chopped. Add remaining 5 tablespoons oil, remaining 1½ teaspoons vinegar, and ½ teaspoon salt; process until well blended.
6. Heat farro according to package directions. Combine beet wedges, farro, and remaining ½ teaspoon salt. Divide farro mixture and Broccolini evenly among 4 plates; top evenly with onion, orange slices, and chicken. Drizzle each serving with about 2 tablespoons parsley sauce; if desired, sprinkle with dill. Serves 4

CALORIES 580; **FAT** 25g (sat 4g, unsat 19g); **PROTEIN** 43g; **CARB** 47g; **FIBER** 8g; **SUGARS** 17g (added sugars 0g); **SODIUM** 811mg; **CALC** 15% DV; **POTASSIUM** 33% DV

Korean Barbecue Pizza

Hands-on: 20 min. **Total:** 30 min.

3 Tbsp. rice vinegar, divided
2 Tbsp. light brown sugar, divided
1 medium carrot, shaved into
   ribbons
1 medium daikon radish, shaved
   into ribbons
3 Tbsp. fresh cilantro leaves
¼ cup water
½ tsp. cornstarch
1 tsp. olive oil
1 tsp. finely chopped garlic
1 tsp. finely chopped peeled fresh
   ginger
1 Tbsp. lower-sodium soy sauce
1 Tbsp. sambal oelek (ground fresh
   chile paste)
4 oz. skinless, boneless rotisserie
   chicken, shredded (about 1 cup)
1 (10-oz.) prebaked whole-wheat
   thin pizza crust (such as Boboli)
3 oz. fresh mozzarella cheese, torn
   into small pieces (about ¾ cup)

1. Preheat oven to 450°F.
2. Combine 1 tablespoon vinegar and 1 tablespoon brown sugar in a bowl. Add carrot and daikon; toss to coat. Let stand 10 minutes. Stir in cilantro.
3. Combine ¼ cup water and cornstarch in a bowl. Heat oil in a small skillet over medium. Add garlic and ginger; sauté 2 minutes. Stir in remaining 2 tablespoons vinegar, remaining 1 tablespoon brown sugar, soy sauce, and sambal oelek; bring to a boil. Reduce heat, stir in cornstarch mixture, and simmer until slightly thickened, 2 to 3 minutes. Remove pan from heat; stir in chicken.
4. Place prepared crust on a baking sheet. Spread chicken mixture over crust, leaving a 1-inch border. Top with mozzarella. Bake at 450°F

for 10 minutes. Top evenly with carrot mixture. Serves 4 (serving size: 2 slices)

CALORIES 351; **FAT** 11g (sat 5g, unsat 5g); **PROTEIN** 20g; **CARB** 13g; **FIBER** 8g; **SUGARS** 10g (added sugars 7g); **SODIUM** 705mg; **CALC** 19% DV; **POTASSIUM** 10% DV

SPEED IT UP

We made this weeknight friendly by using canned black-eyed peas, searing quick-cooking pork tenderloin, and slicing collards into ribbons so they wilt quickly.

Pork Tenderloin and Collards Skillet

Hands-on: 30 min. **Total:** 35 min.
The Southern New Year's tradition of eating black-eyed peas and collard greens is a delicious one—though, until now, not quick enough for a weeknight. Pork is a natural pairing and makes the meal more satisfying.

2½ Tbsp. unsalted butter, divided
1 (1-lb.) pork tenderloin, trimmed
¾ tsp. kosher salt, divided
¾ tsp. black pepper, divided
¾ cup sliced yellow onion
¾ cup chopped red bell pepper
3 garlic cloves, sliced
2 tsp. fresh thyme leaves
4 cups thinly sliced stemmed
   collard greens
1 cup canned unsalted black-eyed
   peas, rinsed and drained
2½ Tbsp. apple cider vinegar

1. Heat 1 tablespoon butter in a large cast-iron skillet over medium-high. Sprinkle pork with ½ teaspoon salt and ½ teaspoon pepper. Add pork to pan; cook, turning to brown all sides, until a thermometer inserted in the center registers 145°F, about 15 minutes.

Place pork on a cutting board; let stand 10 minutes. Cut into 12 slices.
2. Melt remaining 1½ tablespoons butter in skillet over medium. Add onion, bell pepper, garlic, and thyme; sauté 3 minutes. Move onion mixture to one side of pan; add collard greens to other side of pan. Cook 2 minutes. Add black-eyed peas and vinegar to greens; cook 1 minute. Stir together onion mixture and collard mixture. Stir in remaining ¼ teaspoon salt and remaining ¼ teaspoon pepper. Serve with sliced pork. Serves 4 (serving size: 3 oz. pork and about ¾ cup greens mixture)

CALORIES 266; **FAT** 11g (sat 5g, unsat 4g); **PROTEIN** 29g; **CARB** 15g; **FIBER** 5g; **SUGARS** 3g (added sugars 0g); **SODIUM** 442mg; **CALC** 12% DV; **POTASSIUM** 21% DV

---

3 WAYS TO:

MAXIMIZE YOUR SKILLET

1. Cook the pork in one pan entirely on the stovetop, saving preheating and roasting time. Turn it every couple of minutes to brown all sides.

2. No need for a second pan. Divide the skillet into two zones, adding the greens to one side after the veg mix has started to cook on the other.

3. Cast iron holds heat well—it may be hotter than you need at some point. Adjust the heat lower, or move the pan off the burner temporarily.

---

3 WAYS TO USE BABY BOK CHOY

Baby bok choy has crisp-tender ribs that can sear, sauté, and steam without losing their texture. It is also rich in fiber and folate, which can help reduce cancer risk.

Fast • Gluten Free • Vegetarian
Shiitake-and-Sesame Bok Choy

Shiitake mushrooms have a rich, meaty flavor that boosts the bok choy and marries well with the toasted sesame oil. They also brown quickly without releasing much liquid.

1. Heat 2 tsp. toasted sesame oil in a skillet over medium-high. Add 1 lb. quartered baby bok choy; cook until browned, about 4 minutes. Reduce heat to medium; cover and cook until tender, 3 minutes. Remove bok choy from pan. Add 2 tsp. toasted sesame oil and 8 oz. sliced shiitake mushrooms to pan; cook 2 minutes.
2. Stir in 3 sliced scallions and 3 minced garlic cloves; cook 30 seconds. Add cooked bok choy, 2 tsp. fresh lime juice, ½ tsp. kosher salt, and ⅛ tsp. black pepper; cook 1 minute. Top with 1 Tbsp. chopped cilantro and 1 tsp. toasted sesame seeds. Serves 4 (serving size: ⅔ cup)

CALORIES 86; FAT 5g (sat 1g, unsat 4g); PROTEIN 3g; CARB 8g; FIBER 3g; SUGARS 3g (added sugars 0g); SODIUM 201mg; CALC 13% DV; POTASSIUM 14% DV

Fast
Sweet-and-Sour Bok Choy

Oyster sauce and a pinch of sugar add caramel flavor and color to the bok choy. A little butter turns the sauce into a glaze. This side would be excellent with a spicy main like a Szechuan-style stir-fry or a chile-laden meat or fish dish.

1. Combine 2 Tbsp. rice vinegar, 1½ Tbsp. oyster sauce, and ⅛ tsp. sugar in a small bowl. Heat 2 tsp. canola oil in a skillet over medium-high. Add 1 lb. quartered baby bok choy; cook until browned, about 4 minutes.
2. Reduce heat to medium; cover and cook until tender, about 3 minutes. Add 1 Tbsp. thinly sliced garlic; cook 1 minute. Add oyster sauce mixture and 1 Tbsp. unsalted butter; cook, stirring occasionally, 1 minute. Sprinkle with 2 Tbsp. chopped fresh basil. Serves 4 (serving size: ⅔ cup)

CALORIES 68; FAT 5g (sat 2g, unsat 3g); PROTEIN 2g; CARB 4g; FIBER 1g; SUGARS 2g (added sugars 0g); SODIUM 259mg; CALC 13% DV; POTASSIUM 9% DV

Fast • Gluten Free • Vegetarian
Ginger-Chile Bok Choy

Mirin is a sweet rice wine that counters the spice. You can sub 1 tablespoon unseasoned rice vinegar combined with ½ teaspoon sugar.

1. Heat 2 tsp. canola oil in a skillet over medium-high. Add 1 lb. quartered baby bok choy; cook until browned, 4 minutes. Reduce heat to medium; cover and cook until tender, 3 minutes. Remove bok choy from pan. Add 2 tsp. canola oil; 1 Tbsp. minced peeled fresh ginger; 2 sliced, seeded red Fresno chiles; and 1 sliced garlic clove to pan. Cook, stirring often, 2 minutes.
2. Add 1 Tbsp. mirin, stirring to scrape up browned bits. Return bok choy to pan; cook 2 minutes.

Sprinkle with 2 Tbsp. chopped roasted unsalted peanuts and ¼ tsp. kosher salt. Serves 4 (serving size: about ⅔ cup:

CALORIES 68; FAT 5g (sat 0g, unsat 4g); PROTEIN 2g; CARB 5g; FIBER 1g; SUGARS 3g (added sugars 0g); SODIUM 211mg; CALC 9% DV; POTASSIUM 8% DV

3 WAYS TO USE TAHINI

The mild sesame seed paste is far more than just a hummus stir-in. It provides richness to the bulgur bowls on page 43 and has many other delicious uses; try it in these everyday dishes.

Fast • Make Ahead
Double-Sesame Noodles

Creamy tahini and fragrant sesame oil give this simple noodle dish a double dose of nutty flavor. The sauce is similar to Southeast Asian peanut sauce—but more allergy-friendly because it's made with sesame seeds.

1. Cook 6 oz. soba noodles according to package directions; drain and rinse with cold water.
2. Combine ¼ cup tahini (well stirred), ¼ cup water, 2 Tbsp. toasted sesame oil, 1 Tbsp. fresh lime juice, 2 tsp. sambal oelek or Sriracha, and ¾ tsp. kosher salt in a large bowl. Add noodles, 2 cups thinly sliced red cabbage, 1 cup chopped scallions, and 8 oz. shredded skinless, boneless rotisserie chicken breast. Toss gently to combine. Serve at room temperature. Serves 4 (serving size: about 1½ cups)

CALORIES 400; FAT 17g (sat 3g, unsat 14g); PROTEIN 24g; CARB 41g; FIBER 5g; SUGARS 4g (added sugars 0g); SODIUM 621mg; CALC 8% DV; POTASSIUM 16% DV

Fast • Gluten Free
Make Ahead • Vegetarian

Garlicky Lemon-Tahini Dressing

Think of this as an all-purpose dressing, perfect for green salads or whole-grain salads, roasted vegetables or roasted meats. It has citrusy pep and a nice garlic follow-through. We like to grate the garlic on a Microplane-style grater so that it becomes a smooth paste—leaving no crunchy bits, but all the pungent flavor.

1. Place 2 Tbsp. tahini (well stirred) in a medium bowl. Stir in 2 Tbsp. water, 2 Tbsp. fresh lemon juice, 1½ Tbsp. extra-virgin olive oil, ⅜ tsp. kosher salt, ¼ tsp. black pepper, and 1 grated garlic clove. Refrigerate in an airtight container up to 1 week. Serves 4 (serving size: 2 Tbsp.)

CALORIES 92; **FAT** 9g (sat 1g, unsat 7g); **PROTEIN** 1g; **CARB** 2g; **FIBER** 0g; **SUGARS** 0g; **SODIUM** 183mg; **CALC** 1% DV; **POTASSIUM** 1% DV

Fast • Gluten Free
Make Ahead • Vegetarian

Nutty Mashed Sweet Potatoes

If you prefer your sweet potatoes more on the savory side, this dish is for you. Since the tubers are already naturally sweet, we add just a small drizzle of honey to enhance their flavor. The tahini lends a distinct nuttiness and contributes to the overall creaminess of the dish. We use a food processor for the smoothest texture.

1. Place 1½ lb. peeled, cubed sweet potatoes in a large saucepan; cover with water. Bring to a boil; reduce heat and simmer until very tender, about 15 minutes. Drain.
2. Place potatoes, ¼ cup tahini (well stirred), 1 Tbsp. honey, ½ tsp. kosher salt, and, if desired, ½ tsp.

ground ginger in a food processor; process until smooth. Serves 4 (serving size: about ⅔ cup)

CALORIES 206; **FAT** 8g (sat 1g, unsat 7g); **PROTEIN** 4g; **CARB** 31g; **FIBER** 4g; **SUGARS** 12g (added sugars 4g); **SODIUM** 281mg; **CALC** 6% DV; **POTASSIUM** 11% DV

SLOW COOKER
Staff Favorite • Gluten Free
Make Ahead

Slow Cooker Chicken Mole Tacos

Hands-on: 10 min. **Total:** 8 hr. 10 min. This beautifully complex dish is traditionally a labor of love. We've streamlined the dish and made it almost entirely hands-off. The recipe yields about 2 cups extra mole sauce; use this for enchiladas, as a topper for pork chops, or as a phenomenal stir-in for chili.

2 dried ancho chiles
1 (28-oz.) can unsalted whole tomatoes
1 cup chopped yellow onion
½ cup toasted sliced almonds
3 oz. semisweet baking chocolate, finely chopped (about ½ cup)
¼ cup raisins
¼ cup unsalted chicken stock
1 Tbsp. ground cumin
1 Tbsp. canned adobo sauce
1 tsp. ground cinnamon
2 chipotle chiles, canned in adobo sauce
3 garlic cloves, smashed
2 lb. bone-in chicken thighs, skinned
1 tsp. kosher salt
16 (6-in.) corn tortillas

1 oz. Cotija cheese, crumbled (about ¼ cup)
¼ cup fresh cilantro leaves
2 limes, cut into wedges

1. Place ancho chiles in a bowl; cover with water. Let stand 10 minutes. Drain; remove and discard stems and seeds. Process seeded chiles, tomatoes, onion, almonds, chocolate, raisins, stock, cumin, adobo sauce, cinnamon, chipotle chiles, and garlic in a food processor until smooth.
2. Sprinkle chicken with salt; place in a 6-quart slow cooker. Add tomato mixture. Cover and cook on low 8 hours. Place chicken on a cutting board; remove bones. Reserve 2 cups sauce for another use. Shred chicken into large pieces; return to slow cooker.
3. Working with 1 tortilla at a time, heat tortillas over medium-high directly on burner until lightly charred, about 15 seconds per side. Top tortillas with chicken mixture, cheese, and cilantro. Serve with lime wedges. Serves 8 (serving size: 2 tacos)

CALORIES 437; **FAT** 14g (sat 4g, unsat 8g); **PROTEIN** 31g; **CARB** 53g; **FIBER** 9g; **SUGARS** 15g (added sugars 6g); **SODIUM** 477mg; **CALC** 15% DV; **POTASSIUM** 22% DV

20-MINUTE MAINS

Fast

Sesame Shrimp with Ginger Broccoli

Hands-on: 20 min. **Total:** 20 min.
We achieve a deep-fried effect by incorporating sesame seeds into a light panko coating that cooks to perfect crunchiness in just a little oil. A squeeze of Sriracha adds big flavor with minimal effort.

1½ Tbsp. brown sugar
1 Tbsp. Sriracha chili sauce
2 large egg whites
½ cup whole-wheat panko (Japanese breadcrumbs)
¼ cup toasted sesame seeds
1½ lb. large shrimp, peeled and deveined (tails on)
2 Tbsp. canola oil, divided
1 Tbsp. toasted sesame oil, divided
½ tsp. kosher salt, divided
½ tsp. freshly ground black pepper, divided
1 Tbsp. sliced garlic
1 Tbsp. finely chopped peeled fresh ginger
2 (12-oz.) broccoli heads, cut into florets with stems attached
¼ cup water

1. Whisk together brown sugar, Sriracha, and egg whites in a shallow dish. Combine panko and sesame seeds in a shallow dish. Working in batches, add shrimp to egg mixture; dredge in panko mixture.
2. Heat 1½ teaspoons canola oil and 1½ teaspoons sesame oil in a large nonstick skillet over medium-high. Add half of dredged shrimp; cook until golden brown, 2 to 3 minutes per side. Remove from pan. Repeat procedure with 1½ teaspoons canola oil, remaining 1½ teaspoons sesame oil, and remaining half of dredged shrimp. Sprinkle cooked shrimp with ¼ teaspoon salt and ¼ teaspoon pepper.
3. Heat remaining 1 tablespoon canola oil in pan over medium-high. Add garlic and ginger; cook, stirring constantly, 1 minute. Add broccoli; cook until lightly browned, about 2 minutes. Add ¼ cup water; cover and cook until crisp-tender, 2 to 3 minutes. Uncover; sprinkle with remaining ¼ teaspoon salt and remaining ¼ teaspoon pepper. Serve with shrimp. Serves 4 (serving size: about 8 shrimp and 1 cup broccoli)

CALORIES 393; **FAT** 17g (sat 2g, unsat 15g); **PROTEIN** 33g; **CARB** 28g; **FIBER** 6g; **SUGARS** 8g (added sugars 5g); **SODIUM** 681mg; **CALC** 21% DV; **POTASSIUM** 22% DV

HOW TO:
COOK IN BATCHES

1. Bread a few shrimp at a time so the coating doesn't clump. Have a landing plate for breaded shrimp so they don't crowd the panko mixture.

2. Cook shrimp in two batches to not overcrowd the pan; they'll cook more quickly and be crispier. Have a platter nearby for the cooked shrimp.

3. Tent foil over the cooked shrimp to keep them warm while you cook the next batch. Skip the oven; even a low temp could overcook the shrimp.

Fast • Vegetarian

Creamy Tomato Soup with Parmesan Crisps

Hands-on: 20 min. **Total:** 20 min.
We've turned our favorite part of a grilled cheese sandwich—those irresistible lacy, golden crisps that form when the cheese oozes out and hits the hot pan—into a delicious garnish for our quick, creamy tomato soup.

¼ cup extra-virgin olive oil
¾ cup prechopped onion
⅓ cup chopped carrot
6 large garlic cloves, crushed
2 Tbsp. tomato paste
2 (15-oz.) cans unsalted fire-roasted tomatoes
1 cup organic vegetable broth (such as Swanson)
⅓ cup half-and-half
⅜ tsp. kosher salt
½ cup whole-wheat panko (Japanese breadcrumbs)
2 oz. Parmigiano-Reggiano cheese, finely grated (about ½ cup)
½ tsp. paprika
¼ tsp. ground cumin
⅛ tsp. ground red pepper

1. Heat olive oil in a large saucepan over medium-high. Add onion, carrot, and garlic; sauté until onion is golden, about 5 minutes. Stir in tomato paste; cook 1 minute. Add tomatoes and broth; bring to a simmer. Cook 6 minutes. Stir in half-and-half and salt.
2. Place tomato mixture in a blender. Remove center from blender lid (to allow steam to escape); secure blender lid on blender. Cover opening with a kitchen towel; blend until smooth, about 30 seconds.

3. Heat a large nonstick skillet over medium-high. Combine panko, cheese, paprika, cumin, and red pepper in a bowl. Spoon about 2 tablespoons panko mixture in a small mound in pan; repeat 3 times to form 4 mounds. Gently pat mounds with the back of a spoon to flatten into 3-inch discs. Cook until browned and crisp, about 2 minutes per side. Remove from pan; place on a wire rack. Repeat procedure 2 times to yield 12 crisps. Serve crisps with soup. Serves 4 (serving size: about 1¼ cups soup and 3 crisps)

CALORIES 326; FAT 20g (sat 6g, unsat 14g); PROTEIN 9g; CARB 28g; FIBER 4g; SUGARS 11g (added sugars 0g); SODIUM 653mg; CALC 16% DV; POTASSIUM 7% DV

Fast

Quick Chicken Marsala

Hands-on: 20 min. **Total:** 20 min. Marsala wine is a worthy addition to your pantry: It's both dry and sweet without being overpowering, adding depth to sauces. Serve this skillet main over polenta, mashed potatoes, or hot cooked brown rice.

2 Tbsp. olive oil, divided
4 (4-oz.) skinless, boneless chicken breast cutlets
¾ tsp. black pepper, divided
½ tsp. kosher salt, divided
1 (8-oz.) pkg. presliced button mushrooms
4 thyme sprigs
1 Tbsp. all-purpose flour
⅔ cup unsalted chicken stock
⅓ cup Marsala wine
2½ Tbsp. unsalted butter
1 Tbsp. chopped fresh thyme (optional)

1. Heat 1 tablespoon oil in a large nonstick skillet over medium-high. Sprinkle chicken with ½ teaspoon pepper and ¼ teaspoon salt. Add chicken to pan; cook until done, about 4 minutes per side. Remove chicken from pan (do not wipe out pan).
2. Add remaining 1 tablespoon oil to pan. Add mushrooms and thyme sprigs; cook, stirring occasionally, until mushrooms are browned, about 6 minutes. Sprinkle flour over mixture; cook, stirring constantly, 1 minute.
3. Add stock and wine to pan; bring to a boil. Cook until slightly thickened, 2 to 3 minutes. Remove pan from heat. Stir in butter, remaining ¼ teaspoon pepper, and remaining ¼ teaspoon salt. Add chicken to pan, turning to coat. Discard thyme sprigs before serving. Sprinkle with chopped thyme, if desired. Serves 4 (serving size: 1 cutlet and about ¼ cup sauce)

CALORIES 344; FAT 17g (sat 6g, unsat 9g); PROTEIN 28g; CARB 9g; FIBER 1g; SUGARS 7g (added sugars 0g); SODIUM 567mg; CALC 19% DV; POTASSIUM 16% DV

Fast • Vegetarian

Kale-and-Chickpea Grain Bowl with Avocado Dressing

Hands-on: 20 min. **Total:** 20 min. This veggie-heavy bowl provides more than 50% of your daily fiber—key for weight loss, energy, and healthy digestion. Find tasty ways to use up leftover tahini (used in the avocado dressing) on page 40.

1 cup boiling water
½ cup uncooked bulgur
2 (15-oz.) cans unsalted chickpeas, rinsed and drained
1½ Tbsp. canola oil
2 cups finely chopped carrots
4 cups chopped lacinato kale
½ cup vertically sliced shallots
¼ cup fresh flat-leaf parsley leaves
¾ tsp. kosher salt, divided
½ tsp. black pepper
½ avocado, peeled and pitted
2 Tbsp. extra-virgin olive oil
1 Tbsp. fresh lemon juice
1 Tbsp. water
1 Tbsp. tahini (sesame seed paste), well stirred
1 garlic clove
¼ tsp. ground turmeric

1. Combine 1 cup boiling water and bulgur in a medium bowl. Let stand 10 minutes; drain well.
2. Pat chickpeas dry with paper towels. Heat canola oil in a large skillet over high. Add chickpeas and carrots; cook, stirring occasionally, until chickpeas are browned, about 6 minutes. Add kale; cover and cook until kale is slightly wilted and carrots are tender, about 2 minutes. Add chickpea mixture, shallots, parsley, ½ teaspoon salt, and pepper to bulgur; toss.
3. Process avocado, olive oil, juice, 1 tablespoon water, tahini, garlic, turmeric, and remaining ¼ teaspoon salt in a food processor until smooth. Divide bulgur mixture among 4 bowls; drizzle with avocado mixture. Serves 4 (serving size: about 1¼ cups bulgur mixture and 1½ Tbsp. dressing)

CALORIES 520; FAT 20g (sat 2g, unsat 16g); PROTEIN 18g; CARB 68g; FIBER 16g; SUGARS 7g (added sugars 0g); SODIUM 495mg; CALC 26% DV; POTASSIUM 26% DV

Staff Favorite • Fast
Gluten Free

Beef Tenderloin with Horseradish Cream and Glazed Carrots

Hands-on: 20 min. **Total:** 20 min.
Beef tenderloin is a worthy splurge when you want a special entrée in less time; the cut cooks to tender perfection in 8 minutes. Beyond the sauce, try using up horseradish by stirring it into a deviled egg filling, mashed potatoes, or a dressing for slaw.

2 tsp. canola oil
4 (4-oz.) beef tenderloin steaks
1 tsp. kosher salt, divided
¾ tsp. black pepper, divided
½ tsp. smoked paprika
¼ tsp. ground cumin
¼ tsp. garlic powder
4 cups chopped carrots (about 1¼ lb.)
½ cup water
2 Tbsp. unsalted butter
2 tsp. honey
2 Tbsp. finely chopped fresh flat-leaf parsley
2 Tbsp. light sour cream
1 Tbsp. fat-free buttermilk
1 Tbsp. prepared horseradish
1 Tbsp. chopped fresh chives

1. Heat oil in a large skillet over medium-high. Sprinkle steaks with ½ teaspoon salt, ½ teaspoon pepper, paprika, cumin, and garlic powder. Add steaks to pan; cook to desired degree of doneness, 4 to 5 minutes per side for medium-rare. Remove steaks from pan; keep warm. Wipe out pan with paper towels.
2. Add carrots and ½ cup water to pan; bring to a boil over medium-high. Cover and reduce heat to medium; simmer 5 minutes. Uncover, add butter and honey to pan, and cook, stirring occasionally, until liquid has evaporated and carrots are glazed and tender, about 3 minutes. Sprinkle with remaining ½ teaspoon salt, remaining ¼ teaspoon pepper, and parsley.
3. Stir together sour cream, buttermilk, horseradish, and chives in a small bowl. Serve with steaks and carrot mixture. Serves 4 (serving size: 3 oz. beef, ⅔ cup carrots, and about 1 Tbsp. sauce)

CALORIES 326; **FAT** 17g (sat 7g, unsat 8g); **PROTEIN** 27g; **CARB** 17g; **FIBER** 4g; **SUGARS** 9g (added sugars 3g); **SODIUM** 660mg; **CALC** 10% DV; **POTASSIUM** 25% DV

4 GO-WITH-ANYTHING SIDES

Fast • Gluten Free
Vegetarian
Creamed Curried Spinach
Curry powder adds warmth and earthiness to this speedy version of creamed spinach. Serve with steak or seared planks of spice-rubbed tofu.

Cook 1½ Tbsp. extra-virgin olive oil, ¼ tsp. crushed red pepper, and 5 thinly sliced garlic cloves in a large skillet over medium-high until garlic begins to sizzle, about 2 minutes. Add ½ cup thinly sliced shallots and ¾ tsp. curry powder; cook 2 minutes. Add 1 lb. fresh baby spinach to pan in batches, stirring until wilted before adding more. Stir in ½ cup plain whole-milk Greek yogurt and ¼ tsp. kosher salt. Serves 4 (serving size: about ½ cup)

CALORIES 126; **FAT** 7g (sat 2g, unsat 5g); **PROTEIN** 6g; **CARB** 10g; **FIBER** 4g; **SUGARS** 3g (added sugars 0g); **SODIUM** 221mg; **CALC** 15% DV; **POTASSIUM** 4% DV

Fast • Gluten Free
Vegetarian
Sherry-Glazed Parsnips with Pomegranate
Sweet parsnips are an excellent match for the sherry glaze. Try this side with roasted chicken or pork loin.

Bring ½ cup water, ½ cup dry sherry, 1 tsp. chopped fresh thyme, and 1½ lb. peeled parsnips, cut diagonally into 2-in. pieces, to a boil in a large skillet. Reduce heat to medium; cover and simmer until parsnips are tender, about 10 minutes. Uncover; cook until liquid is slightly thickened, about 5 minutes. Stir in 1 Tbsp. unsalted butter, 1 Tbsp. sherry vinegar, ¼ tsp. kosher salt, and ¼ tsp. black pepper. Sprinkle with ¼ cup pomegranate arils. Serves 4 (serving size: 1 cup)

CALORIES 205; **FAT** 3g (sat 2g, unsat 1g); **PROTEIN** 2g; **CARB** 33g; **FIBER** 8g; **SUGARS** 8g (added sugars 0g); **SODIUM** 138mg; **CALC** 6% DV; **POTASSIUM** 18% DV

Gluten Free • Vegetarian
Spanish-Style Roasted Potatoes
Paprika, fresh oregano, and olives turn everyday roasted potatoes into a spectacular side. Serve with a chorizo-flecked frittata or pan-grilled steak or chicken.

Toss together 1 lb. halved small Yukon Gold potatoes, 2 Tbsp. extra-virgin olive oil, 1 Tbsp. chopped fresh oregano, 2 tsp. minced fresh rosemary, and 2 tsp. paprika on a parchment paper–lined baking sheet. Bake at 400°F for 25 minutes, stirring after 10 minutes. Toss with 3 Tbsp. chopped pitted Castelvetrano olives, 1 Tbsp. extra-virgin olive oil, 1 Tbsp. chopped fresh parsley, and ¼ tsp. kosher salt. Serves 4 (serving size: ¾ cup)

CALORIES 190; FAT 12g (sat 1g, unsat 9g); PROTEIN 2g; CARB 19g; FIBER 3g; SUGARS 2g (added sugars 0g); SODIUM 292mg; CALC 1% DV; POTASSIUM 10% DV

Fast • Gluten Free
Vegetarian
Fennel, Tomato, and Feta Skillet Bake
Fresh fennel becomes mellow and sweet once sautéed and braised with tomatoes. Pair this simple, beautiful side with baked fish or lemon-and-herb roasted chicken.

Cut 2 fennel bulbs into 8 wedges each; sprinkle with 2 tsp. ground coriander. Chop fennel fronds to equal 1 Tbsp. Heat 2 Tbsp. olive oil in a large ovenproof skillet over medium-high. Add fennel wedges; cook 4 minutes. Turn; add 1½ cups chopped tomatoes (such as Pomì), 2 Tbsp. sliced garlic, 1 Tbsp. lemon juice, and ¼ tsp. kosher salt. Bake at 375°F for 15 minutes. Sprinkle with 3 Tbsp. crumbled feta and fronds. Serves 4 (serving size: 1 cup)

CALORIES 149; FAT 9g (sat 2g, unsat 7g); PROTEIN 4g; CARB 15g; FIBER 6g; SUGARS 8g (added sugars 0g); SODIUM 250mg; CALC 11% DV; POTASSIUM 15% DV

4 SAUCES FOR ANY PROTEIN
Fast • Vegetarian
Smoked Gouda and Beer Sauce
We save on fat by adding flour straight to the beer rather than making a roux with butter or oil. The result is a thick, velvety cheese sauce with a pleasantly bitter edge from the beer. Spoon over beef burgers or sliced roasted turkey.

Heat 9 Tbsp. pale ale or wheat beer in a small saucepan over low until bubbling, about 1 minute. Stir in 1½ Tbsp. all-purpose flour. Add 3½ oz. shredded smoked Gouda cheese (about 1 cup), stirring with a whisk until smooth. Remove pan from heat; stir in 2 Tbsp. 2% plain reduced-fat Greek yogurt, ¼ tsp. ground mustard, and ¼ tsp. paprika. Serves 8 (serving size: about 2 Tbsp.)

CALORIES 64; FAT 4g (sat 3g, unsat 0g); PROTEIN 4g; CARB 2g; FIBER 0g; SUGARS 0g; SODIUM 116mg; CALC 10% DV; POTASSIUM 0% DV

Fast • Gluten Free
Make Ahead • Vegetarian
Tandoori Yogurt Sauce
The key to this marinade-turned-sauce is to heat the spices in oil to release their fragrance and keep the final mixture from having a gritty texture. Use the sauce on pan-grilled chicken or tofu; garnish with cilantro.

Heat 1 Tbsp. olive oil in a small skillet over medium. Add 2 tsp. paprika, 1 tsp. ground cumin, and ½ tsp. ground turmeric; cook, stirring often, until fragrant, about 30 seconds. Combine oil mixture and 1 cup 2% plain reduced-fat Greek yogurt in a bowl. Stir in 2 tsp. grated peeled fresh ginger, ½ tsp. kosher salt, and 1 minced small garlic clove. Serves 8 (serving size: about 2 Tbsp.)

CALORIES 41; FAT 2g (sat 1g, unsat 1g); PROTEIN 3g; CARB 2g; FIBER 0g; SUGARS 1g (added sugars 0g); SODIUM 132mg; CALC 3% DV; POTASSIUM 0% DV

Fast • Gluten Free
Make Ahead
Pepperoni Tomato Sauce
Turn plain chicken breasts, hamburger steaks, or leftover pot roast into a surefire family favorite with a sauce that tastes like pepperoni pizza. It's also great as a dip for homemade chicken

fingers, grilled cheese sandwiches, or roasted zucchini wedges.

Heat 2 Tbsp. olive oil in a medium skillet over medium-high. Add ½ tsp. dried oregano, ¼ tsp. crushed red pepper, 12 chopped pepperoni slices, and 3 minced garlic cloves; sauté 2 minutes. Add 1 (8-oz.) can unsalted tomato sauce, ¼ tsp. kosher salt, and ⅛ tsp. sugar; cook, stirring occasionally, until slightly thickened, about 4 minutes. Serves 4 (serving size: ¼ cup)

CALORIES 108; FAT 10g (sat 2g, unsat 7g); PROTEIN 2g; CARB 4g; FIBER 1g; SUGARS 2g (added sugars 0g); SODIUM 222mg; CALC 2% DV; POTASSIUM 6% DV

Fast • Gluten Free
Make Ahead • Vegetarian
Pear and White Balsamic Chutney
This sweet, fruity, herby chutney pairs best with pork. Try it on roasted pork tenderloin, seared pork chops, or ham. If you don't have white balsamic on hand, use 1½ tablespoons apple cider vinegar.

Heat 1½ Tbsp. olive oil in a medium skillet over medium-high. Add ⅓ cup finely chopped shallots and 2 tsp. minced peeled fresh ginger; sauté 3 minutes. Add 2 cups chopped peeled Anjou pear (about 2 pears), 1 Tbsp. brown sugar, and ¼ tsp. kosher salt; sauté 4 minutes. Stir in ¼ cup golden raisins and 2 Tbsp. white balsamic vinegar; cook 10 minutes. Stir in 1 tsp. chopped fresh rosemary. Serves 6 (serving size: about 3½ Tbsp.)

CALORIES 100; FAT 4g (sat 0g, unsat 3g); PROTEIN 1g; CARB 18g; FIBER 2g; SUGARS 12g (added sugars 2g); SODIUM 85mg; CALC 1% DV; POTASSIUM 4% DV

Steak with Mixed Olive Tapenade, Butternut Squash, and Green Beans

Hands-on: 20 min. **Total:** 25 min.
Make this elegant meal in a flash with savvy finds: The olive bar is key to the steak topping, frozen squash makes a sweet side, and spiralized beets add a lovely touch.

1 (12-oz.) pkg. steam-in-bag frozen butternut squash
¾ tsp. kosher salt, divided
2 oz. pitted marinated olives, finely chopped (about 3 Tbsp.)
3 Tbsp. minced shallot
3 Tbsp. extra-virgin olive oil, divided
2 Tbsp. fresh orange juice, divided
1 Tbsp. red wine vinegar
1 tsp. grated orange rind
¼ tsp. crushed red pepper
1 (8-oz.) pkg. haricots verts (French green beans)
2 oz. prespiralized red beets
Cooking spray
1 (1-lb.) flank steak, halved lengthwise
½ tsp. black pepper
1 Tbsp. chopped fresh flat-leaf parsley

1. Cook squash according to package directions. Place squash in a bowl; stir in ¼ teaspoon salt.
2. Combine olives, shallot, 2 tablespoons oil, 1 tablespoon juice, vinegar, rind, and crushed red pepper in a bowl.
3. Bring a large saucepan filled with water to a boil. Add haricots verts; cook until crisp-tender, about 4 minutes. Place beets in a colander; drain haricots verts over beets. Place mixture in a bowl. Add remaining 1 tablespoon oil and remaining 1 tablespoon juice; toss.
4. Heat a grill pan or large skillet over high; coat with cooking spray. Sprinkle steak with black pepper and remaining ½ teaspoon salt. Add steak to pan; cook to desired degree of doneness, 4 to 5 minutes per side for medium-rare. Place steak on a cutting board; let stand 5 minutes. Cut across the grain into thin slices.
5. Divide butternut squash, haricots verts mixture, and steak among 4 plates. Top steak with olive mixture. Sprinkle servings with parsley. Serves 4 (serving size: about 3½ oz. steak, 2 Tbsp. olive mixture, 1 cup bean mixture, and ½ cup squash)

CALORIES 341; FAT 19g (sat 4g, unsat 13g); PROTEIN 25g; CARB 19g; FIBER 4g; SUGARS 6g (added sugars 0g); SODIUM 737mg; CALC 8% DV; POTASSIUM 23% DV

Crispy Oven-Fried Chicken

Hands-on: 15 min. **Total:** 8 hr. 15 min.

1 qt. whole buttermilk
1 Tbsp. kosher salt
2 tsp. hot sauce (such as Tabasco)
3 lb. assorted skinless, bone-in chicken pieces (thighs and drumsticks; breasts cut in half crosswise)
Cooking spray
1½ cups panko (Japanese breadcrumbs)
¾ cup whole-wheat flour
2 oz. finely grated fresh Parmigiano-Reggiano cheese (about ½ cup)
1 tsp. garlic powder
1 tsp. onion powder
1 tsp. sweet paprika

1. Combine first 3 ingredients in a large bowl; stir until salt dissolves. Add chicken; submerge in with buttermilk mixture. Cover bowl. Refrigerate 8 hours (or at least 2 hours and up to 24 hours).
2. Preheat oven to 400°F.
3. Place a wire rack on a baking sheet; coat rack with cooking spray. Combine panko and remaining ingredients in a large bowl; stir well. Remove chicken from marinade, one piece at a time, letting excess drip off; dredge in panko mixture to coat. Place coated chicken on prepared rack. Repeat with remaining chicken and panko mixture. Spray coated chicken with cooking spray. Place chicken in oven; bake at 400°F for 30 minutes or until browned and meat is done. Let stand 10 minutes; serve. Serves 8 (serving size: about 3 oz. meat)

CALORIES 290; FAT 7g (sat 2g, unsat 3g); PROTEIN 37g; CARB 18g; FIBER 2g; SUGARS 2g (added sugars 0g); SODIUM 371mg; CALC 7% DV; POTASSIUM 15% DV

THE DIFFERENCE-MAKERS

THESE HELP MAKE OUR OVEN-FRIED CHICKEN AS SOUL-SATISFYING AS DEEP-FRIED.

PARMIGIANO-REGGIANO
This crisps easily, binds the crumbs, and adds umami flavor, so there's no need for salt in the breading.

BUTTERMILK
Its tangy acids tenderize meat. With salt, the milk becomes a brine, seasoning the chicken throughout.

ALLIUM POWDERS
For classic fried chicken flavor. Unlike fresh garlic or onion, these won't scorch or add moisture to the coating.

WHOLE-WHEAT FLOUR
A healthier choice than white flour, its deeper flavor complements roasted meats.

THE BEST SPAGHETTI SQUASH TRICK

Do you halve spaghetti squash to get at the "spaghetti"? Try the ring method instead for long, flowing strands that won't sog out.

Gluten Free

Spaghetti Squash Shrimp Scampi

Hands-on: 20 min. **Total:** 1 hr. 20 min.

1 (2.5-lb.) spaghetti squash
Cooking spray
1½ Tbsp. unsalted butter
1½ Tbsp. olive oil
¼ tsp. crushed red pepper
3 garlic cloves, minced
8 oz. large raw shrimp, peeled and deveined
5 oz. fresh baby spinach
⅜ tsp. kosher salt

1. Preheat oven to 375°F. Trim off squash ends. Cut remaining squash into 1½-inch rings; scoop out and discard seeds and membranes. Arrange rings on a foil-lined baking sheet coated with cooking spray. Coat rings with cooking spray. Bake at 375°F for 45 minutes or until just tender. Cool slightly. Cut through each ring and open slightly to reach strands; carefully scrape out spaghetti-like squash strands.
2. Heat butter and oil in a medium skillet over medium-high. Add pepper and garlic; cook 30 seconds, stirring constantly. Add shrimp; sauté 2 minutes or until almost done. Add spinach, tossing until spinach wilts. Add squash strands; sprinkle with salt. Toss gently to combine. Serves 2 (serving size: about 2 cups)

CALORIES 349; FAT 21g (sat 7g, unsat 12g); PROTEIN 20g; CARB 24g; FIBER 6g; SUGARS 8g (added sugars 0g); SODIUM 638mg; CALC 20% DV; POTASSIUM 25% DV

THE STEPS

1. CUT SQUASH INTO RINGS
The squash's strands run horizontally in circles around the inside of the squash. To get the longest "spaghetti," cut the squash crosswise into rings. First, trim off a small slice from the stem and blossom ends, and discard. Then cut the remaining squash into 1½-inch rings.

2. SCRAPE OUT THE SEEDS
Clean out each squash ring by scraping away and discarding the seeds and stringy membranes in the center. Scoop with the edge of a large spoon, or try scraping with the blunt side of a paring or utility knife.

3. BAKE, COOL, AND SEPARATE
Coat squash rings with cooking spray; bake at 375°F until al dente. Cool slightly, then cut through the outer edge of each ring so that you can open it a bit and get the full length of the strands. Gently scrape out strands (your fingers may work best here since the strands are delicate).

4. LOOK AT THE DIFFERENCE
Squash that's cut lengthwise (at left, above) gives you strands that are half as long as they could be; these shorter strands can overcook and grow soggy faster compared with the longer strands that maintain their texture better.

1 LIST 3 DINNERS

Shop this list to feed four for three nights, all for about $30. Read the recipes first to be sure you have the staples on hand.

5 limes

2 English cucumbers

3 red bell peppers

1 avocado

1 bunch cilantro

2 (5-oz.) pkg. baby kale

1 yellow onion

2 lb. sweet potatoes

Unsalted roasted almonds

Quinoa

1 (13.5-oz.) can light coconut milk

Thai red curry paste

Unsalted almond butter

Cotija cheese

1¾ lb. skinless, boneless chicken breasts

Gluten Free

Almond-Coconut Chicken Satay

Hands-on: 20 min. **Total:** 40 min.
Don't worry about the extra coconut milk in the can; you'll use it up in the next recipe. Wooden skewers can burn on a grill pan, so soak them for 10 to 20 minutes first. You can also use metal skewers (handle with an oven mitt or potholder).

½ cup unsalted almond butter
⅓ cup light coconut milk, well stirred
6 Tbsp. fresh lime juice (about 3 limes), divided
4 tsp. Thai red curry paste
1 lb. skinless, boneless chicken breasts, cut into bite-sized pieces
Cooking spray
8 (8-in.) wooden skewers, soaked in water
½ tsp. kosher salt, divided
3 cups thinly sliced English cucumbers
1 cup thinly sliced red bell pepper
¼ cup minced fresh cilantro
¼ tsp. black pepper
¼ tsp. crushed red pepper
2 Tbsp. unsalted roasted almonds, chopped

1. Combine almond butter, coconut milk, ¼ cup lime juice, and curry paste in a medium bowl, stirring until smooth. Place ½ cup almond butter mixture in a small bowl; reserve. Add chicken to remaining almond butter mixture; toss to coat. Refrigerate 15 minutes.
2. Remove chicken from almond butter marinade; discard marinade. Heat a grill pan over medium-high; coat with cooking spray. Thread chicken evenly onto skewers;

sprinkle with ¼ teaspoon salt. Add chicken skewers to pan; cook, stirring occasionally, until done, about 5 minutes.
3. Combine cucumbers, bell pepper, cilantro, remaining 2 tablespoons lime juice, remaining ¼ teaspoon salt, black pepper, and crushed red pepper in a bowl; toss. Serve salad with chicken skewers and reserved ½ cup almond butter mixture. Sprinkle with almonds. Serves 4 (serving size: 2 chicken skewers, 2 Tbsp. sauce, about 1 cup salad, and 1½ tsp. almonds)

CALORIES 412; **FAT** 25g (sat 3g, unsat 18g); **PROTEIN** 34g; **CARB** 16g; **FIBER** 6g; **SUGARS** 6g (added sugars 0g); **SODIUM** 646mg; **CALC** 15% DV; **POTASSIUM** 24% DV

Gluten Free • Make Ahead

Thai Chicken and Vegetable Curry

Hands-on: 15 min. **Total:** 40 min.
The vegetables make the meat almost secondary; just 12 ounces go far here. If you can't find baby kale, use spinach or lacinato kale cut into 1-inch pieces.

2 tsp. olive oil
12 oz. skinless, boneless chicken breasts, cut into 1-in. pieces
½ tsp. black pepper
¼ tsp. kosher salt
1 lb. diced peeled sweet potatoes (about 3 cups)
1 cup chopped yellow onion
1 cup chopped red bell pepper
1 Tbsp. minced garlic
1½ Tbsp. Thai red curry paste
1 (5-oz.) pkg. baby kale (about 5 cups)
1 cup light coconut milk, well stirred
1 cup unsalted chicken stock
2 cups hot cooked quinoa
3 Tbsp. fresh cilantro leaves

1. Heat the oil in a large Dutch oven over medium-high. Sprinkle chicken with black pepper and salt; cook, turning to brown on all sides, 5 minutes. Place chicken in a bowl (do not wipe out pan).

2. Add potatoes, onion, and bell pepper to pan; cook, stirring occasionally, 3 minutes. Add garlic; cook 1 minute. Stir in curry paste and kale; cook until kale wilts, about 2 minutes. Stir in coconut milk and stock; bring to a boil. Reduce heat, cover, and cook until potatoes are tender, about 15 minutes. Return chicken to pan; cook 5 minutes.

3. Divide quinoa among 4 shallow bowls. Top evenly with chicken mixture and cilantro leaves. Serves 4 (serving size: ½ cup quinoa and 1¼ cups curry)

CALORIES 471; **FAT** 11g (sat 4g, unsat 5g); **PROTEIN** 31g; **CARB** 63g; **FIBER** 10g; **SUGARS** 11g (added sugars 0g); **SODIUM** 681mg; **CALC** 20% DV; **POTASSIUM** 35% DV

Dinner 3 of 3

Gluten Free • Vegetarian

Zesty Kale and Sweet Potato Bowl

Hands-on: 20 min. **Total:** 40 min.
This loaded veggie bowl gets a touch of smoke from the spiced sweet potatoes. Chili powder and lime also give toasted almonds an addictive crust; make extra and enjoy as a snack. If you can't find Cotija cheese, substitute feta.

1 lb. diced peeled sweet potatoes (about 3 cups)
3 Tbsp. olive oil, divided
1 tsp. chili powder, divided
1 tsp. kosher salt, divided
½ tsp. black pepper, divided
1 large red bell pepper, quartered

½ cup unsalted roasted almonds, chopped
2 tsp. grated lime rind, divided
½ tsp. sugar
2 Tbsp. fresh lime juice
1 Tbsp. chopped fresh cilantro
2 cups hot cooked quinoa
4 oz. baby kale, chopped (about 4 cups)
1 oz. Cotija cheese, crumbled (about ¼ cup)
1 ripe avocado, sliced
4 lime wedges

1. Preheat oven to 400°F.

2. Combine sweet potatoes, 1½ teaspoons oil, ½ teaspoon chili powder, ⅛ teaspoon salt, and ¼ teaspoon black pepper in a bowl; toss. Arrange sweet potato mixture on one side of an aluminum foil-lined baking sheet. Place bell pepper on other side of pan; drizzle with 1½ teaspoons oil, and toss to coat. Bake until potatoes are tender and peppers are lightly charred, about 30 minutes, stirring potatoes once halfway through. Remove pan from oven. Cut bell pepper into strips.

3. Cook almonds in a small skillet over medium until toasted, 2 to 3 minutes. Add 1 teaspoon oil, remaining ½ teaspoon chili powder, ⅛ teaspoon salt, 1 teaspoon rind, and sugar; cook, stirring occasionally, 1 minute.

4. Whisk together remaining 5 teaspoons oil, remaining ¾ teaspoon salt, remaining ¼ teaspoon black pepper, remaining 1 teaspoon rind, juice, and cilantro in a bowl. Divide quinoa evenly among 4 bowls; top evenly with kale, sweet potatoes, and bell pepper. Drizzle with juice mixture; top evenly with coated almonds, Cotija, and avocado. Serve with lime wedges. Serves 4 (serving size: about 2 cups)

CALORIES 591; **FAT** 32g (sat 5g, unsat 25g); **PROTEIN** 16g; **CARB** 67g; **FIBER** 15g; **SUGARS** 10g (added sugars 1g); **SODIUM** 680mg; **CALC** 22% DV; **POTASSIUM** 36% DV

CHEERS TO YOUR HEALTH

Fast • Make Ahead Vegetarian

Carrot-Citrus Crush

Hands-on: 5 min. **Total:** 5 min.
Brighten up happy hour or Sunday brunch with this citrusy cocktail. Leafy carrot tops lend an herby backbone similar to parsley, and blood oranges infuse a berrylike sweetness. Plus, this drink boasts half your daily vitamin A and more than a third of your daily vitamin C goal.

Muddle 2 tsp. carrot top leaves and 1 (2-in.) blood orange rind strip in a cocktail shaker using the handle of a wooden spoon. Add ½ cup 100% carrot juice, ⅓ cup fresh blood orange juice, 2 Tbsp. fresh lime juice, 2 oz. vodka, 1 oz. triple sec (orange-flavored liqueur), and a handful of ice cubes to shaker; shake well for 15 seconds. Pour mixture through strainer into 2 ice-filled glasses. Garnish with a blood orange slice and carrot top leaves, if desired. Serves 2 (serving size: about ¾ cup)

CALORIES 153; **FAT** 0g; **PROTEIN** 1g; **CARB** 15g; **FIBER** 0g; **SUGARS** 7g (added sugars 0g); **SODIUM** 39mg; **CALC** 2% DV; **POTASSIUM** 7% DV

MAKE IT A MOCKTAIL

Omit vodka and triple sec. Add 2 more tablespoons blood orange juice and a dash of orange nonalcoholic bitters.

EASIEST-EVER SHEET PAN SUPPERS

Crank up the heat and load on any creative combo of protein, veg, and starch. All the magic happens on one pan, so cleanup is a breeze.

Gluten Free

Roasted Pork with Apples and Potatoes

Hands-on: 20 min. **Total:** 40 min.
This is one-pan cooking at its best. After the meat and produce are done, the browned bits in the pan get scraped up into a buttery finishing sauce.

1 (1-lb.) pork tenderloin, trimmed
3 Tbsp. olive oil, divided
1½ Tbsp. chopped fresh thyme, divided
1½ Tbsp. chopped fresh rosemary, divided
1¼ tsp. kosher salt, divided
¾ tsp. black pepper, divided
1 lb. Yukon Gold potatoes, cut into 2-in. wedges
1 large Braeburn apple, sliced (about 10 oz.)
6 oz. haricots verts (French green beans), trimmed
3 Tbsp. unsalted chicken stock
3 Tbsp. unsalted butter
1½ Tbsp. apple cider vinegar

1. Preheat oven to 500°F. Place a rimmed baking sheet in oven (do not remove pan while oven preheats).
2. Rub pork with 1 tablespoon oil, 2½ teaspoons thyme, 2½ teaspoons rosemary, ½ teaspoon salt, and ¼ teaspoon pepper. Remove pan from oven; add pork, and return to oven. Immediately reduce oven temperature to 450°F. Bake pork 5 minutes.
3. Combine remaining 2 tablespoons oil, remaining 2 teaspoons thyme, remaining 2 teaspoons rosemary, ½ teaspoon salt, remaining ¼ teaspoon pepper, potatoes, and apple in a bowl; toss.
4. Remove pan from oven; add potato mixture to pan with pork. Bake at 450°F until a thermometer inserted in pork registers 140°F, 11 to 13 minutes. Remove pork from pan; place on a cutting board. Add green beans to pan with potato mixture. Bake at 450°F until potatoes are tender, about 10 minutes.
5. Place potato mixture on a platter. Add remaining ¼ teaspoon salt, stock, butter, and vinegar to hot pan. Scrape browned bits loose with a wooden spoon, and stir until butter is melted. Cut pork into 12 slices; arrange over vegetables. Drizzle stock mixture over pork. Serves 4 (serving size: 4 oz. pork and 1 cup potato mixture)

CALORIES 421; FAT 22g (sat 8g, unsat 13g); PROTEIN 27g; CARB 31g; FIBER 4g; SUGARS 10g (added sugars 0g); SODIUM 691mg; CALC 5% DV; POTASSIUM 33% DV

> ### THE ONE SHEET PAN YOU NEED
> Look for an 18- x 13-inch heavy-duty aluminum pan with at least 1-inch sides (called a rimmed baking sheet or jelly-roll pan). The high sides will contain foods and be easier to grip. One we love: Nordic Ware Naturals for Sur la Table, $20, surlatable.com

Fast

Sheet Pan Hawaiian Shrimp

Hands-on: 15 min. **Total:** 20 min.
Rather than spreading the rice to the far edges of the sheet pan, keep it closer to the center and layer the vegetables and shrimp on top. This way their juices seep into the rice, and the teriyaki drizzle coats every bite.

2 (8.8-oz.) pkg. precooked jasmine rice
3 Tbsp. canola oil
2 cups fresh pineapple chunks (about 8 oz.)
1 large red bell pepper, cut into 1-in. pieces
1¼ lb. raw large shrimp, peeled and deveined
3 Tbsp. lower-sodium soy sauce
2 Tbsp. light brown sugar
1½ Tbsp. unseasoned rice vinegar
½ tsp. black pepper
½ cup loosely packed fresh cilantro leaves

1. Preheat oven to 450°F. Place a rimmed baking sheet in oven (do not remove pan while oven preheats).

2. Place rice and oil in a bowl. Using your fingers, break apart rice and coat with oil. Carefully remove pan from oven; spread rice mixture in an even layer in center of pan. Bake in preheated oven for 5 minutes; stir. Top rice with pineapple and bell pepper; bake at 450°F for 5 minutes. Arrange shrimp over rice mixture; bake at 450°F until shrimp are done, about 6 minutes.

3. Place soy sauce, sugar, and vinegar in a microwave-safe bowl. Microwave at HIGH 45 seconds. Whisk until sugar dissolves. Drizzle over pan. Add black pepper; toss. Sprinkle with cilantro. Serves 4 (serving size: about 5 shrimp and 1 cup rice mixture)

CALORIES 505; FAT 14g (sat 1g, unsat 11g); PROTEIN 26g; CARB 68g; FIBER 2g; SUGARS 13g (added sugars 7g); SODIUM 655mg; CALC 12% DV; POTASSIUM 10% DV

Fast · Gluten Free

Sheet Pan Flank Steak with Salsa Verde

Hands-on: 10 min. **Total:** 20 min.
Italian salsa verde, a combo of olive oil, parsley, capers, and crushed red pepper, perks up this simple main. Serve with roasted potatoes or brown rice to complete the meal.

1 (1-lb.) flank steak, trimmed
1 tsp. kosher salt, divided
¾ tsp. black pepper, divided
6 Tbsp. extra-virgin olive oil, divided
1 lb. broccoli heads, cut into florets with stem attached
1 medium-sized red onion, cut into wedges
¼ cup chopped fresh flat-leaf parsley
3 Tbsp. red wine vinegar
1½ Tbsp. chopped fresh oregano
1 Tbsp. capers, chopped
¼ tsp. crushed red pepper

1. Preheat broiler with oven rack in top position. Place a rimmed baking sheet in oven (do not remove pan while oven preheats).

2. Sprinkle steak with ½ teaspoon salt and ½ teaspoon black pepper. Carefully remove pan from oven; add 1 tablespoon oil to pan, tilting pan to coat. Add steak to pan; broil 5 minutes. Remove pan from oven; turn steak over. Add 1 tablespoon oil to pan around steak. Arrange broccoli and onion evenly around steak; sprinkle vegetables with ¼ teaspoon salt and remaining ¼ teaspoon black pepper. Return pan to oven; broil until a thermometer inserted in steak registers 140°F, about 5 minutes. Place steak on a cutting board. Continue to broil vegetables until tender and lightly charred, about 5 minutes.

3. Whisk together remaining ¼ teaspoon salt, remaining ¼ cup oil, parsley, vinegar, oregano, capers, and red pepper in a bowl. Cut steak against the grain into thin slices. Spoon parsley mixture evenly over steak. Serve with vegetable mixture. Serves 4 (serving size: 3 oz. steak and about 1½ cups vegetables)

CALORIES 406; FAT 27g (sat 5g, unsat 21g); PROTEIN 28g; CARB 11g; FIBER 4g; SUGARS 3g (added sugars 0g); SODIUM 635mg; CALC 10% DV; POTASSIUM 23% DV

7 TIPS FOR PERFECT SHEET PAN COOKING

1. ADD IN STAGES
Foods of varying sizes and densities will take different lengths of time in the oven. Start cooking meats first. Add hearty vegetables (like potatoes) a few minutes later and delicate veggies (greens, green beans) last.

2. POSITION WISELY
Place whole proteins in the center of the sheet pan (where they'll absorb the most heat), and scatter the vegetables on both sides.

3. AIM FOR UNIFORM SIZES
Cut vegetables to the same size and shape (too large and they won't cook through, too small and they'll burn). Look for meat cuts of the same thickness so they'll cook evenly.

4. PREHEAT THE PAN
Place the baking sheet in the oven as it preheats to create a sizzling surface for the food; this will create a browned crust.

5. KEEP MOISTURE OUT
Excess water is the enemy of sheet pan cooking because the oven has to work harder to evaporate moisture before it can brown and cook the food. Pat meat and rinsed veggies dry before cooking.

6. DON'T OVERCROWD
Allow room on the pan for air to circulate around the food. If food is packed too tightly, any moisture that's released won't evaporate—giving you soggy results.

7. TEST FOR DONENESS
It's hard to tell when meats are done when you can't prod them throughout cooking as you would on a stovetop. Take their temp with a meat thermometer.

Lemon Chicken with Artichokes and Kale

Hands-on: 10 min. **Total:** 25 min.
Smaller chicken breasts (about 5 ounces each) will cook more easily in the time frame. Trim larger breasts to size and use the remaining chicken for tomorrow's soup or stir-fry.

1 (6-oz.) bunch lacinato kale, stemmed and torn into large pieces
3 Tbsp. olive oil, divided
4 (5-oz.) skinless, boneless chicken breasts
½ tsp. black pepper
¼ tsp. kosher salt
2 (9-oz.) pkg. frozen artichokes, thawed and patted dry
1 lemon, cut into quarters
1 Tbsp. chopped fresh thyme, divided
2 oz. Parmigiano-Reggiano cheese, finely grated (about ½ cup)
¼ tsp. crushed red pepper

1. Preheat broiler to high with oven rack in top position. Place a rimmed baking sheet in oven (do not remove pan while oven preheats).
2. Combine kale and 1 tablespoon oil in a bowl; massage leaves with your hands until slightly wilted.
3. Sprinkle chicken with black pepper and salt. Carefully remove pan from oven. Add 1 tablespoon oil to pan; tilt pan to coat. Add chicken to pan; broil 5 minutes. Add artichokes and lemon quarters to pan. Drizzle with remaining 1 tablespoon oil, and sprinkle with 1½ teaspoons thyme. Broil until chicken is done, 10 to 12 minutes. Place chicken on a cutting board. Add kale mixture to pan; broil until kale is frizzled and edges are crisp, 3 to 5 minutes.
4. Return chicken to pan; sprinkle with remaining 1½ teaspoons thyme, cheese, and red pepper. Squeeze lemon quarters over chicken and vegetables. Serves 4 (serving size: 5 oz. chicken and about 1 cup vegetables)

CALORIES 417; FAT 19g (sat 5g, unsat 12g); PROTEIN 40g; CARB 20g; FIBER 10g; SUGARS 2g (added sugars 0g); SODIUM 560mg; CALC 28% DV; POTASSIUM 15% DV

Sheet Pan Curried Tofu with Vegetables

Hands-on: 10 min. **Total:** 25 min.
Preheating the pan will help the potatoes and tofu achieve a crispy exterior; be careful when adding the vegetable mixture to the hot pan.

1 lb. sweet potatoes, peeled and cut into 1½-in. cubes
1 (14-oz.) pkg. extra-firm water-packed tofu, drained, patted dry, and cut into 1½-in. cubes
3 Tbsp. olive oil, divided
4 tsp. red curry powder or Madras curry powder
1¼ tsp. kosher salt, divided
Cooking spray
8 oz. fresh cauliflower florets
⅓ cup plain 2% reduced-fat Greek yogurt
1½ Tbsp. fresh lime juice
¼ cup torn fresh mint
¼ cup chopped unsalted cashews
¼ cup pomegranate arils

1. Preheat oven to 500°F. Place a rimmed baking sheet in oven (do not remove pan while oven preheats).
2. Combine potatoes, tofu, 2 tablespoons oil, curry powder, and 1 teaspoon salt in a bowl; toss to coat. Carefully remove pan from oven. Coat pan with cooking spray. Arrange potato mixture in a single layer on pan; bake at 500°F for 10 minutes, stirring once after 5 minutes. Add remaining 1 tablespoon oil and cauliflower to pan; toss gently to combine. Bake at 500°F until potatoes are tender, 10 to 12 minutes. Remove pan from oven.
3. Whisk together remaining ¼ teaspoon salt, yogurt, and juice in a small bowl. Drizzle yogurt mixture evenly over tofu mixture. Sprinkle with mint, cashews, and pomegranate arils. Serves 4 (serving size: about 2 cups)

CALORIES 390; FAT 21g (sat 4g, unsat 16g); PROTEIN 16g; CARB 37g; FIBER 6g; SUGARS 7g (added sugars 0g); SODIUM 690mg; CALC 16% DV; POTASSIUM 18% DV

WHY THE WARP?

Metal expands as it heats and contracts as it cools, which explains why the pan may twist with an audible "pop" in the oven or when cold foods hit a preheated pan. Not to worry: It should straighten as the temperature evens out.

CHICKEN + RICE

The World's Best Chicken and Rice Dishes

From Singapore's iconic Hainanese chicken rice, to a poultry-studded paella, to a creamy Minnesota-style chicken and wild rice soup, here's global comfort food to satisfy any craving.

Staff Favorite • Make Ahead

Hainanese Chicken

Hands-on: 30 min. **Total:** 2 hr.
Chicken rice is one of Singapore's most beloved dishes. It's deceptively plain-looking but loaded with flavor.

HOT SAUCE
3 red Fresno chiles, stems removed
1 medium-sized red bell pepper, seeded and coarsely chopped
⅓ cup rice vinegar
¼ cup granulated sugar
1 Tbsp. Sriracha chili sauce
1 Tbsp. lower-sodium soy sauce

CHICKEN
3 oz. peeled fresh ginger, divided
12 cups water
8 cilantro sprigs
1 garlic head, split horizontally
2¼ tsp. kosher salt, divided
1 (3½- to 4-lb.) whole chicken
1 Tbsp. grapeseed oil
1 Tbsp. minced garlic (about 3 garlic cloves)
2 cups uncooked jasmine rice
2 tomatoes, cut into wedges
1 English cucumber, sliced
4 scallions, thinly sliced
2 Tbsp. chopped fresh cilantro
8 tsp. sweet soy sauce (such as ABC)

1. To prepare hot sauce, process all sauce ingredients in a blender until smooth.

2. To prepare chicken, coarsely chop 2 ounces fresh ginger; mince remaining 1 ounce ginger. Bring 12 cups water, chopped ginger, cilantro sprigs, garlic head, and 2 teaspoons salt to a boil in a large Dutch oven over high. Add chicken. Reduce heat to medium and cover. Simmer 20 minutes. Remove from heat. Let chicken stand in broth until cooked through, about 30 minutes. Remove skin. Pick meat from chicken and reserve; discard skin and bones. Pour broth through a fine wire-mesh strainer into a bowl; discard solids. Reserve 4 cups broth; reserve remaining broth for another use.

3. Place oil, minced garlic, and minced ginger in a large saucepan; cook over high, stirring often, until garlic sizzles and ginger turns golden, about 30 seconds. Add rice, 3 cups reserved broth, and remaining ½ teaspoon salt; bring to a boil. Cover and simmer 12 minutes. Remove from heat. Let stand 12 minutes; fluff with a fork.

4. Spread rice on a platter. Top with chicken; pour remaining 1 cup reserved broth over chicken. Arrange tomato wedges and cucumber slices on rice. Sprinkle with the scallions and cilantro. Serve with hot sauce and sweet soy sauce. Serves 8 (serving size: about ½ cup chicken and ¾ cup rice)

CALORIES 514; FAT 8g (sat 2g, unsat 5g); PROTEIN 51g; CARB 55g; FIBER 3g; SUGARS 12g (added sugars 9g); SODIUM 685mg; CALC 6% DV; POTASSIUM 24% DV

Chicken Adobo

Hands-on: 20 min. **Total:** 2 hr. 40 min.

2 lb. bone-in, skin-on chicken thighs (about 8 medium chicken thighs)
1½ cups rice vinegar
¼ cup lower-sodium soy sauce
8 garlic cloves, smashed
3 Thai chiles, split
2 bay leaves
1 Tbsp. canola oil
3 cups hot cooked jasmine rice
¼ cup shaved scallions
2 Tbsp. torn fresh mint
2 Tbsp. torn fresh basil

1. Combine chicken, vinegar, soy sauce, garlic, chiles, and bay leaves in a large ziplock plastic bag; seal and chill 2 hours or up to overnight. Remove chicken from marinade. Pour marinade through a fine wire-mesh strainer into a bowl, and discard solids. Reserve marinade.

2. Heat oil in a Dutch oven over medium-high. Cook half of chicken in hot oil until browned on both sides, about 7 minutes. Remove from pan; repeat with remaining chicken. Discard drippings.

3. Place browned chicken thighs and reserved marinade in pot; bring to a boil over medium-high. Cover and reduce heat to medium-low; simmer until chicken is done, about 25 minutes. Spread rice on a platter, and top with chicken.

4. Increase heat to medium-high; cook sauce until reduced to ½ cup, about 6 minutes. Remove from heat. Skim fat from sauce; discard fat.

5. Drizzle chicken with half of sauce; serve remaining sauce on the side. Sprinkle chicken with scallions, mint, and basil. Serves 6 (serving size: 1⅓ chicken thighs and ½ cup rice)

CALORIES 314; FAT 10g (sat 4g, unsat 5g); PROTEIN 22g; CARB 39g; FIBER 1g; SUGARS 1g (added sugars 0g); SODIUM 474mg; CALC 2% DV; POTASSIUM 9% DV

Chicken Paella

Hands-on: 30 min. **Total:** 55 min.
A Spanish dish from the Valencia region, paella is named for the cooking vessel itself: a round, shallow pan made of carbon steel that heats quickly and evenly. A good paella pan helps develop the socarrat, or crispy layer of rice crust on the bottom that's the most prized part of the dish. A large skillet will work as well if you don't have a paella pan. Look for short-grain Bomba or Valencia rice at specialty markets. Be aware that risotto rice like Arborio won't work here, since paella rice isn't meant to be creamy.

1 tsp. grated lemon rind
2 Tbsp. fresh lemon juice
½ tsp. saffron threads, crushed
3 Tbsp. olive oil
8 (6-oz.) skin-on, bone-in chicken thighs, divided
1 tsp. black pepper
1½ tsp. kosher salt, divided
1½ cups chopped yellow onion
1½ Tbsp. chopped fresh thyme
5 garlic cloves, minced
1½ cups uncooked Bomba rice
⅓ cup dry white wine
3 cups unsalted chicken stock
2 cups frozen green peas
1 red bell pepper, torn into pieces
3 Tbsp. chopped fresh flat-leaf parsley
Lemon wedges

1. Stir together lemon rind, juice, and saffron in a small bowl; set aside.
2. Heat oil in a 13- to 15-inch paella pan or skillet with lid over medium-high. Sprinkle chicken with black pepper and ¾ teaspoon salt. Add 4 chicken thighs to pan; cook, skin side down, until golden brown, about 6 minutes. Turn chicken over; cook until browned, about 3 minutes. Transfer chicken to a plate; repeat with remaining 4 chicken thighs. Add onion, thyme, and garlic to pan; cook, stirring often, 4 minutes. Add rice; cook, stirring often, 2 minutes. Add wine; cook until reduced by about half, about 2 minutes. Stir in lemon juice mixture, stock, and remaining ¾ teaspoon salt. Nestle chicken, skin side up, into rice. Cover and reduce heat to medium; simmer until rice is just al dente, about 18 minutes. Uncover pan.
3. Add peas and red pepper pieces. Increase heat to medium-high; cook until rice begins to brown on the bottom and edges of pan, about 5 minutes. Remove from heat. Sprinkle with parsley; serve with lemon wedges. Serves 8 (serving size: 1 chicken thigh and about ½ cup rice mixture)

CALORIES 459; FAT 18g (sat 4g, unsat 14g); PROTEIN 40g; CARB 38g; FIBER 4g; SUGARS 4g (added sugars 0g); SODIUM 569mg; CALC 2% DV; POTASSIUM 4% DV

Chicken and Wild Rice Soup

Hands-on: 20 min. **Total:** 1 hr. 30 min.
A favorite in Minnesota, a region known for its wild rice, this dish is a bowl of pure comfort. Sherry adds a touch of acidic brightness to balance the creamy, starchy broth. If you can't find celery root, use a russet potato instead.

2 Tbsp. unsalted butter
2 (8-oz.) skinless, boneless chicken breasts
8 oz. sliced fresh cremini mushrooms
½ cup thinly sliced shallots (about 2 large shallots)
1 Tbsp. chopped fresh thyme
¼ cup dry sherry
2 Tbsp. all-purpose flour
6 cups unsalted chicken stock, divided
1 cup uncooked Minnesota wild rice
1 cup chopped carrot
1 cup chopped peeled celery root
1¼ tsp. kosher salt
1 cup green beans, cut into 1-in. pieces
¼ cup heavy cream
¾ tsp. black pepper
1 Tbsp. extra-virgin olive oil
2 oz. Parmesan cheese, grated (about ½ cup)

1. Heat butter in a large Dutch oven over medium-high until foamy. Add chicken and cook, turning occasionally, until browned on both sides, about 8 minutes. Remove from pan; let stand 5 minutes. Cut into bite-sized pieces and set aside.
2. Add mushrooms, shallots, and thyme to Dutch oven; cook, stirring often, until slightly browned, about 7 minutes. Add sherry; cook until reduced by about half, about 1 minute.
3. Whisk together flour and 1 cup stock; stir into sherry mixture. Add remaining 5 cups stock, rice, carrot, celery root, and salt. Cover and increase heat to high; bring to a boil. Reduce heat to medium-low; simmer until vegetables are just tender, about 40 minutes. Add chicken and green beans; simmer until beans are crisp-tender, about 5 minutes. Add cream and pepper.
4. Ladle soup into bowls. Drizzle evenly with oil, and sprinkle with cheese. Serves 8 (serving size: about 1½ cups)

CALORIES 311; FAT 11g (sat 5g, unsat 5g); PROTEIN 23g; CARB 28g; FIBER 3g; SUGARS 5g (added sugars 0g); SODIUM 612mg; CALC 11% DV; POTASSIUM 17% DV

RICE COOKING RATIOS

IF YOU HAVE EXTRA RICE ON HAND THAT YOU'D LIKE TO COOK UP, WE'VE FOUND THAT PACKAGE INSTRUCTIONS DON'T ALWAYS LEAD TO PERFECTLY COOKED GRAINS. HERE ARE THE GUIDELINES OUR RECIPE TESTERS FOLLOW. BRING WATER TO A BOIL, AND STIR IN RICE. REDUCE HEAT TO LOW, COVER, AND SIMMER FOR THE TIME INDICATED.

RICE	AMOUNT	WATER	TIME	YIELD
Long-Grain White	1 cup	1¼ cups	16 minutes	3 cups
Long-Grain Brown	1 cup	2½ cups	40 minutes	3½ cups
Bomba (Short Grain)	1 cup	2½ cups	18 minutes	3 cups
Jasmine	1 cup	1½ cups	18 minutes	3 cups
Basmati	1 cup	1½ cups	18 minutes	3 cups
Wild	1 cup	3 cups	45 minutes	3 cups

Gluten Free

Chicken Biryani

Hands-on: 20 min. **Total:** 2 hr. 45 min. A standard in Indian cuisine, biryani gets plenty of flavor and fragrance from the spice mix, which typically includes turmeric, cardamom, ginger, and cumin. We use basmati rice here, which is a delicate white rice with an almost floral aroma. We particularly like Royal brand basmati, which has extraordinarily long grains.

1 cup plain 2% reduced-fat
 Greek yogurt
1 Tbsp. ground turmeric
2 tsp. ground cumin
¼ tsp. ground red pepper
1½ lb. skinless, boneless chicken
 thighs, cut into 1½-in. cubes
2 Tbsp. olive oil
1 Tbsp. minced peeled fresh ginger
5 garlic cloves, minced
4 cardamom pods, crushed
1½ cups uncooked basmati rice
2 cups unsalted chicken stock
1 cup coarsely chopped carrot
½ cup raisins
1 tsp. kosher salt
1 cinnamon stick
2 Tbsp. heavy cream
¼ cup unsalted dry-roasted
 cashews, chopped
2 Tbsp. chopped fresh cilantro
2 Tbsp. crispy fried onions
1 thinly sliced serrano chile
Lime wedges

1. Stir together yogurt, turmeric, cumin, and red pepper in a large bowl. Add chicken pieces; toss to coat. Cover and chill 2 to 4 hours. **2.** Combine oil, ginger, garlic, and cardamom in a large, high-sided skillet, and cook over medium-high, stirring often, until ginger begins to sizzle and toast, about 1 minute. Add rice; cook, stirring constantly, until rice is toasted, about 1 minute. Add stock, carrot, raisins, salt, and cinnamon. **3.** Remove chicken from marinade; discard remaining marinade. Place chicken in an even layer on rice mixture. Cover and increase heat to high; bring to a boil. Reduce heat to medium-low, and simmer until chicken is done and rice is tender, about 15 minutes. Remove from heat. Remove and discard cinnamon stick. Let stand 5 minutes. Stir in cream. **4.** Serve in shallow bowls. Sprinkle servings evenly with cashews, cilantro, crispy fried onions, and serrano slices. Serve with lime wedges. Serves 6 (serving size: 3 oz. chicken and about 1 cup rice mixture)

CALORIES 508; **FAT** 16g (sat 5g, unsat 9g); **PROTEIN** 33g; **CARB** 63g; **FIBER** 4g; **SUGARS** 11g (added sugars 0g); **SODIUM** 502mg; **CALC** 9% DV; **POTASSIUM** 7% DV

Chicken, Shrimp, and Rice Stew

Hands-on: 30 min. **Total:** 1 hr. 10 min. This stew is based on the savory rice porridge congee, which has roots in Chinese, Thai, and Korean cuisines. This version is inspired by a recipe from North Carolina chef Andrea Reusing.

8 oz. raw large shrimp, peeled and deveined
8 oz. skinless, boneless chicken thighs
2 tsp. kosher salt
½ cup finely chopped shallots (about 2 large shallots)
2 Tbsp. fish sauce
1 tsp. granulated sugar
¾ tsp. black pepper, divided
1 cup uncooked jasmine rice
3 Tbsp. canola oil
2 tsp. minced peeled fresh ginger
2 tsp. minced garlic
8 cups water
4 cups packed baby bok choy leaves or spinach (about 8 oz.)
2 cups frozen small green peas, thawed
1 cup chopped scallions (about 4 scallions)
¾ cup chopped fresh cilantro
¼ cup chopped fresh mint
2 tsp. fresh lime juice

1. Cut shrimp in half lengthwise. Cut shrimp pieces in half crosswise, and place in a large bowl. Cut chicken into 2-inch-wide strips, and add to bowl. Sprinkle with salt, and toss to coat. Let stand 10 minutes; rinse well. Add shallots, fish sauce, sugar, and ½ teaspoon pepper; stir to combine. Let stand at room temperature 30 minutes.

2. Place rice in a mini food processor. Process until rice is broken into very small pieces, about 2 minutes. (This also can be done in a spice grinder or coffee mill in 2 batches.) Set aside.

3. Place oil, ginger, and garlic in a large Dutch oven; cook over medium, stirring often, until fragrant and beginning to brown, 2 to 3 minutes. Add shrimp and chicken mixture and any accumulated juices; cook, stirring often, until shrimp turn pink, 5 to 6 minutes.

4. Stir in rice. Gradually stir in 8 cups water. Cover and increase heat to high. Bring to a boil, and cook 6 to 7 minutes. Uncover and reduce heat to medium. Cook, stirring often, until rice is tender and liquid is thickened, 18 to 20 minutes. Stir in bok choy, peas, and scallions; cook 2 minutes. Remove from heat. Stir in cilantro, mint, lime juice, and remaining ¼ teaspoon pepper. Serves 8 (serving size: 1⅓ cups)

CALORIES 228; **FAT** 7g (sat 1g, unsat 6g); **PROTEIN** 14g; **CARB** 27g; **FIBER** 3g; **SUGARS** 4g (added sugars 1g); **SODIUM** 541mg; **CALC** 8% DV; **POTASSIUM** 9% DV

THE BREAKDOWN: 4 SIMPLE STEPS

After a quick dry brine that lets the salt permeate the shrimp and chicken, marinate them with fish sauce and seasonings.

Process the rice into tiny bits that will release more creamy starch and cook into porridge faster than full grains.

Cook the shrimp and chicken, along with their marinade, just until the shrimp are opaque.

The cracked rice bits simmer to a creamy consistency and become evenly infused with the marinade flavors.

A HEALTHY COOK'S GUIDE TO OILS

Here's the lowdown on the everyday and specialty oils that will elevate your cooking and create healthier, tastier dishes.

Oil is every cook's go-to fat, in part because of its versatility but also for its ability to make food so tasty. Fat tenderizes and conducts heat, letting us cook foods well past the boiling point of water in order to dry out their surface. This is how, with a little oil in the pan, we get a perfectly crusted steak or a crisp shell on a cube of tofu. But despite its workhorse status, oil is often a second-rate ingredient in too many kitchens; too often, what's most affordable and easiest to find determines which varieties end up in our pantries, and quality, taste, and diversity often take a back seat.

Calorie-wise, oils are all about the same (120 calories per tablespoon), as is their fat content (around 14g per tablespoon). And they're devoid of protein, sodium, and fiber. But where oils differ is in their fat composition, with some having more saturated, polyunsaturated, or monounsaturated fats than others. Most oils predominately comprise polyunsaturated and monounsaturated fats, but all oils have a little bit of each type of fat in them. Saturated fat is the one to limit, as it raises your blood cholesterol. The two unsaturated fats are so-called healthy fats because research shows they're good for your heart and brain. You can enjoy them more liberally, but understand that you shouldn't deploy them with wild abandon because calories will skyrocket.

There are other ways fat is good for us, too: It helps our cells "speak" to one another, is key for neurological development, and helps us absorb fat-soluble vitamins (like vitamins A, D, E, and K) and some plant pigments, such as lycopene in red-hued produce. See, you need fat. So dig in: We rounded up our favorite oils and created tasty recipes so you can try them out. We hope you'll find a new oil to add to your pantry.

SESAME OIL

Smoke point: 350°F (toasted); 445°F (refined)

Uniquely equal parts mono- and polyunsaturated fats, sesame oil is packed with lignans, compounds that may help improve cholesterol and blood pressure. In one small study, adults on blood pressure meds who used sesame oil as their exclusive oil for 45 days saw their blood pressure dip to a healthy range. After they stopped? Their pressure returned to their above-average baseline. You'll see two sesame oils: regular/light and toasted/dark. Toasted has a more robust nutty flavor, which we prefer.

Fast • Make Ahead
Vegetarian
Thai-Style Aioli

Hands-on: 5 min. **Total:** 5 min.
Although it's not a typical Thai ingredient, sesame oil adds a savory nuttiness to this aioli. To really get the sauce's consistency creamy, slowly drizzle the oil into the food processor. Use this aioli as a spread on a sandwich, as a dip for sweet potato fries, or pair it with your vegetables for a fresh take on crudités.

1 Tbsp. minced garlic (about 3 cloves)
1 tsp. finely grated peeled fresh
   ginger
1 tsp. minced lemongrass stalk
   (from base only) (optional)
2 Tbsp. lower-sodium soy sauce
1 Tbsp. fresh lime juice (about
   1 lime)
1 tsp. light brown sugar
½ tsp. Sriracha chili sauce
1 large pasteurized egg yolk
¾ cup toasted sesame oil
¼ cup loosely packed fresh cilantro
   leaves

1. Combine garlic, ginger, and, if desired, lemongrass in a mortar and pestle; grind into a paste. Place garlic mixture in bowl of a mini food processor or food chopper. Add soy sauce, lime juice, brown sugar, Sriracha, and egg yolk; pulse until smooth. With processor running, slowly pour oil in a thin stream through food chute, and process until fully blended and creamy. Add cilantro; pulse until blended, about 30 times. Serves 12 (serving size: 1½ Tbsp.)

CALORIES 130; FAT 14g (sat 2g, unsat 12g); PROTEIN 0g; CARB 1g; FIBER 0g; SUGARS 0g (added sugars 0g); SODIUM 101mg; CALC 0% DV; POTASSIUM 0% DV

Coconut Oil Waffles

Hands-on: 30 min. **Total:** 30 min.
Look for unrefined or virgin coconut oil to provide a hint of coconut essence, which gives these waffles a unique flavo. Be sure your coconut oil is melted before adding it to your wet mixture. To continue the tropical theme, top the waffles with mango or kiwi and toasted unsweetened coconut flakes.

7⅞ oz. white whole-wheat flour
  (about 1¾ cups)
3 Tbsp. granulated sugar
2 tsp. baking powder
1 tsp. ground cinnamon
1 cup fat-free buttermilk
2 Tbsp. coconut oil, melted
2 large eggs, lightly beaten
1 large egg white, lightly beaten
Cooking spray

1. Heat a waffle iron to medium-high according to manufacturer's instructions. Stir together flour, sugar, baking powder, and cinnamon in a large bowl. Set aside.
2. Whisk together buttermilk, coconut oil, eggs, and egg white in a separate bowl. Add buttermilk mixture to flour mixture, and stir just until blended.
3. Lightly coat waffle iron with cooking spray. Spoon ⅓ heaping cup batter onto waffle iron. Cook until lightly browned, about 4 minutes. Repeat with remaining batter; serve immediately. (If not serving immediately, keep waffles warm in a 200°F oven.) Serves 4 (serving size: 2 waffles)

CALORIES 337; **FAT** 11g (sat 6g, unsat 3g); **PROTEIN** 13g; **CARB** 45g; **FIBER** 5g; **SUGARS** 10g (added sugars 9g); **SODIUM** 112mg; **CALC** 24% DV; **POTASSIUM** 7% DV

COCONUT OIL

Smoke point: 280°F (virgin); 365°F (refined)

You'll find refined, virgin (unrefined), and liquid coconut oil on store shelves. Virgin delivers bold coconut flavor that's reminiscent of summer beach trips. The refined and liquid versions are milder. Coconut oil has more saturated fat than butter at 11g per tablespoon. Research shows the tropical oil raises your "good" HDL cholesterol, but also boosts your "bad" LDL cholesterol, which ups heart disease risk. Per a 2017 report from the American Heart Association, the benefits don't outweigh the risks—so use it sparingly.

Collard-and-Chickpea Salad

Hands-on: 35 min. **Total:** 35 min.
Look for red palm oil in health-food stores, at Whole Foods, and online.

5½ Tbsp. red palm or coconut oil, divided
1½ cups canned chickpeas, rinsed and drained
¼ tsp. sea salt, divided
¼ tsp. ground red pepper
1 bunch fresh collard greens (about 10½ oz.)
1½ cups matchstick-cut carrots (about 5 carrots)
3 Tbsp. white vinegar
2 tsp. honey
⅔ cup salted dry-roasted pepitas (shelled pumpkin seeds)

1. Preheat oven to 400°F. In a small microwavable bowl, microwave oil on HIGH until melted, 30 to 45 seconds. (Skip if your oil is liquid.)
2. Toss chickpeas with 1½ tablespoons palm oil and ⅛ teaspoon sea salt. Spread on a baking sheet, and roast at 400°F for 25 minutes. Stir in ground red pepper, and roast until crispy, 5 to 10 more minutes.
3. Remove stems and ribs from collards, and thinly slice leaves into ribbons. Place in a large bowl; add carrots, and toss to combine.
4. Whisk together vinegar, honey, remaining ¼ cup liquefied oil, and remaining ⅛ teaspoon sea salt. Toss with collards and carrots; add pepitas and chickpeas. Serve immediately. Serves 6 (serving size: about 1½ cups)

CALORIES 294; **FAT** 20g (sat 8g, unsat 12g); **PROTEIN** 9g; **CARB** 21g; **FIBER** 6g; **SUGARS** 4g (added sugars 2g); **SODIUM** 169mg; **CALC** 17% DV; **POTASSIUM** 12% DV

RED PALM OIL

Smoke point: 450°F

Semisolid with a buttery, mild, carrotlike taste, red palm oil comes from the fleshy fruit of the palm tree. Its red hue is thanks to carotenoids (eye-healthy compounds also in red produce). Because red palm oil has more saturated fat than most oils (about 8g per tablespoon) and also contains squalene, which promotes cholesterol production, it is another oil to limit. Also, much of our palm oil production is environmentally unfriendly, so look for the label "Palm Done Right"—an organization known for sustainable production.

WALNUT OIL

Smoke point: 320°F

With either a bold (roasted walnut oil) or mild (regular) nutty taste, this oil is rich in polyunsaturated fats and one of the few to deliver the heart-healthy omega-3 fat alpha linoleic acid (ALA). Research suggests that walnut oil may improve blood sugar control. In a July 2016 study, adults with type 2 diabetes who added about 1 tablespoon of walnut oil to their daily diet for three months had better blood sugar control than diabetics who didn't eat walnut oil.

Pasta Aglio e Olio

Hands-on: 25 min. **Total:** 25 min.
In this riff on the traditional Italian garlic and oil pasta dish, roasted walnut oil adds an unexpected nutty flavor. Cool the walnut oil slightly before adding water to avoid splatters.

7 oz. uncooked bucatini pasta
½ cup roasted walnut oil
5 garlic cloves, thinly sliced
¼ cup chopped fresh flat-leaf
  parsley
¼ tsp. sea salt
¼ cup grated pecorino Romano
  cheese (optional)
Freshly ground black pepper
  (optional)

1. Cook pasta according to package directions for al dente, omitting salt and fat. Drain in a colander over a bowl, reserving 1 cup cooking liquid.
2. While the pasta cooks, heat walnut oil in a large skillet over medium-high. Add garlic and cook, stirring often, until golden, 3 to 4 minutes. Stir in parsley; remove from heat. Let mixture cool 2 minutes.
3. Add ½ cup reserved cooking liquid to oil mixture, and return to medium-high heat. Cook until sauce has reduced by half, about 5 minutes. Stir in cooked pasta. Add ¼ cup reserved cooking liquid and cook, stirring constantly, until sauce has thickened, about 2 minutes. Stir in remaining ¼ cup cooking liquid as needed to reach desired consistency. Season with salt; if desired, top with cheese and black pepper. Serve immediately. Serves 4 (serving size: 1 cup pasta)

CALORIES 431; **FAT** 29g (sat 2g, unsat 26g); **PROTEIN** 7g; **CARB** 39g; **FIBER** 2g; **SUGARS** 1g (added sugars 0g); **SODIUM** 146mg; **CALC** 2% DV; **POTASSIUM** 4% DV

AVOCADO OIL

Smoke point: 520°F (refined)

This slightly green oil is buttery with a mild avocado flavor. It has a high monounsaturated fat content that's similar to olive oil, but thanks to a higher smoke point, it is quite versatile in the kitchen. Avocado oil also boasts eye-healthy lutein; cholesterol-lowering phytosterols; and—in virgin varieties—chlorophyll, which is good for detoxifying cancer-causing compounds.

Garlic-Soy Chicken Stir-Fry

Hands-on: 15 min. **Total:** 20 min.

1 Tbsp. avocado oil, divided
6 (4-oz.) skinless, boneless chicken
  thighs, cut into 1-in. pieces
1 red bell pepper (about 6 oz.), sliced
6 oz. trimmed fresh green beans
4 oz. trimmed fresh sugar snap peas
¼ cup minced shallot
3 garlic cloves, thinly sliced
1 Tbsp. fish sauce
2½ tsp. lower-sodium soy sauce
2 tsp. honey
1 tsp. sambal oelek (chile paste)
1 tsp. water
½ tsp. cornstarch
¼ cup unsalted dry-roasted peanuts
3 Tbsp. sliced scallions

1. Heat 2 teaspoons oil in a wok or skillet over medium-high. Add chicken; cook, stirring often, until browned and done, 5 to 6 minutes. Remove chicken. Add remaining 1 teaspoon oil, pepper, green beans, snap peas, shallot, and garlic. Cook until crisp-tender, 5 to 7 minutes.
2. Whisk together fish and soy sauces, honey, sambal oelek, 1 teaspoon water, and cornstarch in a small bowl. Add to wok with chicken, stirring to coat chicken and veggies; cook until sauce thickens, about 2 minutes. Remove from heat; add peanuts and scallions. Serves 5 (serving size: about 1¼ cups)

CALORIES 282; **FAT** 13g (sat 3g, unsat 9g); **PROTEIN** 32g; **CARB** 12g; **FIBER** 3g; **SUGARS** 6g (added sugars 2g); **SODIUM** 525mg; **CALC** 6% DV; **POTASSIUM** 6% DV

LABEL DECODER

1. UNFILTERED
Solid elements of the original fruit, seed, nut, etc. remain in the oil. For example, with olive oil, bits of pulp and skin might be floating around or have settled at the bottom. This so-called sediment may have additional health properties, but it also can make the oil spoil faster.

2. ORGANIC
Plants that produce the fruits, seeds, and nuts for oil are grown and processed per USDA organic standards—no synthetic fertilizers or other artificial agents are used. Some say this may enhance the oil's quality, but that's not guaranteed.

3. FIRST PRESSED
As it implies, it's the first pressing of the fruit, seed, or nut to extract oil—and sometimes synonymous with the term "extra-virgin."

4. EXPELLER PRESSED
It's a mechanical way to extract oil from fruits, nuts, or seeds. Essentially, a big screw-press exerts a lot of pressure to squeeze oil out of the fruits, seeds, or nuts. But because it's less efficient—as in, less oil is made—chemical or solvent extraction has become more popular. The process of expeller pressing can also heat the oils quite a bit, upping the chances of some oils turning rancid.

5. COLD PRESSED
Typically means that an oil is extracted at a cooler temperature (and without any chemicals)—and thus may retain more of its health properties. In Europe, there are regulations that a "cold-pressed" oil must not exceed 27°C, or 80–90°F, but in the U.S. such a regulation doesn't exist.

5 MORE OILS TO BUY

THE WORKHORSE CLASS

CANOLA
Smoke point: 468°F*

Canola is a go-to oil at *Cooking Light*. We use it to sauté, oven-fry, and bake due to its neutral taste and high smoke point—the temp at which your oil literally begins to smoke. All cooking fats (butter and lard, too!) have a smoke point. When you cook it to or past its smoke point, it'll taste scorched or rancid—and not only do the good-for-you compounds start to break down, but health-harming ones form. Canola, like walnut oil, is one of the few oils that's rich in the omega-3 fat ALA—and research shows it may help lower total and "bad" LDL cholesterol.

OLIVE
Smoke point: 428°F (refined); 331°F (unrefined)

Well-known for its heart-healthy benefits, extra-virgin olive oil is frequently used in the *Cooking Light* Kitchen, mostly as a finishing oil, meaning you use it to add flavor and texture to a finished dish. (Think: dressing a salad, drizzling on roasted vegetables or fish, etc.) Research shows it can lower your risk of heart disease and death from heart disease. Other research shows it's good for your brain by possibly lowering your risk of Alzheimer's and dementia, improving the speed at which you think, and decreasing your risk of depression.

CORN
Smoke point: 453°F

This underutilized oil deserves a little more attention. Its high smoke point and very mild corn flavor make it an all-purpose oil—use it in baking, grilling, and sautéing. It's also healthier than you might think: Corn oil is the cooking oil richest in phytosterols, which are plant-based micronutrients that can reduce the amount of cholesterol your gut absorbs. One study (funded by Mazola, a company that produces corn oil) showed that people who ate foods made with corn oil lowered their cholesterol more than when they ate the same foods made with olive oil.

THE SPECIALTY CREW

PEANUT
Smoke point: 471°F (refined); 320°F (unrefined)

You're probably most familiar with refined peanut oil; it's very mild in flavor, as it has been bleached and deodorized. Because of its processing, all of the allergenic proteins have been stripped away, so refined peanut oil is safe for people with peanut allergies. Lesser-known gourmet peanut oil adds a delicious roasted peanut aroma and taste to food. It also boasts more good-for-you phytosterols, but it still contains allergenic proteins. Peanut oil also contains resveratrol, the brain- and heart-healthy compound that we associate with red wine.

GRAPESEED
Smoke point: 435°F

A byproduct of winemaking, grape seeds yield a light, neutral-tasting oil, which encourages the flavors of your ingredients to really shine. Its neutral flavor is also good for blending into salad dressings. Its high smoke point makes it ideal for sautéing and stir-frying. Numerous studies have found that grapeseed oil has both cancer-fighting and heart health–promoting benefits (thanks to its phenolic compounds), but the research is still young, and the amount of oil necessary to reap those benefits is often more than what's commonly consumed.

*All smoke points listed here are from common brands and can vary based on processing.

1 LIST 3 DINNERS

Shop this list to feed four for three nights, all for about $30. Read the recipes first to be sure you have the staples on hand.

1 lime

1 avocado

1½ lb. multicolored mini bell peppers

1 (8-oz.) container cremini mushrooms

1 (12-oz.) pkg. broccoli florets

1 (5-oz.) container baby arugula

1 (12-oz.) container refrigerated pico de gallo

1 large yellow onion

2 medium-sized sweet onions

Thyme

White balsamic vinegar

Ancho chile powder

7 large eggs

3½ oz. goat cheese

1 (1-lb.) loaf whole-grain sourdough bread

1 lb. flank steak

Fast

Fajita Panzanella Salad

Hands-on: 15 min. **Total:** 30 min.
If you can't find mini bell peppers, cut one large red and one large orange bell pepper into strips.

5 oz. whole-grain sourdough bread, cut into 1-in. cubes (about 3½ cups)
Cooking spray
1½ tsp. ground cumin, divided
1 (8-oz.) flank steak (about 1 in. thick)
½ tsp. kosher salt, divided
½ tsp. freshly ground black pepper, divided
¼ cup olive oil, divided
1 (1-lb.) pkg. multicolored mini bell peppers, cut into strips
1 large yellow onion, cut into ⅓-in. slices
1½ Tbsp. fresh lime juice
1 tsp. honey
¼ tsp. ancho chile powder
¼ cup refrigerated pico de gallo
2 oz. baby arugula (about 2 cups)

1. Preheat oven to 375°F.
2. Arrange bread in a single layer on a baking sheet; coat with cooking spray. Sprinkle with ½ teaspoon cumin. Bake at 375°F for 18 to 20 minutes or until toasted, stirring once after 10 minutes.
3. Heat a large cast-iron skillet over medium-high. Coat pan with cooking spray. Sprinkle steak with ¼ teaspoon salt and ¼ teaspoon black pepper. Add steak to pan; cook 4 minutes on each side for medium-rare or until desired degree of doneness. Place steak on a cutting board; let stand 10 minutes. Cut into 1-inch pieces.
4. Heat 1 tablespoon olive oil in a medium skillet over medium-high. Add remaining 1 teaspoon cumin, ⅛ teaspoon salt, bell peppers, and onion; cook 8 minutes, stirring occasionally.
5. Combine remaining ⅛ teaspoon salt, remaining ¼ teaspoon black pepper, remaining 3 tablespoons olive oil, lime juice, honey, and chile powder in a large bowl, stirring with a whisk. Add bread, steak, bell pepper mixture, pico de gallo, and arugula; toss to coat. Serves 4 (serving size: 1½ cups)

CALORIES 367; FAT 18g (sat 3g, unsat 13g); PROTEIN 18g; CARB 34g; FIBER 4g; SUGARS 11g (added sugars 1g); SODIUM 586mg; CALC 8% DV; POTASSIUM 17% DV

This hearty salad combines everything we love about classic fajitas—seared steak, sautéed bell peppers, and salsa—with panzanella, a Tuscan bread salad.

continued

Staff Favorite

Steak, Goat Cheese, and Onion Jam Tartine

Hands-on: 25 min. **Total:** 54 min.
We start these tartines (French for topped bread slices, though more familiar to us as open-faced sandwiches) with a caramelized onion and balsamic jam. You can make the jam and cook the steak ahead and refrigerate, then build the toasts later.

3 Tbsp. olive oil, divided
4 cups chopped sweet onion, such as Vidalia (about 2 medium)
⅜ tsp. kosher salt, divided
2 Tbsp. turbinado or light brown sugar
¼ cup white balsamic vinegar
1 tsp. chopped fresh thyme
1 (8-oz.) flank steak (about 1 in. thick)
¼ tsp. freshly ground black pepper
4 (1½-oz.) whole-grain sourdough bread slices, toasted
1 oz. baby arugula (about 1 cup)
2 oz. goat cheese, crumbled (about ½ cup)

1. Heat 2 tablespoons oil in a large skillet over medium-low. Add onions and ⅛ teaspoon salt; cook 25 minutes or until deep golden brown. Add sugar; cook 2 minutes, stirring occasionally. Stir in vinegar and thyme; cook 3 minutes, stirring frequently. Place onion mixture in a bowl.
2. Increase heat to medium-high. Add 2 teaspoons oil to pan. Sprinkle steak with remaining ¼ teaspoon salt and pepper. Add steak to pan; cook 4 minutes on each side for medium-rare or until desired degree of doneness. Place steak on a cutting board; let stand 10 minutes. Cut across the grain into thin slices.
3. Spread about ¼ cup onion mixture over each bread slice. Top evenly with steak, arugula, and goat cheese; drizzle evenly with remaining 1 teaspoon olive oil. Serves 4 (serving size: 1 tartine)

CALORIES 412; **FAT** 19g (sat 5g, unsat 13g); **PROTEIN** 18g; **CARB** 41g; **FIBER** 4g; **SUGARS** 16g (added sugars 7g); **SODIUM** 430mg; **CALC** 9% DV; **POTASSIUM** 14% DV

Fast • Gluten Free Vegetarian

Vegetable and Goat Cheese Frittata

Hands-on: 15 min. **Total:** 25 min.
A veggie-loaded frittata is a great way to use up produce odds and ends. Look for refrigerated pico de gallo in the prepared produce section of the supermarket. Serve with a simple salad made with the remaining arugula you bought.

7 large eggs
¾ tsp. kosher salt
½ tsp. freshly ground black pepper
4 tsp. olive oil
1 (8-oz.) pkg. cremini mushrooms, sliced
4 oz. multicolored mini bell peppers, cut crosswise into ¼-in.-thick rings
4 oz. small broccoli florets (about 2 cups)
1½ oz. goat cheese, crumbled (about ⅓ cup)
1 medium avocado, chopped
¼ cup refrigerated pico de gallo

1. Preheat oven to 400°F.
2. Combine eggs, salt, and black pepper in a medium bowl, stirring with a whisk.
3. Heat oil in a 10-inch ovenproof nonstick skillet over medium-high. Add the mushrooms; sauté 6 minutes. Add bell peppers and broccoli; cook 5 minutes or until tender. Remove pan from heat; pour egg mixture over vegetable mixture in pan. Sprinkle with goat cheese.
4. Bake at 400°F for 8 to 10 minutes or until egg is set. Cut into 4 wedges; top evenly with avocado and pico de gallo. Serves 4 (serving size: 1 wedge)

CALORIES 282; **FAT** 21g (sat 6g, unsat 13g); **PROTEIN** 17g; **CARB** 10g; **FIBER** 4g; **SUGARS** 4g (added sugars 0g); **SODIUM** 588mg; **CALC** 9% DV; **POTASSIUM** 18% DV

COOKING CLASS: WHY INGREDIENTS MATTER

BAKER'S HALF DOZEN

Executive Editor Ann Taylor Pittman shares the tricks to perfecting a quick-bread classic—our best banana bread.

Staff Favorite • Vegetarian Make Ahead

Banana-Walnut Bread

Hands-on: 15 min. **Total:** 1 hr. 35 min.

¾ cup whole buttermilk
½ cup plus 3 Tbsp. quick-cooking oats, divided
6 oz. (about 1⅓ cups) plus 1 Tbsp. white whole-wheat flour, divided

1 tsp. baking powder
¼ tsp. baking soda
⅝ tsp. kosher salt, divided
¾ cup plus 3 Tbsp. packed light
   brown sugar, divided
6 Tbsp. roasted walnut oil, divided
¼ cup chopped walnuts
½ tsp. ground cinnamon
1⅓ cups mashed very ripe bananas
   (about 3)
1½ tsp. vanilla extract
2 large eggs, lightly beaten
Cooking spray

1. Preheat oven to 350°F. Stir buttermilk into ½ cup oats in a bowl; let stand 10 minutes.
2. Place 1½ cups flour in a bowl. Stir in baking powder, baking soda, and ½ teaspoon salt.

3. Combine 3 tablespoons sugar, 2 tablespoons oil, nuts, cinnamon, ⅛ teaspoon salt, and remaining oats and flour in a small bowl.
4. Add bananas, vanilla, eggs, and remaining brown sugar and oil to buttermilk mixture; fold in flour mixture. Spoon batter into a 9- x 5-inch loaf pan coated with cooking spray. Sprinkle walnut streusel over top. Bake at 350°F until a wooden pick inserted in center comes out clean, 55 minutes to 1 hour. Cool in pan on a wire rack 15 minutes. Remove bread from pan; serve warm, or cool completely. Serves 16 (serving size: 1 slice)

CALORIES 190; FAT 8g (sat 1g, unsat 7g); PROTEIN 4g; CARB 27g; FIBER 2g; SUGARS 16g (added sugars 10g); SODIUM 208mg; CALC 5% DV; POTASSIUM 4% DV

BAKER'S HALF DOZEN

THESE SIX INGREDIENTS MAKE ALL THE DIFFERENCE IN PITTMAN'S HOMEMADE QUICK BREAD.

QUICK-COOKING OATS
Oats add some bulk without making the bread dense. Quick oats won't be chewy like rolled oats.

BUTTERMILK
This helps keep the bread moist and lends it an oh-so-subtle tang to balance the sugary overripe bananas.

WALNUT OIL
Fat adds moistness, and here it boosts taste, too: Use roasted walnut oil for deeper nut flavor than walnuts alone.

BAKING SODA
Acidic buttermilk needs a little alkaline baking soda for pH balance and rise. One quarter teaspoon is just right here.

BROWN SUGAR
The touch of molasses in light brown sugar gives the banana bread more complexity than plain white sugar would.

BANANAS
These should be way overripe. One trick: Put bananas in the oven while it preheats and cook them until they're black.

Fast • Make Ahead

Tuna Poke with Mango and Avocado

Hands-on: 13 min. **Total:** 13 min.
Find fresh or frozen wakame seaweed at Asian markets. You can also use fresh or frozen premixed seaweed salad. The tuna and avocado make this dish a potassium powerhouse. Serve the poke atop brown rice, if you like.

1 Tbsp. sesame oil
3 Tbsp. lower-sodium soy sauce
1 lb. sushi-grade yellowfin tuna, cut
   into ½-in. cubes
2 cups cubed mango
1 cup fresh or thawed frozen
   wakame seaweed
2 Tbsp. fresh lime juice
1 Tbsp. shaved shallot
2 tsp. very thinly sliced seeded red
   Fresno chile
1 tsp. sesame seeds, toasted
2 ripe avocados, peeled and cubed

Combine first 3 ingredients in a small bowl. Combine mango and remaining 6 ingredients in a separate medium bowl; toss gently to coat. Place mango mixture in each of 4 shallow bowls. Top each serving with tuna mixture. Serves 4 (serving size: about ¾ cup mango mixture and about ½ cup tuna mixture)

CALORIES 372; FAT 20g (sat 3g, unsat 15g); PROTEIN 30g; CARB 22g; FIBER 8g; SUGARS 9g (added sugars 0g); SODIUM 493mg; CALC 7% DV; POTASSIUM 32% DV

LIGHTEN UP NEW ENGLAND CLAM CHOWDER

An East Coast classic gets a nutritional overhaul with far less sodium and sat fat than the original.

A classic bowl of clam chowder—in all of its creamy, comforting glory—can add up to over half a day's sodium allowance and almost half a day's saturated fat. To build all the great flavor with less sodium, we skip the bottled clam juice and make a quick homemade clam stock to draw lots of flavor from the shells. Seek the freshest clams from your local fishmonger; their shells should be closed or just slightly open before cooking. Your brain will also benefit from every bit of the clams' vitamin B12 goodness (low levels are associated with a higher risk for dementia); one serving of this soup delivers 100% of your daily goal. Just ½ cup of half-and-half adds ample richness; the rest comes from the potatoes. Our chowder is so satisfying, you don't even need oyster crackers.

Staff Favorite • Gluten Free Make Ahead

New England Clam Chowder

Hands-on: 30 min. **Total:** 1 hr. 20 min.

4 lb. littleneck clams (about 4 dozen), scrubbed
4 cups plus 1 Tbsp. water, divided
1 Tbsp. canola oil
1¼ cups chopped yellow onion
1 cup chopped celery
2 garlic cloves, minced
2 lb. Yukon Gold potatoes, peeled and cut into ¼-in. pieces (about 7 cups)
1 Tbsp. white miso
1 Tbsp. chopped fresh thyme
¼ tsp. freshly ground black pepper
1 bay leaf
1 Tbsp. cornstarch
½ cup half-and-half
2 Tbsp. chopped fresh chives

1. Bring clams and 4 cups water to a boil in a large pot over high. Cook until clams open, 8 to 10 minutes. (Discard any clams that do not open.) Using a large slotted spoon, transfer clams to a large baking sheet lined with paper towels; set cooking liquid aside. Let clams stand until cool enough to handle. Pull meat from shells; discard shells. Coarsely chop clam meat and set aside.
2. Heat oil in a Dutch oven over medium. Add onion, celery, and garlic; cook, stirring often, until onion is translucent, about 8 minutes. Add reserved clam cooking liquid, potatoes, miso, thyme, pepper, and bay leaf; cook until potatoes are tender, about 25 minutes.
3. Transfer 2 cups of the chowder to a food processor; pulse until coarsely chopped, about 6 times. Stir mixture into remaining chowder.

4. Whisk together cornstarch and remaining 1 tablespoon water in a small bowl until smooth. Stir cornstarch mixture into chowder; bring to a boil over medium-high. Remove from heat; discard bay leaf. Stir in clam meat and half-and-half until combined. Divide chowder evenly among 6 bowls. Top with chives. Serves 6 (serving size: about 1½ cups)

CALORIES 244; **FAT** 6g (sat 2g, unsat 3g); **PROTEIN** 15g; **CARB** 34g; **FIBER** 5g; **SUGARS** 4g (added sugars 0g); **SODIUM** 647mg; **CALC** 8% DV; **POTASSIUM** 11% DV

DINNER TONIGHT

Fast, fresh, and colorful dishes are proven healthy weeknight winners—that's why we've filled up on crisp-tender vegetables, versatile sauces, and speedy soups.

WEEKNIGHT MAINS

Fast

Herb and Leek "Orzotto" with Fried Eggs

Hands-on: 25 min. **Total:** 30 min.
We give quick-cooking orzo pasta the risotto treatment—toasting the grains first, then slowly incorporating hot liquid until creamy and starchy—for a comforting "orzotto." The rich egg yolk ties it all together.

4 cups unsalted chicken stock (such as Swanson)
1 Tbsp. unsalted butter
2 Tbsp. olive oil, divided
1 cup chopped yellow onion
2 medium leeks, chopped (about 2¼ cups)

1 cup uncooked whole-wheat orzo
⅓ cup dry white wine
¼ cup chopped fresh flat-leaf
   parsley
¼ cup chopped fresh chives, divided
1¼ oz. Parmesan cheese, shaved
   and divided (about ⅓ cup)
½ tsp. kosher salt
⅜ tsp. freshly ground black pepper,
   divided
4 large eggs
1 tsp. grated lemon rind

1. Bring stock to a simmer in a medium saucepan over medium-low. Keep warm.
2. Heat butter and 1½ tablespoons olive oil in a large saucepan over medium-high. Add onion and leeks; sauté 10 minutes. Add orzo; cook 2 minutes, stirring occasionally. Add wine; cook 1 minute or until liquid almost evaporates. Add ⅔ cup warm stock to pan; cook 3 minutes or until liquid is absorbed. Add remaining stock, ⅔ cup at a time, stirring occasionally until each portion is absorbed before adding more. Remove pan from heat; stir in parsley, 3 tablespoons chives, ¼ cup Parmesan, salt, and ¼ teaspoon pepper.
3. Heat a large nonstick skillet over medium. Add remaining 1½ teaspoons oil to pan; swirl to coat. Crack eggs into pan; cook 2 minutes. Cover and cook 2 more minutes or until desired degree of doneness. Divide orzo mixture among 4 bowls; top each serving with an egg. Sprinkle evenly with remaining 1 tablespoon chives, remaining Parmesan, remaining

MAKE IT VEGETARIAN

Swap chicken stock for 2 cups vegetable broth and 2 cups water. If you don't eat eggs, top with sautéed mushrooms and toasted walnuts instead.

⅛ teaspoon pepper, and lemon rind. Serves 4 (serving size: 1 cup)

CALORIES 432; FAT 18g (sat 6g, unsat 10g); PROTEIN 20g; CARB 44g; FIBER 9g; SUGARS 6g (added sugars 0g); SODIUM 586mg; CALC 18% DV; POTASSIUM 8% DV

Fast • Gluten Free
Make Ahead • Vegetarian

Thai Curried Squash Soup

Hands-on: 15 min. **Total:** 25 min. Instead of shaking the coconut milk can to emulsify the cream, reserve the rich "cream" floating to the top and blend with ginger and lime for a decadent swirl on each serving. Silken tofu adds instant body and protein to the soup for a more substantial main dish.

1 Tbsp. olive oil
1 Tbsp. red curry paste (such as
   Thai Kitchen)
2 tsp. grated peeled fresh
   ginger, divided
1 tsp. minced garlic
1 tsp. ground coriander
1 tsp. ground cumin
1 tsp. light brown sugar
¼ tsp. crushed red pepper
1 (13.5-oz.) can light coconut milk,
   unshaken
1½ cups unsalted vegetable stock
2 (10-oz.) pkg. frozen chopped or
   pureed butternut squash, thawed
3 Tbsp. lime juice, divided
½ tsp. kosher salt
1 (16-oz.) pkg. silken tofu, drained
   and cubed
¼ cup chopped scallions
¼ cup chopped fresh basil

1. Heat oil in a large Dutch oven over medium-high. Add curry paste; cook 1 minute, stirring constantly. Add 1 teaspoon ginger and next 5 ingredients (through red pepper); cook 1 minute or until fragrant.

2. Remove 2 tablespoons coconut cream from surface of coconut milk in can; reserve. Place remaining coconut milk in a bowl, and whisk until emulsified. Add whisked coconut milk, stock, and squash to pan; bring to a boil. Reduce heat, and simmer 10 minutes or until slightly thickened.
3. Add 2 tablespoons lime juice, salt, and tofu to pan. Transfer squash mixture to a blender; blend until smooth.
4. Combine remaining 1 teaspoon ginger, reserved coconut cream, and remaining 1 tablespoon lime juice in a small bowl. Divide soup among 4 bowls; top evenly with coconut cream mixture, scallions, and basil. Serves 4 (serving size: about 1½ cups)

CALORIES 250; FAT 11g (sat 5g, unsat 5g); PROTEIN 9g; CARB 33g; FIBER 4g; SUGARS 12g (added sugars 1g); SODIUM 621mg; CALC 15% DV; POTASSIUM 10% DV

3 WAYS TO MAKE THIS SOUP QUICKLY

1. Frozen butternut squash saves you the trouble of peeling, dicing, and parboiling a whole fresh squash; cubes or unseasoned puree will work here.

2. Cooking the spices in a little oil (called "blooming") at the beginning is a fast, simple way to amp up flavor. Just be sure not to burn them.

3. Save yourself a little cleanup and use an immersion blender to puree the soup directly in the pot instead of transferring the soup to a blender.

Mediterranean Chicken and Couscous Bowls

Hands-on: 20 min. **Total:** 40 min.

1 Tbsp. olive oil
1¼ cups uncooked whole-wheat Israeli couscous
2¼ cups water
¼ cup plain whole-milk Greek yogurt
3 Tbsp. whole buttermilk
1½ Tbsp. white vinegar
½ tsp. kosher salt
¼ tsp. freshly ground black pepper
1 garlic clove, grated
1½ Tbsp. chopped fresh dill, divided
12 oz. skinless, boneless rotisserie chicken (white and dark meat), shredded (about 3 cups)
1 small English cucumber, halved lengthwise and sliced (about 1½ cups)
1 cup multicolored cherry tomatoes, halved
¼ cup thinly sliced red onion
1 oz. feta cheese, crumbled (about ¼ cup)

1. Heat oil in a large saucepan over medium-high. Add couscous; cook 3 minutes or until lightly toasted, stirring frequently. Add 2¼ cups water; bring to a boil. Reduce heat; cover and simmer 14 minutes or until done. Drain; rinse with cold water. Drain.
2. Combine yogurt and next 5 ingredients (through garlic) in a bowl. Stir in 1 tablespoon dill. Divide cooked couscous evenly among 4 bowls. Arrange chicken, cucumber, tomatoes, red onion, and feta evenly over couscous. Top each serving with about 3 tablespoons yogurt mixture; sprinkle with remaining 1½ teaspoons dill. Serves 4 (serving size: about 1¾ cups)

CALORIES 473; FAT 14g (sat 4g, unsat 8g); PROTEIN 35g; CARB 55g; FIBER 5g; SUGARS 4g (added sugars 0g); SODIUM 608mg; CALC 11% DV; POTASSIUM 14% DV

Fast • Gluten Free

Chorizo and Bell Pepper Tostadas

Hands-on: 15 min. **Total:** 20 min.
Uncured Mexican chorizo is raw ground pork laced with garlic, cumin, oregano, and chile powder—not the dried, cured links. Try it on a baked potato, too.

1 Tbsp. canola oil, divided
8 oz. ground pork
2 oz. Mexican chorizo
3 cups sliced yellow onion (about 1 large)
1 cup sliced red bell pepper (about 1 medium)
1 cup sliced yellow bell pepper
½ tsp. ground cumin
½ tsp. chili powder
⅜ tsp. kosher salt
4 tostada shells
1 ripe avocado, sliced
3 Tbsp. crumbled queso fresco
2 Tbsp. fresh cilantro leaves
8 lime wedges

1. Heat 1½ teaspoons oil in a large nonstick skillet over medium-high. Add pork and chorizo; cook 5 minutes or until browned, stirring to crumble. Remove pork mixture from pan with a slotted spoon (do not wipe out pan).
2. Add remaining 1½ teaspoons oil to drippings in pan. Add onion, bell peppers, cumin, chili powder, and salt; cook 8 minutes or until tender. Return pork mixture to pan; cook 2 minutes.
3. Spoon bell pepper mixture evenly over tostada shells. Top each evenly with avocado, queso fresco, and cilantro. Serve with lime wedges. Serves 4 (serving size: 1 tostada)

CALORIES 352; FAT 23g (sat 7g, unsat 12g); PROTEIN 17g; CARB 22g; FIBER 6g; SUGARS 6g (added sugars 0g); SODIUM 430mg; CALC 7% DV; POTASSIUM 12% DV

Fast • Gluten Free

Blackened Shrimp with Citrus and Roasted Fennel

Hands-on: 15 min. **Total:** 25 min.
You don't need to grill outdoors to get smoky char on this shrimp dish; you just need a quick spice rub and a hot skillet. The multigrain medley is a fun alternative to brown rice; it includes brown, red, and wild rice, plus quinoa. Can't find it? Use all quinoa instead.

2 small navel oranges
2 medium fennel bulbs with stalks (about 7 oz. each)
¼ cup olive oil, divided
1 tsp. kosher salt, divided
6 small shallots, halved
2 tsp. paprika
1 tsp. chopped fresh thyme
½ tsp. garlic powder
¼ tsp. chopped fresh oregano
¼ tsp. ground red pepper
1 lb. large shrimp, peeled and deveined, tails on
2 (4.4-oz.) pkg. precooked multigrain rice medley (such as Minute)

1. Preheat oven to 425°F.
2. Grate one orange to equal 1 teaspoon rind; reserve. Cut oranges crosswise into ⅓-inch-thick rounds.

Remove stalks from fennel; chop fronds to equal 2 tablespoons and reserve (discard stalks). Cut fennel bulbs into ½-inch-thick wedges. Combine orange slices, 2 tablespoons oil, ½ teaspoon salt, shallots, and fennel wedges in a bowl. Arrange fennel mixture in a single layer on a rimmed baking sheet. Bake at 425°F for 25 minutes or until fennel is tender and lightly charred.

3. Combine remaining ½ teaspoon salt, paprika, and next 4 ingredients (through red pepper) in a ziplock bag. Add shrimp, seal, and shake to coat. Heat remaining 2 tablespoons oil in a large skillet over medium-high. Add shrimp; cook 3 minutes or until done.

4. Heat rice medleys according to package directions; place in a bowl and stir in reserved 1 teaspoon orange rind. Divide rice mixture, fennel mixture, and shrimp among 4 plates; sprinkle evenly with reserved fennel fronds. Serves 4 (serving size: ½ cup fennel mixture, ½ cup rice mixture, and about 7 shrimp)

CALORIES 549; **FAT** 17g (sat 2g, unsat 13g); **PROTEIN** 26g; **CARB** 78g; **FIBER** 8g; **SUGARS** 12g (added sugars 0g); **SODIUM** 723mg; **CALC** 14% DV; **POTASSIUM** 23% DV

DINNER IN AMERICA

Fast

Tomato, Basil, and Chicken Pasta

Hands-on: 15 min. **Total:** 20 min.
Think of this as a lighter, fresher take on chicken Parmesan—we ditch the breading on the poultry, and cherry tomatoes stand in for jarred sauce. Grated carrot adds sweetness to round out the acidity in the tomatoes.

8 oz. uncooked whole-wheat spaghetti
1 Tbsp. olive oil
4 (4-oz.) skinless, boneless chicken breast cutlets
½ tsp. kosher salt, divided
½ tsp. freshly ground black pepper
4 cups cherry tomatoes
¼ cup dry white wine
½ cup thinly sliced fresh basil, divided
1 medium carrot, peeled and grated (about ¼ cup)
3 oz. fresh mini mozzarella cheese balls (about ½ cup)
2 oz. Parmesan cheese, grated and divided (about ½ cup)

1. Cook pasta according to package directions, omitting salt and fat; drain.

2. Heat oil in a large skillet over medium-high. Sprinkle chicken with ¼ teaspoon salt and pepper and add to pan; cook 2 to 3 minutes on each side. Remove chicken from pan; keep warm.

3. Add remaining ¼ teaspoon salt, tomatoes, wine, ¼ cup basil, and carrot to drippings in pan; bring to a boil. Cook 3 minutes or until tomatoes begin to break down, stirring frequently. Reduce heat, and simmer 5 minutes or until slightly thickened. Remove pan from heat; stir in mozzarella and ¼ cup Parmesan.

4. Divide pasta among 4 bowls. Top evenly with chicken, sauce, and remaining ¼ cup basil and ¼ cup Parmesan. Serves 4 (serving size: ⅔ cup pasta, 1 cutlet, and ½ cup sauce)

CALORIES 512; **FAT** 16g (sat 6g, unsat 9g); **PROTEIN** 43g; **CARB** 51g; **FIBER** 7g; **SUGARS** 6g (added sugars 0g); **SODIUM** 598mg; **CALC** 24% DV; **POTASSIUM** 19% DV

1 INGREDIENT, 3 SIDES

3 WAYS TO USE BROCCOLINI

Long, slender stalks and tender florets make this broccoli cousin a great choice for crunchy slaws or quick sautés. Broccolini is also high in immune-boosting vitamin C.

Fast • Gluten Free
Make Ahead • Vegetarian
Broccolini Slaw
Instead of cabbage, this quick slaw gets its crunch from fresh carrots, beets, and Broccolini. Serve with simply baked fish or as an alternative to coleslaw with hamburgers or barbecue.

1. Combine 2 Tbsp. apple cider vinegar, 2 tsp. Dijon mustard, 1 tsp. honey, ¼ tsp. kosher salt, and ¼ tsp. black pepper in a small bowl. Bring ½ cup water and 14 oz. Broccolini, cut into 1-inch pieces (about 5½ cups), to a boil in a large saucepan over medium-high; cover and cook 5 minutes or until tender. Drain; rinse with cold water. Drain.

2. Combine Broccolini, 1 cup matchstick-cut carrots, ½ cup julienne-cut golden beet, ¼ cup thinly sliced red onion, and ¼ cup toasted sunflower seeds in a large bowl. Add vinegar mixture; toss. Let stand 10 minutes. Serves 6 (serving size: about ⅔ cup)

CALORIES 77; **FAT** 3g (sat 0g, unsat 3g); **PROTEIN** 4g; **CARB** 10g; **FIBER** 2g; **SUGARS** 4g (added sugars 1g); **SODIUM** 158mg; **CALC** 6% DV; **POTASSIUM** 10% DV

continued

Fast • Gluten Free
Stir-Fried Broccolini

The Broccolini stays perfectly al dente while picking up a nice bit of sear from the hot pan. Fish sauce and chili garlic sauce (available in the international aisle) give this side a Vietnamese profile. If you don't have fish sauce, use soy sauce. Pair this with seafood or pork.

1. Heat 1 Tbsp. toasted sesame oil in a large skillet over medium-high. Add 14 oz. trimmed Broccolini; stir-fry 1 minute. Add ½ cup water; cook 5 minutes or until crisp-tender, stirring occasionally.
2. Stir in ½ cup sliced scallions, 2 tsp. fish sauce, 1 tsp. chili garlic sauce, 1 tsp. fresh lime juice, ¼ tsp. sugar, and ¼ tsp. crushed red pepper, if desired. Cook 1 to 2 minutes or until liquid evaporates. Serves 6 (serving size: about ⅔ cup)

CALORIES 53; FAT 2g (sat 0g, unsat 2g); PROTEIN 3g; CARB 6g; FIBER 1g; SUGARS 2g (added sugars 0g); SODIUM 223mg; CALC 5% DV; POTASSIUM 7% DV

Fast • Vegetarian
Panko-Crusted Broccolini

This speedy side has all the best parts of a broccoli casserole: crisp-tender Broccolini florets and a golden, cheesy panko topper.

1. Preheat broiler to high. Combine ¼ cup whole-wheat panko (Japanese breadcrumbs), 1 oz. (¼ cup) grated pecorino Romano cheese, 2 Tbsp. chopped fresh flat-leaf parsley, and 1 tsp. grated lemon rind in a small bowl. Bring ½ cup water and 14 oz. trimmed Broccolini to a boil in a large ovenproof skillet.
2. Cover and cook 6 minutes. Uncover and cook 30 seconds. Remove Broccolini from pan. Add 2 tsp. olive oil and 1 tsp. minced garlic to pan; sauté 30 seconds. Stir in Broccolini and ¼ tsp. kosher salt. Sprinkle panko mixture evenly over

Broccolini mixture. Broil 2 minutes or until lightly browned. Serves 6 (serving size: about ⅔ cup)

CALORIES 70; FAT 3g (sat 1g, unsat 1g); PROTEIN 4g; CARB 7g; FIBER 1g; SUGARS 2g (added sugars 0g); SODIUM 200mg; CALC 9% DV; POTASSIUM 6% DV

20-MINUTE MAINS

Fast • Gluten Free
Seared Scallops with Chile-Garlic Spinach

Hands-on: 15 min. **Total:** 20 min.
The trick to perfect scallops is to leave them alone once they hit the pan—they'll stick to the skillet at first but then release once they sear.

Cooking spray
1½ lb. dry sea scallops, patted dry with paper towels
½ tsp. kosher salt, divided
½ tsp. freshly ground black pepper
2 (8.8-oz.) pkg. precooked brown rice (such as Uncle Ben's)
1 Tbsp. olive oil
1 cup thinly sliced red onion
2 red Fresno chiles, seeded and sliced
4 garlic cloves, thinly sliced
1 lb. baby spinach
8 lemon wedges

1. Heat a cast-iron skillet over high. Coat pan with cooking spray. Sprinkle scallops with ¼ teaspoon salt and pepper. Add scallops to pan; cook 2 minutes. Turn and cook 1 minute or until desired degree of doneness. Remove scallops from pan; keep warm.
2. Heat rice according to package directions. Reduce pan heat to medium-high. Add oil to pan. Add

remaining ¼ teaspoon salt, onion, and chiles; cook 2 minutes. Add garlic; cook 2 minutes. Add spinach in batches, stirring to wilt.
3. Serve scallops with rice, spinach mixture, and lemon wedges. Serves 4 (serving size: 5 scallops, ½ cup rice, and ⅔ cup spinach mixture)

CALORIES 368; FAT 7g (sat 1g, unsat 6g); PROTEIN 28g; CARB 50g; FIBER 7g; SUGARS 3g (added sugars 0g); SODIUM 617mg; CALC 14% DV; POTASSIUM 14% DV

Fast
Panko Salmon with Snap Peas

Hands-on: 15 min. **Total:** 20 min.
Tarragon has a sweet, anisey flavor that pairs beautifully with pungent Dijon mustard. You can also try the two together in a simple vinaigrette.

1½ Tbsp. Dijon mustard
1½ Tbsp. canola mayonnaise
¾ tsp. kosher salt, divided
½ tsp. black pepper, divided
4 (6-oz.) skinless salmon fillets
½ cup whole-wheat panko (Japanese breadcrumbs)
1 Tbsp. chopped fresh tarragon
2 tsp. grated lemon rind, divided
2 Tbsp. olive oil, divided
2½ cups sugar snap peas, trimmed
⅓ cup thinly sliced shallots (about 2 medium)
2 tsp. fresh lemon juice

1. Combine mustard, mayonnaise, ½ teaspoon salt, and ¼ teaspoon pepper in a shallow bowl. Spoon mustard mixture evenly over fillets. Combine panko, 1½ teaspoons tarragon, and 1 teaspoon lemon rind in a bowl. Sprinkle panko mixture over fillets, pressing to adhere.
2. Heat 1 tablespoon oil in a large nonstick skillet over medium. Add fillets, panko side down. Cook 3 to 4 minutes or until golden; turn and cook 3 to 4 minutes or until desired

degree of doneness. Remove fillets from pan; keep warm.

3. Increase heat to medium-high. Add remaining 1 tablespoon oil to pan. Add snap peas and shallots; cook 3 minutes, stirring occasionally. Add the remaining ¼ teaspoon salt, remaining ¼ teaspoon pepper, remaining 1½ teaspoons tarragon, remaining 1 teaspoon lemon rind, and juice to pan; cook 2 minutes or until snap peas are crisp-tender. Serve with fillets. Serves 4 (serving size: 1 fillet and about ½ cup peas)

CALORIES 387; **FAT** 18g (sat 3g, unsat 14g); **PROTEIN** 39g; **CARB** 13g; **FIBER** 3g; **SUGARS** 3g (added sugars 0g); **SODIUM** 630mg; **CALC** 4% DV; **POTASSIUM** 20% DV

Fast

Lamb and Beet Meatballs

Hands-on: 20 min. **Total:** 20 min. These meatballs are a great example of using meat as a supporting player rather than the star and getting more veggies and whole grains into your diet.

1 (8-oz.) pkg. vacuum-packed cooked beets (such as Love Beets)
½ cup uncooked bulgur
1 tsp. ground cumin
¾ tsp. kosher salt, divided
¾ tsp. freshly ground black pepper
6 oz. ground lamb
1 oz. almond flour (about ⅓ cup)
1 Tbsp. olive oil
½ cup grated cucumber
½ cup reduced-fat sour cream
2 Tbsp. thinly sliced fresh mint
2 Tbsp. fresh lemon juice
4 cups mixed baby greens (4 oz.)

1. Preheat oven to 425°F.
2. Place beets in a mini food processor; pulse until finely chopped. Combine beets, bulgur, cumin, ½ teaspoon salt, pepper,

lamb, and almond flour in a bowl; divide and shape lamb mixture into 12 meatballs.
3. Heat oil in a large ovenproof skillet over medium-high. Add meatballs to pan; cook 4 minutes or until browned on all sides. Transfer pan to oven; bake at 425°F for 8 minutes or until cooked through.
4. Combine remaining ¼ teaspoon salt, cucumber, sour cream, mint, and juice in a small bowl. Divide greens among 4 plates. Top evenly with meatballs. Serve with cucumber mixture. Serves 4 (serving size: 3 meatballs, 1 cup greens, and about ¼ cup sauce)

CALORIES 338; **FAT** 21g (sat 8g, unsat 13g); **PROTEIN** 14g; **CARB** 25g; **FIBER** 5g; **SUGARS** 8g (added sugars 0g); **SODIUM** 458mg; **CALC** 11% DV; **POTASSIUM** 13% DV

THE SHORTCUT

Staff Favorite · Fast
Vegetarian

Zucchini Noodles with Spicy Peanut Sauce

Hands-on: 15 min. **Total:** 20 min. Precut produce helps this come together in a flash. Spiralized zucchini and summer squash are in the produce section of many supermarkets; you can also spiralize your own or make ribbons with a vegetable peeler.

¼ cup cornstarch
1 (12-oz.) pkg. extra-firm water-packed tofu, drained, patted dry, and cut into 1-in. cubes
1½ Tbsp. canola oil
¼ cup fresh lime juice
3 Tbsp. creamy peanut butter
3 Tbsp. lower-sodium soy sauce

1 Tbsp. unsalted ketchup
1 Tbsp. Sriracha chili sauce
1 Tbsp. water
2 tsp. light brown sugar
1 tsp. grated peeled fresh ginger
2 (16-oz.) pkg. spiralized zucchini or yellow squash and zucchini (about 4 cups total)
3 cups fresh mung bean sprouts (about 5 oz.)
1 cup matchstick-cut carrots
½ cup chopped fresh cilantro
¼ cup unsalted peanuts, finely chopped and divided
¼ cup chopped fresh mint
4 scallions, cut into 1-in. pieces
4 lime wedges

1. Place cornstarch in a dish. Add tofu; toss to coat, shaking off excess. Heat oil in a nonstick skillet over medium. Add tofu; cook 8 to 10 minutes or until tofu is brown and crisp, stirring occasionally.
2. Combine lime juice and next 7 ingredients in a bowl, stirring with a whisk. Combine spiralized squash, sprouts, carrots, ¼ cup cilantro, 2 tablespoons peanuts, and mint in a large bowl. Add tofu and peanut butter mixture to bowl; toss. Sprinkle with remaining ¼ cup cilantro, remaining 2 tablespoons peanuts, and scallions. Serve with lime wedges. Serves 4 (serving size: 1½ cups)

CALORIES 406; **FAT** 22g (sat 3g, unsat 17g); **PROTEIN** 20g; **CARB** 40g; **FIBER** 7g; **SUGARS** 15g (added sugars 3g); **SODIUM** 594mg; **CALC** 15% DV; **POTASSIUM** 30% DV

BRAIN BOOST

The peanuts here may spur activity in the part of your brain responsible for immune response and deep (non-REM) sleep, per a new study conducted by Loma Linda University.

3 WAYS TO USE BULGUR

Whole-grain bulgur (cracked wheat kernels) bulks up the lamb meatballs on p. 69. Try the quick-cooking grain to add nutty flavor and hearty texture to meatless burgers, chili, and quiches.

Make Ahead · Vegetarian
Bulgur and Greens Mini Quiches

1. Preheat oven to 375°F.
2. Boil ⅓ cup water and ⅓ cup uncooked bulgur in a small saucepan; cover, reduce heat to low, and simmer 12 minutes or until water is absorbed.
3. Heat 2 Tbsp. canola oil in a medium skillet over medium-high. Add ⅔ cup chopped onion; sauté 3 minutes. Add 4 cups lightly packed chopped stemmed curly kale (4 oz.); sauté until wilted, about 5 minutes (add 2 Tbsp. water if mixture starts to scorch). Stir in bulgur. Divide mixture among 8 muffin cups coated with cooking spray.
4. Whisk together 1 cup whole milk, 2 tsp. chopped fresh thyme, ½ tsp. kosher salt, ½ tsp. black pepper, and 4 large eggs. Pour ¼ cup into each muffin cup (cups will be very full). Sprinkle 3 oz. (¾ cup) crumbled feta cheese evenly over cups. Bake 20 to 22 minutes, until set. Serves 4 (serving size: 2 quiches)

CALORIES 292; **FAT** 19g (sat 6g, unsat 11g); **PROTEIN** 14g; **CARB** 18g; **FIBER** 3g; **SUGARS** 6g (added sugars 0g); **SODIUM** 546mg; **CALC** 26% DV; **POTASSIUM** 11% DV

Make Ahead · Vegetarian
Bulgur Chickpea Burgers

1. Bring ¾ cup water and ½ cup uncooked bulgur to a boil in a small saucepan; cover, reduce heat to low, and simmer 12 minutes or until water is absorbed. Cool slightly.
2. Place 1 (15-oz.) can drained unsalted chickpeas in a large bowl; mash until almost smooth. Stir in ⅓ cup chopped scallions, 1 tsp. ground cumin, ¾ tsp. kosher salt, ¾ tsp. smoked paprika, 1 large egg, and 1 large egg white. Stir in bulgur. Shape into 4 (¾-in.-thick) patties.
3. Heat 1 Tbsp. olive oil in a large skillet over medium. Add patties to pan; cook 5 minutes on each side or until browned and done.
4. Mash 1 ripe avocado; stir in ⅛ tsp. kosher salt and 1 grated garlic clove. Divide patties and avocado mixture among 4 whole-wheat hamburger buns. Serves 4 (serving size: 1 burger)

CALORIES 409; **FAT** 13g (sat 2g, unsat 9g); **PROTEIN** 11g; **CARB** 56g; **FIBER** 12g; **SUGARS** 4g (added sugars 1g); **SODIUM** 678mg; **CALC** 18% DV; **POTASSIUM** 14% DV

Make Ahead · Vegetarian
Hearty Bulgur Chili

The amount of chipotle we call for yields a medium level of spice; use more or less to suit your family's taste.

1. Heat 2 Tbsp. olive oil in a large Dutch oven over medium-high. Add 1 cup chopped onion and 5 minced garlic cloves; sauté 5 minutes. Add ½ cup uncooked bulgur, 2 Tbsp. chopped canned chipotle chiles in adobo sauce, and 1 tsp. ground cumin; cook 1 minute, stirring constantly. Add 3 cups unsalted vegetable stock, 1 (26.46-oz.) box finely chopped tomatoes (such as Pomì brand), 1 (15-oz.) can drained unsalted kidney beans, and 1¼ tsp. kosher salt. Bring to a simmer; reduce heat to medium-low, and cook 15 minutes or until bulgur is tender.
2. Ladle about 1 cup chili into each of 6 bowls; top each serving with 1 Tbsp. sour cream and 1 Tbsp. cilantro leaves. Serves 6 (serving size: about 1 cup chili)

CALORIES 274; **FAT** 8g (sat 2g, unsat 5g); **PROTEIN** 10g; **CARB** 43g; **FIBER** 11g; **SUGARS** 6g (added sugars 0g); **SODIUM** 636mg; **CALC** 6% DV; **POTASSIUM** 10% DV

4 GO-WITH-ANYTHING SIDES

Vegetarian
Roasted Carrots with Pine Nut Gremolata

Starting the carrots at a high temp gives them a pretty browned exterior; finishing at a lower temp makes them tender. Pair with chicken or fish.

Preheat oven to 450°F. Toss 1 Tbsp. olive oil, ¼ tsp. kosher salt, and ¼ tsp. pepper with 1 lb. trimmed small carrots on a baking sheet. Bake at 450°F for 20 minutes, stirring after 10 minutes. Reduce oven to 325°F (keep pan in oven). Bake for 10 more minutes. Combine 2 Tbsp. chopped fresh flat-leaf parsley, 2 Tbsp. chopped fresh chives, 1 Tbsp. toasted pine nuts, 2 tsp. grated orange rind, and 1 tsp. minced garlic. Add to carrots with 1 Tbsp. malt vinegar; toss. Serves 4 (serving size: about 4 oz.)

CALORIES 90; **FAT** 5g (sat 1g, unsat 4g); **PROTEIN** 1g; **CARB** 10g; **FIBER** 4g; **SUGARS** 6g (added sugars 0g); **SODIUM** 210mg; **CALC** 4% DV; **POTASSIUM** 9% DV

Fast • Gluten Free
Vegetarian
Curried Peas with Mint and Lime

Green peas are a freezer staple, making this side dish that much easier to bring together. Serve this herby side with roast beef or lamb. Stir any leftover peas into an Indian-style curry on another night.

Combine 2 Tbsp. olive oil, 1½ tsp. curry powder, and 4 sliced garlic cloves in a medium skillet over medium. Cook 3 minutes or until garlic is fragrant, stirring frequently. Add 1 cup frozen thawed green peas and 1 (8-oz.) pkg. trimmed fresh sugar snap peas; cook 3 minutes. Stir in ¼ cup torn fresh mint, ½ tsp. grated lime rind, 1 tsp. fresh lime juice, and ¼ tsp. kosher salt. Serve immediately. Serves 4 (serving size: ½ cup)

CALORIES 118; FAT 7g (sat 1g, unsat 6g); PROTEIN 4g; CARB 10g; FIBER 3g; SUGARS 4g (added sugars 0g); SODIUM 165mg; CALC 5% DV; POTASSIUM 6% DV

Fast • Gluten Free
Make Ahead • Vegetarian
Radish, White Bean, and Olive Salad

This quick side is all about texture, from the meaty olives to the creamy beans and crunchy radishes. The mild bean makes the salad a great match for nearly any main.

Place ½ cup thinly sliced radishes, 1 Tbsp. chopped fresh flat-leaf parsley, 1 Tbsp. extra-virgin olive oil, 1 tsp. grated lemon rind, 1 Tbsp. fresh lemon juice, ¼ tsp. kosher salt, ¼ tsp. pepper, 1 oz. pitted chopped Castelvetrano olives, and 1 (15-oz.) can rinsed and drained unsalted cannellini beans in a medium bowl, stirring to combine. Serves 4 (serving size: ½ cup)

CALORIES 128; FAT 6g (sat 1g, unsat 5g); PROTEIN 5g; CARB 15g; FIBER 4g; SUGARS 0g (added sugars 0g); SODIUM 279mg; CALC 4% DV; POTASSIUM 7% DV

Fast • Gluten Free
Braised Fingerling Potatoes with Oregano and Thyme

A stovetop sauté and an oven braise lend the spuds a bronzed exterior and creamy interior. The stock mixture reduces, giving the potatoes their own rich gravy. Serve with a simply roasted chicken or pork loin.

Preheat oven to 375°F. Heat 1 Tbsp. olive oil and 2 tsp. unsalted butter in a large ovenproof skillet over medium-high. Add ½ cup thinly sliced white onion and 1 lb. fingerling potatoes, halved lengthwise; cook 8 minutes. Add ½ cup unsalted chicken stock, 3 oregano sprigs, and 2 thyme sprigs. Cover; bake for 10 minutes. Discard oregano and thyme. Sprinkle with 1 tsp. chopped oregano, 1 tsp. chopped thyme, ¼ tsp. kosher salt, and ¼ tsp. black pepper. Serves 4 (serving size: ⅔ cup)

CALORIES 133; FAT 5g (sat 2g, unsat 3g); PROTEIN 2g; CARB 20g; FIBER 3g; SUGARS 2g (added sugars 0g); SODIUM 137mg; CALC 1% DV; POTASSIUM 14% DV

4 SAUCES FOR ANY PROTEIN

Fast • Gluten Free • Make Ahead
Nuoc Cham

This sweet-and-sour sauce is seriously addictive. We replace traditional white sugar with brown to add a caramel note. Spoon over grilled meats, sautéed shrimp, or ground pork.

Combine ¼ cup water, 5 tsp. light brown sugar, 4 tsp. fresh lime juice (from 1 lime), 1 Tbsp. unseasoned rice vinegar, and 2 tsp. fish sauce in a small bowl, and stir until sugar dissolves. Stir in 2 Tbsp. matchstick-cut carrots and 1 Tbsp. thinly sliced red Fresno chile (from 1 chile). Serves 4 (serving size: 2 Tbsp.)

CALORIES 28; FAT 0g; PROTEIN 0g; CARB 7g; FIBER 0g; SUGARS 6g (added sugars 6g); SODIUM 240mg; CALC 1% DV; POTASSIUM 2% DV

Fast • Gluten Free
Vegetarian
Avocado-Cilantro Sauce

Be sure to include the cilantro stems when blending the sauce; they have even more flavor than the leaves. Add this cool, creamy sauce to pan-grilled chicken or tacos.

Place 1 small garlic clove in a mini food processor; pulse until minced, about 5 times. Add ¼ cup plain 2% reduced-fat Greek yogurt, ½ cup fresh cilantro leaves and stems, 1 Tbsp. water, 1 Tbsp. fresh lime juice (from 1 lime), ¼ tsp. kosher salt, and ½ ripe avocado; process until smooth, about 30 seconds. Serves 4 (serving size: 2 Tbsp.)

CALORIES 54; FAT 4g (sat 1g, unsat 3g); PROTEIN 2g; CARB 3g; FIBER 2g; SUGARS 1g (added sugars 0g); SODIUM 148mg; CALC 2% DV; POTASSIUM 4% DV

Fast • Gluten Free
Caesar Sauce

We took the classic dressing elements and thickened them for a creamy sauce that's delicious on salmon or for reviving leftover rotisserie chicken. Finely grated garlic has a big kick, so start with half a clove.

Place 3 Tbsp. plain 2% reduced-fat Greek yogurt, 2 Tbsp. canola mayonnaise, ½ tsp. grated lemon rind, 1 Tbsp. fresh lemon juice, 1 tsp. grainy Dijon mustard, ½ tsp. anchovy paste, ¼ tsp. ground black pepper, ½ oz. grated Parmesan cheese, and ½ small grated garlic clove in a bowl, stirring to combine. Serves 4 (serving size: 2 Tbsp.)

CALORIES 46; FAT 3g (sat 1g, unsat 2g); PROTEIN 2g; CARB 2g; FIBER 0g; SUGARS 1g (added sugars 0g); SODIUM 199mg; CALC 5% DV; POTASSIUM 0% DV

continued

Quick Barbecue Sauce

The ingredient list for this sauce is short and practical—you likely have most of the ingredients on hand. Use as a glaze for pan-seared pork tenderloin or toss with shredded chicken for sandwiches.

Combine ½ cup unsalted ketchup, 3 Tbsp. water, 1 Tbsp. pure maple syrup, 2 tsp. Dijon mustard, 1 tsp. Worcestershire sauce, 1 tsp. unsalted butter, ½ tsp. smoked paprika, ½ tsp. onion powder, ½ tsp. garlic powder, and ¼ tsp. ground black pepper in a small saucepan over medium heat. Bring to a simmer; cook 3 to 5 minutes, stirring occasionally. Serves 4 (serving size: about 2½ Tbsp.)

CALORIES 78; FAT 1g (sat 1g, unsat 0g); PROTEIN 0g; CARB 16g; FIBER 0g; SUGARS 11g (added sugars 9g); SODIUM 75mg; CALC 1% DV; POTASSIUM 1% DV

SLOW COOKER

Gluten Free • Make Ahead

Tuscan White Bean Soup

Hands-on: 20 min. **Total:** 17 hr. 20 min. The hard rind from a hunk of Parmesan cheese is packed with umami and imparts savory depth as the soup cooks. Keep leftover rinds in a ziplock bag in your freezer for soups and stock.

1 cup dried cannellini beans
4 cups unsalted chicken stock
4 oz. diced pancetta (such as Boar's Head)
1 cup chopped yellow onion
1 cup chopped carrot
1 cup chopped celery
1 Tbsp. minced garlic
1 tsp. finely chopped fresh rosemary
½ tsp. kosher salt
¼ tsp. freshly ground black pepper
1 (14.5-oz.) can unsalted diced tomatoes
1 (2-in.) piece Parmesan cheese rind
1 bay leaf
2 cups chopped kale
2 Tbsp. red wine vinegar
2 Tbsp. chopped fresh flat-leaf parsley (optional)

1. Place beans in a large pot; cover with water 2 inches above beans. Soak at least 8 hours or overnight. Drain beans well; combine with stock in a medium saucepan. Bring to a boil over high. Transfer to a 5- to 6-quart slow cooker.
2. Cook pancetta in a large skillet over medium-high for 5 minutes or until crispy. Remove from pan and set aside. Add onion, carrot, celery, and garlic to drippings in pan; sauté 1 minute. Place veggie mixture, rosemary, and next 5 ingredients (through bay leaf) into slow cooker. Cook on LOW 8 hours. Discard Parmesan rind and bay leaf.
3. Add kale; cover and cook 1 hour. Stir in reserved pancetta and vinegar. Sprinkle with parsley, if desired. Serves 6 (serving size: about 1½ cups)

CALORIES 248; FAT 7g (sat 3g, unsat 2g); PROTEIN 14g; CARB 32g; FIBER 11g; SUGARS 5g (added sugars 0g); SODIUM 602mg; CALC 12% DV; POTASSIUM 24% DV

COOKING LIGHT DIET

Gluten Free • Make Ahead

Baked Chicken Moussaka

Hands-on: 20 min. **Total:** 32 min. This dish is usually layered with eggplant, ground beef or lamb, and a béchamel sauce. Our lightened version calls for ground chicken and a yogurt-based sauce. Brown the chicken well; most of the rich, meaty flavor comes from that step.

1 Tbsp. olive oil
10 oz. ground chicken
2 cups cubed eggplant
1 cup chopped red bell pepper
½ cup chopped yellow onion
1 Tbsp. chopped fresh thyme
1 Tbsp. finely chopped garlic
1 cup canned unsalted white beans, rinsed, drained, and slightly mashed
1 cup chopped tomato
1 cup unsalted tomato sauce (such as Muir Glen)
¼ cup unsalted chicken stock (such as Swanson)
1 tsp. kosher salt
1 tsp. freshly ground black pepper
¾ cup plain 2% reduced-fat Greek yogurt
2 large eggs, lightly beaten
¼ cup chopped fresh flat-leaf parsley
2 Tbsp. pine nuts, toasted

1. Preheat oven to 400°F.
2. Heat olive oil in a large skillet over medium-high. Add chicken; cook 5 minutes or until browned. Add eggplant, bell pepper, onion, thyme, and garlic; cook 6 minutes. Add mashed beans, tomato, tomato sauce, stock, salt, and pepper; bring to a boil. Reduce heat and simmer 5 minutes, stirring occasionally. Spoon vegetable mixture into a 2-quart glass or ceramic baking dish.
3. Combine yogurt and eggs in a bowl. Pour yogurt mixture over dish. Bake at 400°F for 12 to 14 minutes or until bubbly and yogurt mixture is set. Sprinkle with parsley and pine nuts. Serves 4 (serving size: 1¾ cups)

CALORIES 340; FAT 17g (sat 4g, unsat 11g); PROTEIN 26g; CARB 24g; FIBER 7g; SUGARS 10g (added sugars 0g); SODIUM 617mg; CALC 12% DV; POTASSIUM 31% DV

THE PERFECT WAY TO STEAM-BAKE FISH

Baking fish in banana leaves keeps it incredibly moist and adds subtle fragrance. Our simple steps deliver seafood perfection.

Gluten Free

Caribbean-Spiced Fish Wrapped in Banana Leaves

Hands-on: 17 min. **Total:** 37 min. Find fresh or frozen banana leaves at Asian and Latin markets. This preparation is often used for grilled fish since the leaf wrapping protects delicate fillets from harsh, dry heat. But it also works wonders in a hot oven, and the charred citrus infuses the fish with lightly grilled flavor.

6 thin navel orange slices
6 thin blood orange slices
4 (6-oz.) sustainable skinless white fish fillets (such as snapper, halibut, or sea bass)
1 Tbsp. canola oil
½ tsp. kosher salt
¼ tsp. ground coriander
¼ tsp. ground cinnamon
¼ tsp. ground red pepper
⅛ tsp. ground ginger
⅛ tsp. ground nutmeg
4 (12-in.-square) fresh or thawed frozen banana leaf pieces
2 Tbsp. chopped fresh cilantro (optional)

1. Preheat oven to 400°F. Heat a large cast-iron skillet over high. Add orange slices to pan; sear until partly blackened, about 2 minutes on each side. Remove orange slices from pan.

2. Coat fish fillets with oil. Stir together salt, coriander, cinnamon, red pepper, ginger, and nutmeg; sprinkle evenly over tops of fish fillets. Place 3 orange slices, slightly overlapping, in center of each banana leaf piece. Place 1 fish fillet, seasoned side up, on each set of orange slices. Fold each leaf piece to enclose fish. Place packets, folded side down, on a baking sheet. Bake at 400°F until fish is done, about 20 minutes. Serve in packets, or unwrap and transfer fillets and orange slices onto plates. Garnish with cilantro, if desired. Serves 4 (serving size: 1 fish fillet)

CALORIES 210; FAT 6g (sat 1g, unsat 5g); PROTEIN 35g; CARB 2g; FIBER 0g; SUGARS 1g (added sugars 0g); SODIUM 589mg; CALC 6% DV; POTASSIUM 21% DV

THE STEPS

1. PREPARE LEAVES
Thaw leaves if frozen. Trim away any discolored or wilted portions from banana leaves. If your leaves are not already preportioned, cut into 12-inch-square or round pieces.

2. ADD MOISTURE
The packets aren't tightly sealed, so adding wine or broth as you would with a foil or parchment packet won't work here. Instead, the citrus slices give off juice that will steam while the fish roasts.

3. WRAP UP
With the seasoned fish fillet set atop the citrus slices, wrap opposite sides of the leaf over the fish; wrap the remaining sides toward the center. Flip packet; the weight of the fish will hold folds in place.

AN ANCIENT GRAIN YOU SHOULD BE EATING

BY ANDREA NGUYEN

This fiber-rich whole grain, with nearly as much protein as quinoa, is a must-try. Here's why.

I had drizzled sweet sorghum syrup into my muesli, baked gluten-free treats with sorghum flour, done sorghum hooch shots, but strangely, I'd never eaten the whole grain until a pitchman at a food trade show suggested it.

It's a trending grain, he said, that American farmers have mostly grown for animal feed. But with gluten-free diets on the rise, it's becoming more popular for human consumption. He handed me a taste of what looked like Israeli couscous, a round pasta made from wheat. I expected the sorghum to be tender-chewy like the pasta, but it was snappy-chewy, with a wholesome, nutty flavor. The peppercorn-sizes grains pleasantly surprised. When I reacted positively with "*Mmm, yum,*" he went in for the kill: Sorghum is loaded with protein, antioxidants, and fiber; costs less than quinoa; and is grown domestically from SouthDakota to South Texas, the "Sorghum Belt." Having read about the area's water constraints, I asked about sustainability. Sorghum is drought-tolerant, he responded. It's farmed in hot, dry areas and can thrive with minimal water. (During drought, sorghum survives by smartly rolling its leaves to minimize water loss and may go dormant rather than die.)

Excited about a new food discovery, I found the buff-colored, bead-size grains (the plant's actual seeds) at our natural foods store. Eaten like rice with other dishes, sorghum absorbed flavors well. So I began asking food friends how to handle it. Few were excited because the grains aren't as widely sold as the flour. Fellow cookbook author and teacher Molly Stevens, however, was game. She'd spotted whole-grain sorghum at her local markets but hadn't cooked with it much. We agreed to experiment with it for a cooking event that we were both participating in. Not quite sure how to best prepare the grain for 75 people, we each practiced cooking it and compared notes over email.

Our key discovery was this: You can't overcook whole-grain sorghum. Molly gently simmered hers in water. I cooked mine like rice on the stove and in the Instant Pot® (the pressure cooker didn't save much time). You can add water to the pot well into the cooking if you're short or about to burn the grains, like I had to one time. Sorghum—as we pleasantly discovered—is a resilient, no-fail ingredient.

To pair with an eclectic menu for 75 people, we imbued cooked sorghum with miso, butter, shallot, and mushroom. The umami-rich side dish was a hit with guests, and Molly was so pleased with it that she drafted the recipe for her forthcoming cookbook and shared it with me for this column. I tested the recipe a handful of times, refining and polishing some minor technical steps. I tried swapping a few ingredients, but the result didn't taste as good as her original.

The sublime flavors reflect the ingredients and techniques as much as the collaboration between two curious cooks bent on better understanding a delicious and healthy ancient grain.

> It's a trending grain that American farmers have mostly grown for animal feed. But with gluten-free diets on the rise, it's becoming more popular for human consumption.

Gluten Free • Vegetarian

Sorghum with Mushroom and Miso

Hands-on: 30 min. **Total:** 1 hr. 30 min. Be sure to save a few tablespoons of the leftover sorghum cooking liquid, which helps ensure a creamy final product.

3 cups water
1 cup whole-grain sorghum
   (such as Bob's Red Mill)
¼ tsp. plus 1 pinch fine sea salt,
   divided
1 tsp. canola oil, divided
10 oz. cremini mushrooms, cut into
   ¼-in.-thick slices, divided
¼ tsp. black pepper, divided
¼ cup chopped shallots
3 scallions, thinly sliced, white
   and green parts separated (¼ cup
   whites, ⅓ cup greens)
2 ½ Tbsp. unsalted butter, divided
2 Tbsp. plus 1 tsp. white or yellow
   miso

1. Combine 3 cups water, sorghum, and 1 pinch of salt in a 2-quart saucepan. Bring to a boil over high; cook 5 minutes. Reduce heat to low; cover and cook for 1 hour, stirring once after 30 minutes. Remove from heat. Stir sorghum. Cover and let stand until more liquid is absorbed, 15 to 20 minutes. (The sorghum is done when the grains are chewy-firm with a slight snap.)

2. Meanwhile, heat ½ teaspoon oil in a large nonstick skillet over medium-high. Add half of the mushrooms, and spread in an even layer. Season with ⅛ teaspoon salt and ⅛ teaspoon pepper. Sear 3 minutes, stirring when bottoms of mushrooms are browned and tops are glistening with mushroom sweat. Cook, stirring often, until tender and fragrant. Transfer to a bowl. Repeat with remaining ½ teaspoon oil, remaining half of mushrooms, remaining ⅛ teaspoon salt, and remaining ⅛ teaspoon pepper.

3. Reduce heat to medium-low; add shallots, white scallion slices, and 1 tablespoon butter to skillet. Cook until soft and fragrant, about 2 minutes. Add to mushrooms.

4. Drain sorghum, reserving 2 to 3 tablespoons cooking liquid.

5. Melt remaining 1½ tablespoons butter in skillet over medium. Whisk in the miso. Add the sorghum and reserved cooking liquid; stir to combine. (If mixture is too creamy, cook for a few minutes more to evaporate some of the liquid.) Stir in the mushroom mixture. Cook until warmed through. Stir in the green scallion slices. Serve warm or at room temperature. Serves 6 (serving size: about ⅔ cup)

CALORIES 187; **FAT** 7g (sat 3g, unsat 3g); **PROTEIN** 6g; **CARB** 30g; **FIBER** 4g; **SUGARS** 4g (added sugars 0g); **SODIUM** 337mg; **CALC** 3% DV; **POTASSIUM** 11% DV

WHAT IS WHOLE-GRAIN SORGHUM?

AND WHAT ELSE CAN YOU DO WITH IT? PLUS, WHERE CAN YOU BUY IT? WE HAVE ANSWERS.

SORGHUM 101
Sorghum is a grass that looks like corn, but instead of developing ears, sorghum produces fluffy seed heads. There are many sorghum varieties, and certain kinds are for cooking. Whole-grain sorghum (the plant's seeds) has more fiber than pearled, but it takes longer to cook. Regardless of type, sorghum grains are a worthy sub for pearled barley, wheat berries, or Israeli couscous.

ANOTHER WAY TO COOK IT
You can pop sorghum with oil in a covered pan on the stove, but it also can be done fast and oil-free in the microwave: Put about 2 tablespoons of whole-grain sorghum in a small, lunch-sized brown paper bag. Fold the top edge over 4 or 5 times, and then place it, folded edge down, in the microwave. Cook on HIGH for 1 minute and 30 seconds, until the popping noise is barely audible. Let stand 1 to 2 minutes before opening the bag. Check for unpopped grains before eating.

WHERE TO BUY IT
Bob's Red Mill is Nguyen's go-to brand of whole-grain sorghum; it's available at well-stocked supermarkets or on Amazon. Hodgson Mill sells pearled sorghum, which cooks up to be more tender (but isn't a whole grain).

THE EASIEST FISH-COOKING TECHNIQUE

BY BARTON SEAVER

Like our new columnist, Barton Seaver, we think eating more seafood is good for you and the planet. His quick method makes that doable on even the busiest nights.

Broiling is a technique typically used with richer fish—those with more luxurious and healthful fats, such as salmon, tuna, or swordfish—but it also can be used on leaner varieties such as tilapia. Simply put, broiling is the direct application of high heat. But because broiling cooks from one side, cooking the fish evenly can be a challenge. The key is to manage the heat by moderating its intensity and the distance of the fish from the heat source. Thicker fillets are best cooked under medium to medium-high heat a couple of inches below the heat source, whereas thin, lean seafood such as tilapia is best placed directly under the withering heat of a broiler set to high. When done properly, this gives fish the nuanced and complex charisma of a slight char while preserving the succulence and moisture of the underside of the fillet, resulting in a satisfying duality of textures. Fear not—broiling is actually an easily mastered technique that with a little practice (and the few tips at right) you'll be able to apply to nearly any seafood.

Fast · Gluten Free

Broiled Tilapia with Yogurt and Herbs

Hands-on: 5 min. **Total:** 30 min. Parcook the tilapia before slathering on the sauce to brown it slightly. Look for fillets with even thickness, but if you can't find them, fold the thin end of the fillet under itself to encourage even cooking. Serve this with a New Zealand Sauvignon Blanc or American Pinot Gris—both pick up on the floral and herbal notes and accentuate the topping's acidity.

4 skinless tilapia, flounder, or catfish fillets (about 1¼ lb. total)
⅛ tsp. kosher salt
Olive oil or canola cooking spray
2½ Tbsp. plain 0% fat-free Greek yogurt
1½ Tbsp. mayonnaise
1 Tbsp. cooking sherry or Madeira, preferably amontillado sherry or rainwater Madeira
1 Tbsp. chopped fresh herbs, such as tarragon or dill (about 2 sprigs)

1. Season fish with salt and let stand 20 minutes. Pat dry with a paper towel.
2. Grease a baking sheet, or line it with aluminum foil and spray with cooking spray. Place fish on sheet, folding the last 1 inch to 2 inches of the fillet under itself to make the fillet an even thickness.
3. Preheat broiler to high. Combine yogurt, mayonnaise, sherry, and herbs, and stir until fully incorporated.
4. Place fish under the broiler on the highest rack as close to the heat source as possible, ensuring fillets are spread evenly under the heating unit. Broil, rotating if necessary to brown evenly, until browned, 4 to 5 minutes. Remove from oven; spoon sauce over fillets, and spread as thick as possible. Return fish to oven for about 2 minutes. Fish is fully cooked when it flakes easily. Serves 4 (serving size: 1 fillet)

CALORIES 182; FAT 6g (sat 1g, unsat 5g); PROTEIN 29g; CARB 0g; FIBER 0g; SUGARS 0g (added sugars 0g); SODIUM 170mg; CALC 3% DV; POTASSIUM 13% DV

MASTER THE BROILER FOR ANY FISH VARIETY WITH THESE TIPS

PRESEASON
First, all fish headed for the broiler should be preseasoned at least 20 minutes before cooking, preferably 40-plus minutes for thicker fillets. Then, based on the fish you're cooking, pick a method below:

USE A RUB
Steak fish (swordfish, tuna) need a highly seasoned dry rub, such as lemon pepper, and a drizzle of olive oil. Broil a couple inches below the heat source for 12 minutes; check for doneness and add 1 to 2 minutes, if needed.

KEEP THE SKIN ON
Rich fish (salmon, bluefish, mackerel) are best cooked skin-on and broiled for about 10 minutes, skin side up. These need little more than a proper seasoning of salt and a sheen of olive oil to help crisp the skin.

CONSIDER A TOPPER
Lean fish (flounder, tilapia) are best paired with a rich topping, as in the featured recipe (above), or a brightly flavored compound butter (for example, add chopped tarragon and lemon zest to butter). Broil directly under the heat source for about 7 minutes.

COOK ONCE, ENJOY TWICE

BY GINA HOMOLKA

Weeknight cooking is infinitely easier when you can cook extra today and reinvent the leftovers. Whip up a batch of this simple carne molida and take the pressure off a later meal.

I love a dish that I can cook once but use several ways throughout the week. And carne molida, a flavorful Latin classic, fits the bill. This versatile recipe, which can be made many different ways, is easy to execute any night of the week. And the recipe can be doubled to accommodate larger families.

Mine is made with ground turkey (it's leaner and more tender than ground beef), peas, and carrots. It's delicious in tacos or served over brown rice. The leftovers can be the base for a variety of meals. Here are a few of my favorites:

Shepherd's pie (with a Latin twist): Layer the carne molida in the bottom of a casserole dish, top it with mashed potatoes (or mashed cauliflower for a lower-carb option), and bake at 400°F for 20 to 25 minutes.

Savory empanadas: Place 2 tablespoons of carne molida in the center of each empanada dough round (empanada dough rounds can be found in the freezer section of most supermarkets—I use the Goya brand), and then fold and seal the edges. Brush the tops of the empanadas with egg white, and bake at 350°F until golden, about 20 minutes.

Carne molida also makes a perfect filling for baked potatoes, stuffed peppers, and quesadillas. The meal possibilities are almost endless!

Make Ahead

Turkey Carne Molida

Hands-on: 15 min. **Total:** 50 min. This recipe serves four, with 2 cups of carne molida left over for a second meal. It's a simple dish with great flavor thanks to cumin, garlic, and achiote. Achiote is an earthy spice that can be found in well-stocked supermarkets. It's also sometimes labeled as annatto. Frozen peas and carrots make this dish come together quickly. Although we suggest serving the carne molida in tacos, it's also delicious over brown rice, roasted potatoes, or even with tortilla chips. A dollop of sour cream and a squeeze of lime dress it up a little more.

1¼ lb. 93% lean ground turkey
1½ tsp. kosher salt
½ medium-sized yellow onion, minced
4 garlic cloves, minced
1 cup unsalted tomato sauce
1 cup frozen peas and carrots
½ cup water
1 tsp. reduced-sodium Worcestershire sauce
½ tsp. ground cumin
¼ tsp. ground achiote
¼ cup chopped fresh cilantro, plus more for garnish
8 (6-in.) corn tortillas

1. Cook turkey in a large skillet over high, stirring often, until browned, about 5 minutes. Add salt; cook, stirring with a wooden spoon to break meat into small pieces.
2. Reduce heat to medium-low; add onion and garlic, and cook, stirring often, until onion is softened, 4 to 5 minutes. Add tomato sauce, frozen vegetables, ½ cup water, Worcestershire sauce, cumin, and achiote, and stir to combine.
3. Gently stir in ¼ cup chopped cilantro. Cover and reduce heat to low; cook until meat is tender and sauce thickens, about 30 minutes.
4. Place ¼ cup carne molida in each corn tortilla. Garnish with cilantro. Reserve leftover meat mixture for another meal. Serves 4 (serving size: ½ cup carne molida and 2 corn tortillas)

CALORIES 210; FAT 7g (sat 2g, unsat 5g); PROTEIN 20g; CARB 20g; FIBER 3g; SUGARS 2g (added sugars 0g); SODIUM 517mg; CALC 6% DV; POTASSIUM 4% DV

Fast · Gluten Free Vegetarian

Passion Pisco Punch

Hands-on: 5 min. **Total:** 5 min. Zingy passion fruit and mango add a tropical spin to this South American classic. Rich in immune-boosting vitamin C and antioxidants, passion fruit can be found at well-stocked supermarkets or Asian or Latin markets.

Scoop out the flesh from 3 large ripe passion fruit and place into a strainer; use the back of a spoon to press out 1 oz. fresh juice. Add 1 oz. passion fruit juice, 4 oz. fresh mango juice, 3 oz. pisco, 3 oz. coconut water, 1 Tbsp. fresh lemon juice, and 1 large pasteurized egg white to a cocktail shaker. Shake 2 minutes or until frothy. Strain into 2 ice-filled glasses. Garnish with fresh passion fruit. Serves 2 (serving size: about ¾ cup)

CALORIES 158; FAT 0g; PROTEIN 2g; CARB 13g; FIBER 2g; SUGARS 9g (added sugars 0g); SODIUM 36mg; CALC 2% DV; POTASSIUM 5% DV

FLIP YOUR PASTA

Invert the usual pasta-to-vegetable ratio to create fresh, carb-conscious mains packed with produce.

Eating a pasta dinner is a downright soulful experience: comforting, filling, and deeply satisfying. Yet many people clamor for lower-carb options, hence the meteoric rise of recipes using spaghetti squash, zucchini noodles (aka zoodles), or other veggie noodles. While we do love those types of dishes, they sometimes don't truly replicate the joys of eating real pasta. So here's the way to have your noodles and eat them, too: Flip your pasta by going heavy on the produce and far lighter on the starchy stuff, using half (or less) than you typically would. You'll get loads more vegetables into your diet without depriving yourself of those al dente bites you crave.

Staff Favorite • Fast
Vegetarian

Carrot Orecchiette

Hands-on: 25 min. **Total:** 25 min. Large carrots work best here. For faster prep, use a mandoline for slicing.

1 lb. large carrots, peeled and cut into ⅛-inch-thick coins
1 tsp. ground cumin
½ tsp. ground coriander
¾ tsp. kosher salt, divided
½ tsp. black pepper, divided
¼ cup extra-virgin olive oil, divided
4 oz. uncooked orecchiette pasta
1 Tbsp. red wine vinegar
¼ cup chopped fresh cilantro
2 Tbsp. chopped fresh chives
1 Tbsp. chopped fresh dill
3 oz. goat cheese, crumbled (about ¾ cup)

1. Preheat oven to 475°F.
2. Place carrots on a parchment paper–lined rimmed baking sheet; sprinkle with cumin, coriander, ¼ teaspoon salt, and ¼ teaspoon pepper. Drizzle with 2 tablespoons oil; toss to coat. Spread in an even layer (there will be overlap). Bake at 475°F for 8 minutes. Stir carrots. Spread in an even layer; bake until slices curl and are crisp-tender, about 8 minutes.
3. Cook pasta according to package directions, omitting salt and fat. Drain and transfer to a bowl; add vinegar, remaining 2 tablespoons oil, remaining ½ teaspoon salt, and remaining ¼ teaspoon pepper; toss to coat. Add carrot slices; toss gently to combine. Divide pasta mixture evenly among 4 shallow bowls.
4. Combine cilantro, chives, and dill; sprinkle over pasta. Top with cheese. Serves 4 (serving size: about 1¼ cups)

CALORIES 347; **FAT** 21g (sat 6g, unsat 13g); **PROTEIN** 9g; **CARB** 32g; **FIBER** 5g; **SUGARS** 6g (added sugars 0g); **SODIUM** 529mg; **CALC** 11% DV; **POTASSIUM** 12% DV

Fast

Garden Greens Pasta

Hands-on: 20 min. **Total:** 20 min. A little bit of pancetta pulls more than its weight in this recipe. Kale and spinach cook in the rendered drippings for rich, salty flavor, and the crisped pork bits make a delicious finishing touch for the pasta.

5 oz. uncooked whole-grain spaghetti (such as Bionaturae Whole Wheat or Barilla Whole Grain)
2 oz. diced pancetta
3 Tbsp. extra-virgin olive oil
6 garlic cloves, thinly sliced
½ tsp. crushed red pepper
8 cups sliced stemmed lacinato kale (about 12 oz.)
1 (10-oz.) pkg. fresh baby spinach
1 Tbsp. fresh lemon juice
⅝ tsp. kosher salt
¼ cup coarsely chopped unsalted roasted almonds (about 1 oz.)

1. Cook pasta according to package directions, omitting salt and fat. Drain pasta.
2. While pasta cooks, cook pancetta in a large skillet over medium, stirring often, until browned and crisp, about 6 minutes. Using a slotted spoon, transfer pancetta to a plate, reserving drippings in skillet.
3. Add oil, garlic, and crushed red pepper to drippings in skillet; cook, stirring constantly, 30 seconds. Gradually add kale and spinach, tossing with tongs until wilted. Add cooked pasta, lemon juice, and salt; toss gently to combine. Divide among 4 plates. Sprinkle servings evenly with pancetta and almonds. Serves 4 (serving size: 1½ cups)

CALORIES 358; **FAT** 21g (sat 4g, unsat 16g); **PROTEIN** 13g; **CARB** 35g; **FIBER** 7g; **SUGARS** 3g (added sugars 0g); **SODIUM** 579mg; **CALC** 16% DV; **POTASSIUM** 22% DV

Spring Vegetable Pasta Alfredo

Hands-on: 15 min. **Total:** 30 min.
Our seasonal pasta toss is made luscious and rich with a lighter take on alfredo sauce. Instead of using heavy cream, we employ flour-thickened 2% milk enriched with cream cheese. We also switch from traditional Parmesan to more robust pecorino Romano, which allows us to use less cheese while still achieving the same flavor impact. We love the flavor of Bionaturae brand whole-wheat pasta, which is milder than most other brands we've tried and doesn't overpower the vegetables.

8 oz. fresh asparagus, trimmed and
    cut into 1½-inch pieces
8 oz. fresh sugar snap peas,
    trimmed and halved
½ cup frozen green peas
4 oz. uncooked whole-wheat or
    chickpea cavatappi or penne pasta
1 Tbsp. olive oil
3 garlic cloves, minced
1¼ cups 2% reduced-fat milk
1 tsp. all-purpose flour
3 oz. cream cheese
1 tsp. kosher salt
½ tsp. black pepper
2 cups arugula (about 2 oz.)
2 oz. pecorino Romano cheese,
    shaved (about ½ cup)

1. Fill a large Dutch oven with water; bring to a boil over high. Add asparagus, snap peas, and green peas; cook until bright green, about 3 minutes. Using a slotted spoon, transfer vegetables to a colander; rinse vegetables well with cold water.
2. Add pasta to boiling water; cook according to package directions for al dente. Drain pasta.
3. Heat oil in Dutch oven over medium. Add garlic; cook, stirring constantly, until fragrant, about 30 seconds. Whisk together milk and flour in a bowl. Add milk mixture to garlic; bring to a boil. Cook, stirring occasionally, until slightly thickened, about 1 minute. Add cream cheese, salt, and pepper; whisk until cream cheese melts. Reduce heat to low; stir in pasta and pea mixture. Remove from heat; let stand 5 minutes (sauce will thicken upon standing). Top with arugula and shaved cheese. Serves 6 (serving size: about 1⅓ cups)

CALORIES 239; **FAT** 11g (sat 6g, unsat 4g); **PROTEIN** 11g; **CARB** 24g; **FIBER** 4g; **SUGARS** 6g (added sugars 0g); **SODIUM** 520mg; **CALC** 23% DV; **POTASSIUM** 8% DV

Broccoli, Lemon, and Browned Butter Pasta

Hands-on: 20 min. **Total:** 20 min.

1 lb. broccoli crowns
¼ cup canola oil, divided
1 Meyer lemon, sliced crosswise
4 oz. uncooked whole-grain shell
    pasta (such as Ancient Harvest
    Supergrain Pasta Shells)
2 Tbsp. unsalted butter
3 garlic cloves, minced (about
    1 Tbsp.)
¼ tsp. crushed red pepper
¾ tsp. kosher salt
½ tsp. black pepper
2 tsp. Meyer lemon zest
1 oz. pecorino Romano cheese,
    shaved and crumbled (about
    ¼ cup)

1. Place a baking sheet in oven. Preheat oven to 450°F (leave pan in oven as it heats).
2. Cut broccoli into florets. Peel and thinly slice stems. Toss together broccoli and 2 tablespoons oil in a bowl. Arrange broccoli in a single layer on hot baking sheet; arrange lemon slices around broccoli. Bake at 450°F until browned and crisp-tender, about 15 minutes.
3. Meanwhile, fill a Dutch oven with water; bring to a boil. Add pasta; cook according to package directions for al dente. Reserve ½ cup cooking liquid. Drain.
4. Melt butter in Dutch oven over medium-high. Cook until browned and very fragrant, about 3 minutes. Add remaining 2 tablespoons oil, garlic, and red pepper; cook, stirring constantly, 30 seconds. Stir in pasta, salt, and black pepper. Gently stir in broccoli. Stir in ¼ to ½ cup reserved cooking liquid to reach desired consistency. Top with zest and cheese. Serves 4 (serving size: 1½ cups)

CALORIES 356; **FAT** 23g (sat 6g, unsat 15g); **PROTEIN** 7g; **CARB** 33g; **FIBER** 6g; **SUGARS** 3g (added sugars 0g); **SODIUM** 538mg; **CALC** 13% DV; **POTASSIUM** 11% DV

Mostly Mushroom Pasta

Hands-on: 20 min. **Total:** 20 min.
If you're a mushroom lover, then this is the pasta dish for you. We cook the mushrooms in stages so the tougher mushrooms cook longer and the more delicate shiitakes cook less and they hold their shape. The touch of crème fraîche in the sauce gives the dish a stroganoff-like flavor; substitute full-fat sour cream if you can't find it.

4 oz. uncooked whole-wheat or spelt tortiglioni or rigatoni pasta
1 lb. portobello mushrooms
8 oz. shiitake mushrooms
3 Tbsp. olive oil
1½ Tbsp. chopped fresh thyme
5 garlic cloves, minced
8 oz. cremini mushrooms, quartered
1½ Tbsp. lower-sodium soy sauce
¼ cup crème fraîche
¾ tsp. kosher salt
½ tsp. black pepper
¼ cup chopped fresh flat-leaf parsley

1. Cook pasta according to package directions, omitting salt and fat. Reserve ½ cup cooking liquid; drain pasta.
2. While pasta cooks, remove the stems from portobello and shiitake mushrooms; reserve for another use (such as making stock). Scrape out black gills from underside of portobello caps with a spoon, and discard gills. Cut each portobello cap in half; cut each half crosswise into ½-inch slices. Cut the shiitake caps into ½-inch slices.
3. Heat oil in a large skillet over medium-high. Add thyme and garlic; cook, stirring constantly, until fragrant, about 30 seconds.

Add portobello and cremini mushrooms; cook, stirring often, 3 minutes. Add shiitakes; cook, stirring occasionally, until tender and liquid has evaporated, about 5 minutes. Stir in soy sauce; cook until absorbed. Stir in crème fraîche, salt, pepper, and ¼ cup reserved cooking liquid. Add pasta; toss gently to coat. Stir in remaining cooking liquid as needed to reach desired consistency. Sprinkle with parsley. Serves 4 (serving size: 1 ½ cups)

CALORIES 313; FAT 17g (sat 5g, unsat 10g); PROTEIN 10g; CARB 34g; FIBER 6g; SUGARS 7g (added sugars 0g); SODIUM 609mg; CALC 7% DV; POTASSIUM 29% DV

Seared Radicchio and Red Cabbage Pasta with Pickled Raisins

Hands-on: 35 min. **Total:** 35 min.
Gorgeous magenta hues make this dish a beauty. The flavor is a sophisticated blend of slightly bitter radicchio, tart-sweet pickled raisins, and toasty walnuts. We call for chickpea-based pasta, which we love for its mild flavor; you can use another legume-based pasta if you'd like, or noodles made from whole grains. For a lower-carb option, omit the pickled raisins to cut 7g of carbs per serving. When slicing the onion into wedges, try to leave some of the root end intact so the wedges hold together; this will make them easier to turn in the pan.

6 Tbsp. apple cider vinegar
2 Tbsp. water
¼ cup golden raisins
4 oz. uncooked chickpea linguine (such as Banza)

1 small (1½-lb.) head red cabbage
8 oz. radicchio (about 1½ heads)
¼ cup olive oil, divided
1 medium-size red onion (about 10 oz.), cut into 8 wedges
2 Tbsp. balsamic vinegar
1 tsp. kosher salt
½ tsp. black pepper
¼ cup chopped toasted walnuts
1 oz. Parmigiano-Reggiano cheese, shaved (about ¼ cup)

1. Bring apple cider vinegar and 2 tablespoons water to a boil in a small saucepan over high. Add raisins; boil 1 minute. Remove from heat; cool to room temperature. Drain.
2. Cook pasta according to package directions; drain and place in a bowl.
3. Cut cabbage in half lengthwise (reserve 1 half for another use). Cut remaining half into 2 equal wedges. Cut whole head radicchio in half.
4. Heat a large cast-iron skillet over high. Add 1 tablespoon oil; swirl. Add cabbage and radicchio, cut sides down, and cook until well charred, about 5 minutes. Remove radicchio from skillet. Turn cabbage wedges; cook until well charred, about 5 minutes. Remove from skillet.
5. Add 1 tablespoon oil to skillet; swirl to coat. Add onion wedges, cut sides down, and cook until well charred, about 4 minutes. Carefully turn wedges; cook until well charred, about 4 minutes. Remove from skillet.
6. Cut cabbage and radicchio crosswise into slices; separate onion wedges into "petals." Add cabbage, radicchio, onion, balsamic vinegar, salt, pepper, and remaining 2 tablespoons oil to pasta; toss well to combine. Top each serving with nuts, cheese, and pickled raisins. Serves 4 (serving size: 2 cups pasta mixture, 1 Tbsp. nuts, 1 Tbsp. cheese, and 1 Tbsp. pickled raisins)

CALORIES 395; FAT 22g (sat 4g, unsat 18g); PROTEIN 14g; CARB 41g; FIBER 8g; SUGARS 16g (added sugars 0g); SODIUM 650mg; CALC 19% DV; POTASSIUM 22% DV

HOW TO BE A MORE SUSTAINABLE COOK: A BEGINNER'S GUIDE

Making your home kitchen more eco-friendly doesn't have to be overwhelming. Even small steps can lead to meaningful change. Here, we turn to sustainability experts and chefs to give you tips, tricks, and recipes to green up your kitchen.

GROW YOUR OWN ▶

It's hard to get more sustainable than planting your own garden. If you don't have the space or time to tend to a large plot, Douglas Katz, chef-owner of Fire Food and Drink in Cleveland, recommends starting with pots on your patio and filling them with herbs, tomatoes, and peppers: "You can snip herbs like thyme and rosemary for months while keeping the plant looking good."

CHOOSE SEAFOOD WISELY

Knowing which fish is sustainable is easy with the Seafood Watch app. The Monterey Bay Aquarium app's simple red, yellow, and green rating system makes sustainable seafood shopping a snap.

Gluten Free

Steak and Carrots with Parsley Pesto

Hands-on: 30 min. **Total:** 8 hr. 40 min.
Grass-fed beef can be tough, so we use an overnight salt-and-sugar rub to tenderize it.

1 lb. grass-fed flank steak
¾ tsp. fine sea salt, divided
½ tsp. freshly ground black pepper
½ tsp. light brown sugar
1 lb. rainbow carrots
1 Tbsp. canola oil, divided
½ tsp. cumin
½ tsp. ground coriander
1 cup fresh flat-leaf parsley leaves
½ cup chopped fresh mint
¼ cup extra-virgin olive oil
1 Tbsp. apple cider vinegar
½ tsp. crushed red pepper
1 tsp. salted butter

1. Sprinkle steak evenly with ¼ teaspoon salt, black pepper, and sugar; refrigerate, uncovered, 8 houres or overnight.
2. Preheat oven to 400°F. Let steak stand at room temperature while oven heats.
3. Toss carrots in 1 teaspoon canola oil, cumin, coriander, and ¼ teaspoon salt. Spread carrots on a baking sheet, and roast at 400°F until just tender, about 40 minutes.
4. Place parsley, mint, olive oil, vinegar, and red pepper in a food processor, and pulse until chopped. Transfer to a small bowl. Stir in remaining ¼ teaspoon salt; set aside.
5. Heat a large cast-iron skillet over high. Add butter and remaining 2 teaspoons canola oil. Add steak to pan; cook 3 to 4 minutes on each side or until desired degree of doneness.
6. Divide steak and carrots evenly among 4 plates; top each serving with 2 tablespoons pesto. Serves 4

CALORIES 376; FAT 25g (sat 5g, unsat 18g); PROTEIN 26g; CARB 13g; FIBER 4g; SUGARS 6g (added sugars 1g); SODIUM 574mg; CALC 9% DV; POTASSIUM 23% DV

EMBRACE "UGLY" AS BEAUTIFUL

We all have flaws. That holds true for produce, too—from misshapen potatoes to twisted, multi-legged carrots. But most imperfections are only skin deep. Embracing funny-looking fruits and veggies can go a long way in reducing our nation's food waste problem. We toss a jaw-dropping 400 pounds of food per person per year—40% of our food. Look for "imperfect produce" bins at grocers like Whole Foods, Walmart, and Hy-Vee.

SAVE ALL (NUTRITIOUS) BITS

Parmesan rinds, radish tops, turnip greens, leftover bread—keep these nutritious bits out of the trash can, says Kevin Fink, executive chef and owner of Austin's Emmer & Rye. Steep Parmesan rinds into broths. Whiz raw radish tops and turnip greens in a food processor with pine nuts, cheese, and fresh mint, and then use on pasta or grilled vegetables. Carrot tops add fresh flavor and a feathery texture to salads. Or resuscitate leftover bread for a panzanella, says Fink: "Toss in oil, bake, then coat it with oil and vinegar. It saturates [the bread] and is so good."

STOCK UP ON FRIGID FRUIT

The produce aisle isn't the only place to get your fruit on. Registered dietitian Ashley Koff goes to the freezer section for deals on mangoes, berries, peaches, and more. "They're often more nutritious than what you'll find in the produce bin because they're picked and processed at their peak ripeness," she says, and preserving them in your freezer means they're less likely to go bad on your counter.

FRIEND A FARMER

Chef Eric Skokan of Black Cat in Boulder, Colorado, says the best way to make the transition to a sustainably minded home cook is to shop at one of nearly 8,700 farmers markets sprinkled across the U.S. "Farmers are dying to let you in on their secrets," he says. And there's an added benefit: Locally produced food at its seasonal peak is at its most nutritious and delicious.

UP YOUR VEGGIES ▶

One of the easiest ways to eat more sustainably is to downsize that larger center-of-the-plate meat entrée to a side, says chef Amanda Cohen, owner of Dirt Candy in New York: "The more vegetables you eat, the more sustainable your kitchen, period. And the trick to eating more veggies is to make them taste better." If frying eggplant, buttering spring peas, salting your salad, or dipping your crudités gets you to eat more veggies, do it.

EAT PLANT-BASED "MEAT"

Raising animals for food takes vast amounts of land, water, and energy, and those animals are a major source of greenhouse gas emissions. Even worse: Global meat production is expected to increase to a whopping 62.6 million tons in 2018, placing an even heavier environmental burden on our planet. But companies like Impossible Foods and Beyond Meat are working hard to win over even staunch carnivores with mouthwatering plant-based burgers.

OPTIMIZE GRAINS

Oats already have a low carbon footprint, and overnight oats get a sustainability bump: The tasty breakfast requires no heat. But heritage grain legend and Anson Mills founder Glenn Roberts says you can take it one step further: "With heirloom whole grains, nutrition is at its highest if you allow them to soak." He recommends starting with a water-to-grain ratio of 1-to-1 for his famous Carolina Gold rice. "Soak it on the counter for a good 12 hours; 24 is better. Look for bits of foam like Champagne," he says. Then cook the rice in that same liquid.

BUY FROZEN FISH

"Chefs don't like frozen seafood," says Andrea Reusing, chef and owner of Lantern in Chapel Hill, North Carolina. Many think freezing can change its texture and flavor. But the way fish is frozen today is much improved, and that can mean better quality, especially for seafood that travels a long way. Plus, seafood frozen at sea reduces food waste.

Gluten Free • Vegetarian

Creamy Artichoke Dip

Hands-on: 20 min. **Total:** 1 hr.

3 garlic cloves
18 oz. frozen artichoke hearts, thawed
⅔ cup plain 2% reduced-fat Greek yogurt
4 oz. silken tofu
1¼ oz. Parmesan cheese, shredded (about ⅓ cup), divided
4 oz. ⅓-less-fat cream cheese
¾ tsp. kosher salt
¼ tsp. black pepper
⅛ tsp. cayenne pepper

1. Preheat oven to 350°F.
2. Add garlic to food processor and pulse until minced. Add half of artichoke hearts, yogurt, tofu, ⅓ cup Parmesan cheese, and cream cheese. Blend until smooth. Transfer to a medium bowl.
3. Roughly chop remaining artichokes; fold into yogurt mixture. Add salt, black pepper, and cayenne.
4. Divide dip among 4 (8-ounce) ramekins. Top evenly with remaining ⅓ cup Parmesan. Bake at 350°F until bubbly, about 30 minutes. Turn broiler to high; cook until tops are golden, about 5 minutes. Serve warm. Serves 15 (serving size: ¼ cup)

CALORIES 61; **FAT** 3g (sat 2g, unsat 1g); **PROTEIN** 4g; **CARB** 4g; **FIBER** 2g; **SUGARS** 1g (added sugars 0g); **SODIUM** 197mg; **CALC** 7% DV; **POTASSIUM** 1% DV

Vegetarian

Mini Breakfast Pizzas

Hands-on: 1 hr. **Total:** 1 hr.
This glorious all-in-one—pizza and salad—is a tasty dinner or weekend breakfast.

12 oz. whole-wheat pizza dough
1 cup part-skim ricotta cheese
1¼ tsp. lemon zest
¼ tsp. kosher salt, divided
¼ tsp. ground pepper, divided
4 large eggs
1 oz. Parmesan cheese, grated (about ¼ cup)
2 tsp. extra-virgin olive oil
2 tsp. fresh lemon juice
4 cups packed baby arugula

1. Place a pizza stone or large baking sheet in oven; preheat to 450°F (leave stone in oven as it preheats).
2. Let dough stand at room temperature for 30 minutes. Divide dough into 4 pieces.
3. On a lightly floured surface, roll each piece of dough into a 7-inch circle. Pierce liberally with a fork.
4. Arrange 2 dough circles on hot pizza stone. Bake at 450°F for 3 minutes. Remove from oven, and flip so cooked side is up. Set aside. Repeat with remaining 2 dough circles.

5. Stir together ricotta cheese and zest in a medium bowl. Divide ricotta mixture evenly among cooked sides of dough circles; sprinkle evenly with ⅛ teaspoon salt and ⅛ teaspoon pepper. Top each dough circle with 1 egg and 1 tablespoon Parmesan.
6. Working in 2 batches, return topped dough circles to pizza stone. Bake at 450°F until egg whites are set and yolks are still a little runny, about 6 to 8 minutes.
7. Whisk together oil, juice, the remaining ⅛ teaspoon salt, and remaining ⅛ teaspoon pepper in a large bowl. Stir in arugula.
8. Top each cooked pizza with 1 cup dressed arugula. Serves 4

CALORIES 386; FAT 16g (sat 6g, unsat 8g); PROTEIN 21g; CARB 42g; FIBER 3g; SUGARS 1g (added sugars 0g); SODIUM 711mg; CALC 29% DV; POTASSIUM 8% DV

Gluten Free

Roast Chicken with Lentils and Yogurt

Hands-on: 50 min. **Total:** 50 min.
We augment a modest portion of chicken thighs with lentils to satisfy.

4 tsp. canola oil, divided
3 large carrots, sliced
1 shallot, chopped
2 garlic cloves, chopped
1 tsp. fresh thyme leaves, plus more for garnish
¾ tsp. salt, divided
¾ cup dried lentils
1 cup unsalted chicken stock
2 cups water
4 (6-oz.) bone-in, skin-on chicken thighs
⅛ tsp. black pepper
1 cup plain nonfat Greek yogurt
1 tsp. lemon zest

1. Preheat oven to 450°F. Place oven rack in top third of oven.
2. Heat 2 teaspoons oil in a Dutch oven over medium-high. Add carrots and shallot; cook until softened, about 2 minutes. Add garlic; cook until fragrant, about 30 seconds. Stir in thyme and ½ teaspoon salt. Add lentils, stock, and 2 cups water. Bring to simmer, cover partially, and cook until al dente, checking occasionally and adding more water as needed to keep lentils covered, about 25 minutes. Drain, reserving ¼ cup cooking liquid.
3. Heat remaining 2 teaspoons oil in a large cast-iron skillet over medium-high. Sprinkle chicken with pepper and remaining ¼ teaspoon salt. Place chicken in pan, skin side down. Cook until slightly browned, about 3 minutes. Flip and cook until other side is browned, about 3 minutes. Move pan to oven. Bake at 450°F until chicken is done, about 20 minutes.
4. Whisk together yogurt and zest in a medium bowl. Set aside.
5. Spread ¼ cup yogurt mixture onto each of 4 plates; top each with ¾ cup lentil mixture. Top each serving with 1 chicken thigh, drizzle with 1 tablespoon reserved cooking liquid, and garnish with thyme. Serves 4

CALORIES 571; FAT 30g (sat 7g, unsat 21g); PROTEIN 41g; CARB 33g; FIBER 6g; SUGARS 6g (added sugars 0g); SODIUM 639mg; CALC 12% DV; POTASSIUM 24% DV

SEEK OUT THESE SUGARS
Keeping true to his Oglala Lakota roots, Minnesota chef Sean Sherman is best known for his use of regional and indigenous foods. That means refined white sugar derived from sugarcane or GMO beets is off the table. Instead he uses sweet, natural alternatives like honey, maple, and agave that don't rely on intense farming practices. "There are so many cool spectrums of honey," says Sherman. And buying honey from local producers helps keep local bee populations up.

AVOID ANTIBIOTICS
Antibiotic resistance is a serious, looming threat. The routine use of antibiotics in animals raised for food (to promote growth and keep them healthy in often crowded environments) is now propagating antibiotic-resistant "superbugs." We're seeing a global rise in ailments that no longer can be treated by a simple round of antibiotics. One of the best things to do is to buy chicken and other meats raised without antibiotics. "Look for the 'No Antibiotics Ever' label," says Maryn McKenna, author of *Big Chicken.*

DON'T LET LEFTOVERS GO
Eat your leftovers; don't toss them. The Natural Resources Defense Council peeked into trash cans in Denver, Nashville, and New York, and they found that two-thirds of the discarded food could have been eaten—with coffee, milk, apples, bread, potatoes, and pasta topping the list.

GO FOR QUALITY OVER QUANTITY
We love cheese, but it has a hefty environmental footprint. Per the Environmental Working Group, cheese is third on the list of highest emissions (behind lamb and beef). For every pound of cheese eaten, about 13½ pounds of carbon dioxide are emitted. Don't totally ditch cheese, though. Make it a special-occasion item—and indulge in an artisan cheese so it won't feel like sacrificing.

FIND FARMED FISH ▶
Not all farmed fish are unsustainable. "Best Choice"–rated farmed trout is a healthy protein with low environmental impact. It's a favorite of Clayton Chapman, chef-owner of The Grey Plume in Omaha, Nebraska. "Farmed trout is a great entry point for home cooks," he says. It's versatile, affordable, and available year-round. "You can grill or roast it; it takes to different seasonings."

SECOND-GUESS SELL-BY DATES
Sell-by, best-by, use-by, enjoy-by, and best-if-used-before dates are confusing because they don't have a precise legal definition and are often based on the manufacturer's concerns over food freshness, not food safety. That confusion prompts many of us to toss food that's often still perfectly safe to eat. Large retailers are trying to standardize those phrases, but variations still abound. Before tossing an item based on date alone, take a closer look. Except for infant formula, if the date passes during home storage, a product should still be safe until you can see spoilage if it's handled properly, says the USDA.

PICK PASTURED PORK
Try to avoid pork raised in large confinement operations (also known as CAFOs), which often pollute the air and nearby waterways, says Paul Willis, co-founder of Niman Ranch's pork program. Look for animals raised on pasture. And instead of going straight for the bacon, pork chop, or tenderloin, give an underutilized cut a try. Willis' favorite? A pork shoulder roast, because it's rich in flavor-enhancing intramuscular fat.

EAT SEASONALLY
Eating produce in season is tastier, more nutritious, and can be better for the planet: Because fruits and veggies are often harvested in your region, it cuts down on the carbon footprint from long-distance transportation. Even better—buy from nearby growers. Find out what's ready to harvest near you via the new Seasonal Food Guide app, which includes more than 140 types of fruits, veggies, legumes, nuts, and herbs.

Gluten Free • Make Ahead

Smoked Trout Niçoise

Hands-on: 1 hr. **Total:** 1 hr.

8 oz. green beans
2 large eggs
1¼ lb. red potatoes
4½ Tbsp. extra-virgin olive oil
¼ cup white wine vinegar
¼ cup chopped fresh flat-leaf parsley
⅛ tsp. sea salt
¼ tsp. freshly ground black pepper
5½ oz. lacinato kale
1½ tsp. Dijon mustard
2 cups cherry tomatoes, halved
4 oz. radishes, sliced
1½ oz. pitted kalamata olives, halved
4 oz. smoked trout

1. Prepare a bowl of ice water. Bring a medium pot of water to a boil. Add green beans; cook for 2 minutes. Remove with a slotted spoon; plunge into ice water. Return pot of water to a boil. Add eggs; cook 6 minutes. Remove with slotted spoon; add to ice bath. Once cool, peel and halve eggs.
2. Return water to a boil, and add potatoes. Cook until tender, 15 to 17 minutes. Drain, then chop potatoes.
3. Whisk together oil, vinegar, parsley, salt, and pepper in a bowl.
4. Remove stems from kale; roughly tear leaves. Place torn leaves in a bowl; add half of dressing, and use your hands to lightly massage into kale. Whisk Dijon into remaining dressing; set aside.
5. Divide kale among 4 plates. Top with green beans, potatoes, tomatoes, radishes, and olives. Top salad with 1 egg half and 1 ounce trout. Drizzle dressing over salads. Serves 4 (serving size: 2 cups salad)

CALORIES 410; **FAT** 24g (sat 4g, unsat 19g); **PROTEIN** 16g; **CARB** 35g; **FIBER** 6g; **SUGARS** 6g (added sugars 0g); **SODIUM** 629mg; **CALC** 13% DV; **POTASSIUM** 30% DV

FLEX YOUR MUSSELS

For a quick, sustainable weeknight meal, try a steamy bowl of farmed mussels, rated a "Best Choice" by Seafood Watch. Mussels filter the water they're grown in, helping to keep the water clean, and they don't require any added feeds to grow. "You don't have to butcher it, cure it, or braise it. They're really simple," says lauded chef Maria Hines, owner of Tilth in Seattle. When buying, look for shells that are tightly closed.

JOIN A CSF

Americans prefer their seafood in the form of shrimp, salmon, and tuna, but there's more deliciousness to be had if you're open to it. That's the message from Jeremiah Bacon, chef-partner of The Macintosh in Charleston, South Carolina. His advice: Join a community-supported fishery. Much like its CSA cousin, members pay up front and each week share in the bounty of their local fishermen's catch.

OPT FOR GRASS-FED

"Choose foods that actively save the world, not just do less harm," says Anthony Myint, co-chef and co-owner of The Perennial in San Francisco. "Anything that's grown in a way that fosters healthy soil is good." Look for producers who embrace adaptive multi-paddock grazing—meaning cattle graze closer together for shorter periods of time, allowing grass and soil to regenerate. Or buy beef or bison labeled "American Grassfed".

REUSE BAGS

Don't wait for a plastic bag ban; pony up with pretty reusable bags. It's a tiny step that helps reduce the 8 million tons of plastic that reach our oceans each year.

EMBRACE THE WHOLE BIRD

The nose-to-tail movement can be tough for the home cook, but not when it comes to chicken, says cookbook author Molly Watson. Roast one for dinner. Use the bones for soup stock, and sauté the livers in a bit of butter for a quick snack with crackers.

EASTER MADE EASY

Celebrate the first big entertaining occasion of the year with a beautiful spread featuring lots of seasonal flourishes.

Staff Favorite • Fast
Gluten Free • Make Ahead
Vegetarian

Cucumber-Lime-Lavender Spritzer

Hands-on: 5 min. **Total:** 30 min.
This effervescent, nonalcoholic refresher perfectly balances floral, tangy, and sweet flavors. If you'd like to turn it into a tipple, try adding a splash of gin or vodka.

½ cup water
⅓ cup granulated sugar
¼ cup loosely packed fresh mint leaves
1 Tbsp. dried culinary lavender
4 cups chopped peeled cucumber (about 4 cucumbers)
⅔ cup fresh lime juice (from about 4 limes)
6 cups club soda
Mint sprigs and lime wedges (optional)

1. Combine ½ cup water and sugar in a saucepan. Bring to a boil over high, stirring until sugar dissolves. Remove from heat. Add mint leaves and lavender. Steep 12 minutes. Pour through a fine wire-mesh strainer into a bowl; discard solids. Cool completely, about 10 minutes.
2. Combine cucumber and lime juice in a blender; process until smooth.
3. Stir together mint-lavender syrup, cucumber-lime mixture, and club soda in a large pitcher. Serve over ice; garnish with mint sprigs and lime wedges, if desired. Serves 8 (serving size: 1 cup)

CALORIES 46; FAT 0g; PROTEIN 0g; CARB 12g; FIBER 1g; SUGARS 10g (added sugars 8g); SODIUM 39mg; CALC 2% DV; POTASSIUM 3% DV

Our Easter feast celebrates early spring flavors, from asparagus and rhubarb to lamb and mushrooms. Most of the recipes are quick, and we offer get-ahead tips (p. 87), so the meal is a cinch to pull together the day of. The menu serves 8 (with dessert leftovers).

MENU

Our Easter feast celebrates early spring flavors, from asparagus and rhubarb to lamb and mushrooms. Most of the recipes are quick, and we offer get-ahead tips (p. 87), so the meal is a cinch to pull together the day of. The menu serves 8 (with dessert leftovers).

CUCUMBER-LIME-LAVENDER SPRITZER

SWEET-AND-SOUR MUSHROOM TOASTS WITH TARRAGON

ROASTED SPRING LAMB WITH FENNEL, RHUBARB, AND STRAWBERRIES

ASPARAGUS WITH AVOCADO-HERB DRESSING

RHUBARB UPSIDE-DOWN CAKE

Fast • Vegetarian

Sweet-and-Sour Mushroom Toasts with Tarragon

Hands-on: 10 min. **Total:** 10 min.
Be sure to get the skillet very hot before adding the mushrooms; otherwise, you won't get good browning (which is the key to maximum flavor).

2 Tbsp. olive oil
1½ lbs. mixed fresh mushrooms (such as shiitake, oyster, and cremini), quartered if large
¼ cup minced shallot
1 Tbsp. chopped fresh thyme
1 tsp. onion powder
3 garlic cloves, minced
2 Tbsp. light brown sugar
2 Tbsp. sherry vinegar
1½ Tbsp. chopped fresh tarragon, divided
¼ tsp. kosher salt
3 oz. ⅓-less-fat cream cheese, softened
16 (¼-oz.) whole-grain baguette slices, toasted

1. Heat oil in a large high-sided skillet over high. Add mushrooms; cook, stirring often, until well browned, 2 to 3 minutes. Reduce heat to medium. Add shallot, thyme, onion powder, and garlic; cook, stirring often, until mushrooms release their liquid, about 3 minutes.
2. Add sugar, vinegar, half of tarragon, and salt. Increase heat to medium-high, and cook, stirring often, until glazy, 2 to 3 minutes. Remove from heat, and stir in remaining tarragon.
3. Spread cream cheese evenly on toast slices. Top evenly with mushroom mixture. Serves 8 (serving size: 2 toasts)

CALORIES 134; **FAT** 7g (sat 2g, unsat 4g); **PROTEIN** 5g; **CARB** 15g; **FIBER** 2g; **SUGARS** 6g (added sugars 3g); **SODIUM** 179mg; **CALC** 3% DV; **POTASSIUM** 9% DV

Staff Favorite • Gluten Free

Roasted Spring Lamb with Fennel, Rhubarb, and Strawberries

Hands-on: 25 min. **Total:** 1 hr. 15 min.
"Frenched" racks of lamb are trimmed so that the bones are cleaned of fat and meat; if you can't find pre-frenched lamb racks, ask the butcher to french them for you.

3 cups unsalted chicken stock
1 Tbsp. red wine vinegar
¼ cup turbinado sugar, divided
1 lb. fresh rhubarb stalks, trimmed and cut into 3-in. pieces, divided
1 qt. fresh strawberries, divided
3 Tbsp. olive oil, divided
2 (2-lb.) lean racks of lamb, frenched
2 Tbsp. chopped fresh oregano
2 Tbsp. chopped fresh thyme
2 tsp. kosher salt, divided
1¼ tsp. black pepper, divided
2 fennel bulbs, trimmed and cut into 16 wedges
Fennel fronds (optional)

1. Preheat oven to 400°F.
2. Combine stock, vinegar, 2 tablespoons sugar, half of the rhubarb, and half of the strawberries in a saucepan. Cover and bring to a boil over high. Reduce heat to medium-low; cook

15 minutes. Pour mixture through a fine wire-mesh strainer into a bowl; discard solids. Reserve liquid.

3. Heat 2 tablespoons olive oil in a heavy roasting pan over medium-high. Rub remaining 1 tablespoon oil over lamb; sprinkle lamb with oregano, thyme, 1½ teaspoons salt, and 1 teaspoon pepper. Place lamb in pan; cook, turning occasionally, until browned on all sides, 8 to 10 minutes.

4. Scatter fennel around lamb in a single layer. Transfer to preheated oven; roast until a thermometer inserted in thickest portion of lamb registers 130°F and fennel is caramelized and tender, about 20 minutes. Using tongs, transfer lamb to a cutting board; place fennel on a platter, and cover with aluminum foil to keep warm. Reserve 2 tablespoons pan juices in roasting pan; discard remaining pan juices.

5. Add remaining rhubarb and strawberries to roasting pan; toss to coat. Sprinkle with ¼ teaspoon salt and remaining 2 tablespoons sugar; arrange in a single layer. Roast at 400°F until just tender, 4 to 5 minutes. (Do not overcook.) Transfer to platter with fennel.

6. Remove roasting pan from oven; add stock mixture. Cook over high, stirring occasionally, until reduced to about ¾ cup; stir in remaining ¼ teaspoon salt and remaining ¼ teaspoon pepper. Carve lamb; add to platter. Drizzle with ¼ cup sauce; top with fennel fronds, if desired. Serve with remaining sauce. Serves 8 (serving size: about 2 chops, 1 cup vegetables and fruit, and 1 Tbsp. sauce)

CALORIES 342; FAT 16g (sat 5g, unsat 8g); PROTEIN 33g; CARB 19g; FIBER 4g; SUGARS 13g (added sugars 8g); SODIUM 643mg; CALC 10% DV; POTASSIUM 25% DV

Fast • Gluten Free
Make Ahead • Vegetarian

Asparagus with Avocado-Herb Dressing

Hands-on: 10 min. **Total:** 10 min.
If you can find white asparagus, try using half white and half green. The white variety will need to boil a couple minutes longer than the green.

2 lb. fresh asparagus, trimmed
1 ripe avocado, sliced
1 cup whole buttermilk
¼ cup fresh basil leaves, divided
¼ cup sliced fresh chives, divided
1½ oz. goat cheese
1 Tbsp. Champagne vinegar
¾ tsp. ground white pepper
½ tsp. kosher salt
½ tsp. granulated sugar
Coarsely ground black pepper
  (optional)

1. Bring a large pot of water to a boil over high. Add asparagus; boil until crisp-tender, about 3 minutes. Drain; rinse under cool water. Pat dry.

2. Combine avocado, buttermilk, half of the basil, half of the chives, goat cheese, vinegar, white pepper, salt, and sugar in a blender. Process until smooth.

3. Arrange asparagus on a platter. Top with dressing, remaining basil, remaining chives, and, if desired, black pepper. Serves 8 (serving size: ½ cup asparagus and ¼ cup dressing)

CALORIES 105; FAT 6g (sat 2g, unsat 4g); PROTEIN 5g; CARB 9g; FIBER 4g; SUGARS 4g (added sugars 0g); SODIUM 177mg; CALC 9% DV; POTASSIUM 12% DV

MAKE AHEAD
PREPARE A FEW THINGS IN ADVANCE SO THAT EASTER SUNDAY IS AN EASY, BREEZY GATHERING THAT THE COOK CAN ENJOY, TOO.

1. SPRITZERS
Combine ingredients (minus club soda) in a pitcher up to a day ahead and chill; add fizz just before serving.

2. ASPARAGUS
Cook asparagus and blend the dressing the day before. Assemble and leave at room temp an hour before serving.

3. CAKE
Bake the cake in the morning, invert onto a plate or cake stand, and leave at room temperature, loosely covered, until ready to serve.

Rhubarb Upside-Down Cake

Hands-on: 25 min. **Total:** 1 hr. 45 min.
Be patient when turning the cake out of the pan; it may take several minutes for it to fully release. Mayonnaise helps create a super-moist cake.

TOPPING
Cooking spray
1 lb. fresh rhubarb stalks, trimmed and cut into 4-in. pieces
½ cup granulated sugar
2 tsp. cornstarch
¼ cup unsalted butter
¼ cup packed light brown sugar
2 tsp. chopped fresh thyme
½ tsp. ground ginger
½ tsp. ground cardamom
¼ tsp. kosher salt
CAKE
4¼ oz. unbleached cake flour (about 1 cup)
3 oz. white whole-wheat flour (about ¾ cup)
1¼ tsp. baking powder
½ tsp. ground cardamom
½ tsp. ground ginger
½ tsp. kosher salt
¾ cup granulated sugar
⅔ cup canola mayonnaise
2 Tbsp. unsalted butter, softened
3 large eggs
1 tsp. orange zest
1 tsp. vanilla extract
⅔ cup reduced-fat sour cream
ADDITIONAL INGREDIENTS
2 tsp. fresh thyme leaves
¾ cup plain 2% reduced-fat Greek yogurt

1. Preheat oven to 350°F.
2. Prepare the topping: Coat a 9-inch round cake pan with cooking spray. Combine rhubarb, ½ cup granulated sugar, and cornstarch in a bowl. Toss to coat; set aside.
3. Combine ¼ cup butter, brown sugar, chopped thyme, ½ teaspoon ginger, ½ teaspoon cardamom, and ¼ teaspoon salt in a saucepan. Cook over medium, stirring often, until butter is melted. Pour mixture evenly into prepared pan.
4. Prepare the cake: Whisk together flours, baking powder, ½ teaspoon cardamom, ½ teaspoon ginger, and ½ teaspoon salt in a bowl; set aside.
5. Combine ¾ cup granulated sugar, mayonnaise, and 2 tablespoons butter in the bowl of a stand mixer fitted with the paddle attachment; beat on medium speed until well incorporated and smooth, 4 to 5 minutes, stopping to scrape down sides of bowl as necessary. Add eggs, 1 at a time, beating well after each addition. Beat in zest and vanilla until just combined.
6. Add flour mixture and sour cream alternately to granulated sugar mixture, beginning and ending with flour mixture, beating just until combined after each addition.
7. Arrange coated rhubarb pieces in a single layer on butter mixture in pan, including any excess sugar from bowl. Pour batter into pan; smooth with a spatula. Gently drop pan on counter several times to remove air bubbles. Bake at 350°F until a wooden pick inserted in center comes out clean, 55 minutes to 1 hour.
8. Cool in pan on a wire rack 20 minutes. Run a knife around edge of cake to loosen it from sides of pan. Place a serving plate upside down on top of cake; carefully invert pan onto plate. Let stand until cake releases from pan, about 5 minutes; carefully remove pan. Sprinkle cake with thyme leaves. Serve with yogurt.
Serves 12 (serving size: 1 cake slice and 1 Tbsp. yogurt)

CALORIES 304; **FAT** 13g (sat 5g, unsat 6g); **PROTEIN** 6g; **CARB** 42g; **FIBER** 2g; **SUGARS** 28g (added sugars 25g); **SODIUM** 300mg; **CALC** 11% DV; **POTASSIUM** 5% DV

Golden Beet Bloody Mary

Hands-on: 15 min. **Total:** 1 hr. 15 min.
Brighten your brunch-time beverage with a Bloody that delivers on all fronts: brisk and bold with the perfect dose of briny tang. Not to mention its nutritional boost: Tomatoes and beets are excellent sources of potassium, which helps regulate the body's fluid balance and keep blood pressure in check. We'll cheers to that!

Preheat oven to 400°F. Wash and trim 4 (4-oz.) golden beets, and reserve green tops. Wrap the beets separately in aluminum foil, and bake at 400°F for 1 hour. Let stand until cool enough to handle. Peel beets; cut into wedges. Place beet wedges and 1 lb. halved yellow or Sun Gold tomatoes in a blender; process until smooth. Pour mixture through a fine wire-mesh strainer into a bowl; discard solids. Add 3 Tbsp. lemon juice, 2 Tbsp. pickled banana pepper juice, 2 tsp. reduced-sodium Worcestershire sauce, 1½ tsp. prepared horseradish, ½ tsp. ground white pepper, and ¼ tsp. celery salt; mix well. Cover and chill 30 minutes. Fill each of 4 glasses with ice and 1 oz. vodka. Top each with ⅓ cup beet juice mixture. Garnish with reserved beet greens, lemon wedges, and additional peeled and sliced beets, if desired.
Serves 4 (serving size: about ¾ cup)

CALORIES 141; **FAT** 0g; **PROTEIN** 3g; **CARB** 17g; **FIBER** 5g; **SUGARS** 11g (added sugars 0g); **SODIUM** 275mg; **CALC** 3% DV; **POTASSIUM** 19% DV

MAKE IT A MOCKTAIL

The beauty of a Bloody is that it needs no booze to shine. You can simply omit the vodka.

GORGEOUS PASSOVER DESSERTS

Most of the Seder meal is fixed, so the sweet finale is your biggest opportunity to get creative and have fun with flavors. Here are two ways to close out the feast.

Gluten Free • Make Ahead Vegetarian

Orange-Almond Cake

Hands-on: 20 min. **Total:** 1 hr. 30 min. Because traditional versions of almond extract and powdered sugar can contain spirits and cornstarch (respectively), seek out kosher-for-Passover versions.

6 large eggs, yolks and whites separated
1 cup granulated sugar, divided
1½ tsp. orange zest
¼ cup fresh orange juice
½ tsp. kosher salt
½ tsp. kosher-for-Passover almond extract
7 oz. (about 2 cups) almond flour
Kosher-for-Passover cooking spray
¼ cup sliced almonds
1 Tbsp. kosher-for-Passover powdered sugar

1. Preheat oven to 350°F.
2. In an electric mixer fitted with whisk attachment, beat egg whites on medium until foamy, about 1 to 2 minutes. Increase speed to high, and 1 tablespoon at a time, add ½ cup granulated sugar; beat until stiff peaks form, about 3 to 5 minutes. Transfer egg whites to a separate bowl.
3. Beat egg yolks and remaining ½ cup granulated sugar in an electric mixer fitted with paddle attachment on medium until pale and creamy, about 2 minutes. Add zest, juice, salt, and extract; beat until combined. Fold in almond flour. Spoon one-third of egg whites into yolk mixture; gently fold until combined. Add remaining egg whites; gently fold until combined. Spoon mixture into a 9-inch springform pan coated with cooking spray. Sprinkle almonds around outside edge.
4. Bake at 350°F until cake springs back when lightly touched in the middle, 35 to 40 minutes. Run a knife around pan edge. Cool cake in pan on a wire rack 10 minutes; remove pan sides. Cool cake fully on wire rack. Sprinkle with powdered sugar. Serves 10 (serving size: 1 wedge)

CALORIES 271; **FAT** 15g (sat 2g, unsat 13g); **PROTEIN** 9g; **CARB** 27g; **FIBER** 3g; **SUGARS** 22g (added sugars 21g); **SODIUM** 147mg; **CALC** 7% DV; **POTASSIUM** 2% DV

Staff Favorite • Gluten Free Vegetarian

Strawberry, Basil, and Balsamic "Slablova"

Hands-on: 20 min. **Total:** 5 hr. 50 min. Inspired by a pavlova-for-a-crowd "slablova" recipe on Food52, we created our own Passover version. Though potato starch is a go-to for Passover baked goods, we found tapioca starch gives better texture here. For a non-Passover occasion, cornstarch makes a beautiful pavlova.

1¼ Tbsp. kosher-for-Passover tapioca starch
1¾ cups plus 1 Tbsp. superfine sugar, divided
8 large egg whites, at room temperature
2 tsp. fresh lemon juice
½ tsp. kosher salt
3 cups fresh strawberries, hulled and quartered
¼ cup chopped or torn fresh basil
3 Tbsp. kosher-for-Passover white or red balsamic vinegar
1¾ cups heavy cream

1. Preheat oven to 250°F. Line a rimmed baking sheet with parchment paper.
2. Whisk together tapioca starch and 1¾ cups sugar in a small bowl.
3. Beat together egg whites, lemon juice, and salt with an electric mixer on medium speed until frothy, 1 to 2 minutes. Increase speed to medium-high, and gradually add sugar mixture, beating until stiff, glossy peaks form, about 10 minutes.
4. Spread meringue onto prepared baking sheet in an even layer to form a 13- x 10-inch rectangle.

continued

Bake at 250°F until set and firm, about 2 hours and 30 minutes. Turn oven off, and let stand in oven to completely cool, about 3 hours.

5. Combine strawberries, basil, and vinegar in a bowl; let stand 30 minutes.

6. Just before serving, beat together cream and remaining 1 tablespoon sugar with an electric mixer on medium-high speed until soft peaks form. Spread whipped cream evenly over meringue. Top with strawberry mixture. Serve immediately. Serves 15 (serving size: 1 [3-in.] piece)

CALORIES 208; FAT 10g (sat 6g, unsat 3g); PROTEIN 3g; CARB 28g; FIBER 1g; SUGARS 26g (added sugars 23g); SODIUM 102mg; CALC 3% DV; POTASSIUM 3% DV

THE RECIPE MAKEOVER

LIGHTEN UP CLASSIC COFFEE CAKE

Satisfy your café pastry craving for 75% less added sugar and 200 fewer calories.

A tall cup of Joe knows no better match than a wedge of coffee cake. But nutritionally, standard coffee cake does no favors: Packed with up to two sticks of butter, a trio of added sugars, and sour cream, the beloved breakfast classic comes in north of 500 calories with 13g sat fat (more than half the daily recommended limit) and a whopping 40g added sugar in a single slice. To build a better breakfast cake that won't send you into midmorning nap mode, we start by building a whole-grain base bolstered with warm spices and brightened up with citrus juice and zest. The savory notes of olive oil lend complexity, while the oil's characteristic fruitiness is accentuated by the citrus zest. The

finished product: a bakery-quality coffee cake with a fraction of the sat fat and only 333 calories per slice.

Make Ahead • Vegetarian

Orange-Walnut Coffee Cake

Hands-on: 30 min. **Total:** 1 hr. 40 min.

FILLING
1 cup pitted whole dates
1 tsp. vanilla extract
1 tsp. ground cinnamon
⅛ tsp. kosher salt
¼ cup fresh orange juice
CAKE
9 ¼ oz. (about 2⅛ cups) whole-wheat pastry flour
2 tsp. baking powder
½ tsp. baking soda
½ tsp. ground cinnamon
½ tsp. ground cardamom
¼ tsp. kosher salt
⅔ cup plain 2% reduced-fat Greek yogurt
⅔ cup packed light brown sugar
⅔ cup extra-virgin olive oil
2 large eggs
1 Tbsp. orange zest
¼ cup fresh orange juice
1 tsp. vanilla extract
Cooking spray
½ cup chopped walnuts
GLAZE
¼ cup plain 2% reduced-fat Greek yogurt
2 Tbsp. powdered sugar
½ tsp. orange zest
1 Tbsp. fresh orange juice

1. Prepare the filling: Place dates in a small bowl; add hot water to cover. Let stand until softened, about 30 minutes; drain.

2. Place drained dates, 1 teaspoon vanilla, 1 teaspoon cinnamon, and ⅛ teaspoon salt in a food processor. With processor running, add ¼ cup orange juice, 1 tablespoon at a time, until smooth.

3. Prepare the cake: Preheat oven to 350°F. Stir together flour, baking powder, baking soda, ½ teaspoon cinnamon, cardamom, and ¼ teaspoon salt in a medium bowl.

4. Stir together ⅔ cup yogurt, brown sugar, oil, eggs, 1 tablespoon zest, ½ cup juice, and 1 teaspoon vanilla in a separate bowl. Stir yogurt mixture into flour mixture.

5. Coat a 12-cup Bundt pan with cooking spray. Set aside 1 ½ cups batter. Pour remaining batter into prepared pan. Spoon filling over batter; use the back of a spoon to spread evenly. Sprinkle walnuts over date mixture. Pour 1 ½ cups reserved batter over walnuts. Bake at 350°F until a wooden pick inserted in center comes out clean, about 30 minutes. Cool in pan on a wire rack 10 minutes; invert cake onto rack, and cool completely.

6. Prepare the glaze: Whisk together ¼ cup yogurt, powdered sugar, ½ teaspoon zest, and 1 tablespoon juice in a medium bowl. Spread glaze over cake. Serves 14 (serving size: 1 slice)

CALORIES 333; FAT 15g (sat 2g, unsat 12g); PROTEIN 6g; CARB 45g; FIBER 5g; SUGARS 20g (added sugars 11g); SODIUM 116mg; CALC 14% DV; POTASSIUM 7% DV

OLIVE OIL
Swap the butter for heart-healthy olive oil, and you'll shave off 8g sat fat per serving. Bonus: Using a liquid oil keeps the cake moist longer.

DATES
Pureed dates add caramel-like sweetness to the filling, boost fiber, and slash added sugar by 29g (that's 7 teaspoons) per slice.

YOGURT
Protein-packed Greek yogurt does double duty: It adds moisture to the cake for a fraction of the sat fat of sour cream and creates an elegant glaze.

Spring is here! With it comes crisp, fresh-from-the-ground produce such as asparagus, peas, and radishes. Bring the best of the season to your table with these recipes.

20-MINUTE MAINS

Fast

Mussels with Spicy Tomato Sauce

Hands-on: 15 min. **Total:** 15 min.
San Marzano plum tomatoes—known for their pure tomato flavor—are the secret to this quick sauce. Crusty baguette is a must-have to soak up the extra.

1 Tbsp. extra-virgin olive oil
1 Tbsp. unsalted butter
2 Tbsp. finely chopped shallot
1 oz. prosciutto, diced
2 tsp. finely chopped garlic
⅛ tsp. crushed red pepper
1 cup chopped boxed or canned San Marzano tomatoes (such as Pomì)
½ cup dry white wine
1 tsp. granulated sugar
⅜ tsp. kosher salt
2 lb. mussels, scrubbed and debearded
2 Tbsp. chopped fresh flat-leaf parsley, divided
Lemon wedges (optional)
8 (½-oz.) whole-wheat baguette slices, toasted

1. Heat olive oil and butter in a large Dutch oven over medium-high until butter melts and starts to foam, about 1 minute. Add shallot and prosciutto; cook, stirring occasionally, until shallot is translucent and prosciutto is crisp, about 5 minutes. Add garlic and crushed red pepper; cook, stirring often, until fragrant, about 1 minute. Add tomatoes, wine, sugar, and salt; bring to a simmer.
2. Add mussels to sauce. Cover and cook until mussels start to open, 4 to 5 minutes. (Discard any mussels that do not open.) Stir in 1 tablespoon parsley. Lightly toss, and spoon into 4 bowls. Top with remaining 1 tablespoon parsley and, if desired, lemon wedges. Serve with bread. Serves 4 (serving size: 2 cups mussel mixture and 2 slices bread)

CALORIES 376; **FAT** 10g (sat 3g, unsat 5g); **PROTEIN** 38g; **CARB** 26g; **FIBER** 2g; **SUGARS** 4g (added sugars 1g); **SODIUM** 548mg; **CALC** 10% DV; **POTASSIUM** 5% DV

Fast • Gluten Free

Almond-Crusted Trout with Swiss Chard

Hands-on: 20 min. **Total:** 20 min.
Trout is, surprisingly, a good source of heart-and brain-healthy omega-3 fats—and sometimes a more palatable fish if you find salmon too strong in flavor. To make cleanup easier, the fish and greens are cooked in batches in one skillet.

1¾ oz. almond flour (about ½ cup)
4 (4- to 5-oz.) skin-on trout fillets
1 Tbsp. Dijon mustard
2½ Tbsp. grapeseed or canola oil, divided
¾ tsp. kosher salt, divided
½ tsp. black pepper, divided
4 cups thinly sliced Swiss chard leaves and stems (about 5⅜ oz.)
3 garlic cloves, thinly sliced
¼ cup dry white wine
1 Tbsp. fresh lemon juice
1 Tbsp. unsalted butter
1 Tbsp. minced fresh chives
4 lemon wedges

1. Place almond flour in a shallow bowl. Brush flesh side of fish fillets with mustard, and gently press mustard side of each fillet into almond flour, leaving the skin side bare. Heat 1 tablespoon oil in a large nonstick skillet over medium-high. Add 2 fillets, flesh side down, and cook until golden brown and lightly crispy, 2 to 3 minutes. Turn fillets, and cook until the flesh is flaky and cooked through. Transfer to a plate lined with paper towels. Wipe skillet clean, and repeat procedure with 1 tablespoon oil and remaining 2 fillets. Sprinkle cooked fillets evenly with ½ teaspoon salt and ¼ teaspoon pepper.
2. Wipe skillet clean. Add remaining 1½ teaspoons oil to skillet, and heat over medium-high. Add chard; cook, stirring occasionally, until slightly tender, 3 to 4 minutes. Add garlic; cook, stirring often, until fragrant, about 1 minute. Add wine and lemon juice, and cook until slightly reduced, about 1 minute. Stir in butter, and season with remaining ¼ teaspoon salt and remaining ¼ teaspoon pepper. Divide chard mixture among 4 plates; top with fish fillets, and sprinkle evenly with chives. Serve with lemon wedges. Serves 4 (serving size: ½ cup chard mixture and 1 fillet)

CALORIES 368; **FAT** 25g (sat 5g, unsat 19g); **PROTEIN** 27g; **CARB** 6g; **FIBER** 2g; **SUGARS** 1g (added sugars 0g); **SODIUM** 591mg; **CALC** 9% DV; **POTASSIUM** 17% DV

Fast

Greek Turkey Burgers

Hands-on: 20 min. **Total:** 20 min.

1 lb. 93% lean ground turkey
¼ cup canola mayonnaise
2 tsp. dried oregano
1 tsp. ground cumin
¼ tsp. kosher salt
¼ tsp. black pepper, divided
Cooking spray
⅓ cup plain whole-milk Greek
  yogurt
⅓ cup chopped kalamata olives
  (about 1½ oz.)
1 Tbsp. fresh lemon juice
4 whole-wheat hamburger buns
2 cups arugula (about 1 oz.)
½ cup sliced cucumber (about 3¼
  oz.)
½ cup thinly sliced red onion

1. Using clean hands, combine turkey, mayonnaise, oregano, cumin, salt, and ⅛ teaspoon pepper. Shape mixture into 4 equal patties.
2. Heat a large cast-iron skillet or grill pan over high. Lightly coat skillet with cooking spray, and add turkey patties. Cook until a meat thermometer inserted in thickest portion registers 165°F, 4 to 5 minutes per side.
3. Stir together yogurt, olives, lemon juice, and remaining ⅛ teaspoon pepper in a small bowl. Spread yogurt mixture evenly on cut sides of top and bottom buns. Divide arugula evenly among bottom halves of buns; top evenly with cooked patties, cucumber, and red onion. Cover with top halves of buns and serve. Serves 4 (serving size: 1 burger)

CALORIES 375; FAT 17g (sat 3g, unsat 12g);
PROTEIN 29g; CARB 28g; FIBER 4g; SUGARS 6g
(added sugars 3g); SODIUM 699mg; CALC 14%
DV; POTASSIUM 15% DV

Fast • Gluten Free
Vegetarian

Spring Salad with Herbed Goat Cheese

Hands-on: 20 min. **Total:** 20 min.
Make this ahead: Blanch the asparagus and peas, make the herbed goat cheese, and whisk the dressing the day before. Toss with the spinach when you're ready to eat.

8 cups water
8 oz. fresh asparagus, cut into 1-in.
  pieces (about 1½ cups)
1 cup frozen green peas
  (about 5 oz.)
¾ tsp. kosher salt, divided
1 Tbsp. finely chopped fresh flat-leaf
  parsley
1 Tbsp. finely chopped fresh chives
1 (3-oz.) goat cheese log
1 tsp. lime zest
2 Tbsp. fresh lime juice
1 tsp. whole-grain mustard
1 tsp. honey
1 tsp. finely chopped fresh mint
¼ tsp. black pepper
2½ Tbsp. olive oil
6 oz. fresh baby spinach
1 cup thinly sliced radishes (about
  3 oz.)
¼ cup roasted unsalted almonds
1 Tbsp. fresh mint leaves

1. Place a bowl of ice water next to the sink. Bring 8 cups water to a boil in a medium stockpot over high. Add asparagus and peas, and cook until tender, 2 to 3 minutes; drain. Plunge asparagus and peas into ice bath; drain. Transfer to a baking sheet lined with paper towels to dry; sprinkle with ¼ teaspoon salt.

2. Place a 12-inch square of plastic wrap on a work surface. Sprinkle parsley and chives in the middle of the square. Roll goat cheese in herb mixture to coat, and roll plastic wrap around cheese. Gently roll into a 4-inch-long log. Cut log into 8 (½-inch-thick) rounds, cutting through the plastic; discard plastic.
3. Whisk together lime zest, juice, mustard, honey, chopped mint, pepper, and remaining ½ teaspoon salt in a medium bowl. Slowly whisk in oil.
4. Toss dressing with spinach; add asparagus, peas, and radishes; top with almonds, cheese, and mint leaves. Serves 4 (serving size: 2 cups salad and 2 cheese rounds)

CALORIES 245; FAT 18g (sat 5g, unsat 12g);
PROTEIN 10g; CARB 14g; FIBER 5g; SUGARS 5g
(added sugars 1g); SODIUM 541mg; CALC 13%
DV; POTASSIUM 16% DV

WEEKNIGHT MAINS

Fast • Gluten Free

Flank Steak and Vegetables with Green Goddess Sauce

Hands-on: 20 min. **Total:** 20 min.
You can easily turn this into a portable dinner: Chop the steak, toss with veggies and sauce, and roll it all up into a whole-grain wrap or stuff into pitas for a handheld meal on the go.

½ cup canola mayonnaise
⅓ cup thinly sliced scallions
⅓ cup chopped fresh dill
¼ cup plain whole-milk yogurt
    (not Greek-style)
½ cup fresh flat-leaf parsley leaves,
    divided
2 Tbsp. fresh lemon juice
1 Tbsp. water
½ tsp. anchovy paste
⅝ tsp. kosher salt, divided
1 garlic clove
1 Tbsp. canola oil
½ tsp. black pepper
1 lb. flank steak, trimmed
4 cups chopped romaine lettuce
    (from 1 romaine heart)
1 cup thinly sliced English
    cucumber (about 5½ oz.)
¾ cup radishes, cut into wedges
    (about 3 oz.)

1. Combine mayonnaise, scallions, dill, yogurt, ¼ cup parsley, lemon juice, water, anchovy paste, ⅜ teaspoon salt, and garlic in the bowl of a mini food processor; process until smooth, about 1 minute. Set aside.
2. Heat oil in a large cast-iron skillet over high. Sprinkle pepper and remaining ¼ teaspoon salt over steak. Cook steak until well browned on bottom, about 5 minutes; turn steak, and cook to desired degree of doneness, about 5 minutes for medium. Transfer to a cutting board, and let rest 5 minutes before thinly slicing.
3. Meanwhile, toss together romaine, cucumber, radishes, and remaining ¼ cup parsley in a large bowl. Divide among 4 plates. Top with sliced steak; drizzle with dressing. Serves 4 (serving size: about 1½ cups vegetables, 3 oz. steak, and ¼ cup dressing)

CALORIES 300; FAT 18g (sat 3g, unsat 13g); PROTEIN 27g; CARB 6g; FIBER 2g; SUGARS 3g (added sugars 0g); SODIUM 645mg; CALC 9% DV; POTASSIUM 19% DV

Glazed Chicken with Couscous and Green Beans

Hands-on: 35 min. **Total:** 40 min.
Get the oil nice and hot (but not smoking hot) to get a good sear on the chicken thighs. Hot oil prevents sticking and creates a flavorful base for the glaze. Small thighs work best so each person gets two; four larger ones will work, but they'll take longer to cook.

1 Tbsp. olive oil
1¼ lb. skinless, bone-in chicken
    thighs (8 small thighs)
1 tsp. kosher salt, divided
½ tsp. black pepper, divided
½ cup fresh orange juice
½ cup Champagne vinegar
½ cup unsalted chicken stock
1 Tbsp. unsalted butter
½ cup uncooked whole-wheat
    couscous
¼ cup pine nuts, toasted
¼ cup chopped scallions
2 cups fresh green beans, trimmed
1 cup orange segments
Sliced scallions (optional)

1. Heat oil in a large skillet over medium-high. Sprinkle chicken with ½ teaspoon salt and ¼ teaspoon pepper; cook, undisturbed, until browned on one side, 4 to 5 minutes. Stir in orange juice, vinegar, and stock. Turn chicken; cover and cook until chicken is cooked through, about 10 minutes. Transfer chicken to a plate; cover with aluminum foil to keep warm.
2. Reduce heat to low; cook sauce, stirring occasionally, until reduced to about ⅓ cup, 8 to 10 minutes. Stir in butter until melted; remove from heat, and set aside.
3. While sauce cooks, prepare couscous according to package directions. Fluff with a fork. Gently stir in pine nuts and chopped scallions.
4. Fill a saucepan with water, and bring to a boil over high. Add green beans, and cook until tender, 3 to 4 minutes. Using a slotted spoon, transfer beans to a medium bowl. Add orange segments to beans; gently toss. Divide couscous mixture among 4 plates, and add green bean mixture; sprinkle with remaining ½ teaspoon salt and remaining ¼ teaspoon pepper. Top with chicken; drizzle with sauce, and sprinkle with sliced scallions, if desired. Serves 4 (serving size: ½ cup couscous, 2 thighs, ½ cup green bean mixture, and 1½ Tbsp. sauce)

CALORIES 411; FAT 18g (sat 4g, unsat 12g); PROTEIN 34g; CARB 30g; FIBER 6g; SUGARS 9g (added sugars 0g); SODIUM 638mg; CALC 6% DV; POTASSIUM 19% DV

Mushroom and Asparagus Grain Bowl

Hands-on: 25 min. **Total:** 25 min.
Grain bowls are great for fast weeknight meals—just top precooked or leftover grains with veggies. Serve warm on a cool night, or make it ahead and dish it up cold the next day. For a little extra protein, you can top with shredded chicken.

1 Tbsp. extra-virgin olive oil, divided
6 oz. shiitake mushrooms, stemmed and sliced (about 3 cups)
1 tsp. minced fresh garlic
1 large fennel bulb, thinly sliced (about 3 cups), or 2 sweet onions, thinly sliced
8 oz. fresh asparagus, trimmed and cut into 2-in. pieces (about 1½ cups)
2 (8½-oz.) pkg. precooked microwavable farro (such as Simply Balanced; about 4 cups)
1 Tbsp. unsalted butter
1 tsp. lemon zest
2 Tbsp. fresh lemon juice
⅞ tsp. kosher salt
⅓ cup thinly sliced scallions
¼ cup toasted sliced almonds
1 oz. Parmesan cheese, shaved (about ¼ cup)
2 Tbsp. chopped fennel fronds, or 2 Tbsp. chopped fresh dill

1. Heat 1½ teaspoons oil in a large skillet over medium-high. Add mushrooms; cook, stirring occasionally, until browned and liquid has evaporated, about 6 minutes. Add garlic, and cook, stirring occasionally, until fragrant, about 1 minute. Transfer to a plate.
2. Reduce heat to medium; add remaining 1½ teaspoons oil to skillet. Add sliced fennel bulb and asparagus; cook, stirring occasionally, until just tender, about 6 minutes. Transfer to plate.
3. Prepare farro according to package directions; place in a large bowl. Stir in butter, lemon zest, and lemon juice until butter is melted; divide among 4 serving bowls. Top evenly with mushroom mixture, fennel, asparagus, salt, scallions, and almonds. Sprinkle each bowl evenly with Parmesan cheese and fennel fronds. Serves 4 (serving size: 1½ cups)

CALORIES 267; FAT 13g (sat 4g, unsat 8g); PROTEIN 11g; CARB 38g; FIBER 8g; SUGARS 4g (added sugars 0g); SODIUM 554mg; CALC 14% DV; POTASSIUM 14% DV

Thai Poached Cod

Hands-on: 30 min. **Total:** 30 min.
Mildly spicy Thai red curry paste adds a deliciously aromatic flavor and a gorgeous orange hue to the coconut milk broth. If you've bought a jar and don't know what to do with the rest, see p. 95 for three ways to use it.

1 Tbsp. canola oil
½ cup thinly sliced shallots
1 (2-in.) piece fresh ginger, peeled and thinly sliced (about 2 Tbsp.)
2 garlic cloves, minced (about 2 tsp.)
2 tsp. Thai red curry paste
½ cup dry white wine
2 (14-oz.) cans light coconut milk, well shaken
3 Tbsp. fresh lime juice
¾ tsp. fish sauce
¾ tsp. kosher salt, divided
4 (6-oz.) skinless cod fillets
1 Tbsp. sesame oil
5 cups thinly sliced baby bok choy (about 10 oz.)
¼ cup fresh cilantro sprigs
8 lime wedges

1. Heat canola oil in a 4-quart Dutch oven over medium-high. Add shallots, ginger, and garlic; cook, stirring often, until shallots are tender, about 5 minutes. Stir in curry paste, and cook until fragrant, about 1 minute. Stir in wine, and cook until liquid almost evaporates, 2 to 3 minutes. Add coconut milk, lime juice, fish sauce, and ½ teaspoon salt. Cover and cook until the mixture comes just to a simmer, 5 to 7 minutes.
2. Sprinkle remaining ¼ teaspoon salt over fish; place fillets in a single layer in simmering liquid in Dutch oven. Cover and cook until fish flakes easily with a fork, 7 to 9 minutes.
3. Meanwhile, heat sesame oil in a large skillet over medium-high. Add bok choy; cook, stirring often, until browned and tender, about 6 minutes.
4. Using a spatula, transfer fish to 4 bowls. Ladle broth evenly over fish; add bok choy. Garnish with cilantro, and serve with lime wedges. Serves 4 (serving size: 6 oz. cod, 1 cup vegetables, and ¾ cup broth)

CALORIES 283; FAT 11g (sat 3g, unsat 7g); PROTEIN 32g; CARB 9g; FIBER 2g; SUGARS 3g (added sugars 0g); SODIUM 663mg; CALC 11% DV; POTASSIUM 23% DV

3 WAYS TO
RIFF ON THIS RECIPE

1. Cod is a blank canvas, perfect for soaking up all the flavorful brothy goodness. But halibut steaks or a couple pounds of mussels are tasty substitutes.

2. Can't find baby bok choy? Thinly slice white or green Swiss chard and sauté in step 3 for 3 to 4 minutes.

3. If you don't have—or dislike—cilantro, try thinly sliced fresh basil instead. Or, get a little adventurous and garnish with both.

4 SAUCES FOR ANY PROTEIN

Fast · Gluten Free
Make Ahead · Vegetarian
Meyer Lemon Vinaigrette

Meyer lemons, the stars here, are in season late winter through early spring. They taste like a cross between a lemon and an orange—fresh citrus flavor without too much pucker. Drizzle the vinaigrette over grilled chicken or salmon.

Combine 2 Tbsp. white wine vinegar, 1 Tbsp. honey, and 1 Tbsp. minced shallot in a medium bowl; let stand 10 minutes. Add ¼ cup fresh Meyer lemon juice, 3 Tbsp. extra-virgin olive oil, 1½ Tbsp. whole-grain mustard, and ½ tsp. kosher salt; whisk to combine. Serves 6 (serving size: about 2 Tbsp.)

CALORIES 77; **FAT** 7g (sat 1g, unsat 6g); **PROTEIN** 0g; **CARB** 4g; **FIBER** 0g; **SUGARS** 3g (added sugars 3g); **SODIUM** 177mg; **CALC** 0% DV; **POTASSIUM** 1% DV

Fast · Gluten Free
Make Ahead · Vegetarian
Five-Spice Mango Sauce

Look for five-spice powder with other specialty spices in most supermarkets or at an Asian market. For the smoothest texture and best flavor, use a ripe fresh mango (thawed frozen will work in a pinch). Serve with stir-fried shrimp or broiled cod.

Place 1 cup peeled and diced mango, 2 Tbsp. water, 1½ Tbsp. fresh lime juice, 1 Tbsp. toasted sesame oil, 1 garlic clove, 2 tsp. brown sugar, 1 tsp. five-spice powder, and ½ tsp. kosher salt in a blender. Blend until smooth. Serves 6 (serving size: about 3 Tbsp.)

CALORIES 41; **FAT** 2g (sat 0g, unsat 2g); **PROTEIN** 0g; **CARB** 5g; **FIBER** 0g; **SUGARS** 4g (added sugars 1g); **SODIUM** 161mg; **CALC** 1% DV; **POTASSIUM** 2% DV

Fast · Gluten Free
Make Ahead · Vegetarian
Arugula-Mint Pesto

We like the flavor of toasted, skin-on, whole almonds, but any almonds will taste great—just be sure to toast them first for the extra depth of flavor. Serve this sauce over grilled flank steak or lamb chops, or toss with tuna, white beans, and cherry tomatoes.

Pulse 5 cups loosely packed arugula, ½ cup fresh mint, ¼ cup toasted almonds, ½ oz. grated Parmigiano-Reggiano cheese (about 2 Tbsp.), 2 garlic cloves, 1 tsp. lemon zest, 2 Tbsp. fresh lemon juice, and ¾ tsp. kosher salt in a food processor until finely chopped. With processor running, slowly drizzle in ⅓ cup extra-virgin olive oil. Add 2 Tbsp. warm water; process until blended. Serves 8 (serving size: 2 Tbsp.)

CALORIES 121; **FAT** 12g (sat 2g, unsat 10g); **PROTEIN** 2g; **CARB** 2g; **FIBER** 1g; **SUGARS** 1g (added sugars 0g); **SODIUM** 194mg; **CALC** 7% DV; **POTASSIUM** 3% DV

Fast · Gluten Free
Make Ahead · Vegetarian
Zippy Almond Butter Sauce

Almond butter isn't just for toast; it's also a great base for savory sauces. Use this creamy condiment as a dip with chicken satay or baked tofu. Be sure to use plain unsweetened almond milk.

Whisk together ¼ cup creamy almond butter, 3 Tbsp. plain unsweetened almond milk, 1 Tbsp. fresh lemon juice, 1 tsp. maple syrup, 1 tsp. grated peeled fresh ginger, ¼ tsp. kosher salt, and ⅛ tsp. cayenne pepper in a bowl until smooth. Serves 5 (serving size: about 2 Tbsp.)

CALORIES 84; **FAT** 7g (sat 0g, unsat 6g); **PROTEIN** 3g; **CARB** 4g; **FIBER** 2g; **SUGARS** 2g (added sugars 1g); **SODIUM** 103mg; **CALC** 3% DV; **POTASSIUM** 0% DV

USE IT UP

3 WAYS TO USE UP RED CURRY PASTE

Look for red curry paste—a blend of red chiles, lemongrass, garlic, and galangal or ginger—near other Asian ingredients in most supermarkets. Depending on the brand, heat level will vary from relatively mild to has-quite-a-kick.

Fast · Gluten Free
Vegetarian
Thai Salsa

This fresh, bright salsa is slightly spicy from the serrano chile, but not over-the-top. A jalapeño is a good substitute, but taste as you go: Some jalapeños are very mild while others have a lot of heat. Serve the salsa with tortilla chips or over fish or chicken.

1. Whisk together 1½ Tbsp. fresh lime juice, 2 tsp. red curry paste, 1 tsp. toasted sesame oil, and ¼ tsp. kosher salt in a medium bowl.
2. Add 1 pint chopped grape tomatoes and 1 seeded and minced serrano chile; toss well to combine. Stir in 2 Tbsp. chopped fresh cilantro. Let stand 10 minutes before serving. Serves 6 (serving size: about ⅓ cup)

CALORIES 19; **FAT** 1g (sat 0g, unsat 1g); **PROTEIN** 0g; **CARB** 3g; **FIBER** 1g; **SUGARS** 1g (added sugars 0g); **SODIUM** 126mg; **CALC** 1% DV; **POTASSIUM** 4% DV

Fast
Red Curry Shrimp Cakes

Cooking these over medium heat is key to getting the shrimp done without burning the exterior.

1. Whisk together 2 Tbsp. red curry paste, 1 Tbsp. fresh lime juice, and 1 large egg in a medium bowl. Stir in ½ cup whole-wheat panko, ¼ cup chopped scallions, ¼ cup chopped fresh cilantro, and ⅜ tsp. kosher salt. Add 1 lb. peeled, deveined, and chopped raw large shrimp; stir well to combine.
2. Divide mixture into 4 equal portions; shape each into a ball. Place ½ cup whole-wheat panko in a shallow dish; roll balls in panko to adhere.
3. Heat a large nonstick skillet over medium. Add 3 Tbsp. canola oil. Add balls to skillet; using a spatula, flatten each to a 1-inch-thick patty. Cook until browned and cooked through, 3 to 4 minutes per side. Serve over Bibb lettuce leaves, if desired. Serves 4 (serving size: 1 cake)

CALORIES 272; **FAT** 13g (sat 1g, unsat 11g); **PROTEIN** 20g; **CARB** 17g; **FIBER** 3g; **SUGARS** 1g (added sugars 0g); **SODIUM** 587mg; **CALC** 7% DV; **POTASSIUM** 5% DV

Staff Favorite • Fast
Gluten Free
Curry-Roasted Chicken Thighs

Be sure to rub the paste under the skin to keep it from sticking or burning.

1. Preheat oven to 450°F. Combine 1½ Tbsp. red curry paste, 1 tsp. lime zest, and 1 grated garlic clove in a bowl.
2. Pat 4 (6-oz.) bone-in, skin-on chicken thighs dry with paper towels. Loosen skin by gently pushing fingers between skin and meat (do not detach skin). Rub curry paste mixture evenly under skin of each thigh. Combine ⅝ teaspoon kosher salt and ½ teaspoon black pepper; sprinkle over chicken.
3. Heat a large ovenproof skillet over medium-high. Add 1 Tbsp. canola oil. Add chicken, skin side down; cook until skin is browned and crisp, about 8 minutes. Turn thighs. Place skillet in oven; bake until cooked through, 10 to 12 minutes. Serves 4 (serving size: 1 thigh)

CALORIES 265; **FAT** 18g (sat 4g, unsat 12g); **PROTEIN** 23g; **CARB** 2g; **FIBER** 1g; **SUGARS** 0g; **SODIUM** 546mg; **CALC** 1% DV; **POTASSIUM** 7% DV

SLOW COOKER
Staff Favorite • Gluten Free
Make Ahead
Slow Cooker Carnitas Tacos

Hands-on: 20 min. **Total:** 15 hr. 30 min. Pork shoulder becomes meltingly tender as it braises in the chile- and garlic-infused citrus sauce. You can find dried ancho chiles in the produce or bulk spice sections in large supermarkets. For charred tortillas, quickly heat both sides on a hot cast-iron pan.

1¾ lb. boneless pork shoulder, trimmed
1 Tbsp. dark brown sugar
1 tsp. kosher salt, divided
¾ tsp. black pepper, divided
¼ cup fresh lime juice, divided
¼ cup fresh orange juice, divided
2 cups hot water
1 dried ancho chile
4 garlic cloves, smashed
1 white onion, sliced (about 1½ cups)
1 bay leaf
1 cinnamon stick
2 oregano sprigs
1 Tbsp. canola oil
12 (6-in.) corn tortillas, warmed
6 Tbsp. chopped white onion
Cilantro sprigs (optional)
Lime wedges (optional)

1. Cut pork into 3-inch pieces, and place in a large ziplock bag. Sprinkle with brown sugar, ½ teaspoon salt, and ½ teaspoon black pepper. Add 2 tablespoons lime juice and 2 tablespoons orange juice to bag, and seal, removing as much air as possible. Refrigerate 8 to 24 hours.
2. Place 2 cups hot water and dried ancho chile in a bowl, and let stand 10 minutes. Drain, reserving ¼ cup soaking liquid. Transfer pork to a 5- to 6-quart slow cooker, and discard marinade. Add garlic, sliced onion, bay leaf, cinnamon stick, oregano, ancho chile, reserved ¼ cup soaking liquid, remaining 2 tablespoons lime juice, and remaining 2 tablespoons orange juice. Cover and cook on low until meat is very tender, 7 to 8 hours.
3. Remove pork to a bowl, and pour cooking liquid through a fine wire-mesh strainer into a separate bowl. Discard solids. Heat canola oil in a large cast-iron skillet over medium-high. Add pork, and sear 1 minute without stirring. Return pork to bowl. Add ½ cup cooking liquid to skillet. Use a wooden spoon to scrape up any bits of pork stuck to bottom of skillet. Pour over pork; add remaining ½ teaspoon salt and remaining ¼ teaspoon pepper. Shred pork. Divide pork evenly among tortillas; top each with 1½ teaspoons chopped onion. Serve with cilantro and lime wedges, if desired. Serves 6 (serving size: 2 tacos)

CALORIES 392; **FAT** 14g (sat 3g, unsat 9g); **PROTEIN** 30g; **CARB** 40g; **FIBER** 5g; **SUGARS** 6g (added sugars 2g); **SODIUM** 441mg; **CALC** 7% DV; **POTASSIUM** 18% DV

Staff Favorite • Fast

Grilled Chicken Curry Flatbreads

Hands-on: 20 min. **Total:** 20 min. Dinner comes together quickly with some smart convenience products. Cooked flatbreads just need a quick turn on the grill pan, a far speedier process than baking pizza dough. And rotisserie chicken is always great to keep on hand for fast, easy meals.

½ cup shaved carrot
2 tsp. minced fresh ginger
½ cup rice vinegar
¼ cup water
1 tsp. granulated sugar
1½ tsp. curry powder
1½ Tbsp. olive oil, divided
½ cup plain whole-milk yogurt (not Greek-style)
2 tsp. honey
¼ tsp. kosher salt
1 (8.8-oz.) pkg. whole-grain naan
2 cups shredded rotisserie chicken breast (about 8 oz.), warmed
2 oz. fresh snow peas, very thinly diagonally sliced (about ½ cup)
¼ cup fresh cilantro leaves
¼ cup dry-roasted unsalted peanuts, chopped
¼ cup golden raisins

1. Combine carrot, ginger, vinegar, ¼ cup water, and sugar in a saucepan; bring to a simmer over high. Cook 1 minute; remove from heat, and let stand until cool.
2. Combine curry powder and 1 teaspoon oil in a medium microwavable bowl. Microwave on high until fragrant, about 45 seconds. Stir in yogurt, honey, and salt until blended.
3. Heat a grill pan over high. Brush naan evenly with remaining 3½ teaspoons oil. Add naan to pan; cook until well-marked, about 90 seconds on each side. Cut each naan in half, and spread each half evenly with 1 tablespoon yogurt mixture.
4. Drain carrot mixture; top naan evenly with warm carrot mixture, chicken, snow peas, cilantro leaves, peanuts, and raisins. Drizzle evenly with remaining yogurt mixture. Serves 4 (serving size: ½ flatbread)

CALORIES 453; FAT 15g (sat 3g, unsat 11g); PROTEIN 32g; CARB 50g; FIBER 8g; SUGARS 14g (added sugars 4g); SODIUM 608mg; CALC 9% DV; POTASSIUM 13% DV

1 INGREDIENT, 3 SIDES

3 WAYS TO USE UP SUGAR SNAP PEAS

Vibrant, green sugar snap peas are at their peak in the spring, when they're sweetest and most tender. They're best either barely cooked or served raw, which preserves their irresistible crunch.

Fast • Vegetarian
Snap Peas with Breadcrumbs and Pecorino

1. Pulse 2 (1-oz.) slices whole-grain bread in a small (or mini) food processor until coarsely crumbled, about 10 times.
2. Heat 1½ tsp. extra-virgin olive oil in a medium skillet over medium-high. Add 8 oz. trimmed fresh sugar snap peas, and cook, stirring often, until crisp-tender, about 3 to 4 minutes. Transfer peas to a large bowl.
3. Heat 1½ tsp. extra-virgin olive oil in skillet; add breadcrumbs, and cook, stirring often, until golden, about 5 minutes. Remove from heat, and stir in 1½ Tbsp. grated pecorino Romano cheese, 1½ tsp. lemon zest, 2 tsp. fresh lemon juice, ½ tsp. black pepper, and ⅛ tsp. kosher salt. Toss breadcrumb mixture with peas. Sprinkle with 1½ Tbsp. pecorino Romano cheese. Serve warm. Serves 4 (serving size: ¾ cup)

CALORIES 115; FAT 6g (sat 2g, unsat 3g); PROTEIN 5g; CARB 11g; FIBER 3g; SUGARS 3g (added sugars 1g); SODIUM 219mg; CALC 9% DV; POTASSIUM 1% DV

Staff Favorite • Fast
Gluten Free • Vegetarian
Snap Peas with Feta

1. Cook 8 oz. trimmed fresh sugar snap peas in a large saucepan of boiling water, stirring often, until bright green, about 1 minute. Using a slotted spoon, transfer peas to a large bowl of ice water. Let peas stand 5 minutes; drain. Pat peas dry with paper towels.
2. Combine ¼ cup plain 2% reduced-fat Greek yogurt, 2 Tbsp. red wine vinegar, 2 Tbsp. water, 1 tsp. finely minced fresh garlic, 1 Tbsp. fresh lemon juice, 1 oz. crumbled feta cheese, and ¼ cup chopped fresh mint in a blender. Process on high until creamy, 1 to 2 minutes.
3. In a serving bowl, drizzle peas with yogurt mixture; toss well to coat. Sprinkle with 1 tsp. lemon zest, 2 Tbsp. toasted sesame seeds, 1 oz. crumbled feta cheese, and ¼ cup chopped fresh mint. Serves 4 (serving size: 1 cup)

CALORIES 95; FAT 5g (sat 2g, unsat 3g); PROTEIN 6g; CARB 7g; FIBER 2g; SUGARS 3g (added sugars 0g); SODIUM 190mg; CALC 12% DV; POTASSIUM 1% DV

continued

Fast • Gluten Free
Make Ahead • Vegetarian
Pea, Radish, and Carrot Salad

1. Cook 5 oz. trimmed fresh sugar snap peas in a medium saucepan of boiling water, stirring often, until bright green, about 1 minute. Using a slotted spoon, transfer peas to a large bowl of ice water. Let peas stand 5 minutes; drain.

2. Place 1 cup thinly sliced radishes and 2 cups peeled, shaved rainbow carrots in a medium bowl. Sprinkle with ¼ tsp. kosher salt; let stand while you make the dressing.

3. Combine 1 cup chopped orange carrots; 3 Tbsp. water; 2 Tbsp. rice wine vinegar; 2 Tbsp. vegetable oil; 1 Tbsp. plain 2% reduced-fat Greek yogurt; ½ chopped shallot; 1½ tsp. chopped fresh ginger; and 1½ tsp. white miso in a small food processor or blender. Process until smooth.

4. In a serving bowl, place peas and carrot mixture. Drizzle peas and carrot mixture with dressing; sprinkle with 2 Tbsp. toasted walnuts. Serves 4 (serving size: 1 cup)

CALORIES 133; **FAT** 9g (sat 1g, unsat 8g); **PROTEIN** 3g; **CARB** 11g; **FIBER** 3g; **SUGARS** 5g (added sugars 0g); **SODIUM** 234mg; **CALC** 5% DV; **POTASSIUM** 7% DV

COOKING LIGHT DIET
Fast • Gluten Free
Cauliflower Puree with Barbecue Rotisserie Chicken

Hands-on: 23 min. **Total:** 23 min.
Don't rush processing the cauliflower; it's key to giving the puree the consistency of grits. You can also use store-bought riced cauliflower. If it's frozen, you can toss it right into the saucepan unthawed.

12 oz. cauliflower florets
1 cup unsalted chicken stock
½ cup coarsely ground cornmeal
3 oz. sharp cheddar cheese, shredded (about ¾ cup)
½ tsp. black pepper
⅛ tsp. kosher salt
½ cup unsalted tomato sauce
3 Tbsp. water
2 Tbsp. yellow mustard
1 Tbsp. unsalted ketchup
¾ tsp. garlic powder
½ tsp. chipotle chile powder
½ tsp. onion powder
6 oz. shredded rotisserie chicken breast
6 oz. shredded rotisserie chicken thigh
¼ cup sliced scallions

1. Process half of the cauliflower in a food processor until very finely chopped. Transfer to a medium saucepan. Repeat with the remaining cauliflower. Add stock and cornmeal to pan; bring to a boil over high. Cover and reduce heat to medium-low; simmer, whisking often, until cauliflower is cooked and mixture is thickened, about 10 minutes. Remove from heat. Stir in cheese, pepper, and salt. Cover to keep warm.

2. Combine tomato sauce, 3 tablespoons water, mustard, ketchup, garlic powder, chile powder, and onion powder in a small saucepan. Bring to a simmer over medium. Simmer, stirring often, until slightly thickened, about 6 minutes. Stir in shredded chicken. Divide cauliflower mixture among 4 bowls. Top evenly with chicken mixture. Sprinkle with scallions. Serves 4 (serving size: ¾ cup cauliflower, ¾ cup chicken mixture, and about 1 Tbsp. scallions)

CALORIES 339; **FAT** 15g (sat 6g, unsat 7g); **PROTEIN** 31g; **CARB** 21g; **FIBER** 4g; **SUGARS** 4g (added sugars 1g); **SODIUM** 650mg; **CALC** 20% DV; **POTASSIUM** 19% DV

---

3 WAYS WE
MAKE THIS DISH HEALTHIER

1. We add finely chopped cauliflower to the cornmeal mixture to bulk it up without adding many calories—yielding a much lighter version of grits.

2. We make our own mustard-based barbecue sauce, which saves loads of sodium and added sugars compared to store-bought.

3. We opt for a modest amount of chicken (3 oz. per serving) but add in some rich dark meat to ensure the meal satisfies.

---

4 GO-WITH-ANYTHING SIDES

Fast • Gluten Free
Vegetarian

Roasted Spring Vegetables with Mustard-Sherry Vinaigrette

For a fresh pop of flavor, we drizzle roasted spring vegetables with a vinaigrette. If you can find small salad turnips, try them in place of radishes.

Preheat the oven to 450°F. Combine 2½ cups small halved carrots, 1½ cups halved radishes, 1 cup halved shallots, ¼ tsp. kosher salt, 1½ tsp. olive oil, and ¼ tsp. black pepper on a rimmed baking sheet. Roast until vegetables are golden, about 20 minutes. Whisk together 1½ Tbsp. sherry vinegar, 1 Tbsp. chopped fresh oregano, 1½ tsp. olive oil, 1½ tsp. whole-grain mustard, and ¼ tsp. black pepper. Drizzle over vegetables. Serve warm. Serves 4 (serving size: ½ cup)

CALORIES 122; FAT 4g (sat 1g, unsat 3g); PROTEIN 3g; CARB 20g; FIBER 5g; SUGARS 10g (added sugars 0g); SODIUM 253mg; CALC 7% DV; POTASSIUM 17% DV

Fast • Vegetarian

Herby Shallot Toasts

These toasts are an easy starter for any meal or a fun side for steak night. Slightly sweet, nutty Manchego cheese pairs well with the savory shallot flavor, but any hard grating cheese would taste great.

Preheat broiler to high. Broil 4 (½-inch-thick) slices multigrain bread until edges begin to brown. Heat 1 tsp. olive oil in a skillet over medium-high. Add 1½ oz. thinly sliced shallots; cook, stirring often, until crisp and brown, 3 to 5 minutes. Remove from heat; stir in 1½ Tbsp. chopped fresh parsley, 1 Tbsp. chopped fresh tarragon, 1 tsp. white balsamic vinegar, and 1½ oz. grated Manchego cheese.

Divide mixture among toasts. Broil until cheese melts, about 2 minutes. Serves 4 (serving size: 1 toast)

CALORIES 137; FAT 6g (sat 3g, unsat 3g); PROTEIN 7g; CARB 14g; FIBER 2g; SUGARS 2g (added sugars 1g); SODIUM 196mg; CALC 19% DV; POTASSIUM 4% DV

Gluten Free

Millet and Tomatoes

Millet is a naturally gluten-free whole grain with a nutty corn flavor. Look for it in bulk bins or the grains aisle. If you can't find it, substitute quinoa or farro.

Bring ½ cup dry millet, 1 cup unsalted chicken stock, and ¼ tsp. kosher salt to a boil in a saucepan; reduce heat to low, cover, and simmer 25 minutes. Stir in 2 tsp. unsalted butter. Heat 1 Tbsp. olive oil in a large skillet over medium-high. Add 1 minced garlic clove, 1 lb. halved cherry tomatoes, and 3 fresh thyme sprigs; sauté 5 minutes. Add 3 Tbsp. dry white wine; discard thyme sprigs. Top millet with tomato mixture and ¼ cup shaved Parmesan cheese. Serves 4 (serving size: 1 cup)

CALORIES 210; FAT 9g (sat 3g, unsat 5g); PROTEIN 7g; CARB 23g; FIBER 4g; SUGARS 4g (added sugars 0g); SODIUM 264mg; CALC 9% DV; POTASSIUM 9% DV

Fast • Gluten Free
Vegetarian

Radicchio and Chickpea Salad with Lemon-Tahini Vinaigrette

Serve as a side with grilled lamb chops or chicken or double it for a satisfying vegetarian main. For a kid-friendly version, swap chopped romaine or spinach for the radicchio.

Whisk together 1 Tbsp. tahini, 1 Tbsp. fresh lemon juice, 2 Tbsp. water, 1 tsp. minced fresh garlic, 1 tsp. white wine vinegar, ¼ tsp. kosher salt, and ¼ tsp. black pepper in a small bowl. Toss together 2 cups chopped radicchio; 1 (15-oz.) can unsalted chickpeas, drained

and rinsed; 1 cup sliced English cucumber; and ¼ cup chopped fresh mint in a medium bowl. Gently toss with dressing. Serves 4 (serving size: 1 cup)

CALORIES 149; FAT 3g (sat 0g, unsat 2g); PROTEIN 8g; CARB 21g; FIBER 5g; SUGARS 2g (added sugars 0g); SODIUM 156mg; CALC 8% DV; POTASSIUM 11% DV

PLAN. SHOP. COOK.

1 LIST 3 DINNERS

Shop this list to feed four for three nights, all for about $30. Read the recipes first to be sure you have the staples on hand.

4 ripe avocados

1 yellow bell pepper

1 bunch scallions

1 head romaine lettuce

2 limes

2 tomatoes

1 bunch asparagus

1 (12-oz.) pkg. silken tofu

7 large eggs

8 oz. whole-wheat linguine

1 oz. Parmesan cheese

1 (1-lb.) bag frozen green peas (2 ½ cups)

8 center-cut bacon slices

2 whole-wheat English muffins

Smoked paprika

continued

Gluten Free • Vegetarian

Creamy Avocado Soup

Hands-on: 15 min. **Total:** 45 min.
If your blender doesn't get the soup silky-smooth, add up to ¼ cup more water and blend some more. Press a piece of plastic wrap on the surface of the soup as it chills to help prevent browning.

3 ripe avocados, peeled and chopped
1 (12-oz.) pkg. silken tofu, drained
2 cups water
2 cups chopped romaine lettuce
1 cup frozen green peas, thawed
3 Tbsp. fresh lime juice
3 Tbsp. white wine vinegar
1 tsp. kosher salt
¾ tsp. black pepper, divided
¼ cup chopped tomato
¼ cup chopped yellow bell pepper
2 Tbsp. chopped scallions
1 Tbsp. extra-virgin olive oil

1. Combine avocados, tofu, 2 cups water, lettuce, peas, lime juice, vinegar, salt, and ½ teaspoon pepper in a blender, and process until very smooth, about 2 minutes. Transfer to a large bowl; cover with plastic wrap, and chill until ready to serve, up to 30 minutes.
2. Toss together tomato, bell pepper, scallions, and remaining ¼ teaspoon pepper in a small bowl. Ladle soup into 4 bowls. Top with tomato mixture, and drizzle evenly with olive oil. Serve chilled. Serves 4 (serving size: about 1¼ cups)

CALORIES 359; **FAT** 28g (sat 4g, unsat 22g); **PROTEIN** 9g; **CARB** 24g; **FIBER** 13g; **SUGARS** 5g (added sugars 0g); **SODIUM** 535mg; **CALC** 7% DV; **POTASSIUM** 31% DV

Fast

Spring Carbonara

Hands-on: 25 min. **Total:** 25 min.
Fresh asparagus and green peas lend a bright spring flavor to the classic bacon, egg yolk, and Parmesan carbonara sauce.

8 oz. uncooked whole-wheat linguine
4 center-cut bacon slices, chopped
1½ cups finely chopped asparagus
1 garlic clove, thinly sliced
3 large egg yolks
¾ tsp. kosher salt
¾ tsp. black pepper
1 oz. Parmesan cheese, finely grated (about ⅔ cup), divided
2 Tbsp. extra-virgin olive oil
1½ cups frozen green peas, thawed

1. Cook pasta according to package directions, omitting salt and fat. Drain in a colander over a bowl, reserving ¾ cup pasta cooking liquid.
2. While pasta cooks, add bacon to a large skillet over low; cook until crisp, stirring occasionally, 6 to 8 minutes. Using a slotted spoon, transfer bacon to a paper towel-lined plate. Add asparagus and garlic to drippings in skillet; cook, stirring often, until beginning to brown, about 3 minutes. Using a slotted spoon, transfer asparagus and garlic to plate with bacon. Remove skillet from heat.
3. Whisk together egg yolks, salt, pepper, and 2 tablespoons Parmesan in a medium bowl.
4. Add oil, drained pasta, ¼ cup reserved cooking liquid, and egg mixture to skillet, and toss to coat. Heat skillet over medium, and cook, stirring constantly, until sauce has thickened slightly, about 1 minute. Add reserved bacon, asparagus, garlic, peas, and another ¼ cup reserved cooking liquid to skillet, and toss gently to combine. Cook until heated through, about 1 more minute. If necessary, stir in up to ¼ cup more reserved cooking liquid to reach desired consistency. Serve topped with remaining Parmesan. Serves 4 (serving size: about 1¼ cups)

CALORIES 392; **FAT** 16g (sat 4g, unsat 11g); **PROTEIN** 18g; **CARB** 52g; **FIBER** 9g; **SUGARS** 4g (added sugars 0g); **SODIUM** 646mg; **CALC** 13% DV; **POTASSIUM** 6% DV

Fast

Fried Egg– Avocado Sandwiches

Hands-on: 20 min. **Total:** 20 min.
Smoky mayonnaise, avocado, and fried eggs add enough heft to turn an open-faced BLT sandwich into exciting dinner-worthy fare.

¼ cup canola mayonnaise
2 Tbsp. water
¼ tsp. smoked paprika
½ tsp. kosher salt, divided
½ tsp. black pepper, divided
4 center-cut bacon slices
2 whole-wheat English muffins, split
1 ripe avocado, quartered
4 romaine lettuce leaves
4 thick tomato slices
4 large eggs

1. Whisk together mayonnaise, 2 tablespoons water, paprika, ¼ teaspoon salt, and ¼ teaspoon pepper in a small bowl. Set aside.
2. Cook bacon in a large nonstick skillet over medium, turning occasionally, until crisp, about 8 minutes. Using a slotted spoon,

transfer bacon to a paper towel-lined plate. Increase heat to medium-high, and add English muffins, cut sides down, to drippings in skillet. Cook until lightly toasted, about 1 minute. Remove muffins from pan; remove pan from heat.

3. Cut each avocado quarter into 4 slices; arrange on muffins. Sprinkle evenly with ⅛ teaspoon salt and ⅛ teaspoon pepper. Break each bacon slice into 2 pieces; place 2 pieces on each sandwich. Top each with 1 lettuce leaf and 1 tomato slice, and sprinkle evenly with remaining ⅛ teaspoon salt and remaining ⅛ teaspoon pepper.

4. Heat skillet over medium-high. Gently break eggs into hot skillet; cook until whites are mostly set, about 90 seconds. Cover and cook until whites are completely set but yolk is still soft, about 1 minute. Place 1 egg on each sandwich; drizzle each with 1½ tablespoons mayonnaise mixture. Serves 4 (serving size: 1 sandwich)

CALORIES 356; **FAT** 26g (sat 4g, unsat 21g); **PROTEIN** 13g; **CARB** 20g; **FIBER** 6g; **SUGARS** 4g (added sugars 2g); **SODIUM** 624mg; **CALC** 13% DV; **POTASSIUM** 14% DV

THE PICKY EATER GURU

GREEK-INSPIRED FRIES FOR DINNER

BY GINA HOMOLKA

This fresher, lighter, satisfying riff on loaded fries is sure to become a family favorite.

I recently got an air fryer, and I'm borderline obsessed. Making fries like these is only one of the many reasons why. If you're wondering if you need yet another gadget in your kitchen, my answer is: absolutely. The air fryer gives food that crispy layer similar to frying, but with much less oil and in a fraction of the time it would take to bake. In this recipe, the potatoes are seasoned and air-fried until golden with a perfect crust. For those who don't have an air fryer (yet!), I've included oven directions with the recipe, too.

Air fryer aside, it's the toppings that bring this dish together. First, there's feta cheese—I buy a big block of fresh feta and grate it to get fine shreds that soften and melt on the hot potatoes. Next is tzatziki—store-bought or homemade—which is like the gravy to poutine or the chili to chili cheese fries, only it's fresher and lighter. Then shredded chicken turns it into a meal. And for a final, colorful, fresh touch: tomatoes, red onion, and fresh herbs. If loaded fries were actually a thing in Greece, I think they would look a lot like this.

Staff Favorite • Gluten Free

Loaded Greek Feta Fries

Hands-on: 5 min. **Total:** 45 min.
This dish gets tons of flavor from the spices. If your fresh oregano is strong, start with less than what's called for and add more to taste. To speed things up, prep all the ingredients in advance so you can assemble quickly while the fries are still hot.

Cooking spray
2 (7-oz.) Yukon Gold or russet potatoes, scrubbed and dried
1 Tbsp. olive oil
2 tsp. lemon zest
½ tsp. dried oregano
¼ tsp. kosher salt
¼ tsp. garlic powder
¼ tsp. onion powder
¼ tsp. paprika
¼ tsp. black pepper
2 oz. feta cheese, finely grated (about ½ cup)
2 oz. shredded skinless rotisserie chicken breast
¼ cup prepared tzatziki
¼ cup seeded and diced plum tomato
2 Tbsp. chopped red onion
1 Tbsp. chopped fresh flat-leaf parsley and oregano

1. Preheat an air fryer to 380°F. Coat the basket with cooking spray.
2. Cut each potato lengthwise into ¼-inch-thick slices; cut each slice into ¼-inch fries.
3. Toss together the potatoes and oil in a large bowl. Season with zest, dried oregano, salt, garlic powder, onion powder, paprika, and pepper; toss to coat.
4. In 2 batches, cook the seasoned potatoes until crisp, about 15 minutes, flipping fries halfway through cooking time.
5. Return the first batch of fries to the basket, and cook until warmed through, 1 to 2 minutes. Remove from air fryer. Top fries with half of the feta, chicken, tzatziki, remaining feta, tomato, red onion, and fresh herbs. Serves 2 (serving size: 1½ cups)

CALORIES 383; **FAT** 16g (sat 7g, unsat 8g); **PROTEIN** 19g; **CARB** 42g; **FIBER** 4g; **SUGARS** 5g (added sugars 0g); **SODIUM** 654mg; **CALC** 21% DV; **POTASSIUM** 29% DV

NO AIR FRYER?
Spread potatoes on a baking sheet coated with cooking spray; bake at 450°F for 10 minutes. Flip fries, and bake until crisp and brown, 10 to 15 minutes.

THE FOOLPROOF FISH-COOKING METHOD

BY BARTON SEAVER

If you typically fret about overcooking your fish fillets, fear no more with this easy, reliable method. Roasting low and slow is simple and frees you up to pull together the rest of dinner. One of the worries about seafood I hear most often is "How do I not overcook my fish?" My answer? Cook it at a lower temperature.

Thanks to the low heat, it takes a while to go from raw to cooked, but that also means it takes a while to go from cooked to overcooked. Slowly applying a gentle heat yields fish that is delicately textured and full of natural juices. When the fish flakes apart under gentle pressure of your thumb, it's done. Unlike other cooking methods, the color of the fish does not change as drastically, but have confidence that if it flakes, it is cooked. The "5-Minute Rule" gives you more guidance: For ½-inch-thick fillets at 300°F, check for doneness after 10 minutes; for ¾-inch-thick fillets at the same temperature, assess after 15 minutes; for 1-inch-thick fillets, 20 minutes; and for anything larger, add another 5 minutes per ¼ inch of thickness.

Not only does this method alleviate fears, it also gives you time to pull together the rest of the meal. The relaxed pace also allows for (what I think is) the best part of this recipe—a glass of wine for the cook. Slow-roasting can be used for a variety of species ranging from flounder to the perennial favorite, salmon, and it yields custard-like halibut.

Gluten Free

Slow-Roasted Halibut with Herb Salad

Hands-on: 5 min. **Total:** 40 min.
The rich, buttery flavor and firm, flaky texture of halibut shine in this recipe. Chervil is a delicious herb that would be lovely in the salad, but it's not readily available; parsley is a fine substitute. Take this recipe to the next level by putting fresh herbs and lemon slices under the fillets while you cook them in the oven to perfume the fish. (If you'd like, trade herb salad for fresh, crunchy pico de gallo.)

1¼ lb. skinless halibut fillets
¾ tsp. kosher salt
Ground black pepper (optional)
2 Tbsp. olive oil
1 large shallot, very thinly sliced
1½ cups fresh mixed soft herb leaves (such as flat-leaf parsley, chervil, and a small amount of more powerfully flavored tarragon)
1½ Tbsp. fresh lemon juice

1. Preheat oven to 300°F. Season fish with salt and, if desired, pepper, and let stand 20 minutes. Toss fish with oil in a bowl to evenly coat, and place in a baking dish. Drizzle remaining oil from bowl over fish. Bake at 300°F; check doneness after 15 minutes by pressing flesh gently with your thumb. If the fish flakes apart, it is ready. If not, cook an additional 3 to 5 minutes and check again.
2. Rinse shallot under cold running water; pat dry. Once the fish is cooked, mix the warm oil from the baking dish with the shallot, herbs, and juice. Serve with fish. Serves 4

(serving size: about 5 oz. fish and ½ cup salad)

CALORIES 205; **FAT** 9g (sat 1g, unsat 7g); **PROTEIN** 27g; **CARB** 4g; **FIBER** 1g; **SUGARS** 1g (added sugars 0g); **SODIUM** 471mg; **CALC** 5% DV; **POTASSIUM** 22% DV

GIVE THIS SEASONING A STARRING ROLE

BY ANDREA NGUYEN

Let's reinstate pepper's "king of spices" title and add a little pep to our cooking.

In our kitchens, pepper is salt's best friend, but rarely do we ponder the ebony over the ivory. Sure, salt comes in curious textures and subtle flavors, but a sprinkling of fragrant pepper can whet your appetite and deliver a wallop of excitement.

Whereas salt may come from many places, members of the Piper family thrive only in certain tropical climes. Grown in tall, leafy columns, the climbing vines are native to Kerala on the Malabar Coast of South India. People have been harvesting pepper's fruits (called drupes until they're dried into wrinkly peppercorns) since ancient times. Enchanting people with an uncommon scent and pungency, pepper proved its versatility by pairing well with other ingredients and playing a role in medicinal remedies. By 2000 B.C., pepper was widely used in Indian cooking, and traders were introducing it to other parts of the world. It became the most valuable commodity in the spice trade between tropical Asia and Europe. Pepper's sea-and-land journey took months and involved multiple middlemen who drove up prices and made it expensive at the end of the line.

Having pepper signaled riches and power; it was status. Pharaoh Ramses II was mummified with peppercorns in his nose. For the Goths to lift their siege, Romans paid a ransom that included 3,000 pounds of pepper. In the 1400s, Columbus sailed westward from Spain looking for gold and pepper but returned from the Americas with chiles, suggesting that their spicy heat was a great sub for that of pricey peppercorns. As chiles spread, the similarity stuck. People began using "pepper" to mean both peppercorns and chiles, though they're not botanical kin.

The term pepper comes from the Sanskrit *pippali*, which refers to long pepper (*Piper longum*), a slender fruit that was the go-to before round *Piper nigrum* got serious traction.

Nowadays, pepper is readily available, but to experience peppy pepper, forget the blah, pre-ground stuff sold in cans, and buy whole peppercorns and grind them yourself. Robust Tellichery, which you can even find at Costco, is a great all-purpose peppercorn, says Lior Lev Sercarz, author of *The Spice Companion*. To experiment, he suggests buying small quantities of quality white and green peppercorns to try in everyday cooking. I often test-drive pepper by sautéing a mild vegetable like baby bok choy with a splash of oil, pinches of salt, and enough pepper for me to detect a bit of its warmth. Like wine, pepper reflects where it's grown, also known as *terroir*. What we buy mostly comes from India and Southeast Asia. Depending on origin, the pepper may be piney, citrusy, or herbaceous.

At my house, the pepper mill is for garnishing and table use. For prepping and cooking, I reach for a jar of pepper that I've ground in small batches in an electric coffee grinder dedicated to spices. So, start your own peppercorn collection: The perfume of each transports me to a different place, and hopefully it'll do the same for you.

Indian Spice-Rubbed Shrimp

Hands-on: 15 min. **Total:** 45 min.
Pepper was the primary heat source in Indian dishes until the Portuguese introduced chiles in the 1500s. Both are used for this fiery shrimp dish from Goa, a former Portuguese colony, in southern India. Traditionally, *feni* (a Goan cashew fruit or coconut palm liquor) would go into this type of dish. This recipe, inspired by author and Indian food expert Julie Sahni, calls for gin—an aromatic nod to the dish's origins that also helps carry the spice notes.

1 lb. raw jumbo or extra-large
   shrimp, peeled and deveined
2 Tbsp. gin or water
1 Tbsp. minced fresh garlic
1 Tbsp. grated peeled fresh ginger
1½ tsp. light brown sugar
1 tsp. cayenne pepper
1 tsp. black pepper
1 tsp. ground cumin
½ tsp. ground cinnamon
Rounded ¼ tsp. ground turmeric
¼ tsp. ground cloves
2 Tbsp. canola oil, divided
⅛ tsp. fine sea salt
1½ Tbsp. fresh lemon juice, divided
2¼ oz. baby lettuce mix (about
   5 loosely packed cups)

1. Pat shrimp dry with paper towels and place on a plate or shallow dish. Stir together gin, garlic, ginger, sugar, cayenne, black pepper, cumin, cinnamon, turmeric, and cloves in a bowl. Rub spice paste all over shrimp. Let stand at room temperature 30 minutes.

2. Heat a large well-seasoned carbon steel or cast-iron skillet over high. Add 2 teaspoons oil and swirl to coat. When shimmering, add half of the shrimp in a single layer. Cook, without stirring, until shrimp have curled and there are some rich browned spots underneath, about 2 minutes. Turn and cook, stirring often, until spices are fried and shrimp are cooked through, 1 to 2 minutes. Remove shrimp to a plate, scraping out all the spice bits from skillet. Quickly wash the skillet before repeating cooking process with 2 teaspoons oil and remaining shrimp. When done, sprinkle shrimp with salt and 1 tablespoon lemon juice.

3. Toss together lettuce mix, remaining 2 teaspoons oil, and remaining 1½ teaspoons lemon juice in a bowl. Arrange on a platter. Top with the shrimp, and serve. Serves 4 (serving size: about 4 oz. shrimp and 1¼ cups lettuce)

CALORIES 181; FAT 8g (sat 1g, unsat 7g); PROTEIN 16g; CARB 6g; FIBER 1g; SUGARS 2g (added sugars 2g); SODIUM 253mg; CALC 9% DV; POTASSIUM 5% DV

THE STEPS

1. WARM THE OILS

Heat oils slowly in a small saucepan over low to 120°F: hot enough to thicken and lightly cook the egg yolks, but cool enough to keep them from curdling. You can pull the oil mixture from the heat at about 115°F and transfer it into a spouted measuring cup—residual heat will carry it up to 120°F.

2. POUR SLOWLY

You're forming an oil-water emulsion (like with vinaigrette), with the yolks acting as emulsifiers to help it stay smooth and creamy. Pour the oil in a slow, thin stream—forming the emulsion gradually helps it hold together longer than if you combined all the ingredients at once.

3. THIN WITH WATER

Hollandaise is a thick, pourable sauce. The exact thickness is a matter of taste. If you like yours thinner, blend warm water (1 tablespoon at a time) into the mixture until it reaches the consistency you want. Water, along with a pinch of sugar, also balances any bitterness from the oil.

COOKING CLASS: HOW TO MASTER THE METHOD

EASIER, HEALTHIER HOLLANDAISE

No whisk, double boiler, or culinary degree needed: This no-butter sauce blends faster than you can say "emulsification."

Fast • Gluten Free
Make Ahead • Vegetarian

Blender Olive Oil Hollandaise Sauce

Hands-on: 10 min. **Total:** 10 min. Using olive oil instead of butter slashes saturated fat by 70%. For the most delicious flavor, we use a combo of oils; all extra-virgin would yield a bitter sauce, and all pure would taste too mild. Be sure to use a mild-tasting extra-virgin oil here to avoid any harshness.

½ cup mild extra-virgin olive oil
¼ cup pure olive oil
3 large egg yolks
5 Tbsp. warm water (110°F to 120°F), divided
2½ Tbsp. fresh lemon juice
½ tsp. kosher salt
¼ tsp. white pepper
⅛ tsp. granulated sugar
Dash of cayenne pepper

1. Heat both olive oils in a small saucepan over low to 120°F.

2. Combine yolks, 3 tablespoons warm water, lemon juice, salt, white pepper, sugar, and cayenne in a blender. Pulse until combined. Pour heated oil into a spouted measuring cup.

3. With blender running, slowly add oil in a thin, steady stream. If sauce is too thick, add up to 2 tablespoons warm water, 1 tablespoon at a time, and process until desired consistency is reached. Serves 12 (serving size: 5 tsp.)

CALORIES 174; **FAT** 19g (sat 3g, unsat 16g); **PROTEIN** 1g; **CARB** 0g; **FIBER** 0g; **SUGARS** 0g (added sugars 0g); **SODIUM** 82mg; **CALC** 0% DV; **POTASSIUM** 0% DV

Staff Favorite • Gluten Free

Risotto Milanese

Hands-on: 45 min. **Total:** 45 min.
Super-creamy rice and a knob of next-level butter deliver pure comfort in our Milanese-style risotto.

3 ½ cups unsalted chicken stock
1 Tbsp. extra-virgin olive oil
1 cup finely chopped yellow onion (about 1 onion)
1 cup uncooked carnaroli or Arborio rice
½ cup dry white wine
¼ tsp. saffron threads
2 oz. Parmigiano-Reggiano cheese, finely grated (about ½ cup)
1 ½ Tbsp. unsalted pastured cultured butter
½ tsp. kosher salt
½ tsp. freshly ground black pepper

1. Heat stock in a small saucepan over medium-high until simmering; reduce heat to low, and cover to keep warm.
2. Heat oil in a medium saucepan or Dutch oven over medium. Add onion; cook, stirring often, until tender and translucent but not browned, about 7 minutes. Increase heat to medium-high. Add rice, and cook, stirring occasionally, until toasted, about 2 minutes. Add wine and saffron; cook, stirring often, until liquid is almost completely evaporated, about 3 minutes.
3. Add 1 cup of hot stock, and cook, stirring constantly, until liquid is almost absorbed. Repeat procedure 2 times. Add up to remaining ½ cup stock, and cook, stirring constantly, until rice is al dente. (Total cooking time is about 22 minutes.) Remove from heat. Add cheese, butter, salt, and pepper; stir until fully incorporated. Serve immediately. Serves 6 (serving size: about ¾ cup)

CALORIES 238; **FAT** 8g (sat 4g, unsat 3g); **PROTEIN** 8g; **CARB** 30g; **FIBER** 2g; **SUGARS** 2g (added sugars 0g); **SODIUM** 409mg; **CALC** 9% DV; **POTASSIUM** 2% DV

THE ESSENTIALS

SIMPLE DISHES DEMAND QUALITY INGREDIENTS. THESE ITEMS MAKE THIS RISOTTO ONE TO REMEMBER.

CARNAROLI RICE
Though Arborio rice can work just fine here, pros prefer carnaroli's superior creaminess. Find it at gourmet markets.

DRY WHITE WINE
Its acidity cuts through risotto's richness. Pinot Grigio and Sauvignon Blanc work well; avoid oaky Chardonnay.

SAFFRON THREADS
Threads are better quality than saffron powder. You only need a few; too many will give a metallic taste.

PASTURED CULTURED BUTTER
Pricey, but worth it. Butter from grass-fed cows has deeper color, richer flavor, and more healthy fat.

PARMIGIANO-REGGIANO CHEESE
Salty, nutty, and bold: Just a half cup makes the dish taste really cheesy.

CHICKEN STOCK
The flavor backbone of risotto. Among store-bought options, Swanson is hard to beat for full, meaty flavor.

Fast • Gluten Free

Grilled Romaine with Feta and Nuoc Cham

Hands-on: 20 min. **Total:** 20 min.
Chef Bill Kim includes fresh chiles in his nuoc cham in *Korean BBQ*. We use crushed red pepper in a smaller batch for convenience.

3 romaine lettuce hearts, halved lengthwise
2 Tbsp. olive oil
4 tsp. water
2 tsp. light brown sugar
2 tsp. fresh lime juice
2 tsp. fish sauce
¼ tsp. minced fresh garlic
⅛ tsp. crushed red pepper
1 oz. feta cheese, crumbled (about ¼ cup)
¼ cup chopped fresh cilantro

1. Preheat grill to medium-high (about 450°F).
2. Brush romaine halves evenly with oil. Place lettuce, cut sides down, on grates; grill 1 minute and 30 seconds. Turn lettuce; grill until lightly charred, about 1 minute and 30 seconds.
3. Place lettuce on a platter. Stir together 4 teaspoons water and next 5 ingredients (though red pepper) in a small bowl until sugar dissolves. Drizzle over lettuce. Top with cheese and cilantro. Serves 6 (serving size: 1 romaine half)

CALORIES 73; **FAT** 6g (sat 1g, unsat 5g); **PROTEIN** 2g; **CARB** 4g; **FIBER** 1g; **SUGARS** 3g (added sugars 2g); **SODIUM** 206mg; **CALC** 7% DV; **POTASSIUM** 0% DV

CALIFORNIA VEGETABLE COOKING

Inspired by some of California's finest chefs, we offer up a bounty of dishes that—with minimum fuss—maximize the sweet, vibrant flavor and tender texture of spring veggies.

California cooks have long taken a minimalist approach to plant-based cooking. The state's chefs and home cooks have the luxury of using spanking-fresh produce from some of the nation's most bountiful and varied farmland, year-round. And they know veggies that good need little adornment.

"Less is more. The ingredients are such high quality, all you need to do is make it taste like what it is," says Jessica Largey, chef-owner of Simone in Los Angeles and former chef at Manresa, a farm-to-table mecca near San Jose. "You don't need to overmanipulate it. A few drops of acid and a little seasoning are often all you need."

This strategy still leaves room for innovation, though, just not in the form of the foams, spheres, and other modernist wizardry that critics consider overmanipulation. Californian revelations are simple but just as inventive, as with San Francisco chef Daniel Patterson's renowned dish of carrots roasted on coffee beans: An unlikely pairing on the plate proves to be pure bliss on the palate.

"Vegetables are the most important aspect of my cooking," says Patterson, owner of the Michelin-starred Coi restaurant. "People in California have always been more attuned to vegetables. There's an incredible abundance here. In spring, the flavors are more delicate, so they want less seasoning."

"Spring is my all-time favorite season," says Kim Alter, chef-owner of Nightbird and Linden Room in San Francisco. "You have to commit to the prep work," including tedious tasks like shelling peas and double-shucking and blanching fava beans, "but it's going to be some of the best food you've had in your life."

Pristine spring produce easily lends itself to a starring role. Alter's go-to casting choices for an iconic spring veggie, such as asparagus, include featuring it along with peas in pasta or risotto, shaving and wrapping it around fish that's served with juiced asparagus sauce, or grilling it and topping with an avocado-buttermilk green goddess dressing. Like many of his California colleagues, former chef Michael Fiorelli of Manhattan Beach's Love & Salt delights in exploring the potential of a single ingredient within one dish (like with his roasted carrots dressed with carrot-top pesto, or an artichoke plate that includes artichoke puree, roasted artichoke hearts, and shaved raw artichokes tossed in lemon and olive oil). Placing a single vegetable in the spotlight showcases the spectrum of tastes and textures one simple plant can offer.

The key, he says, is knowing when to say when. "Just don't mess it up," he says. "It's already beautiful."

Fast • Vegetarian Hearty

Pasta with Shaved Asparagus and Pea Pesto

Hands-on: 20 min. **Total:** 20 min. Thick asparagus stalks are best here because they're easier to shave. We cook the pasta in as little water as possible so the pasta water turns viscous with starch, making the sauce creamy and helping it cling to the noodles. Unsalted sunflower seed kernels are a cheaper alternative to pine nuts, if you prefer.

1 lb. thick asparagus stalks, trimmed
1½ cups fresh or thawed frozen English green peas
2 Tbsp. chopped fresh mint
1 Tbsp. pine nuts, toasted
1¼ tsp. kosher salt
2 oz. Parmigiano- Reggiano cheese, finely grated (about ½ cup), divided
1 garlic clove, chopped
3 Tbsp. extra-virgin olive oil
12 oz. uncooked fettuccine pasta

1. Use a vegetable peeler to shave asparagus stalks into long, thin strips (about 4 cups shaved asparagus).

2. Combine peas, mint, nuts, salt, half of cheese, and garlic in a food processor; pulse until a chunky puree forms. With motor running, slowly add oil, pouring in a thin, steady stream until a smoother puree forms.

3. Fill a 12-inch high-sided skillet with 2 inches water. Bring water to a boil over high. Add pasta to skillet, and completely submerge; cook until al dente, about 8 to 12 minutes. Reserve ½ cup cooking liquid. Drain pasta; return cooked pasta to pan. Add shaved asparagus to pasta; toss well for 1 minute until asparagus softens slightly. Add pea puree to pasta; toss well to coat. Stir in reserved cooking liquid, 1 tablespoon at a time, until sauce is slightly creamy and thoroughly coats pasta. Top with remaining half of cheese and serve. Serves 6 (serving size: about 1 cup pasta and about 2 tsp. cheese)

CALORIES 363; FAT 12g (sat 3g, unsat 9g); PROTEIN 14g; CARB 52g; FIBER 6g; SUGARS 6g (added sugars 0g); SODIUM 588mg; CALC 12% DV; POTASSIUM 10% DV

Fast • Gluten Free
Vegetarian

Sautéed Radish Salad with Avocado Dressing

Hands-on: 20 min. **Total:** 20 min.
Lightly cooked radishes develop rounder flavor, with less pungency and a touch of sweetness, while staying crisp at the core. If you can't find pea shoots, arugula or watercress would also work well here.

12 medium Easter Egg radishes with tops attached, scrubbed, rinsed, and drained (about 1¼ lb.)
1 Tbsp. olive oil
¾ tsp. kosher salt, divided
1 small ripe avocado, peeled and coarsely chopped
½ cup reduced-fat buttermilk
1 Tbsp. chopped fresh chives
4 cups fresh pea shoots

1. Cut off radish tops, leaving ½-inch stem attached to radishes; reserve tops. Quarter radishes lengthwise. Trim leaves from tops, and discard tops. Coarsely chop radish leaves to equal 4 cups.

2. Heat olive oil in a large skillet over medium-high. Add radish quarters and ¼ teaspoon salt to pan, working in batches if needed to prevent overcrowding. Cook radishes until lightly browned on cut sides, about 4 minutes. Set aside.

3. Combine avocado, buttermilk, chives, and remaining ½ teaspoon salt in a mini food processor; blend until smooth, about 1 minute.

4. Combine pea shoots and radish leaves. Place 1 cup of greens mixture on each of 8 salad plates. Top each with 6 radish quarters. Drizzle each serving with about 2 tablespoons avocado dressing. Serves 8

CALORIES 89; FAT 6g (sat 1g, unsat 5g); PROTEIN 2g; CARB 8g; FIBER 4g; SUGARS 4g (added sugars 0g); SODIUM 237mg; CALC 7% DV; POTASSIUM 9% DV

Gluten Free • Make Ahead

Rice Pilaf with Spring Onion Confit

Hands-on: 5 min. **Total:** 1 hr. 15 min.
A simple brown rice pilaf is the perfect platform for the confit to shine. The slow-roasted aromatics infuse the rice with amazing flavor, while the oil coats the grains and gives the starch a lush mouthfeel. A hit of fresh chives at the end adds a little bright color and fresh, verdant allium flavor.

1 Tbsp. oil from Spring Onion Confit (p. 108)
½ cup strained solids from Spring Onion Confit (p. 108)
1 cup uncooked California brown jasmine rice
2 cups unsalted chicken stock
1 tsp. kosher salt
½ tsp. freshly ground black pepper
¼ cup chopped fresh chives

Heat oil in a medium saucepan over medium-high. Add ½ cup solids from Spring Onion Confit; cook until confit starts to brown, about 3 minutes, stirring occasionally. Stir in rice; cook until rice turns translucent, about 2 minutes, stirring frequently. Stir in stock, salt, and pepper; bring to a boil. Reduce heat to medium-low; cover and simmer until liquid is absorbed and rice is tender, about 55 minutes. Let stand, covered, 10 minutes; fluff with a fork. Stir in chives. Serves 6 (serving size: ½ cup)

CALORIES 157; FAT 5g (sat 1g, unsat 4g); PROTEIN 4g; CARB 25g; FIBER 2g; SUGARS 1g (added sugars 0g); SODIUM 365mg; CALC 1% DV; POTASSIUM 1% DV

Fast • Vegetarian

Fava-and-Ricotta Toasts

Hands-on: 20 min. **Total:** 20 min.
We blend the favas with a little oil from the Spring Onion Confit (at right) to show the confit's versatility, but this recipe is plenty tasty with plain extra-virgin olive oil, too.

½ cup shelled fava beans (about 6½ oz. shell-on beans)
1 Tbsp. oil from Spring Onion Confit (see recipe at right) or extra-virgin olive oil
½ cup whole-milk ricotta
½ tsp. lemon zest
¼ tsp. freshly ground black pepper
⅛ tsp. kosher salt
16 (½-oz.) slices whole-grain baguette, toasted

1. Cook beans in boiling water 1 minute; submerge immediately in ice water. Drain well. Peel membranes; discard. Place peeled favas in a mini food processor with oil; pulse until mostly smooth.
2. Combine ricotta, zest, pepper, and salt in a small bowl. Spread 1½ teaspoons ricotta mixture on top of each toast slice. Top each with 1½ teaspoons fava puree. Serves 8 (serving size: 2 toasts)

CALORIES 143; FAT 5g (sat 2g, unsat 3g); PROTEIN 6g; CARB 18g; FIBER 3g; SUGARS 1g (added sugars 0g); SODIUM 189mg; CALC 4% DV; POTASSIUM 3% DV

Staff Favorite • Gluten Free
Make Ahead • Vegetarian

Spring Onion Confit

Hands-on: 5 min. **Total:** 2 hr. 5 min.
Use the finished dish as a flavoring or condiment for a variety of other dishes. For instance, we flavor the fava mixture with the oil in Fava-and-Ricotta Toasts (at left), and we work the oil and the confited onion into an incredibly flavorful rice pilaf (recipe on p. 107). Use the onion in salads, pasta, and stews. The oil is great for dressing salads; sautéing veggies, meat, or fish; or using as a finishing oil.

2 bunches spring onions, spring garlic, or scallions, trimmed and chopped into 1-inch pieces (about 8 oz. total)
2 garlic cloves, peeled
2 (2- x 1-in.) strips lemon peel
2 cups extra-virgin olive oil

1. Preheat oven to 225°F. Spread spring onion pieces on bottom of a 9- x 13-inch ceramic or glass baking dish. Add garlic and peel to dish. Pour oil over solids to completely cover. Place pan in oven; bake until bulbs are very tender, about 2 hours. Let cool to room temperature before using. Store covered in fridge for up to a week. Makes 3½ cups (serving size: about 5 tsp.)

CALORIES 129; FAT 14g (sat 2g, unsat 12g); PROTEIN 0g; CARB 1g; FIBER 0g; SUGARS 0g; SODIUM 1mg; CALC 1% DV; POTASSIUM 1% DV

Coffee-Roasted Carrots

Hands-on: 10 min. **Total:** 30 min.
This is our take on San Francisco chef Daniel Patterson's renowned dish of carrots roasted on whole coffee beans. For a lighter approach with spring carrots, we use just a little instant coffee and roast the carrots quickly in high heat. The carrots develop wonderfully subtle bittersweet flavor, though their springtime brightness shines through. Fennel pollen adds a hint of anise; you can find it online at amazon.com.

1½ lb. multicolored medium
   carrots, trimmed and peeled
   (halved lengthwise, if large)
1 Tbsp. olive oil
¾ tsp. instant coffee granules,
   crushed
½ tsp. kosher salt
½ tsp. light brown sugar
¼ tsp. freshly ground black pepper
⅛ tsp. fennel pollen (optional)
2 Tbsp. chopped fresh parsley
1 tsp. lemon zest

1. Preheat oven to 425°F. Toss carrots with oil, coffee, salt, sugar, pepper, and, if desired, fennel pollen. Arrange in an even layer on a rimmed baking sheet. Roast at 425°F until browned and tender, 20 to 25 minutes, stirring halfway through cooking. Transfer to a platter, and sprinkle with parsley and lemon zest. Serves 6 (serving size: about 2 carrots)

CALORIES 70; **FAT** 3g (sat 0g, unsat 2g); **PROTEIN** 1g; **CARB** 12g; **FIBER** 3g; **SUGARS** 6g (added sugars 1g); **SODIUM** 239mg; **CALC** 4% DV; **POTASSIUM** 11% DV

SPRING AWAKENING

You've been waiting for these seasonal beauties, and now they're finally here: Artichokes, asparagus, sweet peas, and other tender treasures are popping up at the farmers' market. Put them to delicious use in fresh, light dishes that capture the way you want to eat right now.

Soba, Snow Pea, and Asparagus Toss

Hands-on: 15 min. **Total:** 20 min.
Raw and barely cooked veggies offer lots of crunch in this speedy dinner. The dressing delivers salty, toasty, tangy, and pungent flavors, with the underlying complexity of Chinese hot mustard. If you can't find Chinese mustard, use Dijon for less bite.

2 Tbsp. toasted sesame oil
2 Tbsp. lower-sodium soy sauce
1 Tbsp. rice vinegar
1 tsp. light brown sugar
1 tsp. Chinese hot mustard
1 tsp. grated fresh ginger
½ tsp. kosher salt
1 large garlic clove, finely grated
2 large purple or orange carrots,
   peeled and shaved into ribbons
8 oz. fresh snow peas (about 2 cups)
8 oz. 2-in. fresh asparagus pieces
   (about 2 cups)
8 oz. uncooked soba noodles
¼ cup thinly sliced fresh basil

1. Whisk together first 8 ingredients in a large bowl. Add carrot ribbons to mixture; toss to coat. Set aside.
2. Bring a large pot of water to a boil. Add snow peas and asparagus; cook until crisp-tender, about 2 minutes. Remove vegetables with a slotted spoon to a colander; rinse with cold water until cool. Add snow peas and asparagus to carrot mixture.
3. Add noodles to boiling water; cook until al dente, 5 to 6 minutes. Drain and rinse with cold water. Add to bowl; toss well. Sprinkle with basil. Serves 4 (serving size: 1½ cups)

CALORIES 321; **FAT** 8g (sat 1g, unsat 7g); **PROTEIN** 10g; **CARB** 55g; **FIBER** 7g; **SUGARS** 8g (added sugars 1g); **SODIUM** 578mg; **CALC** 8% DV; **POTASSIUM** 13% DV

Vegetarian • Hearty

Charred Spring Onion and Baby Artichoke Pizza

Hands-on: 25 min. **Total:** 50 min. Overbrowning the edges of the onions and artichokes adds wonderful flavor that makes your home-cooked pizza taste as if it came out of a wood-fired oven. When baby artichokes aren't in season, you can use frozen artichoke hearts; thaw them, quarter them, pat them very dry, and char as directed in step 6. Make sure to zest the lemon before you juice it.

12 oz. fresh prepared whole-wheat pizza dough
6 cups water
2 Tbsp. fresh lemon juice
4 baby artichokes
4 spring onions
3 Tbsp. avocado oil or canola oil, divided
⅔ cup part-skim ricotta cheese
2 Tbsp. 2% reduced-fat milk
1 tsp. lemon zest
1 oz. pecorino Romano cheese, finely grated (about ¼ cup)
2 garlic cloves, grated and divided
¼ tsp. kosher salt
⅛ tsp. crushed red pepper
¼ cup loosely packed fresh flat-leaf parsley leaves
2 Tbsp. torn fresh dill sprigs

1. Let pizza dough rest at room temperature for 30 minutes. (Keep dough covered to prevent drying.)
2. Place a pizza stone or large, heavy baking sheet in oven. Preheat oven to 500°F. (Do not remove pizza stone while oven preheats.)
3. Combine 6 cups water and lemon juice in a large bowl. Trim artichoke stems to within 1 inch of base. Peel remaining stem attached to artichoke. Quarter each artichoke lengthwise; place in lemon water.
4. Trim onions to 6 inches in length; halve each lengthwise. Chop remaining green parts of onions; set aside.
5. Heat a large cast-iron skillet over high. Add 1 tablespoon oil to pan; swirl to coat. Add the onion halves, cut sides down. Cook until lightly charred, about 2 minutes; turn over, and cook 1 minute. Remove onion halves from skillet.
6. Drain artichokes; pat dry with paper towels. Add 1 tablespoon oil to skillet; swirl to coat. Add artichoke quarters; cook until lightly charred on all sides, about 6 minutes, turning occasionally. Remove the artichokes from skillet.
7. Place pizza dough on a lightly floured surface; roll into a 12-inch circle. Combine ricotta, milk, lemon zest, pecorino Romano, chopped green parts of onions, and half of the garlic in a bowl. Spread mixture over dough, leaving a 1-inch border. Arrange charred onions and artichokes, cut sides up, over ricotta mixture. Carefully slide pizza onto hot pizza stone. Bake at 500°F until crust is lightly browned and crisp, 8 to 10 minutes.
8. Combine remaining 1 tablespoon oil and remaining half of garlic in a small microwavable bowl. Microwave on HIGH until fragrant, about 40 seconds. Brush oil mixture on edges of pizza crust. Sprinkle pizza evenly with salt and crushed red pepper; top with parsley and dill. Cut into 8 slices. Serves 4 (serving size: 2 slices)

CALORIES 386; FAT 19g (sat 5g, unsat 13g); PROTEIN 14g; CARB 44g; FIBER 5g; SUGARS 2g (added sugars 0g); SODIUM 692mg; CALC 22% DV; POTASSIUM 7% DV

Staff Favorite • Gluten Free Hearty

Double-Pea Risotto

Hands-on: 35 min. **Total:** 35 min. This veg-forward risotto combines tender garden peas with crisp sugar snaps, both highlighted by the anise notes of fresh tarragon. A tangle of lightly dressed microgreens adorns each serving; see box at left for more info on microgreens.

4 cups unsalted chicken stock (such as Swanson)
1½ Tbsp. olive oil, divided
2 bacon slices, chopped
⅓ cup finely chopped shallot (about 1 large shallot)
3 garlic cloves, minced
1 cup uncooked Arborio rice
⅓ cup dry white wine
8 oz. sugar snap peas, trimmed and cut crosswise into thin slices
1 cup fresh or thawed frozen green peas
1 Tbsp. chopped fresh tarragon
¼ tsp. kosher salt

¼ tsp. black pepper
1 oz. Parmigiano-Reggiano cheese,
  finely grated (about ¼ cup)
2 oz. microgreens (about 2 cups)
1½ tsp. fresh lemon juice

1. Bring stock to a simmer in a saucepan over medium-high (do not boil). Reduce heat to low, and keep warm.
2. Heat a large sauté pan or Dutch oven over medium. Add 1 tablespoon oil; swirl to coat. Add bacon; cook until crisp, 4 to 5 minutes. Remove bacon with a slotted spoon; drain on a paper towel. Add shallot and garlic to drippings in pan; cook, stirring often, 2 minutes. Add rice; cook, stirring constantly, 1 minute. Add wine; cook, stirring constantly, until liquid is absorbed, about 2 minutes.
3. Stir in 1 cup warm stock; cook, stirring often, until liquid is nearly absorbed, about 3 minutes. Add 2 cups stock, ½ cup at a time, and cook, stirring almost constantly, until each portion of stock is absorbed before adding the next. Add snap and green peas and ½ cup stock; cook, stirring constantly, until snap peas are crisp-tender and liquid is absorbed, about 2 minutes. Remove from heat; stir in tarragon, salt, pepper, cheese, and remaining ½ cup stock.
4. Combine microgreens, lemon juice, and remaining 1½ teaspoons oil in a medium bowl; toss to coat. Divide risotto among 4 bowls; top with microgreens and bacon. Serves 4 (serving size: 1½ cups risotto, ½ cup microgreens, and about 2 tsp. bacon)

CALORIES 396; FAT 13g (sat 4g, unsat 9g); PROTEIN 15g; CARB 51g; FIBER 5g; SUGARS 7g (added sugars 0g); SODIUM 599mg; CALC 14% DV; POTASSIUM 4% DV

Vegetarian • Hearty
Chunky Spring Gratin

Hands-on: 15 min. **Total:** 55 min.
This meatless main dish is hearty and cheesy yet light enough for spring. Be sure to use fat asparagus spears; thinner ones will overcook. Feel free to use 4 oblong, shallow gratin dishes for individual portions.

1¼ lb. fingerling potatoes, quartered
Cooking spray
1 lb. fat fresh asparagus spears, trimmed and cut into 3-in. pieces
6 spring onions, trimmed to 5 inches and halved lengthwise
1 cup whole milk
1.1 oz. all-purpose flour (about ¼ cup)
¾ tsp. kosher salt
½ tsp. black pepper
3 oz. aged Gruyère cheese, shredded (about ¾ cup)
2 Tbsp. olive oil
2 garlic cloves, minced
1 oz. multigrain bread, finely chopped or torn
1 Tbsp. chopped fresh parsley

1. Preheat oven to 375°F.
2. Place potatoes in a Dutch oven; cover with cool water. Bring to a boil over high; reduce heat to medium-low, and simmer until almost tender, about 10 minutes. Remove potatoes with a slotted spoon; place in an 11- x 7-inch baking dish coated with cooking spray.
3. Add asparagus to boiling water; cook 1 minute. Add onion halves; cook 1 minute. Reserve ½ cup cooking liquid; drain asparagus mixture. Arrange asparagus and onions in baking dish with potatoes.

4. Whisk together milk and flour in a small saucepan. Add reserved cooking liquid. Bring to a simmer over medium-high; cook until thickened, 4 to 5 minutes. Remove from heat. Add salt, pepper, and cheese; stir until cheese melts. Spoon evenly over vegetables in baking dish. Bake at 375°F until top is bubbly and lightly browned, about 30 minutes.
5. Meanwhile, heat oil in a small skillet over medium. Add garlic; cook until fragrant, about 1 minute, stirring constantly. Add bread and parsley, and toss to combine.
6. Remove gratin from oven. Preheat broiler to high with oven rack in upper middle position. Sprinkle breadcrumb mixture over gratin; broil until browned, 1 to 2 minutes. Serves 4 (serving size: 2 cups)

CALORIES 378; FAT 17g (sat 6g, unsat 10g); PROTEIN 15g; CARB 44g; FIBER 7g; SUGARS 7g (added sugars 0g); SODIUM 598mg; CALC 36% DV; POTASSIUM 29% DV

Roasted Carrots, Radishes, and Chickpeas

Hands-on: 5 min. **Total:** 45 min.
This seasonal side pairs with pretty much any protein, but it's especially good with roast chicken.

1 lb. small carrots with tops, trimmed
8 radishes (about 1 bunch), trimmed and halved
1 (15-oz.) can unsalted chickpeas, drained, rinsed, and patted very dry
1½ Tbsp. avocado oil or canola oil
1½ Tbsp. unsalted butter, melted
½ tsp. kosher salt
¼ tsp. black pepper
2 Tbsp. small fresh mint leaves
2 tsp. lemon zest

1. Preheat oven to 400°F.
2. Place carrots, radishes, and chickpeas on a rimmed baking sheet lined with aluminum foil. Drizzle oil and butter over vegetables; toss to coat. Spread in an even layer. Bake at 400°F until carrots are tender and chickpeas are browned, about 40 minutes, stirring after 20 minutes.
3. Arrange vegetables on a platter; sprinkle with salt and pepper. Stir together mint and lemon zest; sprinkle evenly over vegetables. Serves 4 (serving size: 1½ cups)

CALORIES 240; **FAT** 11g (sat 3g, unsat 6g); **PROTEIN** 7g; **CARB** 29g; **FIBER** 8g; **SUGARS** 6g (added sugars 0g); **SODIUM** 347mg; **CALC** 9% DV; **POTASSIUM** 16% DV

Golden Beet and Roasted Strawberry Salad

Hands-on: 15 min. **Total:** 1 hr. 30 min.
Earthy beets and sweet berries are a lovely match. Roasting the berries softens them and concentrates their flavor, so they taste like strawberries intensified by a factor of 10.

6 small golden beets, scrubbed and trimmed (about 1 lb.)
8 oz. fresh strawberries, hulled and halved
1 tsp. granulated sugar
¼ cup extra-virgin olive oil
3 Tbsp. white balsamic vinegar
1 tsp. Dijon mustard
¼ tsp. kosher salt
¼ tsp. black pepper
6 oz. mixed baby lettuces, torn (about 6 loosely packed cups)
4 very thin prosciutto slices
2 oz. goat cheese, crumbled (about ½ cup)
1 oz. Marcona almonds, coarsely chopped (about ¼ cup)

1. Preheat oven to 375°F.
2. Place beets on a large piece of heavy-duty aluminum foil; wrap tightly. Bake at 375°F for 1 hour to 1 hour and 15 minutes or until tender. Cool slightly; rub off skins with a paper towel. Cut beets into wedges.
3. Line a small baking sheet with parchment paper. Place strawberries in an even layer on prepared baking sheet; sprinkle with sugar, and toss gently to coat. Bake at 375°F for 15 minutes. Remove from oven; transfer strawberries to a plate to cool.
4. Combine oil, vinegar, mustard, salt, and pepper in a jar or bowl; shake or whisk until emulsified.
5. Divide lettuces evenly among 4 plates; top with beets, strawberries, prosciutto, cheese, and almonds. Drizzle evenly with vinaigrette. Serves 4 (serving size: 2 cups)

CALORIES 325; **FAT** 23g (sat 5g, unsat 17g); **PROTEIN** 11g; **CARB** 22g; **FIBER** 6g; **SUGARS** 14g (added sugars 1g); **SODIUM** 600mg; **CALC** 10% DV; **POTASSIUM** 14% DV

Rosé-Poached Berries

Hands-on: 10 min. **Total:** 20 min.
Serve this condiment at breakfast on top of yogurt or oatmeal, or try it for dessert over ice cream. You can also make the recipe with raspberries or blackberries.

2 cups rosé wine
2 Tbsp. honey
2 fresh thyme sprigs
½ vanilla bean pod
1 lb. fresh strawberries, hulled and halved
Fresh thyme leaves (optional)

1. Bring first 3 ingredients to a boil in a saucepan. Reduce heat to medium; cook until syrupy and reduced to about 1 cup, 12 to 15 minutes.
2. Split vanilla pod in half lengthwise; scrape seeds into wine mixture. Add pod to mixture. Stir in berries. Reduce heat to low; cook 2 minutes (mixture will not come to a simmer). Remove from heat; pour mixture into a bowl to cool completely. Discard vanilla pod and thyme sprigs; garnish with thyme leaves, if desired. Serves 8 (serving size: ⅓ cup berries and 2 Tbsp. sauce)

CALORIES 84; **FAT** 0g; **PROTEIN** 1g; **CARB** 11g; **FIBER** 1g; **SUGARS** 9g (added sugars 4g); **SODIUM** 4mg; **CALC** 2% DV; **POTASSIUM** 4% DV

MAD FOR MISO

If you're only using miso in Japanese recipes, you're missing out. This umami bomb is an underutilized secret weapon that adds flavorful depth to savory and sweet dishes.

Staff Favorite • Make Ahead
Vegetarian

Oatmeal-Raisin Skillet Cookie with Miso-Caramel Sauce

Hands-on: 15 min. **Total:** 1 hr.
Chewy in the middle with crispy edges, this easy dessert flavored with browned butter is absolutely irresistible. You can swap any dried fruit for the raisins here. Keep leftovers in the skillet and cover it.

COOKIE
3 Tbsp. unsalted butter
5 Tbsp. canola oil
⅓ cup packed light brown sugar
⅓ cup granulated sugar
1 tsp. vanilla extract
¼ tsp. ground cinnamon
1 large egg
4.25 oz. all-purpose flour (about 1 cup)
¾ tsp. baking soda
1 cup old-fashioned rolled oats
½ cup raisins
Cooking spray

SAUCE
¼ cup packed light brown sugar
2 Tbsp. unsalted butter
3 Tbsp. sweet white miso
1 Tbsp. heavy cream
1 tsp. apple cider vinegar
¾ cup vanilla frozen yogurt

1. Prepare the cookie: Preheat oven to 325°F. Heat butter in a 9-inch cast-iron skillet over medium until butter melts and foam subsides, 3 to 4 minutes. Pour melted butter in a large bowl, but don't wipe out skillet. Add oil to butter. Add sugars, vanilla, and cinnamon; whisk vigorously until smooth. Whisk in egg.
2. Stir together flour and baking soda in a small bowl. Add to sugar mixture, and stir until just incorporated. Fold in oats and raisins. Lightly coat buttered cast-iron skillet with cooking spray. Spread dough in skillet.
3. Bake at 325°F until just done, 25 to 30 minutes. (The cookie will just be cracking at the edges.) Remove skillet from oven, and cool on a wire rack 15 to 20 minutes.
4. Prepare the sauce: Heat sugar and butter in a skillet over medium-high, whisking until sugar dissolves. Whisk in miso until smooth. Remove from heat. Add cream; stir in vinegar. Pour half of sauce over cookie. Cut into wedges.

Top each serving with 1 tablespoon frozen yogurt, and drizzle evenly with remaining sauce. Serves 12 (serving size: 1 slice, 1 ½ Tbsp. sauce, and 1 Tbsp. frozen yogurt)

CALORIES 280; **FAT** 12g (sat 4g, unsat 8g); **PROTEIN** 5g; **CARB** 39g; **FIBER** 2g; **SUGARS** 24g (added sugars 16g); **SODIUM** 230mg; **CALC** 5% DV; **POTASSIUM** 3% DV

Fast • Make Ahead
Vegetarian

Miso Ranch Dip

Hands-on: 5 min. **Total:** 5 min.
Get ready—this dip is about to become your party go-to. It's quick and easy to make, and you can serve it with any type of vegetable (we particularly like it with carrots, radishes, and cucumbers). Be sure not to puree the chives or pepper, as they will discolor your sauce. Use leftover dip as a spread for pulled pork, hamburgers, or other sandwiches, or thin it out with water or another tablespoon or two of buttermilk to dress lettuces.

½ cup canola mayonnaise
½ cup reduced-fat sour cream
¼ cup low-fat buttermilk
2 Tbsp. rice vinegar
2 ½ Tbsp. white miso
1 tsp. garlic powder
1 tsp. onion powder
2 Tbsp. thinly sliced fresh chives
1 tsp. black pepper

1. Combine mayonnaise, sour cream, buttermilk, vinegar, miso, garlic powder, and onion powder in a blender; process until smooth, about 30 seconds. Stir in chives and pepper. Serve immediately, or store in refrigerator for up to 1 week. Serves 8 (serving size: 3 Tbsp.)

CALORIES 73; **FAT** 6g (sat 1g, unsat 4g); **PROTEIN** 2g; **CARB** 4g; **FIBER** 1g; **SUGARS** 1g (added sugars 0g); **SODIUM** 304mg; **CALC** 3% DV; **POTASSIUM** 1% DV

Hearty

Red Miso Shrimp Bisque

Hands-on: 25 min. **Total:** 1 hr. 45 min. This sophisticated bisque is worthy of a special occasion but is also easy to make. Cooking the shrimp shells deepens the flavor.

1 lb. raw large unpeeled shrimp
2 Tbsp. canola oil
6 Tbsp. unsalted tomato paste
2 cups chopped yellow onion
1 cup chopped carrot
1 cup chopped celery
6 cups water
1 bay leaf
4 cups chicken stock
⅓ cup uncooked long-grain white rice
5 Tbsp. red miso
¼ cup cream sherry
2 tsp. sherry vinegar
⅛ tsp. cayenne pepper
¼ cup unsalted butter
2 Tbsp. chopped fresh dill, divided
Coarsely ground black pepper (optional)

1. Peel and devein shrimp, leaving tails on if desired. Refrigerate shrimp until ready to use, and reserve shells.
2. Heat oil in a Dutch oven over high. Add shells; cook, stirring constantly, until bright red and slightly toasty, 3 to 4 minutes. Reduce heat to medium. Add tomato paste, onion, carrot, and celery; cook, stirring constantly, until fragrant, 2 to 3 minutes. Add 6 cups water and bay leaf; increase heat to high. Bring to a boil; cover and reduce heat to medium-low. Simmer until fragrant and rich, about 50 minutes. Pour through a fine wire-mesh strainer into a bowl, pressing slightly to extract liquid. (You should have 4 cups of liquid.) Discard solids.
3. Add shrimp liquid, chicken stock, rice, miso, and sherry to a stockpot. Bring to a boil over high. Cover, reduce heat to medium-low, and simmer until rice is very tender, 25 to 30 minutes. Working in batches if needed, transfer mixture to a blender. Remove center piece of blender lid (to allow steam to escape); secure lid on blender, and place a clean towel over opening in lid. Process until smooth, about 60 seconds. Stir in vinegar and cayenne. Cover and keep warm.
4. Heat butter in a large skillet over high until foamy. Add shrimp; cook, stirring often, until just translucent, about 3 minutes. Add 1 tablespoon dill; cook, stirring often, 1 minute. Serve soup in shallow bowls; top evenly with shrimp, remaining 1 tablespoon dill, and black pepper, if desired. Serves 8 (serving size: 1 cup soup and 5 shrimp)

CALORIES 239; **FAT** 11g (sat 4g, unsat 6g); **PROTEIN** 13g; **CARB** 20g; **FIBER** 2g; **SUGARS** 6g (added sugars 0g); **SODIUM** 641mg; **CALC** 6% DV; **POTASSIUM** 10% DV

KEY TO UMAMI

Soybeans are the main ingredient in miso. Fermenting those beans (how miso is made) breaks down their proteins into amino acids—and it's those amino acids that give miso its umami depth.

Pasta with Miso Cream Sauce

Hands-on: 25 min. **Total:** 25 min.
This recipe is quite flexible: Fusilli, penne, or any whole-wheat pasta works well. You could also use mini mozzarella balls to save time.

8 oz. uncooked casarecce pasta
1½ cups whole milk, divided
¼ cup all-purpose flour
3 Tbsp. plus 2 tsp. white miso
1½ cups unsalted chicken stock
½ tsp. black pepper
1 Tbsp. olive oil
3 cups multicolored grape tomatoes (about 10 oz.)
2 tsp. chopped fresh thyme
3 garlic cloves, sliced
1 (6-oz.) pkg. baby spinach
2 oz. fresh mozzarella cheese, diced (about ½ cup) and divided

1. Cook pasta according to package directions, omitting salt and fat; drain.
2. Place ½ cup milk in a bowl; whisk in flour and miso until smooth. In a saucepan, bring stock and remaining 1 cup milk to a boil over high. Whisk in flour mixture, reduce heat to medium, and simmer until slightly thickened, 4 to 5 minutes. Add pepper.
3. Heat oil in a skillet over high. Add tomatoes, and cook, stirring occasionally, until slightly blistered and beginning to pop, 2 to 3 minutes. Add thyme and garlic; cook 1 minute. Add spinach; cook, stirring constantly, until wilted, 2 to 3 minutes. Remove from heat. Add cooked pasta, sauce, and half of cheese to skillet; toss to combine. Divide pasta mixture among 4 shallow bowls, and top evenly with remaining cheese. Serves 4 (serving size: 1¾ cups)

CALORIES 434; **FAT** 12g (sat 5g, unsat 5g); **PROTEIN** 20g; **CARB** 65g; **FIBER** 7g; **SUGARS** 13g (added sugars 0g); **SODIUM** 665mg; **CALC** 17% DV; **POTASSIUM** 14% DV

KNOW YOUR MISO

You'll see three miso styles in well-stocked groceries: White, or shiro, miso is the mildest and is also called sweet or mellow miso. Red, or aka, miso, fermented longest, is the most pungent. Yellow, or shinshu, miso falls in the middle and is, to some, the most versatile.

Make Ahead • Vegetarian

Miso Deviled Eggs

Hands-on: 15 min. **Total:** 45 min.
This fun twist on deviled eggs is a nice change-of-pace dish for your next picnic or cookout. With just a hint of tang and spice, they'll appeal to all, including folks who aren't particularly adventurous eaters. Try to use older eggs—they will peel more easily. Look for shichimi togarashi in the same place you buy miso.

6 large eggs
3 Tbsp. canola mayonnaise
1½ Tbsp. white miso
1 tsp. shichimi togarashi (Japanese spice blend), plus more for garnish
⅓ cup thinly sliced scallions, divided
2 Tbsp. toasted sesame seeds

1. Place eggs in a saucepan; cover with water. Bring to a boil over high. Remove from heat; let stand 12 minutes. Transfer eggs to a bowl of ice water. Cool completely, about 5 minutes.
2. Peel eggs; halve lengthwise. Carefully remove yolks, reserving whites.
3. Whisk together mayonnaise and miso in a bowl until smooth. Add yolks, shichimi togarashi, and half of scallions. Place egg white halves on a platter; fill with yolk mixture. Sprinkle with sesame seeds, shichimi togarashi, and remaining scallions. Serves 12 (serving size: 1 egg half)

CALORIES 57; **FAT** 4g (sat 1g, unsat 3g); **PROTEIN** 4g; **CARB** 2g; **FIBER** 1g; **SUGARS** 1g (added sugars 0g); **SODIUM** 131mg; **CALC** 2% DV; **POTASSIUM** 1% DV

From herb-loaded pastas and pizzas to taco truck–inspired lettuce wraps, eating your vegetables has never been this fun. Craving fast and easy suppers? You got it.

20-MINUTE MAINS

Fast • Gluten Free
Vegetarian • Hearty

Black Bean Tostadas with Cabbage Slaw

Hands-on: 20 min. **Total:** 20 min.
For even more veggie goodness and an extra punch of flavor, try adding a few slices of creamy avocado and a sprinkle of charred corn kernels.

1 (15.4-oz.) can lower-sodium refried black beans (such as Amy's)
½ cup pico de gallo, drained
4 Tbsp. olive oil
2 Tbsp. red wine vinegar
1 tsp. dried oregano
½ tsp. kosher salt
1 (10-oz.) pkg. shredded cabbage
1 cup thinly sliced radishes
1 cup grape tomatoes, halved
½ cup thinly sliced red onion
6 (5-inch) corn tostada shells
6 oz. queso fresco (fresh Mexican cheese), crumbled (about 1½ cups)
Torn fresh cilantro

1. Combine beans and pico de gallo in a small saucepan. Cook over medium, stirring often, until hot, about 5 minutes. Remove from heat, and cover to keep warm.
2. Whisk together oil, vinegar, oregano, and salt in a bowl. Add cabbage, radishes, tomatoes, and onion; toss. Let stand 5 minutes.

3. Spread each tostada shell with ⅓ cup bean mixture; top each with 1 cup cabbage mixture and ¼ cup queso fresco. Garnish with torn cilantro, if desired. Serves 6 (serving size: 1 tostada)

CALORIES 324; **FAT** 20g (sat 6g, unsat 13g); **PROTEIN** 12g; **CARB** 27g; **FIBER** 6g; **SUGARS** 5g (added sugars 0g); **SODIUM** 664mg; **CALC** 22% DV; **POTASSIUM** 5% DV

Fast • Hearty

Bacon, Arugula, and Egg Wraps

Hands-on: 20 min. **Total:** 20 min.
Precooked potatoes make these wraps quick and easy to whip up.

1⅓ cups refrigerated diced potatoes (such as Simply Potatoes)
6 center-cut bacon slices, chopped
¼ cup diced shallot (about 2 oz.)
6 large eggs
2 Tbsp. water
⅛ tsp. kosher salt
3 Tbsp. canola mayonnaise
2 tsp. Sriracha chili sauce
4 (8-inch) whole-wheat tortillas
1½ cups baby arugula (about 1½ oz.)

1. Place potatoes in a microwavable dish. Microwave at HIGH until potatoes are almost tender, 2 minutes.
2. Place bacon in a large skillet. Cook over medium-high until bacon begins brown, 5 to 6 minutes. Add shallot and potatoes to skillet; reduce heat to medium, and cook, stirring occasionally, until bacon is done and potatoes are soft and beginning to brown, 3 to 4 minutes. Transfer mixture to a bowl; keep warm. (Do not wipe skillet clean.)
3. Whisk together eggs, 2 tablespoons water, and salt in a bowl until combined. Add mixture to skillet. Cook, stirring constantly, until eggs are almost set, 1 to 2 minutes.
4. Stir together mayonnaise and Sriracha in a bowl. Spread sauce evenly over tortillas. Layer potato mixture, scrambled eggs, and arugula evenly down center of tortillas; fold tortillas burrito-style. Serve immediately. Serves 4 (serving size: 1 wrap)

CALORIES 363; **FAT** 19g (sat 4g, unsat 13g); **PROTEIN** 18g; **CARB** 28g; **FIBER** 2g; **SUGARS** 2g (added sugars 0g); **SODIUM** 722mg; **CALC** 11% DV; **POTASSIUM** 5% DV

Staff Favorite • Fast
Hearty

Creamy Chicken-Tomato Skillet

Hands-on: 20 min. **Total:** 20 min.
When a craving for comfort food hits, and you need it in a hurry, this fast take on chicken and rice hits the spot. Stirring chopped baby spinach into warm brown rice is a smart way to get more vegetables and jazz up an otherwise plain starchy side.

1 Tbsp. olive oil
1 lb. skinless, boneless chicken thighs, cut into bite-sized pieces
½ tsp. kosher salt, divided
½ tsp. black pepper, divided
1 cup grape tomatoes
¼ cup sliced white onion
1 garlic clove, grated
1 tsp. chopped fresh rosemary
1½ cups unsalted chicken stock
2 Tbsp. all-purpose flour
1 (8.8-oz.) pkg. precooked microwavable whole-grain brown rice (such as Uncle Ben's Ready Rice)
3 cups fresh baby spinach, chopped
1 tsp. lemon zest
1 Tbsp. fresh lemon juice

1. Heat oil in a large skillet over medium-high. Sprinkle chicken with ¼ teaspoon salt and ¼ teaspoon pepper. Add chicken to skillet; cook, without stirring, until chicken begins to brown, about

4 minutes. Add tomatoes, onion, garlic, and rosemary. Cook, stirring occasionally, until onion is tender and tomatoes soften, about 3 minutes.

2. Whisk together stock and flour in a bowl until combined. Add to chicken mixture; stir and scrape browned bits from bottom of skillet. Bring to a boil. Cook, stirring often, until sauce thickens, 3 to 4 minutes.

3. Heat rice according to package directions. Place hot rice in a bowl; add spinach, lemon zest, lemon juice, remaining ¼ teaspoon salt, and remaining ¼ teaspoon pepper. Toss to coat. Divide rice mixture evenly among 4 plates; top evenly with chicken mixture. Serves 4 (serving size: about 1¼ cups)

CALORIES 296; **FAT** 10g (sat 2g, unsat 7g); **PROTEIN** 29g; **CARB** 26g; **FIBER** 3g; **SUGARS** 2g (added sugars 0g); **SODIUM** 413mg; **CALC** 5% DV; **POTASSIUM** 4% DV

---

3 WAYS TO:
SPEED UP DINNER

1. Cut the chicken into bite-size pieces ahead of time so you can start cooking immediately.

2. While the chicken cooks, microwave the rice and chop the spinach.

3. Cover the rice and spinach mixture with a plate to help the spinach wilt more quickly.

Fast • Hearty

Shrimp and Leek Spaghetti

Hands-on: 20 min. **Total:** 20 min.
Light and lemony, this pasta provides nearly a third of your daily fiber. Thanks to pre-peeled shrimp and frozen peas, it's weeknight-fast. Dress it up with a glass of crisp white wine.

8 oz. uncooked whole-grain spaghetti
1 lb. peeled, deveined raw medium shrimp
½ tsp. black pepper
¾ tsp. kosher salt, divided
1½ Tbsp. olive oil, divided
2 cups chopped leek (from 1 large leek)
1 Tbsp. chopped garlic (from 3 cloves)
2 cups frozen baby sweet peas (about 9 oz.), thawed
¼ cup heavy cream
2 tsp. lemon zest
2 Tbsp. fresh lemon juice
2 Tbsp. chopped fresh dill

1. Cook pasta according to package directions, omitting salt and fat. Drain, reserving ½ cup cooking liquid. Cover pasta to keep warm.
2. While pasta cooks, pat shrimp dry with paper towels; season with pepper and ¼ teaspoon salt. Heat half of the olive oil in a large nonstick skillet over high. Add shrimp; cook, stirring often, until cooked through, 3 to 4 minutes. Transfer to a plate; cover to keep warm. (Do not wipe skillet clean.)
3. Reduce heat to medium-high. Add leek, garlic, remaining oil, and remaining ½ teaspoon salt. Cook, stirring often, until leek is slightly tender, 2 to 3 minutes. Add peas, cream, lemon zest, lemon juice, and reserved ½ cup cooking liquid. Reduce heat to medium; simmer until sauce thickens slightly, 2 to 3 minutes. Add shrimp to skillet; toss to coat.
4. Divide pasta among 4 bowls; top evenly with shrimp and sauce. Sprinkle with dill, and serve. Serves 4 (serving size: 1¼ cups pasta and 1¼ cups shrimp mixture)

CALORIES 446; **FAT** 13g (sat 5g, unsat 7g); **PROTEIN** 28g; **CARB** 59g; **FIBER** 9g; **SUGARS** 8g (added sugars 0g); **SODIUM** 649mg; **CALC** 14% DV; **POTASSIUM** 16% DV

Fast • Hearty

Zucchini-Pesto-Sausage Pizza

Hands-on: 15 min. **Total:** 20 min.
You can make these vegetable-forward pizzas even more colorful by mixing in sliced yellow squash or yellow bell pepper for half of the zucchini. Lose the crushed red pepper if your kids don't like the heat.

3 oz. ground mild Italian turkey sausage
1 cup thinly sliced zucchini
¼ cup refrigerated basil pesto, divided
1 (12-oz.) pkg. of 3 (7-inch) prebaked pizza crusts (such as Mama Mary's)
3 oz. fresh mozzarella cheese, very thinly sliced
⅛ tsp. crushed red pepper
2 Tbsp. fresh basil leaves

1. Preheat oven to 450°F.
2. Heat a small nonstick skillet over medium-high. Add sausage, and cook, stirring and breaking up sausage with a wooden spoon, until cooked through, 4 to 5 minutes. Transfer sausage to a plate. Add zucchini and 1 tablespoon pesto to the skillet; cook, stirring often, until zucchini is slightly tender, about 3 minutes. Remove from heat.
3. Place pizza crusts on a baking sheet, and spread remaining 3 tablespoons pesto evenly over crusts. Top crusts evenly with zucchini mixture, sausage, mozzarella, and red pepper. Bake at 450°F until crusts are crisped on edges and cheese is melted, 7 to 8 minutes. Remove from oven, and sprinkle evenly with basil. Cut each pizza into 4 slices and serve. Serves 4 (serving size: 3 slices)

CALORIES 392; **FAT** 22g (sat 6g, unsat 15g); **PROTEIN** 15g; **CARB** 44g; **FIBER** 6g; **SUGARS** 4g (added sugars 0g); **SODIUM** 782mg; **CALC** 19% DV; **POTASSIUM** 2% DV

WEEKNIGHT MAINS

Staff Favorite · Gluten Free
Make Ahead

Spice-Crusted Flank Steak with Crispy Potatoes

Hands-on: 35 min. **Total:** 35 min.
We recommend doubling the recipe for this smoky tomatillo sauce. It's also fantastic on grilled chicken and shrimp and in the egg-potato wraps on p. 116. Serve with a salad of romaine and radishes with a tart lime dressing.

1 russet potato
1 Tbsp. ground cumin, divided
¾ tsp. kosher salt, divided
2 Tbsp. extra-virgin olive oil, divided
1 cup sliced red onion
2 medium tomatillos, husked and halved
1 small jalapeño, stemmed and halved
¼ cup pico de gallo, drained
1 Tbsp. fresh lime juice, divided
1 lb. flank steak
2 tsp. ground coriander
½ cup chopped fresh cilantro
2 oz. queso fresco (fresh Mexican cheese), crumbled (about ½ cup)

1. Cut potato into 8 (½-inch-thick) wedges. Combine potato wedges, 1½ teaspoons cumin, and ¼ teaspoon salt in a bowl; toss to coat. Heat 1 tablespoon oil in a large nonstick skillet over medium-high; add potatoes. Cook, turning often, until potatoes begin to brown, about 5 minutes. Reduce heat to medium; cook until potatoes are golden brown, about 15 minutes. Add onion; cook, stirring occasionally, 4 minutes. Remove from heat; keep warm.
2. Meanwhile, heat a medium cast-iron skillet over medium-high. Add tomatillos and jalapeño; cook until charred on all sides, about 8 minutes. Remove from heat. Combine tomatillos, jalapeño, pico de gallo, 2 teaspoons lime juice, and ¼ teaspoon salt in the bowl of a mini food processor. Process until finely chopped, about 1 minute.
3. Heat remaining 1 tablespoon oil in cast-iron skillet over medium-high. Season both sides of steak with coriander, remaining ¼ teaspoon salt, and remaining 1½ teaspoons cumin. Add steak to skillet; cook to desired degree of doneness, 4 to 5 minutes per side for medium-rare. Remove to a cutting board; let stand 5 minutes.
4. While steak rests, toss cooked potato wedges and onions in a large bowl with cilantro, queso fresco, and remaining 1 teaspoon lime juice. Cut steak against the grain into thin slices; drizzle with the tomatillo sauce. Serve steak and sauce with potato mixture. Serves 4 (serving size: about 3 oz. steak, 2 potato wedges, and ¼ cup salsa)

CALORIES 426; FAT 21g (sat 7g, unsat 12g); PROTEIN 37g; CARB 22g; FIBER 5g; SUGARS 5g (added sugars 0g); SODIUM 597mg; CALC 13% DV; POTASSIUM 17% DV

Fast · Gluten Free
Hearty

Creamy Artichoke Soup

Hands-on: 25 min. **Total:** 30 min.
This smooth spring soup gets a creamy boost from silken tofu and a dash of half-and-half, plus a veggie bonus from the addition of sweet peas. If frozen artichokes aren't available, use three (14-ounce) cans artichoke hearts, drained and rinsed.

2 Tbsp. extra-virgin olive oil, divided
½ cup chopped shallots
3 garlic cloves, crushed
3 cups unsalted chicken stock
1 (12-oz.) pkg. frozen artichoke hearts
1 (16-oz.) pkg. silken tofu, drained
1 cup frozen sweet peas
¼ cup half-and-half
¾ tsp. kosher salt
½ tsp. black pepper
¼ cup crème fraîche
2 Tbsp. coarsely chopped fresh flat-leaf parsley

1. Heat 1 tablespoon oil in a large saucepan over medium-high. Add shallots and garlic to pan; cook, stirring occasionally, until tender, 3 to 4 minutes. Add stock and artichokes; bring to a boil. Reduce heat to medium, and simmer until artichokes are very tender, about 5 minutes.
2. Combine artichoke mixture, tofu, and peas in a blender. Remove center piece of blender lid (to allow steam to escape); secure lid on blender, and place a clean towel over opening in lid. Process until smooth, about 45 seconds. Return mixture to saucepan; stir in half-and-half, salt, and pepper. Heat over medium until warmed through.
3. Divide soup among 4 bowls. Top each with 1 tablespoon crème fraîche. Drizzle with remaining 1 tablespoon oil, and top with parsley. Serves 4 (serving size: about 1½ cups)

CALORIES 285; FAT 17g (sat 5g, unsat 11g); PROTEIN 13g; CARB 19g; FIBER 8g; SUGARS 5g (added sugars 0g); SODIUM 574mg; CALC 16% DV; POTASSIUM 4% DV

Taco Truck Lettuce Wraps

Hands-on: 25 min. **Total:** 25 min.
Fresh Mexican chorizo (found near the bulk raw sausage) teams up with ground pork to add bold flavor to these wraps; use it instead of dry-cured Spanish chorizo. Leftover pickled carrots and jalapeños make a zesty sandwich topper.

1 cup white vinegar
1 cup water
¼ cup granulated sugar
2 tsp. kosher salt, divided
1 cup matchstick-cut carrots
4 garlic cloves
1 jalapeño, thinly sliced
8 oz. loose fresh Mexican chorizo
4 oz. ground pork
2 Tbsp. olive oil
½ tsp. ground cumin
¼ tsp. chili powder
8 butter lettuce or Bibb lettuce
  leaves
½ cup chopped fresh cilantro
½ cup diced white onion
¼ cup Mexican crema

1. Combine vinegar, 1 cup water, sugar, and ½ teaspoon salt in a medium saucepan. Bring to a boil over medium-high, whisking until sugar is completely dissolved. Remove from heat. Place carrots, garlic, and jalapeño slices in a medium bowl; pour hot vinegar mixture over carrot mixture. Let stand at room temperature 15 minutes, stirring occasionally.
2. Combine chorizo, pork, olive oil, cumin, chili powder, and remaining 1½ teaspoons salt in a medium bowl; stir until well incorporated. Heat a large nonstick skillet over medium-high. Add chorizo mixture to pan; cook, stirring to crumble, until just cooked through, 5 to 7 minutes. Remove from heat; drain drippings from the skillet.
3. Place lettuce leaves on a large serving platter. Divide chorizo mixture evenly among lettuce leaves; sprinkle servings evenly with cilantro and onion.
4. Drain liquid from carrots and jalapeños; discard garlic. Top each wrap evenly with carrot mixture; drizzle each with 1½ teaspoons crema. Serve immediately. Serves 8 (serving size: 1 wrap)

CALORIES 185; **FAT** 16g (sat 6g, unsat 10g); **PROTEIN** 7g; **CARB** 4g; **FIBER** 1g; **SUGARS** 2g (added sugars 1g); **SODIUM** 651mg; **CALC** 1% DV; **POTASSIUM** 1% DV

THE SHORTCUT
Fast • Hearty

Spring Vegetable Shepherd's Pie

Hands-on: 25 min. **Total:** 25 min.
We use cauliflower for the topping instead of the usual mashed potatoes; cauliflower has twice the fiber and about a fourth of the carbs. For a gluten-free version, use 2 tablespoons cornstarch in place of the all-purpose flour in step 3.

2 (12-oz.) pkg. frozen riced
  cauliflower
1 (6.5-oz.) pkg. light garlic-and-
  herb spreadable cheese (such as
  Boursin)
1½ Tbsp. canola oil
1 lb. ground turkey (white and dark
  meat)
2 cups chopped carrots
1¾ cups chopped zucchini
1 cup prechopped yellow onion
1 cup frozen sweet peas
¾ tsp. kosher salt
3 Tbsp. all-purpose flour
1 tsp. fresh thyme leaves, plus more
  for garnish
1¼ cups unsalted chicken stock
¼ tsp. black pepper

1. Preheat broiler to high with oven rack in upper middle position.
2. Microwave cauliflower according to package directions until tender. Combine cauliflower and cheese in a food processor; process until smooth.
3. Heat oil in a large ovenproof skillet over medium-high. Add turkey, and cook, breaking up with a spoon, until turkey begins to brown, about 4 minutes. Add carrots, zucchini, onion, and peas; stir to combine. Add salt, and cook, stirring often, 4 minutes. Add flour and 1 teaspoon thyme; stir to combine. Increase heat to high, and add chicken stock. Cook, stirring constantly, until mixture thickens. Spoon cauliflower mixture over turkey and vegetable mixture in skillet, smoothing top with a spoon; sprinkle with pepper.
4. Broil until cauliflower topping is golden brown in spots, 3 to 4 minutes. Sprinkle with additional thyme leaves. Serve immediately. Serves 6 (serving size: 1¾ cups)

CALORIES 295; **FAT** 14g (sat 5g, unsat 9g); **PROTEIN** 24g; **CARB** 21g; **FIBER** 6g; **SUGARS** 8g (added sugars 0g); **SODIUM** 540mg; **CALC** 7% DV; **POTASSIUM** 20% DV

SHORTCUT ITEMS

To make this dish weeknight-quick, we use no-prep-required frozen riced cauliflower, frozen peas, prechopped onion, and store-bought garlic-herb cheese.

SLOW COOKER

Make Ahead • Hearty

Spicy Tofu Curry

Hands-on: 15 min. **Total:** 6 hr. 15 min.
Look for lemongrass—a long, slender, woody herb with a citrusy, herbal flavor—near the herbs at grocery stores and Asian markets. Refrigerate leftover lemongrass up to one month, or chop and freeze in an airtight container up to six months.

2 (14-oz.) pkg. extra-firm tofu, drained
1 Tbsp. coconut oil
1 (14-oz.) can light coconut milk, well shaken
½ cup unsalted vegetable stock
¼ cup fresh lime juice (from 2 limes)
1 Tbsp. tomato paste
1 Tbsp. roasted red chili paste (such as Thai Kitchen)
1 Tbsp. granulated sugar
1 tsp. fish sauce or lower-sodium soy sauce
1 tsp. curry powder
3 medium-sized red bell peppers, cut into 1½-in. slices
2 small yellow onions, halved and sliced
1 (2-in.) piece lemongrass stalk, halved and smashed
1 (1-in.) piece peeled fresh ginger, thinly sliced
2 garlic cloves, smashed
1 serrano chile, seeded and vertically sliced
2 cups fresh mung bean sprouts
1 cup fresh cilantro leaves
2 limes, cut into wedges

1. Place tofu on a plate lined with paper towels; top with another layer of paper towels and a plate or a skillet. Press and let stand 20 minutes.
2. Heat coconut oil in a large nonstick skillet over medium-high. Add tofu blocks, and cook until lightly browned on all sides, 8 to 10 minutes. Set aside.
3. Whisk together coconut milk, vegetable stock, lime juice, tomato paste, chili paste, sugar, fish sauce, and curry powder in a slow cooker. Add bell peppers, onions, lemongrass, ginger, garlic, and serrano chile; stir to combine. Top with tofu blocks. Cover and cook on low until vegetables are tender, 6 to 8 hours.
4. One hour before serving, carefully transfer tofu blocks to a cutting board, and cut into ½-inch slices. Return sliced tofu to slow cooker. Remove and discard lemongrass. To serve, ladle curry into 8 bowls; top evenly with bean sprouts and cilantro. Serve with lime wedges. Serves 8 (serving size: about 1 cup)

CALORIES 202; FAT 10g (sat 5g, unsat 5g); PROTEIN 11g; CARB 18g; FIBER 3g; SUGARS 7g (added sugars 2g); SODIUM 161mg; CALC 9% DV; POTASSIUM 6% DV

SMART SUBS

Can't track down lemongrass? Substitute 2 tablespoons fresh lemon peel strips in a pinch. To make this vegetarian, go with soy sauce instead of fish sauce.

---

4 GO-WITH-ANYTHING SIDES

Fast • Gluten Free
Vegetarian
Arugula Salad with Lemon and Pine Nuts

Try swapping white wine vinegar or balsamic vinegar for the lemon juice for a tasty twist. Pair this with grilled chicken or steak or top with lemony tuna salad.

Combine ½ tsp. lemon zest, 1 Tbsp. lemon juice, 1 tsp. honey, ⅜ tsp. kosher salt, and ¼ tsp. black pepper in a small bowl. Slowly drizzle in 2 Tbsp. olive oil, whisking constantly, until emulsified. Combine 5 oz. baby arugula and ½ cup shaved fennel in a large bowl. Toss with dressing, and top with ¼ cup pecorino Romano cheese and 3 Tbsp. toasted pine nuts. Serves 4 (serving size: about 1 cup)

CALORIES 135; FAT 12g (sat 2g, unsat 9g); PROTEIN 3g; CARB 5g; FIBER 1g; SUGARS 3g (added sugars 1g); SODIUM 238mg; CALC 10% DV; POTASSIUM 6% DV

Fast • Make Ahead
Vegetarian
Charred Orange-Chile Broccoli

Broccoli stems deliver a hefty helping of fiber; shave them with a vegetable peeler to keep them tender. Trade out the chile-garlic sauce for Sriracha or a sprinkle of crushed red pepper for more heat.

Preheat oven to 425°F .Cut 2 heads broccoli into florets with 2 inches of stem; toss with 2 Tbsp. canola oil on a large baking sheet. Bake at 425°F until tender and charred, 25 to 30 minutes. Bring 2 Tbsp. fresh orange juice, 1 Tbsp. lower-sodium soy sauce, 1 Tbsp. light brown sugar, and 2 tsp. Asian chile-garlic sauce to a boil in a saucepan over high. Reduce to a simmer, and cook until thickened, 2 minutes. Stir in 2 tsp. dark sesame oil. Drizzle over broccoli. Sprinkle with 2 tsp. toasted sesame seeds. Serves 4 (serving size: ¾ cup)

CALORIES 170; FAT 11g (sat 1g, unsat 9g); PROTEIN 5g; CARB 16g; FIBER 5g; SUGARS 7g (added sugars 3g); SODIUM 251mg; CALC 9% DV; POTASSIUM 16% DV

Fast • Gluten Free
Make Ahead
Crispy Potatoes with Chorizo

Parcooking the potatoes is the secret to this quick dish. Place halved potatoes in a microwavable bowl with 2 tablespoons water; cover and microwave at high until almost tender, 4 to 5 minutes.

Cook ¾ cup chopped dry-cured Spanish chorizo in 1 Tbsp. olive oil in a large skillet over medium-high until crispy, 5 to 6 minutes. Remove chorizo; reserve drippings. Add 1½ lb. parcooked halved baby Yukon Gold potatoes, 1 Tbsp. sliced garlic, ⅝ tsp. kosher salt, ½ tsp. paprika, and 1 tsp. chopped fresh oregano to skillet. Cook until golden, 8 to 10 minutes. Add chorizo; top with 1 Tbsp. chopped fresh parsley. Serves 4 (serving size: about ½ cup)

CALORIES 245; **FAT** 10g (sat 3g, unsat 7g); **PROTEIN** 9g; **CARB** 33g; **FIBER** 3g; **SUGARS** 2g (added sugars 0g); **SODIUM** 355mg; **CALC** 13% DV; **POTASSIUM** 1% DV

Fast • Make Ahead
Vegetarian
Strawberry and Cucumber Tabbouleh

Strawberries stand in for tomatoes in this fresh salad. Add rinsed chickpeas to transform this spring side into a satisfying meatless supper.

Bring 1 cup water and ½ cup bulgur to a boil in a saucepan over high. Reduce heat to medium-low; cover and cook until tender, about 12 minutes. Drain and cool. Toss with ¾ cup chopped strawberries, ½ cup chopped cucumber, ¼ cup chopped toasted almonds, 2 Tbsp. olive oil, 1½ Tbsp. chopped fresh mint, 1 Tbsp. chopped fresh parsley, 1 tsp. lemon zest, 1 tsp. fresh lemon juice, ⅝ tsp. kosher salt, and ¼ tsp. black pepper. Serves 4 (serving size: ¾ cup)

CALORIES 185; **FAT** 12g (sat 1g, unsat 10g); **PROTEIN** 4g; **CARB** 18g; **FIBER** 4g; **SUGARS** 2g (added sugars 0g); **SODIUM** 305mg; **CALC** 4% DV; **POTASSIUM** 6% DV

4 SAUCES FOR ANY PROTEIN

Fast • Gluten Free
Make Ahead • Vegetarian
Everything Bagel Aioli

Your favorite bagel flavor just got upgraded to sauce superstar. Try this drizzled over eggs Benedict, spread on a grilled chicken burger, or spooned over grilled red onion wedges.

Whisk together 1 large pasteurized egg yolk and 1 Tbsp. water in a medium bowl. Add ⅓ cup olive oil in a slow, steady stream, whisking constantly, until thickened. Whisk in 2 Tbsp. plain whole-milk Greek yogurt. Add ½ tsp. grated garlic, ½ tsp. poppy seeds, ½ tsp. white sesame seeds, ½ tsp. black sesame seeds, ½ tsp. dried onion flakes, and ¼ tsp. kosher salt; whisk to combine. Serves 6 (serving size: 1½ Tbsp.)

CALORIES 131; **FAT** 14g (sat 2g, unsat 11g); **PROTEIN** 1g; **CARB** 1g; **FIBER** 0g; **SUGARS** 0g (added sugars 0g); **SODIUM** 84mg; **CALC** 1% DV; **POTASSIUM** 0% DV

Fast • Gluten Free
Vegetarian
Strawberry-Shallot Salsa

Sweet strawberries mingle with lime and nutty coriander in this fresh take on salsa. Try this vibrant sauce spooned over pan-seared halibut or sprinkled with feta over grilled pork-and-zucchini kabobs.

Combine 2 Tbsp. minced shallot, 2 Tbsp. fresh lime juice, 2 tsp. honey, 1 tsp. olive oil, and ½ tsp. red wine vinegar in a medium bowl. Let stand 10 minutes. Stir in ½ tsp. ground coriander, ¼ tsp. kosher salt, and 1 Tbsp. chopped fresh mint. Add 1½ cups finely chopped strawberries; gently toss to combine. Serves 6 (serving size: ¼ cup)

CALORIES 31; **FAT** 1g (sat 0g, unsat 1g); **PROTEIN** 0g; **CARB** 6g; **FIBER** 1g; **SUGARS** 4g (added sugars 2g); **SODIUM** 81mg; **CALC** 1% DV; **POTASSIUM** 2% DV

Make Ahead
Kimchi-Bacon Jam

Salty and smoky with a kick from the kimchi, this chunky, chutney-like jam is delicious on grilled burgers and hot dogs, or as a surprise condiment on your next cheese and crudités platter.

Cook 3 center-cut bacon slices in a skillet over medium-high until crisp. Remove bacon; reserve drippings in pan. Reduce heat to medium; add ⅔ cup chopped onion; cook 4 minutes. Add 1 minced garlic clove, 2 tsp. brown sugar, and ¼ tsp. paprika; cook 1 minute. Add ¾ cup amber beer; bring to a boil over medium-high. Cook until beer is reduced to ¼ cup. Remove from heat; stir in bacon and 2 Tbsp. kimchi. Pulse mixture in a food processor until finely chopped. Serves 4 (serving size: 2 Tbsp.)

CALORIES 65; **FAT** 1g (sat 0g, unsat 1g); **PROTEIN** 3g; **CARB** 7g; **FIBER** 1g; **SUGARS** 3g (added sugars 2g); **SODIUM** 110mg; **CALC** 1% DV; **POTASSIUM** 2% DV

Fast • Gluten Free
Make Ahead • Vegetarian
Hot Mustard Sauce

If you love the spicy mustard that's often paired with Chinese egg rolls, whip up this tangy, cayenne-spiked sauce. Serve it with grilled tofu or chicken tenders, or drizzle it over roasted broccoli.

Combine ¼ cup Dijon mustard, 1 Tbsp. rice wine vinegar, 1 minced garlic clove, 2 tsp. fresh lemon juice, 2 tsp. honey, and ½ tsp. cayenne pepper in a small bowl; whisk until smooth. Serve at room temperature or chilled. Serves 8 (serving size: 2 tsp.)

CALORIES 14; **FAT** 0g; **PROTEIN** 0g; **CARB** 2g; **FIBER** 0g; **SUGARS** 1g (added sugars 1g); **SODIUM** 180mg; **CALC** 0% DV; **POTASSIUM** 0% DV

3 WAYS TO USE CHARD

Colorful and quick-cooking chard is a great leafy green for busy weeknights. Use both the leaves and stems to up your side game.

Fast · Vegetarian
Sweet Potato and Chard Salad

This one-pot dish couldn't be easier; top it with rotisserie chicken for a fast supper.

1. Combine 4 cups water and 10 oz. diced sweet potato in a medium saucepan over medium-high. Bring to a boil; reduce heat to medium-low, and cook 3 minutes. Stir in 6 oz. chopped rainbow chard. Cook until wilted, about 2 minutes; drain well.
2. Combine chard mixture, 1 cup hot cooked farro, 2 Tbsp. extra-virgin olive oil, 2 Tbsp. tarragon vinegar, ¼ tsp. kosher salt, and ¼ tsp. black pepper in a medium bowl; toss to combine. Sprinkle with 2 Tbsp. sliced scallions. Serves 4 (serving size: 1 cup)

CALORIES 165; **FAT** 7g (sat 1g, unsat 6g); **PROTEIN** 3g; **CARB** 24g; **FIBER** 4g; **SUGARS** 4g (added sugars 0g); **SODIUM** 251mg; **CALC** 5% DV; **POTASSIUM** 12% DV

Fast · Gluten Free
Vegetarian
Wilted Chard and Shaved Fennel Salad

We love the color of rainbow chard, but any type will work. Swap the fennel for shaved red onion, if you prefer.

1. Coarsely chop leaves from 1 lb. rainbow chard to equal 8 cups; thinly slice stems to equal 1 cup. (Reserve remaining stems for another use.)

2. Heat 1 Tbsp. olive oil in a large skillet over medium-high. Add chard stems and 1 cup thinly shaved fennel bulb; cook, stirring often, until starting to soften, about 3 minutes. Add chard leaves and ¼ cup water. Cover and cook until just starting to wilt, about 1 minute and 30 seconds. Drain. Top servings evenly with ¼ cup chopped pistachios, 2 Tbsp. fennel fronds, 1 Tbsp. apple cider vinegar, ¼ tsp. black pepper, and ⅛ tsp. kosher salt. Serves 4 (serving size: 1 cup)

CALORIES 93; **FAT** 7g (sat 1g, unsat 6g); **PROTEIN** 3g; **CARB** 7g; **FIBER** 3g; **SUGARS** 2g (added sugars 0g); **SODIUM** 239mg; **CALC** 6% DV; **POTASSIUM** 13% DV

Staff Favorite · Fast
Gluten Free · Vegetarian
Charred Chard and Shallots

This recipe uses chard leaves, but don't discard the stems. Chop and add to an omelet, or sauté them in a little olive oil and use as a flavor booster in a grilled cheese sandwich. To turn this side into a vegetarian main dish, top with chickpeas and crumbled feta.

1. Spray 2 rimmed baking sheets with cooking spray. Trim stems from 1 lb. rainbow chard and reserve for another use. Divide chard leaves and ½ cup sliced shallots evenly between prepared pans; lightly coat vegetables with cooking spray. Broil on high, 1 pan at a time, until partially charred, 4 to 5 minutes.
2. Chop chard into large pieces. Place chard mixture on a platter. Top with ¼ cup golden raisins, 2 Tbsp. extra-virgin olive oil, 1 Tbsp. fresh lemon juice, ⅛ tsp. kosher salt, and ⅛ tsp. black pepper. Serves 4 (serving size: 1 cup)

CALORIES 119; **FAT** 7g (sat 1g, unsat 6g); **PROTEIN** 2g; **CARB** 14g; **FIBER** 2g; **SUGARS** 8g (added sugars 0g); **SODIUM** 215mg; **CALC** 5% DV; **POTASSIUM** 12% DV

COOKING LIGHT DIET
Gluten Free · Vegetarian
Hearty

Zucchini-Mushroom Caprese Bowl

Hands-on: 35 min. **Total:** 35 min.
This deconstructed zucchini "noodle" version of lasagna satisfies your craving for Italian at a fraction of the calories. Creamy dollops of cheese up the yummy factor; toss in a handful of yellow cherry tomatoes for an extra helping of vegetables.

1 medium zucchini
¾ tsp. kosher salt, divided
2 Tbsp. olive oil
1 cup chopped yellow onion
1 Tbsp. finely chopped fresh garlic
16 oz. sliced cremini mushrooms
1 Tbsp. unsalted tomato paste
1 (28-oz.) can unsalted diced fire-roasted tomatoes, undrained
1 tsp. freshly ground black pepper
5 oz. fresh baby spinach
4 oz. part-skim ricotta cheese (about ½ cup)
3 oz. preshredded part-skim mozzarella cheese (about ¾ cup)
¼ cup loosely packed fresh basil

1. Using a vegetable peeler, shave zucchini into long, even strips. Toss with ¼ teaspoon salt in a colander. Let stand until ready to use.
2. Heat oil in a Dutch oven over medium-high. Add onion and garlic; cook, stirring often, until tender, about 3 minutes. Add mushrooms; cook, stirring often, until browned, about 5 minutes. Add tomato paste; cook 1 minute. Stir in tomatoes, pepper, and remaining ½ teaspoon salt; bring to a simmer, stirring often. Reduce heat to medium-low, and simmer, stirring occasionally, until slightly reduced, about 6 minutes. Stir

in spinach; cover and cook until spinach wilts, about 3 minutes. Remove from heat. Gently stir in zucchini strips.

3. Stir together ricotta and mozzarella in a microwavable bowl; microwave at HIGH 30 seconds. Dot zucchini mixture with cheese mixture. Sprinkle with basil. Serves 4 (serving size: 1 ½ cups)

CALORIES 276; FAT 13g (sat 5g, unsat 8g); PROTEIN 16g; CARB 26g; FIBER 5g; SUGARS 13g (added sugars 0g); SODIUM 590mg; CALC 33% DV; POTASSIUM 25% DV

USE IT UP

3 WAYS TO USE CILANTRO

This pungent herb amps up the flavor of the potatoes on p. 118 and lettuce wraps on p. 119, but don't let the rest go to waste. The leaves and stems also can add fresh flavor to drinks, sides, and dressings.

Fast • Gluten Free
Vegetarian
Green Cauliflower Rice

If you can't find premade fresh cauliflower crumbles, coarsely chop 1 pound cauliflower; place in a food processor, and pulse in short bursts until small, rice-sized crumbles form.

1. Place 1 cup coarsely chopped fresh cilantro leaves and stems, ½ cup coarsely chopped white onion, 1 garlic clove, and 1 seeded jalapeño in a mini food processor; process until finely chopped and almost paste-like, stopping to scrape down sides as needed.

2. Heat 2 Tbsp. olive oil in a large skillet over medium-high. Add 1 lb. fresh cauliflower crumbles or riced cauliflower (about 4 cups); cook, stirring occasionally, 3 minutes. Stir in cilantro mixture; cook, stirring occasionally, 2 minutes or to desired texture. Stir in 1 tsp. fresh lime juice and ⅜ tsp. kosher salt. Serves 4 (serving size: ½ cup)

CALORIES 99; FAT 7g (sat 1g, unsat 6g); PROTEIN 3g; CARB 8g; FIBER 3g; SUGARS 3g (added sugars 0g); SODIUM 217mg; CALC 3% DV; POTASSIUM 11% DV

Fast • Gluten Free
Vegetarian
Cilantro-Lime Margaritas

Skip the sugary margarita mix and welcome the warmer weather with this twist on a classic margarita. This is a great use for cilantro stems, which have all the flavor of cilantro, but are often overlooked.

1. Combine 1 cup coarsely chopped fresh cilantro leaves and stems, ½ cup water, ½ cup fresh lime juice, and 2 ½ Tbsp. honey in a blender; blend until completely smooth. Skim off and discard foam from top.
2. For each margarita, pour ¼ cup cilantro mixture and 1 ½ oz. tequila into an ice-filled shaker; shake vigorously 10 seconds. Strain into a glass filled with crushed ice. Serve immediately. Serves 4 (serving size: ½ cup)

CALORIES 147; FAT 0g; PROTEIN 0g; CARB 14g; FIBER 0g; SUGARS 11g (added sugars 11g); SODIUM 4mg; CALC 1% DV; POTASSIUM 2% DV

Fast • Gluten Free
Make Ahead • Vegetarian
Crunchy Romaine Salad with Cilantro Ranch

Try this dressing on top of any combo of greens and crunchy vegetables or as a dip for carrots or cucumbers.

1. Whisk together ¼ cup finely chopped fresh cilantro leaves and stems, ¼ cup whole buttermilk, 3 Tbsp. canola mayonnaise, 1 tsp. apple cider vinegar, ½ tsp. black pepper, ¼ tsp. kosher salt, and 1 grated small garlic clove in a medium bowl.
2. Combine 6 cups torn romaine lettuce, ½ cup thinly sliced radishes, and ½ cup matchstick-cut carrots. Divide among 4 plates, and drizzle with dressing. Serves 4 (serving size: 1 ½ cups salad and 2 Tbsp. dressing)

CALORIES 60; FAT 4g (sat 0g, unsat 3g); PROTEIN 2g; CARB 5g; FIBER 2g; SUGARS 3g (added sugars 0g); SODIUM 238mg; CALC 5% DV; POTASSIUM 8% DV

1 LIST 3 DINNERS

Shop this list to feed four for three nights, all for about $30. Read the recipes first to be sure you have the staples on hand.

Fresh cilantro

Fresh flat-leaf parsley

1 small and 2 medium-sized golden beets

1 small carrot

2 lemons

2 (5-oz.) pkg. baby kale and spinach mix

1 small red onion

Unsalted shelled pistachios

Grainy Dijon mustard

2 (32-oz.) containers unsalted chicken stock

1 pkg. whole-wheat spaghetti

Quinoa (red or regular)

1 (1 ½-lb.) and 1 (10-oz.) skin-on salmon fillets

Plain 2% reduced-fat Greek yogurt

Large eggs

Dinner 1 of 3

Gluten Free • Make Ahead Hearty

Salmon and Quinoa Bowl

Hands-on: 30 min. **Total:** 45 min.
Put this recipe on your last-minute-supper list; everything can be made ahead and assembled just before serving. We use red quinoa, but any color or blend will work fine here. Lunch alert: If you have any leftovers, they're just as delicious cold.

1¼ cups unsalted chicken stock
¾ cup uncooked red quinoa
2 cups baby kale and spinach mix, finely chopped
2 Tbsp. finely chopped fresh cilantro
2 Tbsp. finely chopped fresh flat-leaf parsley
6 Tbsp. extra-virgin olive oil, divided
1⅛ tsp. kosher salt, divided
½ tsp. black pepper, divided
1 small golden beet
1 small carrot
1½ Tbsp. apple cider vinegar
2 tsp. minced garlic
1 (10-oz.) skin-on salmon fillet (about 1½ inches thick)
¼ cup plain 2% reduced-fat Greek yogurt

1. Combine stock and quinoa in a small saucepan; bring to a boil over high. Reduce heat to medium-low, and simmer 15 minutes. Remove from heat, and let stand 5 minutes. Fluff with a fork, and stir in kale-spinach mix, cilantro, parsley, 5 tablespoons oil, ¼ teaspoon salt, and ¼ teaspoon pepper.
2. Using a mandoline or a vegetable peeler, slice or peel beet and carrot into very thin slices. Place beet and carrot in a medium bowl; add vinegar, garlic, and ¼ teaspoon

salt. Let stand 15 minutes, stirring occasionally.
3. Heat remaining 1 tablespoon oil in a skillet over medium-high. Sprinkle salmon with remaining ⅝ teaspoon salt and remaining ¼ teaspoon pepper. Add salmon to hot oil, skin side down, and cook 6 minutes. Reduce heat to medium-low; cover and cook until a thermometer inserted in thickest portion reaches 130°F, 6 to 7 minutes. Let stand 5 minutes; flake salmon into large pieces.
4. Divide quinoa mixture among 4 shallow bowls. Top evenly with salmon, beet mixture, and yogurt. Serves 4 (serving size: ⅔ cup quinoa mix, about 2 ½ oz. salmon, ¼ cup beet mixture, and 1 Tbsp. yogurt)

CALORIES 447; FAT 28g (sat 4g, unsat 23g); PROTEIN 22g; CARB 28g; FIBER 4g; SUGARS 5g (added sugars 0g); SODIUM 672mg; CALC 8% DV; POTASSIUM 20% DV

Dinner 2 of 3

Hearty

Broken Pasta with Pistachio and Lemon

Hands-on: 50 min. **Total:** 1 hr.
Just like rice in risotto, this pasta gets a nice toasting followed by ladlefuls of warm broth until it cooks up tender and creamy. Topped with jammy-yolked eggs and ribboned with healthy greens, it's a pasta supper you can be proud of.

4 large eggs
3 Tbsp. finely chopped unsalted pistachios, toasted
1 tsp. lemon zest
3 cups unsalted chicken stock
3 cups water
3 Tbsp. olive oil

8 oz. uncooked whole-wheat spaghetti, broken into 3-inch pieces
3 Tbsp. fresh lemon juice
2 tsp. Dijon mustard
¾ tsp. kosher salt
½ tsp. black pepper
1 (5-oz.) pkg. baby kale and spinach mix (about 6 cups)

1. Bring 2 inches of water to a boil in a medium saucepan over medium-high. Place a steamer basket in pan. Add eggs to steamer basket; cover and cook 6 minutes. (Cook 8 minutes for hard yolks.) Gently transfer eggs to an ice water bath; let stand 3 minutes. Drain and set aside.
2. Combine pistachios and lemon zest in a small bowl; set aside. Bring stock and 3 cups water to a boil in a medium saucepan. Turn off heat, leaving saucepan on burner.
3. Heat oil in a large skillet over medium. Add pasta to the skillet; cook, stirring often, until toasted, 6 to 7 minutes. Add 2 cups stock mixture to the skillet; bring to a boil over high. Cook, stirring often, until most of the liquid is absorbed, 5 to 10 minutes. Repeat once with 2 cups stock mixture. Finish with 1 ½ cups stock mixture, and cook, stirring often, until pasta is tender and liquid is absorbed, 5 to 10 minutes. Reserve remaining ½ cup stock mixture.
4. Whisk together lemon juice, mustard, salt, pepper, and remaining ½ cup stock mixture in a large bowl. Add pasta, and toss to coat. Add kale-spinach mix; stir until greens begin to wilt. Divide pasta evenly among 4 shallow bowls. Peel eggs, and halve lengthwise; place 2 halves in each bowl. Sprinkle evenly with pistachio-lemon mixture. Serves 4 (serving size: about 2 cups)

CALORIES 313; **FAT** 19g (sat 3g, unsat 14g); **PROTEIN** 15g; **CARB** 23g; **FIBER** 4g; **SUGARS** 2g (added sugars 0g); **SODIUM** 637mg; **CALC** 10% DV; **POTASSIUM** 6% DV

This company-worthy supper is a delicious way to work in one of your two recommended weekly servings of heart-healthy omega-3 fatty acids.

Dinner 3 of 3

Fast · Gluten Free Hearty

Roasted Pistachio-Crusted Salmon and Kale Salad

Hands-on: 15 min. **Total:** 30 min.
For even cooking, look for a fillet that's about the same thickness throughout.

2 medium-size golden beets
¼ cup finely chopped unsalted pistachios, toasted
2 tsp. grainy Dijon mustard
1 tsp. lemon zest
1 (1½-lb.) skin-on salmon fillet (about 1¼ in. thick)
⅞ tsp. kosher salt, divided
¾ tsp. black pepper, divided
3 Tbsp. extra-virgin olive oil
2 Tbsp. fresh lemon juice
3 cups baby kale and spinach mix
½ cup thinly sliced red onion

1. Preheat oven to 450°F. Peel beets, and cut into ½-inch wedges. Place in a small baking dish; cover and bake until tender, 25 to 30 minutes.
2. Stir together pistachios, mustard, and lemon zest in a small bowl. Place salmon on a baking sheet lined with aluminum foil, and sprinkle with ½ teaspoon salt and ½ teaspoon pepper. Spoon pistachio mixture on top of salmon; pat into an even layer. Bake at 450°F until a thermometer inserted in thickest portion registers 130°F, 15 to 16 minutes.
3. Whisk together oil, lemon juice, remaining ⅜ teaspoon salt, and remaining ¼ teaspoon pepper in a large bowl; reserve 3 tablespoons of the dressing. Add beets, kale-spinach mix, and onion to bowl with dressing, and toss to coat. Transfer to a platter. Place salmon fillet on salad. Drizzle with reserved 3 tablespoons dressing. Serves 4 (serving size: 5 oz. salmon and about 1 cup kale mixture)

CALORIES 420; **FAT** 23g (sat 4g, unsat 18g); **PROTEIN** 40g; **CARB** 12g; **FIBER** 4g; **SUGARS** 6g (added sugars 0g); **SODIUM** 624mg; **CALC** 8% DV; **POTASSIUM** 26% DV

SUPER-SIMPLE VEGGIE TART

Rustic yet striking, a free-form galette is a gorgeous dish to display. Even better: It's a breeze to make, even if you're not an experienced baker.

Make Ahead • Vegetarian

Beet and Goat Cheese Tart

Hands-on: 15 min. **Total:** 1 hr. 50 min.

3 medium-sized red beets, trimmed
3 medium-sized golden beets, trimmed
½ (16-oz.) pkg. frozen 9-inch whole-wheat pie crust dough (such as Wholly Wholesome), thawed
Whole-wheat flour, for dusting
1½ oz. fresh goat cheese (about ⅓ cup)
1 Tbsp. red wine vinegar
1 Tbsp. honey
½ tsp. kosher salt
¼ tsp. freshly ground black pepper
1 tsp. fresh thyme leaves
1 large egg, beaten

1. Preheat oven to 400°F. Bundle red beets together; wrap in aluminum foil. Bundle golden beets together; wrap in foil. Roast beets at 400°F until tender, about 1 hour. Unwrap beets, and let stand until cool. Peel and slice into ⅛-inch slices.

2. Roll dough round into a 14-inch circle on parchment paper dusted with whole-wheat flour. Carefully transfer dough and parchment to a baking sheet. Spread cheese over dough, leaving a 2-inch border. Beginning in center, arrange beet slices on cheese in overlapping concentric circles. Stir together vinegar and honey in a small bowl until smooth. Drizzle vinegar mixture evenly over beets. Sprinkle with salt, pepper, and thyme. Fold dough edges over beets toward the center. Brush egg over top of folded dough. Bake tart at 400°F until crust is deeply browned, about 30 minutes. Let stand 10 minutes. Slice into 12 wedges. Serves 12 (serving size: 1 wedge)

CALORIES 135; **FAT** 6g (sat 4g, unsat 0g); **PROTEIN** 3g; **CARB** 17g; **FIBER** 2g; **SUGARS** 5g (added sugars 1g); **SODIUM** 239mg; **CALC** 2% DV; **POTASSIUM** 6% DV

HOW TO ASSEMBLE A GALETTE

1. ROLL CRUST
Place a thawed 9-inch pie crust on lightly floured parchment paper. Roll into a 14-inch circle. Press cracks or tears back together with your fingers. Carefully move parchment and dough to a baking sheet.

2. PLACE TOPPING
Starting in the center, arrange roasted beet slices in overlapping concentric circles over goat cheese. Leave a few inches of crust around the perimeter. Drizzle beets with vinegar-honey glaze, and then season.

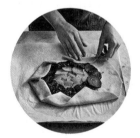

3. FORM GALETTE
The beauty of a galette is that, unlike pie, it doesn't require any fussy crimping. Just fold the edges toward the center. Press any dough cracks closed so beet juice won't seep out.

4. BRUSH AND BAKE
Brush the folded crust evenly with egg wash. This gives the baked crust a gorgeous golden brown sheen. The beets will bubble slightly when it's time to pull from the oven. Let stand before slicing.

ESSENTIAL INGREDIENTS

EVERY ONE OF THE INGREDIENTS PLAYS A KEY ROLE BECAUSE WITH THIS GUACAMOLE, IT'S ALL ABOUT FLAVOR BALANCE.

WHITE ONION
Traditional in Mexican cooking. Gentler than yellow onion, it adds just enough pungency and crunch to the mix.

JALAPEÑO
Just a little—and no fiery seeds—for background heat. Jalapeños without thin brown lines on the skin are usually milder.

CILANTRO
Adds fresh, verdant flavor. Like the other stir-ins, you need only a little so it won't overwhelm the avocado.

LIME JUICE
Aim for a balanced flavor, where the acidic juice subtly cuts through the rich fat without making the guac taste tart.

AVOCADOS
Creamy, rich Hass avocados are best for guac. They should be ripe enough to mash but not browned, bruised, or fibrous.

SALT
We like kosher salt, but the important thing is that fat needs salt (it tastes flat without enough), and guac is a bowl of heart-healthy fat.

COOKING CLASS: WHY INGREDIENTS MATTER
Fast • Gluten Free Vegetarian

No-Frills Guacamole

Hands-on: 10 min. **Total:** 15 min.
This recipe gets back to basics and makes balanced flavor the top priority so no ingredient tramples on the exquisite, subtly nutty, and lightly sweet flavors of avocado. As with all simple recipes, the quality of the ingredients makes or breaks the dish: Be particularly sure to use avocados at peak ripeness. We let the onion and jalapeño macerate with the lime juice and salt to tame their flavors slightly. Serve with your favorite tortilla chips, and set out some crunchy vegetables to dip, too, such as radishes, mini sweet peppers, and jicama slices.

1 ½ Tbsp. finely chopped white onion
1 Tbsp. fresh lime juice
1 tsp. finely chopped seeded jalapeño
½ tsp. kosher salt
2 ripe avocados, coarsely chopped
1 Tbsp. chopped fresh cilantro

1. Combine onion, lime juice, jalapeño, and salt in a medium bowl; let stand 10 minutes. Add avocados; mash to desired consistency. Stir in cilantro. Serves 6 (serving size: about ¼ cup)

CALORIES 109; **FAT** 10g (sat 1g, unsat 8g); **PROTEIN** 1g; **CARB** 6g; **FIBER** 5g; **SUGARS** 1g (added sugars 0g); **SODIUM** 165mg; **CALC** 1% DV; **POTASSIUM** 10% DV

WHAT'S FRESH NOW
Fast • Gluten Free Vegetarian

Shaved Spring Veggie Salad

Hands-on: 15 min. **Total:** 15 min.

2 small heirloom carrots
1 small golden beet, trimmed
3 small French Breakfast radishes, trimmed
4 cups loosely packed spring mix (about 4 oz.)
3 Tbsp. olive oil, divided
3 Tbsp. fresh lemon juice, divided
½ tsp. sumac (optional)
½ tsp. kosher salt, divided
¼ tsp. cracked black pepper
¼ cup tahini (sesame seed paste)
1 tsp. lemon zest
1 small garlic clove, grated
5 Tbsp. warm water
8 pitted Medjool dates, torn into small pieces

1. Using a vegetable peeler or mandoline, shave carrots, beet, and radishes lengthwise into ⅛-inch-thick slices. Submerge slices in a large bowl of ice water for 10 minutes. Drain well; pat dry.
2. Combine shaved vegetables and spring mix in a bowl; toss with 2 tablespoons oil and 2 tablespoons lemon juice. Sprinkle with sumac (if desired), ¼ teaspoon salt, and pepper.
3. Whisk together tahini, zest, garlic, remaining 1 tablespoon oil, remaining 1 tablespoon juice, and remaining ¼ teaspoon salt. Add 5 tablespoons warm water, 1 tablespoon at a time, whisking until smooth. Spread dressing across bottom of a large, shallow bowl. Pile salad on dressing; top with dates. Serves 6 (serving size: about 1 cup)

CALORIES 172; **FAT** 12g (sat 2g, unsat 10g); **PROTEIN** 3g; **CARB** 15g; **FIBER** 3g; **SUGARS** 9g (added sugars 0g); **SODIUM** 208mg; **CALC** 5% DV; **POTASSIUM** 6% DV

WHY YOU SHOULD COOK WITH COCONUT WATER

BY ANDREA NGUYEN

This versatile ingredient is delicious in traditional Asian dishes and modern recipes. Sensing that one of my favorite Whole Foods cashiers was curious about my purchase of five brands of coconut water, I casually said, "I'm doing a little research."

His eyes widened as he launched into telling me about his favorite brand (which I'd fortunately bought), how the packaging was ecological, that the liquid wasn't pasteurized, and how it had electrolytes and antioxidants! When he paused for a breath, I responded, "I'm cooking with this stuff." He raised his eyebrows in surprise as I explained that in certain parts of Asia, coconut water is both a drink and an ingredient. Noting a line of customers behind me, I went on my way.

What I didn't get to explain to the cashier is that for decades, I'd been chasing the fleeting flavors of popular Asian foods such as Vietnamese pork simmered in coconut-caramel sauce, Indonesian fried chicken, and Thai coconut agar jelly. Only recently had I managed to get satisfaction via the proliferation of coconut water in American supermarkets.

Before coconut water came on the scene as healthy hydration, it was a low-key beverage, often sweetened and mostly sold at Asian markets. I longed for the lilt of fresh coconut juice, which adds a subtle sweetness and viscosity to help build umami in savory dishes. Years ago, despite knowing that coconut water comes from young coconuts with green or yellow exteriors, I nevertheless cracked hairy, brown, mature coconuts, thinking I could make milk with the thick, oily flesh then cook with the liquid inside. Wrong. The water was lackluster.

Today's abundance of coconut water is quenching my curiosity. I use the slightly opaque liquid in traditional preparations as well as modern dishes. Sometimes I replace regular water with coconut water to make Vietnamese nuoc cham dipping sauce. If a coconut milk-based curry needs to be thinned out, I'll pour in coconut water to further emphasize coconut goodness. The water's natural sweetness often lets me use less sugar. When I'm sautéing vegetables, I splash in coconut water and cook it down, coating the veggies with a hint of caramelization.

Most recently, I decided to use coconut water instead of coconut milk to make a festive rice. The result was startlingly good. The coconut water didn't weigh down the grains (or turn them gummy) like fattier coconut milk did. The water delicately flavored the rice during the cooking process; adding virgin coconut oil underscored the coconut flavor.

The vibrant rice took me back to a dish that my mom made in Vietnam; I'd long thought those flavors were beyond my reach. Feeling brazen, I used the leftover coconut water in a Julia Child sautéed chicken recipe to serve with the rice. The two made for a great meal.

We cook for different reasons—to explore, create, or reclaim. In the process, we nourish ourselves on many levels. On this occasion, I did it with coconut water.

Fast • Gluten Free Hearty

Chicken and Vegetables with Coconut Water

Hands-on: 15 min. **Total:** 15 min.
This easy chicken sauté is inspired by a recipe in Julia Child's *The Way to Cook.*

2 skinless, boneless chicken breasts (1 to 1¼ lb.)
½ tsp. plus a dash of fine sea salt, divided
⅛ tsp. paprika
1¼ Tbsp. virgin coconut oil, divided
⅓ cup unsweetened pulp-free coconut water, divided
1 small shallot, halved and thinly sliced lengthwise
1 Tbsp. finely chopped fresh garlic
8 oz. sugar snap peas, trimmed
1 (4-oz.) red bell pepper, trimmed and cut diagonally into ½-in.-wide strips
Dash of freshly ground black pepper

1. Pat chicken dry with paper towels, and rub all over with ½ teaspoon salt and paprika. Melt 1 tablespoon coconut oil in a nonstick skillet over medium-high. (I used my 11-inch Mauviel, but a 10-inch All-Clad or Calphalon would be fine.) When oil is shimmering, add chicken, rounded side down. Cook until browned and a meat thermometer inserted in thickest portion registers 160°F, about 4 minutes per side. Remove chicken to a plate, and cover to keep warm. (Do not wipe skillet clean.)
2. Reduce heat to medium-low, sliding skillet off heat to cool if needed, and add ¼ cup coconut water. Cook, without stirring, until liquid reduces to about

2 ½ tablespoons, about 1 minute. Pour pan sauce over chicken. (Do not wipe skillet clean.)

3. Add remaining 1½ teaspoons coconut oil, shallot, and garlic to skillet. Sauté over medium until aromatic, about 30 seconds. Add snap peas and bell pepper. Season with a dash of salt and pepper. Cook, stirring constantly, until hot, about 1 minute. Splash in remaining coconut water to facilitate cooking the vegetables until crisp-tender. Remove from heat.

4. Slice chicken, and serve with vegetables and any accumulated pan juices. Serves 4 (serving size: about 5 oz. chicken and ½ cup vegetables)

CALORIES 243; **FAT** 9g (sat 5g, unsat 2g); **PROTEIN** 31g; **CARB** 9g; **FIBER** 2g; **SUGARS** 4g (added sugars 0g); **SODIUM** 341mg; **CALC** 5% DV; **POTASSIUM** 16% DV

THE PICKY EATER GURU

HOW TO WIN DINNER WITH A WAFFLE IRON

BY GINA HOMOLKA

Skinnytaste founder Gina Homolka transformed her unused, dusty waffle iron into a must-have tool for quick and easy weeknight dinners.

When I have appliances collecting dust, I hate it. That's how I felt about my waffle iron—until recently. It was my most neglected appliance for quite some time, and then I realized the humble waffle iron is capable of making a lot more than just waffles. Now I keep it on my counter to whip up everything from grilled cheese sandwiches and crab cakes to zucchini fritters and chocolate chip cookies—the possibilities really are endless.

Making quesadillas in the waffle iron is perfect for busy weeknights because it only takes a few minutes for each quesadilla to cook, and the kids (and adults!) love them. Plus, they're incredibly versatile: You can swap the chicken for chopped cooked shrimp or make them vegetarian by replacing the chicken with black beans and corn. Because most tortillas are round, this recipe works best with a round waffle maker; just make sure you buy tortillas that aren't larger than your waffle iron.

About the tortillas: You can use any type with this recipe, but my oldest daughter is gluten-free, which led me to discover Siete's Cassava & Coconut Grain-Free Tortillas. I now prefer them to wheat tortillas because not only do they taste great, but they're only 130 calories per tortilla.

Fast • Hearty

Waffle-Iron Chicken Quesadillas

Hands-on: 15 min. **Total:** 30 min. Find precooked chicken in the hot foods section of your grocery store. When assembling, leave a ½-inch border around the fillings so they don't spill over.

2 ripe avocados, peeled and chopped (about 2 cups)
2 Tbsp. chopped red onion
2 Tbsp. fresh lime juice
2 Tbsp. diced tomato
5 tsp. chopped fresh cilantro, divided, plus more for garnish
¼ tsp. kosher salt
Cooking spray
8 (7-inch) whole-wheat or grain-free tortillas

4.2 oz. preshredded part-skim Mexican cheese blend (about 1⅓ cups)
6 oz. shredded cooked skinless chicken breast, divided
Store-bought salsa (optional)
Sour cream (optional)

1. Using a fork, mash avocados in a medium bowl until chunky. Add onion, lime juice, tomato, 1 tablespoon cilantro, and salt; mash to desired consistency. Set aside.

2. Preheat waffle iron to high. Coat interior with cooking spray. Place 1 tortilla on waffle iron. Mound ⅓ cup cheese in the center, and spread cheese evenly, leaving a ½-inch border. Add 1½ ounces chicken and ½ teaspoon cilantro. Place a second tortilla over filling, and close waffle iron. Cook until quesadilla is golden brown and heated through, 2 to 3 minutes, keeping an eye on it so the cheese doesn't ooze out.

3. Remove quesadilla from the waffle iron; repeat 3 times with remaining tortillas, cheese, chicken, and cilantro. Cut into wedges; garnish with cilantro. Serve quesadillas hot with guacamole and, if desired, salsa and sour cream. Serves 4 (serving size: 1 quesadilla and ⅓ cup guacamole)

CALORIES 470; **FAT** 20g (sat 6g, unsat 13g); **PROTEIN** 30g; **CARB** 45g; **FIBER** 7g; **SUGARS** 1g (added sugars 0g); **SODIUM** 699mg; **CALC** 38% DV; **POTASSIUM** 14% DV

THE MUSSEL MATRIX

TRY THE COMBINATIONS BELOW (FOLLOWING THE METHOD IN THE RECIPE BELOW), OR MIX AND MATCH YOUR FAVORITE INGREDIENTS.

LIQUID (1 CUP)	STEP 1: AROMATICS	STEP 2: HERBS	STEP 3: GARNISHES
Red wine	1 fennel bulb, thinly sliced	2 rosemary sprigs and 2 peel strips from 1 orange	2 Tbsp. chopped fresh herbs, such as tarragon and/or parsley
Coconut milk	1 large yellow onion, thinly sliced	1 lemongrass stalk, cut into 1-inch pieces	2 Tbsp. chopped fresh herbs, such as basil and cilantro, and juice of 1 lime
Hoppy beer	⅓ cup diced celery, ⅓ cup diced bell pepper, and ⅓ cup diced onion	½ lb. fresh Mexican chorizo, cooked	1 bunch scallions, thinly sliced
Dark beer	1 fennel bulb or onion, thinly sliced, and 3 garlic cloves, chopped	1 chipotle chile, dried or in adobo	2 Tbsp. chopped fresh herbs, such as tarragon and/or parsley

THE SEAFOOD GUY

CHANNEL YOUR INNER CHEF WITH OUR MUSSEL MATRIX

BY BARTON SEAVER

Mussels are easier to cook than you'd think and go with endless flavor combos, making them a favorite of this seafood guru. Mussels are among my most favorite seafood. The small, blue-black shells guarantee a durable shelf life for the orange-hued omega-3-rich meat inside. You can store them in the fridge covered with a few layers of wet paper towels for several days. They offer home cooks a foolproof way to ensure quality—if the shells are tightly closed, the mussels are worth buying. Plus, mussels are available year-round and can be found at most groceries with a fresh seafood counter.

These affordable delights are excellent cooked with nearly any combination of ingredients you likely have on hand, and most herbs, spices, and liquids can be used to impart delicious flavor (see my suggestions above).

But don't let their practicality limit you; these quick-cooking mollusks are as perfect for date night as they are for Tuesday night. And my favorite thing about mussels? Even though they cook quickly, eating them is slow and deliberate: Bite by bite, each delightful morsel is removed from its shell, dipped in sauce, and savored with crusty bread.

**Fast • Gluten Free
Hearty**

A Perfect Pot of Mussels

Hands-on: 10 min. **Total:** 20 min.

1 large leek, thinly sliced (about 1½ cups)
2 Tbsp. olive oil or unsalted butter, divided
2 lb. mussels, scrubbed and debearded
1 cup seafood stock or water
2 to 3 fresh thyme sprigs
1 bay leaf
2 Tbsp. chopped fresh tarragon
Crusty bread for serving (optional)

1. Heat a heavy pot over medium-high. Add leek (or desired aromatics) and 1 tablespoon oil. Cook, uncovered and stirring often, until leek begins to soften, about 3 minutes.
2. Add mussels, stock (or other liquid), thyme, and bay leaf (or desired herbs). Cover and cook until mussels have opened completely, 3 to 5 minutes.
3. Discard any mussels that have not opened. Toss with tarragon (or desired garnish) and remaining 1 tablespoon oil. Serve with bread, if desired. Serves 4 (serving size: about 12 mussels and ¼ cup broth)

CALORIES 292; FAT 12g (sat 2g, unsat 8g); PROTEIN 29g; CARB 16g; FIBER 1g; SUGARS 2g (added sugars 0g); SODIUM 692mg; CALC 10% DV; POTASSIUM 24% DV

LIGHTEN UP FRENCH ONION DIP

Our savory snack duo slashes a third of the sodium off the classic chip-and-dip combo.

Ditch the sodium-bomb seasoning packets and sour-cream-and-mayonnaise-laden dip (which can pack a small meal's worth of calories and sat fat into a single serving) for our homemade dip. And be patient with the caramelizing process—slowly sizzled onions have noteworthy sweetness and concentrated umami. You'll know the onions are done when they become deep chestnut in color and nearly melt-in-your-mouth tender. And because no dip is complete without a dipper, baked sweet potatoes will satisfy your chip craving for half the calories of most bagged varieties. Dehydrating the potatoes in the oven before roasting helps them develop crispy edges and tender centers. With big flavor and less heft, our healthier ode to the classic is a delicious way to sneak in extra vegetables.

Make Ahead

French Onion Dip with Sweet Potato Chips

Hands-on: 1 hr. **Total:** 2 hr. 10 min.
Try a combination of orange and purple sweet potatoes for a pop of color.

1 lb. sweet potatoes, peeled and ends trimmed
5 tsp. olive oil, divided
1½ tsp. kosher salt, divided
1 (8-oz.) yellow onion, thinly sliced
½ cup finely chopped shallots
1 tsp. chopped fresh thyme
½ tsp. freshly ground black pepper
2 garlic cloves, minced
1½ tsp. lower-sodium Worcestershire sauce
10 oz. soft tofu, drained and patted dry
1 cup plain whole-milk Greek yogurt
1 Tbsp. fresh lemon juice
1 Tbsp. chopped fresh chives

1. Preheat oven to 200°F.
2. Using a mandoline, slice sweet potatoes into ⅛-inch-thick slices. Place in a large bowl; add 2 teaspoons oil, and toss to coat.
3. Place sweet potato slices in a single layer on 2 baking sheets lined with parchment paper; sprinkle evenly with ½ teaspoon salt. Bake at 200°F for 1 hour and 30 minutes. Increase oven temperature to 400°F; bake for 10 minutes. Remove from oven; cool completely.
4. Meanwhile, heat remaining 1 tablespoon oil in a large nonstick skillet over medium-high. Add onion; sauté 8 to 10 minutes or until tender. Reduce heat to medium-low. Stir in shallots, thyme, pepper, and remaining 1 teaspoon salt; cook, stirring occasionally, 40 minutes or until golden brown.
5. Increase heat to medium. Add garlic and Worcestershire sauce; cook, stirring occasionally, 5 minutes. Remove pan from heat, and let cool 15 minutes.
6. Place tofu, yogurt, and juice in a blender; process until smooth. Stir together onion mixture and yogurt mixture in a bowl. Top with chives. Serve with sweet potato chips. Serves 9 (serving size: ¼ cup dip and ½ cup chips)

CALORIES 144; **FAT** 7g (sat 3g, unsat 4g); **PROTEIN** 6g; **CARB** 16g; **FIBER** 2g; **SUGARS** 4g (added sugars 0g); **SODIUM** 369mg; **CALC** 9% DV; **POTASSIUM** 8% DV

Fast • Vegetarian

Pea and Cucumber Cooler

Hands-on: 5 min. **Total:** 5 min.
Celebrate the pea, spring's sweetest vegetable, in a vibrant cocktail that delivers more than 15% of your daily goal for vitamin C, a potent antioxidant linked to more youthful-looking skin. Anise notes from the tarragon balance the sweetness of the elderflower liqueur. Club soda adds an effervescent finish.

Muddle ⅓ cup peeled and sliced cucumber, 2 Tbsp. fresh or thawed frozen green peas, 1 tsp. fresh tarragon leaves, and a dash of kosher salt in a cocktail shaker. Add 2 Tbsp. fresh lemon juice, 1 oz. vodka, ½ oz. St-Germain (elderflower liqueur), 1 tsp. agave nectar, and ½ cup ice; cover and shake 30 seconds. Strain into a coupe glass. Top with 1 oz. club soda. Garnish with additional tarragon, if desired. Serves 1 (serving size: about 5 oz.)

CALORIES 152; **FAT** 0g; **PROTEIN** 1g; **CARB** 15g; **FIBER** 0g; **SUGARS** 12g (added sugars 11g); **SODIUM** 173mg; **CALC** 0% DV; **POTASSIUM** 1% DV

MAKE IT A MOCKTAIL

Replace vodka and elderflower liqueur with 2 ounces brewed and chilled green tea.

GOOD THINGS COME IN PAIRS

Combine prebiotics with probiotics in recipes to form a dynamic duo that boosts your good gut bacteria.

Prebiotics and probiotics are key players in optimizing gut health and managing symptoms of chronic diseases such as type 2 diabetes, obesity, and autoimmune disorders. Prebiotics are components of certain foods (such as garlic and onions) that serve as the fuel for probiotics—the "good" bacteria, or live cultures—found naturally in your gut and also in foods like yogurt and sauerkraut. Prebiotics and probiotics work in tandem, creating a symbiotic effect that fosters the growth and activity of good belly bacteria that can help strengthen immunity, aid in digestion (which in turn improves nutrient absorption), and even boost your mood. You may notice products marketed as "synbiotics" in the cooler case of your health-food store, but there's no need to seek out supplements. With these six delicious recipes that incorporate pre- and probiotic ingredients and are designed to garner all those good-bug benefits, plus the supermarket shopping list on p. 135, we prove that achieving bacterial synergy is easier (and tastier) than you think.

Grilled Caesar Salad with Sourdough Breadcrumbs

Hands-on: 10 min. **Total:** 40 min. Keep the sourdough croutons whole if you don't want to dirty the food processor, or you can lightly crush them in a ziplock bag.

3 cups cubed whole-wheat
   sourdough bread (about 6 oz.)
4 tsp. olive oil, divided
½ tsp. kosher salt, divided
1 cup canned unsalted chickpeas,
   drained and rinsed
¼ tsp. paprika

½ cup plain whole-milk Greek
   yogurt
2 Tbsp. fresh lemon juice
1 tsp. Dijon mustard
1 tsp. reduced-sodium
   Worcestershire sauce
1 tsp. minced fresh garlic
½ tsp. anchovy paste
¼ tsp. freshly ground black pepper
2 large romaine lettuce hearts,
   quartered lengthwise
Cooking spray
1 oz. Parmesan cheese, grated
   (about ¼ cup)

1. Preheat oven to 350°F.
2. Place bread on one half of a rimmed baking sheet. Toss with 1 tablespoon oil and ⅛ teaspoon salt, and spread in a single layer. Place chickpeas on opposite half of baking sheet; toss with paprika, ⅛ teaspoon salt, and remaining 1 teaspoon oil, and spread in a single layer. Bake at 350°F for 20 minutes, tossing once halfway through.
3. Transfer bread to a food processor. Pulse until ground. Set aside.
4. Whisk together yogurt, lemon juice, mustard, Worcestershire sauce, garlic, anchovy paste, pepper, and remaining ¼ teaspoon salt in a bowl. Whisk in water, 1 teaspoon at a time, until dressing reaches desired consistency. Set aside.
5. Preheat a grill to medium-high (about 450°F), or heat a grill pan over medium-high. Coat cut sides of romaine hearts with cooking spray. Place 3 or 4 romaine quarters, cut sides down, on grill grate or in grill pan. Grill until charred, about 2 minutes, turning after 1 minute and watching closely to prevent burning. Repeat with remaining romaine quarters.
6. Place 2 romaine quarters on each of 4 plates. Top with 2 tablespoons Caesar dressing, ¼ cup sourdough breadcrumbs, ¼ cup chickpeas, and 1 tablespoon cheese. Serves 4 (serving size: 1 salad)

CALORIES 310; FAT 11g (sat 3g, unsat 7g); PROTEIN 14g; CARB 35g; FIBER 6g; SUGARS 6g (added sugars 0g); SODIUM 657mg; CALC 19% DV; POTASSIUM 5% DV

Sesame Salmon with Kimchi-Miso Butter

Hands-on: 10 min. **Total:** 40 min.
Serve the salmon over rice or your favorite grain.

1 (1½-lb.) salmon fillet
¼ tsp. kosher salt
2 Tbsp. fresh lime juice
1 Tbsp. lower-sodium soy sauce
1 Tbsp. honey
1 Tbsp. sesame oil
1 Tbsp. minced fresh garlic
2 tsp. grated peeled fresh ginger
1 tsp. sesame seeds
2 Tbsp. unsalted butter, softened
2 Tbsp. finely minced kimchi
2 tsp. white miso
2 Tbsp. sliced scallions

1. Pat salmon dry with paper towels. Sprinkle with salt, and place in a gallon-sized ziplock plastic bag.
2. Stir together lime juice, soy sauce, honey, oil, garlic, ginger, and sesame seeds in a bowl. Pour mixture over salmon in ziplock bag. Seal bag, removing any excess air, and gently massage mixture into salmon. Let stand at room temperature 30 minutes.
3. Preheat broiler to high with oven rack in upper middle position. Stir together butter, kimchi, and miso in a small bowl. Set aside.
4. Place salmon on a rimmed baking sheet lined with aluminum foil. Broil until fish flakes easily when tested with a fork, about 8 to 10 minutes.
5. Top salmon with kimchi-miso butter while salmon is still warm. Scatter scallions evenly over top. Serves 4 (serving size: 6 oz. fish)

CALORIES 366; **FAT** 21g (sat 6g, unsat 13g); **PROTEIN** 35g; **CARB** 7g; **FIBER** 1g; **SUGARS** 5g (added sugars 4g); **SODIUM** 455mg; **CALC** 3% DV; **POTASSIUM** 25% DV

Broccoli-and-Kraut Slaw

Hands-on: 15 min. **Total:** 25 min.
Using fresh broccoli instead of bagged broccoli slaw makes for a sweeter, more flavorful end product. Look for refrigerated sauerkraut in the deli or by the tofu in your local grocery store (canned sauerkraut lacks probiotics).

⅓ cup plain whole-milk Greek yogurt
3 Tbsp. rice vinegar
2 Tbsp. canola oil
1½ Tbsp. honey
1 Tbsp. white miso
2 tsp. minced fresh garlic
¼ tsp. freshly ground black pepper
1 medium head broccoli
2 cups grated red cabbage
1 cup shaved red onion
½ cup thinly sliced scallions
⅓ cup golden raisins
⅓ cup drained refrigerated sauerkraut

1. Whisk together yogurt, vinegar, oil, honey, miso, garlic, and pepper in a small bowl; set aside.
2. Trim and peel broccoli stalk. Cut head in half lengthwise. Starting at the crown, thinly slice both halves, including the stalk. (Or fit food processor with large-hole grating disk. Working with a few pieces at a time, push broccoli pieces and stems through food chute until grated.)
3. Place sliced broccoli, cabbage, red onion, scallions, raisins, and sauerkraut in a large bowl. Add miso-yogurt dressing; toss until coated. Let stand 10 minutes. Serves 6 (serving size: about 1½ cups)

CALORIES 153; **FAT** 6g (sat 1g, unsat 5g); **PROTEIN** 5g; **CARB** 23g; **FIBER** 5g; **SUGARS** 14g (added sugars 4g); **SODIUM** 216mg; **CALC** 9% DV; **POTASSIUM** 14% DV

Kombucha Granita and Berry Parfaits

Hands-on: 15 min. **Total:** 1 hr. 45 min.
This icy dessert is the ultimate summer refresher. Some (limited) research suggests that freezing probiotics for a short time may not actually kill them but rather render them dormant until eaten. You can use any flavor of kombucha you like to complement the lemony berry mixture.

1 (16-oz.) bottle unflavored kombucha
1 lb. mixed raspberries and blackberries
2 Tbsp. granulated sugar
1 tsp. lemon zest
2 tsp. fresh lemon juice
3 cups plain whole-milk Greek yogurt
3 Tbsp. torn fresh basil or mint leaves (optional)

1. Pour kombucha into a 13- x 9-inch glass or ceramic baking dish; freeze 1 hour. Scrape with a fork and stir; return to freezer for 30 minutes. Once fully frozen, scrape and fluff with a fork.
2. Meanwhile, toss berries, sugar, lemon zest, and lemon juice in a large bowl to combine. Let stand at room temperature 45 minutes, stirring occasionally.
3. Place ½ cup yogurt in each of 6 chilled parfait glasses. Top each serving with ½ cup berry mixture and ⅔ cup granita. Top with fresh basil or mint leaves, if desired. Serve immediately. Serves 6 (serving size: 1 parfait)

CALORIES 186; **FAT** 7g (sat 3g, unsat 4g); **PROTEIN** 12g; **CARB** 20g; **FIBER** 4g; **SUGARS** 13g (added sugars 4g); **SODIUM** 49mg; **CALC** 15% DV; **POTASSIUM** 9% DV

Spiced Chicken Tacos with Lime-Cabbage Slaw

Hands-on: 25 min. **Total:** 1 hr.

½ cup cider vinegar
½ cup water
¾ cup very thinly sliced red onion
3 cups thinly sliced red cabbage
1 Tbsp. fresh lime juice
2 Tbsp. olive oil, divided
1 tsp. kosher salt, divided
¾ tsp. chili powder
½ tsp. garlic powder
½ tsp. ground cumin
½ tsp. smoked paprika
12 oz. boneless, skinless chicken breast tenders
8 (6-inch) corn tortillas
1 avocado, peeled and sliced
½ cup plain 2% reduced-fat Greek yogurt
4 tsp. pepitas
Fresh cilantro leaves (optional)
Sliced radishes (optional)

1. Bring vinegar and ½ cup water to a boil in a saucepan. Stir in onion. Remove from heat; let stand 15 minutes. Drain.
2. Combine cabbage, lime juice, 1 tablespoon oil, and ½ teaspoon salt in a large bowl; toss well. Let stand 15 minutes.
3. Combine chili powder, garlic powder, cumin, paprika, and remaining ½ teaspoon salt; rub over chicken. Heat remaining 1 tablespoon oil in a large nonstick skillet over medium-high. Add chicken to pan; cook until well browned and done, about 4 minutes per side. Cool slightly; shred chicken into large pieces.
4. Heat tortillas according to package directions. Divide chicken and slaw among tortillas; top evenly with onion, avocado slices, yogurt, and pepitas. Garnish with cilantro and radishes, if desired. Serves 4 (serving size: 2 tacos)

CALORIES 417; **FAT** 18g (sat 3g, unsat 13g); **PROTEIN** 28g; **CARB** 41g; **FIBER** 8g; **SUGARS** 6g (added sugars 0g); **SODIUM** 586mg; **CALC** 10% DV; **POTASSIUM** 18% DV

Early Summer Salad with Tempeh Croutons and Beet Dressing

Hands-on: 15 min. **Total:** 40 min. Look for beet kvass by the kimchi in well-stocked supermarkets, or substitute beet juice if you can't find it.

1 (8-oz.) pkg. tempeh, cut into 1-in. cubes
2 tsp. minced fresh garlic
¼ tsp. freshly ground black pepper
2 Tbsp. extra-virgin olive oil, divided
5 tsp. fresh lemon juice, divided
¾ tsp. kosher salt, divided
6 oz. asparagus, trimmed
2 Tbsp. beet kvass (such as Harvest Roots)
1½ Tbsp. tahini (sesame seed paste)
1 tsp. granulated sugar
3 cups packed baby arugula
2 cups packed baby kale
1 cup shaved Easter Egg radishes
1 pt. yellow cherry tomatoes, halved

1. Preheat oven to 375°F. Place tempeh, garlic, pepper, 1 tablespoon oil, 1 tablespoon lemon juice, and ½ teaspoon salt in a bowl; toss to combine. Arrange tempeh on a baking sheet. Bake at 375°F for 20 minutes, tossing once halfway through.
2. Meanwhile, bring a large saucepan of water to a boil over medium-high, and prepare a bowl of ice water. Add asparagus to boiling water, and cook until crisp-tender, about 3 minutes. Drain. Plunge asparagus into ice water; let stand 2 minutes. Drain. Cut asparagus diagonally into thirds. Set aside.
3. Combine remaining 1 tablespoon oil, remaining 2 teaspoons lemon juice, and remaining ¼ teaspoon salt in a bowl; whisk in kvass, tahini, and sugar. Add water, 1 teaspoon at a time, until dressing reaches desired consistency.
4. Place arugula, kale, radishes, tomatoes, and asparagus in a large bowl or on a serving platter; gently toss to combine. Top with tempeh croutons. Drizzle evenly with kvass-tahini dressing. Serves 4 (serving size: about 2 cups)

CALORIES 259; **FAT** 17g (sat 3g, unsat 13g); **PROTEIN** 16g; **CARB** 15g; **FIBER** 3g; **SUGARS** 3g (added sugars 1g); **SODIUM** 431mg; **CALC** 19% DV; **POTASSIUM** 25% DV

THE PROS OF PREBIOTICS

ALL TYPES OF FIBER are healthy, but our gut is partial to two: fructans and cellulose. Both bypass digestion in the upper GI tract and reach the colon still intact, where they ferment and feed our good bacteria.

FRUCTANS ARE FOUND in many plants—from artichokes and onions to raspberries. Some food manufacturers add a certain type of fructan called inulin (often extracted from chicory root) to food products to add prebiotics, improve structure and/or taste, and boost fiber.

CELLULOSE IS FOUND in celery and the parts of produce we tend to discard (such as the fibrous stalks of broccoli and stringy bottoms of asparagus).

3-DAY GUT HEALTH MAKEOVER

Want to reboot your microbiome? It's easier and quicker than you might think with our high-fiber, plant-based meal plan, and it's affordable, too, at around just $52 per person.

A few years ago, a study published in the journal *Nature* found that eating a high-fiber, plants-only diet positively shifted people's microbiome makeup in just 24 hours, compared with eating a meat- and cheese-heavy diet—suggesting the former might be a better way of eating for gut health. (Conversely, the animal-based diet rapidly shifted the microbiome in a way that implies it could trigger inflammatory bowel disease.)

Interestingly, one group of gut bacteria—the genus *Prevotella*—that represents microbiome diversity (which you want) did not change on the short-term plants-only diet, suggesting that to see the full benefits, you will need to make a commitment to a high-fiber diet for the long haul.

But to help you quickly reboot your gut flora, we offer this easy-to-follow three-day plan. It's an all-plants (aka vegan) diet based on whole foods, zero added sugars, and lots of fiber to feed the good bugs in your belly. Each day provides around 47g of fiber. That's 88% more fiber than the current daily recommendation for women, so if your usual diet is lacking in fiber, you might want to start slow here to prevent—*ahem*—ill side effects.

We give you a shopping list and some get-ahead recipes to make the plan easier to stick with. It's affordable (about $52 for one person), and servings are generous—so you'll stay satisfied over the three days. Use the plan to jump-start your commitment to better gut health or as a guide to long-term changes. Either way, your gut will thank you.

STOCK A GUT-FRIENDLY KITCHEN
KEEP THESE FOODS IN YOUR PANTRY AND FRIDGE FOR MEALS THAT IMPROVE YOUR MICROBIOME.

PREBIOTICS
Here are some of the most common fiber-rich foods to help good gut bacteria thrive:

Whole-wheat bread
Barley
Oats
Dandelion greens
Onions (including shallots and leeks)
Garlic
Brussels sprouts
Cabbage
Broccoli
Pistachios
Artichokes
Raspberries
Bananas
Asparagus
Celery

PROBIOTICS
Grow your community of good gut bacteria with these probiotic-rich foods.

Sourdough bread
Kefir
Yogurt
Cultured buttermilk
Refrigerated sauerkraut
Kimchi
Miso
Tempeh
Kombucha

MAKE AHEAD

You'll use these two recipes over the course of the one-person meal plan. Each one makes several portions that are spread out over three days.

Fast · Make Ahead
Vegetarian

Simply Seasoned Bulgur

Hands-on: 5 min. **Total:** 30 min.
Make a batch of whole grains ahead of time to enjoy in various forms throughout the three days—as part of breakfast, lunch, and dinner. For a gluten-free option, you can use the same amounts and cook times to make a batch of quinoa. Per serving, the quinoa version will contain 124 calories, 4g fat, 4g protein, and 2g fiber.

1⅓ cups water
⅔ cup uncooked bulgur
2 tsp. olive oil
⅜ tsp. kosher salt

1. Bring 1⅓ cups water to a boil in a small saucepan over medium-high. Stir in bulgur; cover, reduce heat to medium-low, and simmer 12 minutes. Remove from heat, and let stand, covered, 10 minutes. Uncover. Drizzle with oil, and sprinkle with salt. Fluff with a fork to combine. Makes 4 portions (portion size: about ½ cup)

CALORIES 100; **FAT** 3g (sat 0g, unsat 2g); **PROTEIN** 3g; **CARB** 18g; **FIBER** 3g; **SUGARS** 0g; **SODIUM** 184mg; **CALC** 1% DV; **POTASSIUM** 3% DV

Gluten Free · Make Ahead
Vegetarian

Smoky Roasted Chickpeas

Hands-on: 10 min. **Total:** 1 hr.
These crunchy chickpeas will serve you well over the three-day meal plan as both a snack and a crunchy, protein- and fiber-rich topping for salads. For the crunchiest texture, cook them until they're just shy of burning. They'll stay crisp in an airtight container at room temperature for up to a week.

1 (15-oz.) can unsalted chickpeas, rinsed and drained
1½ Tbsp. olive oil
½ tsp. smoked paprika
¼ tsp. kosher salt
¼ tsp. cayenne pepper

1. Preheat oven to 400°F.
2. Spread chickpeas on several layers of paper towels, and pat dry. Spread in an even layer on a small rimmed baking sheet lined with parchment paper. Drizzle with oil, and shake pan to coat. Bake at 400°F 30 minutes.
3. Remove pan from oven. Sprinkle chickpeas evenly with paprika, salt, and cayenne pepper; stir well. Return to oven, and bake at 400°F until chickpeas are very crisp and crunchy (but not burned), 15 to 20 minutes. Cool completely; store in an airtight container up to 1 week. Makes 5 portions (portion size: about ¼ cup)

CALORIES 115; **FAT** 5g (sat 1g, unsat 3g); **PROTEIN** 4g; **CARB** 13g; **FIBER** 3g; **SUGARS** 1g (added sugars 0g); **SODIUM** 114mg; **CALC** 4% DV; **POTASSIUM** 4% DV

DAY 1 MENU

BREAKFAST
Strawberry Bulgur Bowl

A.M. SNACK
5 oz. frozen edamame pods, steamed and tossed with ⅛ tsp. kosher salt (155 calories, 7g fiber)

LUNCH
Tabbouleh with Avocado

P.M. SNACK
3 dates and 12 unsalted roasted almonds (152 calories, 4g fiber)

DINNER
Pasta with Green Peas and Almond Gremolata

DAY 1

TOTAL CALORIES: **1,583**
TOTAL FIBER: **48g**

Fast · Make Ahead
Vegetarian

Strawberry Bulgur Bowl

Hands-on: 10 min. **Total:** 10 min.
While you might not think of turning bulgur into porridge, it's a delicious whole-grain breakfast with a texture similar to instant oatmeal. Mashed dates naturally sweeten and enrich almond milk for a creamy, satisfying, no-added-sugar bowl. You can make the porridge ahead of time and simply reheat before serving; then add the berries and nuts.

½ cup unsweetened almond milk
2 whole dates, pitted and finely chopped
¾ cup Simply Seasoned Bulgur (at left)
¼ tsp. vanilla extract
¾ cup halved small strawberries
2 Tbsp. unsalted roasted almonds, chopped

1. Place almond milk and dates in a small saucepan; mash dates with a fork to break them up and incorporate them into milk. Add Simply Seasoned Bulgur. Cook over medium, stirring often, until mixture just comes to a simmer. Remove from heat, and stir in vanilla.

2. Spoon bulgur mixture into a bowl. Top with strawberries and almonds. Serves 1 (serving size: about 1 cup porridge, ¾ cup berries, and 2 Tbsp. almonds)

CALORIES 352; **FAT** 15g (sat 1g, unsat 12g); **PROTEIN** 10g; **CARB** 50g; **FIBER** 10g; **SUGARS** 16g (added sugars 0g); **SODIUM** 371mg; **CALC** 34% DV; **POTASSIUM** 18% DV

Fast · Make Ahead
Vegetarian

Tabbouleh with Avocado

Hands-on: 10 min. **Total:** 10 min. Crunchy, lemony, fresh, and filling—this hearty tabbouleh makes a fine lunch. If you're packing it up to go, store the chickpeas separately so they'll keep their crunch. Save the other avocado half; you'll use it in the next day's lunch. Keep the pit in the avocado half, and wrap it tightly with plastic wrap to limit browning.

⅔ cup chopped English cucumber

1 medium tomato, chopped (about ⅔ cup)

½ cup Simply Seasoned Bulgur (p. 136)

⅓ cup chopped fresh flat-leaf parsley

¼ cup finely chopped lacinato kale

2 Tbsp. finely chopped red onion

1 Tbsp. fresh lemon juice

1½ tsp. olive oil

⅛ tsp. kosher salt

½ ripe avocado, chopped

⅓ cup Smoky Roasted Chickpeas (p. 136)

1. Combine cucumber, tomato, Simply Seasoned Bulgur, parsley, kale, and onion in a medium bowl. Drizzle with lemon juice and oil, and sprinkle with salt; toss well to combine. Gently fold in avocado. Arrange tabbouleh in a serving bowl or on a plate; sprinkle evenly with Smoky Roasted Chickpeas. Serves 1 (serving size: about 2 ½ cups)

CALORIES 498; **FAT** 27g (sat 4g, unsat 21g); **PROTEIN** 13g; **CARB** 55g; **FIBER** 15g; **SUGARS** 7g (added sugars 0g); **SODIUM** 622mg; **CALC** 14% DV; **POTASSIUM** 35% DV

Fast · Gluten Free
Vegetarian

Pasta with Green Peas and Almond Gremolata

Hands-on: 20 min. **Total:** 20 min. We chose chickpea pasta here for its mild flavor and higher fiber content (when compared with whole-wheat pasta). The gremolata topping truly makes the dish; it's herby, crunchy, fragrant, and citrusy. Serve the pasta immediately for the best texture and taste.

2 oz. uncooked chickpea spaghetti (such as Banza)

¼ cup frozen green peas

1 Tbsp. olive oil

2 garlic cloves, thinly sliced

¼ tsp. black pepper

¼ tsp. plus a dash of kosher salt, divided

2 Tbsp. chopped fresh flat-leaf parsley

1½ Tbsp. chopped unsalted roasted almonds

1 tsp. lemon zest

1. Cook pasta in boiling water until almost al dente, about 5 minutes. Add green peas; cook until peas are warmed through and pasta is tender, about 1 minute. Drain pasta mixture, reserving ½ cup cooking liquid. Cover pasta mixture to keep warm.

2. Heat oil in a small skillet over medium-low. Add garlic; cook until tender, about 2 minutes. Add pasta mixture, pepper, ¼ teaspoon salt, and ¼ cup reserved cooking liquid; toss to combine. If necessary, add up to ¼ cup additional cooking liquid to reach desired consistency.

3. Stir together parsley, almonds, lemon zest, and remaining dash of salt. Sprinkle over pasta, and serve immediately. Serves 1 (serving size: about 1 cup)

CALORIES 426; **FAT** 24g (sat 2g, unsat 20g); **PROTEIN** 19g; **CARB** 42g; **FIBER** 12g; **SUGARS** 7g (added sugars 0g); **SODIUM** 702mg; **CALC** 11% DV; **POTASSIUM** 15% DV

DAY 2

TOTAL CALORIES: **1,597**
TOTAL FIBER: **46g**

Fast • Gluten Free
Vegetarian

Raspberry-Date Smoothie

Hands-on: 5 min. **Total:** 5 min.
You'll often find silken tofu in shelf-stable packages on the Asian foods aisle. We call for Mori-Nu brand because one package will provide exactly what you need for this three-day meal plan. The squeeze pack of almond butter is convenient and contains only what you need for this recipe. If you have almond butter already, just use 2 tablespoons.

¾ cup fresh raspberries (about
   3 oz.), divided
½ cup unsweetened almond milk
½ cup extra-firm silken tofu (such
   as Mori-Nu) (4 oz.)
2 whole dates, pitted
1 (1.15-oz.) packet almond butter
   (such as Justin's)
¾ cup ice cubes

1. Set aside 3 or 4 of the raspberries for garnish, if desired. Process remaining raspberries, almond milk, tofu, dates, and almond butter in a blender until smooth. Add ice; process until smooth. Pour into a serving glass. Garnish with reserved raspberries, if desired. Serves 1 (serving size: about 2 cups)

CALORIES 369; FAT 22g (sat 2g, unsat 18g);
PROTEIN 17g; CARB 31g; FIBER 10g;
SUGARS 15g (added sugars 0g); SODIUM 171mg;
CALC 43% DV; POTASSIUM 16% DV

Staff Favorite • Fast
Make Ahead • Vegetarian

Green Pea Fritters with Avocado Puree

Hands-on: 20 min. **Total:** 20 min.

¼ cup extra-firm silken tofu (2 oz.)
1 Tbsp. all-purpose flour
¼ cup Simply Seasoned Bulgur
   (p. 136)
⅔ cup frozen green peas, thawed
¼ cup chopped scallion whites
½ tsp. ground cumin
¼ tsp. kosher salt, divided
1¼ Tbsp. olive oil, divided
½ ripe avocado
1 small garlic clove, grated
2 tsp. fresh lemon juice, divided
1½ cups torn stemmed lacinato kale
⅓ cup sliced English cucumber
1 thin red onion slice, halved

1. Process tofu and flour in a mini food processor until smooth. Add Simply Seasoned Bulgur; pulse until blended. Add peas, scallions, cumin, and ⅛ teaspoon salt; pulse until combined.
2. Heat 1 tablespoon oil in a medium skillet over medium. Shape pea mixture into 2 patties. (They will be very soft but will firm up as they cook.) Add patties to skillet; gently flatten to ¾-inch

thickness. Cook until browned on bottom, 4 to 5 minutes. Carefully turn fritters, and cook until browned, 4 to 5 minutes.
3. Mash avocado, garlic, 1 teaspoon lemon juice, and salt until smooth.
4. Place kale in a bowl; drizzle with remaining 1½ teaspoons oil. Massage until lightly wilted. Add cucumber, onion, remaining 1 teaspoon lemon juice, and a dash of salt; toss to combine. Serve salad and fritters with mashed avocado. Serves 1 (serving size: 2 fritters, about 2 cups salad, and about ⅓ cup avocado)

CALORIES 512; FAT 34g (sat 5g, unsat 27g);
PROTEIN 14g; CARB 42g; FIBER 13g; SUGARS 8g
(added sugars 0g); SODIUM 733mg; CALC 13% DV;
POTASSIUM 26% DV

Gluten Free • Make Ahead
Vegetarian

Summery Lentil Soup

Hands-on: 30 min. **Total:** 50 min.
This veggie-packed soup serves double duty: Eat some for dinner tonight, and save the rest for breakfast the next day. For a little heat, add a pinch of crushed red pepper.

1 Tbsp. olive oil
½ cup chopped red onion
2 garlic cloves, minced
¼ small yellow bell pepper,
   chopped
2 medium tomatoes, cored and
   chopped (about 2 cups)
1 (4-oz.) eggplant, chopped (about
   1 cup)
2 Tbsp. unsalted tomato paste
2½ cups water
½ cup uncooked dried brown
   lentils
2 bay leaves
1 small zucchini, chopped
½ tsp. kosher salt
½ tsp. black pepper
2 Tbsp. sliced scallion greens

1. Heat a large saucepan over medium. Add oil, and swirl to coat. Add onion, garlic, and bell pepper; cook 3 minutes. Add tomatoes and eggplant; cook, stirring often, 5 minutes. Add tomato paste; cook, stirring constantly, 1 minute. Add 2 ½ cups water, lentils, and bay leaves. Bring mixture to a boil; cover, reduce heat to medium-low, and simmer until lentils are almost tender, about 22 minutes.
2. Stir in zucchini, salt, and black pepper; cook until lentils are tender and zucchini is crisp-tender, about 6 minutes. Discard bay leaves. Ladle 3 cups soup into a large bowl, and top with sliced scallion greens. (Reserve remaining 2 cups soup for Day 3 breakfast.) Serves 1 (serving size: 3 cups [with 2 cups leftovers])

CALORIES 392; FAT 10g (sat 1g, unsat 8g); PROTEIN 19g; CARB 61g; FIBER 13g; SUGARS 14g (added sugars 0g); SODIUM 783mg; CALC 9% DV; POTASSIUM 41% DV

DAY 3 MENU

BREAKFAST
Veggie Bowl with Tofu Scramble

A.M. SNACK
1 medium apple (95 calories, 4g fiber)

LUNCH
Kale Salad with Spiced Chickpeas and Berries

P.M. SNACK
1 cup strawberries and 12 unsalted roasted almonds (138 calories, 5g fiber)

DINNER
Edamame, Okra, and Green Pea Korma

DAY 3

TOTAL CALORIES: **1,585**
TOTAL FIBER: **46g**

Fast · Gluten Free
Vegetarian

Veggie Bowl with Tofu Scramble

Hands-on: 15 min. **Total:** 15 min.
Last night's soup powers this morning's breakfast; just cook off most of the liquid to give the soup a porridge-like texture. The seasoned, sautéed tofu is pretty much a dead ringer for scrambled eggs, especially if you opt to add golden turmeric.

2 cups **Summery Lentil Soup** (p. 138)
1 tsp. olive oil
¼ tsp. ground cumin
⅛ tsp. smoked paprika
⅛ tsp. ground turmeric (optional)
¾ cup extra-firm silken tofu (such as Mori-Nu) (6 oz.)
Dash of kosher salt
1 Tbsp. thinly sliced scallions
1 Tbsp. chopped fresh flat-leaf parsley
Hot sauce (optional)

1. Heat Summery Lentil Soup in a small skillet over medium-high until most of the liquid evaporates, 4 to 5 minutes. Pour into a shallow bowl.
2. Wipe skillet clean with paper towels. Heat oil in skillet over medium-high. Add cumin, paprika, and, if desired, turmeric; cook, stirring constantly, 30 seconds. Crumble tofu; add to skillet, and cook, stirring occasionally, until heated through and tofu looks like scrambled eggs, about 2 minutes. Sprinkle with salt. Top soup with tofu; sprinkle with scallions and parsley. Serve with hot sauce, if desired. Serves 1 (serving size: about 2 ¾ cups)

CALORIES 376; FAT 14g (sat 2g, unsat 11g); PROTEIN 25g; CARB 41g; FIBER 9g; SUGARS 11g (added sugars 0g); SODIUM 703mg; CALC 12% DV; POTASSIUM 34% DV

Fast · Gluten Free
Make Ahead · Vegetarian

Kale Salad with Spiced Chickpeas and Berries

Hands-on: 10 min. **Total:** 10 min.
To make this salad ahead of time, pour the dressing into the bottom of a portable container, and arrange the kale and the toppings (except for the chickpeas) on top without mixing. When you're ready to eat, stir together the salad components to coat with dressing. Bring the chickpeas in a separate container so they'll stay crunchy, and toss them in at the last minute.

1 Tbsp. olive oil
½ tsp. lemon zest
1 ½ tsp. fresh lemon juice
¼ tsp. kosher salt
¼ tsp. black pepper
2 cups torn stemmed lacinato kale (about 2 oz.)
½ cup half-moon English cucumber slices
¼ cup fresh raspberries
¼ cup sliced fresh strawberries
½ yellow bell pepper, thinly sliced
⅓ cup **Smoky Roasted Chickpeas** (p. 136)
2 Tbsp. coarsely chopped unsalted roasted almonds

Whisk together olive oil, lemon zest, lemon juice, salt, and black pepper in a medium bowl. Add kale, and massage gently until kale is lightly wilted. Add cucumber, raspberries, strawberries, and bell pepper; toss well to coat. Arrange salad on a plate; top with Smoky Roasted Chickpeas and almonds. Serves 1 (serving size: about 3 cups)

CALORIES 492; FAT 31g (sat 4g, unsat 25g); PROTEIN 13g; CARB 44g; FIBER 15g; SUGARS 12g (added sugars 0g); SODIUM 669mg; CALC 19% DV; POTASSIUM 25% DV

Edamame, Okra, and Green Pea Korma

Hands-on: 20 min. **Total:** 20 min.
If you have Madras curry powder, use it for slightly more heat and richer flavor; standard curry powder will also be great.

5 oz. frozen edamame pods, thawed
1½ Tbsp. olive oil
½ cup chopped red onion
2 garlic cloves, minced
½ tsp. curry powder
¼ tsp. kosher salt
¼ tsp. cayenne pepper
⅔ cup unsweetened almond milk
1 Tbsp. unsalted tomato paste
3 oz. fresh okra (about 7 pods),
   trimmed and halved lengthwise
¼ cup frozen green peas, thawed
½ cup Simply Seasoned Bulgur
   (p. 136), warmed

1. Shell edamame to equal about ⅓ cup; discard pods; set aside beans. **2.** Heat oil in a medium-sized heavy skillet over medium-low. Add onion and garlic; cook, stirring occasionally, until tender, about 10 minutes. Stir in curry powder, salt, and cayenne; cook, stirring constantly, until fragrant, about 30 seconds. Transfer mixture to a blender. Add almond milk and tomato paste; process until smooth. **3.** Wipe skillet clean with paper towels. Heat skillet over high. Add okra, cut sides down, and cook until slightly charred, 3 to 4 minutes. Turn pods over, and cook 1 minute. Remove from skillet. Remove skillet from heat, and let cool briefly. Return skillet to medium heat. Add curry sauce, green peas, and shelled edamame to skillet; cook until heated through and sauce thickens slightly, about 4 minutes. Spoon Simply Seasoned Bulgur into a bowl; top with curry mixture and okra. Serves 1 (serving size: ½ cup bulgur and about 1¼ cups korma mixture)

CALORIES 484; FAT 27g (sat 3g, unsat 23g); PROTEIN 15g; CARB 49g; FIBER 13g; SUGARS 9g (added sugars 0g); SODIUM 865mg; CALC 50% DV; POTASSIUM 24% DV

SHOPPING LIST

STAPLES YOU HAVE ON HAND

☐ Olive oil
☐ Kosher salt
☐ Black pepper
☐ Smoked paprika
☐ Cayenne pepper
☐ Ground turmeric (optional)
☐ Curry powder (preferably Madras)
☐ Ground cumin
☐ Bay leaves
☐ Vanilla extract
☐ All-purpose flour
☐ Hot sauce (optional)

DRY GOODS

☐ Bulgur (⅔ cup)
☐ Unsalted chickpeas (1 [15-oz.] can)
☐ Whole dates (7)
☐ Unsalted roasted almonds
☐ Chickpea spaghetti (1 [8-oz.] pkg.)
☐ Dried brown lentils (½ cup)
☐ Extra-firm silken tofu (1 [12.3-oz.] pkg., such as Mori-Nu)
☐ Almond butter (1 [1.15-oz.] packet)
☐ Unsalted tomato paste (1 [6-oz.] can)

TOTAL COST

$52.15 (Cost includes three days of breakfast, lunch, dinner, and two daily snacks for one person.)

FROZEN

☐ Green peas (1 [9-oz.] pkg.)
☐ Edamame pods (1 [10-oz.] pkg.)

PRODUCE

☐ Strawberries (1 [16-oz.] pkg.)
☐ Raspberries (1 [6-oz.] pkg.)
☐ Apples (2 medium)
☐ Lemons (3)
☐ English cucumber (1)
☐ Lacinato kale (1 bunch)
☐ Flat-leaf parsley (1 bunch)
☐ Scallions (1 bunch)
☐ Eggplant (4 oz.)
☐ Yellow bell pepper (1 small)
☐ Zucchini (1 small)
☐ Okra (3 oz.)
☐ Red onion (1 large)
☐ Tomatoes (3 medium)
☐ Ripe avocado (1)
☐ Garlic (1 head)

DAIRY CASE

☐ Unsweetened almond milk (1 [32-oz.] carton)

Hello, summer! From glorious grilled seafood to next-level salads, these easy recipes highlight the season's freshest ingredients and show you how to maximize them for a healthier gut.

WEEKNIGHT MAINS

Fast • Make Ahead
Vegetarian

Smoked Tempeh BLT

Hands-on: 15 min. **Total:** 30 min.
Drier than tofu, tempeh roasts up nice and crispy in the oven. Our simple stovetop smoking trick gives it that classic "bacon-y" essence to satisfy your BLT cravings. Artisan whole-grain bread and fresh tomato seal the deal.

1½ Tbsp. reduced-sodium tamari
1 Tbsp. pure maple syrup
2 tsp. smoked paprika
1½ tsp. black pepper, divided
1 (8-oz.) pkg. tempeh, cut into 16 slices
¼ cup wild black cherry wood chips
8 (1-oz.) whole-wheat bread slices
5 tsp. canola mayonnaise
1 heirloom tomato (about 6 oz.), cut into 8 slices
8 romaine lettuce leaves, cut in half horizontally

1. Preheat oven to 400°F. Whisk together tamari, maple syrup, smoked paprika, and 1 teaspoon pepper in a small bowl. Place tempeh slices on a baking sheet, and brush both sides with tamari mixture.
2. Pierce 10 holes on 1 side of bottom of a 13- x 9-inch disposable aluminum foil pan. Place wood chips over holes in pan, and place hole side of pan on stovetop burner over medium-high. Heat until wood chips begin to smoke, about 1 minute. (Turn on vent, if needed.) Remove from heat.
3. Arrange tempeh on opposite side of pan; cover pan with foil. Place pan over medium-high; cook 5 minutes. Remove from heat; uncover.
4. Place tempeh on a wire rack over a baking sheet, and bake at 400°F until slightly crispy and golden-brown, about 20 minutes, flipping once halfway through.
5. Place bread slices on oven rack, and toast until golden brown, 4 to 5 minutes.
6. Spread 1¼ teaspoons mayonnaise on each of 4 toast slices, and sprinkle with remaining ½ teaspoon pepper. Layer each with tomato slices, lettuce, and 4 slices of tempeh, and top with remaining toast. Serves 4 (serving size: 1 sandwich)

CALORIES 328; FAT 13g (sat 2g, unsat 9g); PROTEIN 20g; CARB 36g; FIBER 5g; SUGARS 7g (added sugars 3g); SODIUM 572mg; CALC 17% DV; POTASSIUM 16% DV

FEED YOUR GUT

A more "whole food" cousin of tofu, tempeh goes through a fermentation process, yielding a flavorful, probiotic-rich protein that livens up the good-for-you GI bacteria.

Fast • Gluten Free

Grilled Beef-Mushroom Burgers

Hands-on: 20 min. **Total:** 20 min.
Mushrooms make these burgers extra juicy—and subbing them in for a portion of ground meat is a great way to increase your daily veggie intake. Plus, research shows that vegetable-forward diets help maintain a healthy gut.

4 oz. sliced button mushrooms
1 lb. 90% lean ground sirloin
2 Tbsp. olive oil
⅛ tsp. black pepper
¾ tsp. kosher salt, divided
⅓ cup chopped cucumber
¼ cup plain whole-milk Greek yogurt
2 Tbsp. minced roasted garlic (about 4 large cloves)
1 Tbsp. fresh lemon juice
1 Tbsp. chopped fresh flat-leaf parsley
8 large butter lettuce leaves
4 heirloom tomato slices
4 red onion slices

1. Preheat grill or a grill pan to medium-high (about 450°F). Place mushrooms in a food processor, and process until minced, about 1 minute.
2. Combine mushrooms, ground sirloin, oil, pepper, and ⅜ teaspoon salt in a medium bowl; gently shape into 4 (4-inch) patties, and place on a baking sheet lined with parchment paper.
3. Stir together cucumber, yogurt, garlic, lemon juice, parsley, and remaining ⅜ teaspoon salt in a small bowl; set aside.
4. Place burgers on grill grate, and grill, uncovered, to desired degree of doneness, about 4 minutes per side for medium.
5. Place 2 lettuce leaves on each plate; top each with a burger patty, tomato slice, red onion slice, and 1 heaping tablespoon yogurt mixture. Serves 4 (serving size: 1 burger)

CALORIES 304; FAT 19g (sat 6g, unsat 11g); PROTEIN 26g; CARB 7g; FIBER 1g; SUGARS 3g (added sugars 0g); SODIUM 447mg; CALC 6% DV; POTASSIUM 20% DV

Fast • Gluten Free

Grilled Salmon with Avocado Salsa

Hands-on: 20 min. **Total:** 20 min. Packed with good fats and fiber, this dish is great for heart health. For the crispiest salmon skin (that doesn't stick to the grill), start with clean grill grates and preheat for at least 15 minutes.

2 cups cubed avocado
1 cup halved yellow heirloom cherry tomatoes
2 Tbsp. chopped fresh cilantro
½ tsp. chopped serrano chile
1½ Tbsp. sliced shallot
1 tsp. fresh lime juice
1 tsp. kosher salt, divided
¾ tsp. black pepper, divided
1 Tbsp. olive oil
4 (6-oz.) skin-on salmon fillets

1. Preheat grill to medium-high (about 450°F). Combine avocado, tomatoes, cilantro, serrano, and shallot in a medium bowl. Whisk together lime juice, ¼ teaspoon salt, and ¼ teaspoon pepper in a small bowl; drizzle over avocado mixture, and stir to coat.
2. Brush olive oil on both sides of salmon; sprinkle with remaining ¾ teaspoon salt and remaining ½ teaspoon pepper.
3. Place salmon, skin side down, on grill; cook, flipping once, until salmon is opaque and cooked

through, about 3 minutes per side. Serve salmon topped with salsa. Serves 4 (serving size: 1 salmon fillet and ¾ cup salsa)

CALORIES 408; **FAT** 24g (sat 4g, unsat 18g); **PROTEIN** 38g; **CARB** 9g; **FIBER** 6g; **SUGARS** 1g (added sugars 0g); **SODIUM** 574mg; **CALC** 3% DV; **POTASSIUM** 30% DV

Staff Favorite • Fast

Chicken Curry Stir-Fry

Hands-on: 20 min. **Total:** 25 min. Skip takeout and make this healthier stir-fry instead. Coating the chicken with spices not only seasons the meat—it also allows the spices to toast during cooking to develop richer flavor. Serve with a dollop of plain yogurt and mango chutney.

1¼ lb. boneless, skinless chicken thighs (about 6 thighs), cut into 1-in. pieces
2 tsp. curry powder
½ tsp. kosher salt
⅛ tsp. cayenne pepper
1 Tbsp. olive oil
3 cups broccoli florets with stalks attached (from 1 large head)
2 cups vertically sliced red onion
1 red bell pepper, seeded and cut into strips
1 yellow bell pepper, seeded and cut into strips
2 garlic cloves, minced
½ cup unsalted chicken stock
2 Tbsp. fresh lime juice
2 tsp. lower-sodium soy sauce
2 cups cooked brown rice

1. Toss together chicken, curry powder, salt, and cayenne in a large bowl.
2. Heat oil in a large nonstick skillet over medium-high. Add chicken; cook, stirring occasionally, until cooked through, about 6 minutes. Using tongs, transfer chicken to a medium bowl.

3. Add broccoli, onion, peppers, and garlic to skillet; cook, stirring constantly, until fragrant, about 2 minutes. Add chicken stock; cover and cook until broccoli is crisp-tender, about 4 minutes. Add chicken, lime juice, and soy sauce; stir until heated through, about 1 minute.
4. To serve, place ½ cup rice in each of 4 shallow bowls, and top with about 1½ cups chicken mixture. Serves 4

CALORIES 442; **FAT** 13g (sat 3g, unsat 8g); **PROTEIN** 42g; **CARB** 43g; **FIBER** 6g; **SUGARS** 7g (added sugars 0g); **SODIUM** 532mg; **CALC** 9% DV; **POTASSIUM** 17% DV

1 INGREDIENT, 3 SIDES

3 WAYS TO USE BABY ZUCCHINI

Tender and (let's be honest) adorable, baby zucchini is an attention-grabbing summer side. Whether it's shaved, sautéed, or quick-roasted, it'll be the star of your plate.

Fast • Gluten Free Vegetarian
Baby Zucchini Ribbon Salad
Pull out your vegetable peeler and shave each zucchini into long, thin strips to create a pretty zucchini

"ribbon" salad as the base of this Greek-inspired summer side. Turn this into an easy main dish by adding oil-packed chunk-light tuna or chickpeas.

1. Shave 14 baby zucchini (about 12 oz.) with a vegetable peeler lengthwise into thin strips. Place zucchini, 1 Tbsp. white wine vinegar, ¼ tsp. kosher salt, and ¼ tsp. black pepper in a medium bowl; toss to coat. Let stand 10 minutes.
2. Add ½ cup thinly sliced red bell pepper and 1 tsp. chopped fresh oregano to zucchini mixture; toss to combine. Sprinkle with ¼ cup crumbled feta cheese, and drizzle with 5 tsp. extra-virgin olive oil. Serves 4 (serving size: about ⅔ cup)

CALORIES 98; FAT 8g (sat 2g, unsat 6g); PROTEIN 3g; CARB 4g; FIBER 1g; SUGARS 3g (added sugars 0g); SODIUM 214mg; CALC 6% DV; POTASSIUM 8% DV

Fast · Gluten Free
Make Ahead · Vegetarian
Lemony Zucchini and Radishes
Make this a main dish by broiling salmon fillets for 2 minutes then proceeding with Step 1, adding the vegetables to the pan with the fish.

1. Preheat broiler to high. Halve 12 baby zucchini and 6 small radishes lengthwise. Place, cut sides down, on a rimmed baking sheet. Lightly coat with cooking spray. Broil on high on oven rack in top position until browned and tender, 4 to 5 minutes.
2. Whisk together 2 Tbsp. olive oil, 1 Tbsp. fresh lemon juice, 1 tsp. Dijon mustard, ⅜ tsp. kosher salt, and ⅛ tsp. black pepper in a small bowl. Arrange zucchini mixture on a platter. Drizzle with dressing, and sprinkle with 1 tsp. fresh thyme leaves. Serves 4 (serving size: ½ cup)

CALORIES 85; FAT 8g (sat 1g, unsat 7g); PROTEIN 1g; CARB 3g; FIBER 1g; SUGARS 2g (added sugars 0g); SODIUM 226mg; CALC 2% DV; POTASSIUM 6% DV

Fast · Gluten Free
Vegetarian
Sautéed Baby Zucchini with Pecans and Mint
Cutting zucchini diagonally (also called "on the bias") dresses up the look of this abundant summer veggie. To make this dish more kid-friendly, leave out the turmeric and sauté the zucchini with just butter and salt. The mint will turn brown quickly, so for the prettiest presentation, stir it in just before serving.

1. Cut 14 baby zucchini (about 12 oz.) diagonally into 1-inch pieces. Melt 2 tsp. unsalted butter in a large skillet over medium-high. Add zucchini; cook, stirring occasionally, until crisp-tender, 5 to 6 minutes. Add ½ tsp. kosher salt, ¼ tsp. black pepper, and ⅛ tsp. ground turmeric; cook, stirring often, 1 minute. Spoon zucchini into a bowl. Stir in ¼ cup fresh mint leaves and 2 Tbsp. chopped toasted pecans. Serves 4 (serving size: ½ cup)

CALORIES 57; FAT 5g (sat 1g, unsat 3g); PROTEIN 1g; CARB 4g; FIBER 1g; SUGARS 2g (added sugars 0g); SODIUM 248mg; CALC 2% DV; POTASSIUM 7% DV

WHAT'S FRESH NOW
Staff Favorite · Make Ahead
Cucumber Kimchi

Hands-on: 20 min. **Total:** 7 days
Spicy, zingy fermented cukes deliver plenty of probiotics. The double-sealed water bag helps keep them submerged so they ferment thoroughly.

6 Kirby cucumbers, seeded and cut into 1-in. pieces (5 ½ cups)
1 ¼ tsp. kosher salt
¼ cup sesame oil
2 Tbsp. chopped fresh basil
2 Tbsp. gochujang (Korean red chile paste)
1 Tbsp. minced peeled fresh ginger
1 Tbsp. minced fresh garlic
2 tsp. granulated sugar
½ tsp. fish sauce (such as Red Boat)
1 cup water

1. Toss together cucumbers and salt in a medium bowl. Place cucumbers in a colander; let stand 20 minutes. Rinse and drain well.
2. Combine oil, basil, gochujang, ginger, garlic, sugar, and fish sauce in a bowl. Add cucumbers; toss to coat.
3. Place cucumber mixture in a mason jar. Press down cucumbers firmly, leaving 4 inches of headspace. Place 1 cup water in a small ziplock plastic bag; seal bag. Place inside a second ziplock bag, and seal. Place bags on cucumbers; seal lid. Let stand at room temperature 7 days, opening and resealing lid once per day. Discard water bags before serving. Serves 16 (serving size: ¼ cup)

CALORIES 41; FAT 3g (sat 0g, unsat 3g); PROTEIN 0g; CARB 2g; FIBER 1g; SUGARS 1g (added sugars 1g); SODIUM 56mg; CALC 0% DV; POTASSIUM 0% DV

20-MINUTE MAINS

Spicy Scallops with Watermelon Salsa

Hands-on: 15 min. **Total:** 20 min.
Served over fiber-rich quinoa, scallops shine under a cascade of sweet and minty watermelon salsa.

¼ tsp. dry mustard
¼ tsp. ground coriander
¼ tsp. onion powder
¼ tsp. garlic powder
¼ tsp. cayenne pepper
¼ tsp. black pepper
¼ tsp. kosher salt, divided
1¼ lb. large sea scallops
2 Tbsp. olive oil, divided
2 cups diced watermelon
2 Tbsp. minced red onion
¼ cup chopped fresh mint, divided
2 Tbsp. fresh lime juice, divided
2 cups cooked quinoa
2 Tbsp. pine nuts
¼ cup sliced scallions

1. Combine mustard, coriander, onion powder, garlic powder, cayenne pepper, black pepper, and ⅛ teaspoon salt in a bowl. Pat scallops dry with a paper towel; sprinkle with spice mixture.
2. Heat a large cast-iron skillet over medium-high. Add 2 teaspoons olive oil to skillet; swirl to coat. Add scallops; cook to desired degree of doneness, 1 to 2 minutes per side.
3. Toss together the watermelon, onion, 2 tablespoons mint, 1 tablespoon lime juice, 2 teaspoons olive oil, and remaining ⅛ teaspoon salt in a bowl. Combine quinoa, pine nuts, scallions, remaining 2 teaspoons olive oil, remaining 2 tablespoons mint, and remaining 1 tablespoon lime juice. Serve scallops over quinoa mixture; top with salsa. Serves 4 (serving size: ½ cup quinoa, 4 to 5 scallops, and ½ cup salsa)

CALORIES 330; **FAT** 12g (sat 2, unsat 10g); **PROTEIN** 23g; **CARB** 33g; **FIBER** 4g; **SUGARS** 6g (added sugars 0g); **SODIUM** 358mg; **CALC** 4% DV; **POTASSIUM** 17% DV

Garlic-Miso Pork Noodle Bowl

Hands-on: 15 min. **Total:** 20 min.
Pick up unpasteurized miso—fermented soybean paste—for the best probiotic boost. Look for it near the refrigerated tofu products at your grocery store.

8 oz. uncooked brown rice noodles
8 oz. ground pork
3 Tbsp. grated yellow onion
1 (8-oz.) pkg. sliced fresh mushrooms
2 Tbsp. white miso
1 Tbsp. chili garlic sauce (such as Huy Fong)
2 cups unsalted beef stock
1 cup matchstick-cut carrots
1 Tbsp. lower-sodium soy sauce
¼ cup sliced scallions

1. Cook noodles according to package directions, omitting salt and fat. Drain well, and divide evenly among 4 shallow bowls.
2. Heat a large nonstick skillet over medium-high. Add pork, onion, and mushrooms; cook until pork is cooked through and mushrooms are tender, about 10 minutes. Stir in miso, chili garlic sauce, stock, and carrots; bring to a boil over high. Cook until carrots are crisp-tender, about 3 minutes.
3. Top noodles with pork mixture. Drizzle servings evenly with soy sauce, and top evenly with scallions. Serves 4 (serving size: 2 oz. noodles and 1 cup pork mixture)

CALORIES 404; **FAT** 13g (sat 5g, unsat 7g); **PROTEIN** 18g; **CARB** 54g; **FIBER** 6g; **SUGARS** 6g (added sugars 0g); **SODIUM** 553mg; **CALC** 2% DV; **POTASSIUM** 11% DV

FEED YOUR GUT

Prebiotic-rich leeks are among the best foods for the beneficial bugs that keep your digestive system humming along. Tip: The less you cook them, the bigger prebiotic impact.

Grilled Lemon-Rosemary Chicken and Leeks

Hands-on: 20 min. **Total:** 20 min.
Can't find chicken cutlets? Making your own is easier than you think. Slice two 8-ounce boneless, skinless chicken breasts in half horizontally, and pound them into an even thickness with the smooth side of a meat mallet.

1 Tbsp. lemon zest
2 Tbsp. fresh lemon juice
2 tsp. chopped fresh rosemary, plus more for garnish
½ tsp. kosher salt
¼ tsp. black pepper
2 Tbsp. olive oil, divided
4 (4-oz.) chicken breast cutlets
4 large leeks, trimmed and halved
1 Tbsp. unsalted butter, cubed
2 garlic cloves, sliced
1 lemon, halved

1. Preheat grill or grill pan to medium-high (about 450°F). Combine lemon zest, lemon juice, rosemary, salt, pepper, and 1 tablespoon oil in a large ziplock bag. Add chicken to bag and seal. Turn bag to coat chicken with marinade. Set aside at room temperature.
2. Brush leeks with remaining 1 tablespoon oil. Place leeks, cut sides down, on grill grate; grill, uncovered, until grill marks form, 6 to 7 minutes. Transfer leeks to a large piece of aluminum foil. Sprinkle with butter and garlic; fold up edges of foil to seal.
3. Place chicken, lemon halves, and foil packet on grill grates. Grill chicken until cooked through and grill marks form, 2 to 3 minutes per side. To serve, squeeze lemon over chicken and leeks. Garnish with rosemary. Serves 4 (serving size: 1 cutlet and about ½ cup leeks)

CALORIES 266; **FAT** 11g (sat 3g, unsat 7g); **PROTEIN** 28g; **CARB** 15g; **FIBER** 2g; **SUGARS** 4g (added sugars 0g); **SODIUM** 334mg; **CALC** 6% DV; **POTASSIUM** 5% DV

Fast • Gluten Free Vegetarian

Fig and Greens Salad

Hands-on: 10 min. **Total:** 15 min. Chickpeas, goat cheese, and walnuts pump up the protein in this arugula salad, making it a hearty meatless main. Dried figs add a big fiber boost—more per serving than many other fruits.

½ cup walnut halves
⅛ tsp. cayenne pepper
3 Tbsp. olive oil, divided
¾ tsp. plus ⅛ tsp. kosher salt, divided
2 tsp. balsamic vinegar
1 tsp. honey

1 (15-oz.) can unsalted chickpeas, drained and rinsed
5 oz. fresh arugula
½ cup dried figs, quartered
1 medium carrot, shaved
3 oz. goat cheese, crumbled (about ¾ cup)

1. Preheat oven to 375°F. Toss together walnuts, cayenne, 1 tablespoon oil, and ⅛ teaspoon salt on a small baking sheet. Bake until golden, about 10 minutes. Remove from oven, and set aside.
2. Whisk together balsamic vinegar, honey, remaining 2 tablespoons oil, and remaining ¾ teaspoon salt in a small bowl.
3. Toss together chickpeas, arugula, figs, and carrot in a large bowl. Top with goat cheese and toasted walnuts. To serve, place 2 cups salad in each of 4 bowls; drizzle evenly with dressing. Serves 4

CALORIES 403; **FAT** 24g (sat 5g, unsat 17g); **PROTEIN** 13g; **CARB** 35g; **FIBER** 8g; **SUGARS** 13g (added sugars 1g); **SODIUM** 565mg; **CALC** 18% DV; **POTASSIUM** 16% DV

THE SHORTCUT
Staff Favorite • Fast Gluten Free • Make Ahead

Salmon and Lentil Bowl with Kefir Dressing

Hands-on: 15 min. **Total:** 15 min. This dish is filled with smart shortcut options—pick up a package of precooked lentils, and hit up your grocery's hot bar for cooked salmon (or try smoked). Kefir serves as a probiotic-rich swap for sour cream.

6 Tbsp. whole-milk plain kefir
3 Tbsp. canola mayonnaise
2 tsp. chopped fresh chives

2 tsp. chopped fresh flat-leaf parsley
1 tsp. chopped fresh dill
1 tsp. grated garlic
½ tsp. black pepper
¼ tsp. kosher salt, divided
1 (17.6-oz.) pkg. precooked lentils (about 3 cups)
2 cups shaved fennel (from 1 bulb), divided, fronds reserved
2 Tbsp. olive oil
1 cup thinly sliced English cucumber
2 (4-oz.) baked salmon fillets, flaked, or smoked salmon

1. Stir together kefir, mayonnaise, chives, parsley, dill, garlic, pepper, and ⅛ teaspoon salt in a small bowl.
2. Combine lentils, 1 cup shaved fennel, oil, and remaining ⅛ teaspoon salt in a bowl; toss gently. Divide lentil mixture among 4 bowls. Top with cucumber, salmon, remaining 1 cup shaved fennel, and fennel fronds. Drizzle evenly with dressing, and serve immediately. Serves 4 (serving size: 1 cup lentil mixture, ¼ cup vegetables, 2 oz. salmon, and about 2 ½ Tbsp. dressing)

CALORIES 434; **FAT** 21g (sat 3g, unsat 16g); **PROTEIN** 31g; **CARB** 31g; **FIBER** 11g; **SUGARS** 5g (added sugars 0g); **SODIUM** 275mg; **CALC** 9% DV; **POTASSIUM** 21% DV

FEED YOUR GUT

Kefir—pourable, fermented milk—can contain up to three times more beneficial probiotic cultures than yogurt, including yeasts, which have immune-boosting potential.

3 WAYS TO USE DRY MUSTARD

Don't let that forgotten jar of dry mustard waste away in the back of your pantry—use it to add a kick of flavor and rich, savory undertones to sauces, side dishes, and, yes, even baked goods.

Fast • Gluten Free
Make Ahead • Vegetarian
Garlicky Sweet-Hot Mustard

Similar to the mustard you get in Chinese restaurants, this sinus-clearing condiment has a little honey and vinegar to balance the heat. Serve on sandwiches, burgers, or hot dogs or as a dip for pretzels or pot stickers.

1. Combine ½ cup dry mustard, ¼ cup water, 1 Tbsp. honey, 1 tsp. natural rice vinegar, ½ tsp. kosher salt, and 1 large grated garlic clove in a bowl; whisk until well blended. Let stand at room temperature 15 minutes to "activate" the mustard. Store in refrigerator up to 1 week. Serves 8 (serving size: 1 Tbsp.)

CALORIES 51; **FAT** 3g (sat 1g, unsat 1g); **PROTEIN** 3g; **CARB** 4g; **FIBER** 1g; **SUGARS** 2g (added sugars 2g); **SODIUM** 120mg; **CALC** 2% DV; **POTASSIUM** 0% DV

Fast • Gluten Free
Vegetarian
Broccoli Mac and Cheese

Mustard adds a subtle tang that enhances the cheesy flavor of this gluten-free main.

1. Cook 8 oz. (2 ¼ cups) brown rice macaroni (such as Tinkyada) according to package directions. Add 6 cups broccoli florets during last 3 minutes of cooking. Drain.

2. Whisk together 1 (12-oz.) can evaporated milk, 1 ½ Tbsp. cornstarch, 1 ½ tsp. dry mustard, ¾ tsp. kosher salt, and 1 large grated garlic clove in a large sauté pan over medium; cook, whisking often, until thickened, about 6 minutes. Remove from heat; stir in 4 oz. (about 1 cup) shredded extra-sharp cheddar cheese and pasta mixture. Serves 6 (serving size: 1 cup)

CALORIES 306; **FAT** 8g (sat 4g, unsat 3g); **PROTEIN** 13g; **CARB** 43g; **FIBER** 2g; **SUGARS** 5g (added sugars 0g); **SODIUM** 436mg; **CALC** 32% DV; **POTASSIUM** 13% DV

Make Ahead • Vegetarian
Parmesan-Chive Scones

The tenderest scones are barely fussed with, so don't stir the dough too much after adding the liquids.

1. Preheat oven to 425°F. Combine 7 oz. (about 2 cups) whole-wheat pastry flour, 1 Tbsp. granulated sugar, 2 tsp. baking powder, 2 tsp. dry mustard, ¼ tsp. kosher salt, and ¼ tsp. cayenne pepper in a large bowl. Stir in ¼ cup chopped fresh chives and 2 oz. grated Parmigiano-Reggiano cheese (about ½ cup).

2. Combine ¾ cup fat-free buttermilk, 2 Tbsp. melted unsalted butter, and 2 Tbsp. olive oil, stirring until butter solidifies in clumps. Add buttermilk mixture to flour mixture; stir just until a soft dough forms. Pat dough into a 7-inch circle on a baking sheet lined with parchment paper. Cut into 8 wedges, spacing 2 inches apart. Bake at 425°F until browned, 12 to 15 minutes. Serves 8 (serving size: 1 scone)

CALORIES 190; **FAT** 9g (sat 4g, unsat 4g); **PROTEIN** 6g; **CARB** 22g; **FIBER** 3g; **SUGARS** 3g (added sugars 2g); **SODIUM** 306mg; **CALC** 19% DV; **POTASSIUM** 3% DV

Vegetarian

Roasted Summer Vegetable Plate with Herb Dressing

Hands-on: 35 min. **Total:** 35 min. Farro—a whole-grain hero—adds fiber and heft to this meatless main. We cook it with the green beans to save time and cut down on cleanup. This dish also makes a stellar lunch; dress it just before serving to keep the arugula fresh.

¾ cup uncooked farro
8 oz. fresh green beans, trimmed
5 oz. trimmed fresh asparagus (about ½ bunch)
4 oz. carrot, sliced
2 large shallots, quartered
6 Tbsp. olive oil, divided
⅝ tsp. kosher salt, divided
2 Tbsp. white wine vinegar
1 Tbsp. chopped fresh tarragon
½ tsp. lemon zest
½ tsp. black pepper
1 (5-oz.) pkg. baby arugula
¼ cup unsalted dry-roasted almonds, chopped
1 oz. Parmesan cheese, shredded (about ¼ cup)

1. Preheat oven to 400°F.
2. Bring a medium saucepan of water to a boil over high. Stir in farro, and reduce heat to medium; cook, stirring occasionally, 16 minutes. Add green beans, and cook until beans are tender, 3 to 4 minutes. Drain farro mixture and rinse with cold water.
3. While farro cooks, toss asparagus, carrot, and shallots with 2 tablespoons oil and ⅜ teaspoon

salt. Place in a single layer on a rimmed baking sheet, and roast at 400°F until vegetables are just tender, 18 to 20 minutes. Transfer roasted vegetable mixture to a plate.

4. In a large bowl, whisk together vinegar, tarragon, lemon zest, pepper, remaining ¼ cup oil, and remaining ¼ teaspoon salt.

5. Add farro mixture and arugula to vinegar mixture in bowl. Toss to coat, and divide evenly among 4 plates. Top evenly with roasted vegetable mixture, chopped almonds, and shredded Parmesan. Serves 4 (serving size: about 2 cups)

CALORIES 365; **FAT** 28g (sat 4g, unsat 22g); **PROTEIN** 9g; **CARB** 27g; **FIBER** 6g; **SUGARS** 6g (added sugars 0g); **SODIUM** 462mg; **CALC** 18% DV; **POTASSIUM** 11% DV

4 SAUCES FOR ANY PROTEIN

Fast • Gluten Free
Make Ahead • Vegetarian
Flaxseed and Parsley Pesto

Toasting the flaxseeds and walnuts first brings out their rich, nutty flavor. Serve with steak or chicken, or stir into a pot of steamed mussels and serve with crusty bread.

Process ⅓ cup toasted chopped walnuts, 2 Tbsp. toasted flaxseeds, 2 garlic cloves, ½ tsp. kosher salt, and ½ tsp. black pepper in a food processor 1 minute. Add 4 cups fresh flat-leaf parsley leaves, ⅓ cup grated Parmesan cheese, 2 tsp. lemon zest, and 2 Tbsp. fresh lemon juice; process until smooth. With processor running, gradually add ¼ cup olive oil and 6 Tbsp. water; process until combined. Serves 12 (serving size: 2 Tbsp.)

CALORIES 84; **FAT** 8g (sat 1g, unsat 6g); **PROTEIN** 2g; **CARB** 3g; **FIBER** 1g; **SUGARS** 0g; **SODIUM** 132mg; **CALC** 5% DV; **POTASSIUM** 4% DV

Fast • Gluten Free
Make Ahead • Vegetarian
Fresh Cherry Relish

For the best relish texture and presentation, be sure to evenly and finely chop all of the ingredients. Serve with grilled pork tenderloin, lamb chops, or grilled chicken cutlets. Spoon leftovers on whole-wheat baguette slices spread with goat cheese.

Combine 1 cup pitted and finely chopped fresh cherries, ½ cup finely chopped fennel, ⅓ cup minced celery, ¼ cup finely chopped scallions, 1 Tbsp. honey, 2 tsp. orange zest, 1 tsp. fresh orange juice, 2 tsp. red wine vinegar, 1 tsp. fresh lemon juice, and ¼ tsp. black pepper in a medium bowl; stir gently to combine. Serves 8 (serving size: 3 Tbsp.)

CALORIES 26; **FAT** 0g; **PROTEIN** 0g; **CARB** 6g; **FIBER** 1g; **SUGARS** 5g (added sugars 2g); **SODIUM** 8mg; **CALC** 1% DV; **POTASSIUM** 3% DV

Fast • Gluten Free
Make Ahead • Vegetarian
Tahini Ranch Dressing

Ranch just got a snazzy makeover. Smooth and creamy with a nice jolt of lemon and herbs, this is perfect over kebabs or your favorite pita sandwich.

Combine ¼ cup tahini, 1 Tbsp. canola mayonnaise, and 1 Tbsp. fresh lemon juice in a medium bowl. Gradually whisk in 3 Tbsp. water until smooth. Add 1 tsp. maple syrup, 1 tsp. stone-ground mustard, ½ tsp. minced garlic clove, ¼ tsp. kosher salt, and ⅛ tsp. black pepper; whisk to combine. Stir in 1 Tbsp. chopped fresh flat-leaf parsley, 2 tsp. chopped fresh dill, and 2 tsp. chopped fresh chives. Serves 8 (serving size: 2 tsp.)

CALORIES 53; **FAT** 5g (sat 1g, unsat 4g); **PROTEIN** 2g; **CARB** 2g; **FIBER** 0g; **SUGARS** 1g (added sugars 0g); **SODIUM** 97mg; **CALC** 2% DV; **POTASSIUM** 1% DV

Fast • Gluten Free
Make Ahead • Vegetarian
Carrot-Ginger Turmeric Sauce

Fresh turmeric looks similar to its relative—fresh ginger—but with an orange hue. Drizzle this sauce over roasted lamb or grilled chicken thighs.

Heat 1 Tbsp. coconut oil in a skillet over high. Add 2 chopped carrots, 1 chopped shallot, 2 Tbsp. chopped fresh turmeric, 1 Tbsp. minced garlic, and 1 Tbsp. chopped peeled fresh ginger; cook 30 seconds. Add ¼ cup water; reduce heat. Cover and cook 7 minutes. Place in a blender with ½ cup plain nonfat Greek yogurt, 2 Tbsp. apple cider vinegar, 2 Tbsp. fresh orange juice, ½ tsp. kosher salt, ½ tsp. ground cumin, and ¼ tsp. crushed red pepper; process until smooth. Serves 12 (serving size: 2 Tbsp.)

CALORIES 29; **FAT** 1g (sat 1g, unsat 0g); **PROTEIN** 1g; **CARB** 3g; **FIBER** 0g; **SUGARS** 1g (added sugars 0g); **SODIUM** 91mg; **CALC** 2% DV; **POTASSIUM** 1% DV

4 GO-WITH-ANYTHING SIDES

Fast · Gluten Free
Vegetarian
Early Summer Succotash

This pan-steaming technique cuts down on cooking time and delivers crisp-tender beans and corn—no steamer basket required.

Heat 3 Tbsp. olive oil in a large skillet over medium-high. Add 1 cup sliced shallots and 1 Tbsp. sliced garlic to skillet; cook until softened, about 4 minutes. Add 2 ½ cups chopped green beans, ½ cup fresh corn kernels, and ½ cup water; cover and cook 4 to 5 minutes. Uncover and cook until beans are crisp-tender, about 2 minutes. Stir in ½ cup torn fresh basil, ½ tsp. kosher salt, and ¼ tsp. black pepper. Serves 4 (serving size: ¾ cup)

CALORIES 163; **FAT** 11g (sat 2g, unsat 9g); **PROTEIN** 3g; **CARB** 15g; **FIBER** 4g; **SUGARS** 6g (added sugars 0g); **SODIUM** 252mg; **CALC** 5% DV; **POTASSIUM** 10% DV

Fast · Vegetarian
Nectarine and Bulgur Salad

No nectarines? Sub in your favorite stone fruit, such as peaches or plums. You can make this side dish gluten-free by using quinoa in place of the bulgur.

Cut 3 nectarines into 8 wedges each. Combine with 1 cup cooked bulgur, ½ cup torn fresh basil, ½ cup fresh parsley leaves, ½ tsp. kosher salt, and ¼ tsp. black pepper in a medium bowl. Whisk together 3 Tbsp. olive oil, 2 Tbsp. lemon juice, ½ tsp. poppy seeds, and ½ tsp. honey in a small bowl. Drizzle dressing over nectarine mixture. Serve immediately. Serves 4 (serving size: about 1 cup)

CALORIES 183; **FAT** 11g (sat 1g, unsat 9g); **PROTEIN** 3g; **CARB** 22g; **FIBER** 4g; **SUGARS** 9g (added sugars 1g); **SODIUM** 247mg; **CALC** 3% DV; **POTASSIUM** 8% DV

Fast · Gluten Free
Vegetarian
Spiced Sweet Potato Fries

Here are two tricks for crunchy baked sweet potato fries: Toss them with cornstarch to absorb moisture, and don't crowd the pan—so they'll crisp instead of steam.

Preheat oven to 450°F. Cut 4 sweet potatoes into ¼-inch-thick fries. Combine with 2 Tbsp. cornstarch, 1 tsp. ground cumin, ½ tsp. ground coriander, ½ tsp. kosher salt, and ¼ tsp. black pepper in a ziplock plastic bag; seal bag, and turn to coat. Spread in an even layer on 2 rimmed baking sheets; drizzle each with 1 Tbsp. canola oil, and toss to coat. Bake 22 to 25 minutes, stirring 3 times. Sprinkle with ¼ cup chopped fresh cilantro. Serve with lime wedges. Serves 4 (serving size: ¼ cup)

CALORIES 219; **FAT** 7g (sat 1g, unsat 6g); **PROTEIN** 3g; **CARB** 37g; **FIBER** 5g; **SUGARS** 7g (added sugars 0g); **SODIUM** 331mg; **CALC** 6% DV; **POTASSIUM** 16% DV

Fast · Vegetarian
Squash-Chickpea Crumble

For an Italian-inspired version, use cannellini beans in place of the chickpeas and chopped fresh basil instead of chives. Serve with broiled salmon or grilled shrimp.

Add 2 Tbsp. olive oil, 2 cups diced yellow squash, and 1 (15-oz.) can rinsed and drained unsalted chickpeas to a medium skillet over medium-high. Cook until squash is tender, about 5 minutes. Stir in 1 cup finely diced tomato; cook 1 minute. Stir in 3 Tbsp. chopped fresh chives, ⅜ tsp. salt, and ¼ tsp. black pepper. Top with 1 oz. toasted whole-wheat panko. Serves 4 (serving size: about ¾ cup)

CALORIES 209; **FAT** 8g (sat 1g, unsat 6g); **PROTEIN** 8g; **CARB** 28g; **FIBER** 6g; **SUGARS** 3g (added sugars 0g); **SODIUM** 216mg; **CALC** 8% DV; **POTASSIUM** 13% DV

THE RECIPE MAKEOVER

LIGHTEN UP PECAN BLONDIES

These bars keep every bit of their sweet butterscotch essence for half the added sugar.

Blondies may be lighter in color than their cocoa-based counterparts, but they're not lighter in heft: The classic clocks in at 300 calories and 10g sat fat (55% of your daily recommended limit) per square. Luckily, you don't need 1½ cups of brown sugar and a stick and a half of butter to achieve the coveted chewy texture and crisp, golden edges. We look to the humble chickpea to replace some of the butter, which saves you 3g sat fat per serving (and leaves minimal trace of any beany flavor). White whole-wheat flour's light texture and mild flavor work well with the buttery-sweet profile of these bars, and it yields a tender crumb while adding a few whole grains. With 120 fewer calories and 50% less added sugar than the original, enjoy these for dessert or a midday pick-me-up.

Make Ahead · Vegetarian

Chickpea-Tahini Blondies

Hands-on: 15 min. **Total:** 1 hr. 5 min.

The rich nuttiness of the tahini is amplified in the blondie and matched by the whole-wheat flour. We like Soom brand of tahini; it's unctuous and creamy with no oil slick on top (perfect for stirring into batters). Pecans contribute natural sweetness and indulgent crunch, but feel free to sub in an equal amount of another nut or a few chocolate or butterscotch chips.

3 Tbsp. unsalted butter
¾ cup packed dark brown sugar
2 large eggs
1 tsp. vanilla extract
1 (15-oz.) can unsalted chickpeas,
   rinsed and drained
3 Tbsp. tahini
2 Tbsp. 2% reduced-fat milk
1.3 oz. white whole-wheat flour
   (about ⅓ cup)
½ tsp. baking powder
¼ tsp. kosher salt
⅓ cup chopped pecans
Cooking spray

1. Preheat oven to 350°F.
2. Melt butter in a small saucepan over medium-high. Cook, stirring often, until light brown, 5 to 6 minutes. Transfer butter to a large bowl; cool 15 minutes. Whisk in brown sugar, eggs, and vanilla.
3. Place chickpeas, tahini, and milk in a food processor; process until smooth, about 2 minutes, stopping to scrape down sides of bowl as necessary. Stir chickpea mixture into butter mixture.
4. Place flour, baking powder, and salt in a separate bowl; whisk to combine. Stir flour mixture into chickpea mixture. Fold in pecans.
5. Pour batter into an 8-inch square baking pan coated with cooking spray. Bake at 350°F until a wooden pick inserted in center comes out clean, 25 to 27 minutes. Cool in pan 15 minutes. Slice into 12 bars. Serves 12 (serving size: 1 blondie)

CALORIES 182; FAT 8g (sat 3g, unsat 5g); PROTEIN 4g; CARB 23g; FIBER 2g; SUGARS 14g (added sugars 13g); SODIUM 107mg; CALC 7% DV; POTASSIUM 4% DV

PLAN. SHOP. COOK.

1 LIST 3 DINNERS

Shop this list to feed four for three nights, all for about $30. Read the recipes first to be sure you have the staples on hand.

2 lemons and 2 limes

2 bunches fresh basil

1 bunch fresh cilantro

1 green bell pepper

1 bunch rainbow carrots
(about 12 oz.)

1 small yellow onion

1 bunch radishes

1 large zucchini

2 (5-oz.) pkg. mixed salad greens

1 ⅓ cups whole-wheat panko

Unsalted shelled roasted pistachios

Thai sweet chili sauce

Fish sauce

1 (15-oz.) can unsalted chickpeas

1 cup precooked farro

2 ¼ lb. raw medium shrimp

1 oz. Parmesan cheese

**Staff Favorite • Fast
Make Ahead**

Spicy Thai Shrimp Cakes

Hands-on: 20 min. **Total:** 30 min.
A simple salad rounds out this meal: Whisk together 2 tablespoons olive oil, 1 tablespoon fresh lime juice, 1 minced garlic clove, 2 teaspoons Dijon mustard, and ¼ teaspoon black pepper. Toss with 4 cups mixed greens, top with these cakes, and dinner's done.

1 lb. peeled and deveined raw
   medium shrimp, chopped
1 ⅓ cups whole-wheat panko
   (Japanese breadcrumbs), divided
⅔ cup finely diced green bell pepper
½ cup finely diced yellow onion
¼ cup chopped fresh cilantro
4 tsp. fresh lime juice
2 tsp. fish sauce
2 tsp. Thai sweet chili sauce
2 large eggs, lightly beaten
2 garlic cloves, minced
2 Tbsp. olive oil, divided

1. Combine shrimp, ⅔ cup panko, bell pepper, onion, cilantro, lime juice, fish sauce, chili sauce, eggs, and garlic in a medium bowl. Shape mixture into 8 patties, and dredge patties in remaining ⅔ cup panko.
2. Heat 1 tablespoon oil in a large nonstick skillet over medium-high. Add 4 shrimp patties to skillet, and cook until crispy and well browned, about 4 minutes per side. Repeat procedure with remaining 1 tablespoon oil and remaining 4 shrimp patties. Serves 4 (serving size: 2 cakes)

CALORIES 288; FAT 11g (sat 2g, unsat 7g); PROTEIN 23g; CARB 24g; FIBER 4g; SUGARS 2g (added sugars 0g); SODIUM 482mg; CALC 9% DV; POTASSIUM 8% DV

Dinner 2 of 3

Fast • Gluten Free

Veggie Noodles with Shrimp and Pistachio Pesto

Hands-on: 20 min. **Total:** 20 min.
Creating your own veggie noodles is fast and fun with a spiralizer. If you don't have one, look for pre-spiralized zucchini noodles near the prepared vegetables in your produce department. Pick up peeled and deveined shrimp to save on prep time.

6 Tbsp. unsalted roasted pistachios, divided
1 garlic clove
1 tsp. lemon zest
¼ tsp. kosher salt
¼ tsp. black pepper
2 cups packed fresh basil leaves, plus more for garnish
1 oz. Parmesan cheese, grated (about ¼ cup)
1 Tbsp. fresh lemon juice, plus more for serving
2 Tbsp. plus 1 tsp. olive oil, divided
2 Tbsp. water
1 lb. peeled and deveined raw medium shrimp
1 large zucchini, spiralized
4 rainbow carrots (about 12 oz.), cut into thin ribbons

1. Place ¼ cup pistachios, garlic, lemon zest, salt, and pepper in a food processor; pulse until combined, 6 to 8 times. Add basil, Parmesan, and lemon juice; process until thoroughly combined, about 1 minute. With processor running, drizzle in 2 tablespoons oil and 2 tablespoons water in a steady stream; process until thoroughly combined, about 1 minute. Set pesto aside.
2. Heat remaining 1 teaspoon oil in a large nonstick skillet over medium-high. Add shrimp; cook, stirring occasionally, until cooked through, about 2 minutes. Transfer shrimp to a plate, and cover with aluminum foil to keep warm.
3. Add pesto to skillet, and cook until hot, about 1 minute. Remove from heat. Add zucchini and carrots to skillet, and toss gently to coat. (Do not cook vegetable noodles.) Divide mixture evenly among 4 plates.
4. Return shrimp to skillet, tossing to coat with any remaining pesto. Top vegetable noodles evenly with shrimp. Coarsely chop remaining 2 tablespoons pistachios, and sprinkle evenly over servings. Garnish servings evenly with basil leaves, and serve with lemon juice. Serves 4

CALORIES 301; **FAT** 17g (sat 3g, unsat 12g); **PROTEIN** 22g; **CARB** 17g; **FIBER** 5g; **SUGARS** 7g (added sugars 0g); **SODIUM** 483mg; **CALC** 20% DV; **POTASSIUM** 23% DV

Dinner 3 of 3

**Fast • Make Ahead
Vegetarian**

Superfast Farro and Chickpea Salad

Hands-on: 25 min. **Total:** 25 min.
Anchored by a quick and versatile vinaigrette, this salad is easy to customize with whatever ingredients you have on hand. Swap quinoa or barley for farro, cannellini or black beans for chickpeas, and basil for cilantro.

2 rainbow carrots, thinly sliced
2 radishes, thinly sliced
½ cup rice vinegar
2 tsp. granulated sugar
6 cups mixed salad greens
1 cup precooked farro
1 cup drained and rinsed canned unsalted chickpeas
½ cup plus 1 Tbsp. fresh cilantro leaves, divided
2 Tbsp. olive oil
1½ Tbsp. fresh lime juice
1 garlic clove, minced
1 tsp. honey
¼ cup unsalted shelled roasted pistachios, toasted and roughly chopped

1. Place carrots and radishes in a bowl. Combine vinegar and sugar in a small saucepan. Bring vinegar mixture to a simmer over medium, and pour over carrots and radishes. Let stand 10 minutes.
2. Divide greens, farro, chickpeas, and ½ cup cilantro among 4 plates. Drain carrots and radishes; divide among plates.
3. Chop remaining 1 tablespoon cilantro. Combine oil, lime juice, garlic, honey, and chopped cilantro in a small bowl; whisk to combine. Drizzle over salads. Sprinkle salads with toasted pistachios, and serve immediately. Serves 4 (serving size: 1 ½ cups greens, ¼ cup farro, ¼ cup chickpeas, 1 Tbsp. dressing, and 1 Tbsp. pistachios)

CALORIES 252; **FAT** 11g (sat 1g, unsat 9g); **PROTEIN** 9g; **CARB** 34g; **FIBER** 8g; **SUGARS** 4g (added sugars 1g); **SODIUM** 94mg; **CALC** 10% DV; **POTASSIUM** 9% DV

SLOW COOKER

Gluten Free • Make Ahead

Smoky Brisket with Peppers and Onions

Hands-on: 20 min. **Total:** 8 hr. 20 min.
Don't want to spend a hot summer day tending the smoker? Call on your slow cooker to work its magic. Canned chipotle chiles add smokiness; remove the seeds to tame the heat. For extra flavor and color, try searing the brisket first.

3 Tbsp. minced seeded chipotle chiles in adobo sauce
1 Tbsp. adobo sauce from can
2 Tbsp. olive oil
1 Tbsp. honey
1½ tsp. ground cumin
1¼ tsp. kosher salt
¼ tsp. black pepper
1½ lb. beef brisket, trimmed
2 cups sliced white onions
2 cups sliced red bell pepper
Cooking spray
⅓ cup unsalted beef stock

1. Combine chipotle chiles, adobo sauce, oil, honey, cumin, salt, and black pepper in a small bowl. Rub mixture into brisket, covering all sides.
2. Combine onions and bell peppers in a 5- to 6-quart slow cooker coated with cooking spray. Pour beef stock over onion and pepper mixture. Nestle brisket into mixture. Cover and cook on low until brisket is very tender, about 8 hours.
3. Remove brisket from slow cooker, and shred with 2 forks. Return shredded meat to slow cooker, and toss with vegetables before serving. Serves 6 (serving size: about ¾ cup)

CALORIES 232; **FAT** 10g (sat 2g, unsat 6g); **PROTEIN** 25g; **CARB** 10g; **FIBER** 2g; **SUGARS** 6g (added sugars 3g); **SODIUM** 605mg; **CALC** 4% DV; **POTASSIUM** 15% DV

DINNER IN AMERICA

Fast

Sausage and Tomato Mini Pizzas

Hands-on: 15 min. **Total:** 20 min.
If you've got adventurous palates in the family, punch up the flavor of these personal pizzas with a dash of red pepper flakes and briny kalamata olives. Add a veggie-forward side, like a simple salad or roasted broccoli.

4 whole-wheat pita rounds
1 (4-oz.) link sweet Italian turkey sausage, casing removed
½ cup lower-sodium marinara sauce
4 oz. part-skim mozzarella cheese, shredded (about 1 cup)
1 large plum tomato, thinly sliced
1 (2¼-oz.) can sliced black olives, drained

1. Preheat broiler to high with oven rack in top position.
2. Place pitas on a baking sheet. Broil until lightly browned, about 1 minute. Remove baking sheet from oven; turn pitas over. Do not turn off oven.
3. Heat a medium nonstick skillet over medium-high. Add sausage, and cook, stirring to crumble, until no longer pink, 4 to 5 minutes.
4. Spread 2 tablespoons marinara over each pita. Top evenly with cheese, sausage, tomato, and olives. Broil until cheese melts and browns in spots, 1 to 2 minutes. Serve immediately. Serves 4 (serving size: 1 mini pizza)

CALORIES 292; **FAT** 9g (sat 4g, unsat 3g); **PROTEIN** 19g; **CARB** 35g; **FIBER** 4g; **SUGARS** 3g (added sugars 0g); **SODIUM** 633mg; **CALC** 27% DV; **POTASSIUM** 2% DV

CHEERS TO YOUR HEALTH

Fast • Gluten Free
Vegetarian

Mango-Rum Kefir Lassi

Hands-on: 5 min. **Total:** 5 min.
A little rum-spiration turns the popular Indian yogurt shake into a boozy brunch beverage or cooling poolside cocktail. Kefir offers good lactic acid bacteria that helps fight off harmful bacteria and aids in digestion. Ancho chile powder lends sweet heat.

Place 1 cup plain low-fat kefir, ½ cup coconut water, ¼ cup dark rum, 3 Tbsp. honey, ½ tsp. ground turmeric, ¼ tsp. ground cinnamon, and ⅛ tsp. kosher salt in a blender. Top with 1½ cups frozen chopped mango and 1 ripe banana. Process mixture until smooth. Pour evenly into 3 glasses. Garnish each drink with 1 mint sprig, and, if desired, sprinkle with ancho chile powder. Serves 3 (serving size: about 1 cup)

CALORIES 237; **FAT** 1g (sat 1g, unsat 0g); **PROTEIN** 5g; **CARB** 44g; **FIBER** 3g; **SUGARS** 37g (added sugars 16g); **SODIUM** 126mg; **CALC** 12% DV; **POTASSIUM** 11% DV

MAKE IT A MOCKTAIL

Switch out the rum for ½ cup brewed and chilled orange pekoe or orange spice tea.

ONE SUMMER DISH TO FEED EVERYONE

BY GINA HOMOLKA

Picky palates? Food allergies? A surplus of summer produce? No problem—try this for dinner.

My favorite season is summer: The weather is warmer, the days are longer, and, oh, how I love farm stands and fresh summer produce. Summer is also prime grilling season, and that means one thing: Meals get a lot tastier. We use the grill all summer long; there's just something about a smoky-flavored meal, like these grilled Mexican street food–inspired tacos, that makes dinnertime so satisfying— especially when eaten alfresco.

And when you're looking to please a house full of picky eaters with varying tastes, tacos are a real winner because they offer an easy way to satisfy everyone. They're also great if you're feeding someone with a food allergy; with a few easy tweaks, you can make one dish that makes everyone happy.

My daughter loves corn tortillas, but if your kids don't, try crispy taco shells, lettuce wraps, or flour tortillas. You can swap chicken for steak and grill plain corn on the side for finicky palates. I also set out lots of toppings (cheese, shredded lettuce, tomatoes, and avocado), and let everyone build their own custom tacos.

Fast · Gluten Free

Grilled Steak and Elote Tacos

Hands-on: 20 min. **Total:** 20 min. These tacos are a perfect blend of Mexican street corn and quick-cooking skirt steak. If you only have frozen corn, blister the kernels in a skillet over high heat before making the elote.

2 ears fresh corn
2 Tbsp. canola mayonnaise
2 Tbsp. chopped fresh cilantro, plus more for garnish
1 Tbsp. fresh lime juice, plus wedges for serving
¼ tsp. ancho chile powder
⅝ tsp. kosher salt, divided
1 lb. skirt steak, trimmed
½ tsp. ground cumin
8 (6-inch) corn tortillas
¼ cup finely crumbled Cotija, queso fresco, or feta cheese (about 1 oz.)

1. Preheat grill to medium-high (about 450°F). Place corn on oiled grates; grill corn, turning occasionally, until slightly charred, about 10 minutes. Transfer to a cutting board. When cool enough to handle, cut corn kernels off cobs, discard cobs, and place kernels in a medium bowl. Add mayonnaise, cilantro, lime juice, ancho chile powder, and ⅛ teaspoon salt; stir to combine. Set aside.
2. Sprinkle steak evenly with cumin and remaining ½ teaspoon salt. Increase grill temperature to high (450° to 550°F). Place steak on oiled grill grates, and grill to desired degree of doneness, 1 minute and 30 seconds to 2 minutes per side for medium-rare. Transfer to a cutting board.
3. Grill tortillas until edges become charred, 30 seconds to 1 minute per side. Thinly slice steak across the grain, and divide among tortillas.

Top with corn mixture and cheese; garnish with cilantro, and serve with lime wedges. Serves 4 (serving size: 2 tacos)

CALORIES 417; FAT 15g (sat 5g, unsat 9g); PROTEIN 32g; CARB 45g; FIBER 5g; SUGARS 4g (added sugars 0g); SODIUM 621mg; CALC 11% DV; POTASSIUM 12% DV

PERFECT GRILLED FISH EVERY SINGLE TIME

BY BARTON SEAVER

Use this simple, indirect heat technique to grill flaky fillets with irresistibly crispy skin.

Our attentions turn outdoors and our palates to lighter fare in the warm summer months. This brings us to the union of seafood and the grill, flattering fillets with the smoky charm of a live fire. But it can be intimidating to grill fish, given its fragile texture and the common belief that fish skin inherently sticks to the grill. To avoid mishaps, I like a method called indirect grilling. Indirect grilling uses dual cooking areas, one hot and the other more gentle. For gas grills, simply heat on high. Lay the fish, skin side down, with head-to-tail parallel to the hot grill grate, and sear over high heat for a minute. Then turn off the burner under the fish, cover the grill, and finish cooking. For charcoal grills, place the coals on one side of the kettle, arrange the fillets as described above, and sear them. After a minute, rotate the grill grate 180 degrees, cover, and finish cooking over indirect heat. Notice I don't move or flip the fish, which eliminates the need to touch it until I remove it from the grill. Lastly, a little char is OK—it accentuates the sweet flavor of the fish.

Staff Favorite • Fast Gluten Free

Grilled Rainbow Trout with Chimichurri

Hands-on: 20 min. **Total:** 25 min.
The trout has a nice smoky flavor that is cut by the freshness and acidity of the chimichurri. For a less smoky flavor, seek out thinner fillets (which will take less time to cook).

4 (6-oz.) skin-on trout fillets
1 tsp. kosher salt, divided
Freshly ground black pepper
2 Tbsp. chopped yellow onion
1 garlic clove
1 cup loosely packed fresh cilantro leaves
½ cup loosely packed fresh flat-leaf parsley leaves
1 Tbsp. chopped jalapeño (from 1 small jalapeño)
1 Tbsp. fresh lemon juice (from 1 lemon)
5 Tbsp. olive oil, divided

1. Preheat a gas grill to high (450°F to 550°F), or push hot coals to one side of a charcoal grill. Pat fish dry and season with ¾ teaspoon salt and black pepper to taste. Let seasoned fish rest while grill preheats. (This will help give the fish more structural integrity.) Place onion, garlic, cilantro, parsley, jalapeño, and remaining ¼ teaspoon salt in a food processor; process until smooth. Add lemon juice and ¼ cup olive oil; pulse until combined, about 2 times.
2. When grill is hot, brush fillets with remaining 1 tablespoon olive oil. Place fillets, skin side down,

parallel with the grill grates over one side of grill (or over the hot coals on a charcoal grill). Grill, uncovered, about 1 minute. Turn off burner under fillets, leaving the opposite burner on high. (Or rotate charcoal grill grate 180 degrees using tongs and an oven mitt so fillets sit opposite the coals.) Do not flip fish. Grill, covered, until cooked through, 3 to 5 minutes per inch of thickness. Using a fish spatula, transfer fillets to a platter. Serve with chimichurri. Serves 4 (serving size: 1 fillet and 2 Tbsp. chimichurri)

CALORIES 372; **FAT** 25g (sat 5g, unsat 19g); **PROTEIN** 33g; **CARB** 2g; **FIBER** 1g; **SUGARS** 0g; **SODIUM** 567mg; **CALC** 14% DV; **=POTASSIUM** 21% DV

THE TEACHER

HOW TO PROPERLY MEASURE INGREDIENTS

BY ANDREA NGUYEN

It might seem like an exact, overly fussy science, but measuring contributes to the art of cooking.

Recipes are like road maps that take you on journeys. The starting point lies in the ingredients because without adequate supplies, you might not arrive at your destination in great shape.

That's why each time I develop a recipe, I consider how cooks will measure the ingredients—I ponder their measuring tools and how they might prep and determine appropriate quantities. Do they measure dry ingredients by scooping and sweeping or by pouring and leveling? Do they own a scale? If they're a little off, will the dish be

totally ruined, or will a well-placed tip salvage it?

If I sound fastidious, it's because I am. As a cookbook author, my goal is to help cooks succeed and learn in their kitchens. Because I'm not there with them, my instructions should be clear and precise but with some wiggle room. I never want to come off like, well, my mother.

When she was first teaching me to cook, she'd always be nearby to make sure that I measured things "right" (read: her way). A special melamine cup was our rice scooper. Heaping Chinese soup spoons of sugar were used for certain recipes, while metal serving spoons were used for others.

Those early cooking lessons taught me how good cooks pave their own paths and create personal measuring systems. That's because for most of us, cooking is a craft more than a science. Too much exactitude from the outside can cramp style. Moreover, there can be slight differences between measuring implements. When my husband's aunt Henrietta Hulbert passed, I inherited her vintage set of aluminum measuring cups. She lost a forearm in the 1930s and her husband in World War II, but those setbacks didn't stop her from driving a stick shift and treating loved ones to sensational chile rellenos and pound cakes. I admired her chutzpah and thought the cups would elevate my cooking. Unfortunately, my recipes were always off when I used them. I finally tested her cups against mine and realized that hers held slightly less. Who knows how she measured ingredients, but like my mother, she had a system that worked for her.

Look in my kitchen, and you'll see certain brands of measuring cups and spoons. I've used them to formulate my recipes, and I stick with them to maintain consistency
continued

in my work. That said, a little skepticism is always good. Digital scales supposedly never lie, but I occasionally check the accuracy of mine to keep it honest.

Little vagaries and joyful tweaks are an intrinsic part of cooking. When I overthink ingredient measurements, I remind myself that before 1896, when Fannie Farmer's *Boston Cooking-School Cook Book* introduced exact volume measurements to American cooks, recipes and measurements were fuzzy, and people were still able to put good food on the table.

What's important for you is to decide on certain equipment and methods and nimbly use them to obtain results that satisfy you. In our kitchens, we're the masters of our own delicious destinies.

Make Ahead · Vegetarian

Baby Chocolate Cakes

Hands-on: 25 min. **Total:** 37 min.
For a fun way to check your tools and methods, make a batch of these chocolaty, bite-sized tea cakes, which taste like elegant brownies.

Cooking spray
2 Tbsp. plus 1 tsp. all-purpose flour (20g)
3 Tbsp. almond meal (20g)
¼ cup unsweetened cocoa powder (25g)
¼ cup egg whites (from 2 large eggs) (60g)
⅓ cup plus 1 Tbsp. granulated sugar (80g)
5 Tbsp. unsalted butter, melted (70g)

1. Preheat oven to 375°F with oven rack in the middle. Coat 16 wells of a silicone half-sphere mold or a miniature muffin pan with cooking spray, and set aside. (Place the silicone mold on a baking sheet.) The batter can wait if you need to bake in two batches.

2. Sift flour, almond meal, and cocoa powder into a medium bowl; set aside.

3. Place egg whites and sugar in the bowl of an electric stand mixer fitted with the whisk attachment. Beat on high speed (I use speed 8 on my KitchenAid) until mixture increases in volume and becomes white, very thick, and glossy, 2 to 3 minutes. Stop the machine to check by swiping a bit on a fingertip. The peak should gracefully flop over, and you should barely feel the sugar granules.

4. Return mixer to medium speed, and slowly pour butter down the side of the bowl, scraping down sides of bowl with a spatula as needed. Mix on medium-high until incorporated, 10 to 15 seconds. Reduce speed to low (2 on my KitchenAid).

5. Add half of the flour mixture to egg white mixture; beat on low speed until combined, gently scraping down sides of bowl with spatula. Add remaining half of flour mixture; beat on low speed until combined, about 30 seconds.

6. Spoon 1 tablespoon of batter into each well of the prepared mold to fill one-half to two-thirds full. Bake at 375°F until center of cakes spring back when touched, 12 to 13 minutes. Let cool in the mold for 10 minutes (the cakes will deflate slightly) before removing from mold and cooling completely on a wire rack. Store cakes in an airtight container up to 3 days. Serves 16 (serving size: 1 cake)

CALORIES 68; **FAT** 4g (sat 2g, unsat 1g); **PROTEIN** 1g; **CARB** 7g; **FIBER** 1g; **SUGARS** 5g (added sugars 5g); **SODIUM** 8mg; **CALC** 0% DV; **POTASSIUM** 1% DV

MEASURING TIPS FROM A PRO

In the realm of cooking, baking is where measurements count most. Here's how to measure just right to ensure success.

DRY INGREDIENTS
For ingredients such as flour, use a dry measuring cup. We stir flour a couple times before spooning it into a measuring cup and leveling with a knife. That volume is also weighed for accuracy (1 cup of all-purpose flour weighs 4.25 ounces). If you have a scale, use the weight if it's specified in a recipe.

LIQUID INGREDIENTS
Use a liquid measuring cup for liquids. Place it on your work surface, and then add the ingredient. Bend down to check the meniscus, the surface curvature of a liquid when it's in a container. If the meniscus bottom lies at the target marking, you're golden!

DIGITAL MEASUREMENTS
To check the accuracy of your digital scale, find a shiny new penny or nickel. Set the scale to metric. One penny should weigh 2.5 grams (or 3 grams if the scale cannot register 0.5 grams). One nickel weighs 5 grams.

COOKING CLASS: WHY INGREDIENTS MATTER

Gluten Free • Make Ahead

Chicken Bone Broth

Hands-on: 25 min. **Total:** 3 hr. 55 min.

1 (3-lb.) whole chicken
1 lb. chicken wings, skinless drumsticks, or feet
2 large carrots, cut into 2-in. pieces (about 1⅓ cups)
2 medium leeks, trimmed and cut into 2-in. pieces (about 1⅓ cups)
2 celery stalks, cut into 2-in. pieces (about 1 cup)
1 garlic head, halved crosswise
10 thyme sprigs
5 flat-leaf parsley sprigs
1 bay leaf
9 cups water
1 tsp. kosher salt

1. Preheat oven to 400°F. Debone chicken, reserving breast and thigh meat for another use.
2. Place carcass and wings, drumsticks, or feet on a rimmed baking sheet. Bake in preheated oven until browned, about 1 hour, turning after 30 minutes. Transfer chicken parts to a stock pot or large Dutch oven.
3. Add carrots and next 7 ingredients (through water) to pot. Bring to a boil over high. Reduce heat to medium-low; simmer 2 hours and 30 minutes.
5. Pour broth through a fine wire-mesh strainer into a large bowl; discard solids. Using a ladle, skim fat from top of broth; discard. Stir in salt. Serve hot. Serves 4 (serving size: 1 cup)

CALORIES 32; **FAT** 0g (sat 0g, unsat 0g); **PROTEIN** 5g; **CARB** 3g; **FIBER** 2g; **SUGARS** 2g (added sugars 0g); **SODIUM** 345mg; **CALC** 1% DV; **POTASSIUM** 10% DV

If you choose to use chicken feet, which add collagen to the broth, you'll find them at Asian markets. Ask the butcher to debone the chicken if you don't want to do it at home.

TAKING STOCK

CHOOSE THE RIGHT CHICKEN BONES AND AROMATIC INGREDIENTS FOR THE RICHEST, MOST FLAVORFUL BROTH.

POULTRY PARTS
A mix of carcass bones and high-collagen pieces like wings, drumsticks, or feet is best. Roast until brown for richer flavor.

CELERY STALKS
These bring fresh vegetal taste to mirepoix (a veggie mix that flavors stocks and sauces). Their flavor comes through easily, so we use less than carrots or leeks.

LEEKS
Alliums are traditional in mirepoix. We like leeks because they're mellower than other onion varieties.

CARROTS
The third part of this mirepoix, these lend a touch of sweetness for flavor balance. Less is more; too many carrots can take over the flavor.

GARLIC HEAD
A halved head—versus sliced cloves—adds subtle garlic notes. This delicate flavor is what makes the broth feel complete.

HERB BLEND
A traditional mix of fresh thyme, parsley, and dried bay leaf provides fragrance and refined flavor.

THE STEPS

1. COMBINE AROMATICS

The items you use along with the zucchini transfer their flavors through the pickling liquid. In this batch, we use pungent garlic; floral coriander; spicy chiles; and sweet, grassy fresh dill. We find baby zucchini stays crisper than sliced spears of large zucchini when fermented.

2. COVER WITH BRINE

Cover the solid ingredients with the salted water. From here, the ingredients do the rest of the work as the brine solution slowly ferments the vegetables. Cover the solids completely with the brine so they can ferment evenly and aren't exposed to air.

3. WAIT FOR BUBBLES

The liquid in the covered jars will start to cloud after a day or so once the fermentation process begins and microbes devour the veggie sugar, creating acid and gas. After about five days, the liquid develops bubbles. Loosely lidded jars allow pressure from gas buildup to escape.

COOKING CLASS: HOW TO MASTER THE METHOD

PERFECT PICKLES IN 3, 2, 1…

Waiting to eat them is the hardest part about making these simple fermented pickles.

Gluten Free • Make Ahead Vegetarian

Fermented Zucchini Pickles

Hands-on: 10 min. **Total:** 5 days

For pickles that deliver good gut bacteria, you want fermented—not vinegar—pickles. The brine is the easiest way to spot the difference: If it's cloudy, they're fermented; a clear brine means they're pickled. You can also check the ingredients. For milder spice, remove the chile seeds and membranes. This recipe also works for green beans, pickling cukes, and baby bell peppers.

1½ lb. baby zucchini
1 tsp. coriander seeds
12 dill sprigs
4 Fresno chiles, halved lengthwise
2 garlic cloves, halved
4 cups room-temperature water
2 Tbsp. kosher salt

1. Divide zucchini, coriander, dill, chiles, and garlic between 2 (1-quart) jars.
2. Combine 4 cups water and salt. Stir until salt dissolves fully.
3. Divide liquid between jars to cover zucchini, leaving about ½ inch of space between liquid and top of jar. (Add water as needed to ensure solids are covered.) Cover jars loosely with lids. Let stand in a cool, dry place away from direct sunlight for 5 to 7 days. The liquid will turn cloudy, then bubble and fizz after several days as it develops lactic acid. Once fermented, refrigerate pickles. They will keep in sealed jars for up to 3 months. Serves 20 (serving size: 1 pickle)

CALORIES 7; **FAT** 0g; **PROTEIN** 0g; **CARB** 1g; **FIBER** 0g; **SUGARS** 1g (added sugars 0g); **SODIUM** 74mg; **CALC** 1% DV; **POTASSIUM** 3% DV

SUMMER COOKBOOK: NEW SUMMER ESSENTIALS

The freshest, juiciest produce of the year is abundant right now. Seize the season's best with these inventive takes on summer's most iconic dishes—recipes that modernize, lighten, elevate, and improve upon the classics. The flavors are vibrant, with the best fruits and vegetables of the summer playing a starring role. Whether you're hosting a gathering or looking for tomorrow's dinner, these dishes deliver.

APPETIZERS

Treat your guests—and yourself— to these produce-packed pickups at your next get-together. Our artful appetizers get the party started in real style, from a new take on prosciutto and melon to a fresher bruschetta riff. For an elegant sit-down affair, our creamy, lobster-topped gazpacho is sure to garner raves.

Make Ahead

White Gazpacho with Lobster

Hands-on: 15 min. **Total:** 1 hr. 15 min. Instead of the traditional tomato foundation, this gazpacho uses cucumber and green grapes for bright, fresh flavor. Lobster is a special touch, ideal to kick off a dinner party. You also could omit the lobster or sub shrimp.

3 oz. French bread, crusts removed, cubed
2 cups water, divided
⅓ cup blanched almonds, lightly toasted
2 garlic cloves
12 oz. seedless green grapes (about 2½ cups)
1¼ cups chopped cucumber (from 1 medium), divided
1½ Tbsp. sherry vinegar
2 Tbsp. extra-virgin olive oil, divided
¼ tsp. kosher salt
3 oz. steamed lobster meat, coarsely chopped
1 Tbsp. thinly sliced fresh chives
Ground Aleppo pepper (optional)

1. Combine bread cubes and 1 cup water in a bowl or shallow dish. Let stand until bread has completely absorbed water, about 2 minutes.
2. Process almonds and garlic in a blender on low speed until coarsely chopped. Add bread cubes, remaining 1 cup water, grapes, 1 cup cucumber, vinegar, 1 tablespoon oil, and salt to almond mixture. Process until smooth. Pour mixture into a bowl; chill until cold, about 1 hour.
3. Return bread mixture to blender, and process to redistribute any solids that have settled, about 15 seconds.
4. Ladle about ⅔ cup soup into each of 8 bowls. Divide lobster evenly among bowls. Drizzle evenly with remaining 1 tablespoon oil; top with remaining ¼ cup cucumber and chives. Garnish with Aleppo pepper, if desired. Serve cold. Serves 8 (serving size: about ⅔ cup)

CALORIES 139; **FAT** 7g (sat 1g, unsat 6g); **PROTEIN** 5g; **CARB** 15g; **FIBER** 1g; **SUGARS** 8g (added sugars 0g); **SODIUM** 178mg; **CALC** 4% DV; **POTASSIUM** 5% DV

Double-Serrano Watermelon Bites

Hands-on: 15 min. **Total:** 15 min.
These bites are a step up from classic prosciutto-wrapped melon and provide sweet, spicy, salty, tart, and meaty tastes. If you can't find serrano ham, use prosciutto; you also can use balsamic glaze in place of pomegranate molasses.

1 lb. seedless watermelon, cut into 16 (2-inch) cubes
2 oz. thinly sliced serrano ham, cut into 16 strips
1 serrano chile, cut into 16 slices
1 Tbsp. pomegranate molasses
2 tsp. thinly sliced fresh mint

1. Wrap each watermelon cube with 1 ham slice; top each with 1 chile slice. Place on a serving platter. Drizzle evenly with pomegranate molasses; sprinkle with mint. Serve immediately. Serves 8 (serving size: 2 pieces)

CALORIES 38; **FAT** 1g (sat 0g, unsat 1g); **PROTEIN** 2g; **CARB** 6g; **FIBER** 0g; **SUGARS** 5g (added sugars 0g); **SODIUM** 191mg; **CALC** 0% DV; **POTASSIUM** 2% DV

Ratatouille Zucchini "Bruschetta"

Hands-on: 20 min. **Total:** 55 min.
In this lighter version of bruschetta, crisp zucchini stands in for bread. The ratatouille is delicious left over (even cold), so go ahead and make a double batch to enjoy on pizza or pasta.

2 tsp. olive oil
1 cup chopped yellow onion
2½ cups chopped eggplant
½ cup chopped red bell pepper
1 cup halved grape tomatoes, divided
1 tsp. minced fresh garlic
½ cup lower-sodium vegetable stock
1 Tbsp. white wine vinegar
2 tsp. granulated sugar
⅓ tsp. kosher salt
¼ tsp. black pepper
2 Tbsp. small fresh basil leaves, divided
1 lb. zucchini, cut diagonally into ½-inch-thick slices
1 garlic clove, halved
1 oz. goat cheese, crumbled (about ¼ cup)

1. Heat oil in a medium stockpot over medium-high. Add onion; cook, stirring occasionally, until translucent, 4 to 5 minutes. Add eggplant; cook, stirring occasionally, until softened, 4 to 5 minutes. Add bell pepper, ½ cup tomatoes, and minced garlic to onion mixture; cook, stirring occasionally, until softened, 4 to 5 minutes.
2. Process remaining ½ cup tomatoes in a blender until smooth. Add pureed tomatoes, stock, vinegar, sugar, salt, and black pepper to onion mixture. Bring to a boil, stirring occasionally. Reduce heat to low; cover and simmer until mixture is the consistency of marmalade, about 20 minutes. Remove from heat; cool to room temperature, about 15 minutes. Stir in 1 tablespoon basil.
3. Rub zucchini slices with cut sides of garlic clove; discard garlic. Top each zucchini slice with 1½ tablespoons ratatouille. Top evenly with goat cheese, and sprinkle with remaining 1 tablespoon basil. Serve at room temperature. Serves 8 (serving size: 2 pieces)

CALORIES 56; **FAT** 2g (sat 1g, unsat 1g); **PROTEIN** 2g; **CARB** 8g; **FIBER** 2g; **SUGARS** 5g (added sugars 1g); **SODIUM** 149mg; **CALC** 3% DV; **POTASSIUM** 9% DV

SALADS

Great salads are works of art. More than just greens drizzled with dressing, they're created with intention in order to balance flavors, textures, and colors. Earthy kale melds with sweet cherries, crunchy fried farro tops juicy tomatoes, and red onions pop against a backdrop of green and yellow beans. Look no further for your new favorites.

Four Bean (and One Pea) Salad

Hands-on: 15 min. **Total:** 20 min.
We've updated the tired three-bean staple with a wonderful variety of textures, colors, and shapes. It's a gorgeous salad that you'll be proud to serve at your next backyard barbecue. Charring the snap peas and edamame adds robust flavor notes that complement the zip of the dressing and the mild taste of the green beans.

5 Tbsp. extra-virgin olive oil
5 Tbsp. white wine vinegar
1 Tbsp. granulated sugar
⅝ tsp. kosher salt
¾ tsp. black pepper
8 cups water
4 oz. haricots verts (French green beans), trimmed and halved diagonally
4 oz. yellow wax beans, trimmed and halved diagonally
2 tsp. canola oil
1 cup shelled fresh edamame or fresh chickpeas (garbanzo beans) (about 5½ oz.)
4 oz. sugar snap peas
1 (15-oz.) can unsalted cannellini beans, rinsed and drained
1 cup diagonally sliced celery
1 cup vertically sliced red onion
½ cup coarsely chopped fresh flat-leaf parsley

1. Whisk together olive oil, vinegar, sugar, salt, and pepper in a medium bowl. Set aside.

2. Bring 8 cups water to a boil in a large saucepan over high. Add haricots verts and wax beans; cook until crisp-tender, about 5 minutes. Drain and transfer beans to a bowl of ice water. Let stand until chilled, about 10 minutes. Drain and set aside.

3. Heat canola oil in a large skillet over medium-high. Add edamame and sugar snap peas; cook, stirring occasionally, until lightly charred, about 3 minutes. Cover and cook until peas are tender, about 1 minute.

4. Add edamame mixture, cannellini beans, celery, onion, and parsley to olive oil mixture; toss to coat. Add chilled green beans and wax beans; toss to coat before serving. Serves 6 (serving size: 1 cup)

CALORIES 252; FAT 14g (sat 2g, unsat 11g); PROTEIN 7g; CARB 25g; FIBER 7g; SUGARS 5g (added sugars 2g); SODIUM 252mg; CALC 9% DV; POTASSIUM 11% DV

Make Ahead • Vegetarian

Triple Tomato Salad with Crispy Farro

Hands-on: 25 min.
Total: 1 day, 5 hr. 25 min.
Our salad update is a spectacular platter of tomatoes treated in all the ways that make the most of their flavor: pickled, roasted, and left raw. It does involve a few steps, but you can fry the farro and pickle the green tomatoes a few days in advance to get ahead.

1½ cups white vinegar
1 cup water
2 dill sprigs
1 Tbsp. granulated sugar
¼ tsp. crushed red pepper
12 oz. green tomatoes (2 to 3 inches in diameter), cut crosswise into ½-inch-thick slices
1 lb. grape tomatoes, halved
3 Tbsp. extra-virgin olive oil, divided
½ tsp. black pepper
1 cup canola oil
¼ cup cooked farro, patted very dry
¼ tsp. paprika
1 lb. medium-sized heirloom tomatoes (2 to 3 tomatoes), cut into wedges
2 Tbsp. apple cider vinegar
2 tsp. honey
¾ tsp. kosher salt
½ cup vertically sliced shallots
2 Tbsp. torn fresh dill

1. Combine vinegar, 1 cup water, dill sprigs, sugar, and crushed red pepper in a small saucepan. Bring mixture to a boil over high, stirring occasionally, until sugar dissolves.

2. Place green tomato slices in a 1-quart wide-mouth glass jar. Pour hot vinegar mixture over tomato slices. Cover with lid; chill 1 to 3 days.

3. Preheat oven to 200°F. Place grape tomatoes on a parchment paper-lined rimmed baking sheet. Drizzle with 1 tablespoon olive oil, and toss to coat. Arrange tomato halves cut sides up. Sprinkle with black pepper. Bake at 200°F until very soft and dehydrated, about 5 hours. Cool tomatoes to room temperature, about 10 minutes.

4. Heat canola oil in a large saucepan over medium-high. When oil is very hot but not yet smoking, add cooked farro. Cook, stirring often, until very crispy, about 3 minutes. Using a slotted spoon, transfer farro to a paper towel-lined plate to drain. Let stand 30 seconds; sprinkle with paprika.

5. Drain green tomatoes; discard liquid. Arrange green tomatoes and heirloom tomatoes on a serving platter. Top with roasted grape tomatoes. Whisk together apple cider vinegar, remaining 2 tablespoons olive oil, and honey in a small bowl. Drizzle tomatoes with dressing, and sprinkle with salt, shallots, torn dill, and fried farro. Serves 6 (serving size: about ¾ cup)

CALORIES 165; FAT 12g (sat 1g, unsat 10g); PROTEIN 2g; CARB 14g; FIBER 3g; SUGARS 9g (added sugars 2g); SODIUM 256mg; CALC 3% DV; POTASSIUM 14% DV

Korean Skirt Steak Salad

Hands-on: 25 min. **Total:** 12 hr. 25 min. This dinner salad is an exciting twist on a taco salad: Crisped wonton wedges replace tortilla strips, marinated skirt steak stands in for ground beef, and bok choy subs in for lettuce. Gochugaru—Korean red pepper flakes—is worth seeking out at an Asian market. It has a slightly sweet, deeply roasted flavor and not as much chile heat as you'd expect. Use it anywhere you want some gentle heat and a robust savory note: sprinkled on eggs, kebabs, hummus, roasted vegetables, and grilled corn.

1 small bunch scallions
⅓ cup granulated sugar
¼ cup lower-sodium soy sauce
1½ Tbsp. chili garlic sauce
¼ cup rice vinegar, divided
1 Tbsp. minced fresh garlic
¼ cup toasted sesame oil, divided
1 lb. skirt steak
10 square wonton wrappers
Cooking spray
1 Tbsp. gochugaru (optional)
⅛ tsp. kosher salt
6 (2-oz.) baby bok choy, thinly sliced
    (about 4 cups)
1 cup kimchi (about 5 oz.)
1 cup matchstick-cut daikon radish
    (about 3 oz.)
1 ripe avocado, diced

1. Thinly slice white parts of scallions; set aside green tops. Combine white scallion slices, sugar, soy sauce, chili garlic sauce, 2 tablespoons rice vinegar, garlic, and 1 tablespoon sesame oil in a large ziplock plastic bag. Seal bag, and gently shake to combine. Add steak, and seal bag. Massage bag to coat steak with marinade. Chill 12 hours or up to 1 day. Remove steak from bag; discard marinade.
2. Stack 5 wonton wrappers on top of each other. Using a pizza cutter, cut wonton stack diagonally into quarters to form wedges. Repeat procedure with remaining 5 wonton wrappers.
3. Heat 2 tablespoons sesame oil in a large skillet over medium-high. Place half of wonton wedges in hot oil; cook, stirring occasionally, until crisp and browned, 1 to 2 minutes. Using a slotted spoon, transfer fried wonton wedges to a paper towel–lined plate to drain. Repeat procedure with remaining half of wonton wedges.
4. Heat a grill pan over high, and lightly coat with cooking spray. Add steak to pan; cook to desired degree of doneness, 2 to 4 minutes per side for medium-rare. Let stand at least 5 minutes, and cut against the grain into thin slices.
5. Whisk together remaining 2 tablespoons rice vinegar; remaining 1 tablespoon sesame oil; gochugaru, if desired; and salt in a medium bowl. Cut green scallion tops into 2-inch pieces, and cut each piece in half lengthwise. Add green scallion slices and bok choy to dressing; toss to coat. Divide bok choy mixture evenly among 4 bowls. Top evenly with kimchi and daikon. Divide steak slices, fried wontons, and avocado evenly among bowls. Serves 4 (serving size: 1 salad)

CALORIES 408; FAT 24g (sat 6g, unsat 16g); PROTEIN 29g; CARB 21g; FIBER 4g; SUGARS 5g (added sugars 3g); SODIUM 635mg; CALC 12% DV; POTASSIUM 20% DV

Vegetarian

Kale and Wheat Berry Salad with Fresh Cherry Dressing

Hands-on: 25 min. **Total:** 1 hr. 10 min. Fresh summer touches bring what is typically a cool-weather salad firmly into the season. Fresh cherries perform double duty, featuring in both the dressing (in which they're pureed) and the finished salad. Curly kale has a hearty, slightly tough texture, but massaging it with the salt tenderizes it nicely. If you'd rather use baby kale, you can skip the massage. If you have trouble finding watermelon radishes, any radishes will work beautifully.

6 cups water
¼ cup uncooked wheat berries
1½ cups pitted fresh cherries (about
    9 oz.), divided
2 Tbsp. apple cider vinegar
1½ Tbsp. extra-virgin olive oil
2 tsp. grainy Dijon mustard
½ tsp. black pepper
2 (6-oz.) bunches curly kale,
    stemmed and torn
¼ tsp. kosher salt
½ cup very thinly sliced baby
    watermelon radishes (about 1 oz.)
¼ cup firmly packed small fresh
    mint leaves
2 oz. Marcona almonds

1. Combine 6 cups water and wheat berries in a medium saucepan; bring to a boil over high. Reduce heat to medium-low, and simmer until tender, 50 minutes to 1 hour. Drain well.

2. Place ⅓ cup cherries in a mini food processor. Add vinegar, oil, mustard, and pepper; process until very smooth, about 1 minute.

3. Place kale in a medium bowl; sprinkle with salt. Use your hands to firmly massage salt into kale until leaves are slightly softened, 1 to 2 minutes. Add wheat berries and three-fourths of the dressing to massaged kale; toss to coat. Cut remaining 1 cup cherries in half lengthwise. Add halved cherries, radish slices, and mint leaves to kale mixture; toss gently to combine. Sprinkle with almonds, and drizzle with remaining dressing. Serve immediately. Serves 4 (serving size: about 2 cups)

CALORIES 253; FAT 15g (sat 2g, unsat 12g); PROTEIN 8g; CARB 27g; FIBER 7g; SUGARS 10g (added sugars 0g); SODIUM 362mg; CALC 17% DV; POTASSIUM 15% DV

MAINS

Get out of your dinner rut with these playful summer dishes. We've added a little Chinese takeout flair to backyard-barbecue chicken, piled burgers high with crunchy pickled vegetables and special sauce, and made over a beloved French classic with a hearty, whole-grain base. Just add rosé and dinner is done.

Make Ahead

Tuna Niçoise Whole-Grain Bowls

Hands-on: 30 min. **Total:** 45 min. We combined the classic Niçoise combo of haricots verts, potatoes, hard-cooked eggs, tuna, and olives with whole-grain rye berries, which have a nutty, faintly peppery-tangy flavor. If you can't find them, use farro or wheat berries.

1 cup uncooked rye berries
4 large eggs
8 oz. small red potatoes
8 oz. haricots verts (French green beans) or green beans
1 (8-oz.) tuna steak (½-inch-thick)
Cooking spray
½ tsp. kosher salt
½ tsp. ground fennel seeds
¾ tsp. black pepper, divided
¼ cup plus 1½ tsp. extra-virgin olive oil
3 Tbsp. fresh lemon juice
2 Tbsp. minced shallot
1 Tbsp. chopped fresh thyme
1½ tsp. Dijon mustard
¼ cup firmly packed fresh flat-leaf parsley leaves
1 cup halved grape tomatoes
2 oz. pitted picholine olives, halved (about ½ cup)

1. Place rye berries in a medium saucepan; add water to cover by 1 inch. Bring to a boil over high. Reduce heat to medium; cover and simmer 5 minutes. Carefully add eggs; cover and simmer 7 minutes. Using a slotted spoon, transfer eggs to a bowl of ice water. Cover saucepan, and continue to cook rye berries, stirring occasionally, until tender but still chewy, 18 to 23 minutes. Drain and rinse rye berries. Peel eggs, and halve crosswise.

2. Place potatoes in a saucepan; add water to cover by 2 inches. Bring to a boil over high. Reduce heat to low, and simmer 10 minutes. Add haricots verts; simmer 6 minutes. Using a slotted spoon or tongs, transfer haricots verts to a bowl of ice water. Continue to cook potatoes until tender, 2 to 3 minutes more. Drain and rinse with cold water. Cut potatoes into quarters.

3. Heat a cast-iron skillet over medium-high 5 minutes. Lightly coat tuna with cooking spray; sprinkle evenly with salt, ground fennel, and ½ teaspoon pepper. Coat skillet with cooking spray. Add tuna, and cook to desired degree of doneness, about 1 minute and 30 seconds per side for rare. Remove from skillet.

4. Whisk together oil, lemon juice, shallot, thyme, Dijon, and remaining ¼ teaspoon pepper in a small bowl.

5. Stir together rye berries, parsley, and half of dressing. Divide mixture evenly among 4 bowls. Top with potatoes, haricots verts, tomatoes, and olives. Thinly slice tuna against the grain. Top salads evenly with tuna slices and egg halves. Drizzle with remaining dressing. Serves 4 (serving size: 1 bowl)

CALORIES 521; FAT 24g (sat 4g, unsat 17g); PROTEIN 29g; CARB 51g; FIBER 10g; SUGARS 4g (added sugars 0g); SODIUM 713mg; CALC 10% DV; POTASSIUM 24% DV

Grilled General Tso's Chicken

Hands-on: 45 min. **Total:** 3 hr. 20 min.

1 (4-lb.) whole chicken
3 Tbsp. lower-sodium soy sauce
3 Tbsp. canola oil
¼ cup unsalted ketchup
3 Tbsp. light corn syrup
1¼ Tbsp. apple cider vinegar
1 tsp. grated garlic
½ tsp. crushed red pepper
½ tsp. kosher salt, divided
2 bunches scallions, trimmed
1 red bell pepper
1 yellow bell pepper
Cooking spray
¼ cup firmly packed fresh cilantro
   leaves
1 Tbsp. toasted sesame seeds

1. Place chicken, breast side down, on a cutting board. Using kitchen shears, cut along both sides of the backbone; remove and discard backbone. Turn chicken breast side up; press firmly against breastbone with heel of your hand, splaying chicken open and flattening it slightly, butterfly style. Trim excess fat. Combine soy sauce and oil in a large ziplock plastic bag; add chicken. Seal bag; chill 1 to 2 hours. Drain chicken; discard marinade. Pat chicken dry.
2. Whisk together ketchup, corn syrup, vinegar, garlic, crushed red pepper, and ¼ teaspoon salt until smooth. Set aside.
3. Preheat a gas grill to high (450°F to 550°F) on one side, or push hot coals to one side of a charcoal grill. Place chicken, breast side down, on oiled grates over lit side of grill. Grill chicken, uncovered, rotating (but not flipping) often, until skin is crispy, 6 to 8 minutes. (Make sure to keep rotating chicken to prevent flare-ups.) Place chicken, breast side up, over unlit side of grill, and grill, covered, until a thermometer inserted in thickest portion registers 165°F, about 35 minutes.
4. About 10 minutes before chicken is done, coat scallions and bell peppers with cooking spray. Grill, turning often, until lightly charred, 4 to 5 minutes for scallions and 6 to 7 minutes for bell peppers. Transfer vegetables to a cutting board. Cut scallions into 2-inch pieces, and cut bell peppers into strips.
5. Arrange grilled vegetables on a serving platter; sprinkle with remaining ¼ teaspoon salt. Place chicken on top of vegetables, and brush chicken with ¼ cup sauce. Sprinkle evenly with cilantro and sesame seeds, and serve with remaining sauce. Serves 4 (serving size: ¼ chicken, about ½ cup vegetables, and about 1 Tbsp. sauce)

CALORIES 530; FAT 23g (sat 5g, unsat 16g); PROTEIN 53g; CARB 27g; FIBER 3g; SUGARS 21g (added sugars 15g); SODIUM 541mg; CALC 8% DV; POTASSIUM 20% DV

Staff Favorite

Banh Mi Burgers

Hands-on: 25 min. **Total:** 1 hr.
Here, a basic beef burger takes some cues from the classic Vietnamese sandwich and cranks its flavor up to 10. We enjoy our burgers cooked to medium (140°F) for more juiciness, and we always purchase the meat from a trusted source. You can cook the patties to your desired degree of doneness; the USDA recommends 160°F for ground beef.

½ cup rice vinegar
½ cup water
¼ cup granulated sugar
1 cup shaved English cucumber
1 cup matchstick-cut carrots
6 Tbsp. canola mayonnaise
2 Tbsp. Sriracha chili sauce
1 Tbsp. fresh lime juice
1 lb. 93% lean ground beef
2 Tbsp. olive oil
2 tsp. grated garlic
1 tsp. grated peeled fresh ginger
¾ tsp. black pepper
Cooking spray
4 whole-grain hamburger buns,
   split and toasted
1½ cups loosely packed cilantro
   sprigs
2 serrano chiles, thinly sliced

1. Bring vinegar, ½ cup water, and sugar to a boil in a small saucepan over high. Combine cucumber and carrots in a heatproof bowl; pour hot vinegar mixture over vegetables. Cover and chill at least 15 minutes or up to 3 days.
2. Stir together mayonnaise, Sriracha, and lime juice; set aside.
3. Preheat grill to medium-high (about 450°F). Combine beef, oil, garlic, ginger, and black pepper in a bowl; gently mix just until ingredients are incorporated. Shape mixture into 4 (½-inch-thick) patties. Place patties on a grill grate coated with cooking spray. Grill, covered, until a thermometer inserted in thickest portion registers 140°F, about 3 minutes per side, or to desired degree of doneness. Remove from heat, and keep warm.
4. Spread about 1 tablespoon mayonnaise mixture on each bun half. Place 1 burger patty on each bottom bun half. Drain cucumber mixture; place about ¼ cup on each burger. Divide cilantro sprigs and chiles among burgers. Cover with top halves of buns. Serves 4 (serving size: 1 burger)

CALORIES 407; FAT 20g (sat 3g, unsat 15g); PROTEIN 27g; CARB 32g; FIBER 5g; SUGARS 9g (added sugars 3g); SODIUM 623mg; CALC 7% DV; POTASSIUM 9% DV

SIDES

Impress your friends at the next potluck or picnic gathering by toting along one of these tasty side dishes. Each recipe dusts off a summer classic and deeply infuses it with far more flavor than the traditional version, from smoky beer-poached corn to Indian-spiced baked beans to chargrilled cabbage slaw.

Fast • Gluten Free
Make Ahead • Vegetarian

Cauliflower Salad with Herbs

Hands-on: 30 min. **Total:** 30 min.
You've likely had cauliflower bits as a carb-conscious sub for rice. Now the mild crucifer replaces spuds for a lighter take on potato salad. Turn this into a light meal by upping the egg amount to a whole egg per person.

1 (1½-lb.) head cauliflower, cut into florets
1 Tbsp. apple cider vinegar
1 tsp. grainy mustard
½ tsp. black pepper
⅜ tsp. kosher salt
2 Tbsp. olive oil
4 large eggs
3 Tbsp. finely chopped cornichons (about 8 cornichons) or pickles
1 Tbsp. chopped fresh dill
1 Tbsp. chopped fresh flat-leaf parsley
1 Tbsp. chopped fresh chives

1. Bring 1 inch of water to a boil over medium-high in a large saucepan fitted with a steamer basket. Place cauliflower florets in steamer basket; cover and cook until tender, 8 to 9 minutes. Transfer cauliflower to a bowl of ice water. Let stand 5 minutes; drain well.
2. Whisk together vinegar, mustard, pepper, and salt in a small bowl. Gradually add oil, whisking constantly, until emulsified. Set aside.
3. Bring 1 inch of water to a boil over medium-high in saucepan fitted with steamer basket. Place eggs in steamer basket; cover and cook 8 minutes. Transfer eggs to a bowl of ice water. Let stand until chilled, about 6 minutes. Drain. Peel eggs, and cut in half lengthwise.
4. Combine cauliflower, cornichons, dill, parsley, and chives in a large bowl. Drizzle with vinegar mixture, and toss to coat. Top with egg halves. Serve at room temperature. Serves 8 (serving size: about ½ cup salad and 1 egg half)

CALORIES 90; **FAT** 6g (sat 1g, unsat 4g); **PROTEIN** 5g; **CARB** 5g; **FIBER** 2g; **SUGARS** 2g (added sugars 0g); **SODIUM** 224mg; **CALC** 4% DV; **POTASSIUM** 9% DV

Staff Favorite • Gluten Free

Grilled Wedge-Salad Slaw

Hands-on: 40 min. **Total:** 45 min.
We took the irresistible toppings from a wedge salad—namely bacon and blue cheese dressing—and added them to coleslaw. The cabbage goes onto the grill in wedges to pick up smoky char, then is chopped for the slaw.

6 bacon slices, coarsely chopped
1 head green cabbage (about 2¼ lb.), cut into 8 wedges
Cooking spray
1 pt. cherry tomatoes, halved
2 medium scallions, thinly sliced (about ½ cup)
1 oz. blue cheese, crumbled (about ¼ cup)
¼ cup canola mayonnaise
¼ cup olive oil
2 tsp. white wine vinegar
½ tsp. black pepper
¼ tsp. kosher salt

1. Cook bacon in a skillet over medium, stirring often, until crisp, 10 to 12 minutes. Drain on a paper towel–lined plate.
2. Preheat grill to medium-high (about 450°F). Spray cut sides of cabbage with cooking spray. Grill, uncovered, until charred and tender, 2 to 3 minutes per side. Transfer to a cutting board, and coarsely chop. Transfer to a large bowl. Add bacon, tomatoes, and scallions.
3. Stir together blue cheese, mayonnaise, oil, vinegar, pepper, and salt in a small bowl. (Mixture will look curdled.) Drizzle over cabbage mixture; toss to coat. Serve immediately. Serves 8 (serving size: 1 cup)

CALORIES 163; **FAT** 12g (sat 2g, unsat 9g); **PROTEIN** 6g; **CARB** 13g; **FIBER** 6g; **SUGARS** 6g (added sugars 0g); **SODIUM** 248mg; **CALC** 10% DV; **POTASSIUM** 15% DV

Indian Dal Baked Beans

Hands-on: 20 min. **Total:** 45 min.
The standard backyard-barbecue side takes a global turn with warm spices, but the beans are still perfectly at home alongside burgers and hot dogs.

2 Tbsp. unsalted butter
1½ cups chopped white onion
2 Tbsp. minced fresh garlic
1 Tbsp. cumin seeds
2 tsp. grated peeled fresh ginger
1 tsp. brown mustard seeds
1 tsp. curry powder
1 (26.46-oz.) pkg. chopped tomatoes (such as Pomì)
6 Tbsp. pure maple syrup
1 Tbsp. tomato paste
4 (15-oz.) cans unsalted navy beans, drained and rinsed
3 Tbsp. heavy cream
2 tsp. kosher salt
Cooking spray
¼ cup chopped fresh cilantro

1. Preheat oven to 350°F.
2. Melt butter in a Dutch oven over medium. Add onion; cook, stirring occasionally, until softened, about 4 minutes. Add garlic, cumin seeds, ginger, mustard seeds, and curry; cook, stirring often, until fragrant, about 2 minutes. Add tomatoes, maple syrup, and tomato paste; bring to a boil over medium-high, stirring occasionally. Reduce heat to medium, and simmer, stirring occasionally, until slightly thickened, about 5 minutes. Stir in beans, cream, and salt.
3. Pour mixture into a 13- x 9-inch baking dish coated with cooking spray. Bake at 350°F until bubbly, 25 to 30 minutes. Top with cilantro. Serves 12 (serving size: ⅔ cup)

CALORIES 205; **FAT** 4g (sat 2g, unsat 1g); **PROTEIN** 9g; **CARB** 35g; **FIBER** 9g; **SUGARS** 9g (added sugars 6g); **SODIUM** 354mg; **CALC** 12% DV; **POTASSIUM** 12% DV

Smoky Beer-Poached Grilled Corn

Hands-on: 30 min. **Total:** 30 min.
We took a technique that's typically used for bratwurst and applied it to corn—with amazing results.

1 (½-inch-thick) sweet onion slice
Cooking spray
5 (12-oz.) bottles lager beer
8 ears fresh sweet corn, husks pulled back
3 Tbsp. unsalted butter, softened
2 tsp. grainy mustard
1⅛ tsp. kosher salt
¼ tsp. black pepper
½ cup malt vinegar

1. Preheat grill to medium-high (about 450°F). Coat onion slice with cooking spray; grill, uncovered, until charred and tender, 3 to 4 minutes per side. Transfer to a small bowl, and cover with plastic wrap. Let stand until fully tender, about 10 minutes. Keep grill hot.
2. Meanwhile, bring beer to a boil in a large Dutch oven over medium-high; add corn, and return to a boil. Remove from heat; cover and let stand until corn is mostly tender, 5 to 8 minutes. Drain.
3. Finely chop onion slice. Stir together onion, butter, mustard, salt, and pepper. Shape into a 4-inch log; wrap in plastic wrap, and chill until ready to use.
4. Grill corn, uncovered, turning often, until charred and fully tender, 5 to 6 minutes. Drizzle hot corn with vinegar, and serve with butter mixture. Serves 8 (serving size: 1 ear corn and about 1 ½ tsp. butter mixture)

CALORIES 142; **FAT** 6g (sat 3g, unsat 3g); **PROTEIN** 4g; **CARB** 20g; **FIBER** 2g; **SUGARS** 7g (added sugars 0g); **SODIUM** 320mg; **CALC** 1% DV; **POTASSIUM** 8% DV

DESSERTS

The sweets of summer are always most delicious when they're based on the season's freshest fruit. We use peaches, raspberries—even avocados and fruit-based sorbets—for a lighter approach to time-honored desserts. Bonus: All feed a crowd, so they're perfect for your warm-weather gatherings.

Striped Yogurt-and-Sorbet Sandwiches

Hands-on: 45 min. **Total:** 4 hr. 45 min.

DOUGH
2.6 oz. whole-wheat pastry flour (about ¾ cup)
2.1 oz. all-purpose flour (about ½ cup)
1 tsp. baking powder
1 tsp. ground cinnamon
¼ tsp. kosher salt
⅛ tsp. grated fresh nutmeg
2 Tbsp. cold unsalted butter, cut into pieces
2 Tbsp. honey
2 Tbsp. molasses
2 Tbsp. whole milk
1 tsp. vanilla extract

FILLING
1 cup raspberry sorbet, softened
1 cup vanilla low-fat frozen yogurt, softened
1 cup mango sorbet, softened

1. Prepare the dough: Pulse flours, baking powder, cinnamon, salt, and nutmeg in a food processor until combined. Add butter; pulse until mixture looks like small peas.
2. Whisk together honey, molasses, milk, and vanilla in a small bowl.

Gradually add honey mixture to flour mixture, processing just until combined, about 2 minutes. Wrap dough in plastic wrap, and chill 2 hours or up to 2 days.

3. Preheat oven to 350°F.

4. Unwrap dough, and place on a lightly floured surface. Roll dough out into a 10- x 8-inch rectangle. (You also can make 2 [5- x 4-inch] rectangles.) Cut dough into 20 (2-inch) squares.

5. Place dough squares on 2 parchment paper–lined baking sheets. Using dull end of a wooden skewer, decoratively dot cookies (do not pierce). Use a graham cracker as a template, if desired.

6. Bake at 350°F for 6 minutes. Cool cookies completely on baking sheets on wire racks, about 20 minutes.

7. Prepare the filling: Spread raspberry sorbet in an 11- x 7-inch rimmed baking sheet lined with parchment paper. Freeze 30 minutes. Spread vanilla frozen yogurt over raspberry sorbet; freeze 30 minutes. Spread mango sorbet over vanilla frozen yogurt; freeze until all layers are firm, about 30 minutes.

8. Cut sorbet mixture evenly into 10 rectangles. Sandwich 1 rectangle between 2 cookies; repeat with remaining sorbet mixture and cookies. Wrap each sandwich in plastic wrap, and freeze until ready to eat. Serves 10 (serving size: 1 sandwich)

CALORIES 193; FAT 3g (sat 2g, unsat 1g); PROTEIN 3g; CARB 38g; FIBER 2g; SUGARS 22g (added sugars 13g); SODIUM 164mg; CALC 9% DV; POTASSIUM 5% DV

Gluten Free • Vegetarian

Pavlova Layer Cake with Raspberries and Peaches

Hands-on: 45 min. **Total:** 2 hr.

MERINGUES
6 large egg whites, at room temperature
Dash of kosher salt
1 tsp. cream of tartar
1 vanilla bean pod, halved lengthwise
1⅔ cups granulated sugar
2 Tbsp. plus 2 tsp. cornstarch

FILLING
2 tsp. fresh lemon thyme leaves (or 1½ tsp. thyme leaves and ½ tsp. lemon zest) (optional)
¼ cup granulated sugar, divided
2 large yellow peaches, peeled and thinly sliced (about 8 oz.)
2 cups fresh raspberries
1⅓ cups plain fat-free Greek yogurt
¼ cup crème fraîche
Lemon thyme sprigs (optional)

1. Preheat oven to 250°F.

2. Prepare meringues: Beat egg whites and salt with an electric mixer fitted with whisk attachment on medium-high speed until foamy. Add cream of tartar; beat until soft peaks form.

3. Scrape vanilla bean seeds from pod into a small bowl; discard pod. Whisk together sugar, cornstarch, and half of the vanilla seeds in a second small bowl. Set aside remaining vanilla seeds. Gradually add sugar mixture to egg white mixture, beating on medium-high speed until stiff, shiny peaks form, about 5 minutes (do not overbeat).

4. Line 3 baking sheets with parchment paper, and spread meringue mixture into 3 (8-inch) circles on prepared baking sheets. Bake at 250°F for 1 hour and 15 minutes. Turn oven off, and open oven door just slightly. Let meringues stand in oven 30 minutes.

5. Prepare filling: If using, combine lemon thyme leaves and 2 tablespoons sugar in a small bowl; rub mixture together using your fingertips. Place peach slices in one bowl and raspberries in a second bowl. Sprinkle sugar mixture evenly over peaches and raspberries; toss each to combine.

6. Whisk together yogurt, crème fraîche, remaining vanilla bean seeds, and remaining 2 tablespoons sugar in a small bowl until smooth.

7. Assemble the pavlova cake: Place 1 meringue round on a cake stand or platter. Spread with a thin layer of yogurt mixture, and top with about three-fourths of the peaches. Top with second meringue round. Spread with a thin layer of yogurt mixture and top with about three-fourths of the raspberries. Top with third meringue round. Spread with remaining yogurt mixture, and arrange remaining peaches and raspberries on top of pavlova cake. Garnish with lemon thyme sprigs, if desired. Serve immediately. Serves 16 (serving size: 1 slice)

CALORIES 158; FAT 3g (sat 2g, unsat 0g); PROTEIN 4g; CARB 30g; FIBER 1g; SUGARS 27g (added sugars 24g); SODIUM 38mg; CALC 3% DV; POTASSIUM 4% DV

Make Ahead · Vegetarian

Key Lime Ice Pops

Hands-on: 10 min. **Total:** 4 hr. 10 min. This frozen treat offers all you love about Key lime pie in a neat handheld package. Ripe avocados are the key to making these pops rich and indulgent, and they make the texture creamy and smooth instead of icy. The avocados also plump up the dessert with heart-healthy unsaturated fats, which keep you satisfied. Try to keep the graham cracker crumbs coarse so that the pops have more texture; fine crumbs might end up soggy.

¾ cup water
⅔ cup granulated sugar
4 large lime peel strips
1½ cups chopped ripe avocado (from 2 large avocados)
½ cup plain 2% reduced-fat Greek yogurt
½ cup bottled Key lime juice
2 tsp. lime zest (from 1 lime)
1 tsp. vanilla extract
¼ cup coarse graham cracker crumbs

1. Bring ¾ cup water, sugar, and lime peel strips to a boil in a small saucepan over medium. Reduce heat to medium-low, and cook, stirring constantly, until sugar dissolves, about 5 minutes. Remove from heat, and cool completely, about 30 minutes. Remove and discard lime peel strips.
2. Process lime simple syrup, avocado, yogurt, Key lime juice, lime zest, and vanilla in a blender until smooth. Pour mixture evenly into 7 ice-pop molds. Sprinkle evenly with graham cracker crumbs, pushing some crumbs down slightly into the lime mixture. Freeze 30 minutes.
3. Insert 1 craft stick into each pop. Freeze 3 hours before serving. Serves 7 (serving size: 1 ice pop)

CALORIES 155; FAT 5g (sat 1g, unsat 4g); PROTEIN 3g; CARB 26g; FIBER 2g; SUGARS 21g (added sugars 19g); SODIUM 25mg; CALC 2% DV; POTASSIUM 5% DV

THE TEACHER

THE SUMMER OF HERB LOVE

BY ANDREA NGUYEN

July is an absolute herb fest. Our tips, tricks, and recipe ideas ensure they won't go to waste.

Like clockwork, it happens every year. The weather finally warms up in March, and I'm planting basil, tending to the scrappy mint and tarragon, and nursing volunteer seedlings. I'm a semi-negligent gardener, but come July, things are looking bushy and healthy. Midsummer is when I'm feeling blessed by my homegrown bounty. But what to do with nature's generosity? I can't let my hard-earned herbs go to waste.

The farmers market only complicates matters. Perky parsley, delicate bunches of cilantro with roots intact, and fresh-snipped bundles of mint, thyme, and savory beckon. I'm drawn to the showy displays and load up my tote.

Overbuying and overplanting are inevitable, but consuming a plethora of herbs is in my blood. Raised on mostly Vietnamese food, I learned to treat herbs like raw leafy green vegetables, chopping handfuls for composed salads, pinching leaves off their stems to drop into hot soups, and tucking them into lettuce and rice paper wraps as well as sandwiches. The aromatic leaves are more than mere garnishes—they contribute vibrant flavor, color, and texture to dishes.

My father loved to remind us that mint was great for digestion and lemongrass tea was a powerful detoxifying diuretic, but we didn't focus on the health benefits of herbs. We just knew that they completed our meals. Consequently, I learned to never waste herbs.

Because herbs are incredibly versatile, global ingredients, I eat loads of fresh herbs year-round, but I up my game in the summertime. They're perfect for casual summer cooking. Herb-heavy sauces such as pesto and chimichurri are great for using up multiple herbs by the handful. I tear or snip herb leaves to mix with lettuces for green salads. Chopped herbs enliven make-ahead dishes like potato salad. Whole herb sprigs can be steeped for refreshing shrubs (drinking vinegars) that may be used in mocktails or potent beverages. Any leftover sprigs get bunched together into a bouquet for my guests to enjoy at the dinner table.

To ensure that I always have herbs at the ready, I wash and spin sturdy ones such as cilantro, parsley, and dill before storing them with a paper towel in plastic bags or in recycled plastic boxes that once held salad mixes (be sure to use only food-safe boxes). When wilted basil needs resuscitating, I soak whole sprigs in water for 10 to 15 minutes, then spin them dry before using.

When I've chopped more herbs than I need, I store the leftovers in a small container covered tightly by plastic wrap, and I use them the next day. They might go into an omelet, frittata, or marinade where their browned edges won't be noticed. Lingering robust herbs such as rosemary, savory, or sage may be added to a jar of olive oil in the fridge to create an herb-infused oil for grilling.

At the start of each July, when herbs rush into my life and I wonder how I'll eat them all up, I remind myself that there are innumerable options for savoring this peak herbaceous season.

Gluten Free • Make Ahead

Herb-Scented Rice Salad

Hands-on: 20 min. **Total:** 20 min. Every summer, I revisit this refreshing Malaysian salad called *nasi ulam*. It's what I call an elastic classic—very flexible—so feel free to tinker with the recipe and change up the herbs to create your own twists. The salad tastes good up to 5 hours after you've combined all the ingredients, so it's a nice party or potluck dish. If you can find specialty varieties such as Thai or lemon basil, give them a try.

¼ cup unsweetened finely shredded
   dried coconut
1½ tsp. virgin coconut oil, melted
   and divided
⅓ cup loosely packed fresh basil
   leaves, cut into chiffonade
¼ cup loosely packed fresh mint
   leaves, cut into chiffonade
¼ cup loosely packed fresh cilantro
   leaves, chopped
3 Tbsp. chopped shallot or red
   onion, rinsed to reduce harshness
   and drained well
2 Tbsp. very thinly sliced or minced
   lemongrass (from 1 medium stalk,
   tough outer layers discarded)
2 tsp. lime zest
½ tsp. fine sea salt
¼ tsp. black pepper
3 cups cooked white jasmine rice, at
   room temperature
2 tsp. fish sauce
1 Tbsp. fresh lime juice

1. Place dried coconut and ½ teaspoon coconut oil in a medium skillet over medium. Cook, stirring often, until coconut begins to brown, 2 to 3 minutes. Continue to cook, stirring constantly to ensure even cooking, until coconut is fragrant and golden brown, 2 to 3 more minutes. Remove from heat and cool.

2. Using a large spoon, stir together basil, mint, cilantro, shallot (or onion), lemongrass, lime zest, salt, and pepper in a large bowl until well combined.

3. Add the rice, 3 tablespoons toasted coconut, and remaining 1 teaspoon coconut oil to herb mixture; toss to combine. Add fish sauce and lime juice. Toss, wait 5 minutes, and taste. Aim for a balance of all the flavors. The herbs are subtle, yet their pungent, fragrant selves should shine. Transfer rice mixture to a shallow dish or wide bowl; garnish with remaining toasted coconut. Serves 6 (serving size: ¾ cup)

CALORIES 176; FAT 3g (sat 3g, unsat 0g); PROTEIN 3g; CARB 34g; FIBER 2g; SUGARS 1g (added sugars 0g); SODIUM 351mg; CALC 3% DV; POTASSIUM 2% DV

HERB PREP 101: SIZE MATTERS

WHEN YOU'RE WORKING WITH FRESH HERBS, HOW YOU SERVE THEM VARIES WITH THE DISH AND THE HERB. HERE ARE FOUR COMMON PREP METHODS AND WHEN TO USE THEM.

FINELY CHOPPED
This cut releases the herb's oils into foods faster, dissipating the punch of flavor. Use finely chopped cilantro in pico de gallo.

COARSELY CHOPPED
This preparation allows herbs to stand out, preserving the integrity of their flavors. Perfect for showering over a just-baked pizza.

CHIFFONADE
For an elegant look with prominent flavor, stack broad-leaf herbs like basil and mint, cut into thin strips, and sprinkle over soups.

TORN OR RIPPED
For a casual look, gently tear soft-leaved herbs such as basil, dill, and cilantro for an ethereal yet robust addition to salads.

SAUTÉ YOUR FISH LIKE THIS

BY BARTON SEAVER

Don't be fooled into thinking high heat is a must. This gentle technique yields a juicy fillet and crisp skin.

Craving a restaurant-quality sautéed piece of fish? Try using less heat than what you're probably used to. Aim for medium to medium-high heat—it only takes a few minutes longer than high heat and, in fact, yields crispier skin and a juicier fillet. This gentle approach also has the added benefit of fewer vaporized fish oils filling your home with the not-always-desirable potpourri of the sea.

To successfully employ this technique, you must avoid fiddling. It's the pan that cooks the fish, not impatient pokes and prods from the cook. For the best results, place the fish in the pan skin side down, and leave it to cook undisturbed 90% of the way through. Fat located just under the skin melts to baste the fillet from the bottom up, crisp the skin evenly, and decrease the chance of sticking. Well-rendered fats make each fillet easily flippable, and it will need just another minute to finish cooking before it's ready to serve.

A wedge of seared lemon adds a little extra depth and complexity, as charring caramelizes the lemon's sugars.

Fast • Gluten Free

Sautéed Striped Bass with Lemon and Herb Sauce

Hands-on: 30 min. **Total:** 30 min. Striped bass can be strong-flavored for some, so we remove the pan drippings from the skillet before making the sauce for a milder final product.

4 (5-oz.) skin-on striped bass fillets (either hybrid striped bass or wild), patted dry
¼ tsp. black pepper
1 tsp. kosher salt, divided
1 lemon, halved lengthwise
3 Tbsp. olive oil
2 Tbsp. dry white wine
2 Tbsp. cold unsalted butter
2 Tbsp. chopped fresh parsley

1. Sprinkle fillets with pepper and ¾ teaspoon salt; let stand 20 minutes.
2. Heat a large nonstick skillet over medium-high. Add lemon, cut sides down, and cook until lightly charred, about 5 minutes. Add olive oil, and place fillets, skin sides down, in skillet with lemon. Cook, undisturbed, until sides of skin begin to brown and fish is almost fully opaque, 5 to 7 minutes.
3. When the fillets appear to be approximately 90% cooked through, gently shake skillet. When cooked with patience, the fish will release itself from the pan, allowing you to flip the fillets without sticking. Flip fillets, and cook 1 minute. Transfer fish and lemons to plates. Cut each lemon half into 2 wedges. Wipe skillet clean.

4. Reduce heat to medium-low, and add wine, remaining ¼ teaspoon salt, and butter. As butter melts, whisk to emulsify mixture. Spoon sauce over fillets. Sprinkle with parsley, and serve with a charred lemon wedge. Serves 4 (serving size: 1 fillet, 1 lemon wedge, and 1 Tbsp. sauce)

CALORIES 290; FAT 19g (sat 6g, unsat 12g); PROTEIN 26g; CARB 3g; FIBER 1g; SUGARS 0g; SODIUM 581mg; CALC 4% DV; POTASSIUM 9% DV

---

3 TIPS FOR

A BETTER SAUTÉED FILLET

SCORE THE SKIN
Some fish, particularly thinner fillets, curl over medium heat: Connective tissues just beneath the skin contract, forcing the fillet to arch away from the heat. To prevent curling, use a sharp knife to score the skin with shallow slashes about every inch or so prior to cooking.

USE OLIVE OIL
Striped bass, as well as halibut, mahi-mahi, and sablefish, pair well with olive oil; the oil's green flavors flatter particular characteristics of the fish. And because you're cooking over medium—not high—heat, the olive oil won't burn. Most fish are best friends with butter, so using a mix of the two fats yields a sauce that accentuates the subtle flavors of the fish.

PRACTICE PATIENCE
To properly sauté, you need patience—not manipulation. Cooking the fish nearly completely on the skin side keeps it moist, crisps the skin, and prevents sticking. The fish then can be easily flipped to finish cooking in a minute.

A QUICK DINNER FOR HOT SUMMER NIGHTS

BY GINA HOMOLKA

Refuel and rehydrate after a sticky summer day spent outdoors with this easy, speedy dinner.

You've heard me say it before: My favorite season is summer. There's nothing better than grilling and eating outside after a long day of working indoors. And even though this time of year means that my kids are out of school and I try to work less, I still put in a few full days a week. So when the kids come back to the house starving after playing for hours, I love to grill them something tasty, fresh, and hydrating—and, of course, fast.

This dish checks all of those boxes. It's on the table in less than 30 minutes, and it combines beautiful colors, healthy nutrients, and summer flavors. It's light, it's refreshing, and the colorful melon balls make me giddy because they take advantage of the season's fresh, ripe produce. It's a summer slam dunk!

I use my melon baller to make bite-sized balls (be sure to not use a mini ice cream scoop, which has a release in the scoop). Instead of using a melon baller, you could also cut the fruit into fun shapes with a cookie cutter—like stars for the Fourth of July. Or keep things casual and easy with classic cubes.

Fast • Gluten Free

Shrimp Kebabs with Mint and Melon Salad

Hands-on: 25 min. **Total:** 25 min. The shrimp is balanced with slight sweetness, bitter char, and tangy lime—a combination that complements the refreshing melon. Pick the ripest melons you can find; they should be firm but slightly soft and fragrant, especially near the stem end. Round out this dinner with your favorite grain or the Herb-Scented Rice Salad on page 167.

HONEY-LIME GLAZE
2 Tbsp. fresh lime juice
1 Tbsp. honey

MELON SALAD
1 medium honeydew melon, halved and seeded
1 medium cantaloupe, halved and seeded
1 small seedless watermelon, halved
2 Tbsp. lime zest
2 Tbsp. fresh lime juice
1 tsp. chopped fresh mint

SHRIMP
24 raw jumbo shrimp, peeled and deveined, tails on
4 (10-inch) skewers

1. Prepare the honey-lime glaze: Combine lime juice and honey in a bowl; set aside.
2. Prepare the melon salad: Using a 1¼-inch melon baller, scoop 24 balls of honeydew, 24 balls of cantaloupe, and 24 balls of watermelon, and transfer to a large bowl. Add lime zest, lime juice, and mint; toss to combine. Cover and chill until ready to eat.
3. Prepare the shrimp: Preheat a grill to high (450°F to 550°F), or heat a grill pan over high. Thread 6 shrimp onto each of 4 skewers. Grill shrimp until opaque, about 2 minutes per side. Brush both sides of shrimp with honey-lime glaze, and cook 15 more seconds per side.
4. Divide melon salad among 4 bowls, and serve with shrimp skewers. Serves 4 (serving size: 1 skewer with 8 oz. melon [18 melon balls])

CALORIES 136; FAT 1g (sat 0g, unsat 0g); PROTEIN 8g; CARB 28g; FIBER 2g; SUGARS 23g (added sugars 4g); SODIUM 93mg; CALC 5% DV; POTASSIUM 13% DV

WEEKNIGHT MAINS

From juicy peaches to sweet melon and corn, summer's bounty brings new life to your dinner table. These easy recipes will help you make the most of it all.

Staff Favorite • Make Ahead

Pork Tenderloin with Bourbon-Peach Sauce

Hands-on: 40 min. **Total:** 40 min.

3 Tbsp. olive oil, divided
1 lb. pork tenderloin, trimmed
1 tsp. kosher salt, divided
1 tsp. black pepper, divided
2 cups sliced peeled fresh peaches
2 Tbsp. (1 oz.) bourbon
3 Tbsp. apple cider vinegar, divided
2 Tbsp. honey, divided
1 Tbsp. unsalted butter
1 Tbsp. Dijon mustard
3 cups shredded green cabbage
¼ cup toasted sliced almonds
¼ cup chopped fresh flat-leaf parsley
2 tsp. finely chopped fresh thyme

1. Heat a large cast-iron skillet over medium-high, and add 1 tablespoon oil. Season pork with ½ teaspoon salt and ½ teaspoon pepper. Add to skillet, and cook, turning to brown all sides, until a thermometer inserted in thickest portion registers 140°F, 5 to 6 minutes per side. Transfer to a plate.
2. Add peaches to skillet; cook, stirring often, until lightly browned, 2 to 3 minutes. Add bourbon, 1 tablespoon vinegar, and 1 tablespoon honey; cook, stirring often, until sauce is slightly thickened, about 5 minutes. Remove skillet from heat; add butter, swirling until melted.
3. In a large bowl, whisk together mustard, remaining 2 tablespoons oil, remaining 2 tablespoons vinegar, remaining 1 tablespoon honey, remaining ½ teaspoon salt, and remaining ½ teaspoon pepper. Add cabbage, almonds, parsley, and thyme; toss to coat. Slice pork. Divide slaw and pork among 4 plates; top with peach sauce. Serves 4 (serving size: 4 oz. pork, ¾ cup slaw, and ¼ cup sauce)

CALORIES 411; **FAT** 22g (sat 5g, unsat 16g); **PROTEIN** 28g; **CARB** 22g; **FIBER** 4g; **SUGARS** 16g (added sugars 8g); **SODIUM** 643mg; **CALC** 7% DV; **POTASSIUM** 17% DV

Fast • Gluten Free

Chicken and Honeydew Salad

Hands-on: 25 min. **Total:** 25 min.
Rotisserie chicken and precubed honeydew help get dinner on the table in less than 30 minutes.

7 Tbsp. canola oil, divided
2 (6-inch) corn tortillas, halved and cut into thin strips
6 cups chopped romaine lettuce (about 2 hearts)
1 rotisserie chicken, skin removed, meat picked and shredded (about 3 cups)
3 cups (1-inch) cubed honeydew
2 oz. queso fresco (fresh Mexican cheese), crumbled (about ½ cup)
¼ cup pepitas (shelled pumpkin seeds)
¼ cup fresh lime juice (about 2 limes)
1 red Fresno chile, seeded and thinly sliced
½ tsp. black pepper
⅛ tsp. kosher salt

1. Heat 3 tablespoons oil in a skillet over medium. When oil is shimmering, add tortilla strips, and cook, stirring often, until strips are golden and crisp, 4 to 5 minutes. Drain on paper towels, and let cool 5 minutes.
2. Combine romaine, chicken, honeydew, queso fresco, and pepitas in a large bowl.
3. Whisk together lime juice, Fresno chile, pepper, salt, and remaining ¼ cup oil in a small bowl. Drizzle over salad; toss to combine. Top with crispy tortilla strips. Serves 4 (serving size: 3 cups)

CALORIES 516; **FAT** 34g (sat 6g, unsat 25g); **PROTEIN** 34g; **CARB** 22g; **FIBER** 4g; **SUGARS** 12g (added sugars 0g); **SODIUM** 561mg; **CALC** 16% DV; **POTASSIUM** 18% DV

Gluten Free

Snapper with Corn-Okra Relish

Hands-on: 40 min. **Total:** 40 min.
Snapper sourced from the U.S. southeast Atlantic, Gulf of Mexico, and Hawaii are the best sustainable choices. Learn more at seafoodwatch.org.

2 ears fresh corn
2 cups okra, halved (about 6 oz.)
2 celery stalks
1 bunch scallions
Canola oil cooking spray
¼ cup loosely packed fresh basil leaves
½ tsp. crushed red pepper
2 Tbsp. extra-virgin olive oil
2 Tbsp. Champagne vinegar or white wine vinegar
1⅛ tsp. kosher salt, divided
½ tsp. black pepper, divided
4 (4-oz.) skin-on snapper fillets or other white flaky fish (such as sea bass)

1. Preheat a grill to medium-high (about 450°F), or heat a grill pan over medium-high. Spray corn, okra, celery, and scallions with cooking spray; grill vegetables until slightly charred, 5 to 6 minutes. Place okra in large bowl. When cool enough to handle, cut kernels off corn, slice celery, and chop scallions; add to bowl with okra. Add basil, red pepper, oil, vinegar, ⅝ teaspoon salt, and ¼ teaspoon black pepper; toss to combine.

2. Sprinkle both sides of snapper with remaining ½ teaspoon salt and remaining ¼ teaspoon black pepper. Coat grill grates and fish with cooking spray. Carefully place fish, skin side down, on oiled grates, and grill 5 to 6 minutes. Carefully flip, and grill until cooked through, 4 to 5 more minutes.

3. Divide grilled vegetable mixture among 4 plates; top with fish. Serves 4 (serving size: ¾ cup vegetables and 4 oz. fish)

CALORIES 251; **FAT** 10g (sat 2g, unsat 7g); **PROTEIN** 27g; **CARB** 16g; **FIBER** 4g; **SUGARS** 5g (added sugars 0g); **SODIUM** 650mg; **CALC** 11% DV; **POTASSIUM** 19% DV

Fast • Gluten Free

Beef Kebabs with Cucumber-Mint Salad

Hands-on: 25 min. **Total:** 25 min.
If you can't find fruity, subtly spicy Aleppo pepper, try a blend of 2 teaspoons paprika and ¼ teaspoon cayenne pepper. The refreshing, crunchy cucumber-mint salad cools things down; pack leftovers into whole-wheat pitas for lunch.

1 lb. 90% lean ground sirloin
1 Tbsp. ground Aleppo pepper
2 tsp. ground cumin
1⅛ tsp. kosher salt, divided
¼ tsp. black pepper, divided
2 Tbsp. plus 2 tsp. extra-virgin olive oil, divided
1 English cucumber, halved lengthwise and thinly sliced (about 2½ cups)
1 cup thinly sliced red onion
½ cup chopped fresh mint, divided
2 Tbsp. plus 1 tsp. red wine vinegar, divided
⅓ cup plain whole-milk Greek yogurt

1. Preheat a grill to medium-high (about 450°F), or heat a grill pan over medium-high. Combine ground beef, Aleppo pepper, and cumin in a large bowl. Divide beef mixture into 4 (4-ounce) portions, and gently shape 1 portion around each of 4 (10-inch) skewers, patting the meat flat. Sprinkle evenly with ½ teaspoon salt and ¼ teaspoon black pepper, and brush evenly with 2 teaspoons oil. Place skewers on grates, and grill, uncovered, until a thermometer inserted in thickest portion reads 165°F, 4 to 5 minutes per side.

2. Combine the cucumber, onion, ⅓ cup mint, 2 tablespoons vinegar, ½ teaspoon salt, remaining 2 tablespoons oil, and remaining ¼ teaspoon black pepper in a bowl; stir to combine.

3. Stir together yogurt, remaining mint, remaining 1 teaspoon vinegar, and remaining ⅛ teaspoon salt in a small bowl. Divide cucumber salad among 4 plates, and top each with a skewer. Serve with yogurt sauce for dipping. Serves 4 (serving size: ¾ cup cucumber salad, 1 skewer, and 4 tsp. yogurt mixture)

CALORIES 340; **FAT** 22g (sat 6g, unsat 14g); **PROTEIN** 26g; **CARB** 8g; **FIBER** 2g; **SUGARS** 3g (added sugars 0g); **SODIUM** 625mg; **CALC** 8% DV; **POTASSIUM** 13% DV

SLOW COOKER
Make Ahead • Gluten Free

Easy Vegetable-Ham Frittata

Hands-on: 20 min. **Total:** 2 hr. 5 min.
When it's too hot outside to turn on your oven, your slow cooker is a lifesaver.

2 Tbsp. olive oil
2 medium shallots, chopped
8 oz. broccoli florets
1 medium (6-oz.) zucchini, cut into ½-inch-thick slices
½ cup chopped lower-sodium deli ham
Cooking spray
12 large eggs
1 oz. Parmesan cheese, grated (about ¼ cup)
¼ cup chopped fresh basil or flat-leaf parsley
¼ tsp. kosher salt
¼ tsp. black pepper

1. Heat olive oil in a large skillet over medium. Add shallots, broccoli, and zucchini, and cook, stirring often, until slightly browned, about 3 minutes. Add ham, and cook 2 minutes. Remove from heat, and let cool.

2. Coat bottom and sides of a 5-quart slow cooker with cooking spray; add vegetable mixture.

3. Whisk together eggs, Parmesan, basil, salt, and pepper; pour over vegetables in cooker. Cover slow cooker, and cook on high until frittata is set and the tip of a knife inserted into center comes out clean, about 1 hour and 45 minutes. Cut into 8 slices; lift slices out with a spatula to plates. Serves 8 (serving size: 1 slice)

CALORIES 349; **FAT** 23g (sat 6g, unsat 15g); **PROTEIN** 27g; **CARB** 9g; **FIBER** 2g; **SUGARS** 4g (added sugars 1g); **SODIUM** 610mg; **CALC** 17% DV; **POTASSIUM** 11% DV

4 GO-WITH-ANYTHING SIDES

Gluten Free • Vegetarian
Spicy Tomato-Cucumber Salad

Sunshine-yellow and ruby-red wedges of juicy tomato anchor this dish with a welcome summertime dose of skin-protective lycopene.

Combine 4 red tomatoes, cut into wedges; 1 yellow tomato, cut into wedges; 1 cup sliced English cucumber; ½ cup chopped yellow bell pepper; 1 Tbsp. minced and seeded jalapeño; 2 Tbsp. fresh lemon juice; ¾ tsp. kosher salt; and ¼ tsp. pepper in a large bowl. Cover and chill at least 1 hour. Garnish with 2 Tbsp. fresh basil leaves. Serves 6 (serving size: about 1 ¼ cups)

CALORIES 35; **FAT** 0g; **PROTEIN** 2g; **CARB** 8g; **FIBER** 2g; **SUGARS** 5g (added sugars 0g); **SODIUM** 247mg; **CALC** 3% DV; **POTASSIUM** 9% DV

Gluten Free • Vegetarian
Oven-Fried Smashed Okra

This healthy makeover of a classic *Southern Living* recipe uses a rolling pin to gently break open the okra pods by rolling from the tip to the stem end.

Preheat oven to 450°F with baking sheet in oven. Gently smash 1 lb. fresh okra. Whisk together ¾ cup low-fat buttermilk and 1 large egg in a bowl. Add okra; let stand 3 minutes. Combine 1 cup fine yellow cornmeal, ¾ tsp. kosher salt, and ½ tsp. pepper in a bowl; dredge okra in mixture. Add 2 Tbsp. canola oil to hot pan; tilt pan to coat. Add okra; coat with cooking spray. Bake until crisp, 25 to 30 minutes, turning once. Serves 8 (serving size: ¾ cup)

CALORIES 142; **FAT** 4g (sat 1g, unsat 3g); **PROTEIN** 4g; **CARB** 21g; **FIBER** 2g; **SUGARS** 2g (added sugars 0g); **SODIUM** 237mg; **CALC** 8% DV; **POTASSIUM** 5% DV

Fast • Gluten Free Vegetarian
Fruit and Arugula Salad with Fig Vinaigrette

Make a double batch of this versatile vinaigrette and use it to marinate chicken or brush over salmon before grilling.

Gently mix together 4 cups cubed watermelon, 3 cups fresh peach wedges, and 4 cups baby arugula (4 oz.) in a large bowl. Process 2 Tbsp. fig preserves, 1 ½ Tbsp. fresh lemon juice, ½ Tbsp. white balsamic vinegar, ½ tsp. dry mustard, and ½ tsp. kosher salt in a blender until smooth; add 2 Tbsp. olive oil in a slow, steady stream, processing until blended. Gently toss watermelon mixture with dressing. Serves 6 (serving size: about 1 ½ cups)

CALORIES 125; **FAT** 5g (sat 1g, unsat 4g); **PROTEIN** 2g; **CARB** 20g; **FIBER** 2g; **SUGARS** 16g (added sugars 1g); **SODIUM** 167mg; **CALC** 4% DV; **POTASSIUM** 7% DV

Fast • Gluten Free Vegetarian
Squash-Ribbon Salad with Herbs

Customize this no-cook side with a generous handful of your favorite herbs—it would also be lovely with fresh cilantro and chives.

Shave ¾ lb. zucchini and ¾ lb. yellow squash lengthwise into thin ribbons using a vegetable peeler; combine with 3 cups loosely packed baby spinach and 1 cup loosely packed torn fresh herbs (such as parsley, dill, basil, and mint) in a large bowl. Drizzle with 2 Tbsp. white wine vinegar and 1 Tbsp. extra-virgin olive oil. Sprinkle with ½ tsp. kosher salt and ¼ tsp. pepper. Toss. Serves 6 (serving size: about 1 cup)

CALORIES 45; **FAT** 3g (sat 0g, unsat 2g); **PROTEIN** 2g; **CARB** 5g; **FIBER** 2g; **SUGARS** 3g (added sugars 0g); **SODIUM** 177mg; **CALC** 4% DV; **POTASSIUM** 7% DV

1 INGREDIENT, 3 SIDES

3 WAYS TO USE CORN

Golden and crisp, corn is one of summer's most glorious gifts. Seek out the freshest corn you can find for the sweetest flavor—the sugars begin to turn into starch after it's picked.

Fast • Gluten Free Vegetarian
Smoky Grilled Corn

The trifecta of chili powder, cumin, and paprika creates a spicy, smoky crust that turns this grilled corn into an irresistible side.

1. Preheat a grill to medium-high (about 450°F). Stir together 2 ½ Tbsp. melted unsalted butter, 1 tsp. kosher salt, ½ tsp. chili powder, ½ tsp. smoked paprika, ¼ tsp. ground cumin, and ½ tsp. pepper in a small bowl. Brush mixture evenly over 6 medium-sized fresh corn ears.
2. Place corn on grate, and grill, uncovered, until tender and lightly charred, 10 to 12 minutes, turning often. Sprinkle corn evenly with 3 Tbsp. finely chopped fresh chives. Serves 6 (serving size: 1 ear of corn)

CALORIES 132; **FAT** 6g (sat 3g, unsat 3g); **PROTEIN** 4g; **CARB** 19g; **FIBER** 2g; **SUGARS** 6g (added sugars 0g); **SODIUM** 343mg; **CALC** 1% DV; **POTASSIUM** 6% DV

Staff Favorite • Fast Gluten Free • Make Ahead Vegetarian
Creamed Corn

Corn puree gives this dish its velvety texture without adding loads of cream.

1. Melt 1 Tbsp. unsalted butter in a large skillet over medium-high; add ½ cup minced sweet onion, and cook until softened, about 5 minutes. Stir in 4 cups fresh corn kernels and ½ cup water. Cover and cook 10 minutes.

2. Transfer half of corn mixture to a blender. Remove center of blender lid; secure lid, and place a clean towel over opening. Process until smooth. Add puree to skillet; stir in 3 Tbsp. heavy cream, ½ tsp. kosher salt, ¼ tsp. pepper, and ⅛ tsp. nutmeg. Cook over medium until thickened and heated through. Garnish with chopped fresh parsley. Serves 6 (serving size: about ½ cup)

CALORIES 132; **FAT** 6g (sat 3g, unsat 2g); **PROTEIN** 4g; **CARB** 20g; **FIBER** 2g; **SUGARS** 7g (added sugars 0g); **SODIUM** 177mg; **CALC** 1% DV; **POTASSIUM** 6% DV

Fast • Gluten Free
Make Ahead • Vegetarian
Mexican Corn Salad
This potluck-perfect side is easy to make ahead of time, and it gets even more flavorful when it sits overnight. For easier cleanup, cut the corn off the cobs over a sheet of parchment paper.

1. Whisk together ½ cup chopped fresh cilantro, ¼ cup fresh lime juice (from 2 limes), 1 tsp. kosher salt, and ½ tsp. pepper; gradually whisk in 3 Tbsp. olive oil. Stir together 4 cups fresh corn kernels (from 6 ears); ½ cup chopped scallions; 1 pint multicolored cherry tomatoes, halved; and 1 cup thinly sliced radishes. Gently stir dressing into corn mixture. Sprinkle top with 1 ½ oz. crumbled Cotija cheese (⅓ cup). Serves 8 (serving size: about ¾ cup)

CALORIES 140; **FAT** 8g (sat 2g, unsat 5g); **PROTEIN** 4g; **CARB** 17g; **FIBER** 2g; **SUGARS** 6g (added sugars 0g); **SODIUM** 342mg; **CALC** 9% DV; **POTASSIUM** 7% DV

Turkey Burger Pizza

Hands-on: 15 min. **Total:** 45 min.
If you can't find fresh pizza dough at your grocery, use a prebaked whole-wheat crust instead.

12 oz. whole-wheat pizza dough
1 tsp. canola oil
6 oz. ground turkey
¼ cup chopped scallions
2 garlic cloves, minced
½ cup reduced-sodium marinara sauce
3 oz. shredded reduced-fat colby-Jack cheese (about ¾ cup)
2 plum tomatoes, cut into thin slices (7 oz.)
1¼ Tbsp. canola mayonnaise
1 tsp. pickle juice
1 Tbsp. unsalted ketchup
1 tsp. yellow mustard
2 tsp. water
1 cup shredded iceberg lettuce
7 dill pickle chips

1. Place a pizza stone or baking sheet in oven. Preheat oven to 450°F. Do not remove pizza stone while oven preheats.

2. Let dough stand at room temperature for 30 minutes. Roll dough on parchment paper into a 14-inch circle.

3. Heat oil in a medium nonstick skillet over medium-high. Add turkey, scallions, and garlic to skillet. Cook 5 to 6 minutes or until turkey is browned.

4. Spread marinara sauce over pizza dough, leaving a 1-inch border. Top with cheese, turkey mixture, and tomato slices.

Leaving pizza on parchment paper, place onto pizza stone or baking sheet. Bake 8 to 10 minutes or until browned. Transfer to a wire rack; let cool briefly.

5. Combine mayonnaise, pickle juice, ketchup, mustard, and 2 teaspoons water in a small bowl. Drizzle mixture over top of pizza; top with shredded lettuce and pickle chips. Cut into 8 slices. Serves: 4 (serving size: 2 slices)

CALORIES 391; **FAT** 16g (sat 4g, unsat 12g); **PROTEIN** 21g; **CARB** 44g; **FIBER** 4g; **SUGARS** 4g (added sugars 0g); **SODIUM** 754mg; **CALC** 33% DV; **POTASSIUM** 5% DV

Piled high with classic toppings and a zippy sauce, this burger-and-pizza mash-up is a solid upgrade to takeout— and fun to eat for kids and parents alike.

Staff Favorite · Fast

Pork and Charred Pineapple Sliders

Hands-on: 20 min. **Total:** 20 min.
Pineapple pulls double duty in this recipe—caramelized rings add smoky sweetness while tangy pineapple juice brightens the fast-fix slaw. Pick up a peeled and cored pineapple in the produce section; the flavor is far superior to canned rings.

¼ cup unsalted ketchup
2 tsp. brown sugar
3 Tbsp. pineapple juice, divided
2 Tbsp. apple cider vinegar, divided
8 oz. ground pork
¼ cup sliced scallions, divided
½ tsp. kosher salt, divided
½ tsp. black pepper, divided
Cooking spray
8 (¼-inch-thick) pineapple slices
1 cup shredded red cabbage
8 (1-oz.) whole-wheat rolls, split

1. Stir together ketchup, brown sugar, 1 tablespoon pineapple juice, and 1 tablespoon vinegar in a small bowl. Set aside.
2. Combine pork, ¼ cup scallions, ¼ teaspoon salt, and ¼ teaspoon pepper in a medium bowl; form into 8 patties. Spray a large cast-iron skillet with cooking spray, and heat over high. Add patties, and cook until slightly charred, 2 to 3 minutes. Flip and cook until pork is cooked through, about 1 minute. Transfer to a plate.
3. Add pineapple slices to skillet, and cook on 1 side until lightly charred, 1 to 2 minutes. Top patties with pineapple slices.
4. Combine the cabbage, remaining 2 tablespoons pineapple juice, remaining 1 tablespoon vinegar, remaining ¼ cup scallions, remaining ¼ teaspoon salt, and remaining ¼ teaspoon pepper in a bowl. To assemble sliders, brush bottoms of rolls with ketchup mixture; add a pork patty with a pineapple slice to the bottom of each bun. Top with cabbage mixture and tops of rolls. Serves 4 (serving size: 2 sliders and ¼ cup slaw)

CALORIES 407; **FAT** 15g (sat 5g, unsat 8g); **PROTEIN** 16g; **CARB** 56g; **FIBER** 7g; **SUGARS** 24g (added sugars 3g); **SODIUM** 575mg; **CALC** 10% DV; **POTASSIUM** 11% DV

Fast · Gluten Free

Buffalo Chicken Tacos

Hands-on: 20 min. **Total:** 20 min.
Your favorite appetizer just got upgraded to the dinner menu. These reinvented tacos check every craving box with less than a third of the sodium and half the fat of traditional Buffalo wings.

1 cup thinly sliced celery
1 cup thinly sliced baby bell peppers (from 3 small peppers)
3 Tbsp. fresh lemon juice
½ tsp. kosher salt, divided
½ tsp. black pepper, divided
2 Tbsp. chopped fresh cilantro, plus more for garnish
2 Tbsp. unsalted butter, melted
2 Tbsp. unsalted ketchup
2 tsp. hot sauce (such as Frank's RedHot), plus more for serving
1 Tbsp. extra-virgin olive oil
1 lb. boneless, skinless chicken breasts, thinly sliced
¼ cup reduced-fat sour cream
1 Tbsp. crumbled blue cheese
8 corn tortillas, toasted

1. Combine celery, bell peppers, and lemon juice in a medium bowl. Stir in ¼ teaspoon salt and ¼ teaspoon black pepper. Let stand at room temperature 10 minutes. Toss with cilantro.
2. Meanwhile, stir together butter, ketchup, and hot sauce in a large bowl.
3. Heat oil in a large nonstick skillet over medium-high. Add chicken, and cook until lightly browned on all sides, 3 to 4 minutes. Sprinkle with remaining ¼ teaspoon salt and remaining ¼ teaspoon black pepper. Add chicken to hot sauce mixture; toss to coat.
4. Stir together sour cream and blue cheese. To assemble tacos, spread 1½ teaspoons of the sour cream mixture on each tortilla. Divide chicken and celery mixture evenly among tortillas; top with cilantro and hot sauce. Serves 4 (serving size: 2 tacos)

CALORIES 381; **FAT** 16g (sat 6g, unsat 8g); **PROTEIN** 30g; **CARB** 29g; **FIBER** 4g; **SUGARS** 5g (added sugars 0g); **SODIUM** 435mg; **CALC** 9% DV; **POTASSIUM** 14% DV

3 WAYS TO:

UP YOUR TACO GAME

1. Use metal kitchen tongs to hold the tortillas over your stove's gas burner until they're just barely toasted to add a hint of smoky flavor to the tacos.

2. Make the relish (minus the cilantro) and stir together the blue cheese sauce the night before and stash in the fridge to speed up dinner prep.

3. Toss leftovers with baby arugula, spinach, or romaine lettuce along with rinsed and drained black beans for a quick-fix dinner or lunch salad.

Warm Pasta Salad with Tomatoes and Eggplant

Hands-on: 20 min. **Total:** 20 min.
Buttery burrata cheese has a mozzarella-like exterior with a creamy interior. If you can't track down this dreamy cheese, simply tear 6 ounces of fresh mozzarella into bite-sized pieces. Sub in your favorite whole-wheat pasta for a fiber boost.

8 oz. uncooked casarecce, fusilli, or penne pasta
8 oz. haricots verts (French green beans) or yellow wax beans, trimmed
1 Tbsp. olive oil
2 cups chopped Japanese eggplant (from 1 eggplant)
1 Tbsp. minced fresh garlic
2 pt. cherry tomatoes, halved and divided
¼ cup dry white wine
2 tsp. white wine vinegar
½ tsp. kosher salt
6 oz. burrata
2 tsp. chopped fresh thyme
½ tsp. black pepper

1. Cook pasta according to package directions, omitting salt and fat. Add green beans during last 3 minutes of cooking. Reserve 1 cup of the cooking liquid; drain.
2. Meanwhile, heat oil in a large skillet over medium-high. Add eggplant, and cook, stirring occasionally, until tender, 4 to 5 minutes. Add garlic; cook until fragrant, 1 minute. Add half of tomatoes; cook until juices start to release, about 2 to 3 minutes.
3. Add wine; cook, stirring often, until most of wine evaporates. Add pasta and beans; toss to combine. Add reserved pasta cooking liquid, a couple of tablespoons at a time, if mixture is too dry. Stir in remaining tomatoes, vinegar, and salt. Divide pasta mixture among 4 bowls. Top with burrata; sprinkle evenly with thyme and pepper. Serves 4 (serving size: 1 ½ cups pasta mixture and 1 ½ oz. burrata)

CALORIES 428; FAT 14g (sat 7g, unsat 6g); PROTEIN 17g; CARB 56g; FIBER 6g; SUGARS 9g (added sugars 0g); SODIUM 361mg; CALC 28% DV; POTASSIUM 14% DV

Grilled Heirloom Tomato and Feta Panzanella

Hands-on: 20 min. **Total:** 20 min.
Spring for heirloom tomatoes; their rich flavor and vibrant color add a huge wow factor to this salad. Beans bulk it up with fiber and protein.

2 lb. heirloom tomatoes, halved
4 oz. French bread, cut into 1-inch slices
¼ cup extra-virgin olive oil, divided
1 (3-oz.) block feta cheese
¼ tsp. kosher salt
¼ tsp. black pepper
1 (14.5-oz.) can unsalted cannellini beans, rinsed and drained
½ cup thinly sliced red onion
½ cup chopped fresh basil leaves
2 tsp. red wine vinegar

1. Heat a grill to high (450°F to 550°F). Brush tomatoes and bread with 1 tablespoon oil, and place tomatoes, bread, and feta on grates; grill until charred on both sides, 1 to 2 minutes per side. Transfer to a plate, and sprinkle evenly with salt and pepper. Let cool 5 minutes; cut larger tomatoes and bread into chunks.
2. Combine tomatoes, bread, beans, onion, basil, vinegar, and remaining 3 tablespoons oil in a large bowl; gently toss. Divide salad among 4 plates; crumble feta evenly over top. Serve immediately. Serves 4 (serving size: 1 ½ cups)

CALORIES 381; FAT 21g (sat 5g, unsat 14g); PROTEIN 13g; CARB 39g; FIBER 8g; SUGARS 10g (added sugars 0g); SODIUM 530mg; CALC 19% DV; POTASSIUM 17% DV

WHAT'S FRESH NOW

Easy Peach Hand Pies

Hands-on: 30 min. **Total:** 45 min.

1 (9-inch) frozen whole-wheat piecrust (such as Wholly Wholesome), thawed
¾ cup chopped ripe peaches
3 Tbsp. light brown sugar
1 Tbsp. unsalted butter, softened
¼ tsp. ground cinnamon

1. Preheat oven to 400°F. Shape piecrust into a ball; divide ball into 8 equal portions. Roll each portion into a 4-inch circle on a lightly floured surface. (Cover dough circles with a damp towel to prevent drying.) Stir together peaches, brown sugar, butter, and cinnamon in a medium bowl.
2. Spoon about 1 tablespoon peach mixture onto each dough circle, leaving a ¼-inch border. Moisten dough edges with water; fold circles in half to form half-moons. Crimp edges with a fork to seal; cut slits in top of pies, and place on a parchment paper–lined baking sheet.
3. Bake at 400°F until golden brown, about 14 minutes. Remove and cool 10 minutes before serving. Serves 8 (serving size: 1 hand pie)

CALORIES 46; FAT 9g (sat 5g, unsat 4g); PROTEIN 2g; CARB 15g; FIBER 2g; SUGARS 7g (added sugars 4g); SODIUM 101mg; CALC 1% DV; POTASSIUM 1% DV

1 LIST 3 DINNERS

Shop this list to feed four for three nights, all for about $30. Read the recipes first to be sure you have the staples on hand.

2 red onions

1 heirloom tomato

1 cup cherry tomatoes

2 cups lima beans

1 head romaine lettuce

2 ears fresh corn

4 large zucchini

1 cucumber

1 bunch fresh basil

2 lemons

2 (6-inch) whole-wheat pita rounds

2 cups cooked lentils

12 oz. plain 2% reduced-fat yogurt

3 oz. feta cheese

14 oz. 90% lean ground sirloin

11 oz. ground lamb

Fast

Grilled Lamb and Feta Pita Sandwiches

Hands-on: 20 min. **Total:** 30 min.
Your favorite Mediterranean menu item just got a healthy makeover. Lean ground sirloin teams up with lamb for a lighter patty; lemon and cumin keep the flavor bright and bold. Double the yogurt dip and pair it with veggies for a midafternoon snack.

6 oz. 90% lean ground sirloin
4 oz. ground lamb
3 oz. feta cheese, crumbled (about ¾ cup)
¼ cup finely chopped red onion
1 tsp. lemon zest
1 Tbsp. fresh lemon juice
1 tsp. ground cumin
1 tsp. paprika
½ tsp. black pepper
½ tsp. kosher salt, divided
Cooking spray
3 Tbsp. shredded cucumber
⅓ cup plain 2% reduced-fat yogurt
2 (6-inch) whole-wheat pita rounds, halved
1 heirloom tomato, thinly sliced
4 romaine lettuce leaves

1. Preheat a grill to high (450°F to 550°F), or heat a grill pan over high.
2. Combine beef, lamb, feta, onion, lemon zest, lemon juice, cumin, paprika, pepper, and ¼ teaspoon salt in a bowl; stir well (or use your hands) to incorporate. Divide mixture into 4 equal portions; shape portions into oval patties. Lightly coat grill grate with cooking spray; place patties on oiled grate. Grill to desired degree of doneness, 2 to 3 minutes per side for medium-well.
3. Place shredded cucumber on paper towels to drain 5 minutes. Stir together drained cucumber, yogurt, and remaining ¼ teaspoon salt in a bowl.
4. Place pita halves on grill grates; grill until lightly toasted, about 1 minute per side. Spoon about 2 tablespoons yogurt sauce into each toasted pita. Divide patties, tomato slices, and lettuce evenly among each pita half. Serves 4 (serving size: 1 sandwich)

CALORIES 299; **FAT** 14g (sat 7g, unsat 6g); **PROTEIN** 21g; **CARB** 24g; **FIBER** 3g; **SUGARS** 5g (added sugars 0g); **SODIUM** 663mg; **CALC** 17% DV; **POTASSIUM** 7% DV

**Gluten Free • Make Ahead
Vegetarian**

Succotash Salad with Lentils

Hands-on: 20 min. **Total:** 50 min.
After a long, hot day, this salad refreshes with its hearty crunch and herb-loaded dressing. Prepare the fiber-rich lentils and lima beans the day before, and you can throw this salad together after work without even turning on your stove.

3 cups water
½ medium-sized red onion, cut into ½-inch wedges, plus thin slices for garnish
2 garlic cloves, coarsely chopped
1 dried bay leaf
1 tsp. kosher salt, divided
2 cups fresh or thawed frozen lima beans
¾ cup loosely packed fresh basil leaves
4½ Tbsp. olive oil
1½ Tbsp. white wine vinegar
1½ Tbsp. fresh lemon juice
¾ tsp. honey
½ tsp. black pepper
1 cup fresh corn kernels (from 2 ears)
1 cup cherry tomatoes, halved
1 cup cooked lentils
4 cups chopped romaine lettuce

1. Combine 3 cups water, onion wedges, garlic, bay leaf, and ½ teaspoon salt in a medium saucepan over high; bring to a boil. Add lima beans, and return to a boil. Reduce heat to low, and simmer until beans are tender, 15 to 20 minutes. Drain; discard bay leaf. Spread bean mixture in a single layer on a baking sheet, and refrigerate until cold, about 30 minutes.

2. Place basil, oil, vinegar, lemon juice, honey, pepper, and remaining ½ teaspoon salt in a blender; process until smooth, about 1 minute, scraping down sides of blender as needed.

3. Place lima bean mixture, corn, tomatoes, and lentils in a large bowl; gently toss to combine. Divide lettuce among 4 plates; top with bean mixture. Drizzle with basil vinaigrette; garnish with thin slices of red onion. Serves 4 (serving size: 1 cup lettuce, 1 ¼ cups bean mixture, and about 2 Tbsp. dressing)

CALORIES 341; FAT 17g (sat 2g, unsat 14g); PROTEIN 12g; CARB 39g; FIBER 10g; SUGARS 8g (added sugars 1g); SODIUM 500mg; CALC 8% DV; POTASSIUM 19% DV

Dinner 3 of 3

Gluten Free

Zucchini Stuffed with Lamb and Lentils

Hands-on: 25 min. **Total:** 45 min. If you're still on the fence about lamb, these retro-inspired zucchini boats will win you over. The addition of ground beef and creamy lentils combined with fragrant cinnamon and allspice yield a dish that's exotic and comforting in the same bite.

4 large zucchini (8 oz. each)
2 Tbsp. water
8 oz. 90% lean ground sirloin
7 oz. ground lamb
3 garlic cloves, minced
¼ tsp. ground cinnamon
¼ tsp. ground allspice
¼ tsp. black pepper
½ cup chopped plus 1 Tbsp. minced
   red onion, divided
¾ tsp. kosher salt, divided

1 cup cooked lentils
Cooking spray
1 cup plain 2% reduced-fat yogurt
½ cup minced cucumber, drained on
   paper towels
1 tsp. paprika, divided

1. Preheat oven to 350°F.
2. Halve zucchini lengthwise. Scoop out seeds, leaving ¼-inch-thick sides and bottoms. Place zucchini and 2 tablespoons water in a microwavable bowl. Cover with plastic wrap, and microwave at HIGH until zucchini are crisp-tender, 5 minutes.
3. Heat a large nonstick skillet over medium-high. Add beef, lamb, garlic, cinnamon, allspice, pepper, chopped onion, and ½ teaspoon salt to skillet. Cook, stirring, until meat is browned and crumbly, 6 to 7 minutes. Remove skillet from heat; stir in lentils.
4. Divide mixture evenly among zucchini halves; place stuffed halves on a baking sheet coated with cooking spray. Cover with aluminum foil; bake at 350°F until tender, 10 to 15 minutes.
5. Stir together yogurt, cucumber, ½ teaspoon paprika, remaining 1 tablespoon minced onion, and remaining ¼ teaspoon salt in a bowl. Top each zucchini half with about 2½ tablespoons yogurt sauce, and sprinkle evenly with remaining ½ teaspoon paprika. Serve immediately. Serves 4 (serving size: 2 stuffed zucchini halves)

CALORIES 374; FAT 16g (sat 7g, unsat 8g); PROTEIN 31g; CARB 28g; FIBER 8g; SUGARS 14g (added sugars 0g); SODIUM 494mg; CALC 20% DV; POTASSIUM 29% DV

CHEERS TO YOUR HEALTH

Staff Favorite • Gluten Free
Make Ahead • Vegetarian

Blackberry-Orange Margarita

Hands-on: 10 min. **Total:** 1 hr. 10 min. This fruity sipper has sweet-tart flavor with a subtle burn from the serrano-infused tequila. Tender-tongued? This drink is equally delicious without the chile. Blackberries are fiber-packed and contain antioxidants called polyphenols that might ward off cognitive decline and keep your heart healthy.

Place 4 oz. tequila and 1 small serrano chile, halved lengthwise, in a small bowl or cup. Let stand 1 hour. Strain mixture through a fine-mesh sieve over a cup; discard solids. Blend 12 oz. fresh blackberries, 1 cup fresh orange juice, ½ cup fresh lime juice, 2 Tbsp. agave nectar, and a dash of salt until smooth. Strain mixture into a pitcher; discard solids. Stir in tequila. Divide mixture among 4 ice-filled glasses. Garnish with additional blackberries and a chile, if desired. Serves 4 (serving size: about ¾ cup)

CALORIES 168; FAT 1g (sat 0g, unsat 0g); PROTEIN 2g; CARB 25g; FIBER 5g; SUGARS 18g (added sugars 8g); SODIUM 62mg; CALC 4% DV; POTASSIUM 6% DV

MAKE IT A MOCKTAIL

Omit the tequila and add 4 ounces cactus water (we like True Nopal brand, available at most grocery stores).

3 WAYS TO USE SALSA

That jar of salsa hanging out in the back of your fridge has more in store for it than a date with a bag of tortilla chips. These easy recipes will help you teach that lycopene-rich salsa some tasty new tricks.

Fast • Gluten Free
Chicken Kebabs with Spicy Sauce

1. Preheat grill to medium-high (about 450°F). Combine 8 chicken breast tenders, 2 Tbsp. chopped fresh flat-leaf parsley, 1 Tbsp. olive oil, 1 Tbsp. lemon zest, 1 Tbsp. fresh lemon juice, 3 grated garlic cloves, 1 tsp. pepper, and ¼ tsp. kosher salt in a bowl. Thread tenders onto 8 skewers; grill 5 minutes per side or until done.
2. Stir together 3 Tbsp. salsa, 1 Tbsp. Sriracha chili sauce, and ½ tsp. smoked paprika. Spoon salsa mixture over 1 cup plain 2% reduced-fat Greek yogurt in a small bowl; serve with kebabs. Sprinkle with fresh flat-leaf parsley leaves. Serves 4 (2 skewers and about ⅓ cup sauce)

CALORIES 219; FAT 7g (sat 2g, unsat 4g); PROTEIN 31g; CARB 5g; FIBER 1g; SUGARS 3g (added sugars 0g); SODIUM 349mg; CALC 7% DV; POTASSIUM 9% DV

Staff Favorite • Gluten Free Vegetarian
Salsa-Roasted Potatoes

1. Preheat the oven to 400°F. Place 1 lb. halved baby Yukon Gold potatoes on a rimmed baking sheet lined with aluminum foil. Coat generously with cooking spray. Bake 15 minutes.

2. Combine 1 Tbsp. olive oil, 1 tsp. chili powder, and 1 tsp. ground cumin in a microwavable bowl; microwave at HIGH until fragrant, about 1 minute, stirring after 30 seconds. Add potatoes and ½ cup salsa to olive oil mixture; toss to coat. Return potatoes to baking sheet; bake 15 minutes. Squeeze 4 lime wedges over potatoes; sprinkle with ¼ cup chopped fresh cilantro and ⅛ tsp. kosher salt. Serves 4 (serving size: about ½ cup)

CALORIES 119; FAT 4g (sat 0g, unsat 3g); PROTEIN 2g; CARB 21g; FIBER 4g; SUGARS 3g (added sugars 0g); SODIUM 309mg; CALC 1% DV; POTASSIUM 2% DV

Fast • Gluten Free Vegetarian
Skillet-Charred Green Beans with Salsa

Resist the urge to stir the green beans often—that will prevent them from getting a nice amount of char. For even better flavor, use fresh green beans from your local farmers' market; trim them yourself before steaming in a covered container in the microwave.

1. Microwave 1 (12-oz.) pkg. steam-in-bag green beans at HIGH 2 minutes. Remove green beans from bag; pat dry. Heat 2 tsp. olive oil in a medium skillet over high. Add green beans; cook, stirring once or twice, until slightly charred, 4 to 5 minutes. Remove from heat.
2. Add ¾ cup chopped tomato, ¼ cup salsa, 1 Tbsp. olive oil, 1 Tbsp. fresh lime juice, 1 tsp. honey, and ⅛ tsp. kosher salt to green beans in skillet; stir to combine. Top with ¼ cup roasted salted pepitas. Serves 4 (serving size: about ¾ cup)

CALORIES 136; FAT 10g (sat 1g, unsat 8g); PROTEIN 4g; CARB 11g; FIBER 4g; SUGARS 6g (added sugars 1g); SODIUM 200mg; CALC 5% DV; POTASSIUM 7% DV

THE SHORTCUT
Staff Favorite • Fast Gluten Free • Vegetarian
Black Bean Tostadas

Hands-on: 30 min. **Total:** 30 min.
You'll never miss the meat and cheese in these vegan tostadas. Store-bought refried black beans, quick-steam green beans, and tostada shells make this a breeze to throw together. Look left for three ways to use up the leftover salsa.

½ cup water
½ cup white vinegar
¼ cup granulated sugar
1 cup thinly sliced radishes
1 large (8-oz.) red onion, cut into ½-inch rings
1½ Tbsp. olive oil, divided
2 ears fresh corn
1½ cups lower-sodium refried black beans (such as Amy's Organic)
6½ Tbsp. salsa (such as Frontera Chipotle Salsa), divided
¼ tsp. kosher salt, divided
4 oz. arugula (about 4 cups)
1 (8-oz.) steam-in-bag haricots verts (French green beans), cooked
1 cup cherry tomatoes, halved
8 tostada shells
½ ripe avocado, sliced
1 (2.5-oz.) pkg. plantain strips (such as Tumbis)
½ cup chopped fresh cilantro

1. Preheat broiler with oven rack 6 inches from heat. Place baking sheet in oven (do not remove pan while oven preheats).
2. Add ½ cup water, vinegar, and sugar to a saucepan over high; bring to a boil, stirring to dissolve sugar. Place radishes in a heatproof bowl; add vinegar mixture.
3. Toss onion rings with 1 tablespoon olive oil in a medium bowl. Brush corn with remaining

½ tablespoon oil. Carefully remove pan from oven; add onion and corn to pan, and broil until charred, about 15 minutes, turning halfway through. Adjust oven temperature to 400°F.

4. Combine refried beans, 1½ tablespoons salsa, and ⅛ teaspoon salt in a small saucepan over medium; cook until warm, about 5 minutes.

5. Cut corn kernels off cob; combine with arugula, cooked green beans, tomatoes, remaining 5 tablespoons salsa, and remaining ⅛ teaspoon salt in a large bowl.

6. Bake tostada shells on a baking sheet until warmed, about 1 minute. Spread 3 tablespoons bean mixture on each tostada shell. Top each with 3 onion rings, ½ cup arugula mixture, 2 tablespoons drained pickled radishes, avocado, plantain strips, and 1 tablespoon cilantro. Serves 4 (serving size: 2 tostadas)

CALORIES 536; FAT 23g (sat 6g, unsat 15g); PROTEIN 14g; CARB 74g; FIBER 15g; SUGARS 14g (added sugars 2g); SODIUM 724mg; CALC 17% DV; POTASSIUM 17% DV

4 SAUCES FOR ANY PROTEIN

Gluten Free • Make Ahead Vegetarian • Fast
Peach-Basil Sauce

This fresh sauce combines ripe summer peaches with fennel and toasty pine nuts, making it the perfect pairing for smoky pork chops, flank steak, or shrimp.

Heat 2 Tbsp. olive oil in a large skillet over medium. Add 1 cup chopped fennel and 1 cup chopped onion. Cook until golden brown, about 13 minutes. Stir in ¼ cup toasted pine nuts, 1½ lb. peeled and chopped fresh peaches, 1 tsp. kosher salt, and ¼ tsp. pepper. Cook over medium-low, crushing with a spoon, until jammy, about 15 minutes. Stir in 2 Tbsp. chopped fresh basil and 2 tsp. white wine vinegar. Serves 16 (serving size: 2 Tbsp.)

CALORIES 52; FAT 3g (sat 0g, unsat 3g); PROTEIN 1g; CARB 6g; FIBER 1g; SUGARS 4g (added sugars 0g); SODIUM 123mg; CALC 1% DV; POTASSIUM 3% DV

Fast • Gluten Free
Lemon-Garlic Anchovy Sauce

This flavor bomb from Southern France is guaranteed to take your summer grilling game to the next level. A little goes a long way on charred summer vegetables and mild white fish.

Combine 1 oz. drained and chopped anchovies, 2 minced garlic cloves, and ¼ cup extra-virgin olive oil in a small skillet over medium-low, and cook, stirring constantly, until anchovies are crushed and cooked into a paste, about 5 minutes. Remove from heat; stir in 1 tsp. lemon zest, 1½ Tbsp. fresh lemon juice, and 2 Tbsp. chopped fresh flat-leaf parsley. Serve warm or at room temperature. Serves 12 (serving size: 2 tsp.)

CALORIES 73; FAT 6g (sat 1g, unsat 4g); PROTEIN 5g; CARB 0g; FIBER 0g; SUGARS 0g (added sugars 0g); SODIUM 139mg; CALC 0% DV; POTASSIUM 0% DV

Fast • Gluten Free Make Ahead • Vegetarian
Creamy Zucchini-Lime Dressing

All you need is a blender to whip up this super-simple no-cook sauce. Try it with grilled eggplant or chicken for a hint of Persian flavor.

Place 1 chopped medium zucchini, ½ cup olive oil, 1 small garlic clove, ¼ cup fresh lime juice (from 2 limes), 2 Tbsp. water, 4 tsp. tahini, ¼ tsp. kosher salt, and ¼ tsp. granulated sugar in a food processor or blender. Process until smooth. Serves 16 (serving size: 1½ Tbsp.)

CALORIES 71; FAT 7g (sat 1g, unsat 6g); PROTEIN 0g; CARB 1g; FIBER 0g; SUGARS 0g (added sugars 0g); SODIUM 122mg; CALC 1% DV; POTASSIUM 1% DV

Fast • Gluten Free Make Ahead • Vegetarian
Spicy Tomato Aïoli

This smoky mayonnaise will be your go-to spread this summer. Pair it with your favorite burger, or treat yourself by using it as a decadent dip for sweet potato fries.

Heat 1 Tbsp. olive oil in a medium saucepan over medium-high. Add ¼ cup chopped onion; cook until tender, about 3 minutes. Stir in 2 minced garlic cloves and 1 tsp. crushed red pepper; cook 30 seconds. Add 1 (14.5-oz.) drained can unsalted diced fire-roasted tomatoes and 2 tsp. red wine vinegar. Cook 10 minutes; let cool completely. Process tomato mixture, 1 cup canola mayonnaise, and ¾ tsp. kosher salt in a food processor until smooth. Serves 16 (serving size: 1½ Tbsp.)

CALORIES 116; FAT 12g (sat 1g, unsat 11g); PROTEIN 0g; CARB 2g; FIBER 0g; SUGARS 1g (added sugars 0g); SODIUM 183mg; CALC 0% DV; POTASSIUM 0% DV

Fast • Make Ahead

Fancy Blue Cheese Dressing

Hands-on: 5 min. **Total:** 15 min.
Toast the pepper to add more pungency, and fine-tune the dressing to your taste with extra dashes of Worcestershire or Tabasco. Maybe even sneak in minced anchovies or chives. (Note: You'll likely want more salt than our nutritional guidelines permit.) Spoon over iceberg lettuce, sliced tomatoes, radishes, avocado, or smoked chicken.

3 Tbsp. fresh lemon juice
1 Tbsp. apple cider vinegar
2 tsp. freshly ground black pepper
1 tsp. Worcestershire sauce
½ tsp. hot sauce (such as Tabasco)
¼ tsp. kosher salt
1 garlic clove, minced
1 small shallot, minced
⅔ cup whole buttermilk
3 Tbsp. canola mayonnaise
3 Tbsp. reduced-fat sour cream
3 oz. blue cheese (such as Rogue Creamery or Maytag), crumbled (about ¾ cup)

1. Combine first 8 ingredients (through shallot) in a jar. Stir and let stand 10 minutes to macerate. Add buttermilk, mayonnaise, sour cream, and cheese. Seal jar; shake the dickens out of it before serving. Refrigerate up to 5 days. Serves 10 (serving size: about 2 ½ Tbsp.)

CALORIES 62; **FAT** 4g (sat 2g, unsat 2g); **PROTEIN** 3g; **CARB** 3g; **FIBER** 0g; **SUGARS** 2g (added sugars 0g); **SODIUM** 207mg; **CALC** 8% DV; **POTASSIUM** 2% DV

Gluten Free • Make Ahead Vegetarian

Creamy Potato Salad

Hands-on: 25 min. **Total:** 45 min.

1 ¼ cups chopped red onion
¾ cup chopped multicolored mini bell peppers
4 tsp. olive oil
1 ½ lb. Yukon Gold potatoes, cut into ¾-inch cubes
3 large eggs
⅔ cup olive oil mayonnaise
¼ cup plain whole-milk Greek yogurt
1 Tbsp. grainy or traditional Dijon mustard
2 tsp. fresh lemon juice
¼ cup chopped fresh flat-leaf parsley
2 Tbsp. chopped fresh dill
⅝ tsp. kosher salt
¼ tsp. ground black pepper

1. Preheat oven to 425°F. Combine onion, bell peppers, and oil on a baking sheet. Bake at 425°F until tender and lightly charred, about 15 minutes.
2. Place potatoes in a large saucepan with water to cover by 2 inches; bring to a boil over high. Reduce heat to medium-low; simmer until potatoes are barely tender, about 5 minutes. Add eggs to pan. Cook until potatoes are tender, about 12 minutes. Remove eggs and place in a bowl filled with ice water; let stand 5 minutes. Drain potatoes; cool 5 minutes.
3. Combine mayonnaise, yogurt, mustard, juice, parsley, dill, salt, and pepper in a medium bowl. Peel cooked eggs and chop. Add eggs, potatoes, and onion mixture to mayonnaise mixture; stir gently to combine. Serve immediately, or chill before serving. Serves 8 (serving size: about ⅔ cup)

CALORIES 258; **FAT** 19g (sat 3g, unsat 16g); **PROTEIN** 5g; **CARB** 17g; **FIBER** 3g; **SUGARS** 3g (added sugars 0g); **SODIUM** 344mg; **CALC** 3% DV; **POTASSIUM** 2% DV

DRESS FOR SUCCESS

SILKY, ZESTY DRESSING AND THE RIGHT SPUDS TAKE POTATO SALAD FROM SATISFYING TO SUBLIME.

YUKON GOLDS
Not as starchy as russets, Yukons won't turn gluey. They also hold their shape after cooking and add subtle buttery taste.

OLIVE OIL MAYO
This is the salad's backbone, adding extra richness. Olive oil mayo has less saturated fat than regular.

LEMON JUICE
You need a couple of teaspoons of acid—just enough to brighten flavors without turning the salad tart.

DIJON MUSTARD
A dab delivers plenty of pungency. Choose country-style or grainy Dijon—which is flecked with mustard seeds—for added texture.

WHOLE-MILK GREEK YOGURT
Greek yogurt amps up the creaminess and adds delicious tang to excite your taste buds.

KOSHER SALT
Like all starches, potatoes soak up salt like sponges. You need as much as your healthy diet allows to season them properly.

ICE CREAM WORTH MAKING

Homemade ice cream is easier than you think. Sweet cherries and tangy cheese make this extra special.

Gluten Free • Make Ahead Vegetarian

Cherry–Goat Cheese Ice Cream

Hands-on: 20 min. **Total:** 12 hr. 30 min.

2 ¼ cups fresh Bing cherries, pitted (10 oz.)
4 large egg yolks
¾ cup sugar
1 tsp. vanilla extract
2 ¼ cups half-and-half
1 (12-oz.) can low-fat evaporated milk
1 ½ Tbsp. light corn syrup
½ tsp. kosher salt
2 oz. goat cheese, crumbled (about ½ cup)

1. Preheat oven to 425°F. Place cherries in a single layer in a baking dish. Bake at 425°F until softened, about 15 minutes. Drain; cool completely, about 30 minutes. Place in a small bowl; cover.

2. Whisk together egg yolks, sugar, and vanilla in a large bowl until light and pale. Combine half-and-half, evaporated milk, corn syrup, and salt in a large saucepan over medium-low. Cook, whisking often, until just simmering, about 10 minutes; remove pan from heat. Gradually pour 1 ½ cups hot half-and-half mixture in a steady stream into egg mixture, whisking constantly. Add egg mixture to remaining half-and-half mixture in pan. Return pan to medium-low, and cook, whisking constantly, until mixture is slightly thickened and coats back of a spoon, about 5 minutes. Place in a large bowl; cover. Chill covered bowls of cherries and custard in refrigerator 8 hours or overnight.

3. Pour chilled custard into freezer bowl of a 2-quart electric ice cream maker, and proceed according to manufacturer's instructions. Transfer to an airtight freezer-safe container. Drain chilled cherries to remove any juices that might have accumulated overnight; fold cherries and goat cheese into ice cream. Cover and freeze until firm, at least 4 hours. Serves 10 (serving size: about ¾ cup)

CALORIES 221; **FAT** 10g (sat 5g, unsat 4g); **PROTEIN** 6g; **CARB** 28g; **FIBER** 1g; **SUGARS** 25g (added sugars 18g); **SODIUM** 187mg; **CALC** 16% DV; **POTASSIUM** 4% DV

THE STEPS

1. ROAST CHERRIES
Roasting fresh cherries softens their flesh and evaporates water, concentrating their flavor. Softened cherries also blend better into the custard.

2. TEMPER CUSTARD
The eggs in the custard will curdle if they get too hot. Gradually adding the simmered half-and-half mixture raises the custard temperature slowly.

3. MAKE IT THICK
Cook the custard: Whisk nonstop to heat evenly. The mixture is ready when it reaches *nappe* consistency, thick enough to coat the back of a spoon.

4. FOLD IN FLAVORS
Once the custard has firmed up in the ice cream maker, gently fold in the goat cheese and the cherries, drained to keep the custard from turning pink.

LIGHTEN UP LEMON MERINGUE PIE

Zippy citrus meets 100% whole-grain goodness to deliver a third less saturated fat and added sugar.

Light and fluffy as it might seem, the traditional lemon meringue pie packs up to 30g added sugar (that's nearly 8 teaspoons and more than 60% of the daily recommended limit) into one small slice. To retain the lemony tang and lush mouthfeel with less added sugar and sat fat, we reserve most of the sugar for where it makes the biggest impact (the filling) and deploy a billowy, lightly sweetened meringue to seal the deal. The filling maintains its signature silky sheen even after reducing butter by 75% and using a mix of whole eggs and egg whites (instead of yolks alone), which shave off a total of 20g sat fat from the recipe. With satisfying layers of smooth curd and marshmallowy meringue nestled inside a tender, whole-grain crust, our puckery pie is perfection.

Staff Favorite • Make Ahead Vegetarian

Lemon Meringue Pie

Hands-on: 25 min. **Total:** 3 hr. 40 min.

CRUST
4.38 oz. whole-wheat pastry flour (about 1¼ cups)
1 Tbsp. nonfat dry milk
2 tsp. granulated sugar
¼ tsp. kosher salt
3 Tbsp. vegetable shortening, chilled and cut into small pieces
2 Tbsp. cold unsalted butter, cut into small pieces
¼ cup ice-cold water, divided

FILLING
2 large eggs
1 large egg white
1½ cups water
1 cup granulated sugar
⅓ cup cornstarch
¼ tsp. kosher salt
1½ Tbsp. lemon zest
½ cup fresh lemon juice
2 tsp. unsalted butter

MERINGUE
4 large egg whites
¼ tsp. cream of tartar
2 Tbsp. powdered sugar

1. Prepare crust: Whisk together flour, dry milk, sugar, and salt in a bowl. Add shortening and butter; use your fingers to combine until well distributed and pea-sized clumps form. Stir in 2 tablespoons ice-cold water. Add up to 2 more tablespoons water, as needed, until dough comes together. Knead 2 times on a floured surface. Shape dough into a disk; wrap in plastic wrap. Chill 30 minutes.

2. Preheat oven to 425°F. Unwrap dough; roll into an 11-inch circle on a floured surface. Place inside a 9-inch glass pie plate. Crimp edges of dough; prick all over with a fork. Bake at 425°F until lightly browned, 10 to 12 minutes. Let cool while preparing filling. Reduce oven temperature to 375°F.

3. Prepare filling: Whisk together eggs and egg white in a bowl. Whisk together 1½ cups water, sugar, cornstarch, and salt in a saucepan. Bring to a boil, stirring often. Boil until mixture thickens, 1 minute. Remove from heat; slowly whisk mixture into eggs. Return to pan; cook over medium-low, stirring constantly, 1 minute. Remove from heat; stir in zest, juice, and butter until smooth. Pour into crust.

4. Prepare meringue: Beat egg whites and cream of tartar with a mixer on medium-high speed until soft peaks form, about 2 minutes. Add sugar, increase speed to high, and beat until stiff peaks form, 1 minute.

5. Spread meringue over hot filling to edge of crust. Bake at 375°F until top is golden, about 10 minutes. Cool 2 hours. Serves 12 (serving size: 1 slice)

CALORIES 231; FAT 7g (sat 3g, unsat 3g); PROTEIN 5g; CARB 38g; FIBER 3g; SUGARS 20g (added sugars 19g); SODIUM 118mg; CALC 2% DV; POTASSIUM 3% DV

NO-FUSS SEAFOOD DINNERS

These 12 easy weeknight recipes utilize the four most popular go-to fish and shellfish options: salmon, shrimp, tuna, and tilapia.

SALMON RECIPES

Fast · Gluten Free

Simply Steamed Salmon and Corn with Dill Yogurt

Hands-on: 15 min. **Total:** 15 min.

4 (6-oz.) skin-on salmon fillets
1 tsp. kosher salt, divided
¾ tsp. black pepper, divided
8 oz. trimmed haricots verts
   (French green beans)
2 ears fresh corn, shucked and
   halved crosswise
½ cup plain 2% reduced-fat Greek
   yogurt
1½ Tbsp. chopped fresh dill
1 tsp. lemon zest plus 1 Tbsp.
   fresh juice
1 Tbsp. water

1. Prepare a steamer with 2 stackable bamboo baskets in a large Dutch oven. Line baskets with parchment paper. Add water to Dutch oven to a depth of 1 inch; bring to a boil over high.

2. Sprinkle salmon with ½ teaspoon salt and ¼ teaspoon pepper. Place in 1 bamboo basket. Place haricots verts and corn in second bamboo basket, and stack on salmon basket. Cover and cook until fish flakes with a fork, 8 to 10 minutes.

3. Stir together yogurt, dill, lemon zest and juice, 1 tablespoon water, remaining ½ teaspoon salt, and remaining ½ teaspoon pepper. Drizzle sauce over salmon, corn, and beans. Serves 4 (serving size: 1 salmon fillet, about 2 oz. beans, and 1 corn half)

CALORIES 553; **FAT** 14g (sat 3g, unsat 10g); **PROTEIN** 51g; **CARB** 58g; **FIBER** 17g; **SUGARS** 8g (added sugars 0g); **SODIUM** 591mg; **CALC** 16% DV; **POTASSIUM** 40% DV

Fast · Gluten Free

Sautéed Salmon with Chimichurri and Potatoes

Hands-on: 20 min. **Total:** 30 min.

3 cups small fingerling potatoes,
   halved lengthwise
5 Tbsp. olive oil, divided
1 tsp. kosher salt, divided
¾ tsp. black pepper, divided
⅓ cup finely chopped red onion
¼ cup chopped fresh flat-leaf
   parsley
3 Tbsp. red wine vinegar
1 Tbsp. chopped fresh oregano
½ tsp. crushed red pepper
Cooking spray
4 (6-oz.) skin-on salmon fillets

1. Preheat oven to 425°F.

2. Combine potatoes, 1 tablespoon oil, ¼ teaspoon salt, and ¼ teaspoon black pepper in a bowl; toss to coat. Spread potatoes in a single layer on an aluminum foil–lined baking sheet. Roast at 425°F until tender, 20 to 25 minutes, stirring after 15 minutes.

3. Stir together onion, parsley, vinegar, oregano, red pepper, 3 tablespoons oil, and ¼ teaspoon salt. Set chimichurri aside.

4. Heat a large cast-iron skillet or grill pan coated with cooking spray over high. Rub salmon with remaining 1 tablespoon oil. Sprinkle with remaining ½ teaspoon salt and ½ teaspoon black pepper. Add salmon to pan, skin side down; gently press until skin flattens, about 15 seconds. Cook until skin is browned, about 4 minutes. Flip salmon; cook to desired degree of doneness, about 2 minutes for medium-rare. Serve with chimichurri and potatoes. Serves 4 (serving size: 6 oz. salmon and about 3½ oz. potatoes)

CALORIES 477; **FAT** 28g (sat 4g, unsat 23g); **PROTEIN** 35g; **CARB** 18g; **FIBER** 3g; **SUGARS** 2g (added sugars 0g); **SODIUM** 559mg; **CALC** 4% DV; **POTASSIUM** 19% DV

Staff Favorite

Bourbon-Glazed Salmon with Firecracker Slaw

Hands-on: 30 min. **Total:** 45 min.

3 cups very thinly sliced cabbage
½ cup thinly sliced scallions, divided
¼ cup grated carrot
¼ cup canola mayonnaise
1 Fresno chile, seeded and sliced
2 Tbsp. apple cider vinegar
¾ tsp. granulated sugar
¾ tsp. black pepper, divided
½ tsp. kosher salt, divided
3 Tbsp. dark brown sugar
1 Tbsp. bourbon
1 Tbsp. lower-sodium soy sauce
4 (6-oz.) skin-on salmon fillets

1. Preheat a charcoal grill to medium-high (400° to 450°F).
2. Place cabbage, ¼ cup scallions, carrot, mayonnaise, chile, vinegar, sugar, ¼ teaspoon black pepper, and ¼ teaspoon salt in a bowl. Stir well to combine. Chill until ready to serve.
3. Whisk together brown sugar, bourbon, soy sauce, and remaining ½ teaspoon black pepper. Pour into a shallow dish. Place salmon, flesh side down, in sauce. Chill 15 minutes.
4. Remove salmon from dish. Place marinade in a saucepan; boil 2 minutes. Place salmon, skin side down, on oiled grates; grill, covered, to desired degree of doneness, 10 to 12 minutes for medium, brushing occasionally with reserved marinade. Place on a platter; top with remaining ¼ cup scallions and sprinkle with remaining ¼ teaspoon salt. Serve with slaw. Serves 4 (serving size: 1 salmon fillet and ½ cup slaw)

CALORIES 354; **FAT** 15g (sat 2g, unsat 12g); **PROTEIN** 35g; **CARB** 16g; **FIBER** 2g; **SUGARS** 13g (added sugars 11g); **SODIUM** 585mg; **CALC** 6% DV; **POTASSIUM** 21% DV

SHRIMP RECIPES

Fast

Steamed Shrimp and Watermelon Salad

Hands-on: 30 min. **Total:** 30 min.

3 cups water
1 cup apple cider vinegar

1 lb. peeled and deveined tail-on raw large shrimp
⅓ cup minced shallots
2 Tbsp. lower-sodium soy sauce
2 Tbsp. fresh lime juice
1 Tbsp. honey
3 Tbsp. canola oil
1 Tbsp. toasted sesame oil
3 cups chopped watermelon
2 cups chopped romaine lettuce
2 cups fresh spinach
1 large ripe avocado, cut into wedges
½ cup loosely packed fresh cilantro leaves, divided
1 tsp. shichimi togarashi or crushed red pepper (optional)
½ tsp. black sesame seeds
½ tsp. toasted sesame seeds

1. Fit a steamer basket into a stockpot. Add 3 cups water and vinegar; bring to a boil. Add shrimp; cover and steam 5 minutes. Remove shrimp to a baking sheet; chill 15 minutes.
2. Stir together shallots, soy sauce, lime juice, and honey in a bowl. Let stand 10 minutes. Whisk in canola and sesame oil.
3. Add watermelon, lettuce, spinach, avocado, and ¼ cup cilantro to shallot mixture; toss to combine. Place salad on a large platter, leaving any remaining dressing in bowl. Add shrimp; shichimi togarashi, if desired; and remaining ¼ cup cilantro to bowl. Toss to combine. Place shrimp mixture on salad. Sprinkle with sesame seeds. Serves 4 (serving size: 2 cups)

CALORIES 362; **FAT** 23g (sat 3g, unsat 19g); **PROTEIN** 19g; **CARB** 23g; **FIBER** 5g; **SUGARS** 13g (added sugars 4g); **SODIUM** 476mg; **CALC** 11% DV; **POTASSIUM** 15% DV

Fast • Make Ahead

Thai Pineapple Shrimp Curry

Hands-on: 30 min. **Total:** 30 min.

3 Tbsp. canola oil, divided
2 Tbsp. green curry paste
1 (13.5-oz.) can light coconut milk, well shaken
2 Tbsp. granulated sugar
2 Tbsp. fresh lime juice
1 Tbsp. lower-sodium soy sauce
1¼ lb. peeled and deveined tail-on raw medium shrimp
1½ cups chopped yellow onion
1¼ cups chopped red bell pepper
2 cups fresh pineapple chunks
½ cup chopped fresh cilantro, divided
3 Tbsp. thinly sliced scallions
3 Tbsp. chopped unsalted roasted peanuts

1. Heat 1 tablespoon oil in a medium saucepan over medium-high. Add curry paste; cook, stirring constantly, 1 minute. Add coconut milk and sugar; bring to a boil. Reduce to a simmer; cook until slightly thickened, about 5 minutes. Remove from heat; stir in lime juice and soy sauce.

2. Heat 1 tablespoon oil in a large skillet over high. Add shrimp; cook until opaque, 4 to 5 minutes. Remove to a plate. Add remaining 1 tablespoon oil to pan. Add onion and bell pepper; cook, stirring often, until tender, 2 to 3 minutes. Add curry mixture, shrimp, pineapple, and ¼ cup cilantro; cook until sauce is thickened, about 1 minute.

3. Divide shrimp mixture evenly among 4 bowls. Top evenly with scallions, peanuts, and remaining ¼ cup cilantro. Serves 4 (serving size: 1½ cups)

CALORIES 407; FAT 21g (sat 6g, unsat 12g); PROTEIN 24g; CARB 34g; FIBER 4g; SUGARS 20g (added sugars 6g); SODIUM 521mg; CALC 11% DV; POTASSIUM 11% DV

Fast

Simple Lemon, Shrimp, and Prosciutto Pasta

Hands-on: 20 min. **Total:** 20 min.

8 oz. uncooked vermicelli or angel hair pasta
2 oz. thinly sliced prosciutto
¼ cup extra-virgin olive oil, divided
4 garlic cloves, thinly sliced
2 cups multicolored cherry tomatoes, halved
½ cup thinly sliced fresh basil, divided
½ tsp. kosher salt
¼ tsp. crushed red pepper
12 oz. peeled and deveined tail-on raw large shrimp
2 lemons

1. Cook pasta according to package directions, omitting salt and fat. Drain, reserving 1 cup cooking liquid.

2. Cook prosciutto and 2 tablespoons oil in a large skillet over medium-high, stirring often, until prosciutto is crisp, 3 to 4 minutes. Transfer prosciutto to paper towels to drain. Add garlic to pan; cook, stirring often, until golden, 1 to 2 minutes. Add tomatoes, ¼ cup basil, salt, and red pepper. Cook until tomatoes begin to release their juices, about 4 minutes. Add shrimp; cook until opaque, 3 to 4 minutes. Stir in up to 1 cup reserved cooking liquid to thin sauce to desired consistency.

3. Halve 1 lemon; squeeze juice from both halves into sauce. Stir in pasta and remaining 2 tablespoons oil. Cut remaining lemon into wedges. Divide pasta evenly among 4 plates; top evenly with prosciutto and remaining ¼ cup basil. Serve with lemon wedges. Serves 4 (serving size: 1½ cups)

CALORIES 434; FAT 17g (sat 3g, unsat 13g); PROTEIN 24g; CARB 48g; FIBER 3g; SUGARS 5g (added sugars 0g); SODIUM 586mg; CALC 8% DV; POTASSIUM 8% DV

TUNA RECIPES

Fast • Gluten Free

Grilled Tuna with Chunky Tapenade Salsa

Hands-on: 25 min. **Total:** 25 min.

½ cup halved cherry tomatoes
⅓ cup kalamata olives, chopped
¼ cup thinly sliced fresh basil, divided
¼ cup extra-virgin olive oil, divided
2 Tbsp. balsamic vinegar
2 Tbsp. chopped fresh flat-leaf parsley
2 Tbsp. finely chopped shallot
1 Tbsp. chopped drained capers
½ tsp. kosher salt, divided
4 (6-oz.) tuna steaks
Cooking spray
¾ tsp. black pepper, divided
4 cups arugula
2 tsp. fresh lemon juice

1. Stir together tomatoes, olives, 2 tablespoons basil, 2 tablespoons oil, vinegar, parsley, shallot, capers, and ¼ teaspoon salt in a bowl.
2. Heat a grill pan or cast-iron skillet over high. Coat pan and tuna with cooking spray. Sprinkle tuna with ½ teaspoon pepper. Grill tuna to desired degree of doneness, about 2 minutes per side for medium-rare. Let stand 1 minute. Cut against the grain into ½-inch-thick slices. Sprinkle with remaining ¼ teaspoon salt.
3. Toss arugula in a bowl with lemon juice, remaining 2 tablespoons oil, and remaining ¼ teaspoon pepper.
4. Top tuna steaks evenly with salsa, and sprinkle with remaining 2 tablespoons basil. Serve with salad. Serves 4 (serving size: 1 tuna steak, about 2 Tbsp. salsa, and about 1 cup salad)

CALORIES 352; **FAT** 17g (sat 2g, unsat 14g); **PROTEIN** 43g; **CARB** 5g; **FIBER** 1g; **SUGARS** 3g (added sugars 0g); **SODIUM** 603mg; **CALC** 7% DV; **POTASSIUM** 19% DV

Soy-Marinated Tuna Skewers

Hands-on: 30 min. **Total:** 45 min.

½ cup chopped fresh cilantro, divided
¼ cup lower-sodium soy sauce
3 Tbsp. sesame oil
1 Tbsp. honey
2 tsp. sesame seeds
1 tsp. black pepper
1½ lb. tuna fillet, cut into 24 chunks
16 shishito peppers or mini bell peppers
8 cremini mushrooms, halved
1 medium eggplant, cut into 16 (1-inch) cubes
Cooking spray

1. Soak 8 (12-inch) wooden skewers in water 15 minutes.
2. Stir together ¼ cup cilantro, soy sauce, sesame oil, honey, sesame seeds, and black pepper in a large bowl. Reserve half of marinade. Add tuna to remaining marinade in bowl; toss to coat. Chill 15 minutes.
3. Remove tuna from marinade. Place marinade in a saucepan; boil 2 minutes. Thread tuna, shishito peppers, mushrooms, and eggplant onto skewers, beginning and ending with tuna.
4. Heat a grill pan over medium-high. Coat with cooking spray. Grill skewers until charred, 3 to 4 minutes, turning once. Brush with cooked marinade during last minute of grilling. Place skewers on a plate. Top with reserved marinade and remaining ¼ cup cilantro. Serves 4 (serving size: 2 skewers)

CALORIES 363; **FAT** 12g (sat 2g, unsat 9g); **PROTEIN** 46g; **CARB** 17g; **FIBER** 4g; **SUGARS** 9g (added sugars 4g); **SODIUM** 665mg; **CALC** 4% DV; **POTASSIUM** 28% DV

Gluten Free

Spice-Rubbed Tuna Steaks with Caramelized Fennel

Hands-on: 25 min. **Total:** 35 min.

7 Tbsp. olive oil, divided
2 large fennel bulbs, each cut into 8 wedges, fronds reserved
1½ tsp. black pepper, divided
1 tsp. kosher salt, divided
1 tsp. ground fennel seeds
1 tsp. ground coriander
½ tsp. ground cardamom
¼ tsp. paprika
4 (6-oz.) tuna steaks
1 medium orange
1 tsp. ground Aleppo pepper (optional)

1. Preheat the oven to 425°F. Heat 2 tablespoons oil in an ovenproof skillet over medium-high. Add fennel wedges; cook until one side is caramelized, 4 to 5 minutes. Flip fennel; place pan in oven. Roast at 425°F, stirring occasionally, 12 minutes. Place fennel in a bowl; toss with ½ teaspoon black pepper and ¼ teaspoon salt.
2. Combine fennel seeds, coriander, cardamom, paprika, remaining 1 teaspoon black pepper, and remaining ¾ teaspoon salt. Coat tuna with 1 tablespoon oil, then coat with spice mixture. Heat 2 tablespoons oil in a skillet over

high. Cook tuna to desired degree of doneness, about 2 minutes per side for medium-rare. Cut steaks in half diagonally.

3. Section orange over a bowl; reserve juices for another use. Combine orange sections, 1 tablespoon fennel fronds, and remaining 2 tablespoons oil. Top orange mixture and fennel wedges with Aleppo, if desired, and remaining fennel fronds. Serve with tuna. Serves 4 (serving size: 1 tuna steak and 4 fennel wedges)

CALORIES 464; **FAT** 25g (sat 4g, unsat 20g); **PROTEIN** 44g; **CARB** 16g; **FIBER** 6g; **SUGARS** 9g (added sugars 0g); **SODIUM** 632mg; **CALC** 11% DV; **POTASSIUM** 30% DV

SHOPPING FOR TUNA

LOOK FOR VIBRANCY
Tuna ranges from deep red to pink (tuna closer to the belly will be more pink due to the higher fat content). Regardless of hue, coloring should be vibrant, not muted.

CHECK FOR TIGHT MUSCULATURE
Tightly striated tuna flesh is another marker of freshness. The fish should appear firm and meaty (similar to a steak), not soft and flaky.

BE SELECTIVE ABOUT WHERE YOU BUY
Fishmongers, Asian groceries, and reputable fish counters have higher seafood turnover, so you'll likely find fresher fish—important when you're cooking to rare.

TILAPIA RECIPES

Fast

Blackened Tilapia Po'boys

Hands-on: 20 min. **Total:** 20 min.

¾ tsp. paprika
½ tsp. black pepper
½ tsp. cayenne pepper
¼ tsp. kosher salt
4 (5-oz.) skinless tilapia fillets
2 Tbsp. canola oil, divided
4 (2-oz.) hoagie rolls, split
¼ cup canola mayonnaise
1½ Tbsp. chopped drained capers
1 Tbsp. Creole mustard
1 Tbsp. unsalted ketchup
2 tsp. hot sauce
2 cups thinly sliced romaine lettuce
¼ cup thinly sliced red onion
8 tomato slices

1. Stir together paprika, black pepper, cayenne, and salt in a small bowl. Rub spice mixture evenly over fillets.
2. Heat 1 tablespoon oil in a large nonstick skillet over medium-high. Add half of fish to pan; cook until fish flakes easily with a fork, 2 to 3 minutes per side. Remove fish from pan. Repeat process with remaining 1 tablespoon oil and remaining fish.
3. Preheat broiler to high with oven rack in top position.
4. Arrange rolls, cut sides up, in a single layer on a baking sheet. Broil until golden, 30 to 45 seconds.

5. Stir together mayonnaise, capers, mustard, ketchup, and hot sauce in a bowl. Spread mixture over cut sides of rolls. Place lettuce, onion, and tomato on bottom halves of rolls. Add fish; cover with top halves of rolls. Serves 4 (serving size: 1 sandwich)

CALORIES 387; **FAT** 15g (sat 2g, unsat 12g); **PROTEIN** 34g; **CARB** 30g; **FIBER** 3g; **SUGARS** 6g (added sugars 1g); **SODIUM** 725mg; **CALC** 3% DV; **POTASSIUM** 5% DV

SHOPPING FOR TILAPIA

PURCHASE FROM THE FISH COUNTER
We've noticed that fresh tilapia fillets at the fish counter tend to be thicker and more evenly sized than what you'll find in the freezer case.

SURVEY FOR SIGNS OF FRESHNESS
A red blood line running down the crease of the fillet and seeping into the surrounding flesh is a sure sign of freshness. The blood line will turn brownish-gray the longer the fish sits out and is exposed to oxygen. Look for fillets that are bright and shiny, not dull.

Tilapia and Summer Squash Tacos

Hands-on: 40 min. **Total:** 40 min.

¼ cup olive oil
3 Tbsp. chipotle chiles in adobo
  sauce
1 Tbsp. red wine vinegar
1 tsp. granulated sugar
2 tsp. ground cumin, divided
1½ lb. skinless tilapia fillets
Cooking spray
1 medium-sized yellow squash,
  cut lengthwise into ½-inch-thick
  planks
1 large zucchini, cut lengthwise
  into ½-inch-thick planks
2 serrano chiles
¾ tsp. kosher salt, divided
⅓ cup light sour cream
1½ Tbsp. fresh lime juice
8 (5½-inch) corn tortillas, warmed
¾ cup prepared pico de gallo

1. Process oil, chipotles, vinegar, sugar, and 1 teaspoon cumin in blender until smooth. Add to a bowl with fish. Chill 15 minutes.
2. Heat a grill pan coated with cooking spray over high. Coat the squashes and serranos with cooking spray; sprinkle with ½ teaspoon salt and remaining 1 teaspoon cumin. Grill vegetables until charred, 2 minutes per side for squashes and about 5 minutes for serranos. Roughly chop vegetables.
3. Recoat pan with cooking spray. Cook fish over high until flaky, 2 to 3 minutes per side. Cut into chunks. Season with remaining ¼ teaspoon salt.

4. Stir together sour cream and lime juice. Divide fish and vegetables evenly among tortillas. Top evenly with pico de gallo and sour cream mixture. Serves 4 (serving size: 2 tacos)

CALORIES 498; **FAT** 21g (sat 4g, unsat 15g); **PROTEIN** 40g; **CARB** 42g; **FIBER** 5g; **SUGARS** 8g (added sugars 1g); **SODIUM** 721mg; **CALC** 12% DV; **POTASSIUM** 8% DV

Crispy Fish with Scallions and Peppers

Hands-on: 30 min. **Total:** 30 min.

1¼ lb. skinless tilapia fillets, cut into
  2-inch pieces
½ cup plus 2 tsp. cornstarch, divided
¼ cup unsalted chicken stock
3 Tbsp. lower-sodium soy sauce
1 tsp. sherry vinegar
5 Tbsp. canola oil, divided
5 garlic cloves, minced
1 Tbsp. chopped peeled fresh ginger
1 bunch scallions, halved
1 large red bell pepper, sliced
¾ tsp. crushed red pepper
Hot cooked jasmine rice (optional)

1. Toss fish with ½ cup cornstarch in a bowl, shaking off excess. Place fish on a baking sheet; chill 10 minutes.
2. Whisk together stock, soy sauce, vinegar, and remaining 2 teaspoons cornstarch. Set aside.
3. Heat 2 tablespoons oil in a large nonstick skillet over high. Add half of fish to pan. Cook without stirring, until browned and crispy, about 4 minutes. Turn fish, and cook until fish flakes with a fork,

1 to 2 minutes. Remove fish from skillet. Repeat process with 2 tablespoons oil and remaining fish. Wipe skillet clean.
4. Add remaining 1 tablespoon oil to skillet. Add garlic and ginger; cook over high, stirring constantly, until golden, 5 to 10 seconds. Add scallions and bell pepper; cook 1 minute. Remove skillet from heat. Add soy sauce mixture, crushed red pepper, and fish; stir gently to coat (sauce will thicken). Serve over rice, if desired. Serves 4 (serving size: 1¼ cups)

CALORIES 407; **FAT** 20g (sat 2g, unsat 17g); **PROTEIN** 31g; **CARB** 25g; **FIBER** 3g; **SUGARS** 4g (added sugars 0g); **SODIUM** 523mg; **CALC** 5% DV; **POTASSIUM** 6% DV

SHARE A FRESH SUMMER FEAST

New England chef Ana Sortun's menu features the best seasonal offerings from land and sea. It's perfect for a casual, elegant gathering with friends.

When Boston-area chef Ana Sortun entertains in the summer, the menu focuses on two things: fish and produce. "It's a great time of year to eat—and want to eat—fish," she says. "It's more abundant, with more varieties of species." Fish is simply a natural choice this time of year, lending itself to the type of lighter eating folks crave in the summer, so it's a real crowd-pleaser. On her family's annual two-week summer vacation to Cape Cod, "every night is a dinner party with friends," she explains, "and it's always centered around fish."

The second menu anchor, produce, is something of a family affair. Sortun's husband, Chris Kurth, owns Siena Farms (named for their daughter) and provides most of the produce to Sortun's three restaurants: Oleana, Sofra Bakery and Cafe, and Sarma. For the family's yearly vacation, they "literally bring a truck full of Siena Farms vegetables," she explains. Summertime boasts "the best vegetables you'll eat all year," so now is the time to showcase them. And that's exactly what Sortun does here, with a beautiful menu that celebrates the best you can get from the sea and the farm.

Swordfish Scaloppine with Capers

Hands-on: 35 min. **Total:** 35 min. The garlic sauce, which you can prepare up to two days ahead, is creamy, well seasoned, and wildly delicious.

2 lb. boneless, skinless swordfish loin
1 cup peeled garlic cloves
1 cup whole milk
1½ tsp. kosher salt, divided
1 cup panko (Japanese breadcrumbs)
1 Tbsp. unsalted butter, melted
3 Tbsp. extra-virgin olive oil, divided
2 Tbsp. chopped mixed fresh herbs (such as parsley, thyme, rosemary, oregano, and sage)
2 Tbsp. dried currants
2 Tbsp. pine nuts, lightly toasted
1 Tbsp. capers, drained
½ tsp. finely chopped garlic
1 canned anchovy fillet, minced
Lemon wedges (optional)

1. Place swordfish in freezer for 20 minutes so that it's partially frozen and extremely cold before slicing.
2. Meanwhile, preheat oven to 400°F. Place garlic cloves and milk in a small nonreactive saucepan over medium-low; simmer until very tender, about 20 minutes. Cloves should be squeezable and jammy; the milk will thicken around them. Cool 5 minutes; place in a blender with ¼ teaspoon salt. Process until very smooth and creamy.
3. Combine panko, butter, and 2 tablespoons oil in a bowl. Spread onto a baking sheet; bake at 400°F until toasted, 2 to 3 minutes. Stir in herbs, currants, pine nuts, capers, chopped garlic, and anchovy.
4. Using a sharp knife, cut swordfish loin crosswise into 16 thin slices. Heat remaining 1 tablespoon oil in a large nonstick skillet over high. Season fish with remaining 1¼ teaspoons salt. Working in batches, add fish to pan; cook until lightly browned and cooked through, about 90 seconds per side.
5. Spoon 1½ tablespoons garlic sauce onto each of 8 plates. Arrange 2 slices of fish per plate over the sauce. Top each serving with 3 tablespoons panko mixture; serve with lemon wedges, if desired. Serves 8

CALORIES 294; **FAT** 16g (sat 4g, unsat 11g); **PROTEIN** 23g; **CARB** 14g; **FIBER** 1g; **SUGARS** 3g (added sugars 0g); **SODIUM** 522mg; **CALC** 8% DV; **POTASSIUM** 12% DV

Fast • Vegetarian

Tomato-Cucumber Salad with Whipped Ricotta

Hands-on: 15 min. **Total:** 15 min.
"I've always been inspired by the phrase 'what grows together goes together,'" says Sortun. "This salad is a wonderful way to enjoy what the end of summer offers."

1⅓ cups part-skim ricotta cheese
⅝ tsp. kosher salt, divided
1 cup chopped heirloom tomato
1 cup chopped cucumber
4 sweet mini peppers, stemmed and thinly sliced (about ¾ cup)
2 scallions, finely chopped
2½ Tbsp. extra-virgin olive oil, divided
¾ tsp. sumac
½ tsp. dried mint
3 (6-inch) whole-wheat pita rounds, torn into 8 pieces each

1. Place ricotta and ½ teaspoon salt in a bowl. Using a whisk, whip until cheese is creamy, smooth, and resembles whipped cream but with a stiffer texture. Spread onto a platter to ½-inch thickness.
2. Combine tomato, cucumber, peppers, and scallions in a bowl. Stir in 1 tablespoon oil and remaining ⅛ teaspoon salt. Scatter vegetables over cheese; sprinkle with sumac and mint. Drizzle remaining 1½ tablespoons oil on top. Serve with pita. Serves 8 (serving size: 2½ tablespoons ricotta, ⅓ cup vegetables, and 3 pita pieces)

CALORIES 158; **FAT** 8g (sat 3g, unsat 5g); **PROTEIN** 7g; **CARB** 16g; **FIBER** 2g; **SUGARS** 2g (added sugars 0g); **SODIUM** 242mg; **CALC** 14% DV; **POTASSIUM** 5% DV

Corn and Crab Pita Nachos

Hands-on: 35 min. **Total:** 35 min.
This dish is inspired by the crab melts Sortun's mother made her when she was growing up in the Pacific Northwest.

1 Hungarian wax or banana pepper
3 Tbsp. extra-virgin olive oil, divided
1 Tbsp. fresh lemon juice
1 tsp. finely minced fresh garlic
½ cup plain whole-milk Greek yogurt
3 Tbsp. water
1 tsp. dried mint
4 (6-inch) whole-wheat pita rounds
1 cup finely chopped white onion
1½ cups fresh corn kernels (2 ears)
1½ tsp. ground cumin, divided
½ tsp. black pepper
2 cups sliced romaine lettuce
¾ cup chopped tomato
4 oz. fresh crabmeat, picked
½ ripe avocado, diced
2 tsp. sumac or 1½ tsp. lemon zest
½ tsp. kosher salt

1. Preheat oven to 400°F. Remove stem from wax pepper. Rub pepper with ⅛ teaspoon oil; place on a small baking sheet or piece of aluminum foil. Roast at 400°F until slightly blistered, 10 to 12 minutes. Let pepper stand until cool enough to handle; rub off and discard skin.
2. Combine juice and garlic in a bowl; let stand 5 minutes. Finely chop pepper; add to garlic mixture. Stir in yogurt, 3 tablespoons water, mint, and ¾ teaspoon oil.
3. Reduce oven temperature to 350°F. Split each pita into 2 rounds. Cut pita rounds into wedges, and place in a bowl. Drizzle with 2 tablespoons oil; toss gently to coat. Place in an even layer on 2 baking sheets. Bake at 350°F until browned and crisp, about 10 to 12 minutes.

4. Heat 2 teaspoons oil in a skillet over medium. Add onion; cook until translucent, about 5 minutes. Add corn; cook, stirring often, until tender, about 4 minutes. Stir in 1 teaspoon cumin and black pepper.

5. Arrange pita chips in an even layer on a platter (they can overlap). Spoon corn mixture evenly over chips. Toss lettuce and tomato with remaining ⅛ teaspoon oil and remaining ½ teaspoon cumin; sprinkle over nachos. Drizzle yogurt mixture over nachos, then top with crab and avocado. Sprinkle with sumac and salt. Serves 8 (serving size: about ¾ cup)

CALORIES 194; **FAT** 8g (sat 2g, unsat 6g); **PROTEIN** 9g; **CARB** 26g; **FIBER** 4g; **SUGARS** 4g (added sugars 0g); **SODIUM** 254mg; **CALC** 6% DV; **POTASSIUM** 8% DV

Gluten Free • Make Ahead Vegetarian

Beet Salad with Nectarines and Peppers

Hands-on: 30 min. **Total:** 1 hr. 35 min. "Peaches and sweet peppers are a great combo," says chef Ana Sortun, "so nectarines and shishitos are, too." To get a head start, you can roast the beets and peppers a day ahead. Use baby bell peppers if you can't find shishitos.

4 medium-sized golden beets, trimmed
16 shishito peppers
Cooking spray
3 Tbsp. extra-virgin olive oil
1 Tbsp. fresh lemon juice
½ tsp. kosher salt
½ tsp. dried oregano
¼ tsp. crushed red pepper
3 nectarines, cut into wedges

⅔ **cup coarsely chopped almonds,** toasted
2 oz. barrel-aged or regular feta cheese, crumbled (about ¼ cup)
6 fresh mint leaves, torn

1. Preheat oven to 350°F. Wrap beets in aluminum foil. Roast at 350°F until tender, about 1 hour; let cool. Rub off skins with a paper towel. Cut beets into wedges.

2. While beets cool, coat shishitos with cooking spray. Spread onto a baking sheet, and roast at 350°F until slightly blistered and almost collapsed, about 14 minutes.

3. Whisk together oil, lemon juice, salt, oregano, and red pepper in a large bowl. Add beet and nectarine wedges; toss gently to coat. Arrange on a platter. Top with shishitos, almonds, feta, and mint. Serves 8 (serving size: about ⅔ cup)

CALORIES 169; **FAT** 12g (sat 2g, unsat 9g); **PROTEIN** 4g; **CARB** 14g; **FIBER** 4g; **SUGARS** 9g (added sugars 0g); **SODIUM** 218mg; **CALC** 7% DV; **POTASSIUM** 11% DV

Staff Favorite • Gluten Free Make Ahead • Vegetarian

Milk Chocolate Yogurt with Granola and Blueberries

Hands-on: 45 min. **Total:** 1 hr. 45 min. This dessert is adapted from a recipe in Cheryl Sternman Rule's book *Yogurt Culture.* The yogurt only has three ingredients, so it's important to use the best you can get.

1 cup old-fashioned oats
2 Tbsp. toasted sesame seeds
2 Tbsp. demerara or turbinado sugar

¾ **tsp. ground cinnamon**
1 tsp. flaky sea salt, divided
3 Tbsp. unsweetened cocoa
3 Tbsp. honey
2 Tbsp. extra-virgin olive oil
5 oz. Valrhona or Callebaut milk chocolate, melted over a double boiler
2 cups plain whole-milk Greek yogurt
2 cups fresh blueberries

1. Preheat oven to 300°F. Line a rimmed baking sheet with parchment paper. Combine oats, sesame seeds, sugar, cinnamon, and ½ teaspoon salt in a large bowl.

2. Whisk together cocoa, honey, and oil in a saucepan over medium until honey and cocoa melt together. Pour over oat mixture; stir to coat. Spread onto prepared baking sheet; bake at 300°F for 15 minutes. Stir the granola to break it apart, and bake another 12 minutes. Remove from oven; cool completely. Crumble granola.

3. Place melted chocolate in a medium glass bowl. Gradually whisk in yogurt until smooth. (If chocolate starts to seize up, return bowl to double boiler, and stir constantly over low heat until smooth.) Stir in remaining ½ teaspoon salt. Cover and chill 1 hour or up to 8 hours.

4. Divide yogurt mixture among 8 parfait glasses; top with granola and berries. Serves 8 (serving size: about ⅓ cup yogurt, ¼ cup granola, and ¼ cup blueberries)

CALORIES 299; **FAT** 14g (sat 6g, unsat 7g); **PROTEIN** 9g; **CARB** 37g; **FIBER** 4g; **SUGARS** 26g (added sugars 18g); **SODIUM** 257mg; **CALC** 11% DV; **POTASSIUM** 8% DV

HOW TO COOK FISH (LIKE A PRO)

Seafood savvy comes easier than you may think. Follow our step-by-step guides to four foolproof methods—plus tips on the best fish for each—and start reeling in the praise.

Gluten Free

Flounder Grilled on Banana Leaves

Hands-on: 15 min. **Total:** 35 min.

¼ cup finely chopped fresh cilantro
¼ cup olive oil
3 Tbsp. minced shallot
2 Tbsp. fresh lime juice
1 small Fresno chile, seeded and finely chopped (about 2 Tbsp.)
1 Tbsp. finely chopped lemongrass (from 1 stalk)
1½ tsp. light brown sugar
1 tsp. grated peeled fresh ginger
¾ tsp. fish sauce
4 (6-oz.) skinless flounder fillets
¾ tsp. kosher salt
2 (12-inch-square or round) banana leaves or pieces of heavy-duty foil
4 banana leaves (optional)

1. Preheat grill to medium-high (about 450°F). Stir together cilantro, olive oil, shallot, lime juice, chile, lemongrass, brown sugar, ginger, and fish sauce in a bowl.
2. Sprinkle fillets with salt. Place banana leaves on grill grates; top each leaf with 2 flounder fillets. Spoon ¼ cup shallot mixture evenly over fillets. Grill, covered, until flounder is opaque and cooked through, about 5 minutes.
3. Using 2 spatulas, carefully remove fish-topped banana leaves from grill. Place each fillet on a fresh banana leaf for serving, if desired; divide remaining shallot mixture among fillets. Serves 4 (serving size: 1 fillet and 1 Tbsp. shallot mixture)

CALORIES 261; FAT 17g (sat 3g, unsat 13g); PROTEIN 22g; CARB 6g; FIBER 0g; SUGARS 3g (added sugars 1g); SODIUM 589mg; CALC 4% DV; POTASSIUM 7% DV

GRILL

MANY COOKS ONLY GRILL THICK FISH STEAKS BECAUSE THIN FILLETS BREAK AND FALL INTO THE FIRE. BUT A BANANA LEAF SOLVES THE PROBLEM ELEGANTLY. IT'S NATURALLY NONSTICK, COVERS THE RACK, AND LENDS SUBTLE GRASSY SWEETNESS TO THINNER FILLETS LIKE FLOUNDER, SNAPPER, TILAPIA, AND SOLE, ALONG WITH SMOKY GRILLED FLAVOR.

HANDLE WITH CARE
Cut fresh leaves with scissors. Frozen leaves are more fragile—thaw completely and separate gently so they don't split.

ARRANGE ON GRILL
Place leaves over direct heat; top with fillets. The leaves keep fish from sticking to or falling through the rack.

LIFT THEM AWAY
Keep the leaves under the fish to protect the fragile fillets. Use two spatulas for better leverage and steadiness.

ROAST

ROASTING FISH AT JUST 275°F PRESERVES ITS DELICATE TEXTURE. WITH PINK FISH THAT CAN BE SERVED MEDIUM-RARE OR MEDIUM, SUCH AS ARCTIC CHAR, STEELHEAD TROUT, OR SALMON, THAT MEANS A DELECTABLY SILKY INTERIOR. STILL, IT'S A SMART METHOD FOR MOST ANY FILLETS BECAUSE YOU'RE MUCH LESS LIKELY TO DRY THEM OUT OR OVERCOOK THEM.

BUY FATTY FISH
If you can't find Arctic char, no problem—go with its orange-fleshed cousins like steelhead trout or any variety of fresh salmon.

FLAVOR FEARLESSLY
Basting with savory-sweet sauces is typically done near the end of cooking so they don't burn, but here the low temps don't scorch the sugar.

CHECK THE TEMPERATURE
Use a digital instant-read thermometer to test the internal temperature in the fillet's thickest part. About 120°F means a warm, pink center.

Fast

Slow-Roasted Arctic Char with Soy Glaze

Hands-on: 15 min. **Total:** 20 min.

2 ½ Tbsp. oyster or hoisin sauce
1 Tbsp. lower-sodium soy sauce
1 Tbsp. unseasoned rice vinegar
1 ½ tsp. light brown sugar
½ tsp. crushed red pepper
⅛ tsp. kosher salt
2 (12-oz.) skin-on Arctic char or salmon fillets
1 Tbsp. toasted sesame oil
12 oz. baby bok choy (about 2 inches each), halved lengthwise
2 garlic cloves, smashed
2 Tbsp. water
2 Tbsp. thinly sliced scallions

1. Preheat oven to 275°F. Whisk together first 6 ingredients (through salt) in a small bowl.
2. Place fish, skin side down, on a foil-lined baking sheet. Brush fish with 3 tablespoons oyster sauce mixture; bake at 275°F until a thermometer inserted in thickest portion reaches 120°F, about 12 minutes. Transfer to a serving plate.
3. Heat oil in a large skillet over medium-high. Add bok choy and garlic; cook, stirring often, until slightly softened, about 2 minutes. Add 2 tablespoons water; cover and steam until tender, about 3 minutes. Remove from heat. Add remaining 2 tablespoons oyster sauce mixture; toss to coat. Serve with fish; garnish with scallions. Serves 4 (serving size: 4 ½ oz. fish and 1 cup bok choy)

CALORIES 300; FAT 13g (sat 3g, unsat 10g); PROTEIN 38g; CARB 6g; FIBER 1g; SUGARS 3g (added sugars 3g); SODIUM 648mg; CALC 11% DV; POTASSIUM 13% DV

Stovetop Braised Cod over Couscous

Hands-on: 15 min. **Total:** 35 min.

2 Tbsp. olive oil
1 medium (8-oz.) leek, white and light green parts only, sliced into thin half-moons
1 medium fennel bulb, thinly sliced (about 1½ cups)
1 Tbsp. unsalted tomato paste
2 garlic cloves, chopped
1 (8-oz.) bottle clam juice
½ cup finely chopped tomatoes
1½ oz. (about ⅓ cup) pitted Castelvetrano olives, halved
½ cup water
½ tsp. kosher salt, divided
4 (6-oz.) skinless cod fillets (about ¾ inch thick)
2 cups cooked whole-wheat couscous
Chopped fresh flat-leaf parsley (optional)
Lemon wedges (optional)

1. Heat oil in a 12-inch high-sided skillet over medium-high. Add leek and fennel; cook, stirring often, until softened, about 7 minutes. Add tomato paste and garlic; cook, stirring constantly, until fragrant, about 1 minute. Stir in clam juice, tomatoes, olives, ½ cup water, and ¼ teaspoon salt; bring to a boil. Reduce heat to medium-low; simmer until slightly reduced, about 10 minutes. Adjust heat as needed to maintain a very gentle simmer.

2. Sprinkle cod with remaining ¼ teaspoon salt. Nestle fish into tomato mixture; cover and cook until fish is done, about 10 minutes. Serve cod and tomato mixture over couscous. Garnish with parsley and lemon, if desired. Serves 4 (serving size: ½ cup couscous, 1 fillet, and ½ cup sauce)

CALORIES 313; **FAT** 9g (sat 1g, unsat 6g); **PROTEIN** 31g; **CARB** 25g; **FIBER** 5g; **SUGARS** 5g (added sugars 0g); **SODIUM** 688mg; **CALC** 6% DV; **POTASSIUM** 15% DV

BRAISE

A QUICK BRAISE IS THE BEST WAY TO KEEP LEAN WHITE FISH LIKE COD INCREDIBLY MOIST. THE FILLETS COOK IN A GENTLY SIMMERING SAUCE, BASTED BY AROMATIC STEAM IN THE COVERED PAN. THIS IS AN IDEAL METHOD FOR OTHER LEAN WHITE FISH THAT CAN DRY OUT EASILY, SUCH AS HALIBUT, HADDOCK, STRIPED BASS, OR GROUPER.

SIMMER IT SLOWLY
Adjust the burner heat until the sauce is simmering gently (just a few bubbles). If it boils, the fish will tighten up and dry out.

NESTLE THE FISH
With a braise, you want the protein to be partly in liquid—from one-third to halfway up the sides—but not totally submerged.

TEST WITH A KNIFE
When you can easily insert a paring knife or skewer in the side of the fillet toward the center without resistance, it's done.

SMOKE

YOU DON'T NEED SPECIAL EQUIPMENT TO HOT-SMOKE FISH—A GAS OR CHARCOAL GRILL WORKS JUST FINE IF YOU KEEP AN EYE ON THE TEMPERATURE. MILD, LIGHTLY SWEET ALDER WOOD OR FRUIT WOODS LIKE APPLE OR CHERRY ARE GREAT FOR FISH. FATTIER FISH LIKE TROUT AND SALMON ABSORB SMOKE FLAVOR BETTER THAN LEANER FILLETS.

CURE QUICKLY
Coating the fillets with a salt-sugar-spice mixture flavors the fish and results in fish that has much less sodium than store-bought.

PRESS AND DRY
Weight the fish with a skillet to gently squeeze out water and concentrate flavor. Chill uncovered to dry the flesh even more.

HEAT INDIRECTLY
A low-temp fire topped with fragrant wood chips on one side of the grill cooks the fish slowly over a couple of hours.

Staff Favorite

Hot-Smoked Trout on Sesame Bagels

Hands-on: 40 min. **Total:** 11 hr. 50 min.

⅓ cup kosher salt
¼ cup granulated sugar
1 tsp. ground white pepper
1 tsp. garlic powder
2 (6- to 8-oz.) skin-on butterflied
    rainbow trout fillets
6 cups alder wood chips
8 oz. ⅓-less-fat cream cheese
¼ cup chopped scallions
4 sesame bagels, halved
2 Tbsp. drained nonpareil capers
2 medium tomatoes, thinly sliced
Chopped fresh dill

1. Combine first 4 ingredients (through garlic powder) in a medium bowl. Line a baking sheet with plastic wrap, leaving enough overhang to cover fish. Sprinkle 3 tablespoons salt mixture on plastic; place fish, skin side down, on salt mixture. Sprinkle remaining salt mixture on fish; press to adhere. Tightly wrap plastic around fish. Place a separate baking sheet on fish; weight with a cast-iron skillet. Chill 1 hour.

2. Unwrap and rinse fish; pat dry. Return to pan, and chill overnight.
3. Preheat grill to 180°F; maintain temperature 10 minutes. Push coals to one side; top with wood chips. (Or preheat one side of gas grill and wrap wood chips in foil.) Place fish on oiled grates over indirect heat. Grill, covered, until firm and golden, about 2 hours. Remove from grill; let stand 15 minutes.
4. Combine cream cheese and scallions; spread on bagel halves. Top with capers, tomatoes, fish, and dill. Serves 8

CALORIES 254; **FAT** 11g (sat 5g, unsat 4g); **PROTEIN** 18g; **CARB** 21g; **FIBER** 1g; **SUGARS** 5g (added sugars 2g); **SODIUM** 561mg; **CALC** 13% DV; **POTASSIUM** 9% DV

THE BEST WAY TO MARINATE AND SKEWER MEAT

BY ANDREA NGUYEN

Soak, skewer, grill. Follow these three steps (with a killer marinade) for a no-fail, crowd-pleasing main.

Being a curious, obsessive cook has its pluses and minuses. I often go down a rabbit hole to experiment with something that doesn't really need fixing. Thankfully, along the way, there are valuable lessons learned.

Not long ago, I thought I'd use a favorite beef skewer marinade on a steak. Three rounds of testing and tweaking yielded *meh* results. The marinade just didn't do much to flavor the meat. I was better off with my reliable standby of salt and pepper.

What I realized is that the original recipe worked beautifully because it's better to use a marinade for skewered morsels than large slabs of meat. When you cut up meat, there's more surface area exposed to the marinade, which only penetrates about one-eighth of an inch into the meat. Given that, expecting marinades to season deeply is a fantasy. You're better off ensuring that smallish pieces of protein get well-coated and sufficiently soaked. This ensures that the marinade is absorbed and flavors pop in a bold manner. (If the meat soaks too long in a marinade that's heavy on acidic ingredients like lemon juice or vinegar, the surface of the meat can turn mealy. Those marinades should

only go for 30 minutes to an hour.)

Cultures across the globe grill on skewers—from Mediterranean kebabs and Southeast Asian satays to Japanese yakitori and Peruvian anticuchos. You don't need much protein to satisfy a crowd, and the meat doesn't need to be fancy; it just needs to be cut up small enough to thread onto a skewer. The marinade and grilling take care of the rest.

Aside from flavor payoff, grilling meat on sticks is perfect for entertaining: You must prep in advance to allow the meat to marinate, but the final cooking is relatively fast. To avoid any last-minute hassle, I sometimes coat the meat in marinade, then immediately skewer it so things are ready to go on the grill. When threading the meat, I crowd it to create a compact column. The results are juicier than when there's space between the pieces.

As for the skewers, I dumped the skinny, round bamboo ones long ago. Even after soaking them in water for 30-plus minutes, they'd burn easily, and when loaded with meat, they often bend and droop, making them difficult to maneuver on the grill. Instead, I opt for flat bamboo or metal skewers because food sits more securely on them. (If flat ones aren't available, go for thicker, 3- to 4-millimeter-thick round bamboo skewers—they're sturdier.) Bamboo skewers can be cut down to fit small grills and are disposable (no need to collect empty ones at a party). However, stainless-steel skewers do not require soaking and are reusable.

Depending on my mood and available time, I might grill the skewers over charcoal (fabulous flavor), on a gas grill (easy setup), or a stovetop cast-iron grill pan (simple except for the cleanup). Regardless of marinade, meat, or cooking approach, my summertime grilling has improved simply because I paused to ponder and tinker.

Gluten Free

Harissa Grilled Chicken Skewers

Hands-on: 30 min. **Total:** 4 hr. 30 min. These skewers get a nice, long marinating time due to the low amount of lemon juice. If your marinade is loaded with vinegar or citrus, go for 30 minutes to an hour at most to ensure the best texture.

2 cups plus 1 Tbsp. water, divided
1 dried pasilla chile
¾ cup coarsely chopped yellow onion
3 Tbsp. canola oil, divided
2 Tbsp. spicy or mild harissa
1½ Tbsp. fresh lemon juice
¾ tsp. kosher salt
1½ lb. boneless, skinless chicken thighs, cut into 1-inch chunks
Chopped fresh chives (optional)

1. Microwave 2 cups water in a microwave-safe 1-quart measuring cup on high 3 minutes. Submerge chile in hot water. Let stand until soft and pliable, about 10 minutes. Drain; stem and seed chile.
2. Combine chile, onion, 2 tablespoons oil, harissa, lemon juice, and salt in a blender. Process until smooth and creamy, about 20 seconds. If needed, add 1 tablespoon water to thin.
3. Using a silicone spatula, scrape marinade into a gallon-sized ziplock plastic bag. Add chicken, and stir to coat well. Seal and chill 4 hours or up to 18 hours.
4. Thread chicken onto 4 (8- to 12-inch) skewers (keep chunks close to one another, forming a column of meat, to ensure juicy results); bring to room temperature, about 1 hour.
5. Prepare a hot fire in a charcoal grill or preheat a gas grill to high (450°F to 500°F). Alternatively,

heat a lightly oiled grill pan over high. Gently blot excess marinade from chicken to ensure a nice sear. Brush chicken with remaining 1 tablespoon oil.

6. Grill skewers, turning every 2 minutes, until chicken is lightly charred and cooked through, about 14 minutes. Let rest 5 to 10 minutes. Garnish with chives, if desired. Serves 4 (serving size: 1 skewer)

CALORIES 322; **FAT** 19g (sat 3g, unsat 10g); **PROTEIN** 36g; **CARB** 5g; **FIBER** 1g; **SUGARS** 1g (added sugars 0g); **SODIUM** 540mg; **CALC** 3% DV; **POTASSIUM** 2% DV

THE SEAFOOD GUY

HOW TO SUCCESS-FULLY BLACKEN FISH

BY BARTON SEAVER

Pick a spice blend, and then, literally, burn the fish fillet. Voilà—a fantastic dinner is served.

Blackened fish is steeped not only in flavor but also in culinary legend. In the 1980s, it was blackened redfish that brought Cajun cooking to prominence. Chef Paul Prudhomme introduced this dish at his celebrated New Orleans haunt, K-Paul's Louisiana Kitchen, combining the richness of a well-buttered thin redfish fillet with a spice mixture as spirited as a Mardi Gras krewe in full regalia. The dish proved so popular that redfish, also called red drum, was heavily fished and nearly disappeared from the Gulf of Mexico later that same decade. Redfish is now farmed, so the original dish

endures, but the quick cooking technique has evolved and now is applied to center-of-the-plate stars such as tuna, tilapia, chicken, and cauliflower steaks.

The method is called blackening because the point is to appropriately burn (blacken) the spice coating. (Yes, you have permission to burn your food!) There are as many blackening spice recipes as types of seafood, so pair your chosen blend (or use mine below) with the catch of the day, and make the act of cooking dinner an exciting discovery.

Fast · Gluten Free

Blackened Catfish

Hands-on: 10 min. **Total:** 30 min. Catfish is a perfect partner for the bold flavors of this spice blend, but any thin, white-flesh fillet such as trout, snapper, or perch are worthy substitutions in a pinch. Don't skip the lemon; it adds brightness and acidity to balance the fiery fish and buttery sauce.

½ cup salt-free blackening or Cajun seasoning
1 Tbsp. sweet or smoked sweet paprika
1 Tbsp. freshly ground black pepper
1 tsp. onion powder
1 tsp. garlic powder or garlic salt
1 tsp. ground dried oregano
1 tsp. ground dried thyme or rosemary
Pinch of cayenne pepper
4 (5-oz.) skinless catfish fillets
¾ tsp. kosher salt
1 Tbsp. olive oil
2 Tbsp. unsalted butter
¼ cup loosely packed fresh herb leaves (such as parsley, mint, or chervil)
Lemon wedges

1. Stir together first 8 ingredients (through cayenne pepper) in a small bowl until well combined.
2. Sprinkle fish with salt, and let stand 20 minutes. Drizzle with oil.
3. Heat a large cast-iron or heavy saucepan over high. (And by "heat the pan," I mean get it screaming hot. Turn on your vent to high, and open some windows. You also can heat the pan on a grill outside.)
4. Sprinkle fillets evenly with ¼ cup blackening spice mixture, pressing to adhere. Add butter to skillet, and swirl to coat. Place fillets in hot skillet; cook 2 minutes. Flip fillets and cook 2 to 3 minutes. (The spices will have formed a highly colored crust in varying shades of sunset and midnight black. The fish is done when it flakes apart under the gentle pressure of your finger.)
5. Remove fillets to serving plates, and sprinkle evenly with fresh herbs. Serve with lemon wedges. Serves 4 (serving size: 1 fillet)

CALORIES 251; **FAT** 18g (sat 6g, unsat 15g); **PROTEIN** 22g; **CARB** 0g; **FIBER** 0g; **SUGARS** 0g (added sugars 0g); **SODIUM** 502mg; **CALC** 2% DV; **POTASSIUM** 10% DV

A MAKE-AHEAD DISH FOR EASY SUMMER DINNERS

BY GINA HOMOLKA

Enjoy the dog days of the season with this portable, vegetable-filled dinner pasta salad.

I kick off my late-summer weekends by hitting up my local farmers' market to take advantage of the vegetable bounty. As soon as I get home, I spend a few minutes getting my market haul ready for the grill—stemming, seeding, and seasoning with a little olive oil and salt and pepper. Then I grill all my vegetables at once so they're prepped and ready to quickly add to my weeknight dishes.

This delicious, versatile Mediterranean pasta salad is a great example: Adding already grilled bell peppers and summer squash turns orzo into a meal in minutes. It's a perfectly portable, veggie-loaded summer meal that you can pack for the beach, a picnic, or a weeknight spent at the neighborhood pool. Another plus: It's made without mayo, so it's ideal to take to those hot August afternoon potlucks.

Make a big batch of this on the weekend, and you'll have plenty to serve as a main dish or a side (alongside grilled chicken or fish) in the week ahead. Whether you dish it up hot or cold, it's a delicious solution for fresh and wholesome eating on the go.

Make Ahead · Vegetarian

Grilled Veggie Orzo Salad

Hands-on: 40 min. **Total:** 40 min.
If you have a grill basket, cut the peppers into strips and grill everything together—it's a huge time-saver. Just be sure to stir occasionally so everything cooks evenly and chars nicely.

1 medium-sized red onion, quartered and layers separated
1 red bell pepper, seeded and quartered
1 orange bell pepper, seeded and quartered
1 large zucchini, cut lengthwise into ¼-inch-thick slabs
1 medium-sized yellow squash, cut lengthwise into ¼-inch-thick slabs
Olive oil cooking spray
1½ Tbsp. chopped fresh oregano, divided
10 oz. uncooked whole-wheat or gluten-free orzo
¼ cup sliced pitted kalamata olives
2 Tbsp. plus ½ tsp. red wine vinegar
2 Tbsp. grated Parmesan cheese
2 Tbsp. extra-virgin olive oil
1 tsp. lemon zest plus 2 Tbsp. fresh juice
1 tsp. kosher salt
½ tsp. black pepper
3 oz. feta cheese, crumbled (about ¾ cup)

1. Preheat grill to medium-high (400°F to 450°F).
2. Spritz onion, bell peppers, zucchini, and squash all over with olive oil cooking spray, and sprinkle evenly with 1½ teaspoons oregano. Place vegetables on oiled grates. Grill, uncovered, until soft and edges are browned, about 2 minutes per side for squash and zucchini and 5 minutes per side for onion and bell peppers. Remove from heat, and let cool. Chop vegetables into small pieces, and transfer to a large bowl.
3. Prepare orzo according to package directions for al dente, omitting salt. Reserve ½ cup cooking liquid. Drain and rinse under cold running water; stir orzo into vegetable mixture.
4. Add olives, vinegar, Parmesan, oil, lemon zest and juice, salt, black pepper, and reserved cooking liquid to orzo mixture; stir to combine. Gently stir in feta and remaining 1 tablespoon oregano. Serves 10 (serving size: ¾ cup)

CALORIES 205; FAT 7g (sat 2g, unsat 4g); PROTEIN 7g; CARB 29g; FIBER 7g; SUGARS 3g (added sugars 0g); SODIUM 351mg; CALC 7% DV; POTASSIUM 4% DV

20-MINUTE MAINS

Fast · Make Ahead

Chicken and Bulgur Salad with Peaches

Hands-on: 20 min. **Total:** 20 min.
A quick-cooking whole grain, bulgur is perfect for time-crunched weeknight cooking. If you can't find it on the grains aisle, you can substitute quinoa or whole-wheat couscous.

1⅓ cups water
⅓ cup bulgur
Cooking spray
1 lb. chicken breast cutlets
1 tsp. kosher salt, divided
½ tsp. black pepper
4 cups packed arugula
2 cups halved cherry tomatoes
2 cups sliced fresh peaches
3 Tbsp. extra-virgin olive oil
2 Tbsp. rice vinegar

1. Bring 1⅓ cups water and bulgur to a boil in a small saucepan over high. Reduce heat to medium-low; cover and simmer 10 minutes. Drain and rinse under cold water. Drain well; let dry on paper towels.
2. Meanwhile, heat a grill pan coated with cooking spray over high. Sprinkle chicken with ½ teaspoon salt and pepper. Grill chicken, turning occasionally, until done, 6 to 7 minutes. Remove to a cutting board. Let stand 3 minutes. Slice against the grain into strips.
3. Place bulgur, arugula, tomatoes, and peaches in a large bowl. Add remaining ½ teaspoon salt, oil, and vinegar; toss to coat. Divide mixture among 4 plates; top with chicken. Serves 4 (serving size: 2 cups salad and 4 oz. chicken)

CALORIES 364; FAT 14g (sat 2g, unsat 11g); PROTEIN 31g; CARB 30g; FIBER 6g; SUGARS 9g (added sugars 0g); SODIUM 547mg; CALC 7% DV; POTASSIUM 20% DV

Fast • Gluten Free
Make Ahead

Pork Chops with Corn Relish

Hands-on: 20 min. **Total:** 20 min.
Call on your grill and farmers' market bounty to make summer dinners simple. Keep this relish recipe handy for adding fresh flavor to grilled fish or pasta salad.

2 medium-sized green tomatoes, cut crosswise into ¼-inch-thick slices
4 (6-oz.) bone-in center-cut pork chops (about 1 inch thick)
1 tsp. kosher salt, divided
1 tsp. black pepper, divided
2 large ripe peaches, cut into ½-inch cubes (about 1½ cups)
1 cup fresh corn kernels (from 2 small ears)

¼ cup extra-virgin olive oil
2 Tbsp. chopped fresh flat-leaf parsley
2 Tbsp. white wine vinegar
1 tsp. chopped fresh thyme

1. Heat a grill pan over medium-high. Add tomato slices in a single layer; cook until slightly softened and lightly charred, about 2 minutes per side. Transfer to a cutting board; let cool slightly.
2. Season pork chops on both sides with ½ teaspoon salt and ½ teaspoon pepper. Add chops to grill pan; cook over medium-high until a thermometer inserted in thickest portion registers 145°F, about 3 minutes per side, or to desired degree of doneness. Remove from heat; transfer to a plate, and cover loosely to keep warm.
3. Chop tomato slices; toss together with peaches, corn, oil, parsley, vinegar, thyme, remaining ½ teaspoon salt, and remaining ½ teaspoon pepper in a medium bowl.
4. To serve, place pork chop relish with juices on each of 4 plates. Serves 4 (serving size: 1 pork chop and ¾ cup relish)

CALORIES 353; FAT 21g (sat 4g, unsat 16g); PROTEIN 27g; CARB 16g; FIBER 3g; SUGARS 10g (added sugars 0g); SODIUM 545mg; CALC 4% DV; POTASSIUM 14% DV

Staff Favorite • Fast
Vegetarian

Extra-Crispy Veggie-Packed Pizza

Hands-on: 15 min. **Total:** 20 min.
Our taste testers loved this pizza's crunchy crust and zingy zucchini salad, but the real hero was the halloumi—a dry, salty cheese similar to feta (which you could sub if you can't find halloumi). Sodium amounts vary among brands, so check the label.

1 Tbsp. white wine vinegar
1 Tbsp. canola oil
½ tsp. kosher salt, divided
¼ tsp. black pepper
1 cup shaved zucchini strips (from 1 zucchini)
1 (5-oz.) thin whole-wheat pizza crust (such as 365 Everyday Value)
¼ cup refrigerated basil pesto
2¼ oz. halloumi or feta cheese, crumbled (about ⅔ cup)
2 medium tomatoes, thinly sliced
⅛ tsp. crushed red pepper
1 (2-oz.) pkg. baby spring mix (about 4 cups)
¼ cup thinly sliced red onion
¼ cup chopped fresh basil

1. Preheat oven to 400°F with oven rack in top position. Stir together vinegar, oil, ¼ teaspoon salt, and black pepper in a medium bowl. Stir in zucchini; let stand at room temperature 10 minutes.
2. Meanwhile, place pizza crust on a baking sheet; spread pesto over crust. Sprinkle cheese evenly over pesto, and top with tomatoes and crushed red pepper. Bake on top rack at 400°F until slightly crispy, about 6 minutes. Turn broiler to high, and broil until cheese is bubbly, 1 to 2 minutes. Remove from oven, and let cool 2 minutes.
3. Add baby spring mix, onion, and basil to zucchini mixture; toss to combine. Arrange salad mixture evenly over pizza. Sprinkle with remaining ¼ teaspoon salt. Cut into 8 slices; serve immediately. Serves 4 (serving size: 2 slices)

CALORIES 280; FAT 18g (sat 6g, unsat 10g); PROTEIN 12g; CARB 6g; FIBER 5g; SUGARS 2g (added sugars 0g); SODIUM 738mg; CALC 29% DV; POTASSIUM 5% DV

Meatball and Tomato Salad

Hands-on: 20 min. **Total:** 20 min.
Use ground beef or bison here. Available in most grocery stores, bison is eco-friendly and has fewer calories and less sat fat than beef. Try these meatballs with spaghetti, or pile them on a whole-wheat hoagie for a wholesome take on the classic meatball sub.

1 lb. lean ground sirloin or lean ground grass-fed bison
1 tsp. kosher salt, divided
1 tsp. black pepper, divided
¼ cup canola oil, divided
1 tsp. lemon zest plus 2 Tbsp. fresh juice, divided
¼ cup plain 0% fat-free Greek yogurt
1 Tbsp. water
1 Tbsp. chopped fresh chives
1 Tbsp. chopped fresh dill
4 cups packed arugula
2 cups sliced heirloom tomatoes
1 ripe medium avocado, quartered and sliced

1. Stir together ground meat, ½ teaspoon salt, and ½ teaspoon pepper in a bowl; shape into 12 meatballs. Heat 1 tablespoon oil in a nonstick skillet over medium-high. Add meatballs; cook until browned on all sides, about 12 minutes. Remove from heat.
2. Whisk together the lemon juice, remaining 3 tablespoons oil, remaining ½ teaspoon salt, and remaining ½ teaspoon pepper in a small bowl. Stir together yogurt, 1 tablespoon water, chives, dill, and lemon zest in a separate small bowl.
3. Toss together arugula and 2 tablespoons oil mixture in a large bowl; place 1 cup mixture on each of 4 plates. Toss together tomato slices and 2 tablespoons oil mixture in the same bowl; add ½ cup tomatoes to each plate. Gently toss avocado slices with remaining 1 tablespoon oil mixture in bowl; divide evenly among plates. Place 3 meatballs on each plate; drizzle each with 1 tablespoon yogurt mixture. Serves 4 (serving size: 1 cup arugula mixture, ¾ cup salad, and 3 meatballs)

CALORIES 447; FAT 33g (sat 7g, unsat 24g); PROTEIN 28g; CARB 11g; FIBER 5g; SUGARS 5g (added sugars 0g); SODIUM 582mg; CALC 12% DV; POTASSIUM 20% DV

Chicken and Cucumber Salad with Parsley Pesto

Hands-on: 15 min. **Total:** 15 min.
This hearty supper salad is a lean-protein powerhouse thanks to chicken, chickpeas, and edamame; the parsley pesto delivers bone-boosting vitamin K. Pick up frozen shelled edamame to make this meal extra speedy.

2 cups packed fresh flat-leaf parsley leaves (from 1 bunch)
1 cup fresh baby spinach
2 Tbsp. fresh lemon juice
1 Tbsp. toasted pine nuts
1 Tbsp. grated Parmesan cheese
1 medium garlic clove, smashed
1 tsp. kosher salt
¼ tsp. black pepper
½ cup extra-virgin olive oil
4 cups shredded rotisserie chicken (from 1 chicken)
2 cups cooked shelled edamame
1 (15-oz.) can unsalted chickpeas, drained and rinsed
1 cup chopped English cucumber
4 cups loosely packed arugula

1. Place parsley, spinach, lemon juice, pine nuts, cheese, garlic, salt, and pepper in bowl of a food processor; process until smooth, about 1 minute. With processor running, add oil; process until smooth, about 1 minute.
2. Stir together chicken, edamame, chickpeas, and cucumber in a large bowl. Add pesto; toss to combine.
3. Place ⅓ cup arugula in each of 6 bowls; top each with 1 cup chicken salad mixture. Serve immediately. Serves 6

CALORIES 482; FAT 26g (sat 4g, unsat 18g); PROTEIN 40g; CARB 22g; FIBER 7g; SUGARS 2g (added sugars 0g); SODIUM 465mg; CALC 17% DV; POTASSIUM 13% DV

Gnocchi with Spinach and Pepper Sauce

Hands-on: 15 min. **Total:** 20 min.
Our shortcut version of Spain's beloved romesco sauce boasts all the smoky flavor of the original with a fraction of the prep time.

1 (16-oz.) pkg. whole-wheat potato gnocchi
1 (5-oz.) pkg. baby spinach
1½ oz. Manchego cheese, grated (about 6 Tbsp.) and divided
3 Tbsp. olive oil, divided
½ cup jarred roasted red peppers, chopped
¼ cup smoked almonds
1 plum tomato, chopped
1 baguette slice, torn (about ½ oz.)
2 Tbsp. sherry vinegar
1 garlic clove
½ tsp. paprika
¼ tsp. crushed red pepper

1. Cook gnocchi according to package directions, omitting salt and fat. Drain gnocchi; return to pan. Add spinach, ¼ cup cheese, and 1 tablespoon olive oil; cover and let stand until spinach wilts, 2 to 3 minutes. Gently toss to combine.

2. Pulse red peppers, almonds, tomato, baguette, vinegar, garlic, paprika, crushed red pepper, and remaining 2 tablespoons olive oil in a food processor until smooth, about 1 minute.

3. Divide gnocchi mixture among 5 bowls. Top evenly with sauce and remaining 2 tablespoons cheese. Serves 5 (serving size: about 1 cup gnocchi and ⅓ cup sauce)

CALORIES 324; FAT 16g (sat 4g, unsat 9g); PROTEIN 9g; CARB 34g; FIBER 8g; SUGARS 2g (added sugars 0g); SODIUM 590mg; CALC 14% DV; POTASSIUM 4% DV

4 SAUCES FOR ANY PROTEIN

Fast • Gluten Free
Make Ahead • Vegetarian
Spanish Salsa

This hearty condiment can stand up to just about anything, from charred flank steak to grilled halibut. If you can't find Castelvetrano olives, pick out the mildest green olives you can find.

Stir together ½ cup quartered cherry tomatoes, ¼ cup chopped roasted red peppers, 4 pitted and quartered Castelvetrano olives, 2 Tbsp. golden raisins, 2 Tbsp. chopped fresh parsley, 2 tsp. sherry vinegar, and 2 tsp. extra-virgin olive oil in a bowl. Serves 4 (serving size: about ¼ cup)

CALORIES 50; FAT 3g (sat 0g, unsat 2g); PROTEIN 0g; CARB 5g; FIBER 0g; SUGARS 4g (added sugars 0g); SODIUM 156mg; CALC 1% DV; POTASSIUM 2% DV

Fast • Make Ahead
Vegetarian
Double-Citrus Soy Sauce

A go-to dunking choice for pot stickers, this tangy sauce is also delicious brushed on vegetables during grilling or tossed with lo mein.

Stir together 2 Tbsp. lower-sodium soy sauce, 2 Tbsp. water, 1 Tbsp. fresh orange juice, 1 Tbsp. fresh lemon juice, 1 ½ tsp. rice vinegar, and 1 Tbsp. thinly sliced scallions in a small bowl. Serves 8 (serving size: 2 tsp.)

CALORIES 4; FAT 0g (sat 0g, unsat 0g); PROTEIN 0g; CARB 1g; FIBER 0g; SUGARS 0g (added sugars 0g); SODIUM 144mg; CALC 0% DV; POTASSIUM 0% DV

Fast • Gluten Free
Make Ahead • Vegetarian
Watermelon-Jalapeño Relish

Fresh-cut summer melon is best, but precubed melon will work in a pinch. Spoon this over grilled pork chops or fish, or serve it with tortilla chips for a twist on salsa.

Stir together 1 cup finely chopped watermelon, 2 Tbsp. finely chopped seeded jalapeño, 2 Tbsp. thinly sliced fresh mint, 1 Tbsp. minced shallot, 1 Tbsp. white wine vinegar, 1 Tbsp. extra-virgin olive oil, and ¼ tsp. kosher salt in a medium bowl. Let stand at least 5 minutes before serving. Serves 4 (serving size: about ¼ cup)

CALORIES 46; FAT 4g (sat 1g, unsat 3g); PROTEIN 0g; CARB 4g; FIBER 0g; SUGARS 3g (added sugars 0g); SODIUM 121mg; CALC 1% DV; POTASSIUM 1% DV

Fast • Gluten Free
Make Ahead • Vegetarian
Lemon-Caper Vinaigrette

Salty capers and bright lemon balance with the toasted almond–infused oil, yielding the perfect dressing for sautéed seafood or grilled chicken.

Combine ¼ cup olive oil and 3 Tbsp. sliced almonds in a small nonstick skillet over medium, and cook, stirring often, until lightly toasted, about 2 minutes. Transfer to a small bowl; let cool 5 minutes. Stir in 1½ Tbsp. drained nonpareil capers, chopped; ½ tsp. lemon zest plus 2 Tbsp. fresh juice; 1 Tbsp. finely chopped fresh chives; and ¼ tsp. crushed red pepper. Serves 4 (serving size: 2 Tbsp.)

CALORIES 147; FAT 16g (sat 2g, unsat 13g); PROTEIN 1g; CARB 2g; FIBER 1g; SUGARS 0g (added sugars 0g); SODIUM 76mg; CALC 2% DV; POTASSIUM 1% DV

WEEKNIGHT MAINS

Vegetarian
Chilled Avocado Soup

Hands-on: 10 min. **Total:** 40 min.
This is the perfect dinner for a sweltering summer night. Ice-cold sparkling water is a genius addition to this recipe—its bubbly effervescence provides the perfect lift to buttery ripe avocado. If you're not into tofu, top each serving with three steamed shrimp.

2 ½ cups (20 oz.) cold sparkling water (such as Topo Chico)
3 medium-sized ripe avocados, chilled and chopped (about 2 cups)
1 cup plain fat-free yogurt (not Greek-style)
¼ cup chopped fresh basil
1 Tbsp. apple cider vinegar
1 ¼ tsp. kosher salt
1 tsp. lime zest plus 2 Tbsp. fresh juice
¼ tsp. black pepper
½ (14-oz.) pkg. extra-firm tofu, drained
¼ cup all-purpose flour
¼ cup cornstarch
1 Tbsp. olive oil
2 Tbsp. thinly sliced radishes
Fresh basil leaves

1. Combine sparkling water, avocado, yogurt, chopped basil, vinegar, salt, lime zest and juice, and pepper in a blender; process until smooth. Cover and chill 30 minutes.
2. Meanwhile, place tofu on a paper towel–lined plate. Top with paper towels and a plate; let stand 15 minutes. Cut tofu into ¾-inch cubes.
3. Combine flour and cornstarch in a bowl. Dredge tofu in flour mixture, shaking off excess. Heat oil in a large nonstick skillet over medium-high. Add tofu; cook until browned on all sides, about 5 minutes. Remove cooked tofu from pan.
4. Divide soup among 4 chilled bowls. Top evenly with cooked tofu and radish slices. Garnish with basil leaves; serve immediately. Serves 4 (serving size: about 1 cup soup and 2 oz. tofu)

CALORIES 368; FAT 27g (sat 5g, unsat 21g); PROTEIN 11g; CARB 19g; FIBER 8g; SUGARS 4g (added sugars 0g); SODIUM 616mg; CALC 14% DV; POTASSIUM 11% DV

Gluten Free • Make Ahead
Grilled Hanger Steak with Zucchini Salsa

Hands-on: 15 min. **Total:** 45 min.
We love this low-cost cut for its big, beefy flavor, but feel free to substitute flank or skirt steak in a pinch. Slice medium-rare steak against the grain for melt-in-your-mouth bites. Tuck leftovers into a whole-wheat tortilla for a tasty lunch.

1 (1 ¼-lb.) hanger steak
¼ cup olive oil, divided
1 ¾ tsp. kosher salt, divided
1 tsp. ground cumin
¼ tsp. black pepper
1 ½ lb. zucchini, cut into ¼-inch pieces (about 5 cups)
3 Tbsp. red wine vinegar
1 tsp. lime zest plus 2 Tbsp. fresh juice
¼ cup coarsely chopped fresh cilantro
1 Tbsp. coarsely chopped fresh oregano

1. Drizzle steak with 2 tablespoons oil. Stir together 1 teaspoon salt, cumin, and pepper. Rub mixture into steak; let stand at room temperature 30 minutes.
2. Toss together zucchini, vinegar, lime zest and juice, and remaining 2 tablespoons oil in a bowl. Stir in cilantro, oregano, and remaining ¾ teaspoon salt.
3. Preheat grill to medium-high (400° to 450°F). Place steak on oiled grates. Grill, uncovered, to medium-rare or desired degree of doneness, about 5 minutes per side. Remove from heat; let stand 5 minutes. Cut diagonally against the grain into thin slices. Serve with zucchini salsa. Serves 6 (serving size: 3 oz. steak and ⅔ cup salsa)

CALORIES 248; FAT 16g (sat 4g, unsat 10g); PROTEIN 21g; CARB 4g; FIBER 1g; SUGARS 3g (added sugars 0g); SODIUM 621mg; CALC 3% DV; POTASSIUM 7% DV

Fast
Chicken and Peach Flatbreads

Hands-on: 25 min. **Total:** 25 min.
Premade pizza crusts are a lifesaver for the busy weeknight cook. Here they provide a filling base for these outside-the-box pizzas. To make your own balsamic glaze, simmer down ½ cup balsamic vinegar until thick and syrupy, about 5 minutes.

1 (12-oz.) pkg. of 3 (7-inch) prebaked pizza crusts (such as Mama Mary's)
2 Tbsp. olive oil
2 ½ oz. whole-milk ricotta cheese (about 3 Tbsp.)
1 garlic clove, minced
½ tsp. lemon zest
¼ tsp. black pepper
2 cups shredded skinless rotisserie chicken breast (about 6 oz.)

1 cup sliced ripe peaches
¼ cup thinly sliced sweet cherry peppers (such as Mezzetta; about 1 oz.)
1½ oz. whole-milk mozzarella cheese, torn into small pieces
¼ tsp. kosher salt
⅛ tsp. crushed red pepper
1 Tbsp. bottled balsamic glaze
Fresh basil leaves

1. Preheat oven to 425°F. Brush both sides of crusts evenly with oil, and place on a baking sheet. Combine ricotta, garlic, lemon zest, and black pepper in a small bowl; spread mixture evenly over 1 side of each crust.

2. Top ricotta mixture evenly with shredded chicken, peach slices, cherry pepper slices, and torn mozzarella. Bake until edges of crusts are crisp and cheese is melted, about 15 minutes. Remove from oven, and sprinkle evenly with salt and crushed red pepper. Drizzle with balsamic glaze, and sprinkle with basil leaves. Serves 4 (serving size: 3 slices)

CALORIES 407; **FAT** 18g (sat 5g, unsat 11g); **PROTEIN** 18g; **CARB** 43g; **FIBER** 4g; **SUGARS** 7g (added sugars 0g); **SODIUM** 450mg; **CALC** 10% DV; **POTASSIUM** 3% DV

---

3 WAYS TO:

SPEED UP DINNER PREP

1. Keep a stash of prebaked pizza crusts in your freezer to whip this dish up on a whim. Pro tip: They bake up crispier if you don't thaw them first.

2. Shred the chicken and stir up the ricotta mixture while the oven preheats. Make the ricotta mixture the night before to save even more time.

3. Store-bought balsamic glaze is a quick way to add bold flavor to any dish; look for it next to the vinegars in the grocery store.

---

1 INGREDIENT, 3 SIDES

3 WAYS TO USE EGGPLANT

Enrobed in deep purple skins, meaty eggplants are high in soluble fiber, a key ally for heart health. Enjoy a serving (or two!) over cooked quinoa or fresh greens for a meatless main dish.

Staff Favorite · Fast
Vegetarian · Gluten Free
Spicy Eggplant with Plums

1. Stir together 1 Tbsp. smoked paprika, 1 tsp. cumin, ½ tsp. granulated sugar, ½ tsp. kosher salt, and ⅛ tsp. cayenne pepper. Halve 2 (8-oz.) Japanese eggplants lengthwise; spray cut sides with cooking spray, and sprinkle with spice mix.

2. Heat a grill pan over high; coat with cooking spray. Cook eggplant, cut sides down, 4 to 5 minutes. Turn and cook until tender, 5 to 6 minutes.

3. Stir together ¼ cup plain 2% reduced-fat Greek yogurt, 2 Tbsp. water, 1½ tsp. lemon juice, and ¼ tsp. black pepper; drizzle over eggplant. Sprinkle with 3 Tbsp. chopped fresh parsley and ½ cup chopped pitted fresh plums; drizzle with 2 Tbsp. olive oil. Serves 4 (serving size: 1 eggplant half, 1½ Tbsp. yogurt, and 2 Tbsp. plums)

CALORIES 123; **FAT** 8g (sat 1g, unsat 7g); **PROTEIN** 3g; **CARB** 12g; **FIBER** 4g; **SUGARS** 7g (added sugars 1g); **SODIUM** 251mg; **CALC** 4% DV; **POTASSIUM** 7% DV

Fast · Gluten Free · Vegetarian
Eggplant Caponata
Caponata is a classic Sicilian side typically made with fried eggplant. Our lighter version gets a quick sauté in heart-healthy olive oil.

---

1. Combine 3 Tbsp. golden raisins and 1½ Tbsp. red wine vinegar in a bowl.

2. Heat 2 Tbsp. olive oil in a large nonstick skillet over medium-high. Cut 8 oz. eggplant into ¾-inch cubes. Add 1 cup chopped red bell pepper, ¾ cup chopped white onion, and eggplant cubes to skillet. Cook, stirring occasionally, until softened, 10 to 12 minutes.

3. Stir in 1 cup chopped tomato, 2 Tbsp. chopped drained capers, ¼ tsp. crushed red pepper, and raisin mixture. Simmer until slightly thickened, about 5 minutes. Sprinkle with 2 Tbsp. chopped fresh mint. Serves 4 (serving size: ½ cup)

CALORIES 134; **FAT** 7g (sat 1g, unsat 6g); **PROTEIN** 2g; **CARB** 16g; **FIBER** 4g; **SUGARS** 10g (added sugars 0g); **SODIUM** 218mg; **CALC** 3% DV; **POTASSIUM** 9% DV

Fast · Vegetarian
Miso-Glazed Eggplant Steaks
To quote Robin Bashinsky, the mastermind behind this recipe, "This is a dish full of char and vigor." Savory miso is a natural match for thick eggplant steaks; look for miso in the refrigerated section of your grocery store's produce department.

1. Heat a grill pan over high. Coat with cooking spray. Cut 1 lb. eggplant into ¾-inch-thick rounds; coat eggplant slices generously with cooking spray. Grill eggplant slices, turning occasionally, until charred and tender, 8 to 10 minutes.

2. Whisk together 2 Tbsp. canola oil, 1 Tbsp. light brown sugar, 1 Tbsp. lower-sodium soy sauce, 2 tsp. white miso, and ¼ tsp. crushed red pepper in a large bowl. Add eggplant slices; toss to coat. Sprinkle with 2 Tbsp. chopped fresh cilantro. Serves 4 (serving size: 2 to 3 eggplant slices)

CALORIES 112; **FAT** 7g (sat 1g, unsat 6g); **PROTEIN** 2g; **CARB** 11g; **FIBER** 3g; **SUGARS** 7g (added sugars 3g); **SODIUM** 237mg; **CALC** 1% DV; **POTASSIUM** 6% DV

4 GO-WITH-ANYTHING SIDES

Fast • Vegetarian
Blistered Peppers and Tomatoes

Popping up in more grocery stores these days, shishito peppers are a mild, thin-skinned pepper that have a secret—about one in eight has a surprising kick of heat. For a milder dish, substitute mini bell peppers.

Heat a large skillet over high. Add 2 Tbsp. canola oil and 12 oz. shishito peppers; cook 4 to 5 minutes. Add ½ cup sliced yellow onion and ¼ tsp. five-spice powder; cook 2 minutes. Add 2 cups halved cherry tomatoes; cook 2 minutes. Remove from heat. Stir in 2 Tbsp. sliced fresh basil, 1½ Tbsp. lower-sodium soy sauce, 1 Tbsp. balsamic vinegar, and ½ tsp. black pepper. Sprinkle with 1 tsp. toasted sesame seeds. Serves 4 (serving size: about 1 cup)

CALORIES 113; **FAT** 8g (sat 1g, unsat 7g); **PROTEIN** 2g; **CARB** 10g; **FIBER** 2g; **SUGARS** 3g (added sugars 0g); **SODIUM** 223mg; **CALC** 2% DV; **POTASSIUM** 5% DV

Fast • Gluten Free
Vegetarian
Peach and Celery Salad

The flavors of peach and celery meld beautifully in this no-cook side. Pistachios amp up the crunch factor; recipes for three delicious ways to use up leftover pistachios follow at right and on page 205.

Place 3 cups thinly diagonally sliced celery, 3 cups sliced ripe peaches, 3 cups baby arugula, ¼ cup thinly sliced fresh basil, 2 Tbsp. extra-virgin olive oil, 1 Tbsp. fresh lemon juice, ⅜ tsp. kosher salt, and ¼ tsp. black pepper in a large bowl. Toss gently to coat. Sprinkle ¼ cup chopped roasted salted pistachios over salad. Serves 4 (serving size: 1¼ cups)

CALORIES 171; **FAT** 11g (sat 1g, unsat 9g); **PROTEIN** 4g; **CARB** 17g; **FIBER** 4g; **SUGARS** 12g (added sugars 0g); **SODIUM** 247mg; **CALC** 9% DV; **POTASSIUM** 12% DV

Fast • Vegetarian
Cucumber-Fennel Salad

Any cucumber will do in this salad, but we love the thin-skinned English variety—no peeling or seeding is required.

Toast 3 Tbsp. panko in 1 Tbsp. melted unsalted butter in a skillet over medium. Stir together 3 Tbsp. plain 2% reduced-fat Greek yogurt, 1 Tbsp. prepared horseradish, 2 tsp. fresh lemon juice, ½ tsp. lemon zest, ½ tsp. sugar, ¼ tsp. kosher salt, and ¼ tsp. black pepper in a large bowl. Add 4 cups sliced English cucumber, 2 cups sliced fennel bulb, and 1½ cups sliced bell pepper; toss to coat. Top with panko and 2 tsp. chopped fresh dill. Serves 4 (serving size: 1½ cups)

CALORIES 90; **FAT** 4g (sat 2g, unsat 1g); **PROTEIN** 4g; **CARB** 12g; **FIBER** 3g; **SUGARS** 6g (added sugars 1g); **SODIUM** 175mg; **CALC** 6% DV; **POTASSIUM** 9% DV

Fast • Gluten Free
Vegetarian
Chile-Lime Squash

Charring the squash in a skillet quickly adds smoky flavor without having to fire up the grill. Best served right away, this side pairs well with grilled chicken and brown rice.

Process 1 tomato, 1 seeded Fresno chile, 2 Tbsp. fresh lime juice, 1½ Tbsp. olive oil, and ½ tsp. kosher salt in a blender until smooth. Heat 1½ Tbsp. olive oil in a large skillet over medium-high. Add ½ cup sliced onion; cook 1 minute. Add 2½ cups sliced yellow squash; cook over high until just charred, 7 minutes. Add tomato mixture and 2 Tbsp. sliced fresh mint; bring to a simmer. Cook until slightly thickened, 3 to 4 minutes. Sprinkle with 2 Tbsp. chopped fresh mint. Serves 4 (serving size: 1 cup)

CALORIES 136; **FAT** 11g (sat 2g, unsat 9g); **PROTEIN** 2g; **CARB** 9g; **FIBER** 2g; **SUGARS** 5g (added sugars 0g); **SODIUM** 253mg; **CALC** 3% DV; **POTASSIUM** 10% DV

USE IT UP

3 WAYS TO USE PISTACHIOS

In addition to being the lowest-calorie nut, pistachios pack a balanced mix of heart-healthy fat, gut-friendly fiber, and eye-healthy antioxidants.

Fast • Gluten Free
Pistachio-Crusted Pork Cutlets
Make sure the cutlets are no more than a half-inch thick so they'll cook quickly.

1. Sprinkle 4 (4-oz.) pork cutlets with ½ tsp. kosher salt and ½ tsp. black pepper. Working one at a time, dredge cutlets in ¼ cup cornstarch; dip in a mixture of 1 beaten large egg and 1 Tbsp. water; dredge in a mixture of ¾ cup finely chopped roasted salted pistachios and 2 Tbsp. finely chopped fresh rosemary, pressing to coat.

2. Heat 1 Tbsp. olive oil and ⅛ tsp. cayenne pepper in nonstick skillet over medium-high. Add cutlets to pan; cook until browned, about 3 minutes per side. Toss together 4 cups arugula, 2 Tbsp. fresh lemon juice, and 1 Tbsp. olive oil in a bowl; serve salad with pork. Serves 4 (serving size: 1 cutlet and 1 cup arugula salad)

CALORIES 399; FAT 25g (sat 5g, unsat 18g); PROTEIN 30g; CARB 16g; FIBER 3g; SUGARS 3g (added sugars 0g); SODIUM 421mg; CALC 12% DV; POTASSIUM 12% DV

Gluten Free • Make Ahead
Pistachio Granola with Yogurt

Inspired by the classic Greek dessert baklava, this just-sweet-enough granola also makes a filling, protein- and fiber-rich afternoon snack.

1. Toss together 2 cups regular rolled oats, 2 Tbsp. honey, 2 Tbsp. melted unsalted butter, 2 tsp. orange zest, and 1 tsp. ground cinnamon in a bowl. Whisk 1 large egg white in a small bowl until frothy; stir into oat mixture. Pat mixture to an even ½-inch thickness on a parchment paper–lined baking sheet. (Do not spread out.) Bake at 325°F for 25 minutes, rotating pan halfway through baking time. Let cool.

2. Break into clusters; toss with ½ cup chopped roasted salted pistachios and ⅓ cup chopped dried apricots. Serve with 2 cups plain 2% reduced-fat Greek yogurt. Serves 4 (serving size: ½ cup granola and ½ cup yogurt)

CALORIES 320; FAT 13g (sat 5g, unsat 6g); PROTEIN 18g; CARB 36g; FIBER 5g; SUGARS 16g (added sugars 6g); SODIUM 91mg; CALC 15% DV; POTASSIUM 7% DV

Staff Favorite • Fast
Gluten Free • Vegetarian
Lemony Pistachio-Herb Relish

The beauty of this quick-fix topping is its versatility. The simple, balanced flavors will perk up any savory dish, from grilled chicken to roasted fish— but it's subtle enough to help more delicate foods shine, like freshly shucked raw oysters. Mix it into softened unsalted butter for a fresh take on compound butter.

1. Toss together ¼ cup finely chopped roasted salted pistachios, ¼ cup chopped fresh flat-leaf parsley, 2 Tbsp. chopped fresh mint, 1 Tbsp. minced shallot, 1 Tbsp. lemon zest, ¼ tsp. kosher salt, and ¼ tsp. black pepper in a small bowl. Serve immediately. Serves 4 (serving size: 2 Tbsp.)

CALORIES 49; FAT 4g (sat 0g, unsat 3g); PROTEIN 2g; CARB 3g; FIBER 1g; SUGARS 1g (added sugars 0g); SODIUM 155mg; CALC 2% DV; POTASSIUM 2% DV

COOKING LIGHT DIET
Make Ahead

Grilled Chicken and Vegetable Orzo Salad

Hands-on: 35 min. **Total:** 45 min. The grill is a healthy cook's best friend, allowing you to build big flavor and crispiness with minimal added fat. Make this meal meatless by trading the chicken for steamed edamame or rinsed and drained black beans.

6 oz. uncooked whole-wheat orzo (about 1 cup)
3 (8-oz.) boneless, skinless chicken breasts
1¼ tsp. kosher salt, divided
1 tsp. black pepper, divided
2 ears fresh corn, shucked
1 large zucchini, cut lengthwise into quarters
½ cup olive oil
¼ cup fresh lime juice (from 2 limes)
1 Tbsp. minced shallot
1 tsp. Dijon mustard
½ tsp. honey
2 cups baby arugula
3 oz. goat cheese, crumbled (about ¾ cup)

1. Cook orzo according to package directions, omitting salt and fat. Drain and rinse with cold water.

2. Preheat grill to high (450° to 550°F). Sprinkle chicken with ½ teaspoon salt and ¼ teaspoon pepper. Place chicken on oiled grates. Grill, uncovered, until chicken is done, about 16 minutes, turning after 8 minutes. Let stand 5 minutes; cut into ½-inch-thick slices.

3. Place corn and zucchini on oiled grates, and grill, uncovered, until crisp-tender, about 8 minutes, turning frequently to create grill marks on all sides. Cut kernels off corn, and coarsely chop zucchini.

4. Whisk together oil, lime juice, shallot, mustard, honey, remaining ¾ teaspoon salt, and remaining ¾ teaspoon pepper in a large bowl. Add cooked orzo, corn kernels, chopped zucchini, and arugula; toss well to coat. Divide orzo mixture among 6 plates. Arrange chicken slices over orzo mixture, and top evenly with goat cheese. Serves 6 (serving size: 4 oz. chicken and 1¼ cups orzo mixture)

CALORIES 473; FAT 25g (sat 5g, unsat 18g); PROTEIN 34g; CARB 28g; FIBER 6g; SUGARS 4g (added sugars 0g); SODIUM 549mg; CALC 7% DV; POTASSIUM 14% DV

1 LIST 3 DINNERS

Shop this list to feed four for three nights, all for about $30. Read the recipes first to be sure you have the staples on hand.

4 limes

2 yellow bell peppers

2 medium zucchini

2 bunches scallions

2 heads Bibb lettuce

1 tomato

3 (6-oz.) sweet potatoes

¼ cup unsalted roasted pepitas

6 (6-inch) whole-wheat pita rounds

2 cups uncooked whole-wheat orzo

1 can chipotle chiles in adobo sauce

1 (14.5-oz.) can unsalted chickpeas

8 oz. sour cream

2 lb. boneless, skinless chicken breasts

Chili garlic sauce

Fast • Vegetarian

Spicy Zucchini Salad

Hands-on: 25 min. **Total:** 25 min. Fiber- and protein-packed chickpeas bulk up this late-summer salad.

2 (6-inch) whole-wheat pita rounds, split
¼ cup olive oil, divided
½ tsp. kosher salt, divided
½ tsp. black pepper, divided
1 medium zucchini
1½ Tbsp. finely chopped chipotle chiles in adobo sauce, divided
1 Tbsp. fresh lime juice
4 cups chopped Bibb lettuce
1 (14.5-oz.) can unsalted chickpeas, drained and rinsed
1 cup chopped tomatoes
¼ cup sour cream
¼ cup unsalted roasted pepitas (shelled pumpkin seeds)
2 Tbsp. chopped scallions

1. Preheat oven to 400°F. Brush uncut sides of pita rounds with 1 tablespoon oil, and sprinkle with ¼ teaspoon salt and ¼ teaspoon pepper. Place directly on oven rack, and bake at 400°F until crispy, 5 to 6 minutes. Cool slightly, about 5 minutes. Slice pitas into thin triangles. Set aside.
2. Using a Y-shaped peeler, peel thin strips from zucchini to measure about 1 cup. (Reserve remaining zucchini for another use.) Toss together zucchini strips and 1½ teaspoons chipotle chiles; let stand at room temperature 10 minutes.
3. Whisk together lime juice and remaining 1 tablespoon chipotle chiles in a small bowl. Gradually whisk in remaining 3 tablespoons oil. Toss together lettuce, chickpeas, tomatoes, and dressing.

Season with remaining ¼ teaspoon salt and remaining ¼ teaspoon pepper. Divide among 4 bowls. Top with zucchini strip mixture, pita triangles, sour cream, pumpkin seeds, and scallions. Serves 4 (serving size: 1 cup)

CALORIES 391; **FAT** 21g (sat 4g, unsat 15g); **PROTEIN** 12g; **CARB** 41g; **FIBER** 8g; **SUGARS** 4g (added sugars 0g); **SODIUM** 457mg; **CALC** 11% DV; **POTASSIUM** 14% DV

Fast

Skillet Fajita Pitas

Hands-on: 25 min. **Total:** 25 min. Cooking over high heat without stirring gives the chicken and peppers a smoky, charred crust.

2 Tbsp. fresh lime juice, divided
2 Tbsp. olive oil, divided
1½ Tbsp. chili garlic sauce (such as Huy Fong), divided
4 (6-inch) whole-wheat pita rounds
1 lb. boneless, skinless chicken breasts, thinly sliced
1 yellow bell pepper, thinly sliced
1 medium zucchini, thinly diagonally sliced
¼ cup thinly sliced scallions
½ tsp. kosher salt
¼ tsp. black pepper
¼ cup sour cream
2 cups chopped Bibb lettuce

1. Stir together 1 tablespoon lime juice, 1 tablespoon oil, and 1 tablespoon chili garlic sauce in a small bowl. Set aside.
2. Heat a large cast-iron skillet over medium-high. Working in batches, add pitas to skillet, and toast until lightly browned, about 1 minute per side. Cut in half; set aside.
3. Increase heat to high. When skillet starts to smoke, add

remaining 1 tablespoon oil. Add chicken in a single layer, and cook, undisturbed, until browned, about 1 minute. Stir and cook until browned on both sides, about 1 more minute. Move chicken to sides of skillet. Add bell pepper, and cook, undisturbed, until slightly charred, about 2 minutes. Add zucchini to bell pepper, and cook 1 minute. Add scallions, salt, pepper, and sauce mixture; stir together, and cook 1 minute.

4. Stir together sour cream, remaining 1 tablespoon lime juice, and remaining 1½ teaspoons chili garlic sauce. Fill each pita half with ¼ cup lettuce and ½ cup chicken-and-vegetable mixture. Drizzle with sour cream sauce, and serve immediately. Serves 4 (serving size: 2 pita halves)

CALORIES 389; FAT 13g (sat 3g, unsat 8g); PROTEIN 32g; CARB 38g; FIBER 4g; SUGARS 4g (added sugars 1g); SODIUM 676mg; CALC 5% DV; POTASSIUM 15% DV

Dinner 3 of 3

Chicken and Vegetable Kebabs

Hands-on: 45 min. **Total:** 45 min. Parcooking the potatoes speeds up grill time; pick small potatoes for even cooking.

1 lb. boneless, skinless chicken
   breasts, cut into 1-inch pieces
3 Tbsp. fresh lime juice, divided
1 Tbsp. minced chipotle chiles in
   adobo sauce plus ½ Tbsp. adobo
   sauce
1 tsp. kosher salt, divided
½ tsp. black pepper, divided
3 (6-oz.) sweet potatoes
1 yellow bell pepper, cut into
   1½-inch pieces

2 Tbsp. olive oil, divided
1 bunch scallions
2 cups cooked whole-wheat orzo
¼ cup sour cream

1. Toss chicken with 1 tablespoon lime juice, chipotle chiles, adobo sauce, ½ teaspoon salt, and ¼ teaspoon pepper. Let stand 10 minutes. Thread chicken onto 3 (12-inch) metal skewers.

2. Pierce potatoes with a fork. Wrap with damp paper towels, and microwave at HIGH until slightly tender, about 3 minutes. Cut into ½-inch rounds. Thread sweet potatoes and bell pepper alternately onto 2 (12-inch) metal skewers.

3. Whisk together 1 tablespoon lime juice, 1 tablespoon oil, ¼ teaspoon salt, and remaining ¼ teaspoon pepper. Brush half of dressing on vegetables.

4. Preheat grill to high (450° to 550°F). Place chicken on oiled grates; grill, uncovered, until cooked through, 6 to 8 minutes. Grill vegetables, uncovered, brushing with half of remaining dressing, until tender, 4 to 6 minutes. Brush scallions with remaining dressing; grill, uncovered, until charred, 2 to 3 minutes. Chop scallions; toss with orzo, remaining 1 tablespoon oil, and remaining ¼ teaspoon salt. Combine sour cream and remaining 1 tablespoon lime juice. Serve with skewers. Serves 4 (serving size: ½ cup orzo, 3 oz. chicken, 1 cup vegetables, and 1 Tbsp. sauce)

CALORIES 507; FAT 13g (sat 3g, unsat 8g); PROTEIN 34g; CARB 62g; FIBER 12g; SUGARS 8g (added sugars 0g); SODIUM 640mg; CALC 8% DV; POTASSIUM 21% DV

Fast

Garlic-Parsley Shrimp

Hands-on: 20 min. **Total:** 25 min.

¾ lb. raw large shrimp, peeled and
   deveined
¾ tsp. kosher salt
1 tsp. minced fresh ginger
2 garlic cloves, minced
1 small jalapeño, seeded and
   minced (optional)
2 tsp. olive oil
¼ cup dry white wine
¼ cup chopped fresh parsley
2 Tbsp. unsalted butter
4 (1½-oz.) slices country-style
   bread, grilled or toasted

1. Quarter shrimp by halving lengthwise and then crosswise. Place in a colander, and sprinkle with salt. Massage shrimp with salt; let stand in sink 5 minutes. Rinse shrimp; shake colander to remove excess water. (You'll want a little residual water).

2. Transfer shrimp to a bowl; toss with ginger, garlic, and, if using, jalapeño. Heat oil in a medium skillet over medium-high until it shimmers. Add shrimp mixture; cook, stirring occasionally, until just cooked through, about 3 minutes. Add wine and cook, stirring occasionally, until half of wine has evaporated, about 2 minutes. Stir in parsley and butter; cook until butter melts. Spoon over toast. Serves 4 (serving size: 1 topped toast)

CALORIES 254; FAT 10g (sat 4g, unsat 4g); PROTEIN 17g; CARB 21g; FIBER 6g; SUGARS 4g (added sugars 1g); SODIUM 354mg; CALC 26% DV; POTASSIUM 3% DV

Make Ahead

Slow Cooker Sweet-and-Sour Chicken

Hands-on: 25 min. **Total:** 8 hr.
This may be our easiest slow cooker recipe yet. There's no browning in the skillet, no last-minute stovetop sauce—all the magic happens right in the slow cooker. Craving crunch? Serve it as a wrap in the cabbage of your choice.

1¼ lb. boneless, skinless chicken
   thighs
2 cups chopped red bell pepper
1½ cups unsalted chicken stock
1 cup chopped yellow onion
1 cup thinly sliced carrots
¼ cup lower-sodium soy sauce
2 Tbsp. lower-sodium
   Worcestershire sauce
1 Tbsp. sambal oelek (ground fresh
   chile paste)
¾ cup unsalted ketchup, divided
¼ cup pineapple juice
2 Tbsp. cornstarch
3 cups cooked brown rice
1½ tsp. sesame seeds
1½ tsp. sliced scallions

1. Add chicken, bell pepper, chicken stock, onion, carrots, soy sauce, Worcestershire sauce, sambal oelek, and ½ cup ketchup to a 6-quart slow cooker. Cover and cook on low until chicken shreds easily with a fork, about 7 hours. Remove chicken from slow cooker. Shred chicken, and cover to keep warm.
2. Whisk together pineapple juice and cornstarch in a small bowl. Increase slow cooker heat to high; slowly stir in pineapple juice mixture and remaining ¼ cup ketchup. Cook, uncovered, until sauce is thick enough to coat the back of a spoon, about 30 minutes.

Stir in chicken. Serve over rice, and sprinkle with sesame seeds and scallions. Serves 6 (serving size: about 1⅓ cups chicken mixture and ½ cup rice)

CALORIES 357; **FAT** 5g (sat 1g, unsat 3g); **PROTEIN** 24g; **CARB** 52g; **FIBER** 4g; **SUGARS** 14g (added sugars 2g); **SODIUM** 628mg; **CALC** 4% DV; **POTASSIUM** 12% DV

DITCH THE TAKEOUT

Our version offers the same bold flavor and sticky-sweet sauce as the takeout classic for less than half the calories and 87% less sat fat.

WHAT'S FRESH NOW
Staff Favorite • Fast

Smashed Chili Cheeseburgers

Hands-on: 15 min. **Total:** 15 min.
Our healthier take on a beach-side burger, these patties have a delectable seared crust but are juicy inside, especially if you use a screaming-hot cast-iron skillet.

1 lb. 93% lean ground beef
1 Tbsp. chili powder
½ tsp. black pepper
½ tsp. kosher salt, divided
¼ cup shredded cheddar cheese
4 whole-wheat hamburger buns,
   toasted
2 Tbsp. light sour cream
¼ cup sliced scallions
2 Tbsp. chopped pickled jalapeños

1. Combine beef, chili powder, black pepper, and ⅛ teaspoon salt in a medium bowl. Shape into 4 equal balls.
2. Heat a large cast-iron skillet over high. When the pan is hot enough to release wisps of smoke, add beef balls and press down with a firm

spatula to form patties. Place a slightly smaller skillet directly on patties. Cook until charred, about 1 minute and 30 seconds. Remove top pan, flip patties, replace top pan, and cook until charred, about 1 minute. Remove top pan, sprinkle patties with remaining ⅜ teaspoon salt, and top with cheese. Invert top pan, and cover skillet. Steam until cheese is melted, 30 to 45 seconds. Place patties on buns; top with sour cream, scallions, and jalapeños. Serves 4 (serving size: 1 burger)

CALORIES 335; **FAT** 14g (sat 5g, unsat 8g); **PROTEIN** 29g; **CARB** 25g; **FIBER** 4g; **SUGARS** 4g (added sugars 0g); **SODIUM** 692mg; **CALC** 12% DV; **POTASSIUM** 4% DV

Fast • Make Ahead
Vegetarian

Mint-Lime Pesto
Use this pesto on everything from pineapple to grilled fish.

Place 2 cups packed fresh mint leaves, ¼ cup grated Parmesan cheese, 1 Tbsp. chopped pistachios, and 1 Tbsp. fresh lime juice in a food processor. With processor running, drizzle in 2 Tbsp. canola oil; process until smooth. Serves 8 (serving size: 1 Tbsp.)

CALORIES 50; **FAT** 5g (sat 1g, unsat 4g); **PROTEIN** 1g; **CARB** 1g; **FIBER** 0g; **SUGARS** 0g; **SODIUM** 50mg; **CALC** 4% DV; **POTASSIUM** 1% DV

**Quinoa Breakfast Bowl
with 6-Minute Egg,**
Page 32

**Chickpea
Spinach Salad,**
Page 32

**Slow Cooker Creamy
Lentil Soup,**
Page 33

**Green Goddess
Avocado Sauce,**
Page 30

Salmon with Kale, Walnut, and White Bean Salad,
Page 27

**Avo-Berry
Smoothie Bowls,**
Page 28

**Celery Salad with
Celery Seed Vinaigrette,**
Page 24

Clockwise: **Thai Curried Squash Soup,** Page 65 // **Roasted Carrots with Pine Nut Gremolata,** Page 70
Cumin Lamb Stir-Fry, Page 22 // **Crispy Oven-Fried Chicken,** Page 46

Coconut Oil Waffles,
Page 58

Chicken Paella,
Page 54

Sheet Pan
Hawaiian Shrimp,
Page 50

Clockwise: **Greek Turkey Burgers,** Page 92 **// Millet and Tomatoes,** Page 99
Flank Steak and Vegetables with Green Goddess Sauce, Page 93 **// Red Curry Shrimp Cakes,** Page 96

Clockwise: **Spring Vegetable Pasta Alfredo,** Page 79 **// Rhubarb Upside-Down Cake,** Page 88
Sweet-and Sour Mushroom Toasts with Tarragon, Page 86 **// Asparagus with Avocado-Herb Dressing,** Page 87

Rosé-Poached Berries,
Page 112

**Golden Beet and
Roasted Strawberry Salad,**
Page 112

Grilled Caesar Salad with Sourdough Breadcrumbs, Page 132

Clockwise: **Kale Salad with Spiced Chickpeas and Berries,** Page 139, **Edamame, Okra, and Green Pea Korma,** Page 140, **Veggie Bowl with Tofu Scramble,** Page 139 // **Baby Chocolate Cakes,** Page 154 **Smoky Brisket with Peppers and Onions,** Page 151 // **Grilled Salmon with Avocado Salsa,** Page 142

Pavlova Layer Cake with
Raspberries and Peaches,
Page 165

Double-Serrano Watermelon Bites,
Page 158

**Shrimp Kebabs with
Mint and Melon Salad,**
Page 169

**Cherry–Goat
Cheese Ice Cream,**
Page 181

**Corn and
Crab Pita Nachos,**
Page 190

Roast Beef Hash,
Page 246

**Ultimate
Breakfast Toast,**
Page 257

**Roasted Grape and
Goat Cheese Wheat
Berry Bowl,**
Page 253

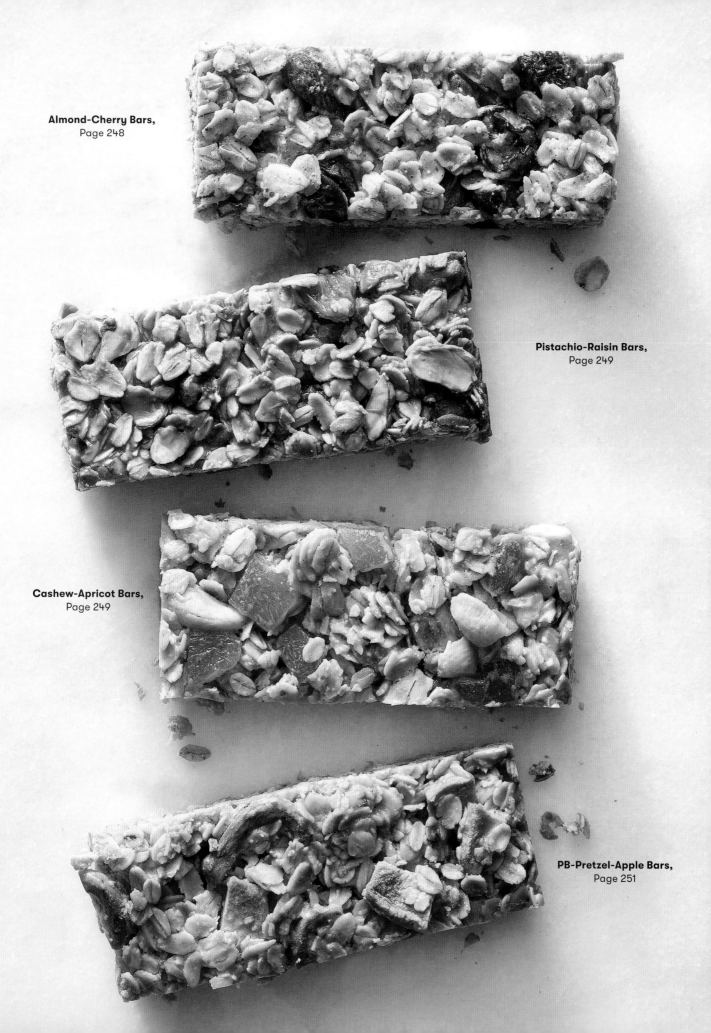

Almond-Cherry Bars,
Page 248

Pistachio-Raisin Bars,
Page 249

Cashew-Apricot Bars,
Page 249

PB-Pretzel-Apple Bars,
Page 251

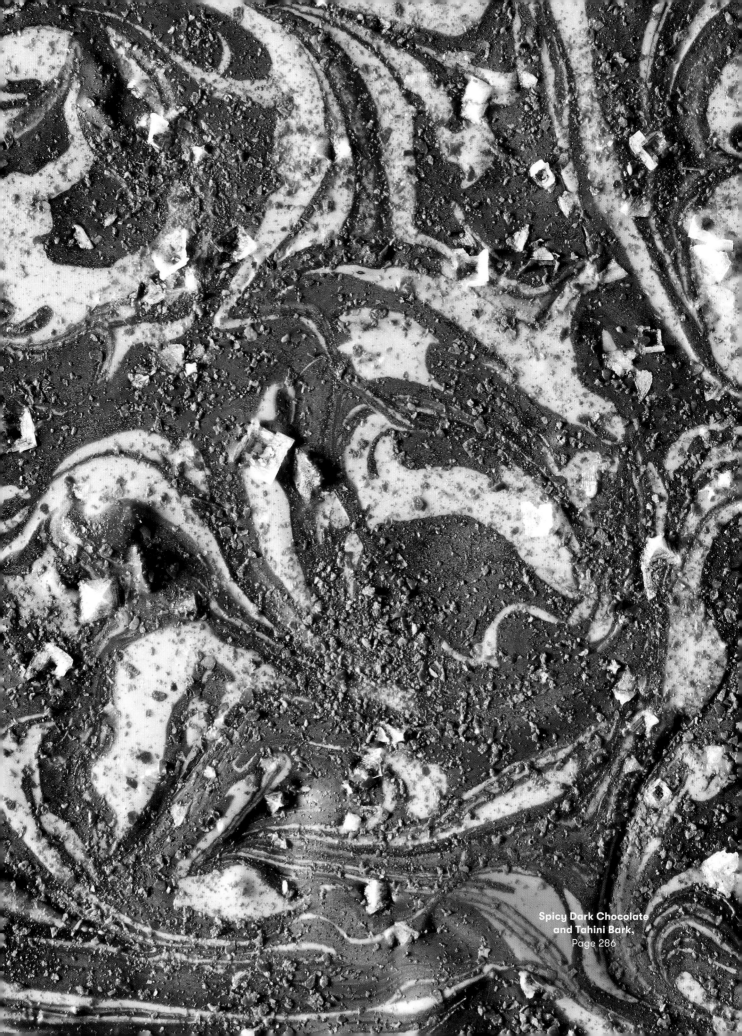

**Spicy Dark Chocolate
and Tahini Bark,**
Page 286

Clockwise: **Brussels and Quinoa Bowl with Orange-Thyme Vinaigrette,** Page 274 **// Ginger-Orange Carrots,** Page 281
Roasted Chickpea Snack Mix, Page 286 **// Beer-Braised Chicken and Root Vegetables,** Page 276

Mushroom and
Marsala-Onion Tartines,
Page 310

**Peppercorn-and-
Coriander-Crusted Roast,**
Page 310

Chocolate-and-
Cream Layer Cake,
Page 361

OUR NEW FAVORITE FRENCH DIP SANDWICH

Our impressive makeover shaves off calories, sat fat, and sodium—and will satisfy even the most devoted meat lover.

A sandwich-shop classic, the French dip—a beef-loaded baguette-and-jus combo—delivers a whopping 1,400mg sodium (more than 60% of your daily recommended limit) plus almost 9g sat fat. To create a healthier handheld without forfeiting its meaty character, we use toothsome mushrooms to mimic meat's heft and enrich the sandwich with noteworthy umami. Caramelized onions get layered on for the perfect alchemy of sweetness and added complexity. And to further infuse each bite with robust flavor, we boost the homemade jus with sherry, thyme, Worcestershire, and soy sauce. Delightfully hearty and a little bit messy, our slimmed-down sandwich provides classic satisfaction (and a full serving of veggies) for one-third fewer calories and 690mg less sodium.

Staff Favorite • Vegetarian

Mushroom French Dip Sandwiches

Hands-on: 1 hr. **Total:** 1 hr. 15 min.

2 tsp. unsalted butter
2½ Tbsp. olive oil, divided
2 large yellow onions, vertically sliced
¼ tsp. kosher salt
1¼ lb. portobello mushroom caps, gills removed, sliced into strips
¾ cup lower-sodium vegetable broth
⅓ cup dry sherry
1 Tbsp. vegetarian or vegan Worcestershire sauce
2 tsp. chopped fresh thyme
1 tsp. lower-sodium soy sauce
¼ tsp. freshly ground black pepper
2 Tbsp. Dijon mustard
½ tsp. prepared horseradish
4 (2-oz.) whole-wheat hoagie rolls, split
4 very thin Swiss cheese slices (such as Sargento Ultra Thin)

1. Heat butter and 1½ teaspoons oil in a large skillet over medium. Add onions; cook, stirring occasionally, 10 minutes. Reduce heat to medium-low; cook, stirring occasionally, until golden, about 30 minutes. Stir in salt; cook 5 minutes.
2. Heat 1 tablespoon oil in a separate large skillet over medium-high. Arrange half of mushrooms in skillet in a single layer and cook, undisturbed, until golden brown, about 3 minutes. Stir and cook, stirring often, until golden brown all over, about 5 minutes. Transfer mushrooms to a bowl. Repeat process with remaining 1 tablespoon oil and remaining mushrooms.
3. Return cooked mushrooms to pan. Add broth, sherry, Worcestershire, thyme, soy sauce, and pepper. Bring mixture to a boil. Reduce to a simmer; cook 5 minutes. Using tongs, remove mushrooms to a bowl. Divide jus evenly among 4 ramekins.
4. Stir together mustard and horseradish in a bowl. Spread on top halves of rolls.
5. Preheat broiler to high. Arrange ¾ cup mushrooms on bottom half of each roll. Top each with ¼ cup onions. Tear each cheese slice in half; place two halves on each sandwich. Place sandwiches on a baking sheet; cover with top halves of rolls. Broil until cheese melts, 1 to 2 minutes. Serve with jus for dipping. Serves 4 (serving size: 1 sandwich and 2 Tbsp. jus)

CALORIES 365; **FAT** 16g (sat 4g, unsat 10g); **PROTEIN** 13g; **CARB** 43g; **FIBER** 7g; **SUGARS** 8g (added sugars 0g); **SODIUM** 742mg; **CALC** 12% DV; **POTASSIUM** 14% DV

HEALTHIER DIY GRAVLAX

Our herby salt-and-sugar mix offers big cured-salmon flavor with half the sodium of store brands.

Make Ahead

Lower-Sodium Gravlax

Hands-on: 15 min. **Total:** 2 days

Be sure to use Morton kosher salt here. Diamond kosher weighs about half as much and will give you dramatically different results. Gin's botanical flavorings subtly season the fish.

1 cup loosely packed fresh dill leaves
⅔ cup granulated sugar
⅓ cup Morton kosher salt
1 tsp. caraway seeds
1 Tbsp. dry gin
1 (1-lb.) skin-on salmon fillet

1. Place dill, sugar, salt, and caraway seeds in a food processor; process until bright green, about 1 minute.
2. Brush gin over flesh side of fish; rub both sides of fish with dill mixture to cover completely. (Use more dill mixture on thicker portions of fish and less on thinner portions.) Wrap fish tightly in several layers of plastic wrap, and place in a baking dish; place another baking dish on top of fish, and refrigerate. Flip fish twice a day; allow fish to cure until it's firm to the touch but not leathery, 1 to 2 days. Scrape dill mixture from fish; rinse fish well with cold water. Pat completely dry with paper towels; cut into very thin slices. Serve cold or at room temperature. Serves 12 (serving size: 1 oz.)

CALORIES 57; **FAT** 2g (sat 0g, unsat 2g); **PROTEIN** 8g; **CARB** 1g; **FIBER** 0g; **SUGARS** 1g (added sugars 1g); **SODIUM** 135mg; **CALC** 1% DV; **POTASSIUM** 4% DV

THE STEPS

1. BLEND EVENLY
Some recipes call for sprinkling dill fronds and cracked spice seeds over the fish. Our method is more uniform, so every bite delivers fully seasoned deliciousness. The key is to process the fresh dill leaves and caraway seeds along with the salt and sugar so all the flavors meld throughout the mixture.

2. APPLY THE CURE
Brush the salmon flesh with gin, and spread the dill mixture evenly over the entire fillet so it's fully covered. Spread less of the mix over thinner sections to avoid overseasoning. When you buy the salmon, ask your fishmonger for a fillet cut toward the head end of the fish, which has more even thickness than the tail end.

3. PRESS AND FLIP
Weighting the fillet lightly with a baking dish squeezes water from the salmon, which intensifies the flavor of both the fish and the seasoning. The dill mixture blends with the extracted liquid, so flipping the fillet regularly helps keep the salmon evenly seasoned.

Make Ahead

Classic Clam Chowder

Hands-on: 45 min. **Total:** 45 min.

2 lb. littleneck clams
3 cups water
1 cup bottled clam juice
1 bacon slice (1 oz.)
1 Tbsp. unsalted butter
1 cup diced yellow onion
1 cup diced celery
2 Tbsp. all-purpose flour
¼ tsp. black pepper
½ cup dry white wine
1½ lb. russet potatoes, peeled and
    chopped
1½ cups half-and-half
1 Tbsp. chopped fresh parsley

1. Combine clams, 3 cups water, and clam juice in a Dutch oven; bring to a boil over high. Cover and reduce heat to medium-low. Simmer 6 minutes or until clams open. Discard unopened clams. Remove clams; let cool. Remove meat; chop. Discard shells. Pour broth through a cheesecloth-lined strainer; discard solids.
2. Add bacon to Dutch oven over medium-high; cook until crisp. Remove bacon and crumble. Add butter, onion, and celery to bacon drippings in pan; sauté 8 minutes. Stir in flour and pepper; sauté 1 minute. Add wine; cook 1 minute. Add potatoes and reserved clam broth; bring to a boil. Cover and reduce heat to low. Simmer until potatoes are tender, 15 minutes.
3. Transfer 1 cup vegetables and liquid to a blender. Remove center piece of lid. Secure lid; place towel over opening. Process until smooth. Return puree to soup; add half-and-half and reserved clams. Return soup to a simmer. Garnish with parsley and bacon. Serves 6 (serving size: 1 ¼ cups)

CALORIES 276; **FAT** 10g (sat 6g, unsat 4g); **PROTEIN** 13g; **CARB** 30g; **FIBER** 2g; **SUGARS** 5g (added sugars 0g); **SODIUM** 496mg; **CALC** 12% DV; **POTASSIUM** 19% DV

THE ESSENTIALS

ENJOY A BOWLFUL OF BRINY CLAM FLAVOR BALANCED WITH A LITTLE LIGHT CREAM, AROMATICS, AND A HINT OF BACON.

LITTLENECK CLAMS
These small hard-shells offer up sweet, tender meat with satisfying chew, plus salty juice.

CLAM JUICE
Bottled juice combines with the juice from the littlenecks to give the broth intense flavor. We like the natural sweetness of Bar Harbor.

CELERY AND ONION
These are the classic chowder aromatics, adding vegetal hints without distracting from clam flavor.

BACON
One slice of mildly smoked bacon does the trick here; smoky pork flavor shouldn't dominate clam chowder.

RUSSET POTATOES
Starchier than red-skinned spuds or Yukon Golds, the russets meld with the half-and-half for a silky texture.

HALF-AND-HALF
It has less sat fat than full-fat cream, which can make the soup too thick, and has a silkier mouthfeel than plain milk.

Fast • Make Ahead
Vegetarian
Thai Peach Punch
Hands-on: 10 min. **Total:** 10 min.
This big-batch-friendly cocktail celebrates summer's juiciest stone fruit and most bountiful herb. Peaches contain two key antioxidants—lutein and zeaxanthin—good for eye health. Lemongrass paste (found near the fresh herbs) imparts aromatic, lemony luster.

Combine 12 oz. peeled and sliced ripe peaches, ½ cup fresh lemon juice, ½ cup water, 2 Tbsp. honey, and, if desired, 1½ tsp. refrigerated lemongrass paste in a blender. Process until smooth, about 1 minute. Pour peach mixture evenly into 4 highball glasses filled with ice. Add 1 oz. bourbon to each, and top each with ¼ cup club soda. Gently stir until combined. Garnish with fresh Thai basil or sweet basil sprigs. Serves 4 (serving size: about 1 cup)

CALORIES 142; **FAT** 1g (sat 0g, unsat 1g); **PROTEIN** 1g; **CARB** 19g; **FIBER** 1g; **SUGARS** 16g (added sugars 8g); **SODIUM** 63mg; **CALC** 1% DV; **POTASSIUM** 4% DV

MAKE IT A MOCKTAIL

Omit bourbon, and use iced tea in place of water. Add a dash of peach non-alcoholic bitters, if desired.

BIG-BATCH COOKING

The transition from long, lazy summer days to action-packed fall schedules can feel overwhelming. But when it comes to feeding your family, we've got you covered. Set yourself up for healthy-eating success with weekend warrior–style, get-ahead recipes for breakfast, lunch, snacks, and dinner.

01. MAKE-AHEAD DINNERS

This is smart meal planning at its best. Two birds—or one big beef roast—power a great meal tonight, plus two more easy, family-friendly dinners later in the week.

Batch cooking brings to mind stews and casseroles, big pans full of several portions. But the batch strategy works even better with roasts and braises: Popping extra meat in the oven when making a delicious roast the first night will save you time and effort later; making a few tweaks yields simple and completely different meals the next two nights. Our juicy roast chicken on a bed of caramelized onions becomes Thai chicken pizza with zesty peanut sauce another night and savory crêpes after that. And extra servings of classic beef pot roast—gently braised until fork-tender and succulent—become herb-sauced tacos and comforting egg-and-potato hash. So crank up the oven, and set yourself up for the week.

ROAST CHICKEN RECIPES
Gluten Free • Make Ahead

French Onion Roast Chicken

Hands-on: 15 min. **Total:** 1 hr. 10 min.

2 Tbsp. olive oil
1½ lb. yellow onions, vertically sliced
2 Tbsp. chopped fresh thyme, divided
1¾ tsp. kosher salt, divided
¼ cup dry white wine
¼ cup unsalted butter, softened
1 tsp. black pepper
2 (3-lb.) whole chickens, spatchcocked (butterflied)

1. Preheat oven to 450°F. Heat oil in a large skillet over medium. Add onions, 1 tablespoon thyme, and ¼ teaspoon salt; cook, stirring occasionally, until onions are lightly browned, about 15 minutes. Add wine; cook, stirring occasionally, until liquid evaporates, about 2 minutes. Spread onion mixture in a rimmed baking sheet.
2. Combine butter, pepper, remaining 1 tablespoon thyme, and remaining 1 ½ teaspoons salt in a bowl. Loosen skin on chickens; spread butter mixture under skin. Place chickens, skin sides up, on onion mixture.
3. Roast chickens at 450°F until a thermometer inserted in thickest portion registers 165°F, about 35 minutes. Let stand 10 minutes. Remove and discard skin; slice meat. Using a slotted spoon, reserve ½ cup onion mixture. Shred meat from 1 chicken; store shredded chicken and remaining onion mixture in separate airtight containers in refrigerator up to 5 days. Serve remaining sliced chicken with reserved ½ cup onion mixture. Serves 4 (serving size: ¼ chicken and 2 Tbsp. onion mixture)

CALORIES 315; FAT 14g (sat 5g, unsat 7g); PROTEIN 36g; CARB 8g; FIBER 2g; SUGARS 4g (added sugars 0g); SODIUM 554mg; CALC 4% DV; POTASSIUM 12% DV

Fast

Thai Chicken Pizza

Hands-on: 15 min. **Total:** 20 min.

10 oz. fresh prepared whole-wheat pizza dough, at room temperature
¼ cup well-shaken and stirred light coconut milk
3 Tbsp. creamy peanut butter
1 Tbsp. fresh lime juice
2 tsp. lower-sodium soy sauce
2 tsp. Sriracha chili sauce
1 tsp. light brown sugar
½ tsp. grated peeled fresh ginger
1½ cups shredded chicken (from French Onion Roast Chicken)

½ cup matchstick-cut carrots
1½ oz. Monterey Jack cheese, finely shredded (about ⅓ cup)
2 scallions, thinly sliced
⅓ cup fresh bean sprouts
¼ cup fresh cilantro leaves

1. Preheat oven to 500°F. Place a pizza stone in oven while it preheats.
2. Place pizza dough on a lightly floured surface; roll into a 14- x 10-inch rectangle. Transfer to parchment paper. Pierce all over with a fork. Transfer dough and parchment to hot pizza stone; bake at 500°F until lightly browned, about 5 minutes.
3. Combine coconut milk and next 6 ingredients (through ginger) in a bowl. Remove crust on parchment from oven. Spread ½ cup coconut milk mixture on crust, leaving a ½-inch border. Top with chicken, carrots, and cheese. Return pizza on parchment to hot pizza stone in oven; bake at 500°F until cheese melts, about 4 minutes. Drizzle with remaining coconut milk mixture; top with scallions, sprouts, and cilantro. Cut into 8 pieces. Serves 4 (serving size: 2 pieces)

CALORIES 353; FAT 16g (sat 5g, unsat 9g); PROTEIN 18g; CARB 39g; FIBER 4g; SUGARS 5g (added sugars 1g); SODIUM 681mg; CALC 10% DV; POTASSIUM 5% DV

Staff Favorite

Chicken and Herb Crêpes

Hands-on: 25 min. **Total:** 1 hr. 20 min.

¾ cup whole milk
3.25 oz. (about ¾ cup) plus 1 Tbsp. all-purpose flour, divided
2 large eggs
3 Tbsp. plus 1 tsp. olive oil, divided
½ tsp. kosher salt, divided
1¼ cups onion mixture (from French Onion Roast Chicken)
¼ cup cream sherry
1¾ cups shredded chicken (from French Onion Roast Chicken)
1 oz. shredded Gruyère cheese (about ⅓ cup)
½ cup chopped fresh herbs (such as parsley and chives), divided

1. Combine milk, ¾ cup flour, eggs, 2 tablespoons oil, and ¼ teaspoon salt in a blender. Process until smooth. Cover and chill 1 hour.
2. Heat onion mixture in a large nonstick skillet over medium-high. Stir in sherry and remaining 1 tablespoon flour; cook, stirring often, 3 minutes. Stir in chicken, cheese, 2 tablespoons herbs, and remaining ¼ teaspoon salt. Keep warm.
3. Whisk ¼ cup herbs into chilled batter. Heat an 8-inch nonstick skillet over medium-low. Brush pan with ½ teaspoon oil; add 3 tablespoons batter to pan. Swirl pan so batter covers bottom. Cook until crêpe is almost set and shakes loose, about 1 minute. Flip crêpe; cook 30 seconds. Remove crêpe from pan; place ⅓ cup chicken mixture down center; roll up. Repeat 7 times with remaining oil, batter, and chicken mixture. Sprinkle with remaining 2 tablespoons herbs. Serves 4 (serving size: 2 crêpes)

CALORIES 421; FAT 24g (sat 6g, unsat 16g); PROTEIN 19g; CARB 27g; FIBER 2g; SUGARS 5g (added sugars 0g); SODIUM 497mg; CALC 17% DV; POTASSIUM 7% DV

ROAST BEEF RECIPES
Gluten Free • Make Ahead

Oven-Braised Pot Roast

Hands-on: 30 min. **Total:** 4 hr.

1½ Tbsp. olive oil
1 (4¼-lb.) boneless chuck roast
1¼ tsp. kosher salt
1 tsp. black pepper
8 oz. frozen pearl onions (about 2 cups), thawed
3 garlic cloves, smashed
2 Tbsp. unsalted tomato paste
¾ cup dry red wine
3 cups unsalted beef stock
¾ lb. Yukon Gold potatoes, peeled and cut into 2-inch pieces
4 large carrots, peeled and cut diagonally into 2-inch pieces
2 rosemary sprigs
¼ cup chopped fresh flat-leaf parsley

1. Preheat oven to 325°F. Heat oil in a Dutch oven over medium-high. Sprinkle beef with salt and pepper. Add to pan; cook until browned on all sides, about 15 minutes. Place beef on a plate.
2. Add the onions and garlic to pan; sauté 2 minutes. Add tomato paste; sauté 1 minute. Add wine; cook, scraping bottom of pan, until liquid is reduced by half. Add stock; bring to boil. Return beef to pan; add potatoes, carrots, and rosemary. Cover; roast at 325°F until beef is tender, about 3 hours and 30 minutes. Transfer beef to a bowl. Place vegetables on a platter; reserve cooking liquid. Discard rosemary sprigs. Shred beef into chunks. Add ½ cup reserved liquid to beef. Transfer 4¾ cups beef to an airtight container with remaining cooking liquid; chill up to 5 days. Serve remaining beef with vegetables; top with parsley. Serves 4 (serving size: about 3 oz. beef and ½ cup vegetables)

CALORIES 284; FAT 9g (sat 3g, unsat 5g); PROTEIN 37g; CARB 10g; FIBER 2g; SUGARS 3g (added sugars 0g); SODIUM 384mg; CALC 6% DV; POTASSIUM 14% DV

Pot Roast Tacos with Chimichurri

Hands-on: 15 min. **Total:** 20 min.

1½ cups loosely packed fresh flat-
  leaf parsley leaves
1 cup fresh cilantro leaves
1½ Tbsp. chopped shallot
1 Tbsp. chopped red Fresno chile
2 garlic cloves, smashed
¼ cup extra-virgin olive oil
2 Tbsp. fresh lemon juice
1 Tbsp. water
¾ tsp. kosher salt
¼ tsp. black pepper
2¾ cups coarsely chopped drained
  cooked chuck roast (from Oven-
  Braised Pot Roast)
8 (6-inch) yellow corn tortillas,
  lightly charred
1 small ripe avocado, sliced
¼ cup thinly sliced radishes (from
  3 radishes)
1 oz. queso fresco (fresh Mexican
  cheese), crumbled (about ¼ cup)

1. Process parsley, cilantro, shallot, Fresno chile, and garlic in a food processor until finely chopped, about 10 seconds. Add olive oil, lemon juice, 1 tablespoon water, salt, and black pepper; process until combined, about 10 seconds.
2. Place chuck roast in a medium nonstick skillet over medium. Cook, stirring occasionally, until heated through, 4 to 5 minutes. Remove from heat. Add ½ cup chimichurri; toss to coat. Top tortillas evenly with meat, avocado, radishes, queso fresco, and remaining chimichurri. Serves 4 (serving size: 2 tacos)

CALORIES 423; FAT 25g (sat 5g, unsat 18g); PROTEIN 17g; CARB 32g; FIBER 7g; SUGARS 4g (added sugars 0g); SODIUM 567mg; CALC 11% DV; POTASSIUM 13% DV

Roast Beef Hash

Hands-on: 25 min. **Total:** 1 hr.

1¾ lb. Yukon Gold potatoes, peeled
  and cut into ½-inch cubes (about
  5 cups)
6 Tbsp. olive oil, divided
2 medium-sized yellow onions,
  thinly sliced (about 3 cups)
1 large red bell pepper, thinly sliced
  (about 1¼ cups)
1 large carrot, peeled and finely
  chopped (about ¾ cup)
2 garlic cloves, chopped
1¼ tsp. kosher salt, divided
¾ tsp. black pepper, divided
2 cups coarsely chopped drained
  cooked chuck roast (from Oven-
  Braised Pot Roast)
4 large eggs, poached
2 Tbsp. chopped fresh chives

1. Preheat oven to 325°F. Toss potatoes with 1 tablespoon oil on a baking sheet; spread evenly. Bake at 325°F until just tender, about 45 minutes.
2. Heat 2 tablespoons oil in a large cast-iron skillet over medium-high. Add onions, bell pepper, carrot, garlic, ½ teaspoon salt, and ¼ teaspoon black pepper; sauté 10 minutes. Place onion mixture in a medium bowl.
3. Heat remaining 3 tablespoons oil in pan over medium-high; add potatoes in a single layer. Sprinkle with ½ teaspoon salt; cook, turning occasionally, until golden, about 8 minutes. Add onion mixture and chuck roast; cook, stirring occasionally, until heated through, about 3 minutes. Sprinkle with remaining ¼ teaspoon salt and remaining ½ teaspoon black pepper. Top with eggs; sprinkle

with chives. Serves 4 (serving size: 1¼ cups hash and 1 egg)

CALORIES 516; FAT 27g (sat 5g, unsat 21g); PROTEIN 19g; CARB 50g; FIBER 9g; SUGARS 11g (added sugars 0g); SODIUM 779mg; CALC 8% DV; POTASSIUM 12% DV

02. LUNCH IS IN

Add a little verve to your workweek with portable, make-ahead lunches. They're packed with flavor and hold up for days.

Here's one great way to win the week: Spend a little time on the weekend prepping your lunches. With healthy meals portioned out in portable containers, your hectic weekday mornings just got a lot easier. Simply grab a container and go.

Here, we offer five make-ahead meals to liven up your midday. Each recipe makes four portions, taking you through the week if you allow for one day for leftovers or dining out. Each meal is around 400 calories, the same as a much-less-exciting PB&J sandwich. We tested how well each lunch held up after two, three, and four days to ensure textures and flavors stayed in their prime. Frankly, that cut out some of our favorite foods—ingredients like shrimp and cauliflower get a little funky come day four. We've taken out the guesswork so that you can enjoy each lunch as much on the last day as you did on the first.

Fast • Make Ahead

Lemon-Dill Salmon Salad

Hands-on: 15 min. **Total:** 15 min.
Canned boneless, skinless salmon is just as tasty and versatile as canned tuna, and it boasts more omega-3 fats—but you could certainly use tuna.

⅓ cup chopped celery
¼ cup chopped scallions
¼ cup canola mayonnaise
1 Tbsp. chopped fresh dill
1 tsp. lemon zest plus 1 Tbsp. fresh lemon juice
½ tsp. black pepper
¼ tsp. kosher salt
2 (6-oz.) cans sustainable boneless, skinless salmon (such as Wild Planet), drained and flaked
⅓ cup chopped unsalted roasted almonds
4 green leaf lettuce leaves
3 cups seedless red grapes
2 cups 3- to 4-inch carrot sticks
2 (6-inch) whole-wheat pitas, each cut into 8 wedges

1. Stir together celery, scallions, mayonnaise, dill, lemon zest and juice, pepper, and salt in a medium bowl. Fold in salmon and almonds. Arrange 1 lettuce leaf in each of 4 (4-cup) containers. Divide salmon salad evenly over lettuce.
2. Divide grapes, carrots, and pita wedges evenly among containers. Serves 4 (serving size: 1 lettuce leaf, ½ cup salmon salad, ¾ cup grapes, ½ cup carrots, and 4 pita wedges)

CALORIES 404; **FAT** 14g (sat 1g, unsat 11g); **PROTEIN** 28g; **CARB** 46g; **FIBER** 6g; **SUGARS** 22g (added sugars 0g); **SODIUM** 674mg; **CALC** 15% DV; **POTASSIUM** 18% DV

Staff Favorite · Gluten Free
Make Ahead

Coriander Chicken and Rice

Hands-on: 40 min. **Total:** 40 min.

2 Tbsp. olive oil, divided
1 cup uncooked brown basmati rice
⅜ tsp. ground turmeric
2 cups unsalted chicken stock

1 tsp. kosher salt, divided
1 lb. boneless, skinless chicken thighs, cut into ¾-inch pieces
¾ tsp. ground coriander
½ tsp. garlic powder
⅛ tsp. cayenne pepper
1 lb. fresh green beans, trimmed
¼ cup plain 2% reduced-fat Greek yogurt
1 Tbsp. fresh lemon juice
1 garlic clove, grated
Lemon wedges, for serving

1. Heat 2 teaspoons oil in a medium saucepan over medium-high. Add rice and turmeric; sauté 1 minute. Add stock and ⅜ teaspoon salt; bring to a boil. Cover, reduce heat to low, and simmer until rice is tender and liquid is absorbed, about 40 minutes.
2. Meanwhile, toss together chicken, coriander, garlic powder, cayenne, and ⅜ teaspoon salt. Heat 1 tablespoon oil in a large skillet over medium-high. Cook chicken, stirring occasionally, until browned, about 12 minutes. Remove chicken. (Do not wipe skillet clean.)
3. Add remaining 1 teaspoon oil to skillet. Add beans; cook, turning every 2 minutes, until charred. Sprinkle with remaining ¼ teaspoon salt.
4. Combine yogurt, lemon juice, and garlic. Serve sauce and lemon wedges with chicken, rice, and green beans. Serves 4 (serving size: about ½ cup chicken, ¾ cup rice, 1¼ cups green beans, and 2 Tbsp. yogurt sauce)

CALORIES 409; **FAT** 14g (sat 3g, unsat 9g); **PROTEIN** 32g; **CARB** 42g; **FIBER** 5g; **SUGARS** 7g (added sugars 0g); **SODIUM** 671mg; **CALC** 8% DV; **POTASSIUM** 11% DV

Fast · Gluten Free
Make Ahead · Vegetarian

Greek Chickpea Salad

Hands-on: 20 min. **Total:** 20 min.
For a heartier salad, you can add 4 ounces of cooked boneless, skinless chicken breast or shrimp; the chicken will add 187 calories and 35g protein, and the shrimp will contribute an extra 135 calories and 26g protein.

6 cups torn romaine lettuce
½ cup vertically sliced red onion
1 (15-oz.) can unsalted chickpeas, drained and rinsed
2 cups halved grape or cherry tomatoes
2 cups half-moon English cucumber slices (from 1 cucumber)
16 pitted kalamata olives (about 2 oz.)
4 oz. feta cheese, cut into 8 slices
¼ cup extra-virgin olive oil
3 Tbsp. red wine vinegar
½ tsp. dried oregano
¼ tsp. black pepper
⅛ tsp. kosher salt
1 garlic clove, grated

1. Arrange 1½ cups lettuce and 2 tablespoons onion in each of 4 (4-cup) bowls or containers. Top each serving with ⅓ cup chickpeas, ½ cup tomatoes, ½ cup cucumber, 4 olives, and 2 cheese slices.
2. Whisk together oil, vinegar, oregano, pepper, salt, and garlic in a small bowl. Serve about 2 tablespoons dressing with each salad. Serves 4 (serving size: about 3 cups)

CALORIES 384; **FAT** 25g (sat 6g, unsat 17g); **PROTEIN** 12g; **CARB** 29g; **FIBER** 7g; **SUGARS** 7g (added sugars 0g); **SODIUM** 584mg; **CALC** 24% DV; **POTASSIUM** 15% DV

Smoky Chicken with Potato Salad and Slaw

Hands-on: 20 min. **Total:** 45 min.

5 cups shredded coleslaw mix
1 tsp. granulated sugar
1¾ tsp. kosher salt, divided
1 lb. new potatoes, quartered
¼ cup plain 2% reduced-fat Greek yogurt
¼ cup chopped fresh chives
3 Tbsp. canola mayonnaise, divided
1 tsp. Dijon mustard
1 tsp. garlic powder
1 tsp. light brown sugar
¾ tsp. smoked paprika
½ tsp. ground cumin
¼ tsp. cayenne pepper
4 (6-oz.) boneless, skinless chicken breasts
2 Tbsp. canola oil, divided
1 tsp. apple cider vinegar

1. Place coleslaw mix in a colander; toss with granulated sugar and 1 teaspoon salt. Let stand 20 minutes. Meanwhile, place potatoes in a saucepan; cover with water. Bring to a boil; cook until tender, about 15 minutes. Drain. Rinse and drain slaw. Combine yogurt, chives, 2 tablespoons mayo, Dijon, and ½ teaspoon salt in a bowl. Stir in potatoes.
2. Combine garlic powder, brown sugar, paprika, cumin, cayenne, and remaining ¼ teaspoon salt. Brush chicken with 1 tablespoon oil; sprinkle with spice rub. Heat a grill pan over medium-high. Add chicken; grill until done, about 6 minutes per side.
3. Stir together vinegar, remaining 1 tablespoon mayo, and remaining 1 tablespoon oil in a bowl. Stir in

slaw. Serve with chicken and potato salad. Serves 4

CALORIES 391; **FAT** 14g (sat 2g, unsat 12g); **PROTEIN** 39g; **CARB** 25g; **FIBER** 4g; **SUGARS** 6g (added sugars 1g); **SODIUM** 644mg; **CALC** 5% DV; **POTASSIUM** 18% DV

Fast • Make Ahead

Glazed Meatballs with Soba Noodles

Hands-on: 30 min. **Total:** 30 min.

12 oz. 90% lean ground sirloin
⅓ cup whole-wheat breadcrumbs
1 large egg
1 garlic clove, grated
⅝ tsp. kosher salt, divided
6 oz. uncooked soba noodles or whole-wheat spaghetti
1 Tbsp. toasted sesame oil, divided
1 Tbsp. rice vinegar, divided
2 cups thinly sliced red cabbage
½ cup chopped scallions
⅓ cup matchstick-cut carrots
1½ Tbsp. lower-sodium soy sauce
1 Tbsp. honey
1 tsp. Sriracha chili sauce

1. Preheat oven to 400°F. Combine beef, breadcrumbs, egg, garlic, and ¼ teaspoon salt in a large bowl; shape into 20 meatballs. Arrange meatballs on a rimmed baking sheet lined with parchment paper. Bake at 400°F until cooked through, 15 to 20 minutes.
2. Meanwhile, bring a saucepan of water to a boil over medium-high. Add noodles; cook until al dente, 4 to 6 minutes for soba. Drain and rinse with cold water; drain. Place noodles in a large bowl. Toss with 2 teaspoons oil, 1½ teaspoons vinegar, and remaining ⅜ teaspoon salt. Add cabbage, scallions, and carrots; toss to combine.

3. Stir together soy sauce, honey, Sriracha, remaining 1 teaspoon oil, and remaining 1½ teaspoons vinegar in a medium skillet. Cook over medium, stirring occasionally, until slightly thickened. Add meatballs; toss to coat. Serve with noodles. Serves 4 (serving size: about 1½ cups noodle mixture and 5 meatballs)

CALORIES 407; **FAT** 12g (sat 4g, unsat 8g); **PROTEIN** 24g; **CARB** 49g; **FIBER** 5g; **SUGARS** 8g (added sugars 4g); **SODIUM** 621mg; **CALC** 6% DV; **POTASSIUM** 11% DV

03. SNACK BAR BASICS

This all-purpose, no-fail, mix-and-match formula is all you need for healthy, customizable, family-friendly treats.

Gluten Free • Make Ahead
Vegetarian

Almond-Cherry Bars

Hands-on: 15 min. **Total:** 1 hr. 40 min.

2 cups old-fashioned oats
⅓ cup almond butter
¼ cup pure maple syrup
1½ Tbsp. coconut oil
1 tsp. vanilla extract
½ tsp. kosher salt
1 large egg white
½ cup coarsely chopped unsalted roasted almonds
⅓ cup chopped unsweetened dried cherries

1. Preheat oven to 350°F. Line an 8-inch square metal baking pan with parchment paper; let excess hang over edge.

2. Spread oats onto a baking sheet. Bake at 350°F until toasted, about 12 minutes. Place in a medium bowl; cool.

3. Place almond butter, maple syrup, and oil in a microwavable bowl. Microwave at HIGH until warm, about 30 seconds; whisk until smooth. Whisk in vanilla, salt, and egg white.

4. Add almonds and cherries to oats. Pour almond butter mixture over oat mixture; stir until well combined. Using a spatula, press mixture very firmly into prepared pan.

5. Bake at 350°F until lightly browned, 20 to 22 minutes. Cool in pan on a wire rack 15 minutes. Remove from pan using parchment paper. Cool completely on rack. Cut into 12 (4- x 1⅓-inch) bars. Serves 12 (serving size: 1 bar)

CALORIES 173; **FAT** 10g (sat 2g, unsat 7g); **PROTEIN** 5g; **CARB** 18g; **FIBER** 3g; **SUGARS** 7g (added sugars 4g); **SODIUM** 103mg; **CALC** 5% DV; **POTASSIUM** 3% DV

---

2. Spread oats onto a baking sheet. Bake at 350°F until toasted, about 12 minutes. Place in a medium bowl; cool.

3. Place sunflower seed butter, agave syrup, and oil in a microwavable bowl. Microwave at HIGH until warm, about 30 seconds; whisk until smooth. Whisk in vanilla, salt, and egg white.

4. Add pistachios and raisins to oats. Pour sunflower seed butter mixture over oat mixture; stir until well combined. Using a spatula, press mixture firmly into prepared pan.

5. Bake at 350°F until lightly browned, 20 to 22 minutes. Cool in pan on a wire rack 15 minutes. Remove from pan using parchment paper. Cool completely on rack. Cut into 12 (4- x 1⅓-inch) bars. Serves 12 (serving size: 1 bar)

CALORIES 174; **FAT** 9g (sat 2g, unsat 6g); **PROTEIN** 4g; **CARB** 21g; **FIBER** 2g; **SUGARS** 9g (added sugars 5g); **SODIUM** 109mg; **CALC** 2% DV; **POTASSIUM** 4% DV

---

2. Spread oats onto a baking sheet. Bake at 350°F until toasted, about 12 minutes. Place in a medium bowl; cool.

3. Place cashew butter, brown rice syrup, and oil in a microwavable bowl. Microwave at HIGH until warm, about 30 seconds; whisk until smooth. Whisk in vanilla, salt, and egg white.

4. Add cashews and apricots to oats. Pour cashew butter mixture over oat mixture; stir until well combined. Using a spatula, press mixture very firmly into prepared pan.

5. Bake at 350°F until lightly browned, 20 to 22 minutes. Cool in pan on a wire rack 15 minutes. Remove from pan using parchment paper. Cool completely on rack. Cut into 12 (4- x 1⅓-inch) bars. Serves 12 (serving size: 1 bar)

CALORIES 181; **FAT** 9g (sat 3g, unsat 6g); **PROTEIN** 4g; **CARB** 22g; **FIBER** 2g; **SUGARS** 9g (added sugars 6g); **SODIUM** 122mg; **CALC** 2% DV; **POTASSIUM** 4% DV

Gluten Free • Make Ahead Vegetarian

Pistachio-Raisin Bars

Hands-on: 15 min. **Total:** 1 hr. 40 min.

2 cups old-fashioned oats
⅓ cup sunflower seed butter
¼ cup agave syrup
1½ Tbsp. coconut oil
1 tsp. vanilla extract
½ tsp. kosher salt
1 large egg white
½ cup coarsely chopped unsalted roasted pistachios
⅓ cup golden raisins

1. Preheat oven to 350°F. Line an 8-inch square metal baking pan with parchment paper; let excess hang over edge.

Gluten Free • Make Ahead Vegetarian

Cashew-Apricot Bars

Hands-on: 15 min. **Total:** 1 hr. 40 min.

2 cups old-fashioned oats
⅓ cup cashew butter
¼ cup brown rice syrup
1½ Tbsp. coconut oil
1 tsp. vanilla extract
½ tsp. kosher salt
1 large egg white
½ cup coarsely chopped unsalted roasted cashews
⅓ cup coarsely chopped dried apricots

1. Preheat oven to 350°F. Line an 8-inch square metal baking pan with parchment paper; let excess hang over edge.

THE MASTER METHOD

WITH OUR EASY INSTRUCTIONS, YOU CAN MIX AND MATCH YOUR FAVORITE FLAVORS TO CREATE YOUR IDEAL COMBO. THE SAME FORMULA WILL GET YOU TO SNACK BAR SUCCESS NO MATTER WHICH NUT BUTTER, SWEETENER, ROASTED NUT, OR DRIED FRUIT YOU CHOOSE. STORE COMPLETELY COOLED BARS IN AN AIRTIGHT CONTAINER AT ROOM TEMPERATURE FOR UP TO TWO WEEKS OR FREEZE UP TO TWO MONTHS.

1. CREATE A BASE
Toast oats in the oven to give them a nutty flavor. Preheat oven to 350°F. Spread 2 cups old-fashioned oats onto a rimmed baking sheet. Bake until lightly browned and fragrant, about 12 minutes. Transfer oats to a bowl, and cool to room temperature.

2. ADD RICHNESS
Creamy nut butter and toasty coconut oil enrich the bars. Liquid sweetener, well, sweetens them. Place ⅓ cup nut butter, ¼ cup liquid sweetener (such as honey, maple syrup, brown rice syrup, or agave), and 1 ½ Tbsp. coconut oil in a bowl. Microwave at HIGH for 30 seconds or until warm.

3. BOOST THE FLAVOR
Add 1 tsp. vanilla extract and ½ tsp. kosher salt to the nut butter mixture to heighten the flavor; whisk until smooth. Whisk in 1 large egg white; it's a key part of the binder that will hold all the ingredients together.

4. ADD CRUNCH AND CHEW
Stir ½ cup unsalted roasted nuts (or broken-up pretzel pieces) into the cooled oats for hearty crunch. Add ⅓ cup dried fruit (chop the pieces if they are large) for bright, sweet flavor and textural contrast.

5. MIX AND PRESS
Pour the nut butter mixture over the oat mixture; stir well until all pieces are evenly coated. Transfer mixture to an 8-inch square metal baking pan lined with parchment paper. Press mixture very firmly into pan; packing tightly helps keep bars from crumbling.

6. BAKE AND COOL
Bake at 350°F until lightly browned around edges, 20 to 22 minutes. Cool in pan on a wire rack 15 minutes. Lift bars out of pan with parchment paper; cool completely on rack before cutting (warm bars might crumble).

Make Ahead • Vegetarian

PB-Pretzel-Apple Bars

Hands-on: 15 min. **Total:** 1 hr. 40 min.

2 cups old-fashioned oats
⅓ cup creamy peanut butter
¼ cup honey
1½ Tbsp. coconut oil
1 tsp. vanilla extract
½ tsp. kosher salt
1 large egg white
½ cup coarsely chopped mini pretzel twists
⅓ cup coarsely chopped dried apples

1. Preheat oven to 350°F. Line an 8-inch square metal baking pan with parchment paper; let excess hang over edge.
2. Spread oats onto a baking sheet. Bake at 350°F until toasted, about 12 minutes. Place in a medium bowl; cool.
3. Place peanut butter, honey, and oil in a microwavable bowl. Microwave at HIGH until warm, about 30 seconds; whisk until smooth. Whisk in vanilla, salt, and egg white.
4. Add pretzels and apples to oats. Pour peanut butter mixture over oat mixture; stir until well combined. Using a spatula, press mixture very firmly into prepared pan.
5. Bake at 350°F until lightly browned, 20 to 22 minutes. Cool in pan on a wire rack 15 minutes. Remove from pan using parchment paper. Cool completely on rack. Cut into 12 (4- x 1⅓-inch) bars. Serves 12 (serving size: 1 bar)

CALORIES 156; **FAT** 7g (sat 2g, unsat 4g); **PROTEIN** 4g; **CARB** 22g; **FIBER** 2g; **SUGARS** 8g (added sugars 6g); **SODIUM** 214mg; **CALC** 1% DV; **POTASSIUM** 2% DV

04. BREAKFAST IN A BOWL

Cook up a big pot of quinoa or wheat berries and you have the foundation for nearly a week's worth of easy morning meals that can go sweet or savory.

QUINOA RECIPES
Fast • Gluten Free
Make Ahead • Vegetarian

Perfect Quinoa

Hands-on: 5 min. **Total:** 25 min.
Rinsing removes this gluten-free pseudo-grain's natural coating, called saponin, which can make it taste bitter. (Quinoa is technically a seed.) Although most boxed quinoa is prerinsed, it doesn't hurt to give it an extra rinse at home. Allowing the quinoa to steam helps it absorb any remaining traces of liquid and plump up.

1 cup uncooked red quinoa
1¾ cups water
¼ tsp. kosher salt

1. Place quinoa in a fine wire-mesh strainer; rinse under running water 1 minute. Drain. Bring quinoa, 1¾ cups water, and salt to a boil in a saucepan over high. Cover and reduce heat to medium. Cook until liquid is mostly absorbed, 12 to 15 minutes.
2. Remove from heat, and let steam, covered, 10 minutes. Drain any excess cooking liquid. Serves 4 (serving size: about ⅔ cup)

CALORIES 156; **FAT** 3g (sat 0g, unsat 2g); **PROTEIN** 6g; **CARB** 27g; **FIBER** 3g; **SUGARS** 1g (added sugars 0g); **SODIUM** 122mg; **CALC** 2% DV; **POTASSIUM** 5% DV

Fast • Gluten Free
Make Ahead • Vegetarian

Apple Quinoa Bowl with Cinnamon Ricotta

Hands-on: 15 min. **Total:** 15 min.
This bowl captures the essence of a warm slice of apple pie but won't send you into midmorning nap mode. Feel free to swap the ricotta for Greek yogurt, if desired.

2 tsp. unsalted butter
10 oz. chopped Granny Smith apples (from 2 medium apples)
¼ tsp. kosher salt
2 tsp. honey
1 cup part-skim ricotta cheese
¼ tsp. ground cinnamon
2⅔ cups Perfect Quinoa (recipe at left)
¼ cup chopped toasted hazelnuts

1. Heat butter in a large nonstick skillet over medium-high. Add apples and salt; cook, stirring occasionally, until apples begin to soften, 8 to 10 minutes. Add honey, and cook, stirring constantly, until apples are tender, 1 to 2 more minutes. Remove skillet from heat.
2. Stir together ricotta and cinnamon in a small bowl.
3. Divide quinoa evenly among 4 bowls. Top each serving with ¼ cup ricotta mixture and ½ cup apples. Top evenly with hazelnuts. Serves 4 (serving size: about 1¾ cups)

CALORIES 357; **FAT** 15g (sat 5g, unsat 9g); **PROTEIN** 15g; **CARB** 44g; **FIBER** 5g; **SUGARS** 12g (added sugars 3g); **SODIUM** 304mg; **CALC** 20% DV; **POTASSIUM** 9% DV

Bacon and Avocado Quinoa Bowl with Buttermilk-Chive Drizzle

Hands-on: 10 min. **Total:** 15 min.
Cook the bacon ahead and this bowl comes together in 5 minutes flat. It's also a great lunch option.

8 center-cut bacon slices, chopped
½ cup whole buttermilk
1 Tbsp. plain whole-milk Greek yogurt
1 Tbsp. chopped fresh chives
¼ tsp. kosher salt
¼ tsp. black pepper
2⅔ cups Perfect Quinoa (recipe on page 251)
2 cups halved cherry tomatoes
1 ripe avocado, sliced

1. Cook bacon in a large nonstick skillet over medium-high, stirring occasionally, until crisp, 5 to 6 minutes. Place bacon on a plate lined with paper towels to drain.
2. Whisk together buttermilk, yogurt, chives, salt, and pepper in a bowl or glass measuring cup.
3. Divide quinoa evenly among 4 bowls. Sprinkle bacon evenly over each serving; top each with ½ cup tomatoes and one-fourth sliced avocado. Drizzle with 2 ½ tablespoons buttermilk-chive dressing. Serves 4 (serving size: about 1¾ cups)

CALORIES 316; **FAT** 13g (sat 3g, unsat 10g); **PROTEIN** 15g; **CARB** 36g; **FIBER** 5g; **SUGARS** 5g (added sugars 0g); **SODIUM** 489mg; **CALC** 7% DV; **POTASSIUM** 14% DV

Perfect Wheat Berries

Hands-on: 5 min. **Total:** 13 hr.
Chewy, nutty, and fiber-rich, wheat berries add satisfying bite and bulk to breakfast. Soaking can help decrease cook time and make for a plumper, more tender grain.

1 cup uncooked wheat berries
1½ cups water, plus more for soaking
¼ tsp. kosher salt

1. Place wheat berries in a bowl with enough water to cover. Soak 12 hours or overnight. Drain.
2. Combine wheat berries, 1½ cups water, and salt in a saucepan over high, and bring to a boil. Cover and reduce heat to medium; cook until tender, 35 to 45 minutes. Remove pan from heat; let steam, covered, 15 minutes. Drain excess liquid. Serves 4 (serving size: ½ cup)

CALORIES 150; **FAT** 1g (sat 0g, unsat 1g); **PROTEIN** 6g; **CARB** 32g; **FIBER** 6g; **SUGARS** 0g (added sugars 0g); **SODIUM** 120mg; **CALC** 2% DV; **POTASSIUM** 0% DV

Wilted Spinach and Fried Egg Wheat Berry Bowl

Hands-on: 10 min. **Total:** 15 min.
Kimchi adds a tangy twist and probiotics to this hearty breakfast bowl. Sprinkle with chile flakes for extra heat.

2 tsp. sesame oil
1 (5-oz.) container baby spinach
1 tsp. lower-sodium soy sauce
4 large eggs
2 cups Perfect Wheat Berries (recipe at left)
¼ cup jarred kimchi (Korean fermented cabbage), chopped
¼ cup chopped scallions
2 Tbsp. roasted unsalted peanuts, roughly chopped

1. Heat oil in a large nonstick skillet over medium. Add spinach; cook, stirring often, until wilted, about 3 minutes. Stir in soy sauce; transfer mixture to a bowl.
2. Crack eggs into skillet; cook 2 minutes. Cover and continue to cook until desired degree of doneness, 2 more minutes for medium.
3. Divide wheat berries evenly among 4 bowls; top each serving with an egg, ¼ cup spinach mixture, and 1 tablespoon kimchi. Top evenly with scallions and peanuts. Serves 4 (serving size: about 1 ½ cups)

CALORIES 281; **FAT** 10g (sat 2g, unsat 7g); **PROTEIN** 15g; **CARB** 35g; **FIBER** 8g; **SUGARS** 1g (added sugars 0g); **SODIUM** 314mg; **CALC** 9% DV; **POTASSIUM** 3% DV

**Fast · Make Ahead
Vegetarian**

Roasted Grape and Goat Cheese Wheat Berry Bowl

Hands-on: 5 min. **Total:** 25 min.
Save time in the morning by preparing the grapes ahead and storing them in a microwave-safe container in the fridge. When ready to use, microwave the grapes for 30 to 45 seconds before spooning them over your grains.

1 lb. red seedless grapes
1 Tbsp. olive oil
¼ tsp. kosher salt
1 tsp. balsamic vinegar
2 cups Perfect Wheat Berries (recipe on page 252)
1 oz. goat cheese, crumbled (about ¼ cup)
¼ cup toasted walnuts, chopped

1. Preheat oven to 400°F. Toss together grapes, oil, and salt in a 12- x 15-inch baking pan. Bake in preheated oven, shaking pan occasionally, until grapes begin to blister, 15 to 17 minutes. Transfer grapes to a bowl, add vinegar, and toss to coat.
2. Divide wheat berries evenly among 4 bowls, and top each serving with ½ cup roasted grapes, 1 tablespoon goat cheese, and 1 tablespoon chopped walnuts. Serves 4 (serving size: about 1 cup)

CALORIES 326; FAT 10g (sat 2g, unsat 8g); PROTEIN 9g; CARB 54g; FIBER 8g; SUGARS 18g (added sugars 0g); SODIUM 275mg; CALC 5% DV; POTASSIUM 5% DV

WEEKNIGHT MAINS

**Fast · Gluten Free
Vegetarian**

Creamy Corn-Mushroom Risotto

Hands-on: 30 min. **Total:** 30 min.
This dish is a stellar way to celebrate the last of the season's corn harvest. Pureeing some of the corn adds a subtly sweet creaminess to the broth that builds as the risotto cooks. If you can't find Arborio rice, feel free to substitute jasmine rice.

4½ cups water
2 cups fresh corn kernels (from 5 ears), divided
2 Tbsp. olive oil
1½ cups chopped fresh mushrooms
1 cup chopped yellow onion
1 cup uncooked Arborio rice
3 garlic cloves, minced
4 tsp. fresh thyme leaves, divided
½ cup dry white wine
2 oz. Parmigiano-Reggiano cheese, grated (about ½ cup) and divided
1½ Tbsp. unsalted butter
⅝ tsp. kosher salt
2 Tbsp. toasted pine nuts

1. Process 4½ cups water and 1 cup corn in a blender until smooth, about 1 minute. Pour through a fine wire-mesh strainer into a large measuring cup; discard solids. Add water, if necessary, to equal 4½ cups. Transfer to a saucepan; bring to a simmer over medium-high. Reduce heat to low.
2. Heat olive oil in a Dutch oven over medium-high. Add mushrooms, onion, and remaining 1 cup corn. Cook, stirring often, until onions are translucent, 4 to 5 minutes. Add rice, garlic, and 2 teaspoons thyme. Cook, stirring constantly, until rice is toasted, 1 to 2 minutes. Add wine; bring to a boil, and cook, stirring occasionally, until liquid is almost evaporated.
3. Stir in 2 cups corn broth; reduce heat to medium-low, and cook, stirring often, until broth is almost absorbed, about 10 minutes. Add 1 cup corn broth, and cook, stirring often, 5 minutes. Repeat with 1 cup corn broth. Remove from heat. Stir in ¼ cup cheese, butter, salt, and remaining ½ cup corn broth. Divide among 4 bowls; top evenly with pine nuts, remaining 2 teaspoons thyme, and remaining ¼ cup cheese. Serves 4 (serving size: 1¼ cups)

CALORIES 456; FAT 20g (sat 6g, unsat 12g); PROTEIN 12g; CARB 60g; FIBER 5g; SUGARS 7g (added sugars 0g); SODIUM 571mg; CALC 14% DV; POTASSIUM 9% DV

Peppery Beef and Broccoli

Hands-on: 35 min. **Total:** 35 min.
Fast-cooking flank steak provides a hefty dose of iron; broccoli's ample vitamin K boosts bone strength.

2 Tbsp. canola oil, divided
1 (1-lb.) flank steak
¾ tsp. kosher salt, divided
¾ tsp. black pepper, divided
1 (12-oz.) pkg. broccoli florets
1 cup sliced red onion
¼ cup water
3 large garlic cloves, thinly sliced
¼ cup canola mayonnaise
1 Tbsp. fresh lemon juice

1. Heat 1 tablespoon oil in a large skillet over high. Pat steak dry; sprinkle with ½ teaspoon salt and ½ teaspoon pepper. Cook until browned and a thermometer inserted in thickest portion registers 135°F, 4 to 5 minutes per side. Remove from skillet; cover to keep warm. Wipe skillet clean.
2. Heat skillet over medium-high. Add broccoli, onion, and remaining 1 tablespoon oil. Cook, stirring occasionally, until broccoli is slightly charred, about 4 minutes. Add ¼ cup water and garlic; cook until water evaporates and broccoli is crisp-tender, about 2 minutes. Sprinkle with remaining ¼ teaspoon salt.
3. Stir together mayonnaise, lemon juice, and remaining ¼ teaspoon pepper in a small bowl. Thinly slice steak against the grain. Serve steak with broccoli and mayonnaise mixture. Serves 4 (serving size: 3 oz. steak, ⅔ cup broccoli, and 1 Tbsp. sauce)

CALORIES 304; **FAT** 17g (sat 3g, unsat 13g); **PROTEIN** 28g; **CARB** 9g; **FIBER** 3g; **SUGARS** 3g (added sugars 0g); **SODIUM** 554mg; **CALC** 8% DV; **POTASSIUM** 16% DV

Chicken Stir-Fry with Bok Choy

Hands-on: 35 min. **Total:** 35 min.

1 lb. skinless, boneless chicken breasts, cut into 1-inch pieces
3 Tbsp. plus 1 tsp. cornstarch, divided
¼ cup canola oil, divided
⅓ cup fresh orange juice
2 Tbsp. lower-sodium soy sauce
2 Tbsp. rice vinegar
1 tsp. honey
½ tsp. crushed red pepper
2 Tbsp. sesame oil, divided
4 (4-oz.) baby bok choy, trimmed and halved lengthwise
¼ cup water
¼ tsp. kosher salt
1½ Tbsp. minced peeled fresh ginger
3 large garlic cloves, minced
1 Tbsp. sesame seeds, toasted
2 Tbsp. sliced red Fresno chile

1. Toss chicken with 3 tablespoons cornstarch; shake off excess. Heat 3 tablespoons canola oil in a large nonstick skillet over high. Add chicken; cook until browned, about 8 minutes. Set aside; wipe skillet clean.
2. Combine orange juice, soy sauce, vinegar, honey, red pepper, and remaining 1 teaspoon cornstarch; set aside. Heat skillet over medium; add 1 tablespoon sesame oil and half of bok choy; cook until browned. Remove from skillet; repeat with remaining 1 tablespoon sesame oil and bok choy. Return all bok choy to skillet. Reduce heat to low; add ¼ cup water. Cover and cook until tender, about 2 minutes. Sprinkle with salt. Set aside.
3. Add ginger, garlic, and remaining 1 tablespoon canola oil to skillet; cook over medium 2 minutes. Add orange juice mixture; cook until thickened.

Stir in chicken. Divide among 4 plates; sprinkle evenly with sesame seeds and chile, and serve with bok choy. Serves 4 (serving size: 3 oz. chicken and 2 bok choy halves)

CALORIES 398; **FAT** 25g (sat 3g, unsat 21g); **PROTEIN** 28g; **CARB** 14g; **FIBER** 2g; **SUGARS** 5g (added sugars 1g); **SODIUM** 525mg; **CALC** 14% DV; **POTASSIUM** 15% DV

Roasted Pork Tenderloin with Cabbage

Hands-on: 40 min. **Total:** 40 min.
This modern twist on hearty German fare gets a fiber boost from savoy cabbage and a crunchy-tart finish from cranberries and almonds. Be sure to let the pork rest atop the cabbage mixture; its juices infuse it with rich, meaty flavor.

4 medium scallions
3 Tbsp. olive oil, divided
1½ lb. pork tenderloin, trimmed
1⅛ tsp. kosher salt, divided
½ tsp. black pepper, divided
8 cups chopped savoy cabbage
½ cup dried cranberries (about 3 oz.)
1½ Tbsp. white wine vinegar
¼ cup toasted sliced almonds

1. Preheat oven to 400°F. Thinly slice scallions; divide green and white parts.
2. Heat 2 tablespoons of the oil in a large cast-iron skillet over high. Sprinkle pork evenly with ¾ teaspoon salt and ¼ teaspoon pepper. Cook until browned, about 3 minutes per side. Transfer to a rimmed baking sheet; roast at 400°F until a thermometer inserted in thickest portion registers 145°F, 10 to 15 minutes.
3. While pork roasts, add remaining 1 tablespoon oil to skillet; heat over medium-high. Add white parts of

scallions; cook, stirring constantly, until translucent, about 1 minute. Add cabbage; cook, stirring often, until slightly softened, about 2 minutes. Reduce heat to medium; add cranberries. Cook, covered, stirring occasionally, until cabbage is tender, about 4 minutes. Stir in vinegar, remaining ⅜ teaspoon salt, and remaining ¼ teaspoon pepper. Remove from heat, and cover to keep warm.

4. Place pork on cabbage in skillet; let stand 5 minutes. Transfer pork to a cutting board; slice. Stir pork juices in skillet into cabbage until well combined. Sprinkle cabbage with sliced almonds and green parts of scallions. Serve with sliced pork. Serves 4 (serving size: 4 oz. pork, and ¾ cup cabbage)

CALORIES 404; **FAT** 17g (sat 3g, unsat 14g); **PROTEIN** 38g; **CARB** 28g; **FIBER** 7g; **SUGARS** 18g (added sugars 8g); **SODIUM** 669mg; **CALC** 9% DV; **POTASSIUM** 23% DV

Fast

Pesto Shrimp and Broccoli Fettuccine

Hands-on: 10 min. **Total:** 25 min.
Put your knife away—store-bought pesto and precut broccoli florets mean no chopping required. Your Dutch oven pulls triple duty in this recipe, cooking the pasta, blanching the broccoli, and bringing the whole dish together.

10 cups water
8 oz. uncooked fettuccine
3 cups broccoli florets (about 7 oz.)
¼ cup refrigerated basil pesto
2 Tbsp. Dijon mustard
1 tsp. lemon zest plus 1 Tbsp. fresh lemon juice
¼ tsp. kosher salt
1 lb. peeled and deveined cooked medium shrimp
3 Tbsp. grated Parmesan cheese

1. Bring 10 cups water to a boil in a Dutch oven over high. Add fettuccine, and cook 6 minutes. Add broccoli florets to pasta; cook until pasta is al dente and broccoli is bright green and crisp-tender, about 3 minutes. Reserve ½ cup cooking liquid, and set aside. Drain pasta mixture.

2. Return pasta and broccoli to Dutch oven; reduce heat to low. Stir in pesto, mustard, lemon zest and juice, and salt. Add shrimp, and cook, stirring constantly, just until heated through, about 2 minutes, adding cooking liquid, 1 tablespoon at a time, if needed for creaminess. Top with the Parmesan; serve immediately. Serves 4 (serving size: about 2 cups)

CALORIES 456; **FAT** 11g (sat 3g, unsat 6g); **PROTEIN** 42g; **CARB** 47g; **FIBER** 4g; **SUGARS** 3g (added sugars 0g); **SODIUM** 723mg; **CALC** 26% DV; **POTASSIUM** 13% DV

PUMP UP THE VOLUME

Boost the veggie volume of this dish by stirring in 1 cup of frozen peas with the broccoli. Sub in whole-wheat pasta for fiber bonus points.

Fast • Gluten Free
Vegetarian

Greek Eggplant Skillet Dinner

Hands-on: 25 min. **Total:** 25 min.
Protein-rich tofu teams up with meaty eggplant in this Greek-inspired vegetarian dinner. San Marzano tomatoes are your best bet here; their sweet flavor and low acidity balance this dish without adding any sugar.

7 Tbsp. olive oil, divided
1 (14-oz.) pkg. extra-firm tofu, cubed
1 large (about 16 oz.) eggplant, cut into ½-inch-thick slices
1 (28-oz.) can whole peeled tomatoes (such as San Marzano), drained and chopped
2 garlic cloves, grated
1 tsp. chopped fresh oregano, plus more for garnish
½ tsp. ground cinnamon
½ tsp. ground cumin
¼ tsp. kosher salt
¼ tsp. crushed red pepper
3 Tbsp. crumbled feta cheese
Chopped fresh mint

1. Preheat broiler with an oven rack 6 inches from heat.

2. Heat a large cast-iron skillet over medium-high. Add 2 tablespoons oil; swirl to coat. Add tofu; cook until browned, about 5 minutes. Remove tofu from skillet. Add ¼ cup oil and eggplant slices in a single layer; cook, without stirring, until browned, about 4 minutes. Flip eggplant slices; cook until tender, about 4 minutes. Remove skillet from heat.

3. Combine tomatoes, garlic, oregano, cinnamon, cumin, salt, and crushed red pepper in a medium bowl.

4. Top eggplant evenly with tofu. Spoon tomato mixture over eggplant and tofu. Drizzle with remaining 1 tablespoon oil; sprinkle with feta. Broil until cheese begins to brown, about 4 minutes. Garnish with chopped mint and oregano. Serves 4 (serving size: 1¼ cups)

CALORIES 397; **FAT** 31g (sat 5g, unsat 25g); **PROTEIN** 14g; **CARB** 20g; **FIBER** 8g; **SUGARS** 11g (added sugars 0g); **SODIUM** 586mg; **CALC** 16% DV; **POTASSIUM** 13% DV

Southwestern-Style Stuffed Sweet Potatoes

Hands-on: 30 min. **Total:** 30 min.
Packed with quinoa and black beans, these spuds make a satisfying meatless main dish with 14g of protein. The quick sheet pan–roasted salsa takes the potatoes over the top with its balance of fresh and charred flavors.

3 small tomatillos, husks removed
3 garlic cloves, unpeeled
1 small jalapeño (about 1½ oz.)
1 (15-oz.) can unsalted black beans, rinsed and drained
½ cup cooked quinoa
1½ Tbsp. fresh lime juice
1 tsp. chopped fresh oregano
½ tsp. ground cumin
½ tsp. kosher salt, divided
4 (8-oz.) sweet potatoes
¼ cup chopped white onion
2 Tbsp. chopped fresh cilantro
¼ cup plain 2% reduced-fat Greek yogurt
1 oz. Cotija cheese, crumbled (about ¼ cup)
1 tsp. hot sauce
Fresh cilantro leaves (optional)
Thinly sliced white onion (optional)

1. Preheat broiler to low with oven rack 6 inches from heat. Place tomatillos, garlic, and jalapeño on a rimmed baking sheet. Broil until well browned, 15 to 18 minutes, flipping vegetables halfway through broiling. Let cool 5 minutes. Remove and discard jalapeño stem and garlic skins.
2. Stir together beans, quinoa, lime juice, oregano, cumin, and ¼ teaspoon salt in a medium bowl; set aside.
3. Prick potatoes all over with a fork. Place on a microwave-safe plate and microwave at HIGH until just tender, 10 to 12 minutes. Pulse broiled tomatillo, garlic, and jalapeño in a food processor 4 times. Transfer to a bowl; stir in chopped onion, chopped cilantro, and remaining ¼ teaspoon salt.
4. Stir together yogurt and cheese in a bowl. Split potatoes lengthwise; fluff flesh with a fork. Top evenly with bean mixture, tomatillo salsa, and yogurt mixture. Drizzle evenly with hot sauce. Top with cilantro leaves and onion slices, if desired. Serves 4 (serving size: 1 potato with toppings)

CALORIES 325; **FAT** 5g (sat 2g, unsat 1g); **PROTEIN** 14g; **CARB** 58g; **FIBER** 11g; **SUGARS** 10g (added sugars 0g); **SODIUM** 487mg; **CALC** 20% DV; **POTASSIUM** 20% DV

4 GO-WITH-ANYTHING SIDES

Bacon-Leek Mashed Potatoes
Pick up Yukon Gold potatoes; their high starch content yields a fluffier, creamier mash. Leeks add gut-friendly prebiotic fiber; a little bit of bacon lends salty flavor.

Cook 1 lb. quartered peeled Yukon Gold potatoes in simmering water until tender, 20 minutes. Cook 2 center-cut bacon slices in a skillet over medium-high until crispy. Remove and crumble bacon; add 1 cup chopped leeks to skillet. Reduce heat to medium-low; cook 8 minutes. Drain potatoes; mash with ¼ cup whole milk, 3 Tbsp. sour cream, ½ tsp. kosher salt, ¼ tsp. black pepper, and leeks. Top with 1 Tbsp. chopped fresh chives and crumbled bacon. Serves 4 (serving size: ⅔ cup)

CALORIES 157; **FAT** 3g (sat 2g, unsat 1g); **PROTEIN** 5g; **CARB** 27g; **FIBER** 3g; **SUGARS** 3g (added sugars 0g); **SODIUM** 322mg; **CALC** 6% DV; **POTASSIUM** 9% DV

Charred Sesame Green Beans
Letting the beans sit in the hot skillet without stirring is the secret to getting a nice char; adding the sauce to the still-hot skillet helps it reduce quickly and cling to the crispy, smoky beans. Serve with roasted pork or salmon.

Stir together 1 Tbsp. lower-sodium soy sauce and 2 tsp. Sriracha in a small bowl; set aside. Heat 2 Tbsp. sesame oil in a large skillet over high; add 8 oz. trimmed fresh green beans. Cook, without stirring, until charred, about 3 minutes. Add ¼ cup chopped scallions; cook until beans are tender, 2 to 3 minutes. Remove from heat. Add sauce mixture; toss to coat. Stir in 1 Tbsp. toasted sesame seeds. Serves 4 (serving size: ½ cup)

CALORIES 98; **FAT** 8g (sat 1g, unsat 6g); **PROTEIN** 2g; **CARB** 6g; **FIBER** 2g; **SUGARS** 2g (added sugars 0g); **SODIUM** 198mg; **CALC** 5% DV; **POTASSIUM** 3% DV

Cheesy Brussels Sprouts and Mushrooms
Cremini mushrooms are often labeled as baby bellas; pick up presliced 'shrooms to cut down on prep time.

Heat 2 Tbsp. olive oil in a large skillet over high. Add 2 cups halved Brussels sprouts (8 oz.); cook until browned, 3 to 4 minutes. Add 2 cups sliced cremini mushrooms (4 oz.); cook until tender, 3 to 4 minutes. Stir in 1 tsp. minced fresh garlic, 1 tsp. chopped fresh thyme, ¼ tsp. kosher salt, and ¼ tsp. black pepper; cook 1 minute. Remove from heat. Stir in 2 Tbsp. whole-wheat panko and 1 Tbsp. white wine vinegar; top with ¼ cup grated Parmesan cheese. Serves 4 (serving size: ½ cup)

CALORIES 122; **FAT** 8g (sat 2g, unsat 6g); **PROTEIN** 4g; **CARB** 9g; **FIBER** 3g; **SUGARS** 2g (added sugars 0g); **SODIUM** 229mg; **CALC** 7% DV; **POTASSIUM** 8% DV

Fast • Gluten Free
Vegetarian
Honey-Ginger Pear Salad

Golden raisins add natural sweetness to this salad. Walnuts deliver crunch and heart-healthy fats. Don't skip the toasting step—it tones down their bitter tannins.

Whisk together 2 tsp. fresh lemon juice, 2 tsp. honey, 1 tsp. Dijon mustard, ½ tsp. grated fresh ginger, ¼ tsp. kosher salt, and ¼ tsp. black pepper in a small bowl; gradually add 1½ Tbsp. olive oil, whisking until blended. Toss together 2 cups baby spinach, 1 (6-oz.) sliced Bartlett pear, and 3 Tbsp. golden raisins in a medium bowl; toss with dressing. Divide salad among 4 plates; top with 3 Tbsp. chopped toasted walnuts. Serves 4 (serving size: ½ cup)

CALORIES 143; **FAT** 9g (sat 1g, unsat 7g); **PROTEIN** 2g; **CARB** 17g; **FIBER** 2g; **SUGARS** 11g (added sugars 3g); **SODIUM** 163mg; **CALC** 3% DV; **POTASSIUM** 3% DV

COOKING LIGHT DIET
Fast • Vegetarian
Ultimate Breakfast Toast

Hands-on: 20 min. **Total:** 30 min. This next-level toast makes a wholesome treat for breakfast, a snack, or breakfast-for-dinner. While store-bought jams are loaded with sugar, this quick microwave version puts you in charge of the sweetness level. Customize it with your favorite fresh or frozen fruit.

2 cups mixed fresh or frozen berries
¼ cup granulated sugar
1 Tbsp. fresh lime juice
1 (¼-inch-thick) slice peeled fresh ginger
½ cup part-skim ricotta cheese
4 (1-oz.) multigrain bread slices, toasted

1 (5-oz.) ripe peach, sliced
½ cup fresh blackberries, halved
5 Tbsp. toasted pecans, chopped
2 Tbsp. honey

1. Stir together berries, sugar, lime juice, and ginger in a medium-sized microwave-safe bowl. Place bowl on a microwave-safe plate (to catch splatters). Microwave 5 minutes; stir. Microwave 5 minutes. Let jam cool to room temperature, 10 to 20 minutes. Remove and discard ginger.
2. Spread 2 tablespoons ricotta on each toasted bread slice. Dollop each slice with 2 tablespoons microwaved fruit jam. Top evenly with peach slices, blackberries, and pecans. Drizzle evenly with honey. Serves 4 (serving size: 1 slice)

CALORIES 307; **FAT** 10g (sat 2g, unsat 7g); **PROTEIN** 9g; **CARB** 50g; **FIBER** 6g; **SUGARS** 33g (added sugars 21g); **SODIUM** 140mg; **CALC** 14% DV; **POTASSIUM** 7% DV

BREAD BUYING TIPS

Be on the lookout when shopping for whole-grain bread; some brands sneak in a lot of extra sodium and added sugars. Pick out a loaf that's packed with as much fiber as you can find.

WHAT'S FRESH NOW
Gluten Free • Make Ahead
Vegetarian
Sweet and Spicy Apple Chips

Hands-on: 10 min. **Total:** 2 hr. 40 min. Long, low-heat baking dehydrates the apple slices so they become wonderfully crunchy once they cool. Ancho chile powder and cayenne pepper lend moderate heat—adjust the amount to suit your taste.

2 (6-oz.) apples (such as Fuji or Pink Lady)
1 Tbsp. light brown sugar
½ Tbsp. honey
½ tsp. water
¼ tsp. ancho chile powder
¼ tsp. kosher salt
¼ tsp. black pepper
⅛ tsp. cayenne pepper

1. Preheat oven to 225°F with 1 oven rack in top third of oven and 1 oven rack in bottom third of oven. Line 2 baking sheets with parchment paper.
2. Remove core from top 1 inch and bottom 1 inch of each apple. Cut apples crosswise into ⅛-inch-thick slices. Arrange slices in a single layer on prepared baking sheets.
3. Stir together brown sugar, honey, ½ teaspoon water, chile powder, salt, black pepper, and cayenne pepper in a small microwavable bowl. Microwave at HIGH until bubbly, about 20 seconds. Stir and brush over tops of apple slices.
4. Bake apple slices at 225°F for 1 hour; flip apple slices, and rotate pans from top rack to bottom rack. Bake until apple slices are firm and not sticky (they should feel like dried fruit), about 1 more hour. Remove baking sheets from oven. Let cool completely on baking sheets. Serves 8 (serving size: 5 chips)

CALORIES 38; **FAT** 0g; **PROTEIN** 0g; **CARB** 9g; **FIBER** 1g; **SUGARS** 8g (added sugars 3g); **SODIUM** 63mg; **CALC** 0% DV; **POTASSIUM** 1% DV

Fast • Gluten Free

Crispy Curry Chicken with Avocado Salad

Hands-on: 20 min. **Total:** 20 min. Inspired by the Thai dish Massaman chicken, this recipe has half the sat fat of typical restaurant renditions. We traded the heavy cream sauce for a velvety avocado salad.

2 tsp. curry powder
1 tsp. kosher salt, divided
¼ tsp. black pepper
4 boneless, skinless chicken thighs (about 1½ lb.)
2 Tbsp. olive oil
1¼ cups chopped tomatoes (about 10 oz.)
⅓ cup plain 2% reduced-fat Greek yogurt
1 Tbsp. fresh lemon juice
2 tsp. honey
4 cups loosely packed baby arugula
1 ripe avocado, sliced
2 Tbsp. toasted cashews, chopped

1. Heat a large skillet over high. Stir together curry powder, ¾ teaspoon salt, and pepper in a small dish. Coat chicken with spice mixture. Add oil to hot skillet. Cook chicken until well-browned, 4 to 5 minutes. Flip chicken; reduce heat to medium-high. Add tomatoes, and cook until chicken is cooked through, 3 to 4 minutes.
2. Whisk together yogurt, lemon juice, honey, and remaining ¼ teaspoon salt in a bowl. Toss arugula, avocado, and cashews with dressing. Divide chicken and salad among 4 plates. Serves 4 (serving size: 1 thigh and about 1 cup salad)

CALORIES 431; **FAT** 27g (sat 6g, unsat 19g); **PROTEIN** 35g; **CARB** 14g; **FIBER** 6g; **SUGARS** 7g (added sugars 3g); **SODIUM** 629mg; **CALC** 11% DV; **POTASSIUM** 19% DV

Fast • Gluten Free

Easy Chicken and Butternut Squash Hash

Hands-on: 20 min. **Total:** 20 min. Smart shortcuts speed up this skillet supper. Precubed butternut squash saves chopping time; parcooking in the microwave shortens the cook time. Center-cut bacon adds smoky flavor with up to 30% less fat than regular bacon.

12 oz. prechopped butternut squash (about 3 cups)
1 Tbsp. water
2 cups Brussels sprouts (about 7 oz.), quartered
3 center-cut bacon slices, chopped (about ¼ cup)
5 oz. shredded rotisserie chicken breast (about 1 cup)
1 cup chopped yellow onion
3 garlic cloves, minced (about 1 Tbsp.)
1 tsp. fresh thyme leaves
¾ tsp. coarsely ground black pepper
5 Tbsp. olive oil, divided
⅜ tsp. kosher salt, divided
2 Tbsp. apple cider vinegar

1. Place squash and 1 tablespoon water in a medium-sized microwavable bowl; cover with plastic wrap. Microwave at HIGH for 2 minutes. Add Brussels sprouts; cover with plastic wrap, and microwave until vegetables are tender, about 2 minutes. Transfer squash and Brussels sprouts to a plate lined with paper towels to drain.
2. Heat a large skillet over medium-high. Add bacon, and cook, stirring often, until just starting to crisp, about 5 minutes. Add chicken, onion, garlic, thyme, pepper, 1 tablespoon oil, and

⅛ teaspoon salt; cook until onion begins to soften, about 2 minutes. Remove skillet from heat; stir in vinegar. Transfer to a bowl. Wipe skillet clean.
3. Increase heat to high. Add remaining ¼ cup oil to skillet; swirl to coat. Add squash mixture; cook, stirring often, until mixture begins to brown, 6 to 8 minutes. Add chicken mixture to squash mixture; stir to combine. Sprinkle with remaining ¼ teaspoon salt. Serves 4 (serving size: 1¼ cups)

CALORIES 365; **FAT** 26g (sat 5g, unsat 20g); **PROTEIN** 16g; **CARB** 19g; **FIBER** 4g; **SUGARS** 5g (added sugars 0g); **SODIUM** 447mg; **CALC** 8% DV; **POTASSIUM** 15% DV

Fast • Gluten Free

Spiced Tilapia with Coconut Rice

Hands-on: 20 min. **Total:** 20 min. Mild-tasting turmeric has powerful anti-inflammatory properties; pair it with black pepper to help your body boost its healing potential. Adding coconut milk to rice is a simple, tasty hack; find three ways to use up the rest of the can on the next page.

1 Tbsp. ground turmeric
¼ tsp. black pepper
1 tsp. kosher salt, divided
4 tilapia fillets (1½ lb.)
2 Tbsp. canola oil, divided
2 (8.8-oz.) pkg. precooked microwavable whole-grain rice (such as Uncle Ben's)
1 cup well-shaken and stirred light coconut milk
1 tsp. granulated sugar
½ cup chopped fresh cilantro, divided
1½ Tbsp. fresh lime juice
1 cup matchstick-cut carrots
¼ cup toasted unsweetened flaked coconut

1. Stir together turmeric, pepper, and ½ teaspoon salt in a small dish. Sprinkle fish with spice mixture.

2. Heat 1 tablespoon oil in a large nonstick skillet over medium. Add half of fillets; cook until golden and fish flakes easily, 2 to 3 minutes per side. Remove from skillet; keep warm. Repeat with remaining 1 tablespoon oil and remaining fillets.

3. Wipe skillet clean with paper towels. Add rice, coconut milk, sugar, and remaining ½ teaspoon salt to skillet; bring to a simmer over high. Cook, stirring often, until thickened, 3 to 4 minutes. Stir in ¼ cup cilantro and lime juice. Divide rice mixture among 4 plates. Top evenly with carrots and fish. Sprinkle evenly with coconut and remaining ¼ cup cilantro. Serves 4 (serving size: about ¾ cup rice and 1 fillet)

CALORIES 487; **FAT** 16g (sat 4g, unsat 10g); **PROTEIN** 41g; **CARB** 48g; **FIBER** 2g; **SUGARS** 3g (added sugars 1g); **SODIUM** 588mg; **CALC** 5% DV; **POTASSIUM** 12% DV

USE IT UP

3 WAYS TO USE LIGHT COCONUT MILK

With up to 60% less fat than regular coconut milk, this pantry staple is a smart, nondairy way to add richness to any recipe. Make sure to shake the can before using for maximum creaminess.

Fast • Vegetarian
Coconut-Cashew Pancakes

1. Heat a nonstick skillet over medium-high. Whisk together 1 cup light coconut milk, 1 large egg, 1 Tbsp. light brown sugar, 1 Tbsp. canola oil, and 1 tsp. vanilla extract in a bowl. Stir in 1 ¼ cups white whole-wheat flour, 3 Tbsp. chopped cashews, 1 tsp. baking powder, and ½ tsp. kosher salt until just combined. Pour about ¼ cup batter per pancake into pan. Cook until tops are covered with bubbles, about 3 minutes. Flip; cook until lightly browned, about 2 minutes. Drizzle with ¼ cup pure maple syrup; sprinkle with 3 Tbsp. toasted unsweetened flaked coconut. Serves 4 (serving size: 3 pancakes)

CALORIES 339; **FAT** 14g (sat 6g, unsat 7g); **PROTEIN** 9g; **CARB** 45g; **FIBER** 5g; **SUGARS** 16g (added sugars 15g); **SODIUM** 279mg; **CALC** 21% DV; **POTASSIUM** 2% DV

Fast • Vegetarian
Coconut-Curry Tempeh Bowls

Be sure to cook the tempeh until golden brown and crisp to add a nice layer of nutty flavor to this dish.

1. Stir together 1 (8-oz.) pkg. tempeh, cubed; 1 Tbsp. lower-sodium soy sauce; 2 tsp. sesame oil; and 1 tsp. curry powder in a bowl. Cook in a skillet over medium until browned, about 5 minutes. Remove tempeh; set aside. Add 1 cup sliced red bell pepper, 1 cup matchstick-cut carrots, 4 tsp. sesame oil, 2 tsp. minced fresh garlic, and 2 tsp. minced peeled fresh ginger to skillet. Cook until crisp-tender, about 3 minutes. Remove from heat; stir in 1 cup light coconut milk and 2 Tbsp. yellow miso until smooth. Divide 3 cups cooked brown rice among 4 bowls; top evenly with vegetable mixture and tempeh. Sprinkle evenly with ¼ cup fresh cilantro leaves. Garnish with lime wedges. Serves 4 (serving size: ¾ cup rice, ½ cup vegetable mixture, and 2 oz. tempeh)

CALORIES 441; **FAT** 16g (sat 5g, unsat 10g); **PROTEIN** 18g; **CARB** 56g; **FIBER** 10g; **SUGARS** 4g (added sugars 0g); **SODIUM** 542mg; **CALC** 9% DV; **POTASSIUM** 9% DV

Staff Favorite • Gluten Free
Make Ahead
Coconut Milk Panna Cotta

Sublimely creamy, this is the perfect make-ahead dessert.

1. Stir together 1 cup cubed mango and 2 tsp. white balsamic vinegar in a bowl; chill. Stir together 2 Tbsp. cold water and 1½ tsp. unflavored gelatin in a bowl; let stand 5 minutes. Bring 1 cup light coconut milk, ¼ cup granulated sugar, 3 Tbsp. unsweetened flaked coconut, and ½ tsp. vanilla extract to a simmer in a saucepan over medium. Remove from heat. Strain; discard solids. Whisk in gelatin mixture; add 1 cup plain 2% reduced-fat Greek yogurt and ¼ cup whole milk. Divide among 4 dishes; chill 6 hours. Top with mango; garnish with mint leaves. Serves 4 (serving size: ½ cup panna cotta and ¼ cup mango)

CALORIES 196; **FAT** 7g (sat 6g, unsat 1g); **PROTEIN** 9g; **CARB** 26g; **FIBER** 1g; **SUGARS** 22g (added sugars 13g); **SODIUM** 46mg; **CALC** 9% DV; **POTASSIUM** 2% DV

SLOW COOKER

Make Ahead

Mediterranean Chicken and Farro

Hands-on: 20 min. **Total:** 7 hr. 20 min. Chicken thighs hold up nicely in the slow cooker, surrendering rich juices that make this fiber-packed farro extra-satisfying.

2 Tbsp. olive oil
4 (6-oz.) bone-in, skin-on chicken thighs
½ tsp. kosher salt, divided
½ tsp. black pepper, divided
Cooking spray
3 cups unsalted chicken stock
1 cup uncooked Italian pearled farro (such as Nature's Earthly Choice)
½ cup chopped shallots
10 pitted Castelvetrano olives, sliced
1½ Tbsp. drained capers
¼ cup finely chopped fresh flat-leaf parsley
¼ cup toasted almonds, finely chopped
1 tsp. lemon zest plus 1 Tbsp. fresh lemon juice
1 garlic clove, grated
¼ tsp. crushed red pepper
Fresh flat-leaf parsley leaves, for garnish

1. Heat oil in a large skillet over medium-high. Sprinkle chicken with ¼ teaspoon salt and ¼ teaspoon black pepper. Cook chicken until browned, about 2 minutes per side. Set aside.
2. Coat a 5-quart slow cooker with cooking spray. Stir together stock, farro, shallots, remaining ¼ teaspoon salt, and remaining ¼ teaspoon black pepper in slow cooker. Top with chicken; sprinkle with olives and capers. Cover and cook on low until a thermometer inserted in chicken registers 165°F, 7 to 8 hours.
3. Remove chicken from slow cooker. Add chopped parsley, almonds, lemon zest and juice, garlic, and red pepper to farro mixture; stir until creamy. Garnish servings with parsley leaves. Serves 4 (serving size: 1 thigh and 1⅛ cups farro)

CALORIES 512; FAT 24g (sat 5g, unsat 17g); PROTEIN 34g; CARB 38g; FIBER 5g; SUGARS 3g (added sugars 0g); SODIUM 665mg; CALC 9% DV; POTASSIUM 9% DV

1 INGREDIENT, 3 SIDES

3 WAYS TO USE CARROTS

Here's looking at you, carrots. In addition to being full of vision-enriching, cancer-fighting antioxidants, the soluble fiber in carrots may help reduce your unhealthy cholesterol (LDL) levels.

Fast • Gluten Free Vegetarian
Carrots Almondine
Traditional versions of glazed carrots can include up to ⅔ cup sugar—our revamped version delivers all the classic flavor with just a tablespoon of honey and a splash of brandy or bourbon.

1. Bring 2 cups thinly sliced carrots and ¼ cup water to a boil in a large skillet over medium-high; cover and reduce heat to low. Cook until just tender, about 6 minutes. Uncover and cook until water evaporates, about 2 minutes. Increase heat to medium-high; add 1 Tbsp. brandy; cook 1 minute. Stir in 1 Tbsp. unsalted butter, 1 Tbsp. honey, ½ tsp. fresh thyme leaves, ¼ tsp. kosher salt, and ¼ tsp. black pepper; cook, stirring often, until tender, 2 to 3 minutes. Remove from heat; stir in ¼ cup toasted slivered almonds. Serves 4 (serving size: ½ cup)

CALORIES 115; FAT 6g (sat 2g, unsat 4g); PROTEIN 2g; CARB 12g; FIBER 3g; SUGARS 8g (added sugars 4g); SODIUM 165mg; CALC 4% DV; POTASSIUM 6% DV

Fast • Gluten Free Vegetarian
Carrot Ribbon Salad
Getting your hands on a Y-shaped vegetable peeler is the secret to long, beautiful carrot ribbons. And if you soak the ribbons in ice water, you'll get nice, distinct curls. Although we used regular carrots here, multicolored carrots would make a vibrant addition. To save time, make the dressing and carrot ribbons in advance.

1. Whisk together 2 Tbsp. fresh lemon juice, 2 tsp. honey, ¼ tsp. kosher salt, and ¼ tsp. black pepper in a small bowl; whisk in 1 Tbsp. olive oil. Toss together 6 oz. carrots, shaved into long strips; 2 cups arugula; ¼ cup coarsely chopped fresh flat-leaf parsley; and lemon juice mixture. Divide among 4 plates. Top evenly with 1 oz. crumbled goat cheese and 3 Tbsp. chopped toasted pecans. Serves 4 (serving size: 1 cup)

CALORIES 119; FAT 9g (sat 2g, unsat 7g); PROTEIN 3g; CARB 9g; FIBER 2g; SUGARS 6g (added sugars 3g); SODIUM 188mg; CALC 6% DV; POTASSIUM 5% DV

Fast • Gluten Free
Vegetarian

Moroccan Spiced Carrots

Small carrots with tops make a great shortcut; just give them a scrub—no need to peel.

1. Preheat oven to 425°F. Toss together 12 oz. trimmed small carrots with tops, 2 tsp. olive oil, ½ tsp. ground cumin, ½ tsp. paprika, ¼ tsp. ground cinnamon, and ¼ tsp. kosher salt in a bowl. Place carrots on a rimmed baking sheet lined with parchment paper. Bake until tender, about 15 minutes. **2.** Combine 3 Tbsp. light sour cream and 1 Tbsp. fresh lime juice in a bowl. Place carrots on a platter; top with sour cream mixture, ¼ cup chopped toasted unsalted pistachios, and 1 Tbsp. chopped fresh cilantro. Serves 4 (serving size: ½ cup)

CALORIES 118; **FAT** 7g (sat 2g, unsat 5g); **PROTEIN** 3g; **CARB** 12g; **FIBER** 3g; **SUGARS** 5g (added sugars 0g); **SODIUM** 190mg; **CALC** 6% DV; **POTASSIUM** 8% DV

4 SAUCES FOR ANY PROTEIN

Fast • Gluten Free
Make Ahead • Vegetarian

Pineapple-Chile Salsa

If you don't want to fuss with a whole pineapple, pick up precubed pineapple in your grocery's produce section. Serve at room temperature over grilled pork or fish.

Stir together 2 cups finely chopped fresh pineapple (about 12 oz.), 2 thinly sliced scallions, 1 seeded and finely chopped red Fresno chile, ½ seeded and finely chopped serrano chile, 1 Tbsp. chopped fresh cilantro, 1 tsp. lime zest, and ¼ tsp. kosher salt in a medium bowl. Serve

immediately, or store covered in refrigerator up to 2 days. Serves 8 (serving size: ¼ cup)

CALORIES 24; **FAT** 0g; **PROTEIN** 0g; **CARB** 6g; **FIBER** 1g; **SUGARS** 4g (added sugars 0g); **SODIUM** 62mg; **CALC** 1% DV; **POTASSIUM** 2% DV

Fast • Make Ahead

Sweet-and-Sour Sauce

We gave your favorite chicken nugget dipping sauce a major flavor upgrade without any junky preservatives. Tasty on nearly everything, it's especially nice on tofu or as a quick starter for a salad dressing; just add a little extra oil or broth to thin it.

Whisk together 3 Tbsp. unsalted ketchup, 2 Tbsp. apple cider vinegar, 2 Tbsp. olive oil, 4 tsp. honey, 1 Tbsp. grated sweet onion, 1 ½ tsp. Asian chili-garlic sauce, 1 tsp. lower-sodium soy sauce, ½ tsp. Worcestershire sauce, and ¼ tsp. paprika in a small bowl. Serve immediately, or store covered in refrigerator up to 3 days. Serves 6 (serving size: about 1 ½ Tbsp.)

CALORIES 67; **FAT** 5g (sat 1g, unsat 4g); **PROTEIN** 0g; **CARB** 7g; **FIBER** 0g; **SUGARS** 6g (added sugars 4g); **SODIUM** 107mg; **CALC** 0% DV; **POTASSIUM** 2% DV

Fast • Gluten Free
Make Ahead • Vegetarian

White BBQ Sauce

Alabama's tangy twist on classic barbecue sauce is a knockout addition to burgers and makes a great dip for veggies. Canola mayo keeps our version nice and light.

Whisk together 1 cup canola mayonnaise, 5 Tbsp. white wine vinegar, 2 tsp. prepared horseradish, 1 tsp. black pepper, ⅜ tsp. kosher salt, and ⅛ tsp. paprika in a medium bowl. Serve

immediately, or store covered in refrigerator for up to 2 weeks. Serves 16 (serving size: 1 Tbsp.)

CALORIES 38; **FAT** 4g (sat 0g, unsat 3g); **PROTEIN** 0g; **CARB** 0g; **FIBER** 0g; **SUGARS** 0g (added sugars 0g); **SODIUM** 154mg; **CALC** 0% DV; **POTASSIUM** 0% DV

Fast • Make Ahead
Vegetarian

Miso-Garlic Vinaigrette

Hit up your grocery's olive bar for roasted garlic cloves, or make your own by roasting unpeeled cloves at 375°F for 25 minutes. The dressing is great with chicken and fish or as a marinade.

Pulse 3 Tbsp. unseasoned rice vinegar, 3 Tbsp. sesame oil, 2 Tbsp. canola oil, 1 Tbsp. white miso, 1 large pasteurized egg yolk, and 3 roasted garlic cloves in a food processor until smooth, about 10 times. Stir in 1 Tbsp. chopped fresh chives. Serve immediately, or store covered in refrigerator up to 1 week. Serves 8 (serving size: about 1 ½ Tbsp.)

CALORIES 88; **FAT** 9g (sat 1g, unsat 8g); **PROTEIN** 1g; **CARB** 1g; **FIBER** 0g; **SUGARS** 0g (added sugars 0g); **SODIUM** 69mg; **CALC** 1% DV; **POTASSIUM** 0% DV

SIMPLIFY DINNER WITH THIS ONE-SKILLET WONDER

BY GINA HOMOLKA

Back-to-school schedules can be complicated—cooking dinner doesn't have to be.

The end of summer means new schedules for everybody, and getting dinner on the table can be a challenge. The secret? Keep it simple. This whole dish—yes, both the meatballs and the sauce—is cooked in one skillet, which makes after-dinner cleanup a breeze.

Plus, there's a bonus: Cooking the meatballs in the skillet first gives the sauce in the next step extra flavor. The combo of ground turkey and turkey sausage (and a little bit of pecorino) yields meatballs that are leaner than traditional beef meatballs yet still juicy and cheesy. If you don't mind doing extra dishes, you can serve these over whole-wheat pasta or cooked spaghetti squash, add a big, crisp salad, and call it a meal.

But the best part of this recipe is that it makes enough to feed a family of four, with plenty of leftovers to pack for school or work lunches. Pop a few hot meatballs in a thermos, tuck a whole-wheat roll in a ziplock plastic bag, and send everyone off with make-your-own meatball sliders. Just be sure to pack plenty of extra napkins—they're going to need them.

Fast • Make Ahead

Cheesy Turkey Meatball Skillet

Hands-on: 30 min. **Total:** 30 min. If you don't have a skillet with a lid, make sure your nonstick skillet is OK to use in the oven—a cast-iron skillet is a safe bet.

MEATBALLS
1 lb. 93% lean ground turkey
12 oz. sweet Italian turkey or chicken sausage, casings removed (about 4 sausages)
½ cup whole-wheat panko (Japanese breadcrumbs)
¼ cup chopped fresh parsley, plus more for garnish
2 Tbsp. grated pecorino Romano cheese (½ oz.)
1 tsp. Italian seasoning
¼ tsp. kosher salt
2 garlic cloves, grated
Cooking spray

SAUCE
1 Tbsp. extra-virgin olive oil
2 garlic cloves, smashed
1 (28-oz.) can unsalted crushed tomatoes
Crushed red pepper to taste
¾ cup fresh mozzarella cheese, torn into pieces

1. Prepare the meatballs: Combine turkey, sausage, panko, parsley, pecorino, Italian seasoning, salt, and grated garlic in a large bowl; form into 18 (2-inch) meatballs.
2. Heat a large nonstick skillet over medium; coat skillet with cooking spray. Working in batches, add meatballs to skillet, and cook until browned on all sides, about 2 minutes per side. Remove meatballs from skillet, and set aside.

3. Prepare the sauce: Reduce heat to medium-low. Add oil and smashed garlic to skillet; cook until garlic is golden, 1 to 2 minutes. Add tomatoes and crushed red pepper; return meatballs to skillet. Cover and simmer until cooked through, about 3 minutes. Uncover; add mozzarella pieces. Cover and cook until cheese is melted, about 2 minutes. If your skillet doesn't have a lid, you can put it under the broiler until cheese is melted, 2 to 3 minutes. Garnish with additional chopped parsley. Serves 6 (serving size: 3 meatballs)

CALORIES 341; FAT 18g (sat 5g, unsat 11g); PROTEIN 30g; CARB 13g; FIBER 3g; SUGARS 5g (added sugars 0g); SODIUM 620mg; CALC 20% DV; POTASSIUM 12% DV

THE SHOW-STOPPING SEAFOOD-COOKING METHOD

BY BARTON SEAVER

A cast-iron griddle delivers a crunchy, flavor-packed crust and irresistible table-side sizzle.

It's hard to beat that sizzling presentation when you bring cooked seafood to the table on a smoking-hot griddle. I refer to the phenomenon as "the fajitas effect." I know you've witnessed it—when someone orders fajitas at a Mexican restaurant, all heads turn as soon as that sputtering pan comes out of the kitchen. A plume of steam fills the room, and soon, everyone's ordering the same thing.

The best griddles are made from heavy metal—typically cast iron—and feature a flat surface (not ridged like a grill pan). They're small enough to fit over one or two burners on a stovetop or a standard grill but big enough to hold a few servings without crowding the portions.

You'll want to marinate your seafood before cooking it on a griddle. The superhot pan turns any marinade into an instant crust, adding both flavor and texture. To finish, drizzle a bit of the reserved sauce over the top; then bring the whole griddle to the table, and witness the fajitas effect in action as your family and friends gobble up these delicious, gorgeous scallops.

Fast • Gluten Free

Seared Scallops with Shallot-Herb Sauce

Hands-on: 10 min. **Total:** 30 min. There are few foods that are as naturally balanced in flavor as scallops, and they pair beautifully with all sorts of seasoning. Salmoriglio—a Southern Italian condiment—serves as both marinade and finishing sauce. Be sure to reserve half of it prior to marinating the scallops for drizzling at the end.

2 shallots, peeled and roughly chopped (about ½ cup)
2 garlic cloves, peeled
½ bunch fresh flat-leaf parsley, leaves only, chopped (about 1 cup)
2 Tbsp. fresh tarragon leaves
1 Tbsp. fresh oregano leaves or 1 tsp. dried oregano
⅛ tsp. kosher salt
¼ cup olive oil
24 dry-packed scallops (about 1¼ lb.)
2 Tbsp. fresh lemon juice
1 tsp. canola oil

1. Combine shallots, garlic, parsley, tarragon, oregano, salt, and olive oil in a food processor; pulse to form a paste. Place scallops in a large bowl, add half of shallot mixture (about ¼ cup), and toss gently to combine. Cover and refrigerate at least 20 minutes or up to 8 hours. Stir lemon juice into remaining half of shallot mixture, and set aside.
2. Thread 3 scallops onto each of 8 (6-inch) wooden skewers. Lightly coat a griddle with canola oil, and heat over high until it is smoking hot. Place skewers on griddle, and cook, undisturbed, until scallops develop a crust, about 3 minutes. Flip skewers, and turn off heat. Allow scallops to sit until just cooked through, about 2 more minutes. Drizzle reserved shallot mixture over top of scallops. Bring sizzling, sauced scallops to the table right on the griddle. Serves 4 (serving size: 6 scallops)

CALORIES 253; FAT 16g (sat 2g, unsat 13g); PROTEIN 18g; CARB 10g; FIBER 1g; SUGARS 2g (added sugars 0g); SODIUM 627mg; CALC 5% DV; POTASSIUM 10% DV

4 WAYS TO BE A SMART SCALLOP SHOPPER

BUY DRY-PACKED SCALLOPS
Some fishermen and wholesalers soak scallops in a salt-based brine (sodium tripolyphosphate, or STP) to add moisture. However, this makes it hard to get a good sear. Sometimes there's even a faint chemical aftertaste. Seek out scallops labeled "dry-packed" or "dry"—they don't contain added brine.

KNOW YOUR SCALLOP SIZES
Retailers describe scallop sizes according to how many are in a pound. The smaller the number, the bigger each scallop is. (U20 means there are under 20 scallops in a pound.) Diver scallops are the largest and most expensive because divers hand-select them for size and quality. Bay scallops are tiny, numbering upward of 100 per pound.

WILD VS. FARMED
Scallop farming is just starting to take off in the U.S.; most scallops sold here are wild-caught (visit seafoodwatch.org for a list of sustainable choices). American farmers are using Japanese techniques to bolster their harvests, so expect to see more farmed scallops in markets soon.

DON'T DISMISS FROZEN
As with many kinds of seafood, high-quality frozen scallops can be a very good choice if you don't have access to fresh scallops. Frozen scallops should be thawed in the refrigerator overnight.

THE AIR FRYER'S DIRTY LITTLE SECRET

BY ANDREA NGUYEN

Miracle gadget or Easy-Bake Oven on steroids? Four days of testing revealed the truth.

When it comes to the "latest and greatest" kitchen gadgets, I'll be the first to admit I have some baggage. A few years ago, my brother nearly ruined Christmas dinner by using an "As Seen On TV" infrared oven (a gimmicky predecessor to the air fryer) to "re-fry" my mom's Vietnamese imperial rolls. Not only did it take forever, but the rice paper wrappers emerged from the "miracle machine" with an extremely unappetizing plastic-like texture. It was a grim meal that my mother has never let him forget.

But after a few trusted colleagues raved about air fryers, I decided to reconsider. At my local home-goods store, I eyed the futuristic, egg-shaped appliance with skepticism. Air fryers are basically compact convection ovens that rapidly blow lots of hot air onto food to cook it. I was intrigued but hesitant to commit due to its small capacity. I went home empty-handed; I needed a little more convincing.

Knowing about my capacity concerns, my editor suggested the Power AirFryer Oven, which boasts a large capacity and multicooker functions. Gearing up for my maiden voyage, I watched the oven's infomercial and perused its user manual. And then I went on an air-frying binge.

During a four-day period, I unleashed the machine on all of my fried favorites. Panko-coated shrimp and onion rings were crunchy, albeit lean tasting, an issue remedied by a dipping sauce. "Fried" Brussels sprout leaves were phenomenal with just a whisper of oil. Chicken wings and tofu developed terrific crispy exteriors. My large machine's five racks allowed for air-frying zucchini sticks and eggplant rounds while also roasting slabs of cauliflower at the same time. That's pretty efficient multitasking, if you ask me.

However, I had to rethink my concept of frying—the major appeal of the oven. With little oil involved, air-frying can dehydrate things quickly and unexpectedly; you're exposing food to a hot windstorm instead of bathing it in oil. For example, within minutes, my slightly limp french fries became dry sticks. You've got to pay attention.

After a week with the oven, I learned a few tricks. Briefly preheating helps avoid overcooking. A bit of fat, such as egg and a spritz of oil, helps coatings adhere to create crisp exteriors. Leaving air-fried morsels to cool slightly in the oven after cooking takes them from damp to crispy.

My ultimate goal was General Tso's chicken, a dish that involves deep-frying the meat in a wok, pouring off the hot oil, then reusing the wok to make a lusty sauce to enrobe the chicken. The air fryer liberated me from the initial frying, and cleanup was much easier than it is with deep-frying—wiping down the oven was a breeze. Many of us adore fried food, but few of us actually want to make it. Air-frying doesn't fully replicate deep-fried flavors and textures, but it's perfect if you want to indulge with less guilt and less mess.

I'm even tempted to bring the air fryer to my mom's house over the holidays and give it a shot at crisping up her imperial rolls. Wish me luck.

Staff Favorite

Air-Fried General Tso's Chicken

Hands-on: 20 min. **Total:** 35 min.

1 lb. boneless, skinless chicken thighs, cut into 1- to 1¼-inch pieces
1 large egg, beaten
⅓ cup plus 2 tsp. cornstarch, divided
¼ tsp. kosher salt
¼ tsp. ground white pepper
1½ Tbsp. canola oil
3 to 4 dried chiles de árbol, seeded and chopped
1 Tbsp. minced peeled fresh ginger
1 Tbsp. minced fresh garlic
7 Tbsp. lower-sodium chicken broth
2 Tbsp. lower-sodium soy sauce
2 Tbsp. ketchup
2 tsp. sugar
2 tsp. unseasoned rice vinegar
2 Tbsp. sliced scallions, divided
1 tsp. toasted sesame oil
½ tsp. toasted sesame seeds

1. Pat chicken dry. Combine chicken and egg in a large bowl; toss to coat. In another bowl, combine ⅓ cup cornstarch, salt, and pepper. Using a fork, transfer chicken to cornstarch mixture; stir to coat.

2. Preheat air fryer to 400°F. Transfer chicken to air fryer oven racks or air fryer basket, leaving space between pieces (work in batches if needed). Cook 12 to 16 minutes, shaking halfway through cooking. Let dry 3 to 5 minutes. If chicken is still damp, cook 1 to 2 more minutes.

3. Heat canola oil and chiles in a large skillet over medium. Add ginger and garlic; cook until fragrant, about 30 seconds.

4. Whisk together broth, soy sauce, ketchup, sugar, rice vinegar, and remaining 2 teaspoons cornstarch; stir into skillet. Increase heat to medium-high, and cook until mixture begins to bubble. Add chicken, and stir to coat. Cook until thickened, about 1 minute and 30 seconds. Turn off heat; stir in 1 tablespoon scallions and sesame oil. Top with sesame seeds and remaining 1 tablespoon scallions. Serves 4 (serving size: about ¾ cup)

CALORIES 302; FAT 13g (sat 3g, unsat 10g); PROTEIN 26g; CARB 18g; FIBER 0g; SUGARS 4g (added sugars 2g); SODIUM 611mg; CALC 3% DV; POTASSIUM 5% DV

THE RECIPE MAKEOVER

BUILD A HEALTHY PLATE OF LOADED NACHOS

We keep the classic meat-and-cheese profile but add a full roster of good-for-you toppings.

Notorious for being a calorie-and-sodium bomb, nachos were overdue for a nutritional overhaul. Ours slashes both calories and sodium by 40% without sacrificing the dish's indulgent nature.

In place of sodium-laden canned refried beans, a blend of unsalted pinto beans, lime juice, adobo sauce, and spices helps the other healthy toppers adhere to our homemade chips. Robust Mexican chorizo packs a big flavor punch, helping a little meat go a long way; look for it in the butcher's case next to the other fresh sausage. And because no tray of nachos is complete without cheese, using a bit of shredded sharp cheddar delivers just enough of a salty kick. Pico de gallo and avocado-tomatillo sauce add a finishing layer of freshness—key for reaching nacho nirvana.

Staff Favorite · Gluten Free

Chili-Chorizo Nachos

Hands-on: 30 min. **Total:** 45 min.

12 (6-inch) corn tortillas, each cut into 8 wedges
Cooking spray
¾ tsp. kosher salt, divided
4 oz. loose fresh Mexican chorizo
1 (15-oz.) can unsalted pinto beans, drained and rinsed
¼ cup fresh lime juice, divided
1 Tbsp. adobo sauce from canned chipotle chiles
1 tsp. chili powder
1 tsp. ground cumin
6 oz. tomatillos, husks removed
½ ripe avocado
½ cup plus 2 Tbsp. fresh cilantro leaves, divided
2 oz. sharp cheddar cheese, shredded (about ½ cup)
1 cup refrigerated pico de gallo, drained

1. Preheat oven to 375°F. Arrange tortilla wedges in a single layer on 2 baking sheets coated with cooking spray. Sprinkle with ¼ teaspoon salt; lightly coat with cooking spray. Bake at 375°F until crisp and lightly browned, 12 to 14 minutes. Combine chips onto 1 baking sheet.

2. Heat a medium nonstick skillet over medium-high. Add chorizo; cook, stirring to crumble, until browned, about 5 minutes. Remove chorizo from pan. Set aside.

3. Combine beans, 2 tablespoons lime juice, adobo sauce, chili powder, cumin, and ¼ teaspoon salt in a food processor. Process until smooth; transfer to a bowl. Wipe food processor clean.

4. Combine tomatillos, avocado, ½ cup cilantro, remaining 2 tablespoons lime juice, and remaining ¼ teaspoon salt in food processor. Process until smooth.

5. Preheat broiler to high. Spoon bean mixture evenly over chips on baking sheet. Sprinkle chorizo evenly over beans, and top with cheese. Broil until cheese is melted, about 2 minutes.

6. Spoon pico de gallo evenly over nachos, and top with avocado-tomatillo sauce. Top with remaining 2 tablespoons cilantro. Serves 6 (serving size: 1 ½ cups)

CALORIES 335; FAT 13g (sat 5g, unsat 6g); PROTEIN 13g; CARB 47g; FIBER 9g; SUGARS 4g (added sugars 0g); SODIUM 678mg; CALC 14% DV; POTASSIUM 7% DV

COOKING CLASS:
HOW TO MASTER
THE METHOD

CREAMY CARBONARA

Our double-boiler technique guarantees smooth success with this curdle-prone egg sauce for pasta.

Fast

Whole-Wheat Pasta Carbonara

Hands-on: 15 min. **Total:** 22 min.

3 large eggs, beaten
1½ oz. pecorino Romano cheese, grated (about ⅓ cup)
¼ tsp. kosher salt
¼ tsp. black pepper
8 oz. uncooked whole-wheat spaghetti
¼ cup diced pancetta or bacon

1. Stir together eggs, cheese, salt, and pepper in a small bowl; set aside.
2. Cook pasta in a pot of boiling water until al dente. Drain pasta in a strainer over a stainless steel bowl large enough to cover the pasta pot. Let cooking liquid stand in bowl 2 minutes. Reserve 1 cup cooking liquid; return remaining cooking liquid to pot. Place bowl on top of pot to create a double boiler; transfer drained pasta to bowl. Heat pot over high. Add egg mixture to pasta; cook, stirring constantly, 2 minutes or until sauce thickens. Stir in reserved 1 cup cooking liquid, ¼ cup at a time, as needed to adjust consistency.
3. Cook pancetta in a small skillet over medium until crisp. Remove pancetta with a slotted spoon; set aside. Stir drippings into pasta mixture. Divide pasta and pancetta among 4 bowls. Serves 4 (serving size: 1 cup)

CALORIES 337; **FAT** 12g (sat 6g, unsat 3g); **PROTEIN** 17g; **CARB** 42g; **FIBER** 5g; **SUGARS** 2g (added sugars 0g); **SODIUM** 556mg; **CALC** 13% DV; **POTASSIUM** 6% DV

THE STEPS

1. CATCH THE COOKING LIQUID
Drain the cooked pasta in a strainer that sits in a large metal bowl. The cooking liquid serves two purposes here: Use some of it to thin the carbonara sauce to the consistency you like; the rest of the liquid creates steam in the makeshift double boiler.

2. SET UP THE DOUBLE BOILER
Your metal bowl should be large enough to cover the top of the pasta pot and rest inside, like the top of a double boiler. A stainless steel bowl conducts heat quickly and evenly, and hot steam won't crack it like untempered glass.

3. THICKEN THE SAUCE
Combine the egg mixture and pasta in the bowl. Gentle steam heat and constant stirring keep the egg sauce from scrambling, as it can when cooked directly over a burner. The sauce will cling to the noodles—and not pool at the bottom of the bowl—as it grows creamy.

4. STIR IN THE TASTY DRIPPINGS
The little bits of pancetta give the pasta a nice salty, meaty crunch here and there, but the drippings spread that delicious flavor through every bite. Make sure the drippings are warm, but not very hot, to keep the sauce from curdling.

Staff Favorite • Make Ahead

Mushroom Meat Loaf

Hands-on: 20 min. **Total:** 1 hr. 30 min.

1 Tbsp. olive oil
1 cup minced yellow onion
1 (8-oz.) pkg. cremini mushrooms, minced
1 Tbsp. reduced-sodium Worcestershire sauce
2 tsp. fresh thyme leaves
1 tsp. finely chopped garlic
1 tsp. kosher salt, divided
½ tsp. black pepper, divided
1½ lb. extra-lean ground beef
½ cup whole-wheat panko
2 large eggs
¼ cup unsalted ketchup
½ Tbsp. light brown sugar
½ Tbsp. apple cider vinegar

1. Preheat oven to 350°F. Place a pan of water on bottom rack.
2. Heat oil in a large skillet over medium-high. Add onion; sauté 3 minutes. Add mushrooms; sauté 3 minutes. Add Worcestershire, thyme, garlic, ½ teaspoon salt, and ¼ teaspoon pepper; sauté 1 minute.
3. Gently combine beef, panko, eggs, mushroom mixture, remaining ½ teaspoon salt, and remaining ¼ teaspoon pepper in a large bowl. For easy cleanup, line an 8 ½- x 4 ½-inch loaf pan with foil; let foil overhang edges. Add meat mixture; lightly press into edges. Bake at 350°F on middle rack until loaf center is 160°F, about 1 hour.
4. Combine ketchup, sugar, and vinegar; brush over loaf top. Increase heat to broil. Broil loaf 10 minutes or until glaze bubbles.

Remove from oven; cool 10 minutes. Lift or remove loaf from pan. Cut into 6 slices. Serves 6 (serving size: 1 slice)

CALORIES 283; FAT 12g (sat 4g, unsat 7g); PROTEIN 28g; CARB 15g; FIBER 1g; SUGARS 6g (added sugars 3g); SODIUM 453mg; CALC 4% DV; POTASSIUM 5% DV

MEATIER THAN MEAT

UMAMI-RICH 'SHROOMS AND TANGY ACCENTS MAKE MEAT LOAF MORE VEGGIE-FORWARD, SAVORY, AND CRAVEABLE THAN EVER.

CREMINI MUSHROOMS
Their meaty flavor and texture let you use less beef. They also help keep the lean meat juicy.

APPLE CIDER VINEGAR
This adds to ketchup's acid for a bright, tart hit of flavor. Think of it like boosting the treble to balance beefy bass notes.

KETCHUP
The traditional meat loaf topper. We use unsalted to keep the sodium in check, then zip it up with smart stir-ins.

BROWN SUGAR
Lends caramel-molasses taste to the zesty topping. It also helps the ketchup mixture melt into a glaze as it bakes.

WHOLE-WHEAT PANKO
These delicate whole-grain breadcrumbs bind the beef mixture without weighing it down.

WORCESTERSHIRE SAUCE
A flavor-bomb condiment with tangy tamarind and savory anchovy to echo the loaf's overall taste.

Vegetarian

Pear-Prosecco Shrub

Hands-on: 10 min. **Total:** 1 hr.
Peak-season pears are super-crisp and nectar-sweet. We keep the skin on for an extra hit of fiber. They also contain an antioxidant called quercetin, a plant flavonoid research shows has heart-health and anti-inflammatory benefits. Fresh lemon juice adds a bright top note and balances the sweetness.

Boil 2 cups water, 12 oz. ripe pear slices, 2 ½ Tbsp. granulated sugar, and 2 Tbsp. apple cider vinegar in a medium saucepan until pears soften, 10 to 12 minutes. Remove from heat; let stand 10 minutes. Transfer to a blender; add 2 Tbsp. fresh lemon juice. Blend until smooth; pour into a large glass measuring cup. Chill 30 minutes. Add ½ oz. gin to each of 6 ice-filled glasses. Add ⅔ cup pear mixture to each glass; top each with ¼ cup chilled prosecco. Garnish with lemon peel strips. Serves 6 (serving size: about 1 cup)

CALORIES 129; FAT 0g; PROTEIN 0g; CARB 16g; FIBER 2g; SUGARS 11g (added sugars 5g); SODIUM 1mg; CALC 1% DV; POTASSIUM 2% DV

MAKE IT A MOCKTAIL

Omit gin and swap prosecco for ¼ cup light ginger beer, such as Fever-Tree Refreshingly Light.

DUTCH OVEN DINNERS

There's something to be said for slowing down with some unhurried, soulful cooking—for braises and stews, for chilis and pot roasts. After the toss-together breeziness of summer meals, now is the time for the magic of a long simmer—the kind that transforms a tough hunk of meat into luscious shreds or dried beans into the rich base for a stew. Here, we offer these kinds of hearty fall meals from the hardest-working pot in your kitchen. Slow cooker instructions included, too.

Just in time for prime comfort food season, we celebrate all that the Dutch oven can do. This piece of kitchen equipment is one we'd argue is worth its weight in gold, especially this time of year, because it's perfect for braised meats, stews, pastas, and more. The Dutch oven is said to get its name from where the molding technique used to make it originated: 18th century Holland. It's a large, heavy, ovenproof, typically cast-iron pot with a tight-fitting lid that doesn't allow steam to escape.

The Dutch oven is sturdy and should last you a lifetime—or more, as many are handed down from generation to generation as heirloom treasures. It will serve you equally well for cooking a Sunday roast as it will a weeknight chicken soup. The recipes here highlight the Dutch oven's versatility, but we also include slow cooker instructions with each recipe if you'd rather go that route—because we understand that sometimes convenience trumps tradition.

Staff Favorite • Gluten Free Make Ahead

Braised Chicken with Olives, Capers, and Prunes

Hands-on: 30 min. **Total:** 1 hr. 30 min. This recipe is inspired by Chicken Marbella, the recipe from *The Silver Palate Cookbook* that went "viral" in the 1980s. It's been updated with far less added sugar (the original recipe calls for a cup of brown sugar) and the welcome addition of citrus.

5 Tbsp. extra-virgin olive oil, divided
¼ cup white wine vinegar
3 Tbsp. drained capers
1 Tbsp. chopped fresh oregano
1 Tbsp. honey
¾ tsp. kosher salt, divided
8 bone-in, skin-on chicken thighs (about 3 lb.), skin removed
¾ tsp. black pepper, divided
16 medium garlic cloves, peeled
1 cup dry white wine
2 bay leaves
24 pitted Castelvetrano olives
1 cup dried pitted plums (prunes)
1 small orange or Meyer lemon, unpeeled, cut into ½-inch slices

1. Preheat oven to 350°F.
2. Whisk together ¼ cup oil, vinegar, capers, oregano, honey, and ¼ teaspoon salt; set aside.
3. Heat remaining 1 tablespoon oil in a Dutch oven over medium-high. Sprinkle chicken with ½ teaspoon pepper and remaining ½ teaspoon salt. Working in batches if necessary, add chicken to pan, meaty side down, and cook until well browned, 6 to 7 minutes. Remove chicken; set aside.
4. Add garlic to drippings in pan; cook, stirring often, until lightly browned and blistered, about 2 minutes. Add

wine and bay leaves; cook until reduced by half, about 4 minutes.
5. Stir in olives and plums. Nestle chicken into mixture; pour vinegar mixture over chicken. Tuck citrus slices into mixture. Cover and bake at 350°F 40 minutes. Uncover and bake until liquid is thick and glossy, 10 to 15 minutes. Discard bay leaves; sprinkle with remaining ¼ teaspoon pepper. Serves 8

CALORIES 339; **FAT** 18g (sat 3g, unsat 13g); **PROTEIN** 22g; **CARB** 19g; **FIBER** 2g; **SUGARS** 11g (added sugars 2g); **SODIUM** 563mg; **CALC** 4% DV; **POTASSIUM** 9% DV

SLOW COOKER METHOD: Omit step 1. Prepare as directed through step 4, substituting a skillet for the Dutch oven. Omit step 5. Pour mixture into a 6-quart slow cooker. Add olives, plums, chicken, vinegar mixture, and citrus. Cover and cook on LOW until chicken is tender, 6 to 7 hours. Discard bay leaves; sprinkle with remaining ¼ teaspoon pepper.

Staff Favorite • Gluten Free Make Ahead

Steak Fajita Chili

Hands-on: 30 min. **Total:** 1 hr. 30 min.

1 Tbsp. olive oil
1½ lb. beef chuck-eye steak, cut into 1-inch pieces
1 medium white onion, thinly vertically sliced, slices halved
8 garlic cloves, minced
2 Tbsp. chili powder
1 Tbsp. chopped canned chipotle chile in adobo sauce
2 tsp. ground cumin
2 (15-oz.) cans unsalted kidney beans, drained and rinsed
1 (28-oz.) can unsalted diced tomatoes, undrained
2 cups unsalted chicken stock
1 (15-oz.) can unsalted pinto beans, drained and rinsed

1¼ tsp. kosher salt
2 cups yellow bell pepper strips, halved crosswise
1¼ cups red bell pepper strips, halved crosswise
½ cup green bell pepper strips, halved crosswise
1 ripe avocado, diced
½ cup plain 2% reduced-fat Greek yogurt
½ cup chopped scallions
½ cup fresh cilantro leaves
Thinly sliced radishes (optional)

1. Heat oil in a large Dutch oven over medium-high. Add half of steak; cook, stirring occasionally, until browned, about 6 minutes. Remove steak from pan. Repeat procedure with remaining steak. Set steak aside. Add onion and garlic to pan; cook, stirring occasionally, until onion is tender, about 6 minutes.
2. Stir in chili powder, chipotle chile, and cumin; cook, stirring constantly, 1 minute. Add kidney beans, tomatoes, stock, pinto beans, and salt; bring to a boil. Return steak to pan; cover, reduce heat to low, and simmer 30 minutes. Stir in bell peppers; cook until steak is tender, about 30 minutes. Ladle chili into bowls; top with avocado, yogurt, scallions, cilantro, and, if desired, radishes. Serves 8

CALORIES 403; **FAT** 18g (sat 6g, unsat 10g); **PROTEIN** 27g; **CARB** 36g; **FIBER** 15g; **SUGARS** 8g (added sugars 0g); **SODIUM** 589mg; **CALC** 15% DV; **POTASSIUM** 25% DV

SLOW COOKER METHOD: Prepare as directed in step 1, substituting a large skillet for the Dutch oven. Transfer steak and onion mixture to a 6-quart slow cooker. Add chili powder, chipotle, cumin, kidney beans, tomatoes, stock, pinto beans, salt, and bell peppers. Cover and cook on LOW until beef is tender, 5 to 6 hours. Serve with avocado, yogurt, scallions, cilantro, and, if desired, radishes.

Gluten Free • Make Ahead

Loaded Cauliflower Soup

Hands-on: 30 min. **Total:** 40 min.
This soup uses low-carb cauliflower in place of spuds for a riff on loaded potato soup.

6 bacon slices, chopped
1 cup chopped leek
½ cup chopped celery
4 garlic cloves, minced
8 cups chopped cauliflower florets and stems (from 1 [2½-lb.] head)
3 cups unsalted chicken stock
1 tsp. kosher salt
¼ tsp. black pepper
¾ cup half-and-half
2 oz. sharp cheddar cheese, shredded (about ½ cup)
3 Tbsp. chopped fresh chives

1. Cook bacon in a Dutch oven over medium, stirring often, until crisp, 5 to 7 minutes. Using a slotted spoon, transfer bacon to paper towels to drain. Reserve 1 tablespoon drippings in pan; discard remaining drippings.
2. Increase heat to medium-high. Add leek, celery, and garlic to hot drippings in pan; cook, stirring often, until crisp-tender, about 5 minutes. Add cauliflower, stock, salt, and pepper; bring to a boil. Cover and reduce heat to medium. Simmer until cauliflower is very tender, about 15 minutes.
3. Remove 1 cup vegetables with a slotted spoon; finely chop.
4. Pour remaining mixture into a blender; add half-and-half. Remove center piece of blender lid (to allow steam to escape); attach lid, and place a clean towel over opening in lid. Process, starting slowly and

continued

increasing speed, until very smooth, 1 minute and 30 seconds to 2 minutes. Return mixture to pan with chopped vegetables; cook over medium until warmed through, about 2 minutes. Ladle soup into bowls; top with bacon, cheese, and chives. Serves 6

CALORIES 200; FAT 13g (sat 6g, unsat 5g); PROTEIN 11g; CARB 12g; FIBER 3g; SUGARS 4g (added sugars 0g); SODIUM 653mg; CALC 15% DV; POTASSIUM 12% DV

SLOW COOKER METHOD: Prepare as directed in step 1, substituting a skillet for Dutch oven. Omit step 2. Combine drippings, leek, celery, garlic, cauliflower, stock, salt, and pepper in a 6-quart slow cooker. Cover and cook on LOW until tender, about 4 hours. Proceed with steps 3 and 4.

Make Ahead

Peppery Beef Stew with Root Vegetables

Hands-on: 45 min. **Total:** 4 hr.
This is how all pot roasts should be: tender meat, lots of flavorful vegetables, and a velvety sauce.

1 Tbsp. olive oil
2 lb. trimmed chuck roast (about 2⅓ lb. untrimmed)
2 tsp. black pepper, divided
1½ tsp. kosher salt, divided
6 garlic cloves, chopped
1 cup dry red wine
2 cups unsalted beef stock
3 Tbsp. all-purpose flour
2 Tbsp. unsalted tomato paste
4 thyme sprigs
2 bay leaves
1 lb. small turnips, peeled and cut into wedges (about 3 cups)
1 lb. carrots, peeled and cut into 2-inch pieces (about 3 cups)
1¼ lb. celery root, peeled and cut into cubes (about 2 cups)

2 cups fresh pearl onions, peeled, or thawed frozen pearl onions (about 8 oz.)
1 cup water
2 Tbsp. chopped flat-leaf parsley

1. Preheat oven to 350°F.
2. Heat olive oil in a Dutch oven over medium-high. Sprinkle roast with ½ teaspoon pepper and ½ teaspoon salt. Add roast to pan; cook until browned, about 5 minutes per side. Remove roast from pan; set aside. Add garlic to pan; cook, stirring constantly, 1 minute. Add wine; cook until reduced by half, about 2 minutes, scraping bottom of pan to loosen browned bits.
3. Whisk together stock and flour in a small bowl. Stir stock mixture into wine mixture; cook, stirring often, until thickened. Stir in tomato paste, thyme, bay leaves, remaining 1½ teaspoons pepper, and remaining 1 teaspoon salt. Nestle roast into stock mixture. Cover and bake at 350°F 1 hour and 30 minutes.
4. Remove pan from oven. Add turnips, carrots, celery root, onions, and 1 cup water; toss carefully with gravy. Cover and bake at 350°F until vegetables are tender and sauce is thick and glazy, about 1 hour. Coarsely shred beef; discard thyme and bay leaves. Top with parsley. Serves 8

CALORIES 382; FAT 18g (sat 6g, unsat 9g); PROTEIN 27g; CARB 24g; FIBER 4g; SUGARS 8g (added sugars 0g); SODIUM 579mg; CALC 9% DV; POTASSIUM 16% DV

SLOW COOKER METHOD: Omit step 1. Prepare as directed in step 2, substituting a skillet for the Dutch oven. Place roast and wine mixture in a 6-quart slow cooker. Omit steps 3 and 4. Stir together stock and flour; pour over roast. Stir in tomato paste, thyme, bay leaves, remaining 1½ teaspoons pepper, and remaining 1 teaspoon salt. Add vegetables and 1 cup water. Cover and cook on LOW until roast is tender, about 7 hours.

Make Ahead

Savory Pork Ragù with Pappardelle

Hands-on: 40 min. **Total:** 2 hr.

Country-style pork ribs typically come from the shoulder (not the ribs). They're boneless and easy to buy in small amounts—unlike a pork shoulder roast (Boston butt)—so they're a great option for recipes that don't use a lot of meat. San Marzano tomatoes have superior flavor and, though not touted as being low in sodium, typically are, with just 20mg per serving.

1 Tbsp. olive oil
1½ lb. boneless country-style pork ribs
1 tsp. kosher salt, divided
2 cups vertically sliced white onion
1 medium fennel bulb, cored and thinly vertically sliced
8 garlic cloves, crushed
1 (28-oz.) can whole peeled San Marzano tomatoes, undrained
4 anchovy fillets, finely chopped
3 oregano sprigs
2 bay leaves
¼ tsp. crushed red pepper
1 lb. uncooked whole-wheat pappardelle or fettuccine
2 oz. percorino Romano cheese, finely grated (about ¼ cup)
Fresh oregano leaves, for garnish

1. Preheat oven to 325°F.
2. Heat olive oil in a Dutch oven over medium-high. Sprinkle pork with ½ teaspoon salt. Add pork to pan; cook until well browned all over, about 8 minutes. Remove pork from pan.
3. Add onion, fennel, and garlic to pan; cook, stirring occasionally, 5 minutes. Add tomatoes and their juices; break tomatoes up with the

back of a spoon or your hands. Stir in anchovies, oregano sprigs, bay leaves, red pepper, and remaining ½ teaspoon salt. Nestle pork into tomato mixture. Cover and bake at 325°F until pork is very tender, about 1 hour and 30 minutes. Carefully remove pork from Dutch oven. Shred pork using 2 forks; stir shredded pork into tomato mixture. Discard bay leaves and oregano sprigs.

4. Cook pasta according to directions, omitting salt. Drain; reserve 1 cup cooking liquid. Add pasta to Dutch oven; toss gently to coat, adding reserved cooking liquid as necessary to reach desired consistency. Sprinkle with cheese and oregano leaves. Serves 8

CALORIES 419; **FAT** 12g (sat 4g, unsat 6g); **PROTEIN** 29g; **CARB** 52g; **FIBER** 8g; **SUGARS** 7g (added sugars 0g); **SODIUM** 554mg; **CALC** 14% DV; **POTASSIUM** 15% DV

SLOW COOKER METHOD: Omit step 1. Brown pork as directed in step 2, substituting a skillet for the Dutch oven. Add pork, onion, fennel, garlic, tomatoes, anchovies, oregano sprigs, bay leaves, red pepper, and remaining ½ teaspoon salt to a 6-quart slow cooker. Cover and cook on LOW until pork is tender, 5 to 6 hours. Shred pork; discard bay leaves and oregano sprigs. Follow recipe as directed in step 4.

Chicken Cassoulet

Hands-on: 45 min. **Total:** 3 hr. 35 min.

1 lb. dried Great Northern beans
3 bay leaves
3¼ Tbsp. extra-virgin olive oil, divided
1 lb. boneless, skinless chicken thighs, cut into bite-size pieces
12 oz. fully cooked Italian chicken sausage, sliced
2 cups chopped white onion
1¼ cups chopped carrots
1 cup chopped celery
2 Tbsp. chopped fresh thyme
2 Tbsp. unsalted tomato paste
6 garlic cloves, minced
⅔ cup dry white wine
1 (14-oz.) can unsalted diced tomatoes, undrained
1 cup unsalted chicken stock
¾ tsp. kosher salt
¾ tsp. black pepper
2 oz. multigrain baguette, torn into small pieces
2 oz. Parmesan cheese, grated (about ½ cup)
2 Tbsp. chopped fresh flat-leaf parsley

1. Place beans in a Dutch oven. Add water to cover by 2 inches; stir in bay leaves. Bring to a boil; boil 1 minute. Remove from heat; cover and let stand 1 hour. Return pan to heat over high (do not drain beans or refresh water); bring to a boil. Reduce heat to medium-low; simmer until beans are almost tender, about 30 minutes. Drain beans; discard bay leaves. Wipe pan dry.

2. Preheat oven to 300°F.

3. Heat 1½ tablespoons oil in pan over medium-high. Add chicken; cook, stirring occasionally, until browned, about 8 minutes. Add sausage; cook, stirring occasionally, until browned, about 5 minutes. Remove chicken and sausage. Add onion, carrots, and celery; sauté 5 minutes. Add thyme, tomato paste, and garlic; sauté 2 minutes. Add wine; cook 1 minute, scraping bottom of pan to loosen browned bits.

4. Add tomatoes, stock, salt, pepper, beans, chicken, and sausage to pan; stir gently to combine. Cover and bake at 300°F 1 hour. Remove pan. Increase oven temperature to 425°F.

5. Scoop out 1 cup bean mixture, avoiding chicken or sausage. Mash with a fork; stir into chicken mixture.

6. Place baguette in a food processor; process until coarse crumbs form. Add cheese, parsley, and remaining 2 tablespoons oil; pulse to combine. Sprinkle breadcrumbs over cassoulet. Bake, uncovered, at 425°F until topping is crusty, 15 to 20 minutes. Let stand 5 minutes before serving. Serves 8

CALORIES 483; **FAT** 15g (sat 4g, unsat 9g); **PROTEIN** 36g; **CARB** 50g; **FIBER** 14g; **SUGARS** 6g (added sugars 0g); **SODIUM** 644mg; **CALC** 23% DV; **POTASSIUM** 26% DV

SLOW COOKER METHOD: Place beans in a 6-quart slow cooker. Omit step 2. Proceed with step 3, substituting a skillet for the Dutch oven. Add chicken mixture and onion mixture to slow cooker. Omit step 4. Add tomatoes, stock, salt, pepper, and 1⅔ cups water. Cover and cook on LOW until beans are tender, 7 to 8 hours. Omit step 5. Make breadcrumb mixture as directed in step 6; toast in a skillet over medium-high about 5 minutes. Sprinkle on cassoulet.

HARVEST BOWLS

These vegetable-forward, brassica-based dinners put our favorite fall produce in the spotlight.

Thick slabs of cauliflower are now taking center plate as hearty "steaks," and kale has cemented its role as the new romaine in Caesar salads in both professional and home kitchens across America. We think it's wonderful how cruciferous veggies are getting their turn in the spotlight. When prepared right (no death-by-boiling, please), brassicas are one of the most delicious and versatile groups of vegetables to cook. They're also nutrition powerhouses, rich in cancer-fighting phytochemicals, gut-healthy fiber, and a slew of vitamins. Here, we celebrate some of our most beloved brassicas for their versatility and ability to take any average grain bowl to next-level status.

Make Ahead • Vegetarian

Crispy Cauliflower with Chili-Tahini Sauce and Farro Pilaf

Hands-on: 15 min. **Total:** 40 min.

5 cups chopped cauliflower florets
2 Tbsp. extra-virgin olive oil, divided
1 tsp. kosher salt, divided
1 tsp. lemon zest plus 2 Tbsp. fresh lemon juice
1½ Tbsp. tahini (sesame seed paste)
½ tsp. chili powder
½ tsp. granulated sugar
4 to 5 tsp. water
3 Tbsp. finely chopped shallot
3 cups cooked farro
2 Medjool dates, finely chopped
2 Tbsp. chopped fresh mint, plus whole leaves for garnish

1. Preheat oven to 425°F. Arrange cauliflower in a single layer on a rimmed baking sheet. Toss with 1 tablespoon oil and ¼ teaspoon salt. Bake at 425°F until tender, 25 to 30 minutes, tossing once after 15 minutes. Set aside.
2. Stir together lemon zest and juice, tahini, chili powder, sugar, and ¼ teaspoon salt in a bowl. Whisk in 1 tablespoon water; add 1 to 2 additional teaspoons water until desired consistency is reached. Set aside.
3. Heat remaining 1 tablespoon oil in a nonstick skillet over medium. Add shallot; cook until softened, about 3 minutes. Stir in farro, dates, chopped mint, and remaining ½ teaspoon salt; cook 2 minutes.
4. Place ⅔ cup farro pilaf in each of 4 bowls. Top each with ¾ cup cauliflower and 1½ tablespoons chili-tahini sauce. Garnish with mint. Serves 4 (serving size: about 1½ cups)

CALORIES 302; **FAT** 12g (sat 2g, unsat 9g); **PROTEIN** 10g; **CARB** 52g; **FIBER** 9g; **SUGARS** 7g (added sugars 1g); **SODIUM** 533mg; **CALC** 5% DV; **POTASSIUM** 10% DV

> **CAULIFLOWER**
> This blank-canvas brassica is diverse enough to be blended into a creamy sauce or soup or blitzed into "rice" as a lower-carb alternative to grains. Roasting brings out its sweeter side, though it takes on just about any flavor you throw its way.

Make Ahead • Vegetarian

Broccoli Rabe and Barley Bowl with Cilantro Pesto

Hands-on: 15 min. **Total:** 40 min.

1½ cups plus 1 Tbsp. water, divided
½ cup uncooked pearled barley
¾ tsp. kosher salt, divided
1 (15-oz.) can unsalted cannellini beans, rinsed and drained
1 cup fresh cilantro leaves
½ cup roasted pepitas (shelled pumpkin seeds)
5 Tbsp. extra-virgin olive oil, divided
1 tsp. lemon zest plus 1½ Tbsp. fresh lemon juice, divided
1 garlic clove
¼ tsp. ground coriander
¼ tsp. black pepper
12 oz. trimmed broccoli rabe
¼ cup grated Parmesan cheese

1. Bring 1½ cups water, barley, and ¼ teaspoon salt to a boil in a saucepan. Reduce heat to medium; cover and cook until barley is tender and water is mostly absorbed, about 25 minutes. Stir in beans.
2. Process cilantro, pepitas, ¼ cup olive oil, lemon juice, garlic, coriander, pepper, remaining 1 tablespoon water, and remaining ½ teaspoon salt in a food processor until smooth.
3. Boil broccoli rabe 2 minutes. Rinse with cold water; drain. Pat dry.

Heat remaining 1 tablespoon oil in a skillet over medium-high. Add broccoli rabe and lemon zest; cook, stirring often, 3 minutes.

4. Place ⅔ cup barley mixture in each of 4 bowls. Top evenly with broccoli rabe, cilantro pesto, and cheese. Serves 4 (serving size: about 1 ½ cups)

CALORIES 462; **FAT** 27g (sat 5g, unsat 21g); **PROTEIN** 16g; **CARB** 41g; **FIBER** 9g; **SUGARS** 2g (added sugars 0g); **SODIUM** 515mg; **CALC** 14% DV; **POTASSIUM** 9% DV

BROCCOLI RABE

This cousin to broccoli is the most calcium-rich of the bunch. Known for its bracing bitterness, a quick blanch followed by pan-searing tames its bite and tenderizes it.

Fast • Make Ahead
Vegetarian

Charred Cabbage with Butternut-Miso Mash

Hands-on: 20 min. **Total:** 30 min.

1 (16-oz.) pkg. peeled and cubed fresh butternut squash
1 Tbsp. unsalted butter
1 Tbsp. white miso
1 garlic clove, grated
¼ tsp. crushed red pepper
1 small head red cabbage
1 Tbsp. canola oil
½ tsp. kosher salt
2 Tbsp. toasted sesame oil
1 Tbsp. fresh lime juice
2 tsp. lower-sodium soy sauce
1 tsp. honey
½ tsp. grated fresh ginger
½ cup fresh cilantro leaves
¼ cup unsalted roasted cashews, roughly chopped

1. Bring a large saucepan of water to a boil. Add squash, and reduce heat to medium; simmer until tender, about 10 minutes. Drain. Combine squash, butter, miso, garlic, and red pepper in a food processor. Process until smooth.

2. Cut cabbage in half lengthwise. Cut each half into 4 equal wedges. Heat canola oil in a large cast-iron skillet over high. Add cabbage, cut sides down; cook until charred, about 5 minutes. Flip cabbage; cook until charred, about 5 minutes. Remove from pan. Sprinkle with salt.

3. Stir together sesame oil, lime juice, soy sauce, honey, and ginger in a bowl.

4. Place ⅔ cup squash mixture in each of 4 bowls. Top evenly with cabbage wedges, sesame oil mixture, cilantro, and cashews. Serves 4

CALORIES 278; **FAT** 18g (sat 4g, unsat 13g); **PROTEIN** 6g; **CARB** 30g; **FIBER** 6g; **SUGARS** 11g (added sugars 1g); **SODIUM** 517mg; **CALC** 13% DV; **POTASSIUM** 18% DV

CABBAGE

Grilled, shredded, or fermented to make kimchi or kraut, the humble cabbage knows no bounds. This stand-out crucifer is also rich in compounds called isothiocyanates, which may help lower cancer risk.

Make Ahead • Vegetarian

Kale and Lentil Bowl with Thai Almond Sauce

Hands-on: 15 min. **Total:** 1 hr. 15 min.

¾ cup apple cider vinegar
½ cup plus 2 Tbsp. water, divided
2 Tbsp. granulated sugar
1½ tsp. table salt, divided
2 cups matchstick-cut carrots

3 cups unsalted vegetable stock (such as Swanson)
1 cup uncooked black lentils
1 (7-oz.) bunch lacinato kale, stemmed and chopped
2 Tbsp. creamy almond butter
1 Tbsp. fresh lemon juice
2 tsp. toasted sesame oil
2 tsp. lower-sodium soy sauce
1 garlic clove, grated
1 ripe avocado, sliced

1. Stir together vinegar, ½ cup water, sugar, and 1 teaspoon salt in a saucepan; bring to a simmer over medium. Place carrots in a glass bowl. Add vinegar mixture; let stand 1 hour.

2. Bring stock, lentils, and remaining ½ teaspoon salt to a boil in a saucepan. Cover, reduce heat to medium, and simmer until lentils are tender, about 45 minutes. Stir in kale. Remove from heat; cover and let stand until kale is slightly wilted, about 5 minutes.

3. Stir together almond butter, lemon juice, sesame oil, soy sauce, and garlic in a bowl. Whisk in 1 tablespoon water. If necessary, whisk in remaining water, 1 teaspoon at a time, until desired consistency is reached.

4. Drain carrots. Place ¾ cup lentil mixture in each of 4 bowls. Top evenly with pickled carrots and avocado. Drizzle with almond sauce. Serves 4 (serving size: about 1 ½ cups)

CALORIES 369; **FAT** 14g (sat 2g, unsat 11g); **PROTEIN** 19g; **CARB** 50g; **FIBER** 11g; **SUGARS** 6g (added sugars 1g); **SODIUM** 651mg; **CALC** 14% DV; **POTASSIUM** 21% DV

KALE

Our reigning leafy green queen is packed with vitamins A, C, and K. The fibrous greens maintain their integrity in long-cooked soups and braises, but we also love them raw in salads (massage the leaves until they start to soften and tenderize).

Brussels and Quinoa Bowl with Orange-Thyme Vinaigrette

Hands-on: 20 min. **Total:** 35 min.

1 cup uncooked tricolor quinoa
¾ tsp. kosher salt, divided
¼ cup fresh orange juice
2 Tbsp. apple cider vinegar
2 Tbsp. extra-virgin olive oil, divided
1 Tbsp. honey
1 tsp. Dijon mustard
1 tsp. chopped fresh thyme
12 oz. Brussels sprouts, trimmed and halved
2 cups chopped radicchio (from 1 head)
1 cup chopped Golden Delicious apple
1½ oz. goat cheese, crumbled (about ⅓ cup)

1. Cook quinoa in water according to package directions. Add ¼ teaspoon salt; stir to combine. Set aside.
2. Whisk together orange juice, vinegar, 1 tablespoon oil, honey, mustard, thyme, and ¼ teaspoon salt in a small bowl.
3. Heat remaining 1 tablespoon oil in a large nonstick skillet over medium-high. Add Brussels sprouts; cook, stirring often, until browned and crisp, 8 to 10 minutes. Sprinkle with remaining ¼ teaspoon salt.
4. Place ½ cup quinoa in each of 4 bowls. Top each with ½ cup radicchio, ¼ cup apple, and ⅔ cup Brussels sprouts. Drizzle each with 2 tablespoons orange-thyme vinaigrette; sprinkle evenly with goat cheese. Serves 4 (serving size: about 2 cups)

CALORIES 333; FAT 12g (sat 3g, unsat 9g); PROTEIN 11g; CARB 47g; FIBER 7g; SUGARS 12g (added sugars 4g); SODIUM 467mg; CALC 8% DV; POTASSIUM 15% DV

BRUSSELS SPROUTS

These petite cabbages transform under heat, turning soft and sweet. Their peppery leaves deliver a hit of vitamin C and also work well shaved raw in salads.

Broccoli Fried Rice with Kimchi Cream

Hands-on: 25 min. **Total:** 25 min.

4 center-cut bacon slices, chopped
4 cups chopped broccoli florets
1 Tbsp. toasted sesame oil
2 (8.8-oz.) pkg. precooked microwavable brown rice
½ cup chopped scallions, plus more for garnish
¼ tsp. granulated sugar
2 large eggs, lightly beaten
2 Tbsp. lower-sodium soy sauce
⅓ cup refrigerated jarred kimchi plus 1 Tbsp. kimchi juice
¼ cup plain whole-milk Greek yogurt
1 Tbsp. canola mayonnaise
⅛ tsp. kosher salt

1. Cook bacon in a large nonstick skillet over medium until crisp, about 5 minutes. Transfer bacon to a plate (do not wipe out skillet). Add broccoli to skillet; cover and cook, stirring occasionally, until broccoli is crisp-tender, about 5 minutes. Transfer to a bowl.
2. Add sesame oil to skillet; increase heat to medium-high. Add rice, scallions, and sugar; cook, stirring occasionally, until warmed through, about 5 minutes. Push rice mixture to edges of skillet to create a hole in center. Add eggs to center; cook, stirring often, until mostly cooked, about 1 minute. Stir in soy sauce, bacon, and broccoli. Remove from heat.
3. Process kimchi and kimchi juice, yogurt, mayonnaise, and salt in a food processor until mostly smooth.
4. Divide fried rice among 4 bowls. Top each with 2 tablespoons kimchi cream; garnish with scallions. Serves 4 (serving size: about 1¾ cups)

CALORIES 294; FAT 11g (sat 3g, unsat 8g); PROTEIN 13g; CARB 36g; FIBER 5g; SUGARS 3g (added sugars 1g); SODIUM 619mg; CALC 9% DV; POTASSIUM 9% DV

BROCCOLI

Coveted for its subtly sweet flowering heads, this everyday veggie delivers crunch and a hefty dose of potassium, which supports blood pressure. Save the stalks for stir-fries or slaws; they're rich in the gut-friendly fiber cellulose.

WEEKNIGHT MAINS

Fast

Loaded Steakhouse Baked Potatoes

Hands-on: 30 min. **Total:** 30 min.
Your family will flock to the kitchen when they get a whiff of these over-the-top spuds. We packed them with a bounty of spinach, plus a savory mushroom blend that would go great spooned over your favorite steak.

4 (5-oz.) russet potatoes
¼ cup 1% low-fat milk
2 Tbsp. unsalted butter, divided
1 tsp. kosher salt, divided
¾ tsp. black pepper, divided
1 Tbsp. olive oil
8 oz. cremini mushrooms, sliced
2 tsp. roughly chopped fresh thyme
½ cup unsalted beef broth
2 tsp. sherry vinegar
2 tsp. lower-sodium Worcestershire sauce
2 garlic cloves, thinly sliced
10 oz. fresh baby spinach
8 oz. shredded smoked brisket, warmed
1 oz. blue cheese, crumbled (about ¼ cup)
¼ cup crispy fried onions (such as French's)

1. Prick potatoes all over with a fork; place on a plate. Microwave potatoes at HIGH in 3 (5-minute) intervals until tender. Halve potatoes; scoop out potato pulp into a large bowl, leaving a ¼-inch border around skin; set halves aside. Add milk, 1 tablespoon butter, ¾ teaspoon salt, and ½ teaspoon pepper to potato pulp; mash until smooth. Cover to keep warm.

2. Heat oil in a medium skillet over medium-high. Add mushrooms and thyme; cook, stirring occasionally, until browned, 6 to 7 minutes. Add broth, vinegar, and Worcestershire; bring to a simmer, and cook until liquid is reduced by half, about 2 minutes. Stir in 1½ teaspoons butter and remaining ¼ teaspoon pepper. Transfer mushroom mixture to a small bowl; cover to keep warm. Wipe skillet clean.

3. Return skillet to heat over medium-high. Add garlic and remaining 1½ teaspoons butter; cook, stirring constantly, until garlic is slightly golden, about 30 seconds. Add spinach in batches, letting each batch cook down slightly before adding the next. Cook, tossing constantly with tongs, until liquid has evaporated, about 2 minutes. Stir in remaining ¼ teaspoon salt. Transfer to bowl with potato pulp; stir to combine.

4. Divide potato mixture evenly among potato halves. Top evenly with brisket, mushroom mixture, cheese, and onions. Serves 4 (serving size: 2 potato halves)

CALORIES 431; **FAT** 19g (sat 8g, unsat 9g); **PROTEIN** 26g; **CARB** 39g; **FIBER** 6g; **SUGARS** 3g (added sugars 0g); **SODIUM** 765mg; **CALC** 17% DV; **POTASSIUM** 26% DV

Fast • Gluten Free

Maple-Miso Salmon with Acorn Squash

Hands-on: 20 min. **Total:** 30 min.
Look for smaller acorn squash; they tend to be less fibrous than larger ones. Red miso is the most potent variety of miso and is a worthy investment for this recipe. In a pinch, lower-sodium soy sauce is a good substitute.

1 (1½-lb.) acorn squash
3 Tbsp. olive oil, divided
½ tsp. ground fennel seeds
¾ tsp. kosher salt, divided
Cooking spray
2 Tbsp. pure maple syrup
2 tsp. red miso
½ tsp. black pepper
4 (6-oz.) skinless salmon fillets
1 (4-oz.) pkg. watercress (about 4 cups)
1½ tsp. fresh lemon juice

1. Preheat oven to 425°F. Cut squash in half vertically; scoop out and discard seeds. Cut squash into 12 wedges; toss with 1½ tablespoons oil, fennel seeds, and ¼ teaspoon salt. Arrange squash in a single layer on an aluminum foil–lined rimmed baking sheet coated with cooking spray. Roast at 425°F 10 minutes. Flip squash. Turn on broiler to high with rack in top third of oven. Broil squash until caramelized and tender, 6 to 7 minutes.

2. Meanwhile, whisk together syrup, miso, and pepper. Heat 1 tablespoon oil in a large nonstick skillet over medium-high. Add salmon, and cook until lightly browned, about 4 minutes. Flip salmon, brush with 1 tablespoon syrup mixture, and cook 2 minutes, brushing with 1 tablespoon syrup mixture. Remove salmon from skillet, and sprinkle with remaining ½ teaspoon salt. Toss watercress with lemon juice and remaining 1 ½ teaspoons oil. Serve salmon with remaining syrup mixture, squash, and watercress. Serves 4

CALORIES 437; **FAT** 22g (sat 3g, unsat 17g); **PROTEIN** 36g; **CARB** 26g; **FIBER** 3g; **SUGARS** 10g (added sugars 6g); **SODIUM** 577mg; **CALC** 13% DV; **POTASSIUM** 33% DV

Beer-Braised Chicken and Root Vegetables

Hands-on: 20 min. **Total:** 50 min.
Parsnips and rutabaga are good sources of soluble fiber, which keeps blood sugar levels in check. Simmering the veggies in beer infuses them with bold flavor; you can use unsalted chicken or vegetable stock.

1 Tbsp. olive oil
4 (6-oz.) boneless, skinless chicken breasts
½ tsp. black pepper
1 tsp. kosher salt, divided
½ rutabaga, peeled and cut into ¾-inch cubes (about 1 cup)
1½ Tbsp. unsalted butter, divided
4 medium parsnips, cut into 2-inch pieces (about 2 cups)
1 cup chopped yellow onion
¾ tsp. caraway seeds
¾ cup wheat beer (hefeweizen)
¾ cup unsalted chicken stock
1 Tbsp. grainy Dijon mustard
1½ Tbsp. chopped fresh tarragon
1½ tsp. apple cider vinegar
3 Tbsp. chopped scallions

1. Heat oil in large, high-sided skillet over medium-high. Sprinkle chicken with pepper and ½ teaspoon salt. Cook chicken until browned on 1 side, 4 to 5 minutes. Remove from skillet.
2. Add rutabaga and 1 tablespoon butter to skillet. Cook, stirring often, until caramelized, 5 to 6 minutes. Add parsnips, onion, and caraway seeds. Cook, stirring occasionally, until browned, 3 to 4 minutes. Add beer, chicken stock, and mustard; bring to a boil over high. Return chicken to skillet, and reduce heat to medium-low. Cover and simmer until a thermometer inserted in thickest portion of chicken registers 155°F, about 10 minutes.
3. Remove chicken from skillet; cover to keep warm. Cook vegetables, uncovered, until tender, 20 to 25 minutes. Stir in tarragon, vinegar, scallions, remaining ½ teaspoon salt, and remaining 1½ teaspoons butter. Serves 4

CALORIES 385; FAT 13g (sat 4g, unsat 7g); PROTEIN 41g; CARB 22g; FIBER 5g; SUGARS 7g (added sugars 0g); SODIUM 691mg; CALC 7% DV; POTASSIUM 22% DV

Roasted Butternut Squash and Poblano Pizza

Hands-on: 35 min. **Total:** 45 min.
This Mexican-inspired twist on flatbread is packed with oven-roasted veggies, delivering almost a third of your daily fiber goal. Buy precubed butternut squash to save time.

2 cups peeled and cubed butternut squash
1 poblano chile, seeded and chopped
1 small red onion, cut into 8 wedges
8 unpeeled garlic cloves
1½ Tbsp. olive oil
¾ tsp. ground cumin
½ tsp. smoked paprika
¼ tsp. ground cinnamon
¼ tsp. kosher salt
⅛ tsp. cayenne pepper
Cooking spray
1 cup 2% reduced-fat milk
1 Tbsp. all-purpose flour, plus more
12 oz. fresh prepared pizza dough, at room temperature
3 oz. queso fresco, crumbled (about ¾ cup) and divided
3 Tbsp. chopped fresh cilantro
2 Tbsp. roasted pepitas (shelled pumpkin seeds)

1. Place an aluminum foil-lined rimmed baking sheet on middle oven rack. Preheat oven to 500°F.
2. Combine squash, poblano, onion, garlic, and oil in a large bowl. Add cumin, paprika, cinnamon, salt, and cayenne; toss to coat. Carefully remove pan from oven; coat with cooking spray. Spread squash mixture on pan. Roast at 500°F for 10 minutes. Stir vegetables; turn on broiler. Broil on middle rack until squash is tender, about 5 minutes. Remove from oven; transfer vegetables to a bowl, and peel garlic cloves. Discard foil; line pan with new foil, and return to oven. Reduce oven temperature to 475°F.
3. Bring milk and 1 tablespoon flour to a boil in a saucepan over high, whisking constantly. Cook, whisking constantly, until reduced to about ¾ cup, 5 to 6 minutes. Remove from heat; let cool 10 minutes.
4. Roll dough out into a 12-inch oval on a floured surface. Coat prepared baking sheet with cooking spray. Place dough on baking sheet; prick all over with a fork. Bake at 475°F until dry, about 4 minutes. Remove from oven; spread milk mixture over pizza, leaving a ½-inch border. Top with vegetables and ¼ cup cheese. Bake at 475°F 10 to 12 minutes. Top with cilantro, pepitas, and remaining ½ cup cheese. Serves 4 (serving size: ¼ pizza)

CALORIES 424; FAT 12g (sat 3g, unsat 7g); PROTEIN 16g; CARB 64g; FIBER 9g; SUGARS 6g (added sugars 0g); SODIUM 572mg; CALC 19% DV; POTASSIUM 10% DV

KNOW YOUR DOUGH

You can keep pizza dough refrigerated for a few days; it develops more flavor. Let the dough come to room temperature before rolling it out.

Poached Sea Bass with Gingery Veggies

Hands-on: 30 min. **Total:** 40 min.
This dish is a nice break from heavier fall flavors thanks to the ginger-and-star-anise–perfumed broth that poaches the fish to the perfect, flaky texture. If you can't score baby bok choy, asparagus or green beans are a smart swap.

1 (3-inch) piece fresh ginger
6 cups water
1 whole star anise (optional)
1 Tbsp. plus ¾ tsp. kosher salt, divided
6 oz. small carrots, tops trimmed, halved lengthwise
2 baby bok choy (about 8 oz.), halved lengthwise
½ cup dry white wine
4 (6-oz.) skinless sea bass fillets
2 Tbsp. unsalted butter
1 cup orange segments
¼ cup packed fresh flat-leaf parsley leaves
Black pepper, for garnish

1. Peel ginger, and grate to equal 1 teaspoon; set grated ginger aside. Slice remaining ginger. Combine sliced ginger, 6 cups water, star anise (if using), and 1 tablespoon salt in a large Dutch oven. Cover and bring to a boil over high. Reduce heat to medium-low; cover and simmer 10 minutes. Remove solids and discard. Add carrots to Dutch oven; simmer 4 minutes. Increase heat to high. Add bok choy; cook until carrots are tender and bok choy is bright green and crisp-tender, 1 to 2 minutes. Using a slotted spoon, transfer vegetables to a colander; rinse under cold water until cool. Drain.
2. Add wine to Dutch oven. Bring to a boil. Reduce heat to medium (only tiny bubbles should appear, and water temperature should be around 160°F). Add fish; cook, without stirring, until fish just flakes with a fork, 6 to 8 minutes. Using a slotted spoon, remove fish from liquid. Sprinkle fish with ½ teaspoon salt.
3. Heat grated ginger and butter in a large skillet over medium 30 seconds. Stir in carrots, bok choy, and remaining ¼ teaspoon salt. Cook, stirring constantly, until heated through, 2 to 3 minutes. Place vegetables on a serving platter. Top with fish, orange segments, and parsley. Garnish with pepper. Serves 4 (serving size: 1 fillet and 1 cup veggies)

CALORIES 287; **FAT** 9g (sat 4g, unsat 4g); **PROTEIN** 33g; **CARB** 12g; **FIBER** 3g; **SUGARS** 7g (added sugars 0g); **SODIUM** 664mg; **CALC** 12% DV; **POTASSIUM** 14% DV

20-MINUTE MAINS
Fast • Gluten Free

Seared Chicken with Shallots and Grapes

Hands-on: 20 min. **Total:** 20 min.
This rustic skillet supper is the ultimate company-worthy comfort food. Juicy, antioxidant-rich red grapes combine with shallots, vinegar, and cardamom to yield an intriguing balance of tart and sweet flavors.

1 Tbsp. olive oil
1½ lb. boneless, skinless chicken thighs (about 6 thighs)
½ tsp. black pepper
¾ tsp. kosher salt, divided
1½ cups seedless red grapes
1 cup thinly sliced shallots
¾ tsp. ground cardamom
½ cup unsalted chicken stock
1½ Tbsp. red wine vinegar
2 Tbsp. chopped fresh flat-leaf parsley
1½ tsp. unsalted butter

1. Heat oil in a large skillet over high. Sprinkle chicken with pepper and ½ teaspoon salt. Add chicken to skillet; cook until browned on one side, 5 to 6 minutes. Remove from skillet.
2. Add grapes to skillet; cook, stirring occasionally, until skins are slightly charred, about 3 minutes. Add shallots and cardamom; cook, stirring often, until shallots are translucent and grapes begin to burst, about 3 minutes. Add chicken, browned side up, stock, and vinegar. Bring to a boil; reduce heat to medium, and simmer until grapes release their liquid, 3 to 4 minutes.
3. Remove chicken from skillet. Add parsley, butter, and remaining ¼ teaspoon salt to skillet; stir to combine. Return chicken to skillet. Spoon sauce over chicken to serve. Serves 4

CALORIES 322; **FAT** 12g (sat 4g, unsat 6g); **PROTEIN** 37g; **CARB** 18g; **FIBER** 2g; **SUGARS** 12g (added sugars 0g); **SODIUM** 532mg; **CALC** 5% DV; **POTASSIUM** 6% DV

TRY THIGHS

If boneless chicken breasts are your go-to cut, give boneless thighs a try. Not only are they more moist and flavorful, they're also much less expensive.

Spicy Shrimp Noodles

Hands-on: 20 min. **Total:** 20 min.
These superfast bowls satisfy with filling brown rice noodles and fresh shrimp. If you can't find brown rice noodles, substitute your favorite whole-grain linguine or fettuccine.

6 oz. uncooked brown rice pad Thai noodles
3 Tbsp. canola oil
2 cups sliced scallions (about 2 bunches)
8 oz. peeled and deveined raw medium shrimp
1 large egg
⅓ cup chopped unsalted peanuts, divided
3 Tbsp. unsalted ketchup
2 Tbsp. fresh lime juice
1½ Tbsp. Sriracha chili sauce
1 Tbsp. fish sauce
1 Tbsp. water
2 Tbsp. chopped fresh cilantro

1. Cook noodles according to package directions.
2. Heat oil in a large cast-iron skillet over high. Add scallions and shrimp. Cook, stirring often, until scallions are bright green, 1 to 2 minutes. Add egg; cook, stirring constantly, until egg and shrimp are cooked, about 1 minute. Add noodles, half of the peanuts, ketchup, lime juice, Sriracha, fish sauce, and 1 tablespoon water. Toss well to combine. Serve in shallow bowls; sprinkle with cilantro and remaining peanuts. Serves 4 (serving size: 1½ cups)

CALORIES 410; FAT 18g (sat 2g, unsat 15g); PROTEIN 14g; CARB 49g; FIBER 3g; SUGARS 5g (added sugars 1g); SODIUM 585mg; CALC 9% DV; POTASSIUM 10% DV

Beef and Cabbage Stir-Fry

Hands-on: 20 min. **Total:** 20 min.
This crunchy and filling skillet meal delivers big flavor with a nutritional punch: Flank steak contains blood-enriching iron, and cabbage has a whopping dose of vitamin C. Microwavable brown rice makes a great time-saver.

½ cup unsalted beef stock
2 tsp. cornstarch
2 Tbsp. canola oil, divided
12 oz. flank steak, cut against the grain into thin strips
3½ Tbsp. lower-sodium soy sauce, divided
1½ tsp. granulated sugar, divided
4 cups chopped red cabbage
1 Tbsp. minced fresh ginger
4 garlic cloves, thinly sliced
1 cup matchstick-cut carrots
¼ cup chopped scallions
1 Tbsp. toasted sesame oil
1 Tbsp. sherry vinegar
2 (8.8-oz.) pkg. precooked microwavable brown rice, warmed
2 tsp. toasted sesame seeds

1. Whisk together stock and cornstarch in a small bowl until smooth.
2. Heat 1 tablespoon canola oil in a large cast-iron skillet over high. Add steak; cook, stirring occasionally, until browned, 2 to 3 minutes. Add 1½ tablespoons soy sauce and 1 teaspoon sugar. Cook, stirring often, until meat is charred, 1 to 2 minutes. Remove steak to a plate. Add cabbage, ginger, garlic, and remaining 1 tablespoon canola oil; cook, stirring often, until cabbage begins to wilt, 2 to 3 minutes. Add stock mixture, remaining 2 tablespoons soy sauce, and remaining ½ teaspoon sugar. Bring to a boil; reduce heat to medium, and simmer until cabbage is crisp-tender, about 2 minutes. Stir in steak, carrots, scallions, sesame oil, and vinegar. Cook 1 minute. Serve over brown rice. Sprinkle with sesame seeds. Serves 4 (serving size: 1½ cups)

CALORIES 428; FAT 17g (sat 3g, unsat 12g); PROTEIN 25g; CARB 43g; FIBER 5g; SUGARS 5g (added sugars 2g); SODIUM 587mg; CALC 7% DV; POTASSIUM 12% DV

Crispy Chicken Milanese

Hands-on: 20 min. **Total:** 20 min.
This simple dredge-dip-dredge method is our go-to trick for adding superb crunch to quick-cooking cutlets. The speedy salad is also a perfect partner for pork and salmon; swap frisée or your favorite bitter greens for a flavor twist.

2.13 oz. all-purpose flour (about ½ cup)
2 large eggs, lightly beaten
1 cup panko
4 (5-oz.) chicken breast cutlets
2 Tbsp. olive oil
½ tsp. kosher salt
¼ cup canola mayonnaise
2 tsp. fresh lemon juice
¾ tsp. granulated sugar
¼ tsp. black pepper
3 cups baby arugula
1 cup thinly sliced red onion
1 cup thinly sliced celery
2 tsp. drained capers, chopped
1 Tbsp. chopped fresh chives

1. Place flour in a shallow dish. Place eggs in a second shallow dish. Place panko in a third shallow dish. Dredge chicken in flour. Dip chicken in egg; shake off any excess. Dredge chicken in panko.

2. Heat oil in a large nonstick skillet over medium-high. Add chicken; cook until golden brown on bottom, 3 to 4 minutes. Flip chicken, and cook until golden brown, 2 to 3 minutes. Remove from pan. Sprinkle with salt.

3. Whisk together mayonnaise, juice, sugar, and pepper in a large bowl. Add arugula, onion, celery, and capers; toss gently to coat. Divide among 4 plates; serve with chicken. Top with chives. Serves 4 (serving size: 1 cutlet and 1 cup salad)

CALORIES 371; FAT 16g (sat 2g, unsat 12g); PROTEIN 36g; CARB 19g; FIBER 2g; SUGARS 3g (added sugars 1g); SODIUM 523mg; CALC 6% DV; POTASSIUM 14% DV

Fast · Gluten Free
Make Ahead · Vegetarian

Fall Veggie Bowls with Charred Avocado

Hands-on: 20 min. **Total:** 20 min.
Packed with whole grains, plant-based protein, and a bounty of fall veggies and fruit, this nutritional knockout is a fresh take on Meatless Monday. Pick up precooked beets and preshredded butternut squash to save big on prep time.

4 cups water
2 (3-oz.) pkg. boil-in-bag quinoa
1 Tbsp. unsalted butter
2 cups grated peeled butternut squash
¼ cup chopped fresh flat-leaf parsley
1 firm-ripe avocado
Cooking spray
2 Tbsp. extra-virgin olive oil
2 Tbsp. rice vinegar
1 Tbsp. agave nectar
¾ tsp. kosher salt
¼ tsp. black pepper

6 oz. peeled cooked beets, quartered
1 medium Bosc pear, thinly sliced
1 cup thinly sliced radishes
2 oz. blue cheese, crumbled (about ½ cup)
¼ cup sliced almonds, toasted

1. Bring 4 cups water to a boil in a saucepan over high. Add quinoa packages; cover and cook 10 minutes. Drain. Empty packages into a large bowl.

2. Heat butter in a large skillet over high until foamy and light brown. Add squash, and cook, stirring often, until crisp-tender, 2 to 3 minutes. Remove from heat. Add squash and parsley to quinoa; toss to combine.

3. Heat a cast-iron skillet over high. Halve avocado and remove pit (do not peel). Cut each half in half lengthwise to make 4 wedges. Coat cut sides with cooking spray, and add to skillet, cut sides down. Cook until charred, 15 to 20 seconds per side. Remove from pan; peel and discard skins.

4. Whisk together oil, vinegar, agave nectar, salt, and pepper in a small bowl.

5. Divide quinoa mixture evenly among 4 bowls; top evenly with avocado, beets, pear, radishes, cheese, and almonds. Drizzle with dressing. Serves 4

CALORIES 511; FAT 27g (sat 7g, unsat 18g); PROTEIN 13g; CARB 58g; FIBER 12g; SUGARS 12g (added sugars 4g); SODIUM 555mg; CALC 17% DV; POTASSIUM 20% DV

RISE AND SHINE

Here's a hearty way to start your day: Hold the blue cheese and top each bowl with a fried egg to transform this easy recipe into a bountiful breakfast.

4 SAUCES FOR ANY PROTEIN

Fast · Gluten Free
Make Ahead · Vegetarian
Toasted Pecan and Kale Pesto
Spread this hearty pesto on pizza, or add a dollop to your favorite comforting fall soup.

Place 2 cups packed stemmed baby kale leaves, 1½ oz. grated Parmesan cheese (about ⅓ cup), 3 Tbsp. chopped toasted pecans, 3 Tbsp. olive oil, 2 tsp. lemon zest plus 1 tsp. fresh lemon juice, ¼ tsp. crushed red pepper, and ⅛ tsp. kosher salt in a food processor. Process until smooth, about 30 seconds, adding 1 to 2 Tbsp. water, if needed, to reach desired consistency. Serves 6 (serving size: 2 Tbsp.)

CALORIES 112; FAT 11g (sat 2g, unsat 8g); PROTEIN 2g; CARB 2g; FIBER 1g; SUGARS 0g; SODIUM 134mg; CALC 7% DV; POTASSIUM 1% DV

Fast · Gluten Free
Make Ahead
Apple Cider–Mustard Sauce
Golden raisins add a layer of jammy natural sweetness that perfectly balances this tangy sauce. Pork loin, turkey, salmon—you name it, this sauce is the perfect partner.

Combine 2 tsp. olive oil, ⅓ cup minced shallots, and 1 Tbsp. chopped fresh sage in a pan over medium-high; cook 2 minutes. Whisk together 1 cup unsalted chicken stock, ½ cup apple cider, 4 tsp. white wine vinegar, 1 Tbsp. Dijon mustard, 2 tsp. maple syrup, and 2 tsp. cornstarch; add to pan. Bring to a boil; stir in ½ cup golden raisins. Reduce heat; whisk 2 minutes. Stir in 1 Tbsp. unsalted butter, ½ tsp. pepper, and ⅛ tsp. kosher salt. Serves 6 (serving size: 3 Tbsp.)

CALORIES 108; FAT 3g (sat 1g, unsat 2g); PROTEIN 1g; CARB 17g; FIBER 1g; SUGARS 12g (added sugars 1g); SODIUM 127mg; CALC 2% DV; POTASSIUM 3% DV

Gluten Free • Make Ahead Vegetarian

Roasted Tomato-Garlic Sauce

Pick up low- or no-sodium canned tomatoes; regular canned varieties can contain a surprising amount of added salt that you won't miss. Use on pizzas or stirred into pasta.

Preheat oven to 425°F. Drain 1 (28-oz.) can unsalted whole tomatoes. Halve tomatoes; place on a foil-lined baking sheet coated with cooking spray. Top with 6 smashed peeled garlic cloves, 1 Tbsp. fresh thyme leaves, 1 Tbsp. fresh oregano leaves, and ¼ tsp. crushed red pepper. Drizzle with 2 Tbsp. olive oil. Roast 30 minutes. Cool 10 minutes. Transfer to blender; blend until smooth. Stir in ⅜ tsp. kosher salt. Serves 6 (serving size: 2 Tbsp.)

CALORIES 62; **FAT** 5g (sat 1g, unsat 4g); **PROTEIN** 0g; **CARB** 5g; **FIBER** 1g; **SUGARS** 3g (added sugars 0g); **SODIUM** 126mg; **CALC** 3% DV; **POTASSIUM** 4% DV

Fast • Gluten Free Make Ahead

Mushroom-Shallot Sauce

This is an easy and elegant sauce you'd expect from a fancy restaurant. Spoon it over steak and mashed potatoes for a solid comfort food upgrade.

Cook ⅓ cup chopped shallots and 1 tsp. chopped garlic in a large skillet coated with cooking spray over medium-high until softened, about 2 minutes. Add 4 cups sliced shiitake mushrooms; cook until browned, 5 minutes. Add ¾ cup unsalted chicken stock, ¼ cup white wine, and 2 tsp. balsamic vinegar; bring to a boil. Reduce heat to medium; cook until reduced by half. Stir in 1 Tbsp. unsalted butter, ¼ tsp. kosher salt, and ¼ tsp. black pepper. Serves 4 (serving size: about ¼ cup)

CALORIES 79; **FAT** 3g (sat 2g, unsat 1g); **PROTEIN** 2g; **CARB** 7g; **FIBER** 2g; **SUGARS** 3g (added sugars 0g); **SODIUM** 153mg; **CALC** 1% DV; **POTASSIUM** 5% DV

1 INGREDIENT, 3 SIDES

3 WAYS TO USE TURNIPS

Raw, roasted, or stir-fried, the humble turnip takes center stage in these easy recipes. The robust root is high in immunity-supporting vitamin C, great for cold and flu season. Pro tip: For milder, sweeter turnips, select small ones.

Fast • Gluten Free Vegetarian

Shaved Turnip Salad

Fruity and just slightly spicy, Aleppo pepper teams up with grapefruit juice in a knockout vinaigrette, providing the perfect balance for the raw turnips in this salad.

Section 1 medium-sized Ruby Red grapefruit; set segments aside. Whisk together 2 Tbsp. olive oil, 1½ Tbsp. grapefruit juice, 2 tsp. honey, ½ tsp. Aleppo pepper, and ⅜ tsp. kosher salt in a small bowl. Toss together 1½ cups shaved peeled turnip, 5 oz. mixed baby greens, 1 oz. crumbled goat cheese, 2 Tbsp. chopped toasted pistachios, reserved grapefruit segments, and vinaigrette in a large bowl. Serve immediately. Serves 4 (serving size: 1½ cups)

CALORIES 160; **FAT** 10g (sat 2g, unsat 8g); **PROTEIN** 4g; **CARB** 16g; **FIBER** 3g; **SUGARS** 10g (added sugars 3g); **SODIUM** 280mg; **CALC** 7% DV; **POTASSIUM** 4% DV

Fast • Gluten Free Vegetarian

Roasted Turnips and Potatoes

Roasting the turnips softens their peppery bite, resulting in a caramelized flavor that goes perfectly with smoked paprika. Pair with roasted pork tenderloin and a salad to make an easy, company-worthy dinner.

Preheat oven to 450°F. Heat 2 Tbsp. olive oil in a small skillet over medium. Add 2 minced garlic cloves and 1 tsp. smoked paprika; cook until fragrant, about 2 minutes. Peel 2 medium turnips, and cut into wedges. Combine turnip wedges, 12 oz. halved baby Yukon Gold potatoes, and garlic oil in a large bowl; toss. Place on a baking sheet lined with parchment paper. Bake until golden, about 20 minutes, stirring halfway through. Toss with 1 Tbsp. chopped fresh parsley, 1 Tbsp. fresh lime juice, and ½ tsp. kosher salt. Serves 4 (serving size: ½ cup)

CALORIES 144; **FAT** 7g (sat 1g, unsat 6g); **PROTEIN** 2g; **CARB** 21g; **FIBER** 3g; **SUGARS** 3g (added sugars 0g); **SODIUM** 309mg; **CALC** 9% DV; **POTASSIUM** 3% DV

Staff Favorite • Fast Make Ahead

Stir-Fried Turnips

This makes a great main if you add stir-fried beef, chicken, or tofu.

Cook 2 chopped thick center-cut bacon slices in a skillet over medium until crisp, about 8 minutes. Remove from skillet and set aside; reserve drippings in pan. Increase heat to medium-high; add 1 Tbsp. sesame oil, 2 cups peeled chopped turnips, and ½ cup chopped scallions. Cook, stirring, until browned, 4 to 5 minutes. Reduce heat to medium; cover and cook, stirring often, until tender, about 4 minutes. Uncover; stir in 3 cups baby spinach, and cook until wilted, about 1 minute. Stir in 1 Tbsp. lower-sodium soy sauce, 1 tsp. Sriracha chili sauce, ½ cup chopped fresh pineapple, and reserved bacon. Serves 4 (serving size: ½ cup)

CALORIES 109; **FAT** 5g (sat 1g, unsat 3g); **PROTEIN** 5g; **CARB** 11g; **FIBER** 3g; **SUGARS** 6g (added sugars 0g); **SODIUM** 360mg; **CALC** 8% DV; **POTASSIUM** 5% DV

Gluten Free

Pork Chops with Orange-Avocado Salsa

Hands-on: 20 min. **Total:** 45 min.
This one-pan dinner makes mealtime easy. The pork marinates while the potatoes and veggies roast, then everything takes a quick trip under the broiler to crisp up and concentrate the zesty flavors.

1 Tbsp. chopped fresh oregano
1 tsp. minced garlic
1 tsp. orange zest plus 1 Tbsp. fresh orange juice
1 tsp. ground cumin
2 Tbsp. olive oil, divided
2 tsp. lime zest, divided, plus 2 Tbsp. fresh lime juice, divided
1⅛ tsp. kosher salt, divided
1 tsp. black pepper, divided
4 (7-oz., 1-inch-thick) bone-in, center-cut pork chops
1 lb. red new potatoes, halved
½ large sweet onion, cut into ½-inch wedges (about 1 cup)
1 cup red bell pepper strips
Canola oil cooking spray
¾ cup cubed ripe avocado
1 cup orange segments
2 Tbsp. chopped fresh cilantro
1 Tbsp. finely chopped seeded jalapeño

1. Preheat oven to 425°F. Stir together oregano, garlic, orange zest and juice, cumin, 1 tablespoon oil, 1 teaspoon lime zest, 1 tablespoon lime juice, ½ teaspoon salt, and ½ teaspoon black pepper in a small bowl. Rub both sides of pork chops with mixture. Set aside.
2. Toss together potatoes, onion, bell pepper, ½ teaspoon salt, ¼ teaspoon black pepper, and remaining 1 tablespoon oil in a bowl. Spread mixture in an even layer on a rimmed baking sheet coated with cooking spray. Bake at 425°F until potatoes are just tender, 20 to 22 minutes, stirring once.
3. Stir together the avocado, orange, cilantro, jalapeño, remaining 1 teaspoon lime zest, remaining 1 tablespoon lime juice, remaining ⅛ teaspoon salt, and remaining ¼ teaspoon pepper. Set aside.
4. Remove pan from oven. Move potato mixture toward the edges, leaving just enough room in center for pork chops. Place pork chops in center of pan, and return to oven. Bake at 425°F for 5 more minutes. Turn on broiler to high, and broil until a thermometer inserted in thickest part of pork registers 140°F, 3 to 4 more minutes. Serve with salsa. Serves 4 (serving size: 1 pork chop, about ¾ cup vegetables, and ½ cup salsa)

CALORIES 505; **FAT** 19g (sat 4g, unsat 13g); **PROTEIN** 48g; **CARB** 34g; **FIBER** 6g; **SUGARS** 7g (added sugars 0g); **SODIUM** 668mg; **CALC** 8% DV; **POTASSIUM** 23% DV

4 GO-WITH-ANYTHING SIDES

Fast • Gluten Free
Make Ahead • Vegetarian
Kohlrabi and Apple Slaw
Kohlrabi is a good source of vitamin C; it makes a great stand-in for celery in this riff on Waldorf salad.

Whisk together ¼ cup canola mayonnaise, 1½ tsp. apple cider vinegar, 1 tsp. honey, and ¼ tsp. black pepper in a large bowl. Add 1 (12-oz.) kohlrabi, peeled and cut into thin strips; 1 small Fuji apple, unpeeled and thinly sliced; and 2 Tbsp. thinly sliced scallions. Toss to coat. Top with 2 oz. shaved aged Gouda cheese. Serves 4 (serving size: 1 cup)

CALORIES 133; **FAT** 8g (sat 3g, unsat 5g); **PROTEIN** 5g; **CARB** 11; **FIBER** 4g; **SUGARS** 7g (added sugars 1g); **SODIUM** 244mg; **CALC** 13% DV; **POTASSIUM** 9% DV

Fast • Gluten Free
Make Ahead • Vegetarian
Ginger-Orange Carrots
This recipe is great for entertaining: Simply roast the carrots ahead of time and broil just before serving.

Preheat oven to 450°F. Cut an unpeeled orange in half. Cut one half into thin half-moons; toss with 12 oz. carrots, 2 Tbsp. olive oil, 4 unpeeled garlic cloves, 6 thyme sprigs, ¾ tsp. ground ginger, ⅛ tsp. cayenne pepper, and ⅛ tsp. kosher salt on a baking sheet. Roast at 450°F 15 minutes, stirring once. Turn on broiler; broil 2 minutes. Discard thyme. Peel garlic; place garlic and carrots on a platter. Squeeze remaining orange half over carrots. Sprinkle with ¼ tsp. kosher salt. Serves 4 (serving size: 3 oz.)

CALORIES 122; **FAT** 7g (sat 1g, unsat 6g); **PROTEIN** 1g; **CARB** 14g; **FIBER** 3g; **SUGARS** 7g (added sugars 0g); **SODIUM** 240mg; **CALC** 5% DV; **POTASSIUM** 8% DV

Fast • Gluten Free
Vegetarian
Frizzled Kale with Chiles
Massaging the kale first helps tenderize it slightly; this technique is also handy when using this fibrous green in raw preparations like salads and slaws. Serve with steak or top with sunny-side up eggs.

Preheat broiler to high with oven rack in middle of oven. Rub ¼ cup olive oil into 6 cups packed torn lacinato kale leaves in a large bowl for 30 seconds. Add 1 thinly sliced unseeded red Fresno chile; toss to coat. Place on a baking sheet lined with aluminum foil; broil until crispy, 3 to 4 minutes, stirring after 2 minutes. Drizzle with 2 tsp. red wine vinegar, and sprinkle with ½ tsp. kosher salt. Serves 4 (serving size: 1 cup)

CALORIES 133; **FAT** 14g (sat 2g, unsat 12g); **PROTEIN** 1g; **CARB** 2g; **FIBER** 1g; **SUGARS** 1g (added sugars 0g); **SODIUM** 250mg; **CALC** 4% DV; **POTASSIUM** 3% DV

Fast • Gluten Free
Vegetarian
Spiced Apples and Cabbage

This tasty spin on skillet apples gets a fiber upgrade thanks to crunchy green cabbage. Pair with roasted pork tenderloin or chicken.

Cook 3 cups apple wedges in 1½ tsp. unsalted butter in a skillet over medium 5 to 6 minutes. Stir in 2 tsp. apple cider vinegar, 2 tsp. light brown sugar, ½ tsp. caraway seeds, and ⅛ tsp. ground allspice; cook 1 minute. Add 3 cups thinly sliced green cabbage, 1½ tsp. unsalted butter, ½ tsp. kosher salt, and ¼ tsp. black pepper; cook 2 minutes. Top with ¼ cup pomegranate arils and 2 Tbsp. chopped fresh dill. Serves 4 (serving size: 1 cup)

CALORIES 90; **FAT** 3g (sat 2g, unsat 1g); **PROTEIN** 1g; **CARB** 16g; **FIBER** 3g; **SUGARS** 12g (added sugars 2g); **SODIUM** 251mg; **CALC** 3% DV; **POTASSIUM** 4% DV

EXCLUSIVE SNEAK PEEK: *EVERYDAY SLOW COOKER*
Make Ahead

Asian Short Ribs

Hands-on: 20 min. **Total:** 8 hr. 20 min. These short ribs are fall-off-the-bone tender. If you can't find short ribs, pick up a boneless chuck roast and cut it into 2-inch chunks instead.

8 lean bone-in beef short ribs (about 2¼ lb.), trimmed
½ tsp. kosher salt
½ tsp. black pepper
1½ Tbsp. canola oil, divided
2 cups sliced fresh shiitake mushroom caps
1 Tbsp. finely chopped garlic
2 tsp. finely chopped fresh ginger
½ cup unsalted beef stock
¼ cup packed light brown sugar
¼ cup rice vinegar
1½ Tbsp. lower-sodium soy sauce
1 tsp. crushed red pepper

1. Sprinkle ribs with salt and pepper. Heat 1 tablespoon oil in a large skillet over medium-high. Add half of the ribs to skillet; cook, turning occasionally, until browned on all sides, about 8 minutes. Transfer ribs to a 6-quart slow cooker; discard drippings in skillet. (Don't wipe skillet clean.) Repeat procedure with remaining ribs. Add remaining 1½ teaspoons oil to skillet; stir in mushrooms, garlic, and ginger. Cook, stirring often, until mushrooms soften slightly, about 4 minutes; transfer mushroom mixture to slow cooker. Add beef stock, brown sugar, vinegar, soy sauce, and red pepper to slow cooker. Cover and cook on low until ribs are tender, about 8 hours.
2. Transfer ribs to a serving platter. Reserve cooking liquid in the slow cooker; skim fat from surface. Drizzle ribs with reserved cooking liquid. Serves 4 (serving size: 2 short ribs and ¼ cup sauce)

CALORIES 334; **FAT** 19g (sat 6g, unsat 11g); **PROTEIN** 24g; **CARB** 16g; **FIBER** 1g; **SUGARS** 14g (added sugars 13g); **SODIUM** 583mg; **CALC** 3% DV; **POTASSIUM** 8% DV

Make Ahead

Braised Pork with Potatoes and Shallots

Hands-on: 20 min. **Total:** 8 hr. 25 min. Use preground fennel and coriander seeds if you're short on time; you'll lose the texture the crushed seeds provide, but you'll get the same great flavor. Substitute 2 teaspoons each of the ground seeds for 1 tablespoon whole.

1 Tbsp. fennel seeds
1 Tbsp. coriander seeds
1 tsp. black pepper
1½ tsp. kosher salt, divided
3 lb. bone-in pork shoulder roast (Boston butt), trimmed
1 Tbsp. olive oil
¾ cup unsalted chicken stock
¼ cup dry white wine
2 Tbsp. lower-sodium soy sauce
1 lb. sweet potatoes, peeled and cut into 1½-inch pieces
1 lb. baby Yukon Gold potatoes, halved
4 large shallots, peeled and halved lengthwise (about 4 oz.)
2 large fresh thyme sprigs
Fresh thyme leaves (optional)

1. Place fennel seeds and coriander seeds in a spice grinder; pulse until coarsely ground. Stir together ground seeds, pepper, and 1 teaspoon salt in a small bowl; sprinkle evenly over pork.
2. Heat oil in a large nonstick skillet over medium-high. Add pork to skillet; cook, turning to brown on all sides, about 8 minutes. Transfer pork to a 5- to 6-quart slow cooker; reserve drippings in skillet.
3. Add chicken stock, wine, and soy sauce to reserved drippings in skillet; bring to a boil over medium-high, stirring to loosen browned bits from bottom of skillet. Pour mixture over pork. Add sweet potatoes, Yukon Gold potatoes, shallots, and thyme sprigs to slow cooker. Cover and cook on LOW until pork and vegetables are tender, about 8 hours.
4. Transfer pork to a cutting board, and let rest 5 minutes. Transfer vegetables to a platter; reserve cooking liquid in slow cooker. Discard thyme sprigs. Break pork into large pieces; discard bone. Place pork on platter with vegetables; sprinkle with remaining ½ teaspoon salt. Garnish with thyme leaves, if desired. Serve with reserved cooking liquid. Serves 8 (serving size: ⅔ cup pork, ⅔ cup vegetables, and ¼ cup sauce)

CALORIES 280; **FAT** 9g (sat 3g, unsat 6g); **PROTEIN** 23g; **CARB** 24g; **FIBER** 4g; **SUGARS** 4g (added sugars 0g); **SODIUM** 627mg; **CALC** 5% DV; **POTASSIUM** 12% DV

NEW-SCHOOL TUNA NOODLE CASSEROLE

A comfort-filled classic, traditional tuna casserole features a cast of hefty characters (cream, cheese, and noodles) and delivers nearly 700 calories and a day's worth of sat fat in one helping.

To introduce fresher ingredients while staying true to the original, we start by bolstering the filling with meaty mushrooms, lots of aromatics, and herbs. Tomato paste adds a tangy counterpoint to the creamy, noodle-coating sauce, while Dijon mustard and lemon zest add zing.

Canned tuna is a pantry staple that takes center stage in our remake (with just as many beneficial omega-3s as fresh). In lieu of a breadcrumb or potato chip topper, we use fresh dill and sharp cheddar to round out this dinner with bright flavor and cheesy goodness for less sodium.

Make Ahead

Tuna Noodle Casserole

Hands-on: 25 min. **Total:** 55 min. Boost the veggies, cut the heavy cream, and drop 250 calories with our modern makeover.

12 oz. uncooked whole-wheat egg noodles
1 Tbsp. canola oil
8 oz. cremini mushrooms, chopped
1 cup chopped yellow onion
1 Tbsp. minced garlic
1 Tbsp. chopped fresh thyme leaves
2 Tbsp. unsalted butter
3 Tbsp. all-purpose flour
2 cups unsalted chicken stock
2½ cups 2% reduced-fat milk
1 Tbsp. tomato paste
2 tsp. Dijon mustard
2 tsp. lemon zest plus 1½ Tbsp. fresh lemon juice
1¼ tsp. kosher salt
½ tsp. freshly ground black pepper
3 (4-oz.) cans unsalted albacore tuna in water, drained
2 Tbsp. chopped fresh dill, plus more for garnish
Cooking spray
2 oz. sharp cheddar cheese, shredded (about ½ cup)

1. Preheat oven to 375°F. Cook noodles according to package instructions until very al dente, omitting salt and fat. Drain and transfer to a large bowl.
2. Heat oil in a large high-sided skillet over medium. Add mushrooms; cook until softened, about 4 minutes. Add onion and garlic; cook until tender, about 4 more minutes. Add thyme; cook until fragrant, about 1 minute, stirring constantly.
3. Add butter; stir to melt. Whisk in flour; cook until roux is golden, about 1 minute. Whisking constantly, add stock; bring to a boil. Reduce to a simmer; whisk in milk, tomato paste, mustard, lemon zest and juice, salt, and pepper. Return to a simmer; simmer 2 to 3 minutes. Pour mixture into bowl with noodles. Stir in tuna and dill.
4. Coat a 13- x 9-inch baking dish with cooking spray. Transfer tuna mixture to baking dish; top with cheese. Bake at 375°F until bubbly and cheese is melted, about 15 minutes. Let stand at room temperature 5 to 10 minutes. Garnish with dill. Serves 6 (serving size: 2 cups)

CALORIES 439; FAT 13g (sat 6g, unsat 5g); PROTEIN 30g; CARB 55g; FIBER 7g; SUGARS 9g (added sugars 0g); SODIUM 640mg; CALC 21% DV; POTASSIUM 11% DV

HEALTHIER TUNA CASSEROLE

OUR LIGHTENED TWIST ON THIS CLASSIC FAMILY FAVORITE CUTS TWO-THIRDS OF THE SATURATED FAT BUT KEEPS ALL OF THE COMFORTING APPEAL.

THE SAUCE
Building a roux-thickened sauce in place of cream of mushroom soup or heavy cream cuts saturated fat and sodium.

THE FILLING
Mushrooms add nutritious heft to the tuna-noodle filling while upping the veggie count. Garlic and herbs add big flavor for few calories.

THE TOPPING
Instead of mixing cheese into the filling, where its flavor might get diluted, we reserve it for the topping, which locks in moisture.

SECRETS FROM A SANDWICH ARCHITECT

BY ANDREA NGUYEN

This Ultimate Vegetarian Club is the result of a lifetime of lessons and sandwich love.

Some people just can't stop baking pies; I'm crazy about sandwiches. My obsession started in the late 1970s. My family had recently fled war-torn Vietnam and didn't have much money, so I qualified for the free school lunch program. However, after trying the cafeteria's pizza and burgers, I began preparing my own lunches. Sandwiches were easy and thrillingly doable for an elementary schooler. Back then, the sandwich that I knew best was the Vietnamese banh mi. We had simple ones for breakfast made from baguette, butter, homemade pâté, cucumber, salt, and pepper. I'd make an extra one with sliced white bread for school; I didn't want to appear too different from my classmates.

It was fun to construct sandwiches, to cut them to reveal their handsome cross sections. The creative bready adventures were departures from making wontons under my mom's watchful eye, and besides, I got to practice my knife skills. My after-school activities sometimes involved tinkering with tiny sandwich snacks made with luncheon meats, saltine crackers, and margarine.

I made mistakes and learned over time. Piling ingredients in the center made a mountain-shaped sandwich that was hard to eat. A too-thick slice of tomato tucked in the middle may slip and slide or even go airborne, causing the sandwich to collapse in your hands. Building a delicious sandwich is a balancing act; the elements should be thoughtfully layered and proportioned so that the flavors pop and the sandwich holds together, bite after bite.

My lessons continued in the early 1990s, when I started dabbling in professional cooking and got a job as a pantry cook at City, a landmark Los Angeles restaurant. Owners Mary Sue Milliken and Susan Feniger had an amazing knack for crafting sandwiches packed with vibrant colors, textures, and flavors. My favorite was the vegetarian club, a tour de force prepared with walnut bread grilled to a light smokiness over an open flame. Layered between the bread was a spread of rich hummus, meaty grilled eggplant, plush roasted red pepper, spicy arugula, salty olive puree, creamy avocado, and refreshing tomato and cucumber, plus a kickin' mustard-horseradish mayo. There was just enough of each item to create a symphonic sandwich experience and hold things together. It blew other restaurants' conventional turkey and bacon club combinations out of the water.

I loved the sandwich but never wrote down the details to replicate it. Mary Sue and Susan kindly emailed a copy of the stained recipe from the restaurant's kitchen binder. They also noted tweaks to help me come up with this version.

With all its moving parts, the recipe seemed complex. But once I prepared the components and got everything in place, there was pure synergy, and I saw the path that led me from my early experiments to sandwich magic. Then I happily lunched on vegetarian clubs for days.

Fast • Vegetarian

The Ultimate Vegetarian Club

Hands-on: 20 min. **Total:** 30 min. Taking time and care with each component—like getting a nice char on the eggplant—is the secret to this standout sandwich.

1 Japanese eggplant, cut into ¼-inch-thick rounds
⅜ tsp. kosher salt, divided
⅜ tsp. freshly ground black pepper, divided
Cooking spray
2 Tbsp. canola mayonnaise
1 Tbsp. stone-ground mustard
1 Tbsp. prepared horseradish
⅓ cup pitted kalamata olives plus 1 tsp. olive brine
8 (¼-inch-thick) slices seeded whole-grain bread
½ cup hummus
1 cup roasted red pepper, sliced
1 ripe avocado, peeled and thinly sliced
1 Roma tomato, sliced
2 Persian cucumbers, thinly sliced
1 to 1½ cups arugula

1. Season eggplant with ¼ teaspoon salt and ¼ teaspoon pepper. Generously coat with cooking spray. Heat a cast-iron grill pan over medium-high. Working in batches, add eggplant, cut sides down, to pan, and grill 2 to 3 minutes, turning 1 or 2 times. Transfer to a plate; let cool.
2. Stir together mayonnaise, mustard, and horseradish in a small bowl. Set aside. Using a small food processor, whirl the olives and brine into a spreadable puree.
3. Grill bread directly over a medium flame, turning often, about 1 minute to slightly char the surface and impart a bit of smokiness. Let cool briefly.

4. Spread about 2 tablespoons hummus on each of 4 bread slices, and top evenly with eggplant, olive puree, roasted red pepper, avocado, tomato, cucumber, and arugula. Spread 1½ teaspoons mayonnaise mixture on each of the remaining 4 bread slices. Sprinkle evenly with remaining ⅛ teaspoon salt and remaining ⅛ teaspoon pepper, and top the sandwiches. If you like, add a little more arugula for bite. Serve sandwiches whole or cut in half. Serves 4 (serving size: 1 sandwich)

CALORIES 421; FAT 39g (sat 2g, unsat 36g); PROTEIN 13g; CARB 48g; FIBER 15g; SUGARS 4g (added sugars 0g); SODIUM 734mg; CALC 7% DV; POTASSIUM 14% DV

THE PICKY EATER GURU

ONE-PAN DINNERS FOR BUSY HOME COOKS

BY GINA HOMOLKA

Simplify your life with recipes from Gina Homolka's new cookbook that trim prep time and dish duties.

Life is busy! Between balancing work, keeping up with kids and their homework, and making time for ourselves, it's a wonder any of us have time to even think about dinner. And yet, it's so important to feed our families meals that are not just healthy but tasty, too. As much as I enjoy cooking, I absolutely hate the cleanup, especially tackling dirty pots and pans. I develop and test recipes all day, almost every day, and then I cook dinner on top of that, so those dishes stack up quickly. When it comes to weeknight meals, I'm always looking for a streamlined

way to get dinner on the table. Quicker cleanup means more time for family or—get ready for this crazy idea—for yourself. That's where one-dish meals come in. The "less is more" strategy of one-pot cooking means you end up with fantastic dinners, such as these sheet pan mini meatloaves or my one-skillet Fiesta Chicken and Carrot Rice, with hardly any fuss at all. My picky kids are huge fans of these comforting recipes, and now that I've given them a one-pan makeover, they're an extra-big hit with me, too.

Gluten Free

Fiesta Chicken and Carrot Rice

Hands-on: 30 min. **Total:** 35 min.

14 oz. carrots, peeled and chopped
4 (4-oz.) boneless, skinless chicken cutlets
1 tsp. kosher salt, divided
¼ tsp. garlic powder
¼ tsp. black pepper, divided
Olive oil cooking spray
2 tsp. olive oil
1 cup chopped white onion
1 small jalapeño, seeded and minced, plus ½ jalapeño, thinly sliced
2 garlic cloves, minced
1½ cups fresh or thawed frozen corn kernels
1 cup canned unsalted black beans, drained and rinsed
¼ cup chopped cilantro, divided
2 Tbsp. fresh lime juice
¼ cup low-sodium salsa
4 slices pepper-Jack cheese
¼ cup chopped fresh tomatoes
2 Tbsp. sliced scallions
4 oz. diced avocado

1. Pulse carrots in a food processor until they resemble rice. Place in a kitchen towel; squeeze out excess liquid.

2. Season chicken with ½ teaspoon salt, garlic powder, and ⅛ teaspoon pepper. Heat a large, deep skillet over high. Coat with cooking spray. Add chicken to skillet, and cook 3 to 4 minutes per side. Set aside.

3. Reduce heat to medium; add olive oil, onion, minced jalapeño, and garlic. Cook, stirring constantly, about 2 minutes. Add carrots; increase heat to high, and add remaining ½ teaspoon salt and remaining ⅛ teaspoon pepper. Cook until carrots are slightly tender, about 6 minutes. Add corn and beans; cook 1 to 2 minutes. Stir in 2 tablespoons cilantro and lime juice.

4. Place chicken on carrots. Top evenly with salsa, jalapeño slices, and cheese. Reduce heat to low; cover and cook until cheese melts, about 5 minutes. Top with tomatoes, scallions, avocado, and remaining 2 tablespoons cilantro. Serves 4 (serving size: 4 oz. chicken and 1 cup vegetable mixture)

CALORIES 471; FAT 18g (sat 6g, unsat 11g); PROTEIN 38g; CARB 43g; FIBER 11g; SUGARS 10g (added sugars 0g); SODIUM 683mg; CALC 9% DV; POTASSIUM 27% DV

Petite Meatloaf Dinner

Hands-on: 10 min. **Total:** 35 min.

Olive oil cooking spray
1 lb. 93% lean ground turkey
⅓ cup quick-cooking oats
6 Tbsp. unsalted ketchup, divided
¼ cup finely chopped onion
1 large egg
1 tsp. dried marjoram
1 tsp. kosher salt, divided
2 tsp. lower-sodium Worcestershire sauce
12 oz. fresh green beans, trimmed
10 oz. small carrots, trimmed
2 Tbsp. olive oil
½ tsp. garlic powder
¼ tsp. freshly ground black pepper

1. Preheat oven to 450°F. Coat a large rimmed baking sheet with cooking spray. Combine turkey, oats, 3 tablespoons ketchup, onion, egg, marjoram, and ½ teaspoon salt in a medium bowl. Divide into 4 (4- x 2 ½-inch) loaves; place, evenly spaced, on prepared pan. Combine Worcestershire sauce and remaining 3 tablespoons ketchup in a small bowl; brush over loaves.
2. Combine green beans, carrots, olive oil, garlic powder, pepper, and remaining ½ teaspoon salt in a large bowl. Scatter vegetables around loaves. Bake at 450°F for 12 minutes. Turn vegetables. Continue to bake until loaves are no longer pink in the center, 12 to 15 more minutes. Serves 4 (serving size: 1 meatloaf and ¾ cup vegetables)

CALORIES 373; **FAT** 17g (sat 4g, unsat 11g); **PROTEIN** 30g; **CARB** 29g; **FIBER** 6g; **SUGARS** 12g (added sugars 1g); **SODIUM** 678mg; **CALC** 12% DV; **POTASSIUM** 11% DV

---

3 WAYS TO USE ALEPPO PEPPER

With a gentle spiciness and a flavor like toasted sun-dried tomatoes, this coarsely ground Middle Eastern spice is great for adding flavor and color to recipes without cranking up the heat too much.

Gluten Free • Make Ahead Vegetarian
Spicy Dark Chocolate and Tahini Bark
This treat will keep you from raiding your kids' stash of Halloween candy.

Microwave 1 cup chopped dark chocolate in a small bowl until melted, about 90 seconds, stirring every 30 seconds. Repeat process in a separate bowl with ¼ cup peanut butter chips and 1 Tbsp. tahini. Spread chocolate in an even layer on a parchment paper–lined baking sheet. Spoon peanut butter mixture over chocolate; swirl together with a knife. Sprinkle with 2 Tbsp. Aleppo pepper and ½ tsp. flaky sea salt. Freeze until firm, about 1 hour. Break into pieces. Serves 10 (serving size: about ⅓ cup)

CALORIES 164; **FAT** 10g (sat 6g, unsat 4g); **PROTEIN** 3g; **CARB** 16g; **FIBER** 2g; **SUGARS** 11g (added sugars 11g); **SODIUM** 173mg; **CALC** 1% DV; **POTASSIUM** 1% DV

Make Ahead
Aleppo-Spiced Meatball Salad
To take this salad to the next level, roast the cherry tomatoes with the meatballs to concentrate their flavor.

Preheat oven to 400°F. Stir together 1 lb. 90% lean ground beef, ⅓ cup uncooked bulgur, ¼ cup minced red onion, 5 tsp. Aleppo pepper, 1 ½ tsp. ground cumin, ½ tsp. kosher salt, and 1 beaten large egg in a bowl. Form into 20 meatballs; arrange evenly on a baking sheet. Bake until cooked through, 13 to 15 minutes. Whisk together 3 Tbsp. water, 2 Tbsp. tahini, 1 Tbsp. canola oil, 2 tsp. fresh lemon juice, ¼ tsp. minced garlic, and ⅛ tsp. kosher salt. Divide 4 cups mixed salad greens, 1 pt. cherry tomatoes, and meatballs among 4 plates; drizzle with dressing. Sprinkle with 1 tsp. Aleppo pepper; serve with 1 whole-wheat pita, cut into 8 wedges. Serves 4 (serving size: 5 meatballs, 1 cup salad, 2 pita wedges, and 1 ½ Tbsp. dressing)

CALORIES 447; **FAT** 22g (sat 6g, unsat 13g); **PROTEIN** 32g; **CARB** 35g; **FIBER** 7g; **SUGARS** 4g (added sugars 0g); **SODIUM** 703mg; **CALC** 10% DV; **POTASSIUM** 17% DV

Gluten Free • Make Ahead Vegetarian
Roasted Chickpea Snack Mix
This fiber-filled, gluten-free snack mix is great sprinkled over salads to give them a little spicy crunch.

Preheat oven to 375°F. Stir together 1 (15-oz.) can drained and rinsed chickpeas, 1 Tbsp. olive oil, 1 Tbsp. Aleppo pepper, 1 tsp. garlic powder, and ½ tsp. kosher salt in a bowl. Transfer to a rimmed baking sheet. Bake 15 minutes. Using the same bowl, stir together 1 ½ cups coarsely chopped walnuts, 1 cup chopped kale, 1 Tbsp. olive oil, 1 Tbsp. Aleppo pepper, 1 tsp. garlic powder, and ½ tsp. kosher salt. Stir into baked chickpeas. Bake until kale is crispy, 18 to 20 minutes. Stir in 2 tsp. lemon zest. Serves 10 (serving size: about ⅓ cup)

CALORIES 172; **FAT** 13g (sat 1g, unsat 11g); **PROTEIN** 5g; **CARB** 10g; **FIBER** 3g; **SUGARS** 1g (added sugars 0g); **SODIUM** 250mg; **CALC** 4% DV; **POTASSIUM** 4% DV

Make Ahead • Vegetarian

Triple-Apple Pie

Hands-on: 30 min. **Total:** 2 hr.

2 (9-inch) refrigerated whole-
    wheat pie doughs (such as
    Wholly Wholesome)
Cooking spray
⅓ cup packed brown sugar
2 Tbsp. unsalted butter
1 Tbsp. water
¼ tsp. kosher salt
2 Tbsp. whole milk
1 tsp. vanilla extract
1 (10-oz.) Braeburn apple, peeled
    and grated
¼ cup all-purpose flour, divided
1½ lb. Fuji apples, peeled, cored, and
    cut into 12 wedges each
1½ lb. Honeycrisp apples, peeled,
    cored, and cut into 12 wedges each
1 large egg white, lightly beaten

1. Preheat oven to 375°F. Roll 1 dough into a 13-inch circle on a floured surface; fit into a 9-inch pie plate coated with cooking spray. Chill until ready to use.

2. Heat sugar, butter, 1 tablespoon water, and salt in a skillet over medium-high; cook 1 minute, stirring constantly. Stir in milk and vanilla. Bring to a boil, and cook, stirring constantly, until thickened, about 1 minute. Remove from heat; let stand 10 minutes.

3. Combine grated apple and 1 tablespoon flour in a bowl. Add apple wedges and remaining 3 tablespoons flour; toss to coat. Pour sugar mixture over apples; toss. Nestle apple mixture into piecrust in pie plate.

4. Roll remaining pie dough into an 11½-inch circle on floured surface. Place over apples in pie plate. Fold dough edge under, flute edges, and trim off any excess. Brush egg white over crust. Cut 6 to 8 (1-inch-long) slits in crust. Bake on bottom rack at 375°F for 1 hour or until browned and bubbling. Tent with foil after 40 minutes to prevent overbrowning, if needed. Remove from oven; cool on a wire rack. Cut pie into 10 wedges. Serves 10 (serving size: 1 slice)

CALORIES 295; **FAT** 13g (sat 5g, unsat 7g); **PROTEIN** 3g; **CARB** 46g; **FIBER** 4g; **SUGARS** 23g (added sugars 10g); **SODIUM** 216mg; **CALC** 3% DV; **POTASSIUM** 0% DV

> **Three kinds of apples give our pie big flavor—so you need less added sugar and butter.**

PIE CHART

HOW NEXT-LEVEL STORE-BOUGHT CRUST, SMART TOUCHES OF FAT AND FLAVORING, AND A TRIO OF APPLES FIT TOGETHER FABULOUSLY

PREMADE CRUST
Convenience doesn't have to be less healthy. We love Wholly Wholesome's grain-forward flavor and crumbly texture.

BROWN SUGAR
The apples deliver plenty of natural sweetness here, so we can use less sugar—brown makes more of a flavor impact.

VANILLA EXTRACT
A teaspoon boosts apple flavor. You don't taste vanilla, but you'd think something was missing without it.

BRAEBURN APPLE
This is a juicy baking apple with great sweet-tart balance. Grating disperses the flavor throughout the filling.

HONEYCRISP AND FUJI
These highly sweet apples don't turn mushy when they're baked, which also helps the wedges keep their juices.

BUTTER
You need just a couple knobs to add richness to the filling. Many recipes use more, but that can mute apple flavor.

LOW-CARB LASAGNA

Silky roasted butternut squash stands in for noodles in this more nutritious take on the starchy pasta casserole.

Make Ahead • Vegetarian

Butternut Squash and Spinach Lasagna

Hands-on: 35 min. **Total:** 1 hr. 35 min.

2 tsp. canola oil
1¼ cups vertically sliced red onion
1½ Tbsp. sliced garlic
1 (6-oz.) pkg. baby spinach
¾ cup plain 0% fat-free Greek yogurt
⅓ cup 1% low-fat milk
3 oz. sliced part-skim provolone cheese, torn into small pieces
1½ Tbsp. all-purpose flour
1 tsp. kosher salt
2 large eggs
1 (20-oz.) butternut squash
Cooking spray
1 cup part-skim ricotta cheese
1½ oz. Gruyère cheese, grated (⅓ cup)

1. Preheat oven to 350°F. Heat oil in a large skillet over medium-high. Add onion and garlic; sauté 4 minutes. Add spinach; sauté until wilted. Remove from heat. Place yogurt, milk, and provolone in a blender; blend 20 seconds. Add flour, salt, and eggs; blend 1 minute.

2. Peel neck of the squash. Cut neck from bulb. Cut neck lengthwise into 24 (⅛-inch-thick) slices using a knife or mandoline. (Use bulb for more slices if needed.)

3. Place squash slices in an 8-inch square microwave-safe glass baking dish; cover with plastic wrap. Microwave until squash slices are almost tender, about 4 minutes. Remove squash from dish. Coat dish with cooking spray; spread ½ cup yogurt mixture in bottom of dish.

4. Shingle one-third of squash over yogurt mixture. Top with one-third of ricotta cheese, one-third of spinach mixture, and one-third of remaining yogurt mixture. Repeat procedure twice, ending with yogurt mixture.

5. Sprinkle lasagna with Gruyère. Cover dish with foil; bake at 350°F for 50 minutes. Remove from oven. Turn on broiler with oven rack about 8 inches from top. Remove foil from dish; broil 4 minutes or until lightly browned. Remove from oven; loosely cover, and let stand 20 minutes. Cut into 6 rectangles. Serves 6 (serving size: 1 rectangle)

CALORIES 252; FAT 12g (sat 6g, unsat 5g); PROTEIN 19g; CARB 17g; FIBER 3g; SUGARS 6g (added sugars 0g); SODIUM 597mg; CALC 43% DV; POTASSIUM 9% DV

THE STEPS

1. BLEND FILLING
Puree the yogurt and provolone mixture. It's thin now, but the flour thickens and stabilizes the dairy while it cooks.

2. SLICE SQUASH
Whether you use a mandoline or knife here, make the slices as uniformly thick as possible so they cook evenly.

3. PRECOOK PLANKS
A quick steam in the microwave makes the squash planks more pliable and better able to absorb flavors.

4. LAYER EVENLY
Shingle the squash slices and spread the ricotta, spinach, and yogurt fillings in even layers to enjoy each in every bite.

Staff Favorite • Gluten Free
Make Ahead • Vegetarian

Butterscotch Crispy Rice Bars

Hands-on: 15 min. **Total:** 45 min.

1 Tbsp. unsalted butter
1 (7-oz.) jar marshmallow creme
½ cup cashew butter
6 cups brown rice crisps cereal (such as Barbara's)
Cooking spray
¼ cup candy-coated milk chocolate pieces
2 oz. bittersweet chocolate, coarsely chopped
2 oz. butterscotch chips
2 tsp. 2% reduced-fat milk

1. Melt butter in a large saucepan over medium, and cook, stirring occasionally, until browned, about 3 minutes. Stir in marshmallow creme and cashew butter. Cook, stirring often, 2 minutes. Remove from heat; stir in cereal until evenly coated.
2. Coat a 13- x 9-inch baking dish with cooking spray. Press cereal mixture into baking dish; top with milk chocolate pieces, pressing to adhere.
3. Bring 2 inches of water to a boil in a medium saucepan over medium-high. Place a heatproof bowl on top of saucepan. (Water shouldn't touch bottom of bowl.) Add bittersweet chocolate to the bowl; cook, stirring occasionally, 1 minute or until chocolate is melted. Drizzle over cereal mixture.
4. Wipe the bowl clean. Add the butterscotch chips to bowl; return to top of saucepan. Reduce heat to low, and cook, stirring often, 4 minutes or until melted. Add milk; whisk until smooth. Drizzle over cereal mixture. Chill, uncovered, 20 minutes. Slice into 16 bars. Serves 16 (serving size: 1 bar)

CALORIES 192; **FAT** 8g (sat 3g, unsat 4g); **PROTEIN** 2g; **CARB** 24g; **FIBER** 1g; **SUGARS** 13g (added sugars 10g); **SODIUM** 40mg; **CALC** 2% DV; **POTASSIUM** 2% DV

NOTE FROM THE EDITOR: AT MY TABLE

Every year when the afternoon sun draws longer shadows, a Pavlovian urge kicks in to text Willis the wood guy. A few days later he backs up his red 1978 Ford pickup truck to the top of my driveway and stacks a payload of seasoned white and red oak into a tidy pile under the magnolia tree. We make small talk as Willis smokes a Pall Mall and rests his elbows on the tailgate, our dog Birdie wagging her tail at his feet. Willis reminds me that he grew up down the road from my house, remembers it being built in 1967, and says that they don't make chimneys as sturdy as mine anymore.

A series of fall rituals ensues, rituals that give comfort and pleasure: Saturday morning pancakes and Sunday braises and stews; the clang of a wooden spoon on an enameled cast-iron pot; supper clubs on the calendar; a pumpkin patch to visit; and fires to build as the sun retreats.

Chicken and Mushroom Stew

Hands-on: 40 min. **Total:** 1 hr. 40 min.

2 oz. chopped bacon
1 Tbsp. olive oil
1¼ lb. boneless, skinless chicken thighs, cut into 2-inch pieces
¾ tsp. kosher salt
½ tsp. black pepper
8 oz. button mushrooms, quartered
1 medium carrot, diced
1 medium onion, diced
3 garlic cloves, chopped
2 bay leaves
¼ cup apple cider vinegar
3 Tbsp. unsalted butter
¼ cup all-purpose flour
1 cup 2% reduced-fat milk
2 cups low-sodium chicken broth
½ tsp. dry mustard
2 Tbsp. chopped fresh parsley
4 cups cooked wild rice

1. Preheat oven to 325°F. Cook bacon and oil in a Dutch oven over medium-high until bacon is crisp. Transfer to a bowl. Add chicken, salt, and pepper to pot; cook until browned. Transfer chicken to bowl with bacon.
2. Add mushrooms to pot; cook 5 minutes. Transfer to bowl with meat. Add carrot, onion, garlic, and bay leaves to pot; cook until softened. Add vinegar; cook until reduced, 2 minutes. Return chicken mixture to pot. Remove from heat.
3. Melt butter in a medium saucepan over medium-high until foamy. Add flour; cook, stirring constantly, 1 minute. Add milk; cook, whisking often, until thickened. Add broth and mustard; cook, whisking constantly, until thickened. Pour over chicken mixture, cover, and cook at 325°F 1 hour. Discard bay leaves. Stir in parsley; serve over rice. Serves 6 (serving size: 2 cups)

CALORIES 434; **FAT** 17g (sat 7g, unsat 9g); **PROTEIN** 36g; **CARB** 34g; **FIBER** 3g; **SUGARS** 5g (added sugars 0g); **SODIUM** 799mg; **CALC** 9% DV; **POTASSIUM** 8% DV

THE ULTIMATE GUIDE TO THANKSGIVING SIDES

And if you need a roast turkey recipe, you'll find a glorious one on p. 309.

This year, we focus our annual holiday cookbook on the dishes you've told us you need help with the most—all the stuffings, vegetables, mashes, salads, sauces, and casseroles that fill out the table with hearty abundance and bring your family great joy. For each dish, we offer a classic rendition for the traditionalists and a next-level version for those of you looking to branch out.

SALADS, STUFFINGS, AND SAUCES

These are not your grandmother's greens and stuffings, but she'll gladly eat them. Each one resembles a traditional take but calls for ingredients that make it more memorable—and give it your own signature, not granny's.

GIVE IT TIME

We like to make our cranberry sauce first thing on Thanksgiving morning (or even better, the night before) to let the ingredients meld together and allow the flavors to deepen.

CLASSIC
Gluten Free • Make Ahead Vegetarian

Simple Cranberry-Orange Sauce

Hands-on: 20 min. **Total:** 2 hr. 30 min. This lower-sugar cranberry sauce is fruity and tart, the perfect complement to the richness of turkey, stuffing, and gravy. Canned whole-berry sauce contains 60% more sugar and lacks the fresh flavor of ours.

3 cups fresh or frozen whole cranberries (12 oz.)
¼ cup granulated sugar
1 Tbsp. agave nectar
⅛ tsp. kosher salt
2 tsp. orange zest plus ¼ cup fresh orange juice (from 1 navel orange), divided

1. Combine cranberries, sugar, agave, salt, and orange juice in a medium saucepan over medium-high, and cook, stirring occasionally, until cranberries burst and liquid starts to reduce, about 15 minutes. Reduce heat to low, and simmer until liquid has a thick, syrupy consistency, about 12 more minutes. Remove from heat, and cool completely, about 2 hours. (Sauce will continue to thicken as it cools.) Sprinkle with orange zest. Serves 12 (serving size: about 2 Tbsp.)

CALORIES 38; **FAT** 0g; **PROTEIN** 0g; **CARB** 10g; **FIBER** 1g; **SUGARS** 7g (added sugars 5g); **SODIUM** 20mg; **CALC** 0% DV; **POTASSIUM** 0% DV

NEXT-LEVEL
Gluten Free • Make Ahead Vegetarian

Roasted Grape, Apple, and Cranberry Sauce

Hands-on: 5 min. **Total:** 1 hr. 30 min. Roasted grapes—especially black grapes (see "Editor's Pick" at right)—are supersweet and slightly tannic, with a concentrated fruit flavor. They help balance the tangy, astringent quality of the cranberries, allowing you to use less added sugar.

Cooking spray
2 cups seedless black grapes (about 10 oz.)
1¾ cups chopped Honeycrisp apple (1 [8-oz.] apple)
2 Tbsp. chopped shallot
1 cup fresh or frozen whole cranberries (about 4 oz.)
1½ Tbsp. unsalted butter
3½ tsp. pure maple syrup
⅛ tsp. kosher salt
¼ tsp. fresh thyme leaves or sprigs (optional)

1. Preheat oven to 425°F. Lightly coat a rimmed baking sheet with cooking spray. Place grapes, apple, and shallot on prepared baking sheet, and lightly coat with cooking spray. Bake at 425°F until shallot begins to soften, about 5 minutes.

2. Add cranberries to baking sheet. Bake at 425°F until cranberries burst, apple is tender, and grape skins are beginning to burst, about 20 more minutes. Remove from oven, and transfer grape mixture to a medium bowl. Stir in butter, maple syrup, and salt. Cool completely, about 1 hour. Sprinkle with thyme, if desired. Serves 12 (serving size: about 2 ½ Tbsp.)

CALORIES 47; FAT 2g (sat 1g, unsat 1g); PROTEIN 0g; CARB 8g; FIBER 1g; SUGARS 6g (added sugars 1g); SODIUM 21mg; CALC 1% DV; POTASSIUM 1% DV

CLASSIC

Staff Favorite • Fast
Gluten Free • Make Ahead
Vegetarian

Winter Greens and Citrus Salad

Hands-on: 15 min. **Total:** 15 min.
If you make the vinaigrette and slice the oranges and onions in advance, this becomes a fast throw-together side on Turkey Day. Though we love the texture and flavor variety of three kinds of greens, you could use all of one type if you'd rather.

⅓ cup olive oil
½ tsp. orange zest plus 2 Tbsp. fresh orange juice
2 Tbsp. fresh lemon juice
1 Tbsp. rice vinegar
2 tsp. Dijon mustard
2 tsp. honey
¾ tsp. black pepper, divided
½ tsp. fresh thyme leaves
½ tsp. finely chopped garlic
¼ tsp. kosher salt
2 small (5 oz. each) blood oranges
1 large (12½-oz.) navel orange
1 (8-oz.) bunch lacinato kale, stemmed and torn into bite-sized pieces (4 cups)
1 (6-oz.) head curly endive, leaves separated and cut in half crosswise (4 cups)
4 oz. fresh baby spinach (4 packed cups)
1 cup thinly sliced red onion
2 Tbsp. torn fresh basil leaves
1½ oz. Manchego cheese, shaved (about ¾ cup)
1 Tbsp. dried Zante currants
½ tsp. flaky sea salt (such as Maldon)

1. Whisk together olive oil, orange zest and juice, lemon juice, rice vinegar, Dijon, honey, ¼ teaspoon pepper, thyme, garlic, and kosher salt in a bowl until smooth and emulsified. Set aside.

2. Remove and discard peel and white pith from oranges. Cut oranges crosswise into ¼-inch-thick slices.

3. Combine kale, endive, and spinach in a large bowl. Add vinaigrette; toss to coat. Transfer mixture to a large platter. Top with orange slices, onion, basil, cheese, currants, flaky salt, and remaining ½ teaspoon pepper. Serves 12 (serving size: 1 cup)

CALORIES 106; FAT 7g (sat 2g, unsat 5g); PROTEIN 2g; CARB 9g; FIBER 2g; SUGARS 5g (added sugars 1g); SODIUM 192mg; CALC 9% DV; POTASSIUM 4% DV

EDITOR'S PICK: ROASTED GRAPE, APPLE, AND CRANBERRY SAUCE

"A fresh partner for roasted turkey, this garnet-hued game-changer can also show off on a cheese board paired with creamy Camembert or funky Roquefort. (It'll kick your day-after-Thanksgiving sandwich up a notch, too.) Pick up the darkest grapes you can find; I love the Midnight Beauty variety for their balanced tannins and intensely jammy flavor."

Josh Miller, Food Editor

Gluten Free • Make Ahead

Shaved Vegetable Salad with Warm Bacon Vinaigrette

Hands-on: 20 min. **Total:** 35 min.
If you can't find golden or Chioggia beets, just use red beets; wear gloves to prevent stains on your hands. Once tossed with the dressing, the vegetables wilt slightly to a crisp-tender texture. You can make the dressing a day ahead and reheat just before tossing with the salad; shave the vegetables (but not the apple) up to a day ahead.

6 bacon slices, cut into ¾-in. pieces
6 Tbsp. grapeseed or canola oil
2 Tbsp. plus 2 tsp. Dijon mustard
2 Tbsp. sherry vinegar or apple cider
  vinegar
2 tsp. dark molasses
¼ tsp. fine sea salt
2 cups thinly sliced fennel
  (1 [13-oz.] bulb)
1 cup thinly sliced peeled red beet
  (1 [5-oz.] beet)
1 cup thinly sliced peeled golden
  beet (1 [5-oz.] beet)
1 cup thinly sliced peeled Chioggia
  beet (1 [5-oz.] beet)
1 cup thinly sliced Honeycrisp apple
  (1 [6-oz.] apple)
½ cup loosely packed fresh tarragon
  leaves
½ cup chopped fresh chives
1 (5-oz.) container arugula (6 cups)

1. Cook bacon in a large skillet over medium-high, stirring occasionally, until crisp, 8 to 10 minutes. Drain on a paper towel–lined plate; reserve 3 tablespoons drippings in a medium bowl. Whisk oil, Dijon, vinegar, molasses, and salt into drippings.

2. Toss fennel, beets, apple, tarragon, chives, arugula, and vinaigrette in a large bowl. Transfer beet mixture to a platter. Sprinkle with cooked bacon; serve immediately. Serves 12 (serving size: 1 cup)

CALORIES 147; **FAT** 12g (sat 2g, unsat 9g); **PROTEIN** 3g; **CARB** 7g; **FIBER** 2g; **SUGARS** 5g (added sugars 1g); **SODIUM** 238mg; **CALC** 4% DV; **POTASSIUM** 6% DV

MAKE IT AHEAD

To get a head start on either the classic or next-level bread stuffings, you can combine all the ingredients up to the point of baking, then cover and refrigerate for up to two days. Let the dish or pan stand at room temperature for an hour or two, then bake as instructed in the recipe (you may need to cook a few additional minutes to reach the desired texture).

CLASSIC

Make Ahead

Sausage, Apple, and Herb Stuffing

Hands-on: 25 min. **Total:** 1 hr. 10 min.
This recipe captures the traditional stuffing vibe with sausage, aromatic vegetables, sage, and thyme. The bread soaks up all the goodness and stays moist inside, with a crispy layer on top. Bulk sausage is ideal, but you could use links and just remove the casings. You can skip the first step if you cut the bread into cubes and let them dry on the counter for 24 hours.

8 oz. sourdough bread, cut into
  1-in. cubes
6 oz. sweet Italian pork sausage
1 Tbsp. unsalted butter
1 cup chopped yellow onion
1 cup chopped celery stalks and
  leaves (about 3 stalks)

2 medium Granny Smith apples, cut
  into 1-in. cubes (3 cups)
1 Tbsp. chopped fresh sage
1 Tbsp. chopped fresh thyme
½ tsp. kosher salt
½ tsp. black pepper
1½ cups unsalted chicken stock,
  divided
3 large eggs
Thyme sprigs

1. Preheat oven to 300°F. Spread bread cubes in an even layer on a rimmed baking sheet. Bake at 300°F until dry and toasted, 12 to 14 minutes. Remove from oven; transfer bread to a bowl. Increase oven temperature to 350°F.
2. While bread cubes bake, cook sausage in a large skillet over medium-high until browned, about 6 minutes, using a spoon to break sausage into small pieces. Transfer sausage to bowl with bread cubes. (Do not wipe skillet clean.) Reduce heat to medium. Add butter, onion, and celery to skillet; cook, stirring occasionally, until vegetables are tender, 6 to 8 minutes. Add apples; cook until soft but not mushy, about 10 minutes. Stir in sage, thyme, salt, and pepper; cook, stirring constantly, until fragrant, about 1 minute. Add 1 cup stock, stirring and scraping bottom of skillet to release browned bits. Transfer apple mixture to bowl with bread cubes and sausage.
3. Whisk together eggs and remaining ½ cup stock in a bowl until combined; stir into bread mixture. Transfer mixture to a 2-quart glass or ceramic baking dish, cover with aluminum foil, and bake at 350°F for 15 minutes. Remove foil, top with thyme sprigs, and continue to bake until stuffing is lightly browned on top and set, 15 to 20 more minutes. Let stuffing stand 5 minutes before serving. Serves 12 (serving size: ⅓ cup)

CALORIES 126; **FAT** 4g (sat 2g, unsat 2g); **PROTEIN** 7g; **CARB** 16g; **FIBER** 2g; **SUGARS** 5g (added sugars 0g); **SODIUM** 318mg; **CALC** 4% DV; **POTASSIUM** 3% DV

Pancetta, Kale, and Raisin Stuffing

Hands-on: 35 min. **Total:** 1 hr. 25 min.

Torn bread gives this stuffing a lovely rustic appearance, but you can cube it. Kale, pancetta, and raisins all provide a flavor update, and there's enough red pepper to give a hint of heat. Ask for a chunk of pancetta at the deli counter, or look for a package of diced pancetta near the salami and cured meats. You could also substitute bacon, which will add a smoky flavor.

8 oz. multigrain bread, torn into
    chunks
4 oz. diced pancetta
2 Tbsp. olive oil, divided
1 (8-oz.) bunch lacinato kale,
    stemmed and roughly chopped
    (4 cups)
½ cup thinly sliced shallots (about
    4 small shallots)
1 Tbsp. minced garlic
¼ tsp. crushed red pepper
½ tsp. kosher salt
½ tsp. black pepper
1 Tbsp. sherry vinegar
1½ cups unsalted chicken stock
¼ cup chopped fresh flat-leaf
    parsley, plus more for garnish
¾ cup golden raisins, divided
2 large eggs

1. Preheat oven to 300°F. Spread bread chunks in an even layer on a rimmed baking sheet. Bake at 300°F until dry and slightly toasted, 12 to 14 minutes. Remove from oven; transfer bread to a large bowl. Increase oven temperature to 350°F.
2. While bread bakes, cook pancetta in a 10-inch cast-iron skillet over medium, stirring occasionally, until crisp and browned, about 8 minutes. Remove with a slotted spoon, and add to bread in bowl. Add 1 tablespoon oil to skillet. Add kale, and cook, stirring occasionally, until wilted and tender, about 10 minutes. Add shallots, garlic, and red pepper, and cook, stirring often, until shallots are tender, 2 to 4 minutes. Sprinkle with salt and black pepper, and stir in vinegar. Cook until vinegar is absorbed, about 1 minute. Add 1 cup stock, stirring and scraping skillet to release browned bits. Transfer vegetable mixture to bowl with bread; add parsley and ½ cup raisins.
3. Whisk together the eggs and remaining ½ cup stock in a bowl until combined; stir into bread mixture. Wipe skillet clean with a paper towel; add remaining 1 tablespoon oil to skillet, and swirl to coat. Transfer bread mixture to skillet. Cover tightly with aluminum foil.
4. Bake at 350°F until set, about 30 minutes. Remove foil, and bake until slightly crispy on top, about 10 more minutes. Remove from oven, and let stand until set, about 10 minutes. Sprinkle with remaining ¼ cup raisins; garnish with parsley. Serve hot or at room temperature. Serves 12 (serving size: about ½ cup)

CALORIES 159; **FAT** 7g (sat 2g, unsat 4g); **PROTEIN** 6g; **CARB** 18g; **FIBER** 2g; **SUGARS** 7g (added sugars 0g); **SODIUM** 337mg; **CALC** 4% DV; **POTASSIUM** 4% DV

POTATOES AND GRAINS

Thanksgiving is when you showcase an assortment of starches—say, two types of potatoes and a bread stuffing on the table. With these delightful options, you might even want more.

Wild Rice– Pecan Stuffing

Hands-on: 25 min. **Total:** 1 hr. 35 min.

2 Tbsp. olive oil
1½ cups chopped yellow onion
1 cup chopped celery (about
    3 stalks), leaves reserved
1 cup chopped carrots
1 cup uncooked wild rice
1 Tbsp. unsalted butter
1 Tbsp. minced garlic
1 Tbsp. chopped fresh sage
1 tsp. chopped fresh rosemary
1 tsp. kosher salt, divided
¾ tsp. black pepper, divided
4 cups unsalted chicken stock
1 cup uncooked long-grain brown
    rice
½ cup sweetened dried cherries
½ cup chopped toasted pecans

1. Heat oil in a Dutch oven over medium. Add onion, celery, carrots, and wild rice; cook, stirring occasionally, until vegetables are tender, about 10 minutes. Add butter, garlic, sage, and rosemary; cook, stirring constantly, 1 minute. Sprinkle with ½ teaspoon salt and ½ teaspoon pepper, and pour in stock. Increase heat to high, and bring to a boil. Cover and reduce heat to low; simmer 10 minutes.
2. Add brown rice; cover and simmer until rice is tender and most of the liquid has been absorbed, about 1 hour. Remove from heat; let stand, covered, 10 minutes. Stir in remaining ½ teaspoon salt and ¼ teaspoon pepper; spoon onto a serving platter. Top with cherries, pecans, and celery leaves. Serves 12 (serving size: about ⅔ cup)

CALORIES 208; **FAT** 7g (sat 1g, unsat 6g); **PROTEIN** 5g; **CARB** 32g; **FIBER** 3g; **SUGARS** 7g (added sugars 2g); **SODIUM** 221mg; **CALC** 3% DV; **POTASSIUM** 5% DV

NEXT-LEVEL
Staff Favorite • Make Ahead

Farro Stuffing with Miso Mushrooms

Hands-on: 25 min. **Total:** 1 hr.
While a miso-flavored whole-grain stuffing might not be traditional, the savory, earthy flavor is right at home on the holiday table.

Cooking spray
1¾ cups uncooked farro
2 Tbsp. unsalted butter
1 lb. mixed fresh mushrooms (such as shiitake caps, cremini, and oyster), chopped
1 cup chopped carrots
2 Tbsp. chopped fresh sage
1½ Tbsp. chopped garlic
¼ cup white miso
1 cup unsalted chicken stock
4 oz. fontina cheese, grated (about 1 cup)
2 tsp. sherry vinegar
1 tsp. black pepper
¼ tsp. kosher salt

1. Preheat oven to 400°F. Lightly coat a 2-quart glass or ceramic baking dish with cooking spray. Cook farro according to package directions to yield about 4 cups; drain and set aside.
2. While farro cooks, melt butter in a large skillet over medium-high. Add mushrooms; cook, stirring occasionally, until lightly browned, 6 to 8 minutes. Add carrots, sage, and garlic; cook, stirring occasionally, until tender, 5 to 6 minutes. Stir in miso; cook, stirring constantly, 1 minute. Add stock; simmer until liquid is reduced by half, about 4 minutes. Remove from heat; cool slightly.
3. Combine cooked farro, mushroom mixture, cheese, vinegar, pepper, and salt in a large bowl. Spoon mixture into prepared baking dish. Bake at 400°F until top is lightly toasted, about 20 minutes. Serves 12 (serving size: ⅔ cup)

CALORIES 150; FAT 6g (sat 3g, unsat 2g); PROTEIN 7g; CARB 23g; FIBER 3g; SUGARS 2g (added sugars 0g); SODIUM 293mg; CALC 7% DV; POTASSIUM 5% DV

EDITOR'S PICK

"What makes the Wild Rice–Pecan Stuffing (page 293) so incredibly satisfying is the whole-grain combo of wild and brown rice. It makes a nutty, toasty, and savory flavor base with delectable chewiness and filling fiber."

Tim Cebula, Senior Food Editor

CLASSIC
Gluten Free • Make Ahead
Vegetarian

Lower-Sugar Sweet Potato Casserole

Hands-on: 20 min. **Total:** 2 hr. 35 min.
Our delicious casserole has 5 fewer teaspoons (20g) of added sugar per serving than traditional versions.

3 lbs. sweet potatoes (5 to 6 medium-sized sweet potatoes)
½ cup evaporated whole milk
2 Tbsp. unsalted butter, melted
2 tsp. vanilla extract
1½ tsp. kosher salt
1 tsp. black pepper
2 large eggs, separated
Cooking spray
¾ cup chopped walnuts
¾ cup old-fashioned rolled oats
2 Tbsp. light brown sugar
½ tsp. ground cardamom

1. Preheat oven to 350°F. Wrap potatoes individually in foil. Arrange on a baking sheet. Roast at 350°F until very tender, 60 to 75 minutes. Set aside until cool enough to handle, about 15 minutes. Peel potatoes; discard skins. Place potatoes in a large bowl; mash until smooth. Cool completely, about 20 minutes. Stir in milk, butter, vanilla, salt, pepper, and egg yolks. Spread mixture evenly in a 2-quart glass or ceramic baking dish coated with cooking spray.

2. Whisk egg whites in a medium bowl until frothy. Stir in walnuts, oats, brown sugar, and cardamom. Sprinkle evenly over sweet potato mixture. Bake at 350°F, uncovered, until top is toasted and edges are bubbling, 40 to 50 minutes. Serves 12 (serving size: about ½ cup)

CALORIES 220; FAT 9g (sat 2g, unsat 6g); PROTEIN 5g; CARB 31g; FIBER 4g; SUGARS 8g (added sugars 2g); SODIUM 327mg; CALC 8% DV; POTASSIUM 10% DV

NEXT-LEVEL

Staff Favorite • Gluten Free Vegetarian

Stuffed Sweet Potatoes with Toasted Meringue

Hands-on: 45 min. **Total:** 1 hr. 55 min. Want to wow your family at the table? These stuffed spuds will do the trick. You can prepare the recipe through step 3 up to two days ahead; reheat potatoes at 375°F, then turn up the heat to brown the topping in step 4.

8 (9- to 10-oz.) sweet potatoes
1 (2-in.) piece fresh ginger, unpeeled
⅓ cup whole milk
5 Tbsp. unsalted butter, softened and cut into pieces
1½ tsp. plus ⅛ tsp. kosher salt, divided
¼ tsp. ground nutmeg
¼ tsp. black pepper
3 large egg whites, at room temperature
⅛ tsp. cream of tartar
½ cup powdered sugar

1. Preheat oven to 375°F. Pierce potatoes all over with a fork, and place on a parchment paper–lined baking sheet. Bake at 375°F until tender, about 1 hour. Let stand on baking sheet at room temperature until cool enough to handle, about 15 minutes.

2. Meanwhile, fold an 8-inch square piece of cheesecloth into quarters to make a 4-layer, 4-inch square. Using medium holes of a box grater, grate ginger; place in center of cheesecloth. Gather edges of cheesecloth, and squeeze over a bowl to equal 1 tablespoon ginger juice. Discard solids.

3. Increase oven temperature to 400°F. Cut potatoes in half lengthwise; carefully scoop potato pulp into a medium bowl, leaving about ¼ inch pulp around shell. Return 12 potato shells to baking sheet; discard remaining 4 shells. Add ginger juice, milk, and butter to pulp in bowl, and mash with a potato masher until smooth; stir in 1½ teaspoons salt, nutmeg, and pepper. Spoon mashed potato mixture evenly into 12 potato shells (about ½ cup per shell).

4. Beat egg whites, cream of tartar, and remaining ⅛ teaspoon salt with a mixer on high speed until foamy, about 20 to 30 seconds. Add powdered sugar, 1 tablespoon at a time, beating at high speed until stiff peaks form, about 2 minutes. Stop mixer; scrape sides of bowl. Spoon meringue evenly onto potatoes on baking sheet. Bake at 400°F until meringue is golden brown, 6 to 7 minutes. Transfer potatoes to a platter; serve immediately. Serves 12 (serving size: 1 stuffed potato half)

CALORIES 177; FAT 5g (sat 3g, unsat 2g); PROTEIN 3g; CARB 30g; FIBER 4g; SUGARS 10g (added sugars 5g); SODIUM 345mg; CALC 5% DV; POTASSIUM 10% DV

EDITOR'S PICK: STUFFED SWEET POTATOES WITH TOASTED MERINGUE

"The beauty of billowy meringue makes this side a true standout. Fresh ginger juice is surprisingly simple to make and introduces unexpected spice to balance the honeyed sweetness of the spuds."

Jamie Vespa, Assistant Nutrition Editor

**Gluten Free • Make Ahead
Vegetarian**

Olive Oil Mashed Potatoes

Hands-on: 25 min. **Total:** 1 hr.
Herb-infused olive oil and Greek yogurt replace much of the butter and milk you'd find in traditional mashed potatoes. The finished dish has a lightly tangy, herbal-fruity flavor that's irresistible. You can make the potatoes a day ahead, but anticipate that you may need to stir in a little milk to restore the creamy texture.

**3 lbs. Yukon Gold potatoes, peeled
    and cut into ½-in.-thick slices
½ cup olive oil
1 (3-in.) rosemary sprig
2 thyme sprigs
1⅓ cups plain 2% reduced-fat Greek
    yogurt
3 Tbsp. unsalted butter, softened
    and cut into pieces
2 tsp. kosher salt
¼ tsp. finely ground black pepper
Coarsely ground black pepper
Fresh thyme leaves
Fresh rosemary leaves**

1. Place potatoes in a Dutch oven, and add cold water to cover by 2 inches. Bring to a boil over high. Reduce heat to medium-high, and simmer, uncovered, until potatoes are fork-tender, 20 to 25 minutes. Drain and let stand at room temperature until potatoes look dry and chalky, about 10 minutes. Return potatoes to Dutch oven.
2. While potatoes simmer, bring olive oil, rosemary, and thyme to a gentle simmer in a saucepan over low. Cook, stirring once, until mixture is fragrant and herbs have darkened, about 10 minutes. Remove from heat, and cool 10 minutes. Using a rubber spatula, press oil mixture through a fine wire-mesh strainer into a small bowl. Discard rosemary and thyme.
3. Mash potatoes with a potato masher until all large chunks are broken down and potatoes are fluffy. Stir in herb-infused oil, yogurt, butter, salt, and finely ground pepper until blended. Garnish with coarsely ground pepper and herb leaves. Serves 12 (serving size: ⅔ cup)

CALORIES 218; **FAT** 12g (sat 3g, unsat 8g); **PROTEIN** 5g; **CARB** 21g; **FIBER** 1g; **SUGARS** 1g (added sugars 0g); **SODIUM** 337mg; **CALC** 3% DV; **POTASSIUM** 0% DV

**Staff Favorite • Fast
Gluten Free • Make Ahead
Vegetarian**

Garlic Mashed Potatoes with Chile-Paprika Butter

Hands-on: 10 min. **Total:** 30 min.
These potatoes are bright with garlic, and the chile butter adds a hint of spice. Leaving the skins on the Yukon Golds adds a slightly rustic texture. Aleppo is a flaky smoked chile pepper you'll find at specialty stores; it's a great spice to keep on hand, but you can omit it here if you don't have it.

**1½ lbs. russet potatoes, peeled and
    cubed
12 oz. Yukon Gold potatoes, cubed
10 medium garlic cloves, peeled
2 bay leaves
5 Tbsp. unsalted butter, divided
¼ cup 2% reduced-fat milk
1½ tsp. kosher salt
1 tsp. paprika
½ tsp. crushed red pepper
1 tsp. Aleppo pepper (optional)**

1. Place potatoes, garlic, and bay leaves in a large saucepan; add cold water to cover by 2 inches. Bring to a boil over high; reduce heat to medium-low, and simmer until potatoes are very tender, about 15 minutes. Drain; discard bay leaves. Return potatoes to pan; mash to desired consistency. Stir in 2 tablespoons butter, milk, and salt; transfer to a serving bowl.
2. Heat remaining 3 tablespoons butter, paprika, and crushed red pepper in a small skillet over medium until butter is melted and sizzling, about 2 minutes. Drizzle over potatoes; sprinkle with Aleppo pepper, if desired. Serves 10 (serving size: about ½ cup)

CALORIES 136; **FAT** 6g (sat 4g, unsat 2g); **PROTEIN** 2g; **CARB** 19g; **FIBER** 2g; **SUGARS** 1g (added sugars 0g); **SODIUM** 296mg; **CALC** 2% DV; **POTASSIUM** 7% DV

VEGETABLES

Here's where things get really exciting—and colorful, beautiful, and absolutely delicious. Sure, an assortment of vegetable-heavy dishes balances your Thanksgiving feast, but these will also steal the limelight from the bird. We've included your favorite seasonal vegetables—Brussels sprouts, green beans, root vegetables, onions, and dark, leafy greens—and featured them all in both a classic and next-level version.

3 MIX-AND-MATCH MENUS

CLASSIC
Fast • Gluten Free Vegetarian

Roasted Brussels Sprouts with Mustard Dressing

Hands-on: 10 min. **Total:** 30 min.
Here's proof that Brussels sprouts can be delicious without bacon. Sherry (or apple cider) vinegar lends complementary sweet-tart notes, and grainy mustard adds peppery tang. High-heat roasting gives the sprouts a little char and the faintest hint of smoky flavor. It's a quick dish that yields fantastic results.

2 lbs. fresh Brussels sprouts, halved lengthwise (about 8 cups)
6 Tbsp. extra-virgin olive oil, divided
½ tsp. plus ⅜ tsp. kosher salt, divided
¾ tsp. black pepper, divided
2 Tbsp. sherry vinegar or apple cider vinegar
1 Tbsp. grainy mustard
2 Tbsp. chopped fresh flat-leaf parsley, divided

1. Preheat oven to 450°F. Toss together Brussels sprouts, 2 tablespoons oil, ½ teaspoon salt, and ½ teaspoon pepper in a large bowl. Transfer to a large rimmed baking sheet lined with aluminum foil. Roast at 450°F until golden and just tender when pierced with tip of a knife, about 20 minutes, stirring once after 10 minutes.
2. Whisk together vinegar, mustard, 1 tablespoon parsley, remaining ⅜ teaspoon salt, and remaining ¼ teaspoon pepper in a large bowl. Add remaining ¼ cup oil in a slow, steady stream, whisking constantly, until emulsified.
3. Add sprouts to dressing; toss to coat. Transfer to serving platter; sprinkle with remaining 1 tablespoon parsley. Serves 8 (serving size: about ⅔ cup)

CALORIES 150; FAT 11g (sat 2g, unsat 9g); PROTEIN 4g; CARB 11g; FIBER 4g; SUGARS 3g (added sugars 0g); SODIUM 254mg; CALC 5% DV; POTASSIUM 10% DV

TIME IT RIGHT

The key to delicious Brussels sprouts is to cook them just enough so their flavor stays earthy-sweet and their texture tender without too much give. Use our "knife test" as described in these recipes to check for doneness. They're best served right away (they're not a great make-ahead option), so plan accordingly.

Vegetarian

Brussels Sprouts Tarte Tatin

Hands-on: 40 min. **Total:** 1 hr. 5 min.

Cooking spray
2 Tbsp. olive oil, divided
1 lb. fresh Brussels sprouts, halved
   lengthwise (4 cups)
¼ cup water
½ cup chopped shallot
2 Tbsp. white balsamic vinegar
2 Tbsp. honey
1 Tbsp. chopped fresh thyme
1 tsp. kosher salt
¼ tsp. black pepper
1 (9-in.) frozen whole-wheat
   pie dough (such as Wholly
   Wholesome), thawed

1. Preheat oven to 400°F. Lightly coat an 8-inch round cake pan with cooking spray. Heat 1 tablespoon oil in a large nonstick skillet over medium-high. Add sprouts, cut sides down; cook, stirring occasionally, until beginning to brown, about 5 minutes. Add ¼ cup water; reduce heat to medium. Cover and cook, undisturbed, until sprouts are tender when pierced with tip of a knife, about 4 minutes. Transfer to prepared cake pan; arrange evenly, cut sides down.
2. Wipe skillet clean. Add remaining 1 tablespoon oil; heat over medium-low. Add shallot; cook, stirring often, until softened, 3 to 4 minutes. Stir in vinegar, honey, thyme, salt, and pepper; cook, stirring constantly, until liquid is slightly syrupy, about 2 minutes. Drizzle over sprouts. Drape dough over sprouts, tucking edges into sides of pan. Prick top all over with a fork or tip of a knife.

3. Bake at 400°F until crust is golden brown, 25 to 30 minutes. Transfer to a wire rack to cool 5 minutes. Carefully invert onto a serving plate. Serves 10 (serving size: 1 slice)

CALORIES 149; FAT 9g (sat 4g, unsat 4g); PROTEIN 3g; CARB 16g; FIBER 3g; SUGARS 6g (added sugars 3g); SODIUM 282mg; CALC 2% DV; POTASSIUM 4% DV

Fast • Gluten Free
Make Ahead • Vegetarian

Green Beans Amandine

Hands-on: 20 min. **Total:** 25 min.
Adding lemon juice and water to the browned butter mixture creates a lovely, glossy sauce that coats the beans beautifully. The overall impression is that there's far more butter than is actually there. You can easily get a head start by completing step 1 up to two days ahead; then the recipe can come together in the last few minutes before the feast.

4 qt. plus 2 to 3 Tbsp. water, divided
4 (8-oz.) pkg. fresh haricots verts
   (French green beans)
2 Tbsp. unsalted butter
1 Tbsp. olive oil
½ cup sliced almonds
¼ cup thinly sliced shallot
1 tsp. minced garlic
2 Tbsp. fresh lemon juice
1 tsp. kosher salt
¼ tsp. black pepper

1. Bring 4 quarts water to a boil in a large Dutch oven over medium-high. Add green beans; cook until crisp-tender, 4 to 5 minutes. Drain beans; plunge into a large bowl filled with ice water to stop the cooking process. Drain beans, and dry thoroughly with paper towels.

2. Wipe Dutch oven clean; add butter and oil, and cook over medium-low until butter is melted. Add almonds, and cook, stirring constantly, until butter has browned and almonds are beginning to brown, about 5 minutes. Add shallot and garlic, and cook, stirring constantly, 1 minute. Stir in lemon juice and 2 tablespoons water. Cook, stirring constantly, until sauce has thickened slightly and has a glossy sheen. (Add up to 1 more tablespoon water if sauce is too thick.) Stir in beans, salt, and pepper. Increase heat to medium; cook, tossing occasionally, until beans are hot and coated with sauce and almonds, 4 to 5 more minutes. Serves 8 (serving size: about 1 cup)

CALORIES 114; FAT 8g (sat 2g, unsat 5g); PROTEIN 3g; CARB 10g; FIBER 4g; SUGARS 4g (added sugars 0g); SODIUM 248mg; CALC 6% DV; POTASSIUM 6% DV

Gluten Free • Make Ahead

Prosciutto– Green Bean Bundles with Crispy Mushrooms

Hands-on: 35 min. **Total:** 45 min.
Though it may look complicated, this recipe is quite easy to prepare. To save prep time, look for bags of prewashed, pretrimmed beans in the produce section. If you can't find the slender haricots verts, use regular green beans—they'll just need to cook a few minutes longer in step 1. You can blanch the beans and prepare the dressing the day before, but wait to combine them; the acid will discolor the beans.

4 qt. water
3 (8-oz.) pkg. fresh haricots verts
  (French green beans)
Cooking spray
3 ½ cups stemmed and thinly sliced
  fresh shiitake mushrooms (about
  4 oz.)
7 Tbsp. extra-virgin olive oil,
  divided
¾ tsp. kosher salt, divided
½ tsp. black pepper, divided
4 tsp. fresh lemon juice
5 prosciutto slices (about 2 oz. total),
  cut in half lengthwise

1. Preheat oven to 450°F. Bring 4 quarts water to a boil in a large Dutch oven over medium-high. Add green beans, and cook until crisp-tender, about 4 to 5 minutes. Drain beans, and plunge into a large bowl filled with ice water to stop the cooking process. Drain beans, and dry thoroughly with paper towels.
2. Line a rimmed baking sheet with aluminum foil; lightly coat with cooking spray. Toss together mushrooms, 3 tablespoons oil, ⅛ teaspoon salt, and ⅛ teaspoon pepper in a bowl; arrange evenly on prepared baking sheet. Roast at 450°F until mushrooms are deep brown and crisped, 12 to 15 minutes, stirring halfway through. Transfer mushrooms to a bowl; set baking sheet aside.
3. Whisk together lemon juice, remaining ¼ cup oil, remaining ⅝ teaspoon salt, and remaining ⅜ teaspoon pepper in a large bowl until blended. Add beans; toss to coat. Gather beans into 10 bundles of about 20 beans each. Place 1 bundle at the end of 1 prosciutto piece; roll up lengthwise. Repeat with remaining 9 bundles and remaining 9 prosciutto pieces.
4. Arrange assembled bundles, seam side down, on reserved baking sheet. Bake at 450°F until beans are warmed and prosciutto begins to brown, 5 to 7 minutes. Transfer green bean bundles to a platter; sprinkle with roasted mushrooms. Serves 10 (serving size: 1 bundle)

CALORIES 128; FAT 11g (sat 2g, unsat 9g); PROTEIN 3g; CARB 6g; FIBER 2g; SUGARS 3g (added sugars 0g); SODIUM 241mg; CALC 3% DV; POTASSIUM 4% DV

PREP IT AHEAD

While you wouldn't want to roast either of these recipes in advance, you can still get a head start: Cut all of the veggies up to two days ahead; store in ziplock bags in the fridge. This will save you up to 30 minutes on Turkey Day.

CLASSIC

**Staff Favorite • Gluten Free
Vegetarian**

Roasted Root Vegetables with Balsamic-Maple Glaze

Hands-on: 30 min. **Total:** 1 hr. 10 min.
These vegetables are so good, they may upstage everything else on the table. The balsamic-maple sauce is particularly delicious (and smartly added at the end to keep all flavors and colors vibrant). Roasting the purple vegetables separately will also help keep all the colors looking their best.

Cooking spray
1 lb. red onions, each cut into 8
  wedges with root intact
1 lb. purple sweet potatoes, cut into
  ¾-in. cubes
1 lb. small multicolored carrots,
  (including purple), cut on an angle
  into 2-in.-long pieces, divided
¼ cup olive oil, divided
1 lb. turnips, each cut into 8 wedges
1 lb. parsnips, cut on an angle into
  2-in.-long pieces
1 tsp. kosher salt
1 tsp. black pepper
6 Tbsp. balsamic vinegar
¼ cup pure maple syrup
1 Tbsp. chopped fresh thyme leaves

1. Preheat oven to 450°F. Line 2 rimmed baking sheets with parchment paper, and lightly coat with cooking spray.
2. Combine onions, purple sweet potatoes, purple carrots, and 2 tablespoons olive oil in a large bowl; toss to coat, and arrange in a single layer on a prepared baking sheet. In the same bowl, combine turnips, parsnips, remaining carrots, and remaining 2 tablespoons olive oil, and toss to coat; arrange in a single layer on the other prepared baking sheet. Sprinkle both baking sheets of vegetables evenly with salt and pepper. Bake purple vegetable mixture at 450°F, without stirring, until tender, about 25 minutes. Bake turnip mixture at 450°F, without stirring, until tender and lightly caramelized, 30 to 35 minutes.
3. While vegetables bake, combine vinegar and syrup in a small saucepan over medium-high. Bring to a boil, without stirring, and cook until mixture is thickened, 6 to 8 minutes. (You should have about ½ cup of liquid.) Remove from heat, and cool to room temperature; sauce will thicken to syrupy consistency upon cooling.
4. Arrange roasted vegetables on a platter, and drizzle with balsamic syrup. Sprinkle with fresh thyme, and serve immediately. Serves 10 (serving size: 1 ¼ cups)

CALORIES 202; FAT 6g (sat 1g, unsat 5g); PROTEIN 3g; CARB 36g; FIBER 7g; SUGARS 16g (added sugars 5g); SODIUM 288mg; CALC 8% DV; POTASSIUM 14% DV

NEXT-LEVEL
Gluten Free • Vegetarian

Roasted Carrot and Parsnip Batons with Tahini Dip

Hands-on: 20 min. **Total:** 45 min.
Deep caramelization from roasting brings out the natural sweetness in carrots and parsnips. Try to cut the vegetables into the size we call for in step 2. If the pieces are too large or too long, they may cook unevenly or end up limp; if they're too small, they will likely burn. You can make the dip a day or two ahead, but bring it to room temperature before serving for the best flavor.

Cooking spray
1 lb. parsnips, peeled
1 lb. carrots, peeled
3 Tbsp. extra-virgin olive oil, divided
1½ tsp. ground coriander, divided
¾ tsp. kosher salt, divided
¼ cup plain fat-free yogurt
2 Tbsp. tahini (sesame seed paste)
2 Tbsp. fresh lemon juice
2 tsp. honey
2 garlic cloves, minced

1. Preheat oven to 475°F. Line 2 rimmed baking heets with parchment paper, and lightly coat with cooking spray.

2. Cut parsnips and carrots into ½-inch-wide x 3½- to 4-inch-long sticks. Toss parsnips with 1 tablespoon oil; place on a baking sheet. Toss carrots with 1 tablespoon oil; place on other baking sheet. Sprinkle vegetables with 1 teaspoon coriander and ½ teaspoon salt. (Make sure pieces are not touching for optimal browning.) Bake at 475°F until tips are lightly charred, 15 to 20 minutes.

3. Whisk together yogurt, tahini, lemon juice, honey, garlic, remaining 1 tablespoon oil, remaining ½ teaspoon coriander, and remaining ¼ teaspoon salt. Serve dip with vegetables. Serves 8 (serving size: ½ cup vegetables and 1 Tbsp. dip)

CALORIES 143; FAT 8g (sat 1g, unsat 7g); PROTEIN 2g; CARB 18g; FIBER 4g; SUGARS 7g (added sugars 1g); SODIUM 230mg; CALC 5% DV; POTASSIUM 8% DV

"I'm the person who always orders the salad or sandwich without onions. And onion rings? No way! But these glazed red pearl onions looked so pretty that I just had to taste them. Well, they were delicious—so much so that I went back for seconds. So this year—for the first Thanksgiving ever—I think I'll be putting pearl onions on the table."

Brierley Horton, Food & Nutrition Director

CLASSIC
Gluten Free • Vegetarian
Make Ahead

Glazed Red Pearl Onions

Hands-on: 20 min. **Total:** 35 min.
Think of this as a relish-type side: You don't need a big serving, but the bright flavor is a welcome addition to roasted meat and hearty casseroles.

2 lbs. unpeeled fresh red pearl onions
2½ Tbsp. unsalted butter
¼ cup packed light brown sugar
½ tsp. ground cumin
¼ tsp. kosher salt
1½ tsp. lime zest, divided, plus ¼ cup fresh lime juice (from 2 limes)
½ tsp. flaky sea salt (such as Maldon)

1. Bring a large pot of water to a boil, and add onions. Boil 30 seconds; drain and immediately plunge into a bowl of ice water. Trim root end of each onion, leaving core intact; squeeze gently from top of each onion to remove tough outer skin. Discard skins, and place peeled blanched onions in a bowl.

2. Heat butter in a large nonstick skillet over medium-high. Once butter is sizzling, add onions in a single layer. Cover and cook, stirring often, until onions are lightly caramelized, 8 to 10 minutes.

3. While onions cook, whisk together brown sugar, cumin, kosher salt, 1 teaspoon lime zest, and lime juice in a small bowl; pour into skillet, and toss to coat onions. Cover and cook over medium, stirring occasionally, until mixture is syrupy and onions are tender, 5 to 6 minutes.

4. Spoon onions and sauce onto a platter; sprinkle with flaky sea salt and remaining ½ teaspoon lime zest. Serve immediately. Serves 10 (serving size: about ⅓ cup)

CALORIES 102; **FAT** 3g (sat 2g, unsat 1g); **PROTEIN** 1g; **CARB** 19g; **FIBER** 0g; **SUGARS** 9g (added sugars 5g); **SODIUM** 182mg; **CALC** 3% DV; **POTASSIUM** 0% DV

NEXT-LEVEL
Staff Favorite • Make Ahead

Sausage, Herb, and Cranberry–Stuffed Onions

Hands-on: 45 min. **Total:** 1 hr.
Here's a gorgeous dish you'll be proud to add to the table. Red onion "blossoms" roast until tender with a savory-sweet bread stuffing. You can par-cook the onions, stuff with the filling, and refrigerate overnight. Bring to room temperature, and then bake at 400°F until the stuffing is hot and lightly toasted (about 20 minutes).

Cooking spray
10 small (3- to 5-oz.) red onions, peeled
2 Tbsp. apple cider vinegar
5 (1-oz.) slices whole-grain sandwich bread, cut into ¼-in. cubes
3 Tbsp. olive oil, divided
8 oz. smoked turkey sausage, diced
1 cup finely chopped celery
¾ cup chopped sweetened dried cranberries
2 large eggs, lightly beaten
¼ cup unsalted chicken stock
2 Tbsp. chopped fresh flat-leaf parsley
½ tsp. black pepper
¼ tsp. kosher salt

1. Preheat oven to 400°F. Lightly coat a 13- x 9-inch baking dish with cooking spray.

2. Place onions on a work surface. Working from stem end of onion, cut in the center toward the root end, leaving ¼ inch uncut. Cut again to form 4 quarters, leaving root end intact. Repeat with all onions, placing root sides down in baking dish. (If they fall over, that's OK.) Coat onions with cooking spray, and drizzle with vinegar. Bake at 400°F until slightly softened, 30 to 35 minutes. Remove from oven, and let stand at room temperature.

3. While onions bake, toss bread cubes with 2 tablespoons oil in a large bowl; spread in an even layer on a baking sheet. Place in oven with onions, and bake until crunchy, about 10 minutes. Remove bread cubes from oven, and place in a large bowl.

4. Heat remaining 1 tablespoon oil in a large skillet over medium-high until shimmering. Add sausage, and cook, stirring occasionally, until beginning to brown, about 6 minutes. Stir in celery and cranberries; cook, stirring often, until celery is slightly softened, about 2 minutes. Add sausage mixture to bowl with toasted bread cubes. Stir in eggs, stock, parsley, pepper, and salt until combined. Let mixture stand at room temperature until liquid is absorbed into bread, about 10 minutes. Lightly pack about ½ cup stuffing into each onion. Lightly spray tops of stuffed onions with cooking spray. Bake at 400°F until stuffing is lightly golden, about 15 minutes. Serves 10 (serving size: 1 stuffed onion)

CALORIES 192; **FAT** 8g (sat 2g, unsat 6g); **PROTEIN** 8g; **CARB** 24g; **FIBER** 3g; **SUGARS** 13g (added sugars 9g); **SODIUM** 345mg; **CALC** 5% DV; **POTASSIUM** 5% DV

Creamed Spinach with Hazelnuts

Hands-on: 40 min. **Total:** 1 hr. 15 min.
Unlike some versions of creamed spinach, here you actually taste the greens. They're enhanced by—but not overwhelmed by—the creamy sauce.

Cooking spray
35 oz. fresh spinach
3 Tbsp. canola oil
3 cups vertically sliced yellow onions (from 2 large onions)
1 oz. all-purpose flour (¼ cup)
½ tsp. plus ⅛ tsp. kosher salt
½ tsp. black pepper
2 cups unsalted chicken stock
¼ cup half-and-half
2 oz. spreadable light garlic-and-herb cheese (such as Boursin)
⅛ tsp. ground nutmeg
½ cup chopped toasted hazelnuts

1. Preheat oven to 375°F. Lightly coat an 8-inch baking dish with cooking spray. Lightly coat a large Dutch oven with cooking spray, and heat over medium-high. Add spinach in 3 batches to pan; cook each batch, stirring occasionally, until wilted before adding more, until all spinach is wilted, 4 to 5 minutes. Drain spinach in a colander; wipe out Dutch oven.
2. Heat oil in Dutch oven over medium-high. Add onion; cook, stirring occasionally, until softened, 9 to 10 minutes. Sprinkle with flour, salt, and pepper; stir to coat onions. Stir in stock and half-and-half, scraping pan with a wooden spoon to release browned bits from bottom. Bring mixture to a boil; cook, stirring constantly, until mixture thickens, about 5 minutes.

Add cheese and nutmeg; stir until smooth. Remove from heat.
3. When spinach has cooled enough to handle, place spinach in a clean kitchen towel and squeeze firmly over sink to remove as much liquid as possible. Add squeezed spinach to cheese mixture, and stir to combine.
4. Spoon spinach mixture into prepared baking dish. Bake at 375°F until set, about 20 minutes. Sprinkle with hazelnuts, and bake until hazelnuts are warmed through and golden, about 5 minutes. Remove from oven; let stand 10 minutes before serving. Serves 10 (serving size: ½ cup)

CALORIES 159; **FAT** 10g (sat 2g, unsat 7g); **PROTEIN** 7g; **CARB** 12g; **FIBER** 4g; **SUGARS** 3g (added sugars 0g); **SODIUM** 254mg; **CALC** 12% DV; **POTASSIUM** 15% DV

Make Ahead • Vegetarian

Collard Greens Panzanella with Hot Sauce Vinaigrette

Hands-on: 1 hr. 10 min.
Total: 1 hr. 20 min.
Collard greens are wonderful in salads; just massage them first (as you would kale) to make them a little more tender. You can prep all the components a day ahead, store separately, and then toss together shortly before serving.

Cooking spray
1 (1-lb.) sourdough loaf, cut into 1-in. cubes
3 Tbsp. olive oil, divided
1 tsp. black pepper, divided
¾ tsp. kosher salt, divided
4 cups prechopped butternut squash
1 cup chopped yellow onion
1 lb. collard greens, well cleaned
¼ cup canola oil, divided
1 cup hot water
½ cup dried sour cherries
1½ Tbsp. hot pepper sauce (such as Tabasco)
1 Tbsp. fresh lemon juice
1 Tbsp. light brown sugar
1½ tsp. minced garlic
2 Tbsp. chopped fresh thyme

1. Preheat oven to 375°F. Line 2 rimmed baking sheets with parchment paper, and lightly coat with cooking spray.
2. Toss together bread, 1 tablespoon olive oil, ½ teaspoon pepper, and ¼ teaspoon salt in a large bowl. Place bread in a single layer on a prepared baking sheet. In the same bowl, toss together butternut squash, onion, 1 tablespoon olive oil, ¼ teaspoon pepper, and ¼ teaspoon salt; place in a single layer on the other baking sheet.
3. Place both baking sheets in oven. Bake at 375°F until bread is golden brown and crisp, about 30 minutes, stirring after 15 minutes. Remove bread from oven. Continue to cook squash mixture at 375°F until lightly caramelized and tender, about 15 more minutes. Cool bread and squash mixture about 10 minutes.
4. Remove ribs from greens; tear greens into 1-inch pieces to equal about 8 cups. Place greens in a large bowl, and massage with 1 tablespoon canola oil. Set aside.
5. Place 1 cup hot water and dried cherries in a small bowl, and let stand until plumped, about 10 minutes; drain and coarsely chop. Add cherries, squash mixture, and toasted bread to bowl with greens; toss to combine.
6. Whisk together hot sauce, lemon juice, brown sugar, garlic, remaining 3 tablespoons canola oil, 1 tablespoon olive oil, ¼ teaspoon pepper, and ¼ teaspoon salt in

a small bowl. About 10 minutes before serving, toss greens mixture with dressing on a large platter, and sprinkle with fresh thyme. Serves 10 (serving size: 1 ½ cups)

CALORIES 256; FAT 13g (sat 1g, unsat 11g); PROTEIN 3g; CARB 32g; FIBER 4g; SUGARS 6g (added sugars 2g); SODIUM 319mg; CALC 10% DV; POTASSIUM 5% DV

CASSEROLES AND GRATINS

Creamy, gooey, cheesy indulgence—every holiday table should include side dishes that hit that nostalgic beat. And it just so happens that these versions are lighter, fresher, and—dare we say—better? (We do dare; they are.)

PLAN IT RIGHT

Design your menu so that your last-minute dishes aren't all competing for the oven. Opt for some smart stovetop options like these 25-minute mac and cheese recipes (the Spanish one just finishes quickly under the broiler).

CLASSIC
Fast · Gluten Free
Vegetarian

Quick Stovetop Mac and Cheese

Hands-on: 10 min. **Total:** 25 min.
We like brown rice pasta here for three reasons: It's whole-grain, it's a dead ringer (taste- and texture-wise) for traditional pasta, and it's gluten-free. You could also use a wheat- or chickpea-based pasta.

4 cups whole milk
2 cups water
1 tsp. kosher salt
1 lb. uncooked brown rice macaroni or penne pasta
8 oz. 2% reduced-fat cheddar cheese, grated (about 2 cups)
2 oz. ⅓-less-fat cream cheese (about ¼ cup)
½ tsp. black pepper, plus more for serving

1. Stir together milk, water, and salt in a Dutch oven; bring to a boil over high. Stir in pasta. Reduce heat to medium-low; simmer, stirring often and gently to loosen pasta from bottom of pot, until just tender, about 12 minutes. (Do not over-stir, or pasta may become mushy.)
2. Remove from heat. Add cheeses and pepper; stir gently until melted. Sprinkle with additional pepper. Serves 16 (serving size: about ½ cup)

CALORIES 188; FAT 7g (sat 4g, unsat 2g); PROTEIN 8g; CARB 24g; FIBER 2g; SUGARS 4g (added sugars 0g); SODIUM 280mg; CALC 17% DV; POTASSIUM 2% DV

NEXT-LEVEL
Fast

Spanish Mac and Cheese

Hands-on: 25 min. **Total:** 25 min.
It's surprising how much flavor you can achieve in such a short amount of time. Little bits of Spanish chorizo (the hard, cured kind) are wonderful in the breadcrumb topping.

12 oz. uncooked short whole-grain pasta (such as penne, farfalle, or rotini)
1 cup frozen butternut squash puree (about 12 oz.), thawed
3 oz. Manchego cheese, shredded (about ¾ cup)
2 oz. ⅓-less-fat cream cheese (about ¼ cup)
1 tsp. kosher salt
⅛ tsp. cayenne pepper
2 oz. dry-cured Spanish chorizo, finely chopped
2 Tbsp. canola oil
½ cup panko (Japanese breadcrumbs)
2 Tbsp. chopped fresh flat-leaf parsley
1 tsp. smoked paprika

1. Preheat broiler to high with oven rack in middle of oven. Cook pasta according to package directions in a Dutch oven. Drain, reserving ¼ cup cooking liquid. Return pasta to pan; add reserved cooking liquid, squash, Manchego cheese, cream cheese, salt, and cayenne. Stir until well combined. Spoon mixture into an ungreased 11- x 7-inch glass or ceramic baking dish.
2. While pasta cooks, heat the chorizo and oil in a skillet over medium-high, stirring occasionally, until chorizo is crispy and oil turns red, 5 to 6 minutes. Stir in panko. Spoon over pasta mixture in baking dish.
3. Broil in preheated oven until lightly toasted, 2 to 3 minutes. Sprinkle with parsley and paprika. Serves 12 (serving size: ½ cup)

CALORIES 209; FAT 9g (sat 3g, unsat 4g); PROTEIN 7g; CARB 25g; FIBER 3g; SUGARS 1g (added sugars 0g); SODIUM 335mg; CALC 10% DV; POTASSIUM 0% DV

Gluten Free • Vegetarian

Parmesan-Crusted Potato Gratin

Hands-on: 25 min. **Total:** 1 hr. 30 min.
Be sure to buy same-sized potatoes so
the slices are uniform.

2 ½ Tbsp. unsalted butter
2 Tbsp. canola oil
2 tsp. fresh thyme leaves
3 lbs. medium russet potatoes
1 oz. Parmesan cheese, grated
　(about ¼ cup)
2 Tbsp. pine nuts
1 tsp. kosher salt

1. Preheat oven to 400°F with oven
rack in middle of oven. Cook butter,
oil, and thyme in a small skillet
over medium until butter is melted
and bubbling, about 1 minute.
Remove from heat; set aside.
2. Peel potatoes; thinly slice each,
keeping slices in order and forming
6 to 8 stacks of slices that taper
toward the top. Arrange stacks of
potato slices in a 10-inch cast-iron
skillet, fanning out stacks as you
place them in skillet.
3. Brush potatoes with half of
butter mixture. Roast at 400°F
until lightly browned, 40 to 45
minutes. Brush with remaining
butter mixture; roast until crispy
edges form on potatoes, about
15 minutes. Turn broiler to high.
Sprinkle potatoes with cheese
and pine nuts; broil until cheese
is melted, 2 to 3 minutes. Sprinkle
with salt. Serves 8 (serving size:
1 wedge)

CALORIES 226; **FAT** 10g (sat 3g, unsat 6g);
PROTEIN 5g; **CARB** 32g; **FIBER** 2g; **SUGARS** 1g
(added sugars 0g); **SODIUM** 313mg; **CALC** 6%
DV; **POTASSIUM** 16% DV

Vegetarian

Potato-Butternut Gratin with Poblano Béchamel

Hands-on: 30 min. **Total:** 2 hr.
The mild sweetness of butternut
squash pairs particularly well with
Mexican flavors of poblano chile
and cumin. Goat cheese brightens
and enriches the flavor, and toasty
almonds offer a welcome textural
contrast. Try to get a squash with a
long neck, as slices from that section
are easiest to work with. It's important
to allow the gratin to rest for 20
minutes after baking so the juices that
accumulate can thicken and absorb
into the vegetables.

4 small poblano chiles (about 3 oz.
　each)
Cooking spray
1 Tbsp. chopped fresh oregano
2 Tbsp. all-purpose flour
1 cup whole milk, divided
1 tsp. kosher salt
½ tsp. ground cumin
¼ tsp. ground nutmeg
Dash of cayenne pepper
5 oz. goat cheese, crumbled (about
　1¼ cups), divided
1 medium butternut squash (about
　20 oz.), peeled, seeded, and cut
　into very thin rounds
2 medium russet potatoes (about
　10 oz. each), peeled and cut into
　very thin rounds
¼ cup sliced almonds

1. Preheat broiler to high with oven
rack in top third of oven. Place
chiles on a baking sheet; coat with
cooking spray. Broil in preheated
oven until just blackened, about

10 minutes, turning once after
5 minutes; remove from oven.
Transfer oven rack to middle of
oven; turn oven temperature to
375°F. Transfer chiles to a bowl,
and cover tightly with plastic wrap.
Let stand at room temperature
15 minutes. Peel off and discard
blackened skins from chiles;
remove and discard stems and
seeds. Tear chiles into ¼-inch
strips; set aside ⅓ cup strips. Place
remaining chile strips in a mini
food chopper or food processor; add
oregano, and process until semi-
smooth, about 10 seconds.
2. Whisk together flour and ¼ cup
milk in a small bowl. Pour remaining
¾ cup milk into a medium saucepan;
bring to a boil over medium.
Add flour mixture; cook, stirring
constantly, until slightly thickened,
about 2 minutes. Stir in chile-oregano
mixture, salt, cumin, nutmeg,
cayenne pepper, and ¾ cup goat
cheese. Remove from heat.
3. Coat an 8-inch square glass or
ceramic baking dish with cooking
spray. Layer half of squash and
potato slices in dish in alternating
layers, beginning and ending
with squash. Top with half of
chile-cheese sauce. Repeat with
remaining squash, potato slices,
and sauce.
4. Cover baking dish tightly with
aluminum foil. Bake at 375°F on
rack in middle of oven until squash
and potatoes pierce easily with a
knife, 50 minutes to 1 hour. Remove
foil; sprinkle with almonds,
reserved ⅓ cup chile strips, and
remaining ½ cup goat cheese. Turn
broiler to high; broil on middle
rack until almonds are toasted and
cheese is melted, 2 to 3 minutes.
Remove from oven; let stand 20
minutes before slicing. Serves 10
(serving size: about ¾ cup)

CALORIES 152; **FAT** 5g (sat 3g, unsat 2g);
PROTEIN 6g; **CARB** 22g; **FIBER** 3g; **SUGARS** 3g
(added sugars 0g); **SODIUM** 274mg; **CALC** 9%
DV; **POTASSIUM** 10% DV

CLASSIC

Make Ahead • Vegetarian

Easy Corn Pudding

Hands-on: 10 min. **Total:** 1 hr. 10 min.
We add just a touch of sugar to enhance the sweetness of the corn and onion. The texture falls somewhere between a pudding and a soufflé—rich and custardy, with bubbles of air within. It's best served piping hot, but cold leftovers are good, too.

Cooking spray
2 ½ Tbsp. unsalted butter
4 cups frozen corn kernels, thawed and patted dry
1 cup chopped yellow onion
1 Tbsp. chopped fresh thyme
1 Tbsp. minced garlic
¼ cup thinly sliced scallions
3 Tbsp. all-purpose flour
1 Tbsp. granulated sugar
2 tsp. baking powder
¾ tsp. kosher salt
¾ tsp. black pepper
3 cups 2% reduced-fat milk
8 large eggs, lightly beaten

1. Preheat oven to 350°F with oven rack in middle of oven. Lightly coat a 13- x 9-inch glass or ceramic baking dish with cooking spray. Melt butter in a large skillet over medium-high until foamy. Add corn, onion, thyme, and garlic; cook, stirring occasionally, until lightly browned, 7 to 9 minutes. Remove from heat; stir in scallions. Let cool slightly, about 10 minutes.
2. Whisk together flour, sugar, baking powder, salt, and pepper in a small bowl. Whisk together milk and eggs in a large bowl until smooth. Whisk flour mixture into milk mixture until smooth. Stir in cooled corn mixture. Pour into prepared baking dish.
3. Bake at 350°F until lightly browned and center is set, 55 minutes to 1 hour. Serves 12 (serving size: ¾ cup)

CALORIES 161; FAT 7g (sat 3g, unsat 3g); PROTEIN 8g; CARB 17g; FIBER 1g; SUGARS 6g (added sugars 1g); SODIUM 279mg; CALC 13% DV; POTASSIUM 6% DV

NEXT-LEVEL

Make Ahead • Vegetarian

Elote Corn Pudding

Hands-on: 25 min. **Total:** 1 hr. 10 min.
This creamy side is inspired by the iconic Mexican street corn snack. It gets lots of flavor from salty Cotija cheese; look for it with other Mexican cheeses in your grocery store.

Cooking spray
3 large scallions
10 ears fresh corn, shucked
1 tsp. canola oil
2 Tbsp. minced garlic
¼ cup water
2 cups whole milk
2 large eggs, lightly beaten
2 Tbsp. unsalted butter, melted
2.13 oz. all-purpose flour (about ½ cup)
1 Tbsp. chopped fresh cilantro
1 ½ tsp. kosher salt
¾ tsp. black pepper
1 ¾ oz. Cotija cheese, crumbled (about 7 Tbsp.)
½ tsp. chili powder
Lime wedges

1. Lightly coat a 13- x 9-inch glass or ceramic baking dish with cooking spray. Preheat broiler to high with oven rack in top third of oven. Finely chop white and light green parts of scallions to equal ⅓ cup. (Discard remaining white and light green parts, or reserve for another use.) Reserve green tops of scallions.
2. Lightly coat corn with cooking spray; arrange on a rimmed baking sheet lined with aluminum foil. Broil, turning occasionally, until slightly charred on all sides, 15 to 20 minutes. Remove from oven; let stand until cool enough to handle, about 10 minutes. Turn oven temperature to 350°F.
3. While corn cools, heat oil in a medium nonstick skillet over medium-high. Add garlic and reserved ⅓ cup chopped white and light green scallion pieces; cook, stirring constantly, until fragrant, 1 minute. Transfer to a large bowl.
4. Cut corn kernels from cobs (about 6 cups); discard cobs. Place ¼ cup water and 2 cups corn kernels in a blender or food processor; process until coarsely ground, about 15 seconds. Transfer mixture to garlic mixture in bowl; stir in milk, eggs, melted butter, and remaining corn kernels. Stir in flour, cilantro, salt, and pepper. Pour into prepared baking dish.
5. Bake at 350°F until bubbly, about 40 minutes. Let cool 5 minutes. Slice reserved green scallion tops to equal 1 cup. (Discard remaining scallion tops, or reserve for another use.) Sprinkle corn pudding with sliced scallion tops, Cotija cheese, and chili powder; serve warm with lime wedges. Serves 12 (serving size: about ½ cup)

CALORIES 180; FAT 7g (sat 3g, unsat 3g); PROTEIN 7g; CARB 25g; FIBER 2g; SUGARS 8g (added sugars 0g); SODIUM 347mg; CALC 10% DV; POTASSIUM 8% DV

Make Ahead • Vegetarian

Creamy Broccoli-Cheddar Casserole

Hands-on: 50 min. **Total:** 55 min.
This fresher take on the traditional broccoli casserole is loaded with vegetables and comes together with a homemade sauce instead of sodium-heavy canned soup.

1 ½ oz. rustic sourdough bread, torn
   into ½-in. pieces (1 cup)
3 Tbsp. canola oil, divided
10 cups chopped broccoli florets
   (from 3 medium heads)
¼ cup water
3 cups chopped fresh cremini
   mushrooms (about 4 oz.)
½ cup finely chopped yellow onion
2 tsp. minced garlic
2 Tbsp. all-purpose flour
2 cups whole milk
¼ cup canola mayonnaise
½ tsp. plus ⅛ tsp. kosher salt
½ tsp. black pepper
⅛ tsp. ground nutmeg
Cooking spray
1 ½ oz. cheddar cheese, finely
   shredded (about ⅓ cup)

1. Preheat broiler to high with oven rack in top third of oven. Place bread pieces in a food processor; process until finely crumbled, about 30 seconds. Transfer to a small bowl; toss with 1 tablespoon oil, and set aside.
2. Combine broccoli and ¼ cup water in a large microwavable glass bowl; cover loosely with plastic wrap. Microwave at high until crisp-tender, about 5 minutes. Drain; set aside.

3. Heat 1 tablespoon oil in a large skillet over medium-high. Add mushrooms; cook, stirring occasionally, until golden, about 8 minutes. Transfer to a bowl; set aside.
4. Wipe skillet clean; add remaining 1 tablespoon oil, and heat over medium. Add onion; cook, stirring occasionally, until softened, about 5 minutes. Add garlic; cook, stirring constantly, until fragrant, about 1 minute. Sprinkle with flour; cook, stirring constantly, until onion pieces are evenly coated, about 1 minute. Whisk in milk; bring to a simmer over medium-high, stirring occasionally. Simmer, stirring occasionally, until thickened, about 4 minutes. Whisk in mayonnaise, salt, pepper, and nutmeg until smooth. Add broccoli and mushrooms; stir to combine. Cook, stirring occasionally, until mixture is hot, about 2 minutes.
5. Transfer broccoli mixture to an 11- x 7-inch glass or ceramic baking dish lightly coated with cooking spray; sprinkle with breadcrumbs and cheese. Broil until golden and bubbling, about 3 minutes. Serves 12 (serving size: about ½ cup)

CALORIES 133; **FAT** 9g (sat 2g, unsat 6g); **PROTEIN** 5g; **CARB** 10g; **FIBER** 2g; **SUGARS** 3g (added sugars 0g); **SODIUM** 256mg; **CALC** 11% DV; **POTASSIUM** 7% DV

Vegetarian

Broccoli-Artichoke Casserole

Hands-on: 1 hr. **Total:** 1 hr. 20 min.

Cooking spray
1 ½ cups plus 1 Tbsp. canola oil,
   divided
2 medium shallots, thinly sliced
   and separated into rings (about 1
   ½ cups)
¼ cup all-purpose flour, divided
8 cups chopped broccoli florets
¼ cup water
½ cup finely chopped yellow onion
2 tsp. minced garlic
¼ cup dry white wine
1 ¾ cups whole milk
2 ¼ oz. Gruyère cheese, shredded
   (about ½ cup plus 1 Tbsp.)
1 tsp. kosher salt
½ tsp. black pepper
1 (9-oz.) pkg. frozen artichoke
   hearts, thawed and chopped
   (about 1 ½ cups)

1. Lightly coat an 11- x 7-inch glass or ceramic baking dish with cooking spray. Preheat oven to 350°F. Heat 1 ½ cups oil in a heavy 2-quart stockpot over medium-high until a deep-fry thermometer reads 350°F.
2. Toss together shallots and 2 tablespoons flour in a small bowl. Add to hot oil; fry, stirring occasionally, until golden and crisp, 3 to 4 minutes. Using a slotted spoon, transfer to a plate lined with paper towels. Set aside.
3. Combine broccoli and ¼ cup water in a large microwavable glass bowl; cover loosely with plastic wrap. Microwave at high until crisp-tender, about 5 minutes. Drain and set aside.
4. Heat remaining 1 tablespoon oil in a large skillet over medium.

Add onion; cook, stirring occasionally, until softened, about 4 minutes. Add garlic; cook, stirring constantly, until fragrant, about 1 minute. Add wine; cook, stirring constantly, until liquid is almost evaporated, about 1 minute. Sprinkle with remaining 2 tablespoons flour; cook, stirring constantly, until onion pieces are coated. Whisk in milk; bring to a simmer over medium. Cook, whisking occasionally, until thickened, 4 to 5 minutes. Stir in cheese, salt, and pepper until melted and smooth, about 1 minute. Remove from heat.

5. Add artichokes to broccoli in bowl. Stir in cheese sauce. Pour into prepared baking dish; top with fried shallots. Bake at 350°F until warmed through, about 20 minutes. Serves 12 (serving size: about ½ cup)

CALORIES 125; FAT 7g (sat 2g, unsat 4g); PROTEIN 5g; CARB 11g; FIBER 3g; SUGARS 4g (added sugars 0g); SODIUM 245mg; CALC 14% DV; POTASSIUM 5% DV

BREADS

Folks may not recall all of the varied dishes you made for the big day, but they will always remember if you treated them to homemade bread. Make a lasting impression and make it easy on yourself with these no-yeast options.

BAKE THESE LAST

Both the Herbed Biscuits and the Stuffing-Flavored Cornbread (page 308) are best served fresh from the oven, so plan to bake them about 15 minutes before go-time. You can get ahead with the biscuits by cutting out the dough and freezing the pucks; bake straight from the freezer, adding an extra 2 to 5 minutes to the cook time.

CLASSIC

Staff Favorite · Fast
Make Ahead · Vegetarian

Herbed Biscuits

Hands-on: 15 min. **Total:** 30 min.
Two key techniques make these whole-grain biscuits light and fluffy: smashing the butter into the flour mixture with your fingers, and folding the dough to create layers.

8.75 oz. whole-wheat pastry flour (about 2⅓ cups)
1 Tbsp. baking powder
1 tsp. kosher salt
¼ tsp. baking soda
¼ tsp. black pepper
½ cup cold unsalted butter (4 oz.), divided
2 tsp. chopped fresh thyme
1 cup 1% low-fat buttermilk

1. Preheat oven to 450°F. Whisk together flour, baking powder, salt, baking soda, and black pepper in a large bowl.
2. Cut 7 tablespoons butter into ½-inch cubes; add to flour mixture, and combine with hands, smashing butter between your fingers until all cubes are mixed into the flour and flattened (you will have noticeable pieces of different sizes). Stir in thyme.

3. Add buttermilk; stir with a rubber spatula until flour is fully absorbed. Shape dough into a rough ball; turn dough out onto a lightly floured surface.
4. Gently pat dough into a ½-inch-thick square; fold dough in half, and pat into a ½-inch-thick square. Fold in half again. Repeat folding-and-patting procedure once more. Pat dough to a thickness of about ¾ inch.
5. Cut dough using a 1¾-inch round cutter. Gather dough scraps, and pat to a ¾-inch thickness 2 more times to yield 20 biscuits. Place biscuits 1 inch apart on a parchment paper–lined baking sheet.
6. Bake at 450°F until golden brown, 12 to 14 minutes. Place remaining 1 tablespoon butter in a small microwavable bowl; microwave at high until melted, 15 to 20 seconds. Brush tops of hot biscuits with melted butter, and serve immediately. Serves 20 (serving size: 1 biscuit)

CALORIES 133; FAT 5g (sat 3g, unsat 1g); PROTEIN 3g; CARB 19g; FIBER 3g; SUGARS 1g (added sugars 0g); SODIUM 214mg; CALC 5% DV; POTASSIUM 2% DV

"As a Southerner, I'm all about cornbread dressing at Thanksgiving. But it's a labor of love and takes more time than I might have to spare. This recipe gives me the flavor of my beloved holiday side in a much faster, easier format. And leftovers—split, toasted, and topped with turkey and gravy—are divine."

Ann Taylor Pittman, Executive Editor

NEXT-LEVEL

Staff Favorite • Vegetarian

Stuffing-Flavored Cornbread

Hands-on: 25 min. **Total:** 45 min. This hearty bread captures the essence of classic cornbread stuffing but is quicker and easier to make.

3 Tbsp. unsalted butter, divided
¼ cup chopped yellow onion
¼ cup chopped celery
2 tsp. chopped fresh sage
6.3 oz. whole-grain coarse-ground cornmeal (about 1½ cups)
1 oz. white whole-wheat flour (about ¼ cup)
1½ tsp. baking powder
1 tsp. baking soda
1 tsp. granulated sugar
1 tsp. poultry seasoning
½ tsp. kosher salt
¼ tsp. black pepper
1¾ cups 1% low-fat buttermilk
2 large eggs

1. Preheat oven to 450°F. Melt 1 tablespoon butter in a 10-inch cast-iron skillet over medium-high. Add onion and celery; cook, stirring often, until softened, about 5 minutes. Add sage; cook, stirring constantly, 1 minute. Transfer mixture to a small bowl, and wipe skillet clean. Place skillet in oven. (Do not remove skillet from oven while preparing batter.)
2. Whisk together cornmeal, flour, baking powder, baking soda, sugar, poultry seasoning, salt, and black pepper in a large bowl. Whisk together buttermilk and eggs in a small bowl.

3. Add remaining 2 tablespoons butter to hot skillet; return to oven until butter is melted, about 1 minute. Stir onion mixture and buttermilk mixture into cornmeal mixture until just combined. Pour melted butter from hot skillet into batter, and quickly stir to incorporate. Pour batter into hot skillet, and immediately place in oven.
4. Bake at 450°F until golden brown and cornbread pulls away from sides of skillet, 15 to 18 minutes. Invert cornbread onto a plate; cool 5 minutes, and serve hot. Serves 12 (serving size: 1 slice)

CALORIES 122; FAT 5g (sat 2g, unsat 1g); PROTEIN 4g; CARB 16g; FIBER 3g; SUGARS 2g (added sugars 0g); SODIUM 305mg; CALC 7% DV; POTASSIUM 1% DV

HOW TO ROAST EVERYTHING

Whether low and slow or hot and fast, roasting builds big flavor in meats and vegetables. This comprehensive guide delivers tips, tricks, and recipes for mastering the art of roasting.

CLASSIC ROAST: THE GOLD STANDARD

BEST FOR CRISPY SKIN AND JUICY MEAT

Roasting is one of a handful of ways to cook with dry heat. Baking is, too, but technically baking is for foods that lack structure until the cooking process is complete (think: batters, doughs). Roasting involves foods that have a solid structure from the start, and roast turkey is a signature example. We start this traditional technique at a high temperature (500°F) then drop down (350°F) for the rest of the cook time. That initial blast of high heat promotes a crisp exterior, while switching to low and slow ensures a moist interior. If you maintained that scorching heat, the turkey's muscle fibers would contract and expel their moisture, leaving you with dry, tough meat.

Gluten Free

Lemon-Herb Turkey

Hands-on: 45 min. **Total:** 13 hr. 55 min. We tried wet-brining, dry-brining, and injection-brining techniques before landing on self-basting as the best method. To keep sodium down, we found that injecting the bird with fat and seasoned liquid gives you the most flavor and juiciest meat.

1 (14-lb.) whole fresh or thawed frozen turkey
¾ cup unsalted chicken stock
½ cup plus 3 Tbsp. unsalted butter
12 thyme sprigs, divided
6 rosemary sprigs, divided
3 medium garlic cloves, smashed
4¾ tsp. kosher salt
2 tsp. granulated sugar
2 tsp. lemon zest
1 small yellow onion, halved
1 lemon, halved
1 medium garlic head, halved

1. Remove giblets and neck from turkey; discard or reserve for another use. Trim excess fat from turkey; pat turkey dry. Place turkey, breast side up, on a rack set inside a rimmed baking sheet. Place, uncovered, in refrigerator. Combine stock, butter, 6 thyme sprigs, 3 rosemary sprigs, and smashed garlic cloves in a small saucepan. Cook over low, stirring occasionally, until butter has melted and flavors are infused, about 10 minutes. Remove from heat. Let stand at room temperature 2 hours. Cover and place in refrigerator. Let turkey and butter mixture chill 8 hours or overnight.

2. Remove turkey from refrigerator. Let stand at room temperature 1 hour; discard any accumulated juices on baking sheet. Preheat oven to 500°F with oven rack in lowest position. Remove butter mixture from refrigerator; reheat over low, stirring occasionally, until melted and warm, about 8 minutes. Strain into a small bowl; discard solids. Add salt and sugar to strained butter mixture, and stir until dissolved. Add zest. Place halved onion, halved lemon, halved garlic head, remaining 6 thyme sprigs, and remaining 3 rosemary sprigs inside body cavity of turkey. Secure legs with kitchen twine. Using a turkey injector, inject butter mixture throughout breast, legs, and thighs.

3. Roast turkey at 500°F until skin is golden, 35 to 40 minutes. Remove from oven, and cover breast with foil. Reduce oven temperature to 350°F. Return turkey to oven immediately, and bake until a thermometer inserted in thickest part of breast registers 160°F, about 1 hour and 20 minutes. Transfer turkey to a cutting board. Let turkey rest, loosely covered with foil, 15 minutes (internal temperature will rise to 165°F). Serves 16 (serving size: about 6 oz. turkey)

CALORIES 164; FAT 5g (sat 2g, unsat 2g); PROTEIN 27g; CARB 0g; FIBER 0g; SUGARS 0g; SODIUM 275mg; CALC 2% DV; POTASSIUM 5% DV

Vegetarian

Mushroom and Marsala-Onion Tartines

Hands-on: 45 min. **Total:** 1 hr.
For the mushrooms, use either a presliced mix of wild mushrooms from the grocery store or seek out more unique varieties at specialty stores or a farmers' market. For the toasts, use a good-quality sourdough.

1 cup drained and unrinsed canned cannellini beans
6 Tbsp. olive oil, divided
1½ Tbsp. red wine vinegar, divided
1 medium garlic clove, smashed
1 tsp. kosher salt, divided
½ tsp. chopped fresh thyme
10 oz. cipollini onions (about 12 onions), peeled
1½ Tbsp. turbinado sugar
1 cup unsalted chicken stock
½ cup sweet Marsala wine
1 lb. fresh wild mushrooms, sliced (about 7 cups)
¼ tsp. black pepper
4 (1½-oz.) sourdough bread slices (about ¾ in. thick), toasted
Fresh thyme leaves

1. Place beans, 2 tablespoons oil, 1½ teaspoons vinegar, garlic, ½ teaspoon salt, and chopped thyme in a high-powered blender. Process until mixture is smooth and has the texture of hummus, adding water, 1 teaspoon at a time, until desired consistency is reached, about 30 seconds. Set aside.
2. Heat 1 tablespoon oil in a medium saucepan over medium-high. Add onions; cook, stirring occasionally, until browned, about 5 minutes. Reduce heat to medium; add sugar and ¼ teaspoon salt. Cook, stirring constantly, until sugar starts to melt, about 20 seconds. Add stock; cook, stirring occasionally, until liquid is reduced by half and onions have softened, about 6 minutes. Stir in wine; cook, stirring occasionally, until liquid is reduced by half, about 6 minutes. Stir in remaining 1 tablespoon vinegar; cook, stirring occasionally, until sauce is syrupy, liquid is reduced to about 3 tablespoons, and onions are glazed, 14 to 16 minutes. Remove from heat, and cover to keep warm.
3. Heat 1 tablespoon oil in a large cast-iron skillet over medium-high. Add just enough mushrooms to cover bottom of skillet (about one-third of mushrooms). Cook, undisturbed, until bottoms are golden brown, 2 to 3 minutes. Flip and cook until softened, 2 to 3 minutes. Transfer to a bowl. Repeat procedure twice with remaining 2 tablespoons oil and remaining mushrooms. Toss cooked mushrooms with pepper and remaining ¼ teaspoon salt.
4. Spread bean mixture evenly over toasted bread slices. Top each slice with about ¼ cup onions and ½ cup mushrooms. Drizzle tartines evenly with onion glaze; sprinkle with thyme leaves. Serves 4 (serving size: 1 tartine)

CALORIES 475; FAT 22g (sat 3g, unsat 18g); PROTEIN 13g; CARB 51g; FIBER 6g; SUGARS 15g (added sugars 5g); SODIUM 798mg; CALC 7% DV; POTASSIUM 14% DV

Staff Favorite · Gluten Free

Peppercorn-and-Coriander–Crusted Roast

Hands-on: 20 min. **Total:** 12 hr. 25 min.

2 Tbsp. black peppercorns
2 Tbsp. coriander seeds
2 Tbsp. Dijon mustard
3½ tsp. kosher salt
1 (4¼-lb.) 2-rib standing beef rib roast, chine bone removed

1. Cook peppercorns and coriander seeds in a small skillet over medium, stirring occasionally, until fragrant, about 4 minutes. Remove from heat; cool 10 minutes. Coarsely crush with a mortar and pestle, or transfer to a ziplock plastic bag and crush with a heavy skillet.

2. Stir together mustard, salt, and crushed spices in a small bowl. Rub mixture evenly over roast. Place roast, fat cap up, on a wire rack set inside a rimmed baking sheet lined with aluminum foil. Chill, uncovered, 8 hours or overnight.

3. Remove roast from refrigerator; let stand at room temperature 1 hour. Preheat oven to 300°F. Cook roast in preheated oven until a thermometer inserted in thickest portion registers 120°F for medium-rare, about 2 hours and 30 minutes (or 130°F for medium), rotating pan after 1 hour and 30 minutes. Remove from oven; discard drippings from baking sheet.

4. Increase oven temperature to 500°F. Let rest while oven preheats, at least 30 minutes. Return roast to oven; cook at 500°F until meat is well browned and a crust has formed, 5 to 8 minutes. Slice and serve immediately. Serves 14 (serving size: 3 oz. beef)

CALORIES 254; FAT 15g (sat 6g, unsat 7g); PROTEIN 27g; CARB 0g; FIBER 0g; SUGARS 0g; SODIUM 588mg; CALC 3% DV; POTASSIUM 7% DV

HIGH HEAT: FOR THE PERFECT CHAR

BEST FOR SUBTLE SMOKE FLAVOR

We love how high-heat roasting—from 425°F and up—imparts a hint of smokiness to foods. A blasting hot oven can perfectly char thin-cut pork chops or—in these particular recipes—yield blistered, but not mushy, peppers. Plus, you can usually get away with far less oil (or none at all) when cranking the heat, saving you a step and a few calories.

Make Ahead • Vegetarian

Romesco

Hands-on: 20 min. **Total:** 1 hr. 15 min. Make this romesco as smooth or chunky as you like—and up to three days ahead. Use leftovers as a sandwich spread or sauce to top meat or pasta. Sunchokes are sometimes labeled as Jerusalem artichokes. If you can't find them, substitute fingerling potatoes.

ROMESCO
⅓ cup hazelnuts
1 (1¼-oz.) country-style bread slice (about ¾ in. thick)
2 large red bell peppers
¼ cup blanched almonds
1 medium garlic clove, smashed
¼ cup sun-dried tomatoes in oil, drained
3 Tbsp. olive oil
2 Tbsp. sherry vinegar
1½ tsp. smoked paprika
1½ tsp. kosher salt
⅛ tsp. cayenne pepper

FRESH AND ROASTED VEGETABLES
12 oz. sunchokes, scrubbed and cut lengthwise into ½-in.-thick slices
1 medium fennel bulb, cut into ½-in. wedges, divided
8 oz. small multicolored carrots, halved lengthwise, divided
2 Tbsp. olive oil
¼ tsp. kosher salt
4 oz. radishes, thinly sliced (about 1 cup)
2 heads Belgian endive or radicchio (about 6 oz.), leaves separated

1. Prepare the romesco: Preheat oven to 325°F with oven rack in middle of oven. Spread hazelnuts and bread in an even layer on a rimmed baking sheet. Bake at 325°F until hazelnuts are toasted and bread is slightly dried, about 8 minutes. Using a towel, rub off hazelnut skins. Set aside hazelnuts and bread.

2. Turn on broiler to high with oven rack in top third of oven. Place bell peppers on a rimmed baking sheet. Broil, turning occasionally, until charred, about 14 minutes. Set oven temperature to 425°F. Transfer peppers to a bowl. Cover tightly with plastic wrap, and let stand 10 minutes. Peel, stem, and seed peppers.

3. Tear toasted bread into small pieces; place in a food processor. Add toasted hazelnuts, almonds, and garlic; process until finely chopped, about 20 seconds. Add charred bell peppers, sun-dried tomatoes, oil, vinegar, paprika, salt, and cayenne. Process until almost smooth, about 30 seconds. Set aside.

4. Prepare the fresh and roasted vegetables: Toss together sunchokes, half of fennel, half of carrots, oil, and salt on a rimmed baking sheet. Roast at 425°F until tender, 30 to 35 minutes.

5. Spoon romesco into a serving bowl. Serve with roasted vegetable mixture, radish, endive, and remaining fresh fennel and carrots. Serves 16 (serving size: 2 Tbsp. Romesco and about 2½ oz. vegetables)

CALORIES 190; FAT 13g (sat 3g, unsat 9g); PROTEIN 8g; CARB 20g; FIBER 9g; SUGARS 11g (added sugars 0g); SODIUM 318mg; CALC 20% DV; POTASSIUM 15% DV

Harissa-Spiked Hummus

Hands-on: 30 min. **Total:** 40 min.

1 large red bell pepper
1 medium serrano chile
3 medium garlic cloves, unpeeled
3 Tbsp. olive oil, divided
1½ Tbsp. fresh lemon juice
1 Tbsp. ground Aleppo pepper
1½ tsp. ground cumin
¾ tsp. plus ⅛ tsp. kosher salt
¾ tsp. ground coriander
1 (10-oz.) container hummus
1 Tbsp. chopped fresh flat-leaf
    parsley
Fresh and Roasted Vegetables (p. 311)

1. Preheat broiler to high with oven rack in middle of oven. Place pepper, chile, and garlic on a rimmed baking sheet. Broil, turning occasionally, until pepper and chile are charred and garlic is softened, removing chile after 6 minutes, garlic after 10 minutes, and pepper after 14 minutes. Transfer pepper and chile to a bowl; cover tightly with plastic wrap. Let stand 10 minutes. Peel, stem, and seed pepper and chile. Peel garlic cloves.
2. Place pepper, chile, garlic, 2 tablespoons oil, lemon juice, Aleppo pepper, cumin, salt, and coriander in a food processor. Process until smooth.
3. Spoon hummus into a serving bowl. Spoon harissa over hummus; drizzle with remaining 1 tablespoon oil, and sprinkle with parsley. Serve hummus with Fresh and Roasted Vegetables. Serves 16 (serving size: 2 Tbsp. hummus and about 2 ½ oz. vegetables)

CALORIES 121; **FAT** 8g (sat 1g, unsat 4g); **PROTEIN** 3g; **CARB** 12g; **FIBER** 4g; **SUGARS** 4g (added sugars 0g); **SODIUM** 249mg; **CALC** 3% DV; **POTASSIUM** 7% DV

COAL ROAST: FOR DRAMATIC RESULTS

BEST FOR BOLD, SMOKY FLAVOR

This is a fairly hands-off approach to roasting. It also requires less oil than oven-roasting or sautéing. Use natural lump charcoal (no chemicals), because your food is cooked straight in the embers. Coal-roasting works well with vegetables that have a protective outer layer that can be peeled off, such as russet and sweet potatoes, beets, eggplant (if you're only using the scooped-out flesh), corn (in the husk), and onions. If you want to tone down the smoke flavor, wrap the food in aluminum foil before roasting.

Cabbage Wedge Salad

Hands-on: 30 min. **Total:** 4 hr.

1 medium head red cabbage
    (about 3 lbs.)
2 Tbsp. olive oil, divided
¼ cup plain whole-milk Greek
    yogurt
3 Tbsp. mayonnaise
3 Tbsp. whole buttermilk
2⅓ tsp. fresh lemon juice
1 medium garlic clove, grated
½ tsp. kosher salt
2 oz. feta cheese, crumbled
    (about ½ cup)
¼ cup chopped fresh chives
⅓ tsp. ground sumac or Aleppo
    pepper

1. Light a charcoal chimney starter filled with all-natural lump charcoal; let burn until completely gray, about 30 minutes. Dump charcoal into a fire pit or grill (under grill grate); let burn, uncovered, until smoldering, about 30 minutes. Fan the outer layer of ash off coals. Rub cabbage with 1 tablespoon oil; place directly on hot coals. Cover and cook, turning occasionally, until tender and charred on all sides, 2 hours and 30 minutes to 3 hours. Remove from coals; let stand until cool enough to handle, about 30 minutes. Discard outer charred leaves. Cut cabbage into 6 wedges; remove core.
2. Whisk together yogurt, mayonnaise, buttermilk, lemon juice, garlic, salt, and remaining 1 tablespoon oil in a bowl until smooth. Drizzle over wedges. Sprinkle with feta, chives, and sumac. Serves 6 (serving size: 1 wedge and 2 Tbsp. dressing)

CALORIES 190; **FAT** 13g (sat 3g, unsat 9g); **PROTEIN** 8g; **CARB** 20g; **FIBER** 9g; **SUGARS** 10g (added sugars 0g); **SODIUM** 318mg; **CALC** 20% DV; **POTASSIUM** 15% DV

SLOW ROAST: TO COAX OUT SWEETNESS

BEST FOR CONCENTRATING FLAVORS

Slow-roasting is how pros liven up out-of-season produce. It draws out moisture and concentrates flavors while slowly caramelizing the natural sugars for a sweeter bite. We tried slow-roasting tomatoes at 200°F in a convection oven and a conventional oven. Convection was faster—after 3 hours and 30 minutes the tomatoes were comparable to the conventional ones at the 5-hour mark. But the convection ones were drier and more chewy, while the conventional ones retained a pop of moisture with their concentrated sweetness.

Aglio e Olio with Roasted Tomatoes

Hands-on: 25 min. **Total:** 5 hr. 25 min.
This pasta looks special, but it's doable for a weeknight dinner if you roast and refrigerate the tomatoes in advance. You can store them in an airtight container up to two days.

12 oz. grape tomatoes, halved (about 2 cups)
5 Tbsp. olive oil, divided
1 small bunch Swiss chard (about 8 oz.)
8 oz. uncooked bucatini pasta
4 medium garlic cloves, thinly sliced (about 3 Tbsp.)
1¼ tsp. kosher salt
⅛ tsp. crushed red pepper
½ cup whole-milk ricotta cheese
2 Tbsp. pine nuts, toasted

1. Preheat oven to 200°F. Toss together tomatoes and 2 teaspoons oil on a rimmed baking sheet lined with parchment paper. Arrange tomatoes cut sides up. Roast at 200°F until softened and dehydrated, about 5 hours. Set aside.
2. Remove stems from chard, and thinly slice stems to equal 1 cup. Discard remaining stems, or reserve for another use. Tear leaves into 1-inch pieces.
3. Bring a large pot of water to a boil over high. Add pasta; cook 4 minutes. Add sliced chard stems; cook until pasta is al dente and stems are tender, about 3 minutes, adding chard leaves during last 20 seconds. Reserve 1 cup cooking liquid. Drain pasta mixture.
4. Heat garlic and ¼ cup oil in a large skillet over medium. Cook, stirring often, until garlic is light golden brown, about 4 minutes. Add pasta-chard mixture, roasted tomatoes, salt, crushed red pepper, and reserved cooking liquid. Cook, tossing constantly, until sauce thickens and pasta is coated, 3 to 4 minutes. Divide pasta among 4 shallow bowls. Top evenly with ricotta, pine nuts, and remaining 1 teaspoon oil. Serves 4 (serving size: 1¼ cups)

CALORIES 472; FAT 25g (sat 5g, unsat 18g); PROTEIN 14g; CARB 54g; FIBER 4g; SUGARS 3g (added sugars 0g); SODIUM 766mg; CALC 11% DV; POTASSIUM 9% DV

**Staff Favorite • Gluten Free
Make Ahead • Vegetarian**

Beet and Citrus Salad with Almond Gremolata

Hands-on: 20 min. **Total:** 1 hr. 20 min.

2 cups kosher salt
3 large egg whites
3 medium-sized red or golden beets (about 1¼ lbs.), trimmed
Cooking spray
¼ cup finely chopped unsalted roasted almonds
¼ cup chopped fresh flat-leaf parsley
1 Tbsp. lemon zest (from 2 lemons)
1 small garlic clove, minced (about ¾ tsp.)
⅓ cup plain 2% reduced-fat Greek yogurt
3 Tbsp. crème fraîche
2 medium oranges (about 14 oz.), peeled and cut into ½-in. wedges
1 Tbsp. Champagne vinegar
1½ tsp. extra-virgin olive oil
⅛ tsp. black pepper

1. Preheat oven to 400°F. Whisk salt and egg whites in a large bowl until mixture is the texture of wet sand. Coat beets generously with cooking spray. Using your hands, pack salt mixture onto beets, completely encasing each beet. Place beets 2 inches apart on a baking sheet, and roast at 400°F until salt crust is golden brown and beets are tender when pierced with a knife, about 50 minutes. Cool beets 10 minutes; remove salt crust. Peel beets, and cut into ½-inch wedges.
2. Stir together almonds, parsley, zest, and garlic in a small bowl. Mix yogurt and crème fraîche in another small bowl.
3. Spread yogurt mixture onto a serving platter; top with beets and oranges wedges. Drizzle with vinegar and oil. Sprinkle with almond mixture and pepper. Serves 6 (serving size: ¾ cup)

CALORIES 149; FAT 8g (sat 2g, unsat 4g); PROTEIN 5g; CARB 17g; FIBER 5g; SUGARS 12g (added sugars 0g); SODIUM 232mg; CALC 9% DV; POTASSIUM 9% DV

SALT CRUST: FOR SUPER SEASONING
TO LOCK IN MOISTURE

Salt-crusting pulls double duty by locking in moisture while thoroughly seasoning. The crust insulates the vegetable or protein inside, slowing evaporation and cooking the food gently and evenly. It's also healthier than you might think; only a small amount of sodium is absorbed into the food. Use this method with other root veggies like rutabaga, carrots, parsnips, and turnips, as well as with whole fish and chicken.

REINVENT YOUR THANKSGIVING LEFTOVERS

Create a little breathing room in your fridge by incorporating your extra celery, herbs, carrots, and more into recipes that are fresh, bright, and—best of all—easy to make.

These five recipes approach the idea of Thanksgiving leftovers in a simple way. Instead of jumping through hoops to repurpose fully realized dishes, such as mashed potatoes or stuffing (which is probably the last thing you want to do after a day on your feet cooking), we're sharing easy ideas that use up the leftover ingredients you might have bought for the meal—that half-bunch of celery, for example, or the lone sweet potato on the counter. Each recipe offers zippy flavors to offset the richer ones from the holiday—also most welcome in the days after feasting.

1. Preheat oven to 375°F. Line a 12-cup muffin pan with baking cups.
2. Toss together carrot, apple, and brown sugar in a medium bowl. Let stand 10 minutes.
3. Whisk together flour, baking powder, garam masala, salt, and baking soda in a large bowl.
4. Add buttermilk, oil, vanilla, egg, and 1 teaspoon orange zest to carrot mixture; stir until well combined. Add buttermilk mixture and pecans to flour mixture; stir until well combined. Divide mixture evenly among prepared muffin cups. Bake at 375°F until a wooden pick inserted in center of muffins comes out clean, 18 to 20 minutes. Cool in pan on a wire rack 5 minutes. Remove muffins from pan, and cool slightly, about 10 minutes.
5. Combine powdered sugar, orange juice, and remaining ½ teaspoon orange zest in a medium bowl. Drizzle evenly over muffins. Serves 12 (serving size: 1 muffin)

CALORIES 189; FAT 8g (sat 1g, unsat 6g); PROTEIN 3g; CARB 26g; FIBER 2g; SUGARS 16g (added sugars 14g); SODIUM 197mg; CALC 8% DV; POTASSIUM 2% DV

MUFFINS USE UP

Carrots, apple, orange, and pecans

Make Ahead • Vegetarian

Carrot-Apple Muffins with Orange Glaze

Hands-on: 20 min. **Total:** 45 min.
Look for garam masala in the spice aisle; large spice brands make it. If you don't have it or can't find it, you can substitute an equal amount of cinnamon.

¾ cup finely shredded carrot (about 2 medium carrots)
¾ cup shredded peeled apple (about 1 medium apple)
½ cup packed light brown sugar
6 oz. white whole-wheat flour (about 1½ cups)
1½ tsp. baking powder
1 tsp. garam masala
½ tsp. kosher salt
¼ tsp. baking soda
¾ cup whole buttermilk
3 Tbsp. canola oil
1 tsp. vanilla extract
1 large egg, lightly beaten
1½ tsp. orange zest, divided, plus 1 Tbsp. fresh orange juice, divided
½ cup chopped toasted pecans
½ cup (about 2 oz.) powdered sugar

SOUP USES UP

Sourdough, shallots, garlic, carrot, chicken stock, wine, thyme, and half-and-half

Make Ahead

Silky Garlic Soup with Sourdough Soldiers

Hands-on: 15 min. **Total:** 40 min.
If you've never had garlic soup before, don't be scared off by the idea. The garlic flavor is present, but it's quite

mellow and sweet after cooking. The soup is barely thick, with more of a "coats the back of a spoon" texture than, say, the thickness of a creamy potato soup—making it perfect for dunking toasted breadsticks into.

5 oz. sourdough bread, divided
1 Tbsp. unsalted butter, melted
3 Tbsp. olive oil, divided
1 cup halved shallots, or quartered if large (about 3 medium shallots)
1 medium garlic head, cloves peeled and halved, or quartered if large (about 10 cloves)
1 medium carrot, coarsely chopped (about ⅓ cup)
⅓ cup dry white wine
2 cups unsalted chicken stock
¾ tsp. kosher salt
3 thyme sprigs
⅔ cup half-and-half
Cracked black pepper (optional)

1. Preheat oven to 375°F. Finely chop 1 ounce bread, and set aside. Cut remaining 4 ounces bread into 16 sticks, or soldiers. Stir together butter and 1 tablespoon oil in a small bowl; brush evenly over all sides of breadsticks. Set aside any remaining butter-oil mixture. Arrange breadsticks in a single layer on an aluminum foil–lined baking sheet. Bake at 375°F, turning occasionally, until evenly toasted, about 12 minutes.
2. Meanwhile, heat remaining 2 tablespoons oil and any remaining butter-oil mixture in a large saucepan over medium-low. Add shallots, garlic, and carrot. Cover and cook, stirring occasionally, until vegetables are tender when pierced with a fork, 10 to 15 minutes. Increase heat to medium-high. Add the wine; cook until liquid is mostly evaporated, about 2 minutes. Add chopped bread, stock, salt, and thyme; bring to a boil. Reduce the heat to medium-low; simmer,

uncovered, until vegetables are very tender and bread has dissolved, about 10 minutes.
3. Discard thyme sprigs. Pour chicken stock mixture into a blender; add half-and-half. Remove center piece of blender lid (to allow steam to escape); secure lid on blender. Place a clean towel over opening in blender lid (to avoid splatters). Process until very smooth, about 1 minute. Return chicken stock mixture to pan over medium, and cook, stirring occasionally, until warmed through, about 2 minutes. Ladle soup into each of 4 bowls; garnish with pepper, if desired. Serve with breadsticks. Serves 4 (serving size: 1 cup soup and 4 toast soldiers)

CALORIES 327; **FAT** 19g (sat 6g, unsat 11g); **PROTEIN** 8g; **CARB** 31g; **FIBER** 3g; **SUGARS** 5g (added sugars 0g); **SODIUM** 660mg; **CALC** 11% DV; **POTASSIUM** 5% DV

SALAD USES UP

Raisins, sherry (or other wine), lemon, celery, parsley, and Parmigiano-Reggiano

---

Staff Favorite • Fast
Gluten Free • Make Ahead
Vegetarian

Celery-and-Parsley Salad with Wine-Soaked Raisins

Hands-on: 10 min. **Total:** 30 min.
This easy salad is zippy, crunchy, light, and fresh—an antidote to an overindulgent Thanksgiving. And it happens to pair especially well with a leftover turkey-and-cranberry-sauce sandwich. We love the depth that the wine-soaked raisins add, but you could also omit the wine and instead use raisins straight out of the box.

⅓ cup golden raisins
3 Tbsp. dry or cream sherry, Madeira, Marsala, or white wine
2 Tbsp. extra-virgin olive oil
2 Tbsp. fresh lemon juice (from 1 lemon)
¼ tsp. kosher salt
¼ tsp. black pepper
2 cups thinly diagonally sliced celery plus ½ cup celery leaves (about 5 to 6 stalks), divided
2 cups fresh flat-leaf parsley leaves (about ½ large bunch)
1 oz. Parmigiano-Reggiano cheese, shaved (about ⅓ cup)

1. Place raisins and wine in a microwavable bowl. Microwave at high until mixture boils vigorously, about 1 minute. Let stand 10 minutes or until most of liquid is absorbed.
2. Whisk together oil, lemon juice, salt, and pepper in a medium bowl. Stir in sliced celery; let stand 10 minutes. Add raisin mixture (including any wine that hasn't been absorbed), parsley, and celery leaves; stir well. Divide mixture among 4 plates. Top with cheese. Serves 4 (serving size: about 1 cup salad and 4 tsp. cheese)

CALORIES 164; **FAT** 9g (sat 2g, unsat 6g); **PROTEIN** 4g; **CARB** 16g; **FIBER** 2g; **SUGARS** 9g (added sugars 0g); **SODIUM** 278mg; **CALC** 16% DV; **POTASSIUM** 9% DV

Fast · Gluten Free
Make Ahead · Vegetarian

Curried Sweet Potato–Yogurt Dip

Hands-on: 10 min. **Total:** 10 min.
Sweet potatoes make a wonderful base for a creamy dip, creating a smooth texture and faintly sweet flavor. Toasting the curry paste in the first step helps to deepen the flavor and is worth the extra couple of minutes.

¾ tsp. curry powder
1 cup mashed cooked sweet potato (about 1 medium sweet potato)
½ cup plain 2% reduced-fat Greek yogurt
½ cup water
¼ cup tahini (sesame seed paste)
2 Tbsp. fresh lemon juice
2 tsp. grated peeled fresh ginger
¾ tsp. kosher salt

1. Heat a small skillet over medium. Add curry powder; cook, stirring constantly, until toasted and fragrant, about 1 minute and 30 seconds. Remove from heat.
2. Place sweet potato, yogurt, ½ cup water, tahini, lemon juice, ginger, salt, and curry powder in a blender or food processor (blender will yield very creamy results; food processor will yield a coarser texture); process until smooth. Serve cold or at room temperature with crudités. Serves 8 (serving size: ¼ cup)

CALORIES 88; FAT 4g (sat 1g, unsat 3g); PROTEIN 3g; CARB 10g; FIBER 1g; SUGARS 3g (added sugars 0g); SODIUM 200mg; CALC 4% DV; POTASSIUM 3% DV

Fast · Gluten Free
Vegetarian

Mushroom-Potato Tacos with Scallion Relish

Hands-on: 20 min. **Total:** 20 min.
Cubed potatoes make a great taco filling. They crisp up nicely and take on the smokiness and faint heat of the spices. Kale adds a little toothsome chew; you can use any hearty green you have on hand (such as Swiss chard, collard greens, or spinach). The scallion relish is a fresh, tangy condiment that brightens the earthy flavor of the mushrooms and kale. It would also be delicious with your next batch of fish tacos.

3 Tbsp. olive oil, divided
1 large (8- to 10-oz.) russet potato, cut into ½-in. cubes (2 cups)
½ cup chopped white or yellow onion
¾ tsp. smoked paprika
¼ tsp. cayenne pepper
¾ tsp. kosher salt, divided
2 cups thinly sliced fresh mushrooms (about 8 oz.)
2 cups chopped lacinato kale or other hearty green
½ cup chopped scallions (about 4 scallions)
1 Tbsp. fresh lime juice
1 jalapeño, seeded and chopped (about 1½ Tbsp.)
8 (6-in.) corn tortillas
2 oz. queso fresco (fresh Mexican cheese), crumbled (about ½ cup)
1 medium-sized ripe avocado, sliced

1. Heat 2 tablespoons oil in a large nonstick skillet over medium-high. Add potato cubes in a single layer; cook, without stirring, 5 minutes. Stir in onion, paprika, cayenne pepper, and ½ teaspoon salt. Cook, stirring occasionally, until potatoes are crisp on the outside and tender inside, about 5 minutes. Remove potatoes from skillet. (Do not wipe skillet clean.)
2. Add remaining 1 tablespoon oil to skillet; swirl to coat. Add mushrooms; cook, stirring occasionally, until lightly browned, about 5 minutes. Add kale and ⅛ teaspoon salt; cook, stirring occasionally, 5 minutes. Return potato mixture to skillet; stir to combine. Keep warm.
3. Stir together scallions, lime juice, jalapeño, and remaining ⅛ teaspoon salt in a small bowl.
4. Heat tortillas according to package directions. Spoon a scant ⅓ cup potato mixture onto each tortilla; top each with 1 tablespoon cheese. Divide avocado slices evenly among tortillas, and serve with scallion relish. Serves 4 (serving size: 2 tacos)

CALORIES 408; FAT 21g (sat 4g, unsat 15g); PROTEIN 10g; CARB 52g; FIBER 9g; SUGARS 5g (added sugars 0g); SODIUM 502mg; CALC 16% DV; POTASSIUM 16% DV

SUPER SIMPLE SOUPS

During one of the busiest times of the year, we help you turn out easy, nourishing soups with the slow cooker.

Gluten Free • Make Ahead

Tex-Mex Chicken and Black Bean Soup

Hands-on: 15 min. **Total:** 5 hr. 15 min.

1¼ lbs. boneless, skinless chicken thighs (about 4 thighs)
4 cups unsalted chicken stock (such as Swanson)
1 (15-oz.) can unsalted black beans, drained and rinsed
1 (14.5-oz.) can unsalted diced tomatoes
1 cup chopped yellow onion
1 cup chopped red bell pepper
1 cup fresh or frozen corn kernels
2 Tbsp. chopped canned chipotle chiles in adobo sauce
2 garlic cloves, minced
2 tsp. chili powder
2 tsp. ground cumin
¾ tsp. kosher salt
¼ tsp. black pepper
2 Tbsp. fresh lime juice
½ cup plain whole-milk Greek yogurt
½ cup fresh cilantro leaves

1. Combine chicken, stock, beans, tomatoes, onion, bell pepper, corn, chiles, garlic, chili powder, cumin, salt, and black pepper in a 5- to 6-quart slow cooker. Cover and cook on low until chicken is very tender, 5 to 6 hours.
2. Transfer chicken to a cutting board; shred into small pieces, and return to slow cooker. Stir in lime juice. Divide soup among 5 bowls. Top with yogurt and cilantro.

Instant Pot® Method
Hands-on: 15 min. **Total:** 25 min.

1. Combine chicken, stock, beans, tomatoes, onion, bell pepper, corn, chiles, garlic, chili powder, cumin, salt, and black pepper in Instant Pot®. Cover with lid, and turn to manual. Turn lid valve to seal, and set to high pressure for 10 minutes.
2. Release valve with a towel (be careful of the pressurized steam), and release steam until it stops. Carefully uncover, and transfer chicken to a cutting board. Shred chicken into small pieces; return to Instant Pot®. Stir in lime juice.
3. Divide soup evenly among 5 bowls. Top evenly with yogurt and cilantro. Serves 5 (serving size: about 2 cups soup, 1½ Tbsp. yogurt, and 1½ Tbsp. cilantro)

CALORIES 315; **FAT** 8g (sat 2g, unsat 4g); **PROTEIN** 35g; **CARB** 29g; **FIBER** 7g; **SUGARS** 7g (added sugars 0g); **SODIUM** 615mg; **CALC** 11% DV; **POTASSIUM** 11% DV

Gluten Free • Make Ahead
Vegetarian

Curried Coconut-Pumpkin Soup

Hands-on: 15 min. **Total:** 7 hr. 15 min.

4 cups ½-in.-cubed peeled fresh pumpkin or butternut squash
3 cups lower-sodium vegetable broth
1 large Granny Smith apple, cut into ½-in. cubes (about 1½ cups)
¾ cup chopped shallots
1 (1-in.) piece fresh ginger, peeled and thinly sliced
2 garlic cloves, chopped
2 tsp. curry powder
1 tsp. kosher salt
¼ tsp. crushed red pepper, plus more for garnish
1 cup plus 4 tsp. canned light coconut milk, well shaken
1 Tbsp. fresh lime juice
¼ cup raw pumpkin seed kernels

1. Combine pumpkin, broth, apple, shallots, ginger, garlic, curry powder, salt, and red pepper in a 5- to 6-quart slow cooker. Cover and cook on low until vegetables are very tender, about 7 hours. Stir in 1 cup coconut milk and lime juice.
2. Place half of pumpkin mixture in a blender; remove center piece of lid to allow steam to escape. Secure lid on blender. Place a clean towel over blender lid to avoid splatters; process until smooth. Place soup in a bowl. Repeat with remaining pumpkin mixture.
3. Divide soup among 4 bowls. Swirl 1 teaspoon coconut milk into each serving; garnish with pepitas and additional red pepper.

continued

Instant Pot Method

Hands-on: 15 min. **Total:** 25 min.

1. Combine pumpkin, broth, apple, shallots, ginger, garlic, curry powder, salt, and red pepper in Instant Pot. Cover with lid, and turn to manual. Turn lid valve to seal, and set to high pressure for 10 minutes.

2. Release valve with a towel (be careful of the pressurized steam), and release steam until it stops. Carefully uncover, and stir in 1 cup coconut milk and lime juice.

3. Place half of pumpkin mixture in a blender; remove center piece of blender lid to allow steam to escape. Secure lid on blender. Place a clean towel over opening in blender lid to avoid splatters; process until smooth. Place soup in a medium bowl. Repeat with remaining pumpkin mixture.

4. Divide soup among 4 bowls. Swirl 1 teaspoon coconut milk into each; garnish with pepitas and red pepper. Serves 4 (serving size: 1¼ cups soup and 1 Tbsp. pumpkin seeds)

CALORIES 201; **FAT** 7g (sat 4g, unsat 3g); **PROTEIN** 5g; **CARB** 34g; **FIBER** 6g; **SUGARS** 13g (added sugars 0g); **SODIUM** 658mg; **CALC** 9% DV; **POTASSIUM** 13% DV

Staff Favorite • Make Ahead

Lazy Lasagna Soup

Hands-on: 15 min. **Total:** 6 hr. 45 min.

1 lb. 90% lean ground chuck
8 oz. cremini mushrooms, quartered
1 cup chopped yellow onion
1 cup chopped red bell pepper
2 garlic cloves, minced
4 cups unsalted chicken stock
1 (14.5-oz.) can unsalted crushed tomatoes
1 (6-oz.) can tomato paste
2 tsp. dried oregano
1 tsp. kosher salt
¼ tsp. black pepper
8 oz. whole-wheat lasagna noodles, broken into pieces
¼ cup half-and-half
4 oz. preshredded mozzarella cheese (about ½ cup)
½ cup fresh basil leaves

1. Cook beef in a large nonstick skillet over medium-high, stirring to crumble, until browned, about 5 minutes. Transfer to a 5- to 6-quart slow cooker. Add mushrooms, onion, bell pepper, and garlic, and stir to combine. Add stock, tomatoes, tomato paste, oregano, salt, and black pepper; stir to combine. Cover and cook on low 6 hours.

2. Stir noodles into soup, making sure to submerge all noodles in liquid. Cover and cook on low until noodles are al dente, about 30 minutes. Stir in half-and-half. Divide soup among 8 bowls. Top with mozzarella and basil.

Instant Pot Method

Hands-on: 15 min. **Total:** 30 min.

1. Turn Instant Pot to sauté; heat for 1 minute. Add beef; cook, stirring occasionally, until browned, about 5 minutes. Stir in mushrooms, onion, bell pepper, and garlic. Stir in stock, tomatoes, tomato paste, oregano, salt, and pepper. Cover with lid; turn to manual. Turn valve to seal, and set to high pressure for 10 minutes.

2. Release valve with a towel (be careful of the pressurized steam), and release steam until it stops. Carefully uncover; set to sauté. Bring mixture to a boil; add lasagna noodles, and cook, stirring often, until tender, about 9 minutes. Turn off; stir in half-and-half. Divide soup evenly among 8 bowls. Top with mozzarella and basil. Serves 8 (serving size: 1¼ cups soup, 2 Tbsp. cheese, and 1 Tbsp. basil)

CALORIES 276; **FAT** 8g (sat 3g, unsat 3g); **PROTEIN** 23g; **CARB** 33g; **FIBER** 6g; **SUGARS** 7g (added sugars 0g); **SODIUM** 618mg; **CALC** 11% DV; **POTASSIUM** 9% DV

Gluten Free • Make Ahead
Vegetarian

Tuscan White Bean and Lentil Soup

Hands-on: 10 min. **Total:** 7 hr. 10 min.

4 cups lower-sodium vegetable broth
2 (15-oz.) cans unsalted Great Northern beans, drained and rinsed
1 cup uncooked brown or green lentils, rinsed
1 cup water (increase to 2 cups for Instant Pot)
1 cup chopped yellow onion
¾ cup chopped carrot
1 (2-in.) Parmesan cheese rind
2 garlic cloves, minced
1 tsp. fresh thyme leaves
½ tsp. black pepper
¼ tsp. kosher salt
1 bay leaf
4 cups coarsely rainbow chard
2 Tbsp. fresh lemon juice
2 oz. Parmesan cheese, grated (about ½ cup)

1. Combine broth, beans, lentils, 1 cup water, onion, carrot, Parmesan rind, garlic, thyme, pepper, salt, and bay leaf in a 5- to 6-quart slow cooker. Cover and cook on low until lentils are tender, 7 to 8 hours.

2. Stir in chard and lemon juice. Cover and cook on low until chard is wilted, about 30 minutes. Remove and discard cheese rind and bay leaf. Divide soup among 6 bowls. Sprinkle with Parmesan.

Instant Pot Method

Hands-on: 10 min. **Total:** 25 min.

1. Combine broth, beans, lentils, 2 cups water, onion, carrot, Parmesan rind, garlic, thyme, pepper, salt, and bay leaf in Instant Pot. Cover with lid, and turn to manual. Turn lid valve to seal, and set to high pressure for 15 minutes.

2. Release valve with a towel (be careful of the pressurized steam), and release steam until it stops. Carefully uncover, and add chard and lemon juice. Stir until chard is wilted, about 2 minutes. Remove and discard cheese rind and bay leaf.

3. Divide soup among 6 bowls. Sprinkle evenly with Parmesan. Serves 6 (serving size: about 1 ½ cups)

CALORIES 308; **FAT** 5g (sat 2g, unsat 3g); **PROTEIN** 17g; **CARB** 50g; **FIBER** 15g; **SUGARS** 5g (added sugars 0g); **SODIUM** 502mg; **CALC** 23% DV; **POTASSIUM** 16% DV

Gluten Free • Make Ahead

Jambalaya Soup

Hands-on: 15 min. **Total:** 6 hr. 30 min. Look for andouille near the smoked sausages in the refrigerated section of your grocery store.

6 oz. smoked andouille sausage, chopped
4 cups unsalted chicken stock (such as Swanson)
2 (10-oz.) cans unsalted diced tomatoes and green chiles (such as Rotel)
1 cup chopped yellow onion
1 cup chopped yellow bell pepper
¼ cup chopped celery
3 Tbsp. tomato paste
1 Tbsp. salt-free Creole seasoning (such as Tony Chachere's)
2 garlic cloves, chopped
½ tsp. kosher salt
⅔ cup uncooked brown rice
12 oz. raw medium shrimp, peeled and deveined
¼ cup chopped fresh flat-leaf parsley

1. Heat a large nonstick skillet over medium-high. Add sausage; cook, stirring occasionally, until browned, about 4 minutes. Transfer to a 5- to 6-quart slow cooker. Add stock, tomatoes and chiles, onion, bell pepper, celery, tomato paste, Creole seasoning, garlic, and salt. Cover and cook on low 4 hours.

2. Stir in rice. Cover and cook on low until rice is tender, about 2 hours.

3. Stir in shrimp. Cover and cook on low 8 minutes. Divide soup evenly among 6 bowls. Sprinkle servings with parsley.

Instant Pot Method
Hands-on: 15 min. **Total:** 35 min.

1. Turn Instant Pot to sauté; heat 1 minute. Add sausage; cook, stirring often, until browned, about 4 minutes. Add stock, tomatoes and chiles, onion, bell pepper, celery, tomato paste, Creole seasoning, garlic, and salt. Stir in rice. Cover with lid, and turn to manual. Turn lid valve to seal, and set to high pressure for 22 minutes.

2. Release valve with a towel (be careful of the pressurized steam) and release steam until it stops. Carefully uncover; add shrimp, and cook, uncovered, until shrimp are opaque, about 3 minutes. Divide soup among 6 bowls. Sprinkle servings with parsley. Serves 6 (serving size: about 1 ⅔ cups)

CALORIES 247; **FAT** 6g (sat 2g, unsat 4g); **PROTEIN** 19g; **CARB** 28g; **FIBER** 4g; **SUGARS** 6g (added sugars 0g); **SODIUM** 623mg; **CALC** 7% DV; **POTASSIUM** 11% DV

Gluten Free • Make Ahead

Mediterranean Chicken and Quinoa Stew

Hands-on: 15 min. **Total:** 6 hr. 45 min.

1¼ lbs. boneless, skinless chicken thighs (about 4 chicken thighs)
4 cups chopped peeled butternut squash
4 cups unsalted chicken stock
1 cup chopped yellow onion
2 garlic cloves, chopped
1 bay leaf
1¼ tsp. kosher salt
1 tsp. dried oregano
1 tsp. ground fennel seeds
½ tsp. black pepper
½ cup uncooked quinoa
1 oz. pitted Castelvetrano olives, sliced

1. Combine chicken, squash, stock, onion, garlic, bay leaf, salt, oregano, fennel seeds, and pepper in a 5- to 6-quart slow cooker. Cover and cook on low until chicken is very tender, about 6 hours.

2. Place chicken on a cutting board. Add quinoa to slow cooker. Cover and cook on low until quinoa is cooked, about 30 minutes. Shred chicken; stir into stew. Discard bay leaf. Divide soup among 6 bowls. Sprinkle evenly with olives.

Instant Pot Method
Hands-on: 20 min. **Total:** 30 min.

1. Combine chicken, squash, stock, onion, garlic, bay leaf, salt, oregano, ground fennel seeds, and pepper in Instant Pot. Cover with lid, and turn to manual. Turn lid valve to seal, and set to high pressure for 8 minutes.

2. Release valve with a towel (be careful of the pressurized steam), and release steam until it stops. Carefully uncover, and transfer chicken to a cutting board. Stir quinoa into stew. Turn to sauté, and cook, stirring occasionally, until quinoa is tender, about 15 minutes. Shred chicken, and stir into stew. Discard bay leaf. Divide soup among 6 bowls. Sprinkle evenly with olives. Serves 6 (serving size: about 1⅓ cups)

CALORIES 243; **FAT** 6g (sat 1g, unsat 4g); **PROTEIN** 25g; **CARB** 24g; **FIBER** 4g; **SUGARS** 4g (added sugars 0g); **SODIUM** 658mg; **CALC** 7% DV; **POTASSIUM** 15% DV

MOROCCAN VEGETABLE COOKING

From amlou to zaalouk, cookbook author Nargisse Benkabbou's seemingly exotic comfort foods taste surprisingly familiar.

When you dream about your favorite comfort foods, it's likely that *bakoula*, *chermoula*, and *zaalouk* don't pop into your head—but Nargisse Benkabbou wants them to.

"Twenty years ago, hummus was a specialty food that few people outside the Middle East knew about; now it's everywhere," explains the 31-year-old London-based blogger turned author. "I want to do that for *zaalouk* [an eggplant-based Moroccan dip]. People have to understand a food before they can begin to crave it."

That dip and a bounty of bright salads, comforting stews, and cozy desserts pepper the pages of her new cookbook, *Casablanca: My Moroccan Food*. And while hearty, meat-based tagines may be the first dishes that come to mind when you think of Moroccan food, plant-based cooking is the true backbone of this North African country's cuisine.

"When I wrote the first two chapters of my cookbook, it was pure coincidence that they were almost completely vegan," Benkabbou says. Meat shows up in most Moroccan main dishes, but it's used more as a seasoning, to add richness and depth. "It's the ratio of meat to vegetables that's the difference," she explains. "Most Moroccan dishes have three to four times more vegetables than meat."

The majority of the vegetable-based dishes in her cookbook came untouched from the kitchens of her mother and grandmother, but Benkabbou did treat a handful of traditionally meat-heavy recipes to a vegetarian makeover. Her favorite is the Root Vegetable and Dried Plum Tagine—a dish that's typically made with lamb. "People tend to be very skeptical when you tell them something that's usually made with meat is now vegetarian, but in this tagine it works very well," Benkabbou says. "I think it's magical when you can be completely fulfilled and not even realize there's no meat on your plate."

Ever since she began cooking her favorite Moroccan foods for her roommates in college, Benkabbou's goal has been to help people connect with her native cuisine. "When people are unfamiliar with something, they need a guide," she explains.

The recipes that Benkabbou shares may sound unfamiliar, but the flavors speak a language your palate understands. Barring a few notable exceptions (see "The Moroccan Pantry" on page 323), the foundational components of Moroccan cooking are ones most of us encounter every day.

"One of the main ingredients we use for tagines are onions. We also eat a lot of carrots, potatoes, tomatoes, fava beans, and squash," Benkabbou says. "As for spices, we use a lot of cumin, turmeric, ginger, and cinnamon. Basically, if you've ever made a curry or stew, you can make a tagine."

But there is one exotic, exclusively Moroccan ingredient Benkabbou says is a must-have addition to your spice cabinet: *ras el hanout*. "There's no other spice that captures the melting pot of flavors and cultures that make up Moroccan cuisine," she says. "It's a great secret weapon to keep in your pantry—it turns heads with very little effort."

Gluten Free • Vegetarian

Baked Apples with Amlou

Hands-on: 20 min. **Total:** 1 hr.
Amlou is a rich, nutty spread similar to chunky almond butter that's made from ground toasted almonds and argan oil.

⅔ cup almonds (about 3 oz.)
3 ½ Tbsp. argan oil or walnut oil
3 Tbsp. honey
6 Tbsp. old-fashioned rolled oats
¼ tsp. kosher salt
¼ tsp. ground cinnamon
4 medium-size red apples (such as Braeburn)

1. Preheat oven to 400°F. Spread almonds on a baking sheet. Toast at 400°F until golden, 5 to 6 minutes, stirring once after 3 minutes. Remove from oven.

2. Pulse toasted almonds in a food processor until finely ground, about 10 times (take care not to over-grind them or they could turn into almond butter). With processor running, gradually add oil and honey, and process until combined, 2 to 3 seconds. Transfer to a medium bowl, and stir in oats, salt, and cinnamon.

3. Reduce oven temperature to 350°F. Remove core from apples with a sharp knife or an apple corer; transfer apples to an aluminum foil–lined baking dish.

4. Stuff apples evenly with amlou mixture (about 2 tablespoons each). Bake at 350°F until apples are blistered and soft, about 40 minutes. Serves 4 (serving size: 1 stuffed apple)

CALORIES 309; FAT 17g (sat 1g, unsat 14g); PROTEIN 5g; CARB 39g; FIBER 7g; SUGARS 26g (added sugars 9g); SODIUM 84mg; CALC 6% DV; POTASSIUM 7% DV

Gluten Free • Vegetarian

Harissa-Roasted Carrots with Pistachios

Hands-on: 10 min. **Total:** 40 min.
Available in most supermarkets, *harissa* comes in mild and hot varieties; if you want to play it safe, go with mild, then bump up the heat with a dash of cayenne pepper if you like. To make after-dinner cleanup easier, line your roasting pan with aluminum foil before adding the carrot mixture.

3 Tbsp. harissa
2 Tbsp. olive oil
2 Tbsp. pure maple syrup
2 garlic cloves, crushed
¼ tsp. kosher salt
21 oz. small carrots with tops, trimmed and peeled
⅓ cup unsalted pistachios, coarsely ground

1. Preheat oven to 425°F. Stir together harissa, olive oil, maple syrup, garlic, and salt in a large bowl. Add carrots; toss until well coated.

2. Spread carrots in an even layer in a roasting pan, cover with aluminum foil, and roast at 425°F until tender, about 20 minutes. Remove foil, and cook until caramelized, 5 to 10 more minutes. Sprinkle with pistachios; serve immediately. Serves 4 (serving size: about 5 carrots)

CALORIES 206; FAT 12g (sat 2g, unsat 10g); PROTEIN 3g; CARB 23g; FIBER 6g; SUGARS 14g (added sugars 6g); SODIUM 283mg; CALC 7% DV; POTASSIUM 10% DV

Fast • Gluten Free
Vegetarian

Swiss Chard Salad with Spiced Hazelnuts

Hands-on: 20 min. **Total:** 20 min.
Called *bakoula* in Morocco, this side salad is great with grilled meats or on a charcuterie board. Don't throw away the Swiss chard stems; thinly slice them, then follow the method for the pickled onions in the Chermoula Smashed Potatoes (page 322).

⅓ heaping cup blanched hazelnuts
1¾ tsp. paprika, divided
Pinch of cayenne pepper
¼ cup olive oil

2 lbs. Swiss chard, stemmed, leaves cut into 1-in.-wide strips (about 10 cups)
3 Tbsp. finely chopped fresh flat-leaf parsley
3 Tbsp. finely chopped fresh cilantro
4 garlic cloves, crushed
¾ tsp. ground cumin
⅜ tsp. kosher salt
3 Tbsp. plain whole-milk Greek yogurt
2 Tbsp. fresh lemon juice

1. Preheat oven to 400°F. Place hazelnuts on a baking sheet, and bake until toasted, 5 to 6 minutes. Coarsely chop nuts; place in a bowl. Stir in ¼ teaspoon paprika and cayenne. Set aside.

2. Heat oil in a large saucepan over medium. Add chard, parsley, cilantro, garlic, remaining 1½ teaspoons paprika, cumin, and salt; cover and cook until chard is soft, about 8 minutes. Remove pan from heat.

3. Stir together yogurt and lemon juice in a small bowl. Serve chard mixture at room temperature with a drizzle of yogurt sauce and a generous sprinkle of hazelnuts. Serves 4 (serving size: about ¾ cup)

CALORIES 241; FAT 22g (sat 3g, unsat 18g); PROTEIN 5g; CARB 8g; FIBER 4g; SUGARS 2g (added sugars 0g); SODIUM 381mg; CALC 9% DV; POTASSIUM 11% DV

Chermoula Smashed Potatoes with Pickled Onions

Hands-on: 25 min. **Total:** 1 hr. 20 min. You'll want to make a double batch of both the chermoula and the pickled onions—their bold flavors are a great way to jazz up leftover Thanksgiving turkey.

2 ½ cups water
1 ½ cups thinly sliced red onion
¾ cup white wine vinegar
1 ¼ Tbsp. granulated sugar
1 ¾ tsp. kosher salt, divided
2 lbs. baby Yukon Gold potatoes
½ cup finely chopped fresh cilantro leaves and stems, divided
5 Tbsp. finely chopped fresh flat-leaf parsley, divided
¼ cup olive oil, divided
3 garlic cloves, minced
2 tsp. paprika
1 ¼ tsp. ground cumin
2 Tbsp. fresh lemon juice
Pinch of cayenne pepper

1. Bring 2 ½ cups water to a boil in a medium saucepan over high. Place red onion slices in a fine wire-mesh strainer over a bowl, and pour boiling water over onions. Let drain.
2. Stir together vinegar, sugar, and 1 teaspoon salt in a saucepan. Bring to a boil over medium-high; remove from heat.
3. Transfer drained onions to a clean jar with lid; pour hot vinegar mixture over onions. Use a spoon to press onions down so they are submerged in liquid. Seal jar, and let stand 30 minutes. (Refrigerate up to 1 week.)
4. Preheat oven to 400°F. Place potatoes in a large saucepan, and add cold water to cover. Bring to a boil over high. Reduce heat to medium-low; cover and simmer until a knife slides into potatoes with ease, about 20 minutes. Drain potatoes; let cool.
5. Stir together ¼ cup cilantro, 3 tablespoons parsley, 3 tablespoons oil, garlic, paprika, cumin, and remaining ¾ teaspoon salt in a large bowl. Add potatoes; using your hands, toss to coat potatoes with cilantro mixture.
6. Arrange potatoes on an aluminum foil–lined baking sheet; firmly press each potato to smash it, being careful not to break it. Bake at 400°F until crispy and golden, 25 to 30 minutes.
7. Stir together lemon juice, cayenne, remaining ¼ cup cilantro, remaining 2 tablespoons parsley, and remaining 1 tablespoon oil. Spoon over potatoes; top with drained pickled onions. Serves 6 (serving size: about ½ cup)

CALORIES 202; **FAT** 9g (sat 1g, unsat 7g); **PROTEIN** 3g; **CARB** 29g; **FIBER** 5g; **SUGARS** 4g (added sugars 0g); **SODIUM** 284mg; **CALC** 2% DV; **POTASSIUM** 2% DV

Make Ahead • Vegetarian

Root Vegetable and Dried Plum Tagine

Hands-on: 30 min. **Total:** 1 hr. 20 min. Homemade vegetable stock is best in this recipe. If using store-bought stock, upgrade the flavor by adding a bay leaf while the broth simmers in step 2.

3 Tbsp. olive oil
3 large onions, sliced (about 9 cups)
2 cups vegetable stock
4 garlic cloves, crushed
1 ¼ tsp. ground turmeric
1 ¼ tsp. ground ginger
¾ tsp. kosher salt, plus more to taste
Pinch of saffron threads
11 oz. turnips, peeled and cut into 1-in. chunks (about 2 cups)
11 oz. baby potatoes, scrubbed and halved (about 2 cups)
11 oz. celery root, peeled and cut into 1-in. chunks (about 2 ½ cups)
11 oz. parsnips, peeled and cut into 1-in. chunks (about 2 cups)
11 oz. dried pitted plums (about 1 ¾ cups)
3 Tbsp. honey
1 tsp. ground cinnamon
4 cups cooked couscous
Fresh cilantro leaves

1. Heat olive oil in a large saucepan over medium. Add onions; cover and cook, stirring occasionally, until soft and translucent, about 15 minutes.
2. Stir in stock, garlic, turmeric, ginger, salt, and saffron. Bring to a boil over high. Cover and reduce heat to low; simmer gently 30 minutes.
3. Add turnips, and bring mixture to a boil over high. Cover, reduce heat to medium-low, and cook 10 minutes. Add potatoes, celery root, and parsnips, and stir to combine. (There should be enough liquid in pan to almost cover the vegetables; if not, pour in just enough water to do so.) Bring to a boil over high. Cover and reduce heat to medium-low; cook until vegetables are cooked through and softened, about 20 to 25 minutes.
4. Meanwhile, place dried plums in a heatproof bowl, and add boiling water to cover. Let stand until plums are softened, about 5 minutes; drain.
5. Remove saucepan from heat, and use a ladle to transfer ¾ cup broth to a small saucepan over medium. Add drained plums, honey, and cinnamon to broth. Simmer mixture, stirring occasionally, until sauce has thickened and reduced by half, about 15 minutes.

6. Divide the couscous evenly among 6 shallow bowls. Top with vegetables, plum mixture, and cilantro leaves. Serves 6 (serving size: 1½ cups vegetable mixture and ⅔ cup couscous)

CALORIES 541; FAT 8g (sat 1g, unsat 7g); PROTEIN 11g; CARB 112g; FIBER 15g; SUGARS 38g (added sugars 9g); SODIUM 531mg; CALC 19% DV; POTASSIUM 26% DV

Staff Favorite • Fast
Gluten Free • Make Ahead
Vegetarian

Smoky Eggplant Zaalouk

Hands-on: 30 min. **Total:** 30 min.
"I became familiar with smoked paprika at cookery school," Benkabbou says. "I am so grateful for discovering this flamboyant spice because it gives my *zaalouk* the smokiness I didn't know it was missing. Serve this with grilled meat or fish, or as a spread in a sandwich."

¼ cup olive oil
1 medium eggplant (about 18 oz.), peeled and cut into 1-in. chunks
2 medium tomatoes (about 14 oz.), seeded and cut into 1-in. chunks
3 garlic cloves, smashed
2 Tbsp. chopped fresh cilantro
1 Tbsp. fresh lemon juice
1½ tsp. honey
1 tsp. smoked paprika
¾ tsp. kosher salt
½ tsp. ground cumin
½ tsp. paprika
⅛ tsp. cayenne pepper
Fresh cilantro leaves

1. Heat olive oil in a medium saucepan over medium-low. Add eggplant, tomatoes, garlic, cilantro, lemon juice, honey, smoked paprika, salt, cumin, paprika, and cayenne pepper. Cover and cook, stirring occasionally, until vegetables are softened, 25 to 30 minutes.
2. Uncover pan, and crush vegetables with a potato masher to desired consistency.
3. Garnish with a sprinkling of cilantro leaves; serve warm or cold with grilled bread, if desired. Serves 6 (serving size: about ½ cup)

CALORIES 112; FAT 9g (sat 1g, unsat 8g); PROTEIN 2g; CARB 10g; FIBER 3g; SUGARS 6g (added sugars 1g); SODIUM 246mg; CALC 2% DV; POTASSIUM 8% DV

BEAUTIFULLY BITTER

Learn how to complement, balance, soften, and harness the power of the most sophisticated—and underappreciated—flavor.

The first time I ever tasted a Negroni, the slow-sipping cocktail made from Campari, gin, and red vermouth, was a revelation. A friend had ordered one and offered me a taste—and my world blossomed at such a bold celebration of overt bitterness. It's a flavor that instantly elevates food (and drink) to elegant heights, lending complexity and verve. Consider the role of burned sugar in a flan: It takes what would otherwise be a straight-forward sweet custard and gives it more depth.

As a cook, when you play with bitterness—when you embrace it and learn how and when to tame it—you can create dishes that beguile, with an impact that lingers on your palate and your memory. The recipes here show how to make the most of bitter ingredients. Some highlight that pungency; others balance it to varying degrees with other foods that soften the bite. Get ready: It's time to get bitter.

DRIED CHILES

Ancho and pasilla chiles make Chile Colorado robust and spicy with a decidedly—and deliciously—bitter flavor. We soften the effect slightly with the addition of sweet butternut squash, but the traditional taste still dominates. If you'd like to tame the bitterness further, you could add a dollop of sour cream.

**Staff Favorite • Gluten Free
Make Ahead**

Beef-and-Butternut Chile Colorado

Bitterness rating: 8⁄10

Hands-on: 25 min. **Total:** 2 hr.

1 ¾ lb. chuck roast, trimmed and cut into 1-in. cubes
1 ½ tsp. kosher salt, divided
1 Tbsp. olive oil
8 garlic cloves, coarsely chopped
6 cups unsalted chicken stock (such as Swanson), divided
2 tsp. ground cumin
1 tsp. dried oregano
2 bay leaves
5 ancho chiles
3 pasilla negro chiles
3 ½ cups (1-in.) cubed peeled butternut squash (about 1 lb.)
¼ cup fresh cilantro leaves (optional)

1. Heat a Dutch oven over medium-high. Sprinkle beef with ½ teaspoon salt. Add oil to pan. Add half of beef; cook, turning occasionally, until browned, about 6 minutes. Transfer browned beef to a plate. Repeat with remaining beef.
2. Add garlic to drippings in pan; cook, stirring constantly, 1 minute. Add 3 cups stock, scraping bottom of pan to loosen browned bits. Return beef to pan; stir in cumin, oregano, and bay leaves. Bring to a simmer over medium. Partially cover; simmer 1 hour.
3. While beef cooks, bring remaining 3 cups stock to a boil in a saucepan over medium-high. Working with 1 chile at a time, hold over a blender; gently pull stem to remove, letting seeds fall into blender. Discard stems; place chiles in blender. Pour boiling stock over chiles. Cover with blender lid; let stand 30 minutes. Process until smooth, about 1 minute. Set aside until beef has finished simmering.
4. Add chile mixture, squash, and remaining 1 teaspoon salt to beef in Dutch oven. Simmer over medium, partially covered, until liquid is thickened and beef is very tender, about 45 minutes. Sprinkle with cilantro, if desired. Serves 8 (serving size: 1 cup)

CALORIES 305; FAT 18g (sat 6g, unsat 10g); PROTEIN 21g; CARB 17g; FIBER 5g; SUGARS 2g (added sugars 0g); SODIUM 529mg; CALC 6% DV; POTASSIUM 17% DV

Make Ahead • Vegetarian

Matcha Biscotti with Bittersweet Drizzle

Bitterness rating: ³⁄10

Hands-on: 20 min. **Total:** 2 hr.
If the dough's stickiness makes it difficult to work with, dampen your hands slightly before shaping it.

7.5 oz. whole-wheat pastry flour (about 2 cups plus 2 Tbsp.)
¾ cup granulated sugar
1 Tbsp. matcha powder
½ tsp. baking powder
½ tsp. table salt
¾ cup unsalted roasted almonds
3 large eggs
1 tsp. vanilla extract
½ tsp. almond extract
3 oz. bittersweet chocolate, chopped
1 tsp. instant espresso granules

1. Preheat oven to 350°F. Whisk together flour, sugar, matcha, baking powder, and salt in a large bowl. Stir in almonds. Add eggs and extracts. Beat with an electric mixer on medium speed until a sticky dough forms, about 2 minutes.
2. Divide dough in half. Shape each half into an 8-in.-long log on a baking sheet lined with parchment paper. Pat each log to a width of 3 inches. Bake at 350°F until set, about 20 minutes. (Dough will be cracked.)
3. Remove biscotti logs from oven; cool on pan 5 minutes. Using a wide spatula, carefully transfer biscotti logs to a wire rack; cool 15 minutes. Reduce oven temperature to 300°F.
4. Place biscotti logs on a cutting board. Cut each diagonally into 12 slices. Return slices to parchment-lined baking sheet. Bake at 300°F 20 minutes, flipping slices after 10 minutes. Cool completely on a wire rack, about 30 minutes.
5. Place chocolate in a microwavable bowl. Microwave on medium until melted, about 1 minute and 30 seconds, stirring every 30 seconds (be careful not to overheat chocolate so it doesn't scorch or seize). Stir in espresso granules. Drizzle over biscotti. Let stand until chocolate mixture sets, about 10 minutes. Makes 2 dozen (serving size: 1 biscotto)

CALORIES 113; FAT 4g (sat 1g, unsat 3g); PROTEIN 3g; CARB 15g; FIBER 2g; SUGARS 7g (added sugars 6g); SODIUM 68mg; CALC 2% DV; POTASSIUM 2% DV

Fast • Vegetarian

Grapefruit Gin and Tonic

Bitterness rating: ⁴⁄10

Hands-on: 10 min. **Total:** 10 min.
Though we love the blushing pink color from Ruby Red grapefruit, you also can use a yellow-fleshed variety, which will likely be less sweet. We find that a London-style gin works best here; the floral flavors of more botanical styles (such as new-wave gins) are likely to overpower the taste of the grapefruit.

3 (2-in.) Ruby Red grapefruit peel strips, plus ⅔ cup fresh juice (from 2 medium grapefruit), divided
1 (2-in.) rosemary sprig, plus more for garnish
1 tsp. granulated sugar
⅓ cup (2⅔ oz.) London dry gin (such as Beefeater)
⅔ cup tonic water, chilled

1. Place grapefruit peel strips and rosemary sprig in a 2-cup glass measuring cup or a sturdy glass; sprinkle with sugar. Muddle mixture with a muddler or wooden spoon until the peels release some liquid, 30 seconds to 1 minute.
2. Add grapefruit juice and gin; stir until sugar dissolves. Remove and discard the grapefruit peel strips and rosemary sprig. Stir in tonic water. Pour into 2 ice-filled collins glasses; garnish with additional rosemary sprigs, if desired. Serves 2 (about ¾ cup)

CALORIES 154; FAT 0g; PROTEIN 0g; CARB 17g; FIBER 0g; SUGARS 16g (added sugars 9g); SODIUM 11mg; CALC 1% DV; POTASSIUM 3% DV

BROCCOLI RABE

Though it looks quite similar to Broccolini, broccoli rabe is very different. It ranges from moderately to seriously bitter, a quality that is mellowed here by first blanching the vegetable in boiling water. Tossing it with neutral-flavored pasta and a rich, creamy cheese sauce further balances the pungency.

Fast • Vegetarian

Garlic-and-Herb Pasta with Broccoli Rabe

Bitterness rating: ⁵⁄₁₀

Hands-on: 30 min. **Total:** 30 min. Boursin is the key to the quick and easy sauce; the triple-cream cheese comes in a box and is found in most grocery stores with the specialty cheeses or in the deli. After blanching and cooling the broccoli rabe, it's important to lightly squeeze out the water. That way, you won't dilute the flavors in the sauce.

1 lb. broccoli rabe, trimmed and cut into 2-in. pieces
8 oz. uncooked orecchiette pasta
2 Tbsp. extra-virgin olive oil
¼ cup thinly sliced garlic (4 to 5 large garlic cloves)
¼ tsp. crushed red pepper
¾ tsp. plus ⅛ tsp. kosher salt, divided
½ (5.2-oz.) pkg. garlic-and-herb spreadable cheese (such as Boursin)
1 tsp. lemon zest

1. Bring a large saucepan of water to a boil over high. Add broccoli rabe; boil until crisp-tender, about 2 minutes. Using tongs or a slotted spoon, transfer broccoli rabe to a colander. Rinse under cold water (or dunk in a bowl of ice water) to cool to room temperature; squeeze gently to remove excess water. Set aside.
2. Return water in pan to a boil over high. Add pasta; cook until al dente, about 12 minutes. Reserve ⅔ cup cooking liquid. Drain pasta; set aside.
3. Heat oil in a large skillet over medium-low. Add garlic, red pepper, and ⅛ teaspoon salt; cook, stirring often, until garlic is tender, about 5 minutes. Add cheese and reserved ⅔ cup cooking liquid; stir until cheese melts. Stir in broccoli rabe and pasta; cook until warmed, about 2 minutes. Sprinkle with zest and remaining ¾ teaspoon salt. Toss well to combine. Serves 4 (serving size: about 1 ½ cups)

CALORIES 374; FAT 16g (sat 6g, unsat 8g); PROTEIN 12g; CARB 48g; FIBER 5g; SUGARS 3g (added sugars 0g); SODIUM 573mg; CALC 15% DV; POTASSIUM 6% DV

RADICCHIO

Radicchio is one of the most iconic bitter foods. If you can find different varieties, use a mix for lovely shapes and colors. Try supermarket classic Chioggia, elongated Treviso, or mottled Castelfranco. A sweet balsamic dressing and floral blood oranges offset the leaves' bitterness.

**Fast • Gluten Free
Vegetarian**

Radicchio Salad with Angostura Vinaigrette

Bitterness rating: ⁷⁄₁₀

Hands-on: 10 min. **Total:** 20 min. Angostura bitters lend depth to the dressing, a tip we learned from friend and bitters expert Mark Bitterman.

3 Tbsp. olive oil
2 Tbsp. white balsamic vinegar
2 tsp. minced shallot
1 tsp. honey
1 tsp. Dijon mustard
1 tsp. Angostura bitters
⅜ tsp. kosher salt
¼ tsp. black pepper
1 (8-oz.) head radicchio, leaves separated
2 medium blood oranges, peeled, sliced crosswise, and slices cut into half-moons

1. Whisk together first 8 ingredients (through pepper); let stand 10 minutes.
2. Divide radicchio and oranges evenly among 4 plates. Drizzle with vinaigrette. Serves 4 (serving size: 2 oz. radicchio, ½ orange, and about 1 ½ Tbsp. vinaigrette)

CALORIES 158; FAT 10g (sat 1g, unsat 8g); PROTEIN 2g; CARB 15g; FIBER 2g; SUGARS 9g (added sugars 1g); SODIUM 226mg; CALC 4% DV; POTASSIUM 6% DV

Fast • Vegetarian

Pear-Topped Toast with Honey-Tahini Ricotta

Bitterness rating: ³⁄₁₀

Hands-on: 5 min. **Total:** 5 min. For the most satisfying toast, pick up a hearty whole-grain loaf from a bakery; a hefty sandwich loaf or boule shape will offer nice-sized slices with more surface area for the toppings. Our favorite brands of tahini, all worth seeking out or making a special trip to pick up, are Soom (soomfoods.com), Seed + Mill (seedandmill.com), and 365 Everyday Value (available at Whole Foods).

½ cup part-skim ricotta cheese
1½ tsp. honey
1½ Tbsp. tahini (sesame seed paste), divided
2 (1½-oz.) whole-grain bread slices, toasted
½ firm-ripe medium-size pear, unpeeled and thinly sliced
1 Tbsp. chopped walnuts
⅛ tsp. flaky or kosher salt

1. Stir together ricotta cheese, honey, and 1 ½ teaspoons tahini in a bowl. Spread about ¼ cup ricotta mixture evenly over each toast slice. Top evenly with pear slices; sprinkle with walnuts. Drizzle each toast with 1 ½ teaspoons tahini, and sprinkle evenly with salt. Serves 2 (serving size: 1 toast)

CALORIES 330; **FAT** 15g (sat 4g, unsat 9g); **PROTEIN** 15g; **CARB** 36g; **FIBER** 5g; **SUGARS** 12g (added sugars 4g); **SODIUM** 348mg; **CALC** 24% DV; **POTASSIUM** 6% DV

> "Bitter is a flavor that instantly elevates food (and drink) to elegant heights, lending complexity and verve."
>
> Ann Taylor Pittman, Executive Editor

PIES OF MANY SIZES

For every holiday dessert table

Make Ahead • Vegetarian

Butternut Squash and Cardamom Pie with Crème Fraîche

Hands-on: 45 min. **Total:** 5 hr.
Butternut squash is lighter in flavor and texture than pumpkin, making this spin on the classic a version that might be better after a super-filling Thanksgiving meal. Boil your squash a day or two ahead. Store in an airtight container in the fridge for up to three days before using (it's OK to use it cold). The pie can be made a day ahead, but make the topping just before you serve it.

CRUST

4.25 oz. white whole-wheat flour (about 1¼ cups)
1 Tbsp. nonfat dry milk powder
¼ tsp. kosher salt
¼ cup vegetable shortening (such as Spectrum), chilled
3 Tbsp. cold unsalted butter, cut into ¼-in. pieces
3 to 4 Tbsp. ice-cold water

FILLING

2 (10-oz.) pkg. frozen cubed butternut squash (such as Stahlbush Island Farms)
3½ Tbsp. light brown sugar
¼ tsp. ground cardamom
½ tsp. kosher salt
⅛ tsp. ground cinnamon
⅛ tsp. freshly grated nutmeg
⅛ tsp. ground allspice
1 (14-oz.) can fat-free sweetened condensed milk (such as Borden Eagle Brand)
2 large eggs, lightly beaten
2 Tbsp. unsalted butter

TOPPING

¼ cup crème fraîche
¼ cup heavy cream
2 Tbsp. powdered sugar
2 Tbsp. candied pecans, finely chopped

1. Prepare the crust: Whisk together flour, milk powder, and salt in a large bowl. Using a pastry blender or 2 knives, cut in shortening and cold butter until shortening and butter are well distributed and small clumps begin to form. Stir in 1 tablespoon ice-cold water; add up to 3 more tablespoons water, 1 teaspoon at a time, stirring just until dough begins to come together. Turn dough out on a lightly floured surface, and gently knead 1 or 2 times. Form dough into a disk. On a lightly floured surface, roll disk into a 12-inch circle. Fit dough circle into a 9-inch pie plate, fold dough edges under, and flute. Refrigerate piecrust at least 45 minutes or up to 1 day.

2. Prepare the filling: Place a baking sheet on bottom rack of oven, and preheat oven to 400°F. (Do not remove baking sheet while oven preheats.) Place butternut squash in a medium saucepan, and add water to cover squash. Cover and bring to a boil over medium-high. Reduce heat to medium, and cook, covered, until squash is very tender, 10 to 12 minutes. Drain and place squash in a large bowl. Using a potato masher, mash squash until smooth. Let squash cool to room temperature, about 30 minutes. Add brown sugar, cardamom, salt, cinnamon, nutmeg, allspice, sweetened condensed milk, and eggs to cooled butternut squash. Stir well to combine.

3. Melt butter in a small saucepan over medium. Cook until butter turns brown and has a nutty aroma. Remove saucepan from heat, and stir butter into squash mixture. Pour filling into chilled piecrust. Place pie in oven on preheated baking sheet. Reduce oven temperature to 350°F, and bake until filling is mostly set with a slightly jiggly center, 35 to 38 minutes. Let pie cool completely on a wire rack, 2 hours and 30 minutes to 3 hours.

4. Prepare the topping: Place crème fraîche in a medium bowl, and set aside. Place heavy cream in a large bowl, and beat with an electric mixer on medium-high speed until foamy. Gradually add powdered sugar to heavy cream, and beat until stiff peaks form. Very gently fold heavy cream mixture into crème fraîche. To serve, cut pie into 12 slices. Dollop slices with crème fraîche mixture; top with chopped candied pecans. Serves 12 (serving size: 1 slice)

CALORIES 342; FAT 14g (sat 7g, unsat 5g); PROTEIN 7g; CARB 47g; FIBER 3g; SUGARS 34g (added sugars 20g); SODIUM 189mg; CALC 15% DV; POTASSIUM 2% DV

GO BIGGER

Although this recipe calls for two mini muffin pans, you can make it work with a standard 12-cup muffin tin, too. Bake the 12 larger crusts the same amount of time. Then, in step 2, increase the amount of filling you put in each muffin cup—you'll likely have a little extra filling left over (or at least we did).

Gluten Free • Make Ahead Vegetarian

Mini Chocolate-Nut Pies

Hands-on: 25 min. **Total:** 1 hr. 15 min.
Gooey and sticky-sweet, these mini pies cram all the goodness of a traditional full pecan pie into a couple of rich, indulgent bites. The mix of cashews, macadamia nuts, and almonds adds fantastic crunch. The date syrup replaces traditional corn syrup, and the "crust" is made from nuts and an egg white; both of these swaps help reduce the amount of processed sugars and saturated fat.

CRUST
2 ½ cups cashew, almond, and macadamia nut mix (such as Planters NUT-rition Wholesome Nut Mix), divided
¼ tsp. kosher salt
1 large egg white

FILLING
2 Tbsp. miniature semisweet chocolate chips
¼ cup packed light brown sugar
¼ cup granulated sugar
5 Tbsp. date syrup
3 Tbsp. half-and-half
1 Tbsp. unsalted butter
1 tsp. vanilla extract
2 large eggs
2 oz. bittersweet chocolate, chopped

1. Prepare the crust: Preheat oven to 350°F. Grease and flour 2 (12-cup) mini muffin pans. Process 1 ¼ cups nut mix in a food processor until very finely chopped, about 30 seconds. Place finely chopped nuts in a medium bowl; add salt. Place egg white in a medium bowl; beat with an electric mixer on high speed until stiff peaks form, 1 to 2 minutes. Fold beaten egg white into finely chopped nut mixture. (Mixture will be sticky.) Spoon about 1 teaspoon nut mixture into each cup of prepared muffin pans. With floured fingers, press nut mixture in bottom and up sides of muffin cups to form a crust. Bake at 350°F until beginning to brown around the edges, about 5 minutes. (Egg white will bubble up while baking.) Remove from oven, and let cool in pans to room temperature.
2. Prepare the filling: Pulse remaining 1 ¼ cups nut mix in food processor until coarsely chopped, about 7 times. Transfer coarsely chopped nuts to a medium bowl; add miniature chocolate chips. Spoon about 1 tablespoon nut mixture into each muffin cup. Heat brown sugar, granulated sugar, and date syrup in a small saucepan over medium until sugars are completely dissolved, about

5 minutes. Remove from heat. Stir in half-and-half, butter, and vanilla. Let cool to room temperature, about 20 minutes. Lightly beat eggs with a fork. Add eggs to cooled sugar mixture, whisking well to combine. Pour about 1 tablespoon sugar mixture over each filled cup. Bake on bottom rack of oven at 350°F until just set, 12 to 14 minutes. Let cool in muffin pans 10 minutes. Run a knife around edges of each pie, and remove pies to wire racks to cool completely, about 20 minutes. Place bittersweet chocolate in a microwavable bowl. Microwave at high until melted, about 1 minute, stopping to stir halfway through. Drizzle chocolate over pies. Refrigerate at least 30 minutes. Serve chilled or at room temperature. Serves 12 (serving size: 2 pies)

CALORIES 275; FAT 18g (sat 4g, unsat 14g); PROTEIN 7g; CARB 22g; FIBER 3g; SUGARS 18g (added sugars 7g); SODIUM 127mg; CALC 5% DV; POTASSIUM 1% DV

Make Ahead • Vegetarian

White Chocolate– Raspberry Tart

Hands-on: 15 min. **Total:** 1 hr. 45 min.
This is a tastier version of those strawberry shortcake bars from the ice cream truck. The crust is salty, buttery, and slightly tart—a perfect crunchy match to the creamy and sweet white chocolate filling. This super-simple recipe also has minimal ingredients, which is a nice contrast to labor-intensive Thanksgiving pies. Be sure to fold the cream into the chocolate before folding in the yogurt, otherwise the mixture may seize.

1 (2-oz.) pkg. freeze-dried raspberries
4 oz. saltine crackers (1 sleeve)
1 large egg white
2 ½ Tbsp. unsalted butter, melted
⅓ cup whipping cream
5 ½ oz. white chocolate baking bar, chopped
½ cup vanilla fat-free yogurt (not Greek-style)
½ tsp. powdered sugar
1 ½ cups fresh raspberries (5 oz.)

1. Preheat oven to 350°F. Place freeze-dried raspberries in a food processor, and process until very finely ground, about 30 seconds. Sift raspberry powder into a small bowl; discard seeds.
2. Pulse saltines in food processor until very finely crumbled, about 10 times; transfer to a medium bowl, and set aside.
3. Place 1 teaspoon raspberry powder and egg white in a medium bowl. Beat with an electric mixer on high speed until stiff peaks form, about 1 minute; add to crumbled saltines. Add 2 tablespoons raspberry powder and melted butter to saltine mixture, and stir with a spatula to combine. Press mixture in bottom and up sides of a 13 ½- x 4 ¼-inch fluted rectangular tart pan with a removable bottom. Bake crust at 350°F until crisp and slightly golden, about 10 minutes. Cool completely on a wire rack, about 40 minutes.
4. Place whipping cream in a medium bowl. Beat with electric mixer on medium-high speed until stiff peaks form, about 2 minutes. Place chopped chocolate in a medium microwavable bowl. Microwave at high until melted, about 1 minute and 30 seconds, stirring at 30-second intervals. Let chocolate cool 15 minutes, stirring often. Gently fold whipped cream into melted chocolate. Gently fold yogurt into chocolate mixture; pour into cooled crust. Chill 1 hour.
5. Stir together 1 teaspoon raspberry powder and powdered sugar and in a small bowl. Using a fine wire-mesh strainer, dust powdered sugar mixture over tart.

Arrange fresh raspberries on top of tart. Cut into 12 slices. Serves 12 (serving size: 1 slice)

CALORIES 188; **FAT** 10g (sat 6g, unsat 3g); **PROTEIN** 3g; **CARB** 22g; **FIBER** 2g; **SUGARS** 12g (added sugars 4g); **SODIUM** 114mg; **CALC** 6% DV; **POTASSIUM** 2% DV

Make Ahead • Vegetarian

Pear and Goat Cheese Pie

Hands-on: 1 hr. **Total:** 6 hr.
We precook the pears before adding them to the filling to keep them from releasing too much liquid (which might prevent the filling from setting or create a soggy crust). Avoid Bartlett pears, as they turn to mush when baked. Be sure to add cooled filling to cool dough; a hot filling will warm the butter, and the crust won't be flaky.

CRUST

4.25 oz. white whole-wheat flour (about 1¼ cups)
4 oz. whole-wheat pastry flour (about 1 cup)
2 Tbsp. nonfat dry milk powder
¼ tsp. baking powder
¼ tsp. kosher salt
6 Tbsp. vegetable shortening (such as Spectrum), chilled
3 Tbsp. cold unsalted butter, cut into ¼-in. pieces
5 to 6 Tbsp. ice-cold water

FILLING

3 oz. goat cheese, softened
3 oz. ⅓-less-fat cream cheese, softened
1 large egg yolk
2 Tbsp. honey

½ tsp. lemon zest plus 2 tsp. fresh lemon juice, divided

3 large Anjou pears (26 oz.), peeled, cored, and cut into ⅛-in.-thick slices

3 large Bosc pears (26 oz.), peeled, cored, and cut into ⅛-in.-thick slices

Cooking spray

5 Tbsp. light brown sugar

2 Tbsp. cornstarch

¼ tsp. kosher salt

¼ tsp. ground cinnamon

¼ tsp. freshly grated nutmeg

1 tsp. chopped fresh sage

2 Tbsp. pear nectar

1 Tbsp. unsalted butter, cut into ¼-in. pieces

TOPPING

1 large egg white

1 Tbsp. water

1 Tbsp. turbinado sugar

1. Prepare the crust: Whisk together white whole-wheat flour, pastry flour, milk powder, baking powder, and salt in a large bowl. Using a pastry blender or 2 knives, cut in shortening and cold butter until shortening and butter are well distributed and small clumps begin to form. Stir in ¼ cup ice-cold water, and add up to 2 more tablespoons water, 1 teaspoon at a time, stirring just until dough begins to come together. Turn dough out onto a lightly floured surface, and gently knead 1 or 2 times. Divide dough into 2 pieces. (One piece should be just slightly larger than the second, about 8 ounces for the first piece and 7 ounces for the second.) Shape each portion into a disk. Lightly flour surface, and roll slightly larger disk into a 12-inch circle;

fit into a 9-inch pie plate. Trim dough to edge of pie plate. Roll remaining dough disk into an 11-inch circle. Using a pizza cutter or scalloped dough cutter, cut circle into 16 (½-inch-wide) strips. Weave dough strips into a lattice pattern on a parchment paper–lined baking sheet. Chill dough in pie plate and on baking sheet 45 minutes or up to 1 day.

2. Prepare the filling: Preheat oven to 350°F. Place goat cheese, cream cheese, egg yolk, honey, and lemon zest in a medium bowl, and beat with an electric mixer on medium speed until smooth and creamy, 1 to 2 minutes. Spread mixture in an even layer over dough in pie plate; chill until ready to use.

3. Arrange pear slices in a single layer on a parchment paper–lined baking sheet. Lightly coat with cooking spray. Bake at 350°F until pears start to soften and release some of their juices, 22 to 25 minutes. (You should have about 3½ cups cooked pear slices.) Remove pears from oven, and cool completely, about 20 minutes.

4. Place an empty baking sheet on bottom rack of oven. Increase oven temperature to 400°F. (Do not remove pan while oven preheats.)

5. Place pear slices in a large bowl. Add brown sugar, cornstarch, salt, cinnamon, nutmeg, sage, pear nectar, and lemon juice. Toss gently to coat. Spoon pear mixture over goat cheese mixture in pie plate. Top pear mixture evenly with butter. Place parchment paper with dough lattice over pear mixture; gently remove parchment from under lattice. (Or invert lattice onto pear mixture and peel off parchment.) Lightly whisk together

egg white and 1 tablespoon water. Brush egg wash around edge of pie, and press lattice into edges to secure. Brush egg wash over lattice; sprinkle with turbinado sugar. Chill pie 15 minutes. Place pie on hot baking sheet on bottom rack of oven, and reduce oven temperature to 350°F. Bake until edges of crust are golden brown, 48 to 50 minutes. Loosely cover pie with aluminum foil to prevent overbrowning, and continue to bake until pears are tender and crust is golden, 15 to 20 more minutes. Cool completely on a wire rack, 3 to 4 hours. Cut into 12 slices. Serves 12 (serving size: 1 slice)

CALORIES 318; FAT 14g (sat 6g, unsat 7g); PROTEIN 6g; CARB 45g; FIBER 6g; SUGARS 23g (added sugars 10g); SODIUM 152mg; CALC 7% DV; POTASSIUM 5% DV

WEEKNIGHT MAINS

PROTEIN BOOST

To bulk up this main dish with more protein, top it with rotisserie chicken or leftover shrimp from the sheet pan fajitas on page 335.

Fast • Vegetarian

Smoky Mushroom and Barley Salad with Poblano

Hands-on: 30 min. **Total:** 30 min.
If barley isn't a pantry staple for you, this Mexican-spiced mushroom dish will change that. For this fast-fix recipe, be sure to pick up pearl barley; it cooks in almost half the time of regular barley.

1¼ cups pearl barley
2 Tbsp. olive oil
3 cups chopped fresh cremini mushrooms
3 cups sliced fresh shiitake mushroom caps
½ tsp. ground cumin
1 tsp. kosher salt
4 garlic cloves, minced
1 shallot, thinly sliced
1 small poblano chile, seeded and thinly sliced
½ cup unsalted vegetable stock
⅓ cup reduced-fat sour cream
1 Tbsp. fresh lime juice
¼ cup thinly sliced scallions
¼ tsp. paprika (optional)

1. Prepare barley according to package directions; drain.

2. Heat oil in a large nonstick skillet over medium-high. Add mushrooms; cook, stirring often, until browned, 7 to 8 minutes. Add cumin; cook, stirring constantly, 1 minute. Add salt, garlic, shallot, and poblano, and cook, stirring often, until poblano is softened slightly, 3 to 4 minutes. Stir in barley and stock. Bring to a simmer; cook until absorbed, 2 to 3 minutes.

3. Stir together sour cream and lime juice. Spoon mushroom mixture into 4 bowls, and top servings with sour cream mixture and scallions. Sprinkle with paprika, if desired. Serves 4 (serving size: 1 ½ cups salad and 2 Tbsp. sauce)

CALORIES 353; **FAT** 11g (sat 3g, unsat 7g); **PROTEIN** 11g; **CARB** 57g; **FIBER** 11g; **SUGARS** 4g (added sugars 0g); **SODIUM** 535mg; **CALC** 7% DV; **POTASSIUM** 13% DV

Staff Favorite • Fast
Gluten Free

Chicken Schnitzel with Grapefruit- Celery Slaw

Hands-on: 20 min. **Total:** 20 min.
Nutty almond flour keeps this crispy chicken gluten free; make your own by pulsing ¼ cup almonds in a food processor until finely ground. Pro tip: Segment the grapefruit over a bowl to collect the juice for the slaw's tangy dressing.

¼ cup almond flour, divided
2 Tbsp. cornstarch
1 large egg white, lightly beaten
3 Tbsp. Dijon mustard, divided
½ cup raw almonds, finely crushed
4 (4-oz.) chicken breast cutlets
2 Tbsp. olive oil, divided
1 cup thinly sliced red cabbage
1 cup thinly sliced yellow onion
½ tsp. black pepper
2 cups grapefruit segments plus 2 Tbsp. fresh grapefruit juice (from 3 grapefruit), divided
1 cup thinly sliced celery
2 cups chopped fresh flat-leaf parsley
2 tsp. honey

1. Whisk together 2 tablespoons almond flour and cornstarch in a shallow bowl. Whisk together beaten egg white and 2 tablespoons mustard in a second shallow bowl. In a third shallow bowl, combine crushed almonds and remaining 2 tablespoons almond flour.

2. Dredge chicken cutlets in the cornstarch mixture; shake off the excess. Dip in the egg mixture; let the excess drip off. Dredge in crushed almond mixture.

3. Heat 1 tablespoon oil in a large nonstick skillet over medium. Add chicken; cook until golden brown and cooked through, 5 to 6 minutes per side.

4. Wipe skillet clean; add remaining 1 tablespoon oil, and increase heat to high. Add cabbage and onion; cook, stirring occasionally, until lightly browned, 3 to 4 minutes. Sprinkle with pepper; transfer to a large bowl. Add grapefruit segments, celery, and parsley; toss to combine. Whisk together grapefruit juice, honey, and remaining 1 tablespoon mustard. Drizzle two-thirds of dressing over slaw mixture; toss. Drizzle remaining dressing over chicken and serve. Serves 4 (serving size: 1 chicken cutlet and ¾ cup slaw)

CALORIES 448; **FAT** 21g (sat 2g, unsat 17g); **PROTEIN** 35g; **CARB** 30g; **FIBER** 7g; **SUGARS** 15g (added sugars 3g); **SODIUM** 404mg; **CALC** 16% DV; **POTASSIUM** 14% DV

Fast • Gluten Free

Extra-Crispy Chicken Thighs with Potatoes and Chard

Hands-on: 30 min. **Total:** 30 min.
One-skillet dinners like this one make weeknight cooking a breeze. Starting the chicken in a cold skillet renders flavorful fat that crisps up the chicken and potatoes to golden perfection. Use a cast-iron skillet; its even heat distribution delivers delicious results.

4 (8-oz.) bone-in, skin-on chicken thighs
Cooking spray
½ tsp. kosher salt
1 lb. small red potatoes, halved
1 cup sliced leeks (white parts only)
4 garlic cloves, smashed
4 cups chopped Swiss chard
1 Tbsp. Dijon mustard
2 tsp. apple cider vinegar
¼ tsp. crushed red pepper

1. Preheat oven to 425°F. Place chicken thighs, skin sides down, in a large cast-iron skillet lightly coated with cooking spray; sprinkle salt over chicken. Arrange potatoes around chicken. Cook over medium, stirring potatoes occasionally, until chicken skin is browned and crisp, 14 to 16 minutes.
2. Flip chicken thighs; place skillet in oven. Bake at 425°F until chicken is done, 8 to 10 minutes. Transfer chicken and potatoes to a plate, keeping as much of the drippings in the skillet as possible.
3. Add leeks and garlic to skillet. Cook over medium-high, stirring often, until fragrant, 3 to 5 minutes. Add Swiss chard, mustard, and vinegar; cook just until wilted, 2 to 3 minutes. Sprinkle with crushed red pepper. Serve with chicken and potatoes. Serves 4 (serving size: 1 chicken thigh, 3 oz. potatoes, and 1 cup chard)

CALORIES 288; **FAT** 6g (sat 2g, unsat 3g); **PROTEIN** 31g; **CARB** 26g; **FIBER** 2g; **SUGARS** 1g (added sugars 0g); **SODIUM** 548mg; **CALC** 5% DV; **POTASSIUM** 11% DV

Fast • Gluten Free
Make Ahead • Vegetarian

Roasted Carrot and Coconut Soup

Hands-on: 30 min. **Total:** 30 min.
Avocado and coconut milk give this vegetarian soup a decadent, buttery texture; fiber-rich lentils and beans make it surprisingly filling. Keep your pantry stocked with these staples to help you throw this soup together in no time.

1¼ lbs. carrots, roughly chopped (about 3½ cups)
1 Tbsp. olive oil, divided
½ tsp. plus ⅛ tsp. kosher salt, divided
2 cups chopped yellow onion
2 Tbsp. red curry paste
2 tsp. grated peeled fresh ginger
1 tsp. crushed red pepper
1 (15-oz.) can unsalted cannellini beans, drained
3 cups unsalted vegetable stock
1 (15-oz.) can light coconut milk
3 Tbsp. fresh lime juice
½ tsp. black pepper
1 cup chopped fresh cilantro
1 cup cooked lentils
2 ripe avocados, thinly sliced

1. Preheat oven to 450°F. Toss together carrots, 1½ teaspoons oil, and ½ teaspoon salt on a large foil-lined baking sheet. Roast at 450°F until carrots are fork-tender, about 20 minutes, stirring once.
2. Meanwhile, heat remaining 1½ teaspoons oil in a Dutch oven over medium. Add onion; cook, stirring often, until lightly browned, 10 to 15 minutes.
3. Add curry paste, grated ginger, and crushed red pepper to Dutch oven, and cook, stirring constantly, until fragrant, 1 minute. Add cooked carrots, cannellini beans, vegetable stock, coconut milk, and remaining ⅛ teaspoon salt. Bring to a boil over high. Reduce heat to medium, and simmer 5 minutes.
4. Pour mixture into a blender. Remove center of blender lid to allow steam to escape; secure lid on blender. Place a clean kitchen towel over opening in blender lid. Process until smooth, about 1 minute.
5. Stir in the lime juice and black pepper. Divide soup among 6 bowls; top evenly with cilantro, lentils, and avocado. Serves 6 (serving size: about 2 cups soup, ¼ cup lentils, and ⅓ avocado)

CALORIES 363; **FAT** 17g (sat 5g, unsat 10g); **PROTEIN** 11g; **CARB** 47g; **FIBER** 16g; **SUGARS** 10g (added sugars 0g); **SODIUM** 482mg; **CALC** 10% DV; **POTASSIUM** 22% DV

Sausage and Mushroom Pasta with Butternut Squash

Hands-on: 30 min. **Total:** 30 min.
How's this for a hack? Here we slice refrigerated lasagna noodles to get silky ribbons of pasta that look homemade.

6 oz. reduced-fat ground pork sausage (such as Jimmy Dean)
1 (8-oz.) pkg. sliced fresh cremini mushrooms
1 cup chopped yellow onion
1 cup ¼-in.-cubed butternut squash
3 Tbsp. chopped fresh sage
1½ Tbsp. chopped garlic
⅓ cup dry white wine
8 oz. refrigerated fresh lasagna sheets, cut into ¾-in.-wide strips
1 cup unsalted chicken stock
3 Tbsp. heavy cream
½ tsp. kosher salt, divided
½ tsp. black pepper, divided
½ cup finely chopped fresh flat-leaf parsley
3 Tbsp. unsalted roasted pumpkin seed kernels (pepitas), chopped
2 Tbsp. pecorino Romano cheese, grated
1 tsp. lemon zest

1. Cook sausage, mushrooms, onion, squash, sage, and garlic in a large skillet over medium-high, stirring often, until sausage is cooked through and crumbled, 8 to 9 minutes. Add wine; cook until almost absorbed, 1 to 2 minutes.
2. Meanwhile, cook pasta in a large pot of boiling water 4 minutes, or to desired degree of doneness. Drain.
3. Stir stock into sauce; bring to a boil. Reduce heat to medium; cook 1 minute. Stir in pasta, cream, ¼ teaspoon salt, and ¼ teaspoon pepper. Cook until heated through, 1 to 2 minutes.
4. Stir together parsley, pepitas, cheese, zest, remaining ¼ teaspoon salt, and ¼ teaspoon pepper in a bowl. Divide pasta among 4 bowls; top with parsley mixture. Serves 4 (serving size: 1¼ cups pasta and 1½ Tbsp. parsley mixture)

CALORIES 333; **FAT** 16g (sat 7g, unsat 6g); **PROTEIN** 16g; **CARB** 28; **FIBER** 3g; **SUGARS** 4g (added sugars 0g); **SODIUM** 666mg; **CALC** 11% DV; **POTASSIUM** 11% DV

20-MINUTE MAINS

Fast • Gluten Free

Balsamic Chicken with Oranges and Radicchio

Hands-on: 20 min. **Total:** 20 min.

1 cup fresh orange juice
¾ cup balsamic vinegar, divided
3 Tbsp. pure maple syrup
3 Tbsp. olive oil, divided
4 (6-oz.) boneless, skinless chicken breasts
1 tsp. kosher salt, divided
1 tsp. black pepper, divided
2 small (7-oz.) heads radicchio, quartered lengthwise
2 navel oranges, unpeeled and quartered lengthwise
½ oz. pecorino Romano cheese, shaved (about ¼ cup)
3 Tbsp. chopped walnuts
1 Tbsp. unsalted butter

1. Whisk together orange juice, ½ cup balsamic vinegar, and maple syrup in a bowl. Set aside.
2. Heat 1 tablespoon oil in a large skillet over medium-high. Season chicken with ½ teaspoon salt and ½ teaspoon pepper. Add to skillet; cook until browned, about 5 minutes. Turn chicken over; pour balsamic mixture into skillet. Cook, turning chicken every few minutes, until a thermometer inserted in the thickest portion registers 165°F, about 12 minutes.
3. While chicken cooks, heat a grill pan over high. Drizzle 1 tablespoon oil over radicchio. Place on grill pan; cook until charred on all sides, turning occasionally, about 3 minutes. Transfer to a cutting board; let cool 3 minutes. Place oranges on grill pan; cook until charred, about 3 minutes. Transfer to a platter. Roughly chop radicchio; add to oranges. Add cheese, walnuts, remaining 1 tablespoon oil, remaining ½ teaspoon salt, and remaining ½ teaspoon pepper; toss.
4. Remove cooked chicken from balsamic mixture; arrange on salad. Continue cooking balsamic mixture, stirring often, until reduced to ¼ cup. Whisk in ¼ cup balsamic vinegar. Remove from heat; whisk in butter. Drizzle over chicken and salad. Serves 4 (serving size: 1 chicken breast, 1 cup salad, and 2 Tbsp. sauce)

CALORIES 542; **FAT** 23g (sat 6g, unsat 16g); **PROTEIN** 43g; **CARB** 39g; **FIBER** 3g; **SUGARS** 28g (added sugars 9g); **SODIUM** 663mg; **CALC** 13% DV; **POTASSIUM** 26% DV

Staff Favorite • Fast
Gluten Free

Coffee-Rubbed Steak with Brussels Sprouts Salad

Hands-on: 20 min. **Total:** 20 min.

1 Tbsp. ground coffee beans
¾ tsp. kosher salt, divided
¾ tsp. black pepper, divided
1 lb. hanger steak

¼ cup olive oil, divided
1 Tbsp. apple cider vinegar
2 tsp. Dijon mustard
1 tsp. honey
3 cups shredded Brussels sprouts
⅓ cup chopped toasted pecans
1 oz. blue cheese, crumbled

1. Heat a large cast-iron skillet over medium-high. Stir together the coffee, ⅝ teaspoon salt, and ½ teaspoon pepper in a bowl. Sprinkle mixture over steak, pressing gently to adhere. Add 1 tablespoon oil to skillet. Add steak; cook, without moving, until bottom forms a crust, about 3 minutes. Turn steak over; cook until a thermometer inserted in thickest portion registers 120°F, 6 to 7 minutes. Remove from skillet; set aside.
2. Whisk together vinegar, mustard, honey, remaining 3 tablespoons olive oil, ¼ teaspoon pepper, and ⅛ teaspoon salt in a large bowl. Add Brussels sprouts, pecans, and blue cheese; toss to coat.
3. Slice steak against the grain, and serve with Brussels sprouts salad. Serves 4 (serving size: about 3 oz. steak and ¾ cup salad)

CALORIES 427; FAT 31g (sat 7g, unsat 21g); PROTEIN 29g; CARB 9g; FIBER 4g; SUGARS 3g (added sugars 1g); SODIUM 593mg; CALC 8% DV; POTASSIUM 7% DV;

Fast

Lemony Greek Chicken Soup

Hands-on: 20 min. **Total:** 20 min.
To ensure a velvety texture, whisk some of the hot broth into the eggs before adding them to the pot to prevent curdling.

1 Tbsp. olive oil
¾ cup cubed carrot
½ cup chopped yellow onion
2 tsp. minced fresh garlic
¾ tsp. crushed red pepper
6 cups unsalted chicken stock

½ cup uncooked whole-wheat orzo
3 large eggs
¼ cup fresh lemon juice
3 cups shredded rotisserie chicken
3 cups chopped baby spinach
1¼ tsp. kosher salt
½ tsp. black pepper
3 Tbsp. chopped fresh dill

1. Heat oil in a Dutch oven over medium-high. Add carrot and onion; cook, stirring often, until softened, 3 to 4 minutes. Add garlic and red pepper; cook, stirring constantly, until fragrant, about 1 minute.
2. Add stock to Dutch oven; increase heat to high, and bring stock to a boil. Add orzo, and cook, uncovered, until orzo is al dente, about 6 minutes.
3. Whisk together eggs and lemon juice in a bowl until frothy. Once orzo has cooked 6 minutes, remove 1 cup boiling stock from Dutch oven. Gradually add stock to egg–lemon juice mixture, whisking constantly to temper the eggs, about 1 minute. Pour egg mixture back into Dutch oven, and combine.
4. Reduce heat to medium-low; stir in chicken, spinach, salt, and pepper. Cook, stirring constantly, until spinach wilts, about 1 minute. Divide soup among 6 bowls; sprinkle servings evenly with dill. Serves 6 (serving size: 1¼ cups)

CALORIES 261; FAT 8g (sat 2g, unsat 4g); PROTEIN 32g; CARB 16g; FIBER 3g; SUGARS 3g (added sugars 0g); SODIUM 641mg; CALC 5% DV; POTASSIUM 8% DV

Fast • Gluten Free

Sheet Pan Shrimp Fajitas

Hands-on: 15 min. **Total:** 20 min.
Mild poblano chiles and bell peppers get a nice char under the broiler and deliver more than double a day's worth of vitamin C.

1¼ lbs. peeled and deveined raw large shrimp
1 red bell pepper, sliced
1 orange bell pepper, sliced
1 cup sliced poblano chile
1 cup sliced red onion
3 Tbsp. olive oil
1 Tbsp. chili powder
1 tsp. ground cumin
¾ tsp. kosher salt, divided
½ tsp. ground coriander
¾ cup reduced-fat sour cream
1 Tbsp. chopped fresh cilantro
1 Tbsp. finely chopped seeded jalapeño
¼ tsp. lime zest plus 1 Tbsp. fresh lime juice
1 small garlic clove, grated
8 (6-in.) warm corn or flour tortillas
¼ cup packed fresh cilantro leaves
2 limes, cut into wedges

1. Place oven racks in center and upper third positions of oven. Preheat oven to 400°F. Toss together shrimp, bell peppers, poblano, onion, oil, chili powder, cumin, ⅝ teaspoon salt, and coriander on a baking sheet lined with aluminum foil. Place on middle rack of oven; roast until shrimp are cooked through, 9 to 10 minutes. Transfer shrimp to a plate, reserving remaining vegetable mixture on baking sheet. Cover shrimp with foil to keep warm.
2. Turn broiler to high. Broil vegetables on upper oven rack until slightly charred, 3 to 4 minutes, and set aside. Stir together sour cream, chopped cilantro, jalapeño, lime zest and juice, garlic, and remaining ⅛ teaspoon salt in a medium bowl.
3. Spoon shrimp and vegetables onto warm tortillas; top with sour cream mixture. Sprinkle with cilantro; serve with lime wedges. Serves 4 (serving size: 2 fajitas)

CALORIES 446; FAT 20g (sat 5g, unsat 13g); PROTEIN 26g; CARB 45g; FIBER 7g; SUGARS 10g (added sugars 0g); SODIUM 676mg; CALC 21% DV; POTASSIUM 11% DV

Pomegranate-Glazed Chicken

Hands-on: 20 min. **Total:** 20 min.
Sweet and tangy pomegranate juice gives the chicken a gorgeous garnet-hued glaze. Three tasty ways to use up any leftover juice follow this recipe. Dress up the quinoa pilaf by adding a sprinkle of crumbled feta cheese for a pop of salty flavor.

1 cup refrigerated pomegranate
   juice
1 Tbsp. light brown sugar
2 Tbsp. water
1 tsp. cornstarch
1 Tbsp. grainy mustard
1 Tbsp. unsalted butter
4 (4-oz.) boneless, skinless chicken
   thighs
1 tsp. kosher salt, divided
1 tsp. black pepper, divided
2 Tbsp. olive oil, divided
3 cups hot cooked quinoa
¼ cup unsalted roasted pistachios
¼ cup pomegranate arils
1 Tbsp. chopped fresh mint
Fresh mint leaves

1. Bring pomegranate juice and sugar to a boil in a small saucepan over high, and cook, whisking occasionally, until reduced by half, about 16 minutes. Whisk together 2 tablespoons water and cornstarch in a small bowl; add to pomegranate mixture. Boil, whisking constantly, until thickened, about 1 minute. Remove from heat; whisk in mustard and butter until smooth.
2. Meanwhile, heat a grill pan over medium-high. Season chicken with ¾ teaspoon salt and ¾ teaspoon pepper. Brush 1 tablespoon oil on pan. Cook chicken until browned, about 6 minutes. Turn and cook until a thermometer inserted in thickest

portion registers 165°F, about 6 minutes, turning if necessary to prevent burning. Remove from pan; cover to keep warm.
3. Place the quinoa, pistachios, pomegranate arils, chopped mint, remaining 1 tablespoon oil, remaining ¼ teaspoon salt, and remaining ¼ teaspoon pepper in a bowl; stir until combined. Divide quinoa mixture and chicken among 4 plates. Spoon 2 tablespoons pomegranate sauce over each serving; garnish with mint leaves. Serves 4 (serving size: 1 thigh, ⅓ cup quinoa, and 2 Tbsp. sauce)

CALORIES 496; FAT 21g (sat 5g, unsat 14g); PROTEIN 30g; CARB 48g; FIBER 5g; SUGARS 14g (added sugars 3g); SODIUM 656mg; CALC 6% DV; POTASSIUM 13% DV

USE IT UP

3 WAYS TO USE POME-GRANATE JUICE

Packed with polyphenols (aka antioxidant powerhouses), pomegranate juice has been shown to help tame inflammation throughout the body. It brings a touch of tartness and a pop of color to any recipe.

Fast • Gluten Free
Vegetarian
Glazed Brussels Sprouts
Tangy white balsamic vinegar teams up with pomegranate juice to rev up this twist on the classic Thanksgiving side dish.

1. Heat 3 Tbsp. olive oil, ¼ tsp. ground cardamom, and ⅛ tsp. crushed red pepper in a large skillet over medium-high. Add

1 lb. trimmed and halved Brussels sprouts, cut sides down. Cook until browned, about 7 minutes. Add ¼ cup pomegranate juice and 3 Tbsp. white balsamic vinegar. Cook, tossing often, until sauce is syrupy, another 5 to 6 minutes. Top evenly with 1 oz. crumbled feta cheese (about ¼ cup) and 3 Tbsp. chopped toasted pecans. Serves 4 (serving size: ¾ cup)

CALORIES 208; FAT 16g (sat 3g, unsat 12g); PROTEIN 6g; CARB 14g; FIBER 5g; SUGARS 5g (added sugars 0g); SODIUM 116mg; CALC 10% DV; POTASSIUM 10% DV

Fast • Gluten Free
Vegetarian
Pomegranate-Poached Pears
Mixing low-fat Greek yogurt with crème fraîche yields a decadent-tasting topping with less saturated fat.

1. Peel, halve, and core two firm pears. Melt 1 Tbsp. unsalted butter in a medium skillet over medium-high. Add pears, cut sides down; cook until browned, about 5 minutes. Add 1 cup Pinot Noir, 1 cup pomegranate juice, ¼ cup maple syrup, 1 Tbsp. vanilla extract, and 1 cinnamon stick. Cover and simmer until tender, about 15 minutes. Let cool slightly. Stir together ½ cup plain 2% reduced-fat Greek yogurt, 3 Tbsp. crème fraîche, and 1 tsp. maple syrup in a small bowl. Spoon over pears; garnish with 2 tsp. lemon zest. Serves 4 (serving size: 1 pear half and 1 ½ Tbsp. yogurt mixture)

CALORIES 210; FAT 8g (sat 5g, unsat 2g); PROTEIN 4g; CARB 30g; FIBER 5g; SUGARS 20g (added sugars 4g); SODIUM 22mg; CALC 8% DV; POTASSIUM 4% DV

Fast • Gluten Free
Vegetarian
PB&J Smoothies
These two-toned smoothies are incredibly filling thanks to substantial servings of protein and fiber.

1. Place 1½ frozen bananas, 2 pitted Medjool dates, 2 Tbsp. peanut butter, 2 tsp. honey, ½ cup 2% reduced-fat milk, and 1 cup plain 2% reduced-fat Greek yogurt in a blender. Process until smooth; divide between 2 glasses, reserving ½ cup mixture in blender. Add 1½ cups frozen raspberries, ⅔ cup pomegranate juice, and 2 tsp. honey to blender; process until smooth. Pour over peanut butter mixture in glasses. Top with frozen raspberries. Serves 2 (serving size: about 2 cups)

CALORIES 435; FAT 12g (sat 4g, unsat 7g); PROTEIN 18g; CARB 72g; FIBER 8g; SUGARS 52g (added sugars 12g); SODIUM 75mg; CALC 22% DV; POTASSIUM 14% DV

4 SAUCES FOR ANY PROTEIN

Fast • Gluten Free
Vegetarian
Spicy Parsley-Cilantro Sauce
A blender is the best tool for achieving the smooth texture of this sauce. Serve over grilled or roasted chicken, pork, beef, or lamb, or spoon it on eggs.

Place 1 cup packed fresh cilantro leaves, ¼ cup packed fresh cilantro stems, ¼ cup packed fresh flat-leaf parsley leaves, ¼ cup sliced unseeded serrano chiles, 1 Tbsp. fresh lemon juice, 1 garlic clove, ¾ tsp. kosher salt, ¼ tsp. ground cumin, ⅛ tsp. ground coriander, and ⅛ tsp. ground cardamom in a blender. Pulse until finely chopped, about 7 times. With blender running, gradually add ⅔ cup canola oil until smooth. Serve immediately. Serves 12 (serving size: 1 Tbsp.)

CALORIES 112; FAT 12g (sat 1g, unsat 11g); PROTEIN 0g; CARB 0g; FIBER 0g; SUGARS 0g; SODIUM 122mg; CALC 0% DV; POTASSIUM 0% DV

Fast • Gluten Free
Make Ahead • Vegetarian
Mango-Coconut Chutney
This condiment uses up mango that's gotten a little too ripe. Delicious in curries and vinaigrettes, it's also a stunning addition to a cheese board; see "Cooking Class" (page 348).

Heat 1 tsp. coconut oil in a skillet over medium. Add ½ cup chopped onion; cook 4 minutes. Add 1½ cups chopped mango, 2 Tbsp. brown sugar, 2 Tbsp. apple cider vinegar, 2 tsp. minced garlic, 2 tsp. minced ginger, 1 tsp. curry powder, 1 tsp. honey, and ¼ tsp. mustard seeds; cook 15 minutes. Transfer to a food processor; add 2 Tbsp. water, 1 Tbsp. unsweetened shredded coconut, and ⅜ tsp. kosher salt. Pulse until combined. Stir in ⅛ tsp. crushed red pepper. Serves 12 (serving size: 4 tsp.)

CALORIES 35; FAT 1g (sat 1g, unsat 0g); PROTEIN 0g; CARB 7g; FIBER 1g; SUGARS 6g (added sugars 3g); SODIUM 62mg; CALC 0% DV; POTASSIUM 1% DV

Fast • Gluten Free
Make Ahead • Vegetarian
Creamy Feta Sauce
If you're a fan of Greek tzatziki, you'll love this version that gets nice briny flavor from feta cheese. Fresh mint softens the garlic. Try it on lamb, chicken, or salmon.

Smash 1 garlic clove on a cutting board with the broad side of a chef's knife. Sprinkle with ⅛ tsp. kosher salt; rub salt into garlic with the knife, forming a paste. Transfer garlic to a small bowl; add 1 cup plain whole-milk Greek yogurt, 1 oz. crumbled feta cheese (about ¼ cup), 4 tsp. chopped fresh mint, 4 tsp. fresh lemon juice, 1 Tbsp. chopped fresh dill, 1 Tbsp.

water, and ⅜ tsp. kosher salt. Stir to combine. Serves 12 (serving size: 1½ Tbsp.)

CALORIES 25; FAT 1g (sat 1g, unsat 0g); PROTEIN 2g; CARB 1g; FIBER 0g; SUGARS 1g (added sugars 0g); SODIUM 108mg; CALC 3% DV; POTASSIUM 0% DV

Fast • Gluten Free
Make Ahead • Vegetarian
Homemade Hoisin
This easy make-at-home sauce is great with roasted salmon, riced cauliflower, or a veggie stir-fry. Substitute low-sodium soy sauce for the tamari, if you prefer.

Whisk together 1 Tbsp. dark brown sugar, 1 Tbsp. tamari, 1 Tbsp. natural creamy peanut butter, 3½ tsp. rice vinegar, 2½ tsp. white miso, 1 tsp. Sriracha chili sauce, 1 tsp. toasted sesame oil, 1 tsp. honey, and ¼ tsp. five-spice powder in a small bowl. Serve immediately, or store in an airtight container in the refrigerator up to 3 weeks. Serves 12 (serving size: 1 tsp.)

CALORIES 21; FAT 1g (sat 0g, unsat 1g); PROTEIN 1g; CARB 2g; FIBER 0g; SUGARS 2g (added sugars 1g); SODIUM 141mg; CALC 0% DV; POTASSIUM 0% DV

4 GO-WITH-ANYTHING SIDES

Fast • Gluten Free
Make Ahead • Vegetarian
Fall Fruit Salad

Thanks to the hearty greens, you can assemble the salad ingredients ahead of time—just wait to drizzle with the mustardy vinaigrette until right before serving.

Combine 1 (2½-oz.) head Belgian endive (leaves separated), 2 cups torn radicchio, 1 cup mixed salad greens, ½ thinly sliced Bartlett pear, and 1 peeled and sliced navel orange on a platter. Whisk together 2 Tbsp. white balsamic vinegar, 2 Tbsp. olive oil, 2 tsp. grainy Dijon mustard, ½ tsp. kosher salt, and ¼ tsp. black pepper until combined. Top salad with ¼ cup chopped pecans; drizzle with vinaigrette. Serves 6 (serving size: 1 cup)

CALORIES 111; **FAT** 8g (sat 1g, unsat 7g); **PROTEIN** 1g; **CARB** 9g; **FIBER** 2g; **SUGARS** 5g (added sugars 0g); **SODIUM** 208mg; **CALC** 4% DV; **POTASSIUM** 4% DV

Gluten Free • Vegetarian
Baked Sweet Onions

Keep this recipe around for adding big flavor to burgers, steaks, and winter salads. For the best balance of tenderness and crunchiness, shop for onions that are the same size so they cook evenly.

Toss together 5 quartered red onions (about 2½ lbs.), 2 Tbsp. extra-virgin olive oil, 2 Tbsp. balsamic vinegar, ½ tsp. kosher salt, and ¼ tsp. black pepper in a 12-inch cast-iron skillet; add 6 thyme sprigs. Cover tightly with foil. Bake at 450°F 15 minutes. Uncover and stir. Bake, uncovered, until caramelized, 15 to 20 minutes. Serves 4 (serving size: about ½ cup)

CALORIES 128; **FAT** 7g (sat 1g, unsat 6g); **PROTEIN** 2g; **CARB** 15g; **FIBER** 3g; **SUGARS** 7g (added sugars 0g); **SODIUM** 248mg; **CALC** 4% DV; **POTASSIUM** 5% DV

Vegetarian
Panko-Crusted Acorn Squash

Crunchy and tender in the same bite, these squash wedges are a good source of soluble fiber, which can help lower cholesterol. Roast on the middle oven rack for best results.

Stir together ¼ cup panko (Japanese breadcrumbs), ¼ cup grated Parmesan cheese, 2 tsp. chopped fresh thyme, 1 tsp. chopped fresh sage, 1 tsp. minced garlic, ½ tsp. lemon zest, ½ tsp. kosher salt, ¼ tsp. black pepper, and ¼ tsp. crushed red pepper. Halve 2 (1½-lb.) acorn squash lengthwise; discard seeds. Cut halves into thirds; place on a baking sheet. Brush with 1 Tbsp. olive oil; sprinkle with panko mixture. Bake at 425°F until golden brown, about 35 minutes. Serves 6 (serving size: 2 wedges)

CALORIES 102; **FAT** 3g (sat 1g, unsat 2g); **PROTEIN** 3g; **CARB** 17g; **FIBER** 2g; **SUGARS** 3g (added sugars 0g); **SODIUM** 232mg; **CALC** 8% DV; **POTASSIUM** 11% DV

Fast • Gluten Free
Vegetarian
Roasted Parsnips with Olives

Mild and buttery Castelvetrano olives add a pop of briny flavor; sub in your favorite pitted green olive if you can't find them at your grocery's olive bar.

Toss together 2 lbs. peeled and coarsely chopped parsnips, 1 Tbsp. olive oil, ½ tsp. kosher salt, and ¼ tsp. black pepper until combined. Spread on a large rimmed baking sheet. Bake at 450°F until tender, 20 to 25 minutes, stirring after 15 minutes. Drizzle with 1 Tbsp. fresh lemon juice and 1 Tbsp. olive oil; top with 8 crushed pitted Castelvetrano olives and 2 Tbsp. chopped fresh flat-leaf parsley. Serves 6 (serving size: ⅔ cup)

CALORIES 149; **FAT** 6g (sat 1g, unsat 5g); **PROTEIN** 2g; **CARB** 23g; **FIBER** 6g; **SUGARS** 6g (added sugars 0g); **SODIUM** 280mg; **CALC** 5% DV; **POTASSIUM** 10% DV

1 INGREDIENT, 3 SIDES

3 WAYS TO USE CAULI-FLOWER

Riced, roasted, or even raw cauliflower shows off as a side dish and makes a great vegetarian main. Low in carbs and packed with fiber and vitamins C and B6, it's a nutritional workhorse for the healthy cook.

Fast • Gluten Free
Vegetarian
Cauliflower Salad with Tahini Dressing

Make this recipe even easier by picking up riced cauliflower from the store; you'll usually find it in the freezer section and sometimes with the prepped produce. This is a great dish to make ahead of time; add the fresh herbs just before serving.

1. Grate 1 medium (1½-lb.) head cauliflower into a large microwavable bowl. Stir in 1 tsp. olive oil and ¼ tsp. kosher salt. Cover with plastic wrap, and microwave 3 minutes. Spread on a baking sheet; let cool 10 minutes. Stir together ¼ cup finely chopped shallot and 3 Tbsp. fresh lemon juice. Let stand 10 minutes; stir in 2 Tbsp. tahini. Place the cooled cauliflower in a large bowl; stir in tahini mixture, ½ cup chopped fresh flat-leaf parsley, ¼ cup chopped dried cherries, 1 Tbsp. chopped fresh mint, and ¼ tsp. kosher salt. Sprinkle with 3 Tbsp. chopped salted roasted pistachios. Serves 4 (serving size: 1 cup)

CALORIES 165; **FAT** 8g (sat 1g, unsat 7g); **PROTEIN** 6g; **CARB** 20g; **FIBER** 5g; **SUGARS** 9g (added sugars 0g); **SODIUM** 317mg; **CALC** 7% DV; **POTASSIUM** 13% DV

Fast • Gluten Free

Curried Cauliflower Gratin

Serve this hearty side over cooked brown rice for a meatless main dish.

1. Heat 2 tsp. olive oil in a 9-inch ovenproof skillet over medium-high. Add 1½ tsp. curry powder, 1 tsp. grated peeled fresh ginger, and 2 thinly sliced garlic cloves. Cook, stirring constantly, 1 minute. Stir in 4 cups cauliflower florets, ⅔ cup light coconut milk, ¼ cup lower-sodium chicken broth, and ½ tsp. kosher salt. Bake at 450°F until bubbly, about 20 minutes. Turn on broiler to high; broil until browned, about 6 minutes. Sprinkle with 3 Tbsp. chopped fresh cilantro and 2 Tbsp. sliced red Fresno chiles. Serves 4 (serving size: 1 cup)

CALORIES 88; FAT 5g (sat 3g, unsat 2g); PROTEIN 3g; CARB 9g; FIBER 4g; SUGARS 3g (added sugars 0g); SODIUM 286mg; CALC 4% DV; POTASSIUM 8% DV

Gluten Free

Cauliflower Steaks

1. Cut 1 (2-lb.) head cauliflower into 4 (1½-inch-thick) slices; place on a rimmed baking sheet. Add ⅓ cup unsalted chicken stock, 1 Tbsp. chopped fresh sage, 4 thyme sprigs, 4 crushed garlic cloves, ½ tsp. ground fennel seeds, and 1 bay leaf. Cover tightly with foil. Bake at 425°F 15 minutes. Remove and discard foil. Brush cauliflower with 1 Tbsp. olive oil. Bake until browned, about 10 minutes. Carefully flip; brush with 1 Tbsp. olive oil. Bake until browned, about 10 minutes. Place cauliflower on a platter; sprinkle with ½ tsp. kosher salt and ¼ tsp. crushed red pepper. Serves 4 (serving size: 1 steak)

CALORIES 131; FAT 8g (sat 1g, unsat 7g); PROTEIN 5g; CARB 13g; FIBER 5g; SUGARS 4g (added sugars 0g); SODIUM 315mg; CALC 7% DV; POTASSIUM 15% DV

COOKING LIGHT DIET

Staff Favorite • Gluten Free

Seared Scallops with Fennel and Citrus

Hands-on: 35 min. **Total:** 35 min. Scallops are the perfect choice for an effortless date-night dinner. To get the best golden, crispy sear, let your scallops come to room temperature and pat them dry before cooking. Track down dry-packed scallops; they're lower in sodium.

12 large sea scallops (about 1 lb.)
3 cups thinly sliced fennel bulb (from 1 [1-lb.] fennel bulb), divided
1 cup sliced peeled Yukon Gold potato
1 cup water
2 Tbsp. unsalted butter
1 tsp. fresh lemon juice, divided
½ tsp. kosher salt, divided
3 tangerines, peeled
2 Tbsp. finely chopped shallot
2 Tbsp. olive oil
4 pitted kalamata olives, finely chopped
4 tsp. chopped fresh tarragon
½ tsp. ground coriander
1 small garlic clove, pressed
3 Tbsp. canola oil, divided

1. Pat scallops dry with paper towels. Set aside. Bring 2 cups fennel, potato, and 1 cup water to a boil in a small saucepan. Reduce heat to low; simmer, partially covered, until potato is tender, about 15 minutes. Drain, pressing to remove excess liquid.
2. Transfer fennel mixture to a food processor. Add butter, ½ teaspoon lemon juice, and ⅜ teaspoon salt. Process until smooth. Cover to keep warm.

3. Gently break apart segments of 2 tangerines; set aside. Squeeze juice from remaining tangerine into a medium bowl. Whisk in the shallot, olive oil, olives, tarragon, coriander, garlic, and remaining ½ teaspoon lemon juice. Add the tangerine segments and remaining 1 cup fennel slices; toss to coat.
4. Heat 1½ tablespoons canola oil in a large cast-iron skillet over high until shimmering. Add 6 scallops; press gently with a spatula. Cook until sides are lightly browned, about 3 minutes. Turn scallops; cook 30 seconds or to desired degree of doneness. Transfer cooked scallops to a plate; wipe skillet clean. Repeat with remaining canola oil and remaining scallops. Sprinkle scallops with remaining ⅛ teaspoon salt. Serve with puree and salad. Serves 4 (serving size: 3 scallops, ¼ cup puree, and ¼ cup salad)

CALORIES 385; FAT 25g (sat 6g, unsat 19g); PROTEIN 16g; CARB 26g; FIBER 4g; SUGARS 10g (added sugars 0g); SODIUM 518mg; CALC 7% DV; POTASSIUM 16% DV

1 LIST, 3 DINNERS

Shop this list to feed four for three nights (or two with great leftovers). Read the recipes first to be sure you have the staples on hand.

2 pt. grape tomatoes

2 ½ lbs. baby yellow potatoes

2 (8-oz.) pkgs. haricots verts

7 cups baby spinach

2 English cucumbers

1 bunch fresh flat-leaf parsley

1 yellow onion

3 lemons

1 red bell pepper

1 shallot

1 cup uncooked quinoa

4 (5-oz.) and 4 (6-oz.) skin-on salmon fillets

5 large eggs

3 oz. feta cheese

Fast • Gluten Free

Salmon with Green Beans and Smashed Potatoes

Hands-on: 25 min. **Total:** 25 min.
Smart timing makes this sheet pan supper easy and keeps your dishes-to-clean count down. Briefly microwave the potatoes first to help them cook up perfectly tender with the salmon; add the green beans last to keep them bright and crunchy.

12 oz. baby yellow potatoes
1 cup water
Cooking spray
4 (6-oz.) skin-on salmon fillets
1 ½ Tbsp. olive oil
¾ tsp. kosher salt
½ tsp. black pepper
1 (8-oz.) pkg. haricots verts
¼ cup canola mayonnaise
2 Tbsp. chopped fresh flat-leaf parsley
1 Tbsp. chopped shallot
1 Tbsp. fresh lemon juice
2 tsp. Dijon mustard
1 lemon, cut into 4 wedges

1. Preheat oven to 425°F. Place potatoes and 1 cup water in a microwavable bowl; cover. Microwave at high 6 minutes. Transfer to a plate; let cool 5 minutes.
2. Spray a rimmed baking sheet with cooking spray. Place fillets on one side of baking sheet; coat with cooking spray. Place potatoes in middle of baking sheet. Using the flat side of a measuring cup, gently crush potatoes. Drizzle potatoes with oil. Stir together salt and pepper in a small bowl; sprinkle two-thirds of mixture over salmon and potatoes. Bake at 425°F for 5 minutes; remove from oven.
3. Add haricots verts to baking sheet; season with remaining salt mixture. Bake at 425°F for 10 minutes. Turn on broiler to high; broil until salmon is browned, about 2 minutes.
4. Stir together mayonnaise, parsley, shallot, lemon juice, and mustard in a small bowl. Serve salmon, potatoes, and haricots verts with sauce and lemon wedges. Serves 4 (serving size: 1 salmon fillet, ½ cup green beans, ½ cup potatoes, and 1 Tbsp. sauce)

CALORIES 410; FAT 19g (sat 3g, unsat 14g); PROTEIN 39g; CARB 21g; FIBER 5g; SUGARS 3g (added sugars 0g); SODIUM 613mg; CALC 6% DV; POTASSIUM 16% DV

Gluten Free • Vegetarian

Potato Quiche with Spinach

Hands-on: 25 min. **Total:** 40 min.
Part custardy quiche, part potato gratin, this breakfast-for-dinner dish gets a golden crust thanks to a generous amount of heart-healthy olive oil.

1 ½ lbs. baby yellow potatoes, thinly sliced
1 cup thinly sliced yellow onion
1 ⅛ tsp. kosher salt, divided
Cooking spray
7 Tbsp. olive oil, divided
3 large eggs
2 large egg whites
1 ½ oz. feta cheese, crumbled (about ⅓ cup), divided
1 Tbsp. red wine vinegar
1 Tbsp. fresh lemon juice

1 tsp. honey
4 cups baby spinach leaves
2 cups halved grape tomatoes
1 cup sliced English cucumber
1 cup sliced red bell pepper

1. Preheat oven to 375°F. Place potatoes, onion, and ½ teaspoon salt in a large microwavable bowl; spray lightly with cooking spray, and toss to coat. Cover with plastic wrap; microwave at high 3 minutes. Heat a 9-inch cast-iron or ovenproof skillet over medium-high. Add 1 tablespoon oil and half of potato mixture; cook, stirring occasionally, until potatoes are almost cooked through, 6 to 8 minutes. Transfer to a rimmed baking sheet. Repeat with 1 tablespoon oil and remaining potato mixture. Let cool 6 minutes.
2. Whisk together eggs, egg whites, and ½ teaspoon salt in a medium bowl. Gently fold in cooled potato mixture, being careful to keep potatoes intact.
3. Wipe skillet clean. Add 3 tablespoons oil; heat over medium-high 30 seconds. Add potato mixture; press in an even layer. Sprinkle with 3 tablespoons feta; cook until a crust forms on bottom, about 2 minutes. Transfer to oven, and bake at 375°F until golden brown, 20 to 23 minutes.
4. Whisk together the vinegar, lemon juice, honey, remaining 2 tablespoons oil, and remaining ⅛ teaspoon salt in a large bowl. Add spinach, tomatoes, cucumber, and bell pepper; toss to combine. Cut quiche into 8 wedges; top evenly with spinach salad and remaining feta. Serves 4 (serving size: 2 wedges)

CALORIES 492; **FAT** 30g (sat 6g, unsat 22g); **PROTEIN** 15g; **CARB** 42g; **FIBER** 9g; **SUGARS** 10g (added sugars 1g); **SODIUM** 808mg; **CALC** 16% DV; **POTASSIUM** 9% DV

Fast · Gluten Free
Make Ahead

Easy Greek Salmon Bowls

Hands-on: 20 min. **Total:** 20 min. Heart-hero salmon teams up with protein- and fiber-forward quinoa to fill you up; spinach delivers a hit of iron, while green beans and cucumber up the veggie count. Great warm or at room temperature, this also makes a standout packed lunch.

4 (5-oz.) skin-on salmon fillets
½ tsp. dried dill
½ tsp. dried oregano
1 tsp. kosher salt, divided
5 Tbsp. canola oil, divided
1 (8-oz.) pkg. haricots verts
3 cups packed baby spinach leaves, finely chopped
1½ cups cooked quinoa
½ cup chopped fresh flat-leaf parsley
¼ cup fresh lemon juice
1 tsp. honey
2 cups halved grape tomatoes
2 cups chopped English cucumber
¼ cup crumbled feta cheese

1. Sprinkle salmon with dill, oregano, and ¼ teaspoon salt. Heat 1 tablespoon oil in a large nonstick skillet over medium-high. Add salmon, skin side up, to skillet; cook 2 to 3 minutes per side for medium. Set aside.
2. Fill a large bowl with ice water. Cook haricots verts according to package directions; place in ice water until completely cool, about 1 minute. Pat dry.
3. Toss together spinach, quinoa, and parsley in a bowl. Whisk together lemon juice, honey, and remaining ¼ cup oil in a small bowl. Add ¼ cup lemon dressing to spinach mixture; toss to combine.
4. To serve, spoon ¾ cup spinach mixture into each of 4 bowls. Arrange ½ cup tomatoes, ½ cup cucumber, and ⅓ cup cooked haricots verts in each bowl. Drizzle with remaining dressing; sprinkle with remaining ¾ teaspoon salt. Top each bowl with 1 flaked salmon fillet and 1 tablespoon feta cheese. Serves 4

CALORIES 527; **FAT** 29g (sat 5g, unsat 24g); **PROTEIN** 39g; **CARB** 29g; **FIBER** 7g; **SUGARS** 8g (added sugars 1g); **SODIUM** 683mg; **CALC** 16% DV; **POTASSIUM** 21% DV

Make Ahead

Vietnamese Beef and Noodle Soup

Hands-on: 40 min. **Total:** 8 hr. 40 min. Traditional Vietnamese pho recipes require hours of hands-on cooking; this slow cooker version lets you off the hook in 40 minutes. Toast the spices and sear the short ribs first to add layers of flavor to this beautifully brothy soup.

3 whole star anise
1 cinnamon stick
2 medium-sized sweet onions
3 Tbsp. minced peeled fresh ginger
1½ lbs. bone-in beef short ribs
1 cup water
4 cups unsalted beef stock
¼ tsp. kosher salt
2¼ tsp. fish sauce
2 tsp. hoisin sauce
4 oz. brown rice vermicelli noodles
4 oz. top sirloin steak, thinly sliced
2 cups fresh bean sprouts
1 cup roughly torn fresh basil
¼ cup roughly torn fresh mint
1 lime, cut into 4 wedges
Thinly sliced red Fresno chile

1. Cook star anise and cinnamon in a large skillet over medium until fragrant, about 2 minutes. Transfer to a 6-quart slow cooker. Cut 1 onion in half; place in skillet, cut side down; add ginger. Thinly slice remaining onion, and set aside. Cook onion and ginger over medium, undisturbed, until onion is charred on cut side, 5 to 7 minutes. Transfer to slow cooker. Increase heat under skillet to medium-high. Add short ribs; cook until browned on all sides, 14 to 16 minutes. Transfer to slow cooker.

Remove skillet from heat; discard drippings. Pour 1 cup water into skillet, scraping to loosen browned bits. Pour through a strainer into slow cooker; discard solids. Stir in beef stock and salt. Cover and cook on low 8 hours.

2. Remove short ribs from slow cooker. Pour broth through a strainer lined with cheesecloth into a bowl; discard solids. Skim and discard fat from surface of broth; pour broth back into slow cooker. Remove meat from bones of short ribs; shred meat, and return to slow cooker. Stir in fish sauce and hoisin sauce. Turn slow cooker to high; cover to keep hot.

3. Cook noodles according to package directions. Place ½ cup cooked noodles in each of 4 bowls. Top each with 1 ounce raw sirloin and 1¼ cups hot broth (broth will cook meat). Top each with ⅓ cup short rib meat and ¼ cup thinly sliced onion. Sprinkle with bean sprouts, basil, and mint. Serve with lime wedges; garnish with Fresno chile. Serves 4

CALORIES 337; **FAT** 9g (sat 4g, unsat 5g); **PROTEIN** 26g; **CARB** 38g; **FIBER** 7g; **SUGARS** 7 (added sugars 0g); **SODIUM** 650mg; **CALC** 8% DV; **POTASSIUM** 13% DV

THE RECIPE MAKEOVER

LIGHTEN UP PUMPKIN BREAD

With two-thirds less sugar, this whole-grain loaf is as much breakfast as it is dessert.
A fall favorite, the classic pumpkin loaf might look the part of a healthy breakfast, but it packs 400 calories and nearly 40g sugar into a single dense slice. In the spirit of the season, we developed a lighter loaf that still delivers the treasured fall flavors for 200 fewer calories.

Quick oats and white whole-wheat flour add a double dose of whole grains while still keeping the loaf light and tender. Dark-colored maple syrup (formerly called Grade B) packs a strong maple punch with caramel undertones that complement the fall spices. A sprinkle of toasted pumpkin seeds adds a crunchy finish.

Lots of pureed pumpkin helps keep the loaf moist for days, so let the bake-ahead bonus liberate you (and your oven) during the holidays.

Make Ahead • Vegetarian

Pumpkin-Maple Loaf

Hands-on: 15 min. **Total:** 1 hr. 35 min. For breakfast on the go, spin this pumpkin bread recipe into individually portioned muffins by dividing the batter among 12 muffin cups coated with cooking spray and baking at 375°F for 22 minutes. To freeze muffins, let cool completely, and place in ziplock plastic bags. Reheat in the microwave for 30 seconds.

Cooking spray
¾ cup whole buttermilk
½ cup quick-cooking oats
1 cup canned pumpkin puree
½ cup dark-colored maple syrup
⅓ cup canola oil
¼ cup dark brown sugar
1 tsp. vanilla extract
2 large eggs
6 oz. white whole-wheat flour (about 1¼ cups)
1 Tbsp. pumpkin pie spice
1 tsp. baking powder
½ tsp. kosher salt
¼ tsp. baking soda
2 Tbsp. roasted unsalted pumpkin seed kernels (pepitas)

1. Preheat oven to 350°F. Coat a 9- x 5-inch loaf pan with cooking spray.

2. Place buttermilk and oats in a bowl; stir to combine. Let stand 15 minutes.

3. Whisk together pumpkin, maple syrup, oil, brown sugar, vanilla, and eggs in a large bowl. Stir in oat mixture. Set aside.

4. Whisk together flour, pumpkin pie spice, baking powder, salt, and baking soda in a bowl. Add flour mixture to pumpkin mixture; whisk just until combined. Pour batter into prepared pan; sprinkle with pumpkin seed kernels.

5. Bake at 350°F until a wooden pick inserted in center comes out clean, 55 to 65 minutes. Cool in pan on a wire rack 10 minutes. Remove bread from pan; cool completely. Cut into 12 slices. Serves 12 (serving size: 1 slice)

CALORIES 200; FAT 9g (sat 1g, unsat 7g); PROTEIN 5g; CARB 28g; FIBER 2g; SUGARS 13g (added sugars 11g); SODIUM 146mg; CALC 10% DV; POTASSIUM 3% DV

THE PICKY EATER GURU

DUMPLING SOUP IN A THIRD OF THE TIME

BY GINA HOMOLKA

A big batch of this soup is a healthy way to satisfy your comfort food cravings—and use up leftovers.

When the weather turns cooler, it's comfort foods that folks crave—the kinds of dishes that stick to your bones and warm you up like a big hug or your favorite cozy sweater. But unfortunately, these beloved comfort foods are often loaded with calories and fat that make them hard to squeeze into a healthy eating plan.

My solution to this dilemma is simple—I make a big pot of brothy (calorie-conscious) soup. This hearty turkey and dumpling soup is filling, soothing, light, and delicious, and it pleases everyone in my home—kids included. My daughter, Madison, loves this soup so much, she even asks for leftovers to pack for her school lunch. It's just as tasty with ground chicken, or you can add leftover Thanksgiving turkey instead.

If you don't have a pressure cooker, that's no problem. Simply simmer the soup in a Dutch oven about an hour before adding in the dumplings—just be sure the soup is boiling when you add them so that they don't stick together or to the bottom of the pot. You'll know the dumplings are ready when they are puffed and floating on the top. This, I promise, is comfort food at its best.

Make Ahead

Instant Pot® Turkey And Sage Dumpling Soup

Hands-on: 30 min. **Total:** 1 hr.
Can't find turkey cutlets? Use chicken cutlets or breasts. Serve the soup with a crunchy salad and citrus vinaigrette.

1 Tbsp. unsalted butter
1 cup chopped celery
1 cup chopped carrots
½ cup diced onion
1 garlic clove, minced
4.25 oz. (about 1 cup) plus 2 Tbsp.
all-purpose flour, divided
7 cups water
1¼ Tbsp. reduced-sodium turkey or chicken bouillon (such as Better Than Bouillon)
1¼ lbs. boneless, skinless turkey breast cutlets
4 tsp. minced fresh sage, divided
2 bay leaves
¼ tsp. black pepper, divided, plus more for garnish
1 tsp. baking powder
½ tsp. kosher salt
1 large egg yolk, beaten
½ cup fat-free milk
Chopped fresh flat-leaf parsley

1. Melt butter in an Instant Pot set to sauté. Add celery, carrots, onion, and garlic; cook until soft and fragrant, 5 to 8 minutes. Sprinkle 2 tablespoons flour over vegetables, stir, and cook 1 minute.

2. Add 7 cups water, bouillon, turkey, 1 tablespoon sage, bay leaves, and ⅛ teaspoon pepper. Cover and cook on high pressure 20 minutes. Release pressure with quick or natural release. Remove turkey; shred or chop. Discard bay leaves; return turkey to pot. Turn Instant Pot to sauté; bring back to a boil.

3. Combine remaining 1 cup flour, baking powder, remaining 1 teaspoon sage, salt, and remaining ⅛ teaspoon pepper. Whisk together egg yolk and milk; stir into flour mixture until just blended. Form dough into dumplings using a teaspoon, and drop into soup. (They will expand.) Partially cover; cook until dumplings are cooked through and tender, about 3 minutes. Garnish with pepper and parsley. Serves 6 (serving size: 1½ cups soup and 3 dumplings)

CALORIES 250; FAT 5g (sat 2g, unsat 2g); PROTEIN 27g; CARB 24g; FIBER 2g; SUGARS 3g (added sugars 0g); SODIUM 666mg; CALC 10% DV; POTASSIUM 11% DV

THE ONLY STOCK RECIPE YOU'LL EVER NEED

BY ANDREA NGUYEN

This speedy and versatile chicken stock covers a lot of territory in a short amount of time. Store-bought stock is a modern convenience that simplifies life for home cooks. But I'll let you in on a secret that you probably already know: Your food will taste good with purchased stock, but it'll be over-the-top with homemade stock.

Go ahead and roll your eyes while you open a can of Swanson, my (and *Cooking Light*'s) go-to brand. I buy it by the case for lazy days, but I also keep a stash of frozen homemade stock—aka pure freezer gold.

Although the terms stock and broth are often used interchangeably, stocks are the heavyweight players in the kitchen. They are richer-tasting, versatile building blocks for sauces and other dishes. Thanks to a long simmer with lots of bones, stocks often gel when chilled. Broths tend to be lighter (due to shorter cook times and fewer bones) and are typically used to add depth to soups and sides. So in a nutshell, think of broths as flavored water and stocks as diluted sauce.

I used to simmer big pots of stock for hours—a half-day project if you include butchering the chicken. Nowadays, I whip up delicious batches in a pressure cooker in less than an hour and a half. Pressure cookers are game changers for homemade stock— they quickly extract intense flavor from ingredients. Multifunction cookers like the Instant Pot are programmable pressure cookers, so you can set it to cook and walk away.

Good stock isn't as simple as simmering a hodgepodge of ingredients. For the best flavor, combine meaty parts (such as thighs) with scraps (like the carcass). Add chicken feet to inject the wonderful richness of gelatin; ask a butcher for them, or make a trip to an Asian market.

Since there are only a few ingredients that go into stock, make sure they're all of good quality. Use water that you like to drink. Add aromatics and herbs, but limit the vegetables since they can suppress the chicken flavor. The beauty of my East-West Chicken Stock is you can tweak the direction with a few simple swaps. Keep it Western by sticking with bay leaf and parsley; use this version for everything from killer gravies and sauces to risotto. Or take it in an Asian direction (East) by trading those herbs for ginger and cilantro, and use it to transform a wimpy wonton soup into a soul-warming dish. Regardless, add a Fuji apple, which lends a natural sweet edge to amplify the stock's umami depth. That's a trick I devised for making pho broth, and it totally works for both versions.

To ensure a clear stock with a clean flavor, take a two-step approach: Initially parboil the chicken scraps, then filter the finished stock through paper towels or cheesecloth to remove most of the scum (technically denatured proteins) without robbing the stock of its highly coveted rich flavor.

Since homemade stock freezes beautifully, make a couple of batches to keep on hand for the holidays. Trust me: This stock will help your dishes sparkle all season long. And thanks to your pressure cooker, you can whip it up in record time.

East-West Chicken Stock

Hands-on: 15 min. **Total:** 1 hr. 30 min. Opt for bay leaf and parsley for a Western-style stock, or employ ginger and cilantro to tilt the flavor toward the East.

1 (4-lb.) whole chicken
4 chicken feet (optional)
1 cup chopped yellow onion
½ cup chopped peeled Fuji apple
1 bay leaf or 1 (1-in.) piece fresh
   ginger, peeled, cut into thick
   slices, and smashed
¾ cup chopped fresh flat-leaf
   parsley or cilantro
1½ tsp. kosher salt
7½ cups water

1. Use a sharp boning knife to remove the breasts, drumsticks, and thighs from chicken. Set aside. Remove the wings, and cut the carcass in half through back-bone; place wings and both halves of carcass in a 6- to 8-quart stovetop pressure cooker or electric multifunction cooker, such as an Instant Pot. Add water to barely cover. Bring to a boil over high (adjust the sauté function on an Instant Pot or use a similar setting on other multifunction cookers). After foamy scum appears, remove from the heat, and turn off the cooker. Drain chicken parts; discard liquid. Rinse chicken parts with cold water, and return to cooker. Add reserved breasts, drumsticks, and thighs, chicken feet, onion, apple, bay leaf, parsley, salt, and 7 ½ cups water.

2. Secure pressure cooker lid. Heat over medium-high to bring to high pressure, and cook for 40 minutes. Remove from heat, and naturally depressurize for 25 minutes. (In a multifunction cooker, lock on the lid, and program the machine to cook on high pressure for 40 minutes. Turn off, and let depressurize for 25 minutes.)
3. Release residual pressure on pressure cooker. Remove and discard large solids from stock mixture. Set a fine wire-mesh strainer lined with paper towels, cheesecloth, or muslin over a pot, and pour stock through strainer. (There should be some fat remaining for flavor. If there's too much fat for your taste, refrigerate overnight and remove the solidified fat the next day.) The stock will keep in the refrigerator for up to 5 days or frozen for up to 3 months. Serves 8 (serving size: 1 cup)

CALORIES 32; **FAT** 0g; **PROTEIN** 5g; **CARB** 3g; **FIBER** 2g; **SUGARS** 2g (added sugars 0g); **SODIUM** 601mg; **CALC** 1% DV; **POTASSIUM** 10% DV

STOCK-MAKING MADE SIMPLE

PREPARING HOMEMADE STOCK IS A LABOR OF LOVE THAT HAS HUGE PAYBACKS IN FLAVOR. HERE'S HOW YOU CAN MAXIMIZE YOUR STOCK-MAKING EXPERIENCE.

LEAN ON YOUR BUTCHER
If you're uncomfortable with the idea of breaking down a whole chicken into parts, ask for help at the butcher counter. Most are happy to do the knife work for you.

FREEZE STRATEGICALLY
Fill plastic freezer bags about ⅔ full with stock, then freeze them on baking sheets so they freeze flat. To use, partially thaw to loosen the stock, then break the stock into pieces that will slide into a pot easily. For smaller portions, freeze your stock in ice cube trays.

MAXIMIZE LEFTOVERS
The leftover chicken is somewhat devoid of flavor; season it aggressively with curry powder or chopped, fresh cilantro and use the meat for chicken salad or tacos.

THE STEAMY SECRET TO PERFECTLY COOKED FISH

BY BARTON SEAVER

Enriched with fresh herbs and spices, a gently simmering broth infuses seafood with subtle yet alluring flavor.

Just like marinating packs meat with bold flavor, steaming perfumes seafood with enticing aromas. In this moist-heat cooking method, fish fillets rest above a small amount of scented, simmering liquid. When the pot is covered, captive aromatic heat gently cooks the seafood.

Surprisingly simple, this is a practical and fun method for home cooks. Start with your favorite aromatics—ginger, herbs, and citrus peel provide a fresh punctuation mark; spices like cinnamon, clove, and star anise add complexity. Place in a large pot with a tight-fitting lid, and add liquid to measure ½ inch. Bring the liquid to a simmer. Set a rack (or build a vegetable "raft" from celery or fennel stalks) above the simmering liquid, and place seasoned fish on top. Cover and steam until the fish is cooked through, about 7 minutes per ½ inch of thickness.

There's just one more tip you should know—be sure to season fish well with salt before cooking. Unlike poaching, the steaming process doesn't flavor the fish with any salt.

Fast • Gluten Free

Steamed Cod With Watercress-Orange Sauce

Hands-on: 30 min. **Total:** 30 min. This recipe works with various fish: Try delicate flatfish like sole, flounder, and dab; flaky whitefish like cod, sablefish, and Pacific rockfish; or even fish high in omega-3 fats like salmon. Feel free to play with the aromatics in the steaming liquid, but avoid using sulfurous vegetables like cabbage or broccoli; their strong flavors can overpower the broth. And don't use carrots or potatoes—they don't add any aromatic flavor and are best saved for another purpose.

4 (5-oz.) skinless cod fillets
1 tsp. kosher salt, divided
¼ cup white wine
1 Tbsp. orange zest plus ⅓ cup fresh orange juice
6 garlic cloves, peeled and smashed
3 celery stalks
1 cup watercress, plus more for garnish
2 Tbsp. olive oil
¼ tsp. granulated sugar
⅛ tsp. ground coriander
1 orange, sectioned

1. Sprinkle fillets with ½ teaspoon salt. Combine wine, orange zest and juice, and garlic in a 10-inch pot. Place celery in a single layer in the pot, making a "raft" for the fish. Bring to a boil over medium-high. Place fillets on celery raft; reduce heat to medium to maintain a simmer. Cover; steam fillets until cooked through, about 7 minutes. Transfer fish to a plate.

2. Place the steaming liquid, 2 cooked garlic cloves (discard remaining garlic), watercress, cooked celery, and olive oil in a blender, and puree until smooth. Add sugar, coriander, and remaining ½ teaspoon salt. Divide sauce among 4 shallow bowls. Top with fish, orange sections, and watercress. Serves 4 (serving size: 5 oz. fish and about ⅔ cup sauce)

CALORIES 245; **FAT** 8g (sat 1g, unsat 6g); **PROTEIN** 27g; **CARB** 11g; **FIBER** 2g; **SUGARS** 7g (added sugars 0g); **SODIUM** 585mg; **CALC** 7% DV; **POTASSIUM** 18% DV

YOUR NEW GO-TO GRAVY

Skip the drippings and cook roasted turkey wings in broth to create a lean sauce with incredibly meaty flavor.

Make Ahead

Double-Stock Turkey Gravy

Hands-on: 15 min. **Total:** 2 hr. 25 min.

If you prepare stock up to a week ahead, you can make the gravy in just a few minutes. Simmering the turkey wings in chicken stock makes the resulting liquid twice as meaty tasting as it would be if you used plain water.

1 ¼ lbs. turkey wings (about 4 wings)
2 qt. unsalted chicken stock
1 large yellow onion, chopped
1 large carrot, chopped
2 celery stalks, chopped
1 garlic head, halved crosswise
6 Tbsp. quick-mixing flour (such as Wondra)
½ cup water
½ tsp. kosher salt

1. Preheat oven to 425°F. Place turkey wings on a wire rack set on a sheet pan. Bake at 425°F until well browned and crisp, about 1 hour.

2. Transfer wings to a large Dutch oven. Add stock, onion, carrot, celery, and garlic; bring to a boil over high. Reduce heat to low, and simmer until reduced by half, about 1 hour. Pour liquid through a fine wire-mesh strainer into a bowl; discard solids. Return liquid to pan; bring to a boil.

3. Whisk together flour and ½ cup water in a bowl; whisk into stock mixture until combined. Boil until thickened, about 5 minutes. Stir in salt; serve immediately. Serves 16 (serving size: ¼ cup)

CALORIES 30; FAT 0g; PROTEIN 4g; CARB 3g; FIBER 0g; SUGARS 1g (added sugars 0g); SODIUM 129mg; CALC 0% DV; POTASSIUM 0% DV

THE STEPS

1. BROWN THE WINGS
Wings have stronger flavor and more collagen (a kind of gelatin that adds body) than other turkey parts. Roast them until deep golden brown. The more color you get on the wings, the richer your stock will taste—the liquid absorbs the caramelization on the turkey while simmering.

2. REDUCE AND STRAIN
Combine roasted wings, mirepoix (onion, carrot, and celery), and aromatics in the pot. Cover with store-bought chicken stock, then simmer to reduce liquid and intensify flavor. Pass finished stock through a fine wire-mesh strainer to catch tiny bits of sediment; discard solids.

3. ACTIVATE THE THICKENER
Instead of regular flour or cornstarch, we use Wondra flour, which blends almost instantly and resists clumping. The mixture needs to come to a boil for a few minutes while you whisk to activate its thickening power. When the gravy can coat the back of a spoon, it's ready.

BUILD YOUR BEST CHEESE BOARD

Offer selections from these 10 essential categories to make your party platter a guaranteed crowd-pleaser.

1. SOFT-RIND CHEESE
Soft rinds on Brie and Camembert wheels (shown) are edible and lend funky flavor contrast to the supremely rich, creamy cheese.

2. FIRM CHEESE
Sliceable cheeses like cheddar (shown), Manchego, or Gruyère have been aged for months or years, developing structured texture and nuanced flavors.

3. FRESH CHEESE
Light-textured, milky, and tangy cheeses like goat (shown) or feta are best to taste first because their mild flavors won't overwhelm the palate.

4. HONEY
A little dab is a heavenly pairing with tangy goat cheese and robust, salty blue cheese. Mild, light-colored honeys like clover and alfalfa are best for cheese boards.

5. BREAD
An alternative to crunchy crackers, bread makes a soft, starchy vehicle for the cheese. Cut small slices from bakery-fresh crusty whole-grain or wild-yeast loaves.

6. FRESH FRUIT
Robust blue cheeses love a sweet fruit pairing for flavor balance. Select what's in season, like fall grapes. Avoid fruit with flesh that turns brown, like apples or pears.

7. NUTS
Another textural contrast, nuts amplify the meaty umami flavor in cheese. Roasted unsalted walnuts, pistachios, and almonds are all good choices.

8. BLUE CHEESE
Soft yet sliceable, creamy, tangy, salty, and pungent, mold-veined blues like Stilton (shown) or Roquefort deliver pungent flavor, so taste them last.

9. CRACKERS
Whole-grain and seeded crackers are good choices, but avoid strongly flavored options that might mask or fight with the taste of the cheese.

10. DRIED FRUIT
Choose those that would be out of season if they were fresh so it's even more of a treat. Apricots (shown), figs, and cherries are great for fall or winter spreads.

We food-media types keep strange calendars. While many of you were out of the office sipping margaritas, we were testing turkey recipes when the summer sun shone brightest. And maybe that's appropriate, given that the bird is the sun of the Thanksgiving solar system. An entire day—heck, several days—revolves around coddling and embellishing a relatively flavorless oblong creature and precisely timing what pies and sides can be baked, stewed, or made ahead to accommodate it. Our editors have more than 200 years of collective Thanksgiving wisdom under their belts, which translates to a whole lot of expert advice and a whole lot of turkey—braised; spice-rubbed; stuffed; confited; deep-fried; stewed; and, one of my favorite methods, a cumin-spiced, grilled, spatchcocked number redolent of wood smoke and bedecked with crispy skin. I grill it to free up oven room for the sides, which, if we're all being honest, are the best part of the feast. That's why we serve them up in "The Ultimate Guide to Thanksgiving Sides," (page 290) one of many features you'll find useful in this special double holiday issue. Happy Thanksgiving, dear readers.

Gluten Free

Grill-Smoked Turkey

Hands-on: 30 min. **Total:** 10 hr. 30 min.

2 tsp. kosher salt
2 tsp. ground cumin
1 tsp. dried sage
½ tsp. crushed red pepper
2 tsp. lemon zest
1 (12-lb.) turkey, backbone removed, breastbone flattened
1 Tbsp. olive oil
1 cup applewood chips, soaked in water 30 minutes

1. Combine salt, cumin, sage, red pepper, and lemon zest in a bowl. Rub turkey skin with oil; season skin and cavity with salt mixture. Place turkey, skin side up, on a rack set in a rimmed baking sheet. Refrigerate uncovered overnight to season it and air-dry skin.
2. Preheat grill to medium-high (400° to 450°F). (If using charcoal grill or clay oven like a Big Green Egg, let charcoal burn down to glowing embers). Place turkey, skin side down, on oiled grates, and grill, covered, until skin is light golden, about 30 minutes. Put wood chips in aluminum foil to make a loose packet; place directly on heating element. (Throw wood chips directly on coals, if using.) Reduce heat to low (maintain grill temperature of 300° to 350°F). Cover and grill until a thermometer inserted into thickest part of thigh registers 165°F, about 1 more hour. Let rest 20 minutes before serving. Serves 14 (serving size: about 5 oz. turkey with skin)

CALORIES 371; **FAT** 13g (sat 4g, unsat 8g); **PROTEIN** 59g; **CARB** 0g; **FIBER** 0g; **SUGARS** 0g; **SODIUM** 413mg; **CALC** 5% DV; **POTASSIUM** 11% DV

Make Ahead • Vegetarian

Cider-Bourbon-Honey Punch

Hands-on: 10 min. **Total:** 3 hr. 30 min.
Make this cocktail the morning of—or the night before—the feast, then let guests ladle out cups as they arrive. We like to keep the punch chilled using an ice ring with lemon and apple slices frozen inside.

5½ cups apple cider
4 cinnamon sticks, plus more for garnish (optional)
½ tsp. ground nutmeg
2 large Honeycrisp apples, 1 cut into wedges and 1 thinly sliced, divided
¾ cup wildflower honey
3⅛ cups (25 oz.) bourbon
1 cup fresh lemon juice (from about 6 lemons)
3 cups seltzer water

1. Place apple cider, cinnamon sticks, nutmeg, and apple wedges in a medium saucepan, and bring to a boil over medium-high. Remove from heat, and let stand, uncovered, 20 minutes. Pour cider mixture into a large bowl, and whisk in honey until dissolved. Cover and refrigerate at least 3 hours and up to overnight.
2. Strain cider mixture into a punch bowl; discard solids. Stir in bourbon and lemon juice. To serve, stir in seltzer and apple slices. Garnish with cinnamon sticks, if desired. Serves 20 (serving size: ¾ cup)

CALORIES 160; **FAT** 0g; **PROTEIN** 0g; **CARB** 21g; **FIBER** 0g; **SUGARS** 11g (added sugars 10g); **SODIUM** 1mg; **CALC** 0% DV; **POTASSIUM** 0% DV

THE AMAZING, NO-FAIL, ONE-HOUR DINNER PARTY

With this detailed game plan and 60 minutes on the clock, you can cook an impressive meal for eight—complete with cocktails and dessert.

MENU

POMEGRANATE SPRITZER

BEEF TENDERLOIN WITH MADEIRA-DIJON SAUCE

RED WINE AND PARMESAN FARROTTO

ROASTED BROCCOLINI

DULCE DE LECHE BREAD PUDDINGS

THE GAME PLAN

This might be the most efficiently executed dinner you've ever made. And you don't need eight arms, two ovens, or a culinary degree: A little planning, smart prep, and basic multitask cooking—with dishes in the oven and on the stovetop at the same time—get the job done. You'll be busy for sure; there's no time wasted waiting for bread to toast or beef to roast. Just follow our plan, and take this dazzling menu from "to-do" to "ta-da" in 60 minutes flat.

1. MIX THE SPRITZER
Make the pomegranate syrup; combine everything but the wine and arils in a pitcher, and chill it. Now you can pour a drink for any early guests right away.

2. MACERATE STRAWBERRIES
Combine strawberries, vanilla, and vinegar for the dessert in a bowl. Place in fridge to chill.

3. CUBE BREAD
Cut into cubes with a serrated knife, and spread cubes in a single layer on a sheet pan.

4. PREHEAT OVEN
Set it to 450°F, with one rack near the top and a second toward the bottom. Place pan of bread cubes inside. Set timer; remove pan after 5 minutes.

5. PREP BROCCOLINI
While bread toasts, toss the trimmed Broccolini with the oil and seasonings on a sheet pan, and set aside until you're ready to roast it.

6. MAKE BREAD PUDDINGS
Combine milk, dulce de leche, eggs, and sugar; add toasted bread cubes. Spoon mixture into ramekins or baking dish set on a baking sheet; bake on top oven rack. Set a timer for 20 minutes.

7. START FARROTTO
Chop onion, garlic, and herbs for farrotto. Chop and tear extra thyme and parsley to use for the beef dish. Begin cooking farro. Microwave stock as farro toasts in pan. Stir initial 2 ½ cups of hot stock into pan. Stir the pot occasionally, and add stock as needed for the next 25 minutes.

8. START BEEF
Place a sheet pan on the bottom rack to preheat. Sear seasoned tenderloins on stovetop, turning occasionally to brown all over. Transfer browned tenderloins to hot sheet pan; insert probe thermometer in one tenderloin portion. Set thermometer for an alert at 120°F to 125°F.

9. REMOVE PUDDINGS
Check consistency of bread pudding. Remove from oven once custard is set.

10. ROAST BROCCOLINI
Place sheet pan of Broccolini on top rack (while beef is on bottom rack). Set timer for 15 minutes. Place Broccolini on a serving platter when done and loosely tent with foil.

11. START SAUCE
Sauté aromatics (in the large skillet you used to brown the beef), and reduce liquids until sauce is syrupy. Remove pan from heat, cover, and set aside.

12. FINISH FARROTTO

Stir in remaining stock, cheese, butter, and pepper. Sprinkle with parsley and shaved cheese. Remove from heat, cover; set aside. Transfer to a serving bowl when you're ready to set it out.

13. PULL BEEF

Remove beef from oven once thermometer registers 120°F to 125°F; set pan aside to rest.

14. GARNISH PUDDINGS

Top with strawberry mixture, and dust with powdered sugar.

15. FINISH COCKTAIL

Remove pitcher from fridge. Stir in sparkling wine.

16. FINISH SAUCE

Stir in butter and remaining ingredients until butter is melted. Transfer sauce to a gravy boat.

17. SLICE BEEF

Thinly slice the rested tenderloins. Place slices alongside the Broccolini on the serving platter.

Fast • Gluten Free
Vegetarian

Pomegranate Spritzer

Hands-on: 10 min. **Total:** 30 min.
This is a wonderfully festive beverage to open a dinner party: Sweet-tart pomegranate juice is balanced by bitters and spiked with vodka and fizzy rosé. Find pomegranate arils in the refrigerated area of the supermarket produce section; they'll save you at least 10 minutes because you won't need to pull the arils from a whole pomegranate.

½ cup pomegranate juice
¼ cup granulated sugar
½ cup (4 oz.) chilled vodka
2 Tbsp. fresh lime juice
1½ tsp. Angostura bitters
5 cups (40 oz.) chilled sparkling rosé wine
⅓ cup pomegranate arils

1. Combine pomegranate juice and sugar in an 8-cup microwavable measuring cup. Microwave at high until warmed, about 2 minutes; stir until sugar dissolves. Stir in vodka, lime juice, and bitters; chill 20 minutes. Gently stir in rosé. Serve in Champagne glasses; top each with 4 to 5 pomegranate arils. Serves 8 (serving size: ¾ cup)

CALORIES 187; **FAT** 0g; **PROTEIN** 0g; **CARB** 14g; **FIBER** 0g; **SUGARS** 10g (added sugars 5g); **SODIUM** 3mg; **CALC** 0% DV; **POTASSIUM** 0% DV

SLICE. SAUCE. DONE.

Dinner is served! The beef roasts while you whip up the simple pan sauce, making this recipe an easy "wow" moment.

Staff Favorite • Gluten Free

Beef Tenderloin with Madeira-Dijon Sauce

Hands-on: 40 min. **Total:** 40 min.
As simple as this dish is to make, it looks, feels, and tastes like a special-occasion meal. Ask your butcher for the Chateaubriand cut, which is an evenly sized portion taken from the heart of the tenderloin.

3 Tbsp. olive oil, divided
2 (1-lb.) center-cut beef tenderloin fillets (about 4 inches in diameter)
1½ tsp. kosher salt, divided
1½ tsp. black pepper, divided
¼ cup minced shallot
1 large thyme sprig
½ cup Madeira or dry sherry
3 cups unsalted beef stock
2 Tbsp. unsalted butter
2 Tbsp. torn fresh flat- leaf parsley
1 Tbsp. Dijon mustard

1. Preheat oven to 450°F. Place a rimmed baking sheet in oven (do not remove pan while oven preheats).
2. Heat 1½ tablespoons oil in a large skillet over high. Sprinkle fillets with 1¼ teaspoons salt and 1¼ teaspoons pepper. Cook fillets in hot oil, turning occasionally, until browned on all sides, 6 to 8 minutes.
3. Transfer fillets to hot baking sheet. Do not wipe skillet clean. Roast fillets at 450°F on bottom rack until a thermometer inserted in thickest portion registers 120°F to 125°F for medium-rare, about 10 minutes. Remove from oven; let stand 5 minutes.
4. While the beef roasts, add shallot and thyme to skillet. Cook over medium-high, stirring often, until lightly browned, 1 to 2 minutes. Add wine. Bring to a boil; simmer until reduced by half, 2 to 3 minutes. Add stock, and bring to a boil; boil, stirring occasionally, until slightly syrupy and reduced to ⅔ cup, about 15 minutes. Remove from heat. Stir in butter, parsley, mustard, remaining 1½ tablespoons oil, remaining ¼ teaspoon salt, and remaining ¼ teaspoon pepper; stir until the butter melts. Remove thyme sprig.
5. Thinly slice beef; serve with sauce. Serves 8 (serving size: about 3 oz. beef and 1½ Tbsp. sauce)

CALORIES 268; **FAT** 15g (sat 5g, unsat 9g); **PROTEIN** 26g; **CARB** 3g; **FIBER** 0g; **SUGARS** 1g (added sugars 0g); **SODIUM** 527mg; **CALC** 4% DV; **POTASSIUM** 9% DV

YOU'VE GOT THIS, HOT STUFF!

The Madeira-Dijon sauce is best served warm. If it cools off at all, pop it in the microwave just before serving.

Staff Favorite

Red Wine and Parmesan Farrotto

Hands-on: 40 min. **Total:** 40 min. We use the standard risotto cooking method, adding warm stock to the grains gradually while stirring. This approach takes longer than boiling, so quick-cooking farro saves time.

5 cups unsalted chicken stock
1½ Tbsp. olive oil
1½ cups prechopped yellow onion
6 garlic cloves, chopped
1 large thyme sprig
2 cups uncooked 10-minute farro (such as Trader Joe's)
1 cup dry red wine
3 oz. Parmigiano-Reggiano cheese, divided (2 oz. grated and 1 oz. shaved)
2 Tbsp. unsalted butter
¾ tsp. black pepper
2 Tbsp. torn fresh flat-leaf parsley

1. Place stock in a microwavable measuring cup or glass bowl. Microwave at high until hot, about 2 minutes.
2. Heat oil in a large Dutch oven over high. Add onion, garlic, and thyme; cook, stirring occasionally, 2 minutes. Add farro; cook, stirring occasionally, until toasted, about 4 minutes. Stir in wine. Bring to a boil; cook until nearly evaporated, about 1 minute. Add 2½ cups hot stock; bring to a boil. Reduce heat to medium; simmer until farro is very tender, adding hot stock, 1 cup at a time, stirring until incorporated after each addition, about 25 minutes total. (You may have leftover stock.)
3. Remove from heat. Stir in the grated cheese, butter, and pepper. Remove thyme sprig. Sprinkle with parsley and shaved cheese. Serves 8 (serving size: ¾ cup)

CALORIES 293; FAT 9g (sat 3g, unsat 5g); PROTEIN 13g; CARB 41g; FIBER 6g; SUGARS 2g (added sugars 0g); SODIUM 460mg; CALC 10% DV; POTASSIUM 2% DV

IT'S TOTALLY OK TO KEEP IT SIMPLE.

In a meal full of superstars, you need backup singers. This easy and flavorful side delivers big results without stealing the show.

Gluten Free • Vegetarian

Roasted Broccolini

Hands-on: 10 min. **Total:** 35 min. Mild Broccolini is a crowd-pleasing vegetable; its longer stems give it a more elegant feel than regular broccoli. If you're serving a more adventurous bunch, try swapping in broccoli rabe, broccoli's pleasantly bitter, leafy cousin. Red pepper brings a touch of heat, and lemon zest adds a bright flavor boost. To prep, just trim the bottom inch or so from the stalks.

2 lb. Broccolini, stems trimmed
3 Tbsp. olive oil
2 tsp. lemon zest
¾ tsp. kosher salt
½ tsp. crushed red pepper

1. Preheat oven to 450°F. Toss together Broccolini and olive oil on a rimmed baking sheet. Sprinkle with zest, salt, and red pepper; toss well. Roast at 450°F on top oven rack until slightly crispy and stalks are tender, about 15 minutes. Remove from oven. Serves 8 (serving size: ¾ cup)

CALORIES 70; FAT 6g (sat 1g, unsat 4g); PROTEIN 4g; CARB 3g; FIBER 3g; SUGARS 0g; SODIUM 218mg; CALC 12% DV; POTASSIUM 4% DV

Dulce De Leche Bread Puddings

Hands-on: 15 min. **Total:** 40 min. Strawberries add a fruity pop to the puddings. If you can't find fresh ones, add the same amount of frozen berries to a saucepan with about 2 tablespoons water, plus the vanilla and vinegar; bring to a boil over high, then reduce heat and simmer 5 minutes.

1 (12-oz.) French bread loaf, crusts removed, cut into ¾-in. cubes
1 cup whole milk
¾ cup canned dulce de leche
3 large eggs
¼ cup powdered sugar, divided
1 qt. fresh strawberries, hulled and chopped
1 tsp. vanilla extract
1 tsp. apple cider vinegar

1. Preheat oven to 450°F. Arrange bread on a baking sheet; let warm in oven 5 minutes as oven preheats.
2. Whisk together milk, dulce de leche, eggs, and 3 tablespoons powdered sugar in a large bowl. Stir in bread. Divide bread mixture evenly among 8 (6-ounce) ramekins, or spoon into an 11- x 7-inch baking dish. Place ramekins or baking dish on baking sheet, and bake at 450°F on top oven rack until egg mixture is set, about 20 minutes for ramekins and 20 to 25 minutes for baking dish.
3. Meanwhile, combine berries, vanilla, and vinegar in a bowl; let stand at least 10 minutes before serving.
4. Top bread pudding with strawberry mixture; dust with remaining 1 tablespoon powdered sugar. Serves 8 (serving size: 1 bread pudding)

CALORIES 270; **FAT** 5g (sat 2g, unsat 2g); **PROTEIN** 10g; **CARB** 46g; **FIBER** 2g; **SUGARS** 23g (added sugars 18g); **SODIUM** 345mg; **CALC** 11% DV; **POTASSIUM** 2% DV

Bread puddings are the ultimate low-stress dessert: If you can toast bread and whisk eggs, then you can pull this dish together with ease. Simplify your life even more and bring the strawberries and extra powdered sugar to the table and let your guests garnish their own desserts. The prettiest one gets a prize!

MAKE-AHEAD APPETIZERS

Treat your guests to a spread of fork-free, two-bite treats that come together as a balanced meal on the plate.

Holiday parties tend to go one of two ways: The menu is either laden with so many heavy dips and fried accoutrements that you leave miserably stuffed and lusting for a New Year's diet, or the offerings are so dainty that you need to pick up a pizza on the way home. Here, we serve a delicious middle ground. We overhauled the standard assortment and created a festive cocktail party menu abundant with crunchy, fresh produce yet also adorned with plenty of the meaty, cheesy, indulgent goodness that you look forward to this time of year. Our spread is balanced with protein and carbs, and half of your plate will be filled with vegetables (you even get 16g satiating fiber). This menu gives you, the host, permission to skip a sit-down affair in favor of mingling with your guests. To ensure you get that well-deserved catch-up time, we've tried to make your job as easy as possible and worked in plenty of make-ahead tips so you can spread out the work. Now all you need are cute cocktail napkins and some wine, and your party will be just as stylish and memorable as it is delicious.

Staff Favorite • Make Ahead
Saucy Mini Meatballs

Hands-on: 50 min. **Total:** 50 min.
Adding cinnamon gives these meatballs a slight Moroccan feel. You can make this a day ahead and reheat on the stovetop before the party. Using different types of beef adds moisture to the meatballs while keeping sat fat in check.

1 medium-sized yellow onion
½ lb. 90% lean ground sirloin
½ lb. 85% lean ground beef
⅓ cup whole-wheat panko (Japanese breadcrumbs)
½ cup chopped fresh flat-leaf parsley, divided
2 Tbsp. extra-virgin olive oil
2½ tsp. minced garlic, divided
1 tsp. ground cumin
¾ tsp. kosher salt, divided
½ tsp. black pepper, divided
1 Tbsp. unsalted butter
¼ tsp. crushed red pepper
¼ tsp. ground cinnamon
2 Tbsp. unsalted tomato paste
1 (15-oz.) can unsalted crushed tomatoes
½ tsp. granulated sugar

1. Halve onion lengthwise. Finely grate 1 onion half to equal ¼ cup. Finely chop remaining onion half to equal ½ cup; set aside. (Reserve any remaining onion for another use.)

2. Combine sirloin, ground beef, panko, ¼ cup grated onion, ¼ cup parsley, oil, 1¼ teaspoons garlic, cumin, ¼ teaspoon salt, and ¼ teaspoon black pepper in a large bowl; use hands to gently combine. Shape beef mixture into 36 small meatballs (about 1 tablespoon each).
3. Heat butter in a large skillet over high. Add meatballs, and cook, turning occasionally, until lightly browned, 6 to 7 minutes. Transfer to a plate lined with a paper towels.
4. Reduce heat to low; add crushed red pepper, cinnamon, ½ cup chopped onion, remaining 1¼ teaspoons garlic, remaining ½ teaspoon salt, and remaining ¼ teaspoon black pepper to skillet; cook, stirring often, until onion mixture is softened, about 5 minutes. Add tomato paste; cook, stirring constantly, until onion mixture is well coated, 1 minute. Add crushed tomatoes and sugar. Bring to a boil over medium-high; add meatballs to sauce, and cook until just cooked through, 4 to 5 minutes. Top with remaining ¼ cup parsley. Serves 12 (serving size: 3 meatballs)

CALORIES 133; FAT 8g (sat 3g, unsat 5g); PROTEIN 9g; CARB 5g; FIBER 1g; SUGARS 2g (added sugars 0g); SODIUM 151mg; CALC 3% DV; POTASSIUM 6% DV

Fast • Make Ahead
Cheesy Crab-Artichoke Toasts

Hands-on: 25 min. **Total:** 25 min.
Save time the day of the party by preparing the crab mixture one day ahead. Cut and store the sliced bread in an airtight container until ready to assemble, and then broil as the recipe instructs shortly before party time.

1 (12-oz.) pkg. frozen artichoke
 hearts, thawed and roughly
 chopped
4 oz. fresh lump crabmeat, drained
 and picked
½ cup chopped fresh flat-leaf
 parsley
½ cup plain whole-milk Greek
 yogurt
2 oz. preshredded part-skim
 mozzarella cheese (about ½ cup)
1 oz. Parmesan cheese, grated
 (about ¼ cup)
1 tsp. lemon zest plus 1 Tbsp. fresh
 lemon juice
1 garlic clove, minced
¼ tsp. black pepper
1 (10-oz.) whole-wheat baguette, cut
 into 24 (¼-in.-thick) slices

1. Preheat broiler to high with
oven rack in top position. Combine
artichoke hearts, crabmeat, parsley,
yogurt, mozzarella, Parmesan,
lemon zest and juice, garlic, and
black pepper in a large bowl; stir
well to combine.
2. Spread about 2 tablespoons crab
mixture on each baguette slice.
Place on a baking sheet lined with
aluminum foil. Broil until cheese
begins to melt, 3 to 4 minutes (be
careful not to burn toasts). Serves
12 (serving size: 2 toasts)

CALORIES 106; **FAT** 3g (sat 1g, unsat 1g);
PROTEIN 8g; **CARB** 13g; **FIBER** 2g; **SUGARS** 1g
(added sugars 0g); **SODIUM** 206mg; **CALC** 6%
DV; **POTASSIUM** 2% DV

**Fast • Gluten Free
Make Ahead • Vegetarian**

Chickpea Salad Boats

Hands-on: 20 min. **Total:** 20 min.
This recipe captures all the bright,
fresh appeal of a salad in a pretty,
portable bite. Sturdy endive leaves
have a nice cup shape for filling; you
also could use Little Gem or small
Bibb lettuce leaves. To get a head

start, make the filling (minus the
pears) up to a day in advance. About
an hour before guests arrive, gently
stir in the pear and fill the leaves.

6 Tbsp. plain whole-milk Greek
 yogurt
1 Tbsp. extra-virgin olive oil
1 Tbsp. honey
1½ tsp. lemon zest plus 1½ Tbsp.
 fresh lemon juice
¾ tsp. kosher salt
⅜ tsp. black pepper
3 medium pears, cut into thin strips
1 (15-oz.) can unsalted chickpeas,
 rinsed and drained (about 1½
 cups)
¾ cup finely chopped celery
⅓ cup fresh flat-leaf parsley leaves
⅓ cup chopped red onion
24 Belgian endive leaves (from 5
 heads)
⅓ cup sliced almonds, toasted

1. Whisk together yogurt, olive oil,
honey, lemon zest and juice, salt,
and pepper in a large bowl. Add
pears, chickpeas, celery, parsley,
and onion; stir gently to coat.
2. Spoon mixture evenly into
endive leaves. Arrange on a
serving platter, and top evenly
with almonds. Serves 12 (serving
size: 2 salad boats)

CALORIES 136; **FAT** 4g (sat 1g, unsat 3g);
PROTEIN 6g; **CARB** 22g; **FIBER** 10g; **SUGARS** 7g
(added sugars 1g); **SODIUM** 184mg; **CALC** 15%
DV; **POTASSIUM** 18% DV

**Staff Favorite • Gluten Free
Make Ahead • Vegetarian**

Smoky Red Lentil Hummus

Hands-on: 15 min. **Total:** 1 hr. 15 min.
Use this fun riff on classic chickpea
hummus to anchor a tray of fresh,
seasonal vegetable dippers—we
recommend multicolored carrots,
radishes, and cauliflower florets.
You can prepare the hummus up to

three days ahead; wash and trim the
crudités a day in advance, and store
them in ziplock plastic bags lined with
paper towels.

3 cups water
1 cup dried red lentils
2 Tbsp. tahini
1½ Tbsp. fresh lemon juice
1 Tbsp. extra-virgin olive oil, plus
 more for garnish (optional)
1 Tbsp. unsalted tomato paste
2 garlic cloves, smashed
1¼ tsp. kosher salt
1 tsp. smoked paprika
½ tsp. ground cumin
Fresh flat-leaf parsley leaves
 (optional)

1. Bring 3 cups water and lentils
to a boil in a medium saucepan
over medium-high. Cover, reduce
heat to low, and simmer, stirring
occasionally, until lentils have split
and are mushy, about 30 minutes.
Drain and spread in an even layer
on a small baking sheet; chill 30
minutes.
2. Process lentils, tahini, lemon
juice, oil, tomato paste, garlic,
salt, paprika, and cumin in a food
processor until smooth, about 30
seconds, stopping to scrape down
sides as needed. Spoon into a
serving bowl. If desired, garnish
with parsley and olive oil. Serve
with crudités or pita wedges.
Serves 12 (serving size: ¼ cup)

CALORIES 85; **FAT** 3g (sat 0g, unsat 2g);
PROTEIN 5g; **CARB** 11g; **FIBER** 3g; **SUGARS** 1g
(added sugars 0g); **SODIUM** 204mg; **CALC** 1%
DV; **POTASSIUM** 4% DV

THUMBPRINTS AND SNOWBALLS AND SHORTBREAD, OH MY!

The gang's all here: Your favorite treats of the season are healthier, tastier, and more festive than ever.

The holidays simply don't feel complete without a merry assortment of freshly baked cookies around. Stacked in heirloom tins or piled into kitschy cookie jars, they're a surefire way to spread some serious cheer. We wanted to pay tribute to the beloved treats of the season, but in a healthier way. Without compromising flavor or texture, we crafted these recipes (all of which are whole-grain) to be even more delicious than the cookies you grew up with. That means fun ingredient updates, such as five-spice powder in an otherwise classic spice cookie—a tweak that pays homage to tradition while taking it to a new level. We make subtler moves, too, such as sprinkling flaky salt on chocolate-coated shortbread or adding rosemary to a fruity jam bar. Look no further for your new favorite sweets.

Staff Favorite • Make Ahead
Vegetarian

Almond-Currant Linzer Cookies

Hands-on: 35 min. **Total:** 2 hr. 20 min. We like the more updated look of off-center cutouts, but you can go more traditional by keeping the cutouts centered.

8 oz. whole-wheat pastry flour (about 2 ¼ cups)
3.13 oz. almond flour (about 1 cup)
¼ tsp. baking powder
¼ tsp. kosher salt
⅔ cup granulated sugar
¼ cup unsalted butter, softened
3 Tbsp. canola oil
1 tsp. lemon zest
1 large egg
2 Tbsp. powdered sugar
6 Tbsp. red or black currant jelly

1. Whisk together both flours, baking powder, and salt in a medium bowl; set aside.
2. Beat together sugar, butter, oil, and zest in a large bowl with an electric mixer on medium speed until light and fluffy, about 3 minutes. Beat in egg. Add flour mixture; beat on low speed just until combined. Divide dough in half. Roll each half between 2 sheets of parchment paper or plastic wrap to a thickness somewhere between ⅛ and ¼ inch. Place dough halves on a baking sheet, and freeze until firm, about 20 to 30 minutes.
3. Preheat oven to 350°F. Remove parchment from 1 dough half. Working quickly, cut with a 2-inch round cutter to form 30 rounds, rerolling scraps as necessary. (Refreeze dough if it gets too soft.) Arrange cookies 2 inches apart on 2 baking sheets lined with parchment paper. Bake at 350°F until lightly browned around edges, 8 to 10 minutes. Cool on baking sheets set on a wire rack for 2 minutes. Transfer cookies directly to wire rack to cool completely, about 30 minutes.
4. Uncover remaining dough half. Working quickly, cut with a 2-inch round cutter to form 30 rounds, rerolling scraps as necessary. Cut out center of each round with a 1-inch round cutter, off-center for a more modern appearance if you like. (Refreeze dough if it gets too soft.) Discard center dough circles, or bake to enjoy later. Arrange cookies on 2 baking sheets lined with parchment paper. Bake at 350°F until lightly browned around edges, 8 to 10 minutes. Cool on baking sheets set on a wire rack for 2 minutes. Transfer cookies directly to wire rack to cool completely, about 30 minutes.
5. Dust cut-out cookies evenly with powdered sugar. Spread about ½ teaspoon jelly on each solid cookie; top each with a cut-out cookie. Store in an airtight container up to 2 days. Serves 30 (serving size: 1 sandwich cookie)

CALORIES 120; FAT 7g (sat 2g, unsat 4g); PROTEIN 2g; CARB 14g; FIBER 1g; SUGARS 8g (added sugars 5g); SODIUM 45mg; CALC 2% DV; POTASSIUM 1% DV

Chocolate-Peppermint Thumbprints

Hands-on: 25 min. **Total:** 1 hr. 25 min. Using tahini in the filling instead of heavy cream helps keep sat fat in check. And tahini's subtle flavor won't overwhelm the chocolate in the way many nut butters might—though cashew butter would be a good, mild substitute if you have it on hand.

7 oz. whole-wheat pastry flour (about 2 cups)
½ cup unsweetened cocoa
½ tsp. kosher salt
⅔ cup granulated sugar
¼ cup unsalted butter, softened
1 Tbsp. canola oil
1 tsp. vanilla extract
1 large egg
⅔ cup semisweet chocolate chips
⅓ cup tahini (sesame seed paste)
6 hard peppermint candies, crushed

1. Preheat oven to 350°F. Whisk together flour, cocoa, and salt in a medium bowl; set aside.
2. Beat together sugar, butter, oil, and vanilla in a large bowl with an electric mixer on medium speed until well blended, about 3 minutes. Add egg, and beat until combined. Add flour mixture; beat on low speed until just combined.
3. Shape dough into 36 balls (1 tablespoon each). Arrange dough balls 2 inches apart on 2 baking sheets lined with parchment paper. Lightly press each dough ball to flatten slightly, and make a "thumbprint" impression in dough balls by gently pressing your thumb or the handle of a wooden spoon in center of each ball. Bake at 350°F until set, about 10 minutes. Remove from oven, and cool on baking sheets set on a wire rack for 3 minutes. Transfer cookies directly to wire rack to cool completely, about 30 minutes.
4. Meanwhile, place chocolate chips in a medium microwavable bowl. Microwave at high until chocolate melts, about 1 minute, stirring after 30 seconds. Whisk tahini into melted chocolate until smooth. Spoon about 1 teaspoon chocolate mixture into impression of each cookie. Sprinkle with crushed peppermints. Let stand until set, about 1 hour (or chill 20 minutes to quickly set filling). Store in an airtight container up to 3 days. Serves 36 (serving size: 1 cookie)

CALORIES 98; FAT 5g (sat 2g, unsat 3g); PROTEIN 2g; CARB 12g; FIBER 1g; SUGARS 6g (added sugars 6g); SODIUM 30mg; CALC 1% DV; POTASSIUM 1% DV

Salted Chocolate-Topped Shortbread

Hands-on: 25 min. **Total:** 2 hr. 55 min. These whole-wheat cookies have the expected "short" texture of classic shortbread, plus an irresistible buttery flavor. Cultured butter is worth seeking out here; the richer flavor really comes through in a cookie like this where the butter is front and center. You can also use regular unsalted butter for a still delicious but slightly less complex flavor.

9 oz. whole-wheat pastry flour (about 2¼ cups)
½ cup powdered sugar
¼ cup cornstarch
½ tsp. kosher salt
½ cup unsalted cultured butter, softened
⅓ cup plus 1 Tbsp. canola oil
¼ cup granulated sugar
1½ tsp. vanilla extract
4 oz. 60% to 70% cacao bittersweet chocolate, chopped
1 tsp. flaky sea salt (such as Maldon)

1. Preheat oven to 325°F. Whisk together flour, powdered sugar, cornstarch, and salt in a medium bowl.
2. Beat together butter, oil, and granulated sugar in a large bowl with an electric mixer on medium speed until well blended, about 3 minutes. Beat in vanilla. Add flour mixture; beat on low just until combined.
3. Pat or roll dough into a 10½-inch square on a baking sheet lined with parchment paper. Bake at 325°F until set and lightly browned around edges, about 30 minutes. Remove from oven, and immediately cut into 36 (1¾-inch) squares (a pizza cutter and ruler make this go quickly). Cool cookies completely on baking sheet, about 1 hour.
4. Place chocolate in a small microwavable bowl. Microwave at high until melted, about 1 minute, stirring after 30 seconds. Using a spoon, butter knife, or small offest spatula, spread chocolate over half of top side of each cookie, and sprinkle flaky salt evenly over chocolate. Let stand until chocolate sets, about 1 hour. Store in an airtight container up to 3 days. Serves 36 (serving size: 1 cookie)

CALORIES 106; FAT 6g (sat 2g, unsat 3g); PROTEIN 1g; CARB 11g; FIBER 1g; SUGARS 4g (added sugars 4g); SODIUM 77mg; CALC 0% DV; POTASSIUM 1% DV

KEY INGREDIENTS FOR COOKIE SUCCESS

WHEN IT COMES TO BAKING HEALTHIER TREATS, CERTAIN ITEMS WILL HELP ENSURE YOU END UP WITH PERFECT RESULTS.

1. WHOLE-WHEAT PASTRY FLOUR
All these recipes use whole-wheat pastry flour. It's lower in protein and finer in texture than regular whole-wheat flour, which translates to cookies with a fine, tender texture almost identical to treats made with refined all-purpose flour—but with the nutritional goodness of whole wheat. If you can't find it, order from bobsredmill.com.

2. KOSHER SALT
It may seem odd to see kosher salt in cookie recipes; traditionally, they would use small-grained table salt. But we use kosher salt (specifically Morton brand) so often that we wanted to see how it would perform. The results are great—flavor enhancement with an occasional, delicious burst of mild salinity. If you substitute table salt, use half the amount called for.

3. CULTURED BUTTER
We've sung its praises before, but we hadn't really experimented with cultured butter in baking. We tried these recipes side-by-side using regular unsalted butter and cultured. The latter had a richer flavor, which was particularly noticeable in the shortbread on page 357. Either butter will work fine, but cultured made for tastier cookies.

4. ALL THE SUGARS
Whenever you prepare yourself (and your kitchen) for holiday baking, you have to stock up on different types of sugars. We use granulated for straight-up sweetness; brown for molasses notes and increased moisture; powdered to create a "short," crisp texture; and coarse sparkling or turbinado for a hearty finishing crunch.

5. MERINGUE POWDER
If you're going to decorate sugar cookies, you should incorporate a little meringue powder in the icing. This product, which you'll find in craft stores, helps the icing set up hard and firm—so you can stack and pack your colorful, edible works of art without any worry of smudges or dents.

6. PARCHMENT PAPER
OK, this isn't really an ingredient, but parchment paper is worth its weight in gold when it comes to baking cookies. It helps promote more uniform baking by evening out any hot spots on the pan, and its nonstick surface helps your treats glide right off the pan. You can also reuse each sheet several times—perfect for a baking marathon.

Make Ahead • Vegetarian

Decorated Whole-Wheat Sugar Cookies

Hands-on: 40 min. **Total:** 2 hr. 40 min. You'll often see rolled cookie recipes that call for chilling the dough for an hour or two and then rolling it out. But it's far easier to roll the dough out when it's soft, just after mixing it together. Then you can pop it in the freezer, where—because it's rolled thinly—it firms up quickly. Meringue powder, found in craft stores or the crafting section of big-box stores, helps the icing set firmly so your cookies don't smudge.

8 oz. whole-wheat pastry flour
   (about 2 ¼ cups)
½ tsp. kosher salt
⅔ cup granulated sugar
¼ cup unsalted butter, softened
3 Tbsp. canola oil
1 ¾ tsp. vanilla extract, divided
1 large egg
1 cup powdered sugar
1 ½ to 2 Tbsp. water
2 tsp. meringue powder
Natural food coloring (such as India
   Tree) (optional)

•

1. Whisk together flour and salt in a medium bowl; set aside.
2. Beat together sugar, butter, oil, and 1 ½ teaspoons vanilla in a large bowl with an electric mixer on medium speed until light and fluffy, about 3 minutes. Beat in egg. Add flour mixture; beat on low speed just until combined. Divide dough in half. Roll each half between 2 sheets of plastic wrap to ¼-inch thickness. Place dough

halves on a baking sheet, and freeze until firm, about 20 to 30 minutes.

3. Preheat oven to 350°F. Remove plastic wrap from 1 dough half. Working quickly, cut dough with a 2 ½-inch cutter of desired shape to form 16 cookies, rerolling scraps as necessary. (Refreeze dough if it gets too soft.) Repeat procedure with remaining dough half. Arrange cookies on 2 baking sheets lined with parchment paper. Bake at 350°F until lightly browned around edges, about 10 minutes. Cool on baking sheets set on a wire rack for 2 minutes. Transfer cookies directly to wire rack to cool completely, about 30 minutes.

4. Place powdered sugar, 1 ½ tablespoons water, meringue powder, and remaining ¼ teaspoon vanilla in a medium bowl. Beat with an electric mixer on low speed just until moistened, about 20 seconds; beat on high speed until thick, bright white, and smooth, about 5 minutes. Beat in additional water, ½ teaspoon at a time, if needed, to reach desired consistency. Stir in food coloring, if desired. Spread or pipe icing evenly over cookies. Let stand at room temperature until icing is set, 1 to 2 hours. Store in an airtight container up to 3 days. Serves 32 (serving size: 1 cookie)

CALORIES 97; FAT 4g (sat 2g, unsat 2g); PROTEIN 1g; CARB 13g; FIBER 1g; SUGARS 8g (added sugars 8g); SODIUM 33mg; CALC 1% DV; POTASSIUM 1% DV

Make Ahead • Vegetarian
Five-Spice Cookies

Hands-on: 20 min. **Total:** 1 hr.
Look for five-spice powder on the spice aisle or with the Asian foods in your grocery. We love the sparkle of sanding sugar coating the outside of the cookies; find it in craft stores. Supermarket turbinado works, too.

7 oz. whole-wheat pastry flour (about 2 cups)
1 ½ tsp. five-spice powder
¼ tsp. kosher salt
½ tsp. baking soda
⅔ cup packed dark brown sugar
½ cup unsalted butter, softened
1 large egg
¼ cup coarse sparkling sugar or turbinado sugar

1. Preheat oven to 350°F. Whisk together flour, five-spice powder, salt, and baking soda in a medium bowl. Set aside.

2. Beat together brown sugar and butter in a large bowl with an electric mixer at medium speed until fluffy, about 2 minutes. Beat in egg. Add flour mixture, and beat at low speed just until combined.

3. Place sparkling sugar in a medium bowl. Roll dough into 25 balls (1 tablespoon each); roll in sugar to coat.

4. Arrange dough balls 2 inches apart on 2 baking sheets lined with parchment paper. Bake at 350°F until set and starting to brown around edges, about 12 minutes. Cool on baking sheets set on a wire rack for 2 minutes. Transfer cookies directly to wire rack to cool completely. Store in an airtight container up to 3 days. Serves 25 (serving size: 1 cookie)

CALORIES 92; FAT 4g (sat 2g, unsat 1g); PROTEIN 1g; CARB 13g; FIBER 1g; SUGARS 7g (added sugars 7g); SODIUM 67mg; CALC 1% DV; POTASSIUM 1% DV

Classic chewy spice cookies get a flavor update with five-spice powder, which lends notes of star anise, fennel, and Szechuan peppercorns along with traditional cinnamon and cloves.

Raspberry-Rosemary Jam Bars

Hands-on: 20 min. **Total:** 2 hr.

2 ½ cups fresh raspberries
⅓ cup granulated sugar
¼ cup water
2 Tbsp. cornstarch
2 (3-in.) rosemary sprigs
Cooking spray
1 ⅓ cups uncooked old-fashioned
    regular rolled oats
4 oz. whole-wheat pastry flour
    (about 1 ⅛ cups)
¾ cup packed light brown sugar
¾ tsp. kosher salt
½ cup unsalted butter, melted
¾ tsp. vanilla extract

1. Stir together first 5 ingredients (through rosemary) in a medium saucepan. Bring to a boil over medium, mashing berries to break them down. Reduce heat to medium-low; cook, stirring often, until thickened, about 6 minutes. Remove from heat; cool slightly, about 10 minutes. Discard rosemary sprigs.
2. Preheat oven to 350°F. Coat an 11- x 7-inch glass baking dish with cooking spray. Stir together oats, flour, brown sugar, and salt in a medium bowl. Add butter and vanilla, and stir until all flour is moistened. Reserve ⅔ cup oat mixture.
3. Pat remaining oat mixture in an even layer in prepared dish. Top with raspberry mixture, spreading to edges. Sprinkle reserved oat mixture over raspberry mixture. Bake at 350°F until lightly browned, about 35 minutes. Cool completely on a wire rack. Cut into 16 (3 ½- x 1 ⅓-inch) bars. Store in an airtight container up to 2 days. Serves 16 (serving size: 1 cookie bar)

CALORIES 173; **FAT** 7g (sat 4g, unsat 2g); **PROTEIN** 2g; **CARB** 28g; **FIBER** 3g; **SUGARS** 15g (added sugars 14g); **SODIUM** 94mg; **CALC** 2% DV; **POTASSIUM** 2% DV

Pine Nut–Meyer Lemon Snowballs

Hands-on: 20 min. **Total:** 1 hr. 30 min. If you can't find Meyer lemons, use 1 teaspoon regular lemon zest. Take care not to underbake these cookies; they need to crisp up a bit in the oven.

8 oz. whole-wheat pastry flour
    (about 2 ¼ cups)
½ tsp. kosher salt
½ cup unsalted butter, softened
3 Tbsp. olive oil
2 tsp. vanilla extract
1 ½ tsp. Meyer lemon zest
1 ¼ cups powdered sugar, divided
1 large egg yolk
½ cup toasted pine nuts, roughly
    chopped

1. Preheat oven to 350°F. Whisk together flour and salt in a medium bowl. Set aside.
2. Beat together butter, oil, vanilla, zest, and ¾ cup powdered sugar in a large bowl with an electric mixer on medium speed until light and fluffy, 2 to 3 minutes. Beat in egg yolk. Add flour mixture; beat on low speed just until combined. Stir in nuts.
3. Shape dough into 32 balls (1 tablespoon each). Arrange dough balls 2 inches apart on 2 baking sheets lined with parchment paper. Bake at 350°F until set and lightly browned on bottom, 12 to 14 minutes. Cool on baking sheets set on a wire rack for 3 minutes. Transfer cookies directly to wire rack to cool completely.
4. Place remaining ½ cup powdered sugar in a medium bowl. Gently roll cookies in sugar to coat. Store in an airtight container up to 3 days. Serves 32 (serving size: 1 cookie)

CALORIES 97; **FAT** 6g (sat 2g, unsat 3g); **PROTEIN** 1g; **CARB** 10g; **FIBER** 1g; **SUGARS** 5g (added sugars 5g); **SODIUM** 31mg; **CALC** 0% DV; **POTASSIUM** 1% DV

These buttery cookies take on a little Mediterranean flair with the addition of rich pine nuts, fruity olive oil, and floral Meyer lemon zest.

SWEET CENTERPIECE

With its glossy ganache glaze, deep chocolate layers, rich and creamy filling, and fresh fruit topping, this impressive dessert is guaranteed to steal the show.

Make Ahead • Vegetarian

Chocolate-and-Cream Layer Cake

Hands-on: 40 min. **Total:** 1 hr. 40 min. Save room for dessert—this is one you don't want to miss. It certainly has its virtues: It's made with whole-grain flour, gets topped with fresh fruit, and contains 6g of fiber per serving. But what makes this cake so spectacular, truly, is how good it tastes.

CAKE
Cooking spray
7.33 oz. whole-wheat pastry flour (about 1¾ cups)
¾ cup unsweetened cocoa
1½ tsp. baking powder
¼ tsp. table salt
¼ tsp. baking soda
1¼ cups granulated sugar
½ cup canola oil
2 large eggs
1 cup fat-free buttermilk
⅓ cup warm water
1½ tsp. vanilla extract

GLAZE
½ cup powdered sugar
¼ cup unsweetened cocoa
1 oz. semisweet chocolate chips
2 Tbsp. 2% reduced-fat milk
1 Tbsp. unsalted butter
Dash of table salt

YOGURT CREAM
½ cup heavy whipping cream
⅓ cup powdered sugar
½ cup plain 2% reduced-fat Greek yogurt
¼ tsp. vanilla extract

FRUIT TOPPING
1 cup fresh blackberries
1 (6-oz.) container fresh raspberries
1 cup small strawberries
2 Tbsp. pomegranate arils (optional)

1. Preheat oven to 350°F.
2. Prepare cake: Coat 2 (9-inch) round cake pans with cooking spray; line bottoms of pans with parchment paper. Coat paper with cooking spray; set aside.
3. Weigh or lightly spoon flour into dry measuring cups; level with a knife. Place flour, cocoa, baking powder, salt, and baking soda in a bowl; whisk to combine.
4. Place granulated sugar, oil, and eggs in a large bowl; beat with a handheld mixer on medium speed until well blended, about 2 minutes. Beat in buttermilk, ⅓ cup warm water, and vanilla. Add flour mixture; beat on low speed just until combined. Increase speed to medium, and beat 1 minute.
5. Divide batter evenly between prepared pans. Bake at 350°F until a wooden pick inserted in center comes out clean, 23 to 25 minutes. Cool cake layers in pans on a wire rack 10 minutes. Invert cakes onto rack; remove parchment paper. Let cake layers cool completely.
6. Prepare glaze: Combine powdered sugar, cocoa, chocolate chips, milk, butter, and salt in a small saucepan. Cook over low, stirring constantly, until butter and chocolate melt, about 3 minutes. Let cool slightly.
7. Prepare yogurt cream: Place cream and powdered sugar in a large bowl; beat with a handheld mixer on high speed until stiff peaks form, about 1 minute and 30 seconds. Add yogurt and vanilla; beat on high speed until combined.
8. Place 1 cake layer on a cake stand or plate; top evenly with yogurt cream, leaving a ½-inch border. Top with second cake layer. Carefully pour chocolate glaze over top of cake, spreading to edges. Arrange berries and, if using, arils on top. Serves 16 (serving size: 1 slice)

CALORIES 308; FAT 13g (sat 4g, unsat 8g); PROTEIN 6g; CARB 47g; FIBER 6g; SUGARS 25g (added sugars 23g); SODIUM 203mg; CALC 7% DV; POTASSIUM 4% DV

WEEKNIGHT MAINS

Fast • Vegetarian

Winter Greens Pesto Pizza

Hands-on: 25 min. **Total:** 25 min.
Hearty collard greens pack this pesto with vitamin K, an essential nutrient for bone health. Buttery Castelvetrano olives make any extra pesto perfect for adding big flavor to pasta and grilled cheese sandwiches; substitute any green olive if you can't find them.

1 cup sliced red onion
Cooking spray
1 cup chopped stemmed collard greens
¼ cup pitted Castelvetrano olives
4 ½ Tbsp. grated Parmesan cheese, divided
5 ½ tsp. olive oil
2 Tbsp. canola oil, divided
¼ tsp. lemon zest plus 1 tsp. fresh lemon juice
1 medium garlic clove
⅜ tsp. kosher salt, divided
¼ (10-oz.) pkg. whole-wheat thin and crispy pizza crusts (such as 365 Everyday Value Organic)
4 oz. fresh mozzarella cheese, torn into 2-in. pieces
1 Tbsp. balsamic glaze
2 Tbsp. torn fresh basil
¼ tsp. crushed red pepper

1. Place racks in upper third and middle of oven. Place a baking sheet on top rack; place a pizza stone on middle rack. Preheat oven to 500°F.
2. Spread onion on hot baking sheet; spray with cooking spray. Bake at 500°F until browned, 8 to 9 minutes. Set aside.
3. Process collard greens, olives, 3 ½ tablespoons Parmesan cheese, olive oil, 1 tablespoon canola oil, lemon zest and juice, garlic, and ⅛ teaspoon salt in a food processor until smooth. Brush crust with remaining 1 tablespoon canola oil. Spread pesto mixture on crust. Top with mozzarella and onion.
4. Transfer pizza to hot pizza stone. Bake at 500°F until cheese is melted, 5 to 7 minutes. Drizzle with balsamic glaze; sprinkle with basil, red pepper, remaining 1 tablespoon Parmesan, and remaining ¼ teaspoon salt.
Serves 4 (serving size: 2 slices)

CALORIES 265; FAT 21g (sat 5g, unsat 14g); PROTEIN 10g; CARB 10g; FIBER 1g; SUGARS 2g (added sugars 0g); SODIUM 579mg; CALC 30% DV; POTASSIUM 2% DV

Fast • Vegetarian

Potato Pancakes with Apple Butter

Hands-on: 20 min. **Total:** 25 min.
Frozen hash browns make it possible to whip up latkes in minutes. Enjoy the combo of crisp potato pancakes and a simple green salad for a light entrée, or serve alongside roast chicken or beef for a protein punch.

1 Tbsp. finely chopped shallot
1 Tbsp. finely chopped fresh chives
1 Tbsp. finely chopped fresh tarragon
1 Tbsp. white wine vinegar
1 ½ tsp. Dijon mustard
1 medium garlic clove, grated
⅜ tsp. black pepper, divided
5 Tbsp. canola oil, divided
¾ cup grated yellow onion
3 cups frozen shredded hash browns, thawed
1 large egg, separated
1 ½ Tbsp. all-purpose flour
¾ tsp. kosher salt, divided
4 cups loosely packed baby spring mix
¼ cup apple butter

1. Stir together shallot, chives, tarragon, vinegar, mustard, garlic, and ⅛ teaspoon pepper in a small bowl. Gradually add 3 tablespoons oil, whisking constantly, until blended. Set dressing aside.
2. Place grated onion in center of a clean kitchen towel; twist towel to squeeze liquid from onion. Stir together onion, hash browns, and egg yolk in a medium bowl. Whisk egg white in a small bowl until frothy; stir into potato mixture. Add flour, ½ teaspoon salt, and remaining ¼ teaspoon pepper; stir until combined.
3. Heat 1 tablespoon oil in a large nonstick skillet over medium; swirl to coat. Drop ⅓ cup potato mixture into skillet, and flatten with a spatula. Repeat 3 times to equal 4 pancakes in skillet. Cook until bottoms are crispy, 4 to 5 minutes. Flip pancakes; cook until bottoms are golden brown and crispy, about 2 minutes. Transfer to a plate. (Do not wipe skillet clean.) Repeat with remaining 1 tablespoon oil and potato mixture.
4. Toss together spring mix and dressing in a large bowl; divide salad among 4 plates. Top each potato pancake with 1 ½ teaspoons apple butter; sprinkle evenly with remaining ¼ teaspoon salt. Place 2 potato pancakes on each salad.
Serves 4 (serving size: 2 potato pancakes and 1 cup salad)

CALORIES 280; FAT 19g (sat 2g, unsat 17g); PROTEIN 5g; CARB 25g; FIBER 3g; SUGARS 8g (added sugars 0g); SODIUM 474mg; CALC 5% DV; POTASSIUM 6% DV

Chicken Tetrazzini

Hands-on: 30 min. **Total:** 30 min. If you'd like to make this comforting dish ahead of time, you can freeze the unbaked casserole up to three months. Let it thaw completely; top with Parmesan and panko, then bake at 350°F until browned and bubbly, about 45 minutes.

8 oz. uncooked whole-wheat thin spaghetti
1½ tsp. canola oil
¼ cup chopped yellow onion
¼ cup chopped celery
8 oz. sliced fresh cremini mushrooms (about 2 cups)
1 Tbsp. sherry
1 Tbsp. unsalted butter
1½ Tbsp. all-purpose flour
1 cup unsalted chicken broth
3 oz. Parmesan cheese, grated (about ¾ cup), divided
3 oz. ⅓-less-fat cream cheese (about 6 Tbsp.)
¾ tsp. kosher salt
2 cups shredded rotisserie chicken breast (about 10 oz.)
½ cup panko (Japanese breadcrumbs)
Chopped fresh flat-leaf parsley

1. Bring a large pot of water to boil over high. Add pasta; reduce heat to medium-low, and cook until noodles are al dente, 8 to 9 minutes.
2. Meanwhile, heat oil in a 5- to 6-quart Dutch oven over medium-high. Add onion and celery; cook, stirring occasionally, until softened, about 5 minutes. Add mushrooms; cook, stirring occasionally, until liquid has evaporated, 7 to 8 minutes. Reduce heat to medium.
3. Drain pasta, reserving ¼ cup cooking liquid; set aside. Stir sherry into mushroom mixture, gently scraping to loosen browned bits; stir in butter until melted. Add flour; cook, stirring constantly, until smooth, 1 to 2 minutes. Add broth and reserved cooking liquid; cook, stirring, until liquid begins to thicken, about 3 minutes. Stir in ½ cup Parmesan, cream cheese, and salt; cook, stirring constantly, until smooth, about 2 minutes. Remove from heat. Add chicken and cooked pasta; stir to coat.
4. Preheat broiler to high. Transfer pasta mixture to a deep 3-quart baking dish. Top with the panko and remaining ¼ cup Parmesan. Broil until top is golden, 2 to 3 minutes. Remove from oven; garnish with parsley. Serves 6 (serving size: 1¼ cups)

CALORIES 337; **FAT** 12g (sat 6g, unsat 4g); **PROTEIN** 20g; **CARB** 39g; **FIBER** 4g; **SUGARS** 3g (added sugars 0g); **SODIUM** 615mg; **CALC** 16% DV; **POTASSIUM** 10% DV

Rosemary-Crusted Pork with Mushrooms

Hands-on: 20 min. **Total:** 30 min. Feeding a crowd this season? This recipe's a cinch to double—simply brown the pork in batches, then proceed as directed. If you can't find instant polenta, regular is fine; start cooking it before you prep the pork so it's ready on time.

1 lb. pork tenderloin
2 Tbsp. canola oil, divided
1 Tbsp. chopped fresh rosemary
1¼ tsp. kosher salt, divided
1 tsp. black pepper, divided
12 oz. mixed fresh mushrooms, stemmed and coarsely chopped (about 3 cups)
1 cup sliced leeks
2 Tbsp. chopped fresh flat-leaf parsley
2 Tbsp. unsalted butter, divided
¾ cup uncooked instant polenta
2 Tbsp. plus 2 tsp. shredded Parmesan cheese

1. Preheat oven to 400°F. Pat pork dry; rub with 2 teaspoons oil. Stir together rosemary, ½ teaspoon salt, and ½ teaspoon pepper in a small bowl; sprinkle over pork. Heat an ovenproof skillet over medium-high. Add pork; cook until browned on all sides, about 4 minutes. Transfer skillet to oven; roast at 400°F until a thermometer inserted in thickest portion reaches 145°F, 14 to 16 minutes. Transfer pork to a cutting board, reserving drippings in skillet. Let pork rest 10 minutes.
2. While pork rests, add remaining 4 teaspoons oil to drippings in skillet; heat over medium-high. Add mushrooms, ½ teaspoon salt, and remaining ½ teaspoon pepper; cook, stirring often, until mushrooms begin to brown, 4 to 5 minutes. Add leeks; cook, stirring often, until mushrooms are deeply browned and leeks are tender, about 6 minutes. Stir in parsley and 1 tablespoon butter until melted. Remove from heat; cover to keep warm.
3. Prepare polenta according to package directions, omitting salt and fat. Whisk Parmesan, remaining 1 tablespoon butter, and remaining ¼ teaspoon salt into warm polenta.
4. Cut pork into 12 slices. Spoon ½ cup polenta onto each of 4 plates; top each with 3 pieces of pork and ½ cup mushroom mixture. Serves 4 (serving size: ½ cup polenta, ½ cup mushrooms, and 3 slices pork)

CALORIES 425; **FAT** 18g (sat 6g, unsat 11g); **PROTEIN** 35g; **CARB** 22g; **FIBER** 4g; **SUGARS** 2g (added sugars 0g); **SODIUM** 735mg; **CALC** 8% DV; **POTASSIUM** 18% DV

Mini Chicken Potpies

Hands-on: 40 min. **Total:** 1 hr.
Filled with tender sweet potato, meaty mushrooms, and shredded chicken, these personal potpies are a one-dish meal your family will love. Let the puff pastry thaw in the fridge for about 45 minutes before using.

1 Tbsp. canola oil
4 cups chopped fresh mushrooms
1¼ cups chopped yellow onion
½ cup chopped celery
1½ cups ½-in.-cubed peeled sweet potato
2 tsp. chopped fresh thyme, plus more for garnish
1.5 oz. all-purpose flour (about ⅓ cup)
1¼ cups unsalted chicken stock
½ cup whole milk
8 oz. rotisserie chicken breast, shredded (about 2 cups)
¾ cup frozen lima beans
½ tsp. kosher salt
1 frozen puff pastry sheet, thawed

1. Preheat oven to 425°F. Heat oil in a Dutch oven over medium-high. Add mushrooms, onion, and celery; cook, stirring often, until softened, 7 to 8 minutes. Add sweet potato and thyme; cook until tender and liquid has evaporated, 6 to 7 minutes. Stir in flour to coat. Add stock and milk; bring to a boil, stirring constantly. Boil 1 minute. Remove from heat; stir in chicken, lima beans, and salt. Let cool 20 minutes.
2. Cut puff pastry into 4 (4¼-inch) rounds. Place 4 (10-ounce) ramekins on a baking sheet; fill with chicken mixture. Top with dough rounds; bake at 425°F until golden brown, 17 to 19 minutes. Garnish with thyme. Serves 4

CALORIES 576; **FAT** 25g (sat 4g, unsat 19g); **PROTEIN** 33g; **CARB** 57g; **FIBER** 6g; **SUGARS** 9g (added sugars 0g); **SODIUM** 697mg; **CALC** 11% DV; **POTASSIUM** 25% DV

Fast

Crispy Chicken Cutlets with Lemon-Butter Carrots

Hands-on: 20 min. **Total:** 25 min.
Tossed in a simple lemon-tarragon butter, these tender baby carrots are the perfect partner for quick-cooking chicken cutlets. If you can't track down steam-in-bag carrots, microwave baby carrots until just tender, about 5 minutes.

½ (1-lb.) pkg. steam-in-bag carrots
4 (6-oz.) chicken breast cutlets
1 large egg, lightly beaten
2 Tbsp. water
1½ cups whole-wheat panko
¾ tsp. kosher salt, divided
2 Tbsp. canola oil, divided
¼ cup sliced shallot
½ cup lower-sodium fat-free chicken broth
1 tsp. lemon zest plus 2 Tbsp. fresh lemon juice
2 Tbsp. unsalted butter
1 Tbsp. chopped fresh tarragon, plus more for garnish

1. Preheat oven to 325°F. Cook carrots according to package directions, reserving remaining carrots for another use; set aside.
2. Pat chicken dry. Whisk together egg and 2 tablespoons water in a shallow bowl. Place panko on a plate. Dip cutlets into egg mixture, letting excess drip off. Sprinkle each cutlet with ⅛ teaspoon salt; dredge cutlets in panko to coat.
3. Heat 1 tablespoon oil in a large nonstick ovenproof skillet over medium-high. Cook chicken until browned, 2 to 3 minutes per side. Transfer skillet to oven; bake at 325°F until cooked through, 6 to 8 minutes.

4. Meanwhile, heat remaining 1 tablespoon oil in a skillet over medium-high. Add shallot; cook, stirring often, until tender and golden, about 3 minutes. Stir in broth and lemon zest and juice. Bring to a simmer over medium-high; cook, stirring occasionally, until reduced to ¼ cup, 3 to 4 minutes. Whisk in butter, tarragon, and remaining ¼ teaspoon salt until smooth. Add carrots; toss to coat. Divide carrots and chicken among 4 plates; spoon sauce over carrots. Garnish with tarragon. Serves 4 (serving size: 1 chicken cutlet and ⅔ cup carrots with sauce)

CALORIES 475; **FAT** 19g (sat 5g, unsat 12g); **PROTEIN** 46g; **CARB** 29g; **FIBER** 5g; **SUGARS** 5g (added sugars 0g); **SODIUM** 601mg; **CALC** 4% DV; **POTASSIUM** 17% DV

Sausage Baguette Pizzas

Hands-on: 25 min. **Total:** 40 min.
Your favorite throwback after-school snack gets a healthy makeover from a whole-grain baguette crust and vitamin A–packed spinach. Use mild sausage to make it kid-friendly.

1 (10-oz.) whole-wheat baguette, split lengthwise
¼ cup refrigerated basil pesto
2 Tbsp. canola mayonnaise
1 tsp. olive oil
6 oz. hot Italian turkey sausage
4 cups chopped spinach
2 tsp. sherry vinegar
2 oz. preshredded low-moisture part-skim mozzarella cheese (about ½ cup)

1. Preheat broiler to high. Scoop out the interior of the baguette and discard. Place hollowed baguette halves, cut sides up, on a baking sheet. Broil until lightly toasted, about 1 minute. Stir together pesto

and mayonnaise in a small bowl; spread evenly on baguette halves.

2. Heat oil in a large skillet over high. Cook sausage, stirring, until browned and crumbly, about 4 minutes. Add spinach to sausage; cook, stirring often, until wilted and bright green, about 2 minutes. Stir in vinegar. Remove from heat.

3. Transfer toasted baguette halves to a cutting board, and spoon sausage mixture evenly into baguette. Cut each half into 4 equal pieces. Top evenly with cheese. Place on baking sheet; return to oven, and broil until cheese is melted and lightly browned, 1 to 2 minutes. Serves 4 (serving size: 2 pieces)

CALORIES 394; **FAT** 17g (sat 4g, unsat 11g); **PROTEIN** 21g; **CARB** 39g; **FIBER** 6g; **SUGARS** 3g (added sugars 0g); **SODIUM** 746mg; **CALC** 20% DV; **POTASSIUM** 3% DV

Gluten Free • Vegetarian

Mushroom Quiche with Sweet Potato Crust

Hands-on: 25 min. **Total:** 40 min. Sweet potatoes make the perfect gluten-free crust for this custardy quiche. Brown the mushrooms with garlic to deepen their meaty flavor.

Canola oil cooking spray
1 (10-oz.) sweet potato, peeled and cut into ⅛-in.-thick slices
1 Tbsp. olive oil
4 cups sliced fresh wild mushrooms
2 Tbsp. thinly sliced garlic
5 large eggs
½ cup whole milk
2 oz. part-skim mozzarella cheese, shredded (about ½ cup)
1 cup thinly sliced Swiss chard
½ tsp. kosher salt
¼ tsp. black pepper
3 Tbsp. refrigerated basil pesto

1. Preheat oven to 400°F. Spray a 9-inch pie plate with cooking spray; line with sweet potato in overlapping circles. Bake at 400°F until tender, about 15 minutes. Remove from oven; press sweet potato into dish. Reduce oven temperature to 375°F.

2. Heat olive oil in a large skillet over medium-high; swirl to coat. Add mushrooms; cook, stirring occasionally, 5 minutes. Add garlic, and cook until mushrooms are browned and tender, 2 to 3 minutes. Remove from heat; set aside.

3. Whisk together eggs, milk, cheese, Swiss chard, salt, and pepper in a medium bowl. Place mushrooms in an even layer in sweet potato crust. Pour egg mixture over mushrooms. Dollop with the pesto; swirl into egg mixture with a knife. Bake at 375°F until set in center, about 20 minutes. Let cool slightly. Cut into 8 slices. Serves 4 (serving size: 2 slices)

CALORIES 305; **FAT** 18g (sat 5g, unsat 10g); **PROTEIN** 16g; **CARB** 21g; **FIBER** 3g; **SUGARS** 7g (added sugars 0g); **SODIUM** 563mg; **CALC** 26% DV; **POTASSIUM** 14% DV

HOLIDAY SAUCES FOR ANY PROTEIN

Fast • Make Ahead
Bacon-Shallot Gravy

Center-cut bacon infuses this rich gravy with flavor yet has 25% less saturated fat than regular bacon. If you make this ahead of time, whisk in a tablespoon or two of chicken stock before reheating.

Cook 4 center-cut bacon slices in a skillet over medium-low until crispy. Set bacon aside, reserving drippings in skillet. Add ¼ cup sliced shallot to skillet; cook over medium 2 minutes. Add 1 Tbsp. all-purpose flour; cook, stirring, 1 minute. Add 1 cup unsalted chicken stock and 2 Tbsp. sherry vinegar;

simmer until thickened, 3 to 5 minutes. Remove from heat; stir in 1 Tbsp. unsalted butter, 1 tsp. fresh thyme leaves, and crumbled bacon. Serves 4 (serving size: ¼ cup)

CALORIES 78; **FAT** 5g (sat 2g, unsat 1g); **PROTEIN** 5g; **CARB** 4g; **FIBER** 0g; **SUGARS** 1g (added sugars 0g); **SODIUM** 130mg; **CALC** 0% DV; **POTASSIUM** 0% DV

Fast • Gluten Free
Vegetarian
Port-Cherry Sauce

This elegant and easy sauce is a simple way to elevate your go-to roast pork tenderloin recipe. The sweet and tangy balance also makes it a show-stopping topping for baked Brie or vanilla gelato.

Melt 1 Tbsp. unsalted butter in a small saucepan over medium-low. Add 2 Tbsp. minced shallot; cook until softened, about 2 minutes. Stir in 1 cup ruby port, ¾ cup halved frozen pitted cherries, 3 Tbsp. balsamic vinegar, and 1 ½ Tbsp. pure maple syrup. Bring to a boil; cook until thickened and reduced by half, 15 to 20 minutes. Remove from heat. Stir in 1 Tbsp. unsalted butter and ¼ tsp. kosher salt. Serves 8 (serving size: 2 Tbsp.)

CALORIES 98; **FAT** 3g (sat 2g, unsat 1g); **PROTEIN** 0g; **CARB** 7g; **FIBER** 0g; **SUGARS** 6g (added sugars 2g); **SODIUM** 63mg; **CALC** 1% DV; **POTASSIUM** 1% DV

ROAST THESE

Fresh-roasted chestnuts are an old-timey holiday tradition that's firing back up. Home cooks are rediscovering the meaty taste of warm roasted Italian chestnuts. Go the open-fire route, or score an "X" on the rounded side through the skin, and bake in the oven at 425°F for 10 minutes or so.

Fast • Gluten Free
Make Ahead • Vegetarian

Spiced Winter Squash Soup

Hands-on: 20 min. **Total:** 20 min.
Smooth silken tofu blends perfectly with the butternut squash and pumpkin to create the ultimate velvety texture. And thanks to its protein and fiber, the dish is quite filling—your family won't know it's completely vegan.

2 Tbsp. olive oil, divided
1 cup chopped yellow onion
1 small Honeycrisp apple (about 6 oz.), peeled and chopped
1 tsp. grated peeled fresh ginger
½ tsp. chopped garlic
¼ tsp. curry powder
¼ tsp. grated fresh nutmeg
¼ tsp. ground cinnamon, plus more for garnish
⅛ tsp. ground cardamom
1½ cups lower-sodium vegetable broth
1 (14½-oz.) can butternut squash puree
1 (14½-oz.) can pumpkin puree
2 tsp. creamy natural peanut butter
2 tsp. light brown sugar
1 (14-oz.) pkg. silken tofu, drained
1 tsp. kosher salt
¼ cup unsalted roasted pumpkin seed kernels (pepitas)

1. Heat 1 tablespoon oil in a 5- to 6-quart Dutch oven over medium-high. Add onion and apple; cook, stirring occasionally, until softened, 5 to 6 minutes. Add ginger, garlic, curry powder, nutmeg, cinnamon, and cardamom; cook, stirring often, until fragrant, about 1 minute. Stir in broth, squash, pumpkin, peanut butter, and brown sugar; cook until smooth and heated through, about 5 minutes.
2. Transfer mixture to a blender; add tofu and salt. Remove center piece of blender lid; secure lid on blender, and place a clean kitchen towel over opening in lid. Process until smooth, about 45 seconds. Divide evenly among 4 bowls. Sprinkle with pepitas, and drizzle with remaining 1 tablespoon oil. Sprinkle with cinnamon. Serves 4 (serving size: 1 ½ cups)

CALORIES 295; **FAT** 15g (sat 2g, unsat 12g); **PROTEIN** 10g; **CARB** 34g; **FIBER** 9g; **CALC** 14% DV; **POTASSIUM** 11% DV

Staff Favorite • Fast
Gluten Free

Filet Mignon with Apple-Fennel Slaw

Hands-on: 15 min. **Total:** 20 min.
Ask your butcher to cut evenly sized fillets to ensure the steaks cook at the same rate.

4 (4-oz.) beef tenderloin fillets
1 tsp. ground fennel seeds
1½ tsp. black pepper, divided
1¼ tsp. kosher salt, divided
3 Tbsp. olive oil, divided
2 Tbsp. red wine vinegar
1 Tbsp. canola oil
2 cups thinly sliced fennel bulb, fronds saved for garnish (optional)
1½ cups thinly sliced unpeeled Fuji apple
½ cup thinly sliced red onion
1 cup torn fresh flat-leaf parsley

1. Preheat oven to 425°F. Coat fillets on both sides evenly with ground fennel seeds, 1 teaspoon pepper, and ¾ teaspoon salt. Heat 1 tablespoon olive oil in a large ovenproof skillet over medium-high. Add fillets; cook until browned on both sides, about 2 minutes per side. Transfer skillet to oven; cook at 425°F until a thermometer inserted in thickest portion registers 130°F to 135°F, 3 to 5 minutes. Transfer fillets to a plate; let rest 5 minutes.
2. Meanwhile, whisk together the vinegar, canola oil, remaining 2 tablespoons olive oil, remaining ½ teaspoon pepper, and remaining ½ teaspoon salt in a large bowl. Add sliced fennel, apple, onion, and parsley; toss to coat. Divide slaw among 4 plates. Slice fillets; divide among plates. Garnish with fennel fronds, if desired. Serves 4 (serving size: 4 oz. beef and ¾ cup slaw)

CALORIES 322; **FAT** 20g (sat 4g, unsat 15g); **PROTEIN** 24g; **CARB** 13g; **FIBER** 3g; **SUGARS** 7g (added sugars 0g); **SODIUM** 677mg; **CALC** 7% DV; **POTASSIUM** 13% DV

Fast • Gluten Free
Vegetarian

Creamy Four-Cheese Pasta with Spinach

Hands-on: 10 min. **Total:** 15 min.

8 oz. uncooked quinoa or chickpea pasta (such as rigatoni, penne, farfalle, or rotini)
1 Tbsp. olive oil
8 cups baby spinach
1 Tbsp. chopped garlic
2 oz. fontina cheese, shredded (about ½ cup)
½ cup low-fat ricotta cheese
1 oz. ⅓-less-fat cream cheese, softened
¼ tsp. kosher salt
⅛ tsp. cayenne pepper
¼ cup finely grated Parmesan cheese

1. Prepare pasta in a large stockpot according to package directions, omitting salt and fat. Drain pasta, reserving ¼ cup cooking liquid. Return pasta and reserved cooking liquid to stockpot.
2. Heat oil in a large saucepan over medium-high. Add spinach and

garlic; cook, stirring often, until spinach wilts and garlic is slightly softened, about 3 minutes. Add fontina, ricotta, and cream cheese; cook, stirring constantly, until cheeses melt and mixture is creamy, about 30 seconds. Immediately remove from heat; add to pasta in stockpot. Add salt and cayenne. Stir gently to coat pasta with sauce.

3. Divide pasta among 4 bowls; top with Parmesan. Serve immediately. Serves 4 (serving size: 1 cup)

CALORIES 409; **FAT** 15g (sat 7g, unsat 6g); **PROTEIN** 17g; **CARB** 54g; **FIBER** 7g; **SUGARS** 2g (added sugars 0g); **SODIUM** 507mg; **CALC** 34% DV; **POTASSIUM** 2% DV

Fast · Gluten Free

Sweet Potato and Bacon Frittata

Hands-on: 20 min. **Total:** 20 min. Smart shortcuts deliver a frittata that's perfect for a busy weeknight or weekend brunch. Microwaving the sweet potatoes helps them cook faster; Canadian bacon adds flavor with half the saturated fat of regular bacon.

2 cups chopped peeled sweet potato
Cooking spray
5 Canadian bacon slices (about 3 oz.), chopped
2 Tbsp. canola oil, divided
1 cup thinly sliced shallots
6 large eggs
1 oz. Gruyère cheese, shredded (about ¼ cup)
1 Tbsp. chopped fresh sage
½ tsp. black pepper
¼ tsp. kosher salt
1 oz. goat cheese, crumbled (about ¼ cup)
2 Tbsp. chopped fresh chives

1. Preheat broiler to high with oven rack in top position. Place sweet potato in a microwavable bowl; add water to a depth of ½ inch. Cover with a plate and microwave until slightly tender, 5 to 6 minutes. Drain sweet potato, and transfer to a plate. Pat sweet potato dry, and lightly coat with cooking spray.

2. Heat a 9-inch cast-iron skillet over medium-high. Add Canadian bacon and 1 tablespoon oil; cook, stirring often, until bacon is lightly browned, 4 to 5 minutes. Drain bacon on paper towels, reserving drippings in skillet. Add shallots and sweet potato to skillet; cook, stirring often, until lightly browned, about 5 minutes.

3. Whisk together eggs, Gruyère, sage, pepper, and salt in a bowl. Add remaining 1 tablespoon oil to sweet potato mixture in skillet; pour egg mixture into skillet. Cook over medium, gently pulling eggs in from sides of skillet with a spatula, until eggs are partially set, about 2 minutes. Sprinkle with goat cheese and reserved bacon.

4. Transfer skillet to oven; broil until eggs are completely set and toppings are golden, 3 to 4 minutes. Remove from oven; sprinkle with chives. Serves 4 (serving size: 2 wedges)

CALORIES 331; **FAT** 19g (sat 6g, unsat 13g); **PROTEIN** 18g; **CARB** 21g; **FIBER** 3g; **SUGARS** 7g (added sugars 0g); **SODIUM** 565mg; **CALC** 16% DV; **POTASSIUM** 11% DV

Fast · Gluten Free

Crispy Salmon Salad with Roasted Butternut Squash

Hands-on: 20 min. **Total:** 20 min. Small touches like the charred lemon vinaigrette and tart pomegranate arils elevate this speedy salad into a showstopping main dish. Preheat your sheet pan to get a jump-start on cooking the squash and onions.

2½ cups chopped butternut squash
2¼ cups sliced red onion
1 medium lemon, halved crosswise
¼ cup olive oil
1 Tbsp. rice vinegar
2 tsp. pure maple syrup
1¼ tsp. Dijon mustard
½ tsp. orange zest
¾ tsp. black pepper, divided
¾ plus ⅛ tsp. kosher salt, divided
1 Tbsp. canola oil
4 (6-oz.) skin-on salmon fillets
4 cups torn curly kale
4 cups baby spinach
½ cup pomegranate arils

1. Place a baking sheet on rack in upper third of oven; preheat broiler to high. Once hot, carefully remove baking sheet from oven; place squash, onion, and lemon (cut side down) on baking sheet. Broil until charred, 7 to 8 minutes. Let cool; squeeze juice from lemon halves into a small bowl.

2. Whisk together olive oil, vinegar, maple syrup, mustard, orange zest, 1 teaspoon lemon juice, ½ teaspoon pepper, and ¼ teaspoon salt in a medium bowl; set aside.

3. Heat canola oil in a large nonstick skillet over medium-high. Sprinkle salmon flesh with remaining ¼ teaspoon pepper and remaining ⅝ teaspoon salt. Cook salmon, skin side down, until skin is crisp, 3 to 4 minutes. Flip fillets; cook 2 to 3 minutes.

4. Place kale, spinach, pomegranate arils, squash, and onion in a large bowl. Add vinaigrette; toss to coat. Divide salad and salmon among 4 bowls; spoon ½ teaspoon lemon juice over each fillet. Serves 4 (serving size: 2½ cups salad and 6 oz. salmon)

CALORIES 507; **FAT** 28g (sat 4g, unsat 23g); **PROTEIN** 38g; **CARB** 26g; **FIBER** 5g; **SUGARS** 7g (added sugars 2g); **SODIUM** 606mg; **CALC** 23% DV; **POTASSIUM** 29% DV

Staff Favorite • Make Ahead

Pasta with Italian Sunday Sauce

Hands-on: 40 min. **Total:** 7 hr. 40 min. Known as "Sunday Gravy" to many, this meaty tomato sauce is like marinara but with a major upgrade. Short ribs and turkey sausage add flavor; whole-wheat pasta brings heart-healthy fiber to the table.

1 Tbsp. olive oil
1½ lb. bone-in beef short ribs
12 oz. hot Italian turkey sausage
    (about 3 sausage links)
2 cups finely chopped yellow onion
½ cup finely chopped celery
3 Tbsp. minced garlic
5 Tbsp. unsalted tomato paste
¼ cup dry red wine
1 (28-oz.) can unsalted crushed
    tomatoes
1 rosemary sprig
1 tsp. dried thyme
1 tsp. dried oregano
⅛ tsp. crushed red pepper
14 oz. uncooked whole-wheat
    spaghetti
4 tsp. red wine vinegar
1⅛ tsp. kosher salt

1. Heat oil in a large skillet over medium- high. Add short ribs and sausage in batches; cook, turning occasionally, until browned on all sides. Transfer to a plate. (Do not wipe out skillet.)
2. Reduce heat to medium; add onion, celery, and garlic to skillet; cook, stirring often, until lightly browned, about 5 minutes. Add tomato paste; cook, stirring constantly, 1 minute. Remove from heat; add red wine, scraping bottom of skillet with a wooden spoon to loosen browned bits. Pour mixture into a 6-quart slow cooker. Stir in tomatoes, rosemary, thyme, oregano, and red pepper. Add short ribs and sausage, submerging in tomato mixture. Cover and cook on low until short ribs are tender, about 7 hours.
3. Transfer short ribs and sausage links to a cutting board. Skim and discard fat from surface of tomato sauce in slow cooker. Discard rosemary. Let short ribs and sausage links cool 10 minutes.
4. Meanwhile, prepare pasta according to package directions, omitting salt and fat. Cover to keep warm until ready to serve.
5. Remove meat from bones of short ribs; shred meat, and return to slow cooker. Discard bones. Cut sausage links crosswise into ½-inch-thick slices; return to slow cooker. Stir in vinegar and salt. Serve sauce over pasta. Serves 8 (serving size: ¾ cup pasta and ¾ cup meat sauce)

CALORIES 400; **FAT** 12g (sat 2g, unsat 9g); **PROTEIN** 23g; **CARB** 52g; **FIBER** 9g; **SUGARS** 7g (added sugars 0g); **SODIUM** 604mg; **CALC** 4% DV; **POTASSIUM** 10% DV

3 GO-WITH-ANYTHING SIDES

Fast • Gluten Free Vegetarian
Smoky Brussels Sprouts

Since there's a touch of sugar in this recipe, stir the Brussels sprouts often to prevent burning. If you're feeling decadent, top this side with a little grated Manchego cheese.

Heat 1 Tbsp. olive oil in a large skillet over medium-high. Add 1 lb. trimmed and halved Brussels sprouts; cook, stirring often, until browned, 10 to 12 minutes. Add 1 Tbsp. chopped garlic, 2 tsp. light brown sugar, 1 tsp. smoked paprika, and ¼ tsp. kosher salt. Cook, stirring often, 1 minute; remove from heat. Stir in 3 Tbsp. apple cider vinegar. Sprinkle with 2 Tbsp. chopped salted smoked almonds. Serves 4 (serving size: about ½ cup)

CALORIES 122; **FAT** 6g (sat 1g, unsat 4g); **PROTEIN** 5g; **CARB** 14g; **FIBER** 5g; **SUGARS** 5g (added sugars 2g); **SODIUM** 178mg; **CALC** 5% DV; **POTASSIUM** 10% DV

Gluten Free • Make Ahead Vegetarian
Roasted Acorn Squash with Thyme

To make cutting acorn squash easier, place a kitchen towel on your cutting board to keep the squash from slipping. Pair these tender wedges with pork tenderloin, pan-seared fish, or your favorite roast chicken.

Cut a 2-lb. acorn squash into 16 wedges; discard seeds. Place on a baking sheet. Spray with cooking spray; sprinkle with ⅜ tsp. kosher salt and ½ tsp. black pepper. Roast at 450°F 20 minutes. Whisk together 2 Tbsp. sherry vinegar, 2 Tbsp. olive oil, 1 Tbsp. canola oil, 1 tsp. Dijon mustard, ¼ tsp. kosher salt, and ½ tsp. black pepper. Top squash with vinaigrette, ½ cup pomegranate arils, and 1 Tbsp. fresh thyme. Serves 4 (serving size: 4 wedges)

CALORIES 188; **FAT** 11g (sat 1g, unsat 10g); **PROTEIN** 2g; **CARB** 23g; **FIBER** 4g; **SUGARS** 7g (added sugars 0g); **SODIUM** 336mg; **CALC** 6% DV; **POTASSIUM** 14% DV

Fast • Gluten Free
Roasted Potatoes with Smoked Trout

Canned smoked trout is a pantry staple you must try; it has a very mild, almost bacon-y flavor that enriches every dish you add it to.

Cut 12 oz. fingerling potatoes in half lengthwise; place in a microwavable bowl with ¼ cup water. Cover with plastic wrap, and pierce with a fork to vent. Microwave until tender, 6 to 7 minutes; drain. Combine potatoes, ¼ cup thinly sliced red onion, ¼ cup fresh flat-leaf parsley leaves, 1 ½ Tbsp. olive oil, 1 Tbsp. chopped fresh rosemary, ½ tsp. black pepper, and ⅜ tsp. kosher salt in a bowl. Flake 2 oz. smoked trout into large pieces; gently fold into potato mixture. Serves 4 (serving size: ¾ cup)

CALORIES 136; FAT 6g (sat 1g, unsat 5g); PROTEIN 5g; CARB 15g; FIBER 3g; SUGARS 1g (added sugars 0g); SODIUM 183mg; CALC 1% DV; POTASSIUM 3% DV

1 INGREDIENT, 3 SIDES

3 WAYS TO USE HARICOTS VERTS

These slender, quick-cooking green beans look and feel a little fancy, perfect for dressing up holiday-worthy side dishes. You can also use regular green beans; they'll just need to cook a few minutes longer.

Fast • Gluten Free
Vegetarian
Lemon-Feta Green Beans
Searing lemons is one of our favorite tricks for upping the ante on any dish. The tart juice mellows out, providing the perfect balance for the briny capers and feta in this skillet side. If you have any leftovers, try adding halved cherry tomatoes and enjoying as a cold salad; some cooked chicken or shrimp would turn it into a lovely main dish.

1. Combine 12 oz. haricots verts and ¼ cup water in large microwavable bowl; cover with plastic wrap. Microwave at high for 5 minutes; drain. Heat 1 tsp. olive oil in a large skillet over medium-high. Halve 2 small lemons; cook, cut sides down, until lightly charred, about 2 minutes. Remove from heat; set lemons aside. Combine 5 tsp. olive oil, 1 Tbsp. drained and chopped capers, and haricots verts in skillet. Squeeze lemons over mixture; toss to coat. Sprinkle with 2 Tbsp. crumbled feta cheese, 2 Tbsp. chopped fresh chives, and ¼ tsp. black pepper. Serves 4 (serving size: ¾ cup)

CALORIES 113; FAT 8g (sat 2g, unsat 6g); PROTEIN 3g; CARB 9g; FIBER 3g; SUGARS 4g (added sugars 0g); SODIUM 154g; CALC 6% DV; POTASSIUM 5% DV

Fast • Gluten Free
Vegetarian
Green Beans with Mustard-Tarragon Sauce
Substitute fresh thyme or dill for the tarragon, if you prefer. To blanch haricots verts, cook them in boiling water 2 minutes, and immediately transfer to an ice bath to cool.

1. Heat a small skillet over medium-high. Add 2 Tbsp. sliced almonds; cook, stirring, until golden, about 4 minutes. Set aside. Heat 2 tsp. canola oil in same skillet over medium-high. Add 2 tsp. chopped garlic; cook 1 minute. Remove from heat; stir in 2 Tbsp. white wine vinegar, 2 Tbsp. heavy cream, 1 Tbsp. Dijon mustard, 2 tsp. honey, and ¼ tsp. kosher salt. Return skillet to heat; cook sauce over medium-high until slightly thickened, about 1 minute.

Stir 1 Tbsp. chopped fresh tarragon into sauce. Arrange 12 oz. blanched haricots verts on a serving platter. Drizzle with sauce; sprinkle with almonds. Serves 4 (serving size: ½ cup)

CALORIES 106; FAT 7g (sat 2g, unsat 4g); PROTEIN 3g; CARB 10g; FIBER 3g; SUGARS 6g (added sugars 3g); SODIUM 218mg; CALC 5% DV; POTASSIUM 5% DV

Fast
Green Bean Casserole
We've given the classic casserole an upgrade by swapping sodium-heavy canned soup for a rich and chunky homemade mushroom sauce. For bean blanching instructions, see the note on the recipe at left.

1. Trim and blanch 12 oz. haricots verts; place in an 11- x 7-inch baking dish. Heat 2 Tbsp. canola oil in a large skillet over medium-high. Add 3 cups sliced fresh mushrooms and ½ cup chopped onion; cook until browned, 6 to 8 minutes. Add 1 Tbsp. all-purpose flour; cook, stirring constantly, 1 minute. Add 1 cup unsalted chicken stock, 2 Tbsp. heavy cream, ½ tsp. black pepper, and ⅜ tsp. kosher salt; cook, stirring, until thick and smooth, 1 to 3 minutes. Spoon over haricots verts; sprinkle with ¼ cup whole-wheat panko and 3 Tbsp. grated Parmesan cheese. Spray with cooking spray; broil until golden brown, 1 to 2 minutes. Serves 4 (serving size: 1 cup)

CALORIES 171; FAT 11g (sat 3g, unsat 7g); PROTEIN 6g; CARB 16g; FIBER 4g; SUGARS 5g (added sugars 0g); SODIUM 254mg; CALC 7% DV; POTASSIUM 11% DV

Fast

Shrimp and Grits

Hands-on: 30 min. **Total:** 30 min. This rich and creamy dish proves eating healthier can still feel indulgent at times. The hefty servings satisfy your appetite and keep you full longer. To time this just right, start the vegetables after the grits have been cooking for 10 minutes.

3 cups lower-sodium chicken broth

3 cups water

1½ cups uncooked stone-ground yellow grits

1 Tbsp. canola oil

1 cup chopped yellow onion

1 cup chopped poblano chile

2 tsp. minced garlic

2 cups unsalted fire-roasted diced tomatoes

1 tsp. lower-sodium Worcestershire sauce

½ tsp. black pepper

1 tsp. kosher salt, divided

¼ cup unsalted butter, divided

1 lb. peeled and deveined raw medium shrimp

2 oz. Parmesan cheese, grated (about ½ cup), divided

2½ Tbsp. half-and-half

3 Tbsp. thinly sliced scallions

½ tsp. hot sauce

1. Bring chicken broth and 3 cups water to a boil in a medium saucepan over high. Whisk in grits; reduce heat to medium. Cover and cook, stirring occasionally, until tender, 20 to 23 minutes.

2. Meanwhile, heat oil in a large nonstick skillet over medium-high. Add onion and poblano; cook, stirring often, until onion is softened, 8 to 9 minutes. Add garlic; cook 1 minute. Stir in diced tomatoes, Worcestershire, black pepper, and ¼ teaspoon salt. Simmer 5 minutes. Add 1 tablespoon butter; cook, stirring often, until butter is melted. Add shrimp, and cook until just pink, 3 to 4 minutes.

3. Add 6 tablespoons Parmesan, half-and-half, remaining 3 tablespoons butter, and remaining ¾ teaspoon salt to grits; stir to combine. Divide grits among 6 bowls; top with shrimp mixture. Sprinkle with scallions and remaining 2 tablespoons Parmesan; drizzle evenly with hot sauce. Serves 6 (serving size: 1 cup grits and 1 cup shrimp mixture)

CALORIES 369; **FAT** 15g (sat 7g, unsat 6g); **PROTEIN** 20g; **CARB** 38g; **FIBER** 3g; **SUGARS** 4g (added sugars 0g); **SODIUM** 698mg; **CALC** 14% DV; **POTASSIUM** 3% DV

THE PICKY EATER GURU

HOW TO USE UP HOLIDAY LEFTOVERS

Forget sandwiches—transform that leftover ham into a crispy, cheesy, family-friendly supper.

BY GINA HOMOLKA

I grew up eating (and loving) potato croquettes. My mom always made them with whatever she had left over from the night before—chicken, turkey, fish, you name it. So when I was looking for a new way to use up leftover holiday ham, I knew it would find a happy home in croquettes. My kids might turn their noses up at fish croquettes, but ham is always a winner in my house.

My mom deep-fried her croquettes, but I opt to make my version lighter (and less messy) by cooking them in the oven. I also couldn't resist making mine a little healthier, so I snuck in some extra vegetables. I mashed some cooked carrots with the potatoes, but you can add any leftover cooked vegetables you have on hand, such as broccoli or peas. Trust me—the kids won't even notice.

Here's a helpful prep tip—freeze the croquettes for a few minutes before the final breading. It's not necessary but helps them hold together better during the breading process. Pair these crispy croquettes with roasted vegetables or a green salad for a well-rounded meal.

Ham Croquettes

Hands-on: 50 min. **Total:** 1 hr. 15 min.
Nobody complains about eating leftovers when these are on the menu. Addictively crunchy, these crispy, cheesy croquettes make a great dinner or an afternoon snack. To make them gluten-free, substitute gluten-free baking mix for the all-purpose flour and use gluten-free breadcrumbs.

1 lb. russet potatoes
1 large carrot, peeled and cut into
   small cubes
2 tsp. olive oil
1 small onion, chopped
½ cup chopped fresh parsley
3 garlic cloves, minced
8 oz. leftover smoked ham, minced
2 oz. part-skim cheddar cheese,
   shredded (about ½ cup)
½ tsp. black pepper
¼ tsp. kosher salt
2 Tbsp. all-purpose flour
Olive oil cooking spray
2 large eggs, beaten
⅔ cup whole-wheat or gluten-free
   breadcrumbs

1. Prick potatoes all over with a fork; microwave at high 5 minutes. Turn and cook until potatoes can be easily pierced with a fork all the way to the center, 5 to 7 more minutes. Carefully transfer to a cutting board to cool.
2. Bring a medium pot of water to a boil. Add carrot; cover and cook until tender, 10 to 12 minutes. Drain and transfer to a large bowl. Scoop flesh from cooked potatoes; add to carrot (discard potato skins). Mash with a potato masher.
3. Heat oil in a large skillet over medium. Add onion, parsley, and garlic; cook until soft, about 4 minutes. Stir in ham. Remove from heat; add to potato mixture. Stir in cheese, pepper, and salt.

4. Divide ham mixture into 18 portions (about 3 tablespoons each); roll each portion into a log. Place flour on a large plate; roll logs in flour, pressing to flatten slightly. Shake off excess flour; freeze for 30 minutes.
5. Preheat oven to 450°F. Coat a large rimmed baking sheet with cooking spray. Dip logs in egg wash; dredge in breadcrumbs. Transfer logs to prepared pan. Spritz generously with cooking spray. Bake at 450°F until golden and heated through, 20 to 23 minutes. Serves 6 (serving size: 3 croquettes)

CALORIES 296; **FAT** 9g (sat 3g, unsat 5g);
PROTEIN 15g; **CARB** 37g; **FIBER** 4g; **SUGARS** 3g
(added sugars 0g); **SODIUM** 571mg; **CALC** 11%
DV; **POTASSIUM** 14% DV

THE SEAFOOD GUY

ONE-POT FEAST OF THE SEVEN FISHES

This Catholic holiday tradition gets a streamlined makeover with make-ahead ease.

BY BARTON SEAVER

Starring at least seven (and usually more!) seafood-centric dishes, the Feast of the Seven Fishes is an Italian-American tradition that I love. But the last thing my bustling holiday house needs is a lot of prep work to get dinner on the table. So I transformed this complicated meal into a convenient stew that can be cooked ahead of time, gently warmed, and served in its cooking vessel at the center of the table with loaves of crusty bread. You can even make it a day ahead; simply reheat gently without stirring to keep the delicate fish intact.

The success of this dish lies in using quality seafood and employing the best cooking method for each type. Searing scallops gives them texture when they are nestled back into the stew; the caramelized bits left behind add flavor to the liquid that steams clams and mussels. The shellfish add their juices to the broth as they open; that broth gently poaches the shrimp and flaky fish. The layering of flavors makes these ingredients better for being brought together—just as generations gathering around the table make the holidays more delightful.

Gluten Free • Make Ahead

Feast of the Seven Fishes Stew

Hands-on: 50 min. **Total:** 1 hr. 10 min.
Don't skip the anchovies; these tiny umami bombs add an extra layer of rich flavor to this hearty stew.

½ lb. medium dry-packed scallops
½ lb. skinless salmon fillet, cut into
   1½-oz. pieces
½ lb. white-fleshed fish, cut into
   1½-oz. pieces
1 Tbsp. olive oil
½ cup white wine
¼ cup water
12 littleneck clams, scrubbed
1 lb. mussels, cleaned
1 oz. canned anchovy fillets,
   chopped, oil reserved
1 medium fennel bulb, cored and
   sliced, fronds reserved
4 garlic cloves, chopped
1 tsp. orange zest
1 (28-oz.) can unsalted crushed San
   Marzano tomatoes
1 tsp. crushed red pepper
½ lb. peeled and deveined raw
   medium shrimp

continued

1. Let scallops, salmon, and fish come to room temperature. Heat oil in a large Dutch oven over medium-high. Add scallops; cook until they develop a golden-brown crust on one side, about 2 minutes. Remove from pan, and set aside.

2. Add wine, ½ cup water, and clams to pan. Cover, increase heat to high, and cook until clams open, 5 to 7 minutes. Transfer clams to a large bowl (discard any unopened clams). Add mussels to pan; cover and cook until they open, 3 to 4 minutes. Turn off heat. Remove mussels; set aside. Pour cooking liquid through a fine-mesh sieve over a bowl; set aside.

3. Add reserved oil from anchovies to pan over medium-high. Add anchovies; cook until dissolved, about 2 minutes. Stir in fennel; cook until tender, 5 minutes. Add garlic and orange zest; cook 1 minute. Stir in reserved cooking liquid, tomatoes, and crushed red pepper. Reduce heat to medium; simmer, uncovered, until sauce has thickened slightly, 12 to 15 minutes.

4. Nestle fish and shrimp into broth. Cover and reduce heat to low. Cook until seafood is opaque, 6 to 8 minutes. Add mussels, clams, and scallops, cooked sides up. Heat until warmed through. Top with reserved fennel fronds. Serves 6 (serving size: about 1½ cups)

CALORIES 318; FAT 8g (sat 1g, unsat 5g); PROTEIN 39g; CARB 18g; FIBER 4g; SUGARS 2g (added sugars 0g); SODIUM 712mg; CALC 9% DV; POTASSIUM 17% DV

THE TEACHER

WHY YOU SHOULD TAKE THE TIME TO SOUS VIDE

How a seemingly chef-y kitchen gadget can simplify life for the busy home cook

BY ANDREA NGUYEN

Until quite recently, my feelings toward sous vide were a bit tepid. In case you aren't familiar, sous vide is a French technique in which vacuum-sealed food (think DIY boil-in-bags) is slowly cooked to the perfect doneness in a temperature-regulated water bath. The cooked items may then be seared or grilled to add color and texture to their exteriors.

Preparing food in a tiny Jacuzzi is a godsend to those wanting reliable results; if you're a stickler for doneness, it's definitely the gadget for you. However, it requires time. Pan-frying a 1-inch-thick steak takes less than 10 minutes; cooking it sous vide requires an hour in a burbling water bath, followed by searing or frying.

That's why my first sous vide device—the ultra-sleek Joule model by ChefSteps—sat idle in its artful black box in my garage for nearly two years after I first played around with it. The steaks and pork chops it yielded were great but not life-changing—why would I use a gadget that doesn't save me any time?

Then I met Buffy Poon at one of my cooking classes. I was surprised to hear that this super-busy mom of three cooks sous vide three or four times a week to feed her family. Her

sister-in-law, too. These weren't aspiring chefs or food-gadget nerds; they were busy women cooking for their families. Suddenly, sous vide wasn't mere novelty.

After perusing websites and cookbooks devoted to the method, I spent a full Saturday cooking food sous vide for the following week. My plan included pork satay (cooking in the marinade created a flavorful sauce base), skirt steak (eight hours yielded unbelievably tender results for tacos and sandwiches), and shrimp (the succulent, sweet shellfish flesh was great for salads and rice paper rolls).

What about vegetables? Mushrooms developed a meaty texture and intense umami flavor. It wasn't a game changer for broccoli, but slow cooking asparagus was great for monitoring doneness. Sweet potato cubes were firm-tender but didn't express their natural sweetness much.

Satisfied with my meat and veggie tests, I decided to tackle the last experiment on my list—Eggs Benedict, the one I was most skeptical about. All told, from boiling water to cooking, poaching eggs the traditional way takes barely 10 minutes. The sous vide recipe I was using as a guide called for only a slightly longer cook time. But they were going to have to be some damn fine eggs to justify the extra piece of equipment. And guess what? They were—the custardy texture was otherworldly. Plus, putting the egg poaching on sous vide autopilot transforms a stressful project like eggs Benedict into a dish that's much easier to tackle for a hungry crowd.

Impressed by the week's end, I happily moved Joule from its garage-shelf banishment to a brand-new home—its very own kitchen drawer. After all, it was about time.

Make Ahead

Sous Vide Eggs Benedict

Hands-on: 20 min. **Total:** 1 hr.
To keep the finished eggs for up to five days, cool them in an ice water bath for 10 minutes; refrigerate in an airtight container. Reheat at 140°F for 15 minutes.

9 large eggs
4 slices whole-grain bread
4 (1-oz.) slices lower-sodium ham
3 Tbsp. unsalted butter, divided
2 Tbsp. minced shallot
8 cups baby spinach
Black pepper to taste
2 tsp. fresh lemon juice
¾ cup plain 2% reduced-fat Greek
   yogurt, at room temperature
1 Tbsp. canola mayonnaise
¼ tsp. kosher salt
Pinch of cayenne pepper, plus more
   for garnish (optional)
2 Tbsp. chopped fresh flat-leaf
   parsley

1. Prepare a sous vide water bath in a 6- to 8-quart stockpot. Heat the water to 167°F. Using a slotted spoon, lower eggs into the pot. Cover as much as possible with plastic wrap or a cookie sheet; cook 12 minutes. Lower water temperature to 140°F to hold the eggs until you're ready to start serving, up to 2 hours.

2. Preheat oven to 175°F to 200°F. Meanwhile, toast bread in a toaster oven or toaster. Divide toast slices among 4 plates; transfer to oven to keep warm. (Breakfast is always best served hot, after all.)

3. Place ham in a large skillet over medium- high, and cook, turning once, until brown, 3 to 4 minutes total. Place 1 ham slice on each toast slice, and return to oven.

4. Add 2 tablespoons butter and shallot to skillet over medium. When butter is foamy, add spinach and black pepper. Cook, stirring constantly, until spinach is just wilted and beginning to release liquid, about 1 minute. Transfer to a plate; keep warm.

5. Melt remaining 1 tablespoon butter. Crack 1 sous vide egg into a blender. Add melted butter, lemon juice, yogurt, mayonnaise, and salt. Process on high speed to emulsify. If sauce is too thick, add water, 1 teaspoon at a time, and process until desired consistency is reached. Season with a pinch of cayenne and extra lemon juice, if needed.

6. Divide spinach among toast slices, forming a ring to cradle eggs. Working with one at a time, crack remaining sous vide eggs onto a plate. Place 2 eggs inside each spinach ring. Drizzle warm hollandaise over each serving; garnish with parsley, black pepper, and cayenne, if desired. Serves 4 (serving size: 1 piece)

CALORIES 457; **FAT** 24g (sat 10g, unsat 11g); **PROTEIN** 33g; **CARB** 27g; **FIBER** 6g; **SUGARS** 7g (added sugars 0g); **SODIUM** 796mg; **CALC** 27% DV; **POTASSIUM** 6% DV

BETWEEN THE LINES OF GOGO'S RECIPE CARDS

Best-selling author Ann Hood puzzles over a cherished recipe handed down from her late mother.

BY ANN HOOD

When my mother, Gogo, died in February, she left me her never-used wedding china, a lifetime of her good advice and wisdom, and her confidence in me that I could do anything I put my mind to. What she didn't leave me were her recipes. Or, I should say, she didn't leave me recipes that I could actually read and follow to reproduce my family's generations-old Italian meals.

Easter arrived just six weeks after my mother's unexpected death. Still in a haze of grief, my husband, Michael, and I prepared to make the breakfast specialties. What we found when we looked at the recipes were two, three, or four versions of each, all with different amounts of ingredients, different cooking times, and illegible marginalia. One recipe called for a dozen eggs on one card, two dozen on another, and instructions to both pour butter over the top and not pour butter over the top. Somehow we managed a semblance of the Easter breakfasts I'd eaten for six decades, adding our own scribbled notes to the stained cards.

But then Christmas loomed. It was easy to update the Christmas Eve Feast of the Seven Fishes with its eel, smelt, and baccalà. But what

of Christmas lunch, my favorite of all Gogo's holiday meals? The antipasto platter with prosciutto, pickled peppers, and chunks of Parmesan and provolone was simple. We started deciphering the lasagna recipe in May. The real challenge was the dish I liked best, a rich soup with escarole and tiny meatballs we called Soup a Sundale, likely a bastardization of zuppa something, perhaps Sunday or special. Surely we weren't supposed to drain the broth and then add the ingredients? To what? How much?

As I puzzled over the recipe, I remembered my mother doing the same thing when she tried to make spaghetti sauce after her mother died. How much was a handful of parsley? How long did you cook it "until it was ready"? Gogo complained and swore as she made pot after pot until eventually it was her sauce with its tweaks and interpretations that we craved. This, I realize now, was what these hieroglyphics of recipes are meant to do. By leaving so much out, my mother is telling me I can make Christmas lunch on my own. Even though she isn't here anymore, I can still feel her hand on my shoulder, still hear her voice whispering, "You can do it, baby. Now do it." I take a breath, line up the ingredients, and begin.

Make Ahead

Soup a Sundale

Hands-on: 35 min. **Total:** 35 min.
For convenience, Hood sometimes makes the meatballs ahead of time, freezes them, and thaws them before adding to the soup. She likes to make her own chicken stock for even richer flavor: She puts the picked carcass bones of a roast chicken (or a picked rotisserie chicken) in a Dutch oven, covers it with water, then adds three carrots before simmering.

1¼ lb. ground turkey
1 cup plain breadcrumbs
3 large eggs
2 Tbsp. chopped fresh flat-leaf parsley
3 garlic cloves, crushed and minced
1 tsp. kosher salt, divided
1 tsp. freshly ground black pepper, divided
½ cup canola oil, divided
2 qt. unsalted chicken stock (such as Swanson)
2½ lb. escarole, trimmed and chopped
1½ cups shredded rotisserie chicken
6 hard-cooked eggs, peeled and quartered lengthwise

1. Combine turkey, breadcrumbs, eggs, parsley, and garlic in a large bowl. Add ½ teaspoon salt and ½ teaspoon pepper; mix gently with your hands until mixture doesn't stick to your hands and ingredients are well blended. Place a half-dollar-sized portion of turkey mixture in your palm; roll with both hands until you form a firm, bite-sized ball. Repeat procedure to make about 40 meatballs.
2. Heat a large nonstick skillet over medium-high; add 2 tablespoons oil. Add about 10 meatballs to pan; cook until well browned all over, about 3 minutes. Place on a baking sheet lined with paper towels. Repeat procedure 3 times with remaining oil and remaining meatballs.
3. Bring stock to a simmer in a large Dutch oven over medium. Add escarole; cook until tender, about 3 minutes. Add meatballs, chicken, quartered eggs, remaining ½ teaspoon salt, and remaining ½ teaspoon pepper; serve immediately. Serves 10 (serving size: 1¼ cups)

CALORIES 371; FAT 22g (sat 4g, unsat 17g); PROTEIN 31g; CARB 13g; FIBER 4g; SUGARS 2g (added sugars 0g); SODIUM 570mg; CALC 11% DV; POTASSIUM 13% DV

MAKE-AHEAD FRENCH TOAST CASSEROLE

This easy, crowd-pleasing breakfast is also whole-grain, and a generous single serving clocks in at under 300 calories.

A surefire way to satisfy brunch guests, classic French toast casserole achieves its cozy profile from two sticks of butter plus a pint of half-and-half (not to mention more than 1 cup of sugar), delivering a day's worth of sat fat in a single serving.

We use a mix of whole eggs and egg whites and embellish the custardy filling with creamy mashed banana—all to keep calories in check without sacrificing richness. We reserve the butter for the walnut-studded topping for a decadent streusel effect. Frozen berries add a jammy, pie-like filling to the casserole while slipping in vitamins and antioxidants (which studies show are comparable to or higher than those of fresh berries). This healthy, one-pan breakfast slashes almost 300 calories, and better yet, is perfect for holiday hosting.

Staff Favorite • Make Ahead Vegetarian

Berry-and-Walnut French Toast Casserole

Hands-on: 15 min. **Total:** 8 hr. 55 min. This overnight casserole saves you the trouble of standing over a griddle flipping individual slices of French

toast. If using a fresh baguette, cut it up the day before, and let it sit in the bag overnight to become slightly stale, which helps prevent sogginess when the casserole is baked.

1 (8-oz.) day-old whole-grain crusty baguette, cut into 1-in. cubes
Cooking spray
1 ripe banana
1 cup 2% reduced-fat milk
3 large eggs
3 large egg whites
2 Tbsp. pure maple syrup
1 tsp. vanilla extract
1 tsp. ground cinnamon
¼ tsp. kosher salt
1 (10-oz.) pkg. frozen mixed berries, thawed
⅓ cup chopped walnuts
2 Tbsp. light brown sugar
2 Tbsp. cold unsalted butter, cut into small cubes

1. Arrange bread cubes in a 13- x 9-inch glass or ceramic baking dish coated with cooking spray. Using a fork, mash banana in a large bowl until smooth. Whisk in milk, eggs, egg whites, maple syrup, vanilla, cinnamon, and salt until combined. Pour mixture over bread cubes; toss to coat. Sprinkle berries over mixture. Cover with aluminum foil; chill 8 hours or overnight.
2. Preheat oven to 375°F.
3. Combine walnuts and brown sugar in a bowl. Add butter; using your fingers, mix until crumbly. Remove foil from chilled bread mixture; sprinkle bread mixture with walnut mixture. Replace foil cover.
4. Bake at 375°F until casserole is set, about 30 minutes. Remove foil; bake until golden brown, about 10 minutes. Let stand at room temperature 5 minutes. Serves 6 (serving size: about 1 ¼ cups)

CALORIES 290; FAT 12g (sat 4g, unsat 7g); PROTEIN 11g; CARB 37g; FIBER 3g; SUGARS 16g (added sugars 7g); SODIUM 324mg; CALC 9% DV; POTASSIUM 6% DV

Make Ahead • Vegetarian

Gingerbread Loaf

Hands-on: 15 min. **Total:** 1 hr. 10 min.

Cooking spray
5.4 oz. all-purpose flour (about
   1¼ cups plus 1 tsp.), divided
4 oz. whole-wheat flour (about 1 cup)
2 tsp. ground ginger
1 tsp. baking soda
1 tsp. ground cinnamon
½ tsp. kosher salt
½ tsp. black pepper
¼ tsp. ground cloves
¾ cup unsulfured molasses
¾ cup boiling water
½ cup unsalted butter, softened
½ cup light brown sugar
1 large egg
1 tsp. lemon zest
¼ cup finely chopped crystallized
   ginger

1. Preheat oven to 325°F. Coat a
9- x 5-inch loaf pan with cooking
spray. Whisk together 1¼ cups
all-purpose flour, whole-wheat
flour, ground ginger, baking soda,
cinnamon, salt, pepper, and cloves
in a bowl. Whisk together molasses
and boiling water in a second bowl.
2. Beat butter and brown sugar in
a bowl with a mixer on medium-
high speed until fluffy. Beat in
egg and zest. With mixer running
on low speed, add flour mixture
alternately with molasses mixture.
Stir together crystallized ginger
and remaining 1 teaspoon flour;
fold into batter. Pour batter into
prepared pan.

3. Bake at 325°F until a wooden pick
inserted in center comes out clean,
about 55 minutes. Cool in pan on a
wire rack. Serves 18 (serving size:
1 slice)

CALORIES 176; **FAT** 6g (sat 3g, unsat 2g);
PROTEIN 2g; **CARB** 30g; **FIBER** 1g; **SUGARS** 17g
(added sugars 16g); **SODIUM** 136mg; **CALC** 5%
DV; **POTASSIUM** 5%

GINGERBREAD ESSENTIALS

A ROSTER OF SPICES AND DEEPLY FLAVORED SUGARS MAKE THIS QUICK BREAD HOLIDAY-WORTHY.

CRYSTALLIZED GINGER
Candied pieces of young and
tender fresh ginger root lend hits
of pungent, peppery taste
throughout the loaf.

GROUND GINGER
It's vital to this recipe, so make
sure it's really fresh; if yours
doesn't have a strong aroma,
splurge on a new jar.

MOLASSES
This deeply caramelized, funky
sugar syrup is key to gingerbread.
Look for unsulfured, as it's
slightly milder.

BROWN SUGAR
Light brown sugar contains just
enough molasses to up the ante
on the complex, dark-rum
sweetness.

CINNAMON
When paired with ginger and
clove, it's like a spoonful of
holiday flavor. Remember,
fragrance equals freshness.

LEMON ZEST
A little freshly grated lemon rind
adds a hit of floral brightness to
balance the earthy spices.

BEEF STEW TO BRAG ABOUT

Classic technique layers flavors
for rich, robust broth, and a late
veggie add-in preserves texture.

**Staff Favorite • Gluten Free
Make Ahead**

French-Style Beef Stew

Hands-on: 1 hr. 15 min.
Total: 3 hr. 15 min.

1 Tbsp. canola oil
2½ lb. boneless chuck roast,
   trimmed and cut into 1½-in. pieces
2 tsp. black pepper
1½ tsp. kosher salt
3½ cups sliced yellow onions (from
   2 onions)
½ lb. carrots (about 4 carrots), peeled
   and cut into 2-in. pieces
4 large garlic cloves, smashed
1 (28-oz.) can unsalted whole plum
   tomatoes, undrained
2 cups dry red wine
2 cups lower-sodium beef broth
1 bunch fresh thyme, tied with
   kitchen twine
2 bay leaves
Cooking spray
1 lb. cremini mushrooms, sliced
10 oz. frozen pearl onions (about
   1¾ cups), thawed
2 Tbsp. red wine vinegar

1. Preheat oven to 275°F. Heat oil in a large Dutch oven over high. Sprinkle beef with pepper and salt. Add beef to Dutch oven in batches, and cook, stirring often, until browned on all sides, 8 to 10 minutes. Transfer browned beef to a plate. Set aside.

2. Reduce heat to medium-high. Add sliced onions and carrots to pan. Cook, stirring occasionally and scraping browned bits from bottom of pan, until onions begin to brown, about 10 minutes. Add garlic; cook, stirring often, until fragrant, about 1 minute. Add tomatoes; use a wooden spoon to break them into chunks. Stir in wine, broth, thyme, bay leaves, and beef. Bring to a boil.

3. Cover pan. Transfer to oven, and bake at 275°F until beef is tender, about 2 hours.

4. Meanwhile, spray a large nonstick skillet with cooking spray. Add mushrooms in 2 batches; cook over medium-high, stirring often, until browned, about 5 minutes. About 15 minutes before end of cook time, stir mushrooms, pearl onions, and vinegar into beef mixture. Cook, uncovered, over medium-low, stirring occasionally, until pearl onions are tender, about 15 minutes. Remove from heat. Remove thyme bundle and bay leaves. Serves 8 (serving size: 1½ cups)

CALORIES 298; **FAT** 9g (sat 3g, unsat 5g); **PROTEIN** 25g; **CARB** 18g; **FIBER** 4g; **SUGARS** 8g (added sugars 0g); **SODIUM** 562mg; **CALC** 8% DV; **POTASSIUM** 174% DV

THE STEPS

1. BROWN THE BEEF

Sear the meat in the same pan the stew cooks in so none of the meaty flavor gets lost. Brown in batches; if you crowd the pan, the meat will steam.

2. DEGLAZE THE PAN

The sliced onions and carrots will give off liquid as they sauté. Use it to scrape up the browned bits, which will add richness to the stew.

3. SIMMER IN OVEN

A slow simmer makes the chuck roast fork-tender. We do this in the oven, which prevents any scorching on the bottom of the pan.

4. ADD VEGGIES

Because the mushrooms and pearl onions would suffer if they simmered for two hours, we stir them in toward the end of the cook time.

WHAT'S FRESH NOW

Gluten Free • Make Ahead Vegetarian

Vegan Eggnog

Hands-on: 5 min. **Total:** 2 hr. 35 min. Cashew milk is one of the thickest nut milks, with a mild flavor that makes it ideal as a plant-based swap in this classic sipper. Compared to store-bought versions, our nog has about half the calories and ⅔ less sugar per serving.

4 cups unsweetened cashew milk
⅔ cup well-shaken and stirred canned unsweetened coconut milk (such as Thai Kitchen)
6 pitted Medjool dates
½ tsp. vanilla bean paste
¼ tsp. ground nutmeg
Whole nutmeg (optional)

1. Place cashew milk, coconut milk, and dates in a blender; let stand 30 minutes.

2. Add vanilla bean paste and nutmeg to blender. Process on high until smooth, about 2 minutes, stopping to scrape down sides as needed. Pour mixture through a fine wire-mesh strainer into a pitcher; discard solids. Chill at least 2 hours or up to overnight. If desired, grate whole nutmeg over servings for garnish. Serves 6 (serving size: about ¾ cup)

CALORIES 92; **FAT** 7g (sat 5g, unsat 1g); **PROTEIN** 1g; **CARB** 8g; **FIBER** 1g; **SUGARS** 6g (added sugars 0g); **SODIUM** 110mg; **CALC** 31% DV; **POTASSIUM** 3% DV

A few years back, my nephew, Henry, came home from school to the savory fragrance of Beef Daube Provençal, a favorite *Cooking Light* recipe of my sister-in-law/best friend, Becky. "It smells like the past," Henry said dreamily. His phrasing was both prophetic and symbolic: After this issue, *Cooking Light* magazine—the monthly editions chock-full of new, kitchen-tested recipes; nutrition coverage; and engaging stories—will be a thing of the past. And it will always have a special place in so many people's lives, a source of deep nostalgia for great memories shared with family and friends.

That's what *Cooking Light* has meant to Becky and me. We became fans in the mid-'90s, when graduate school choices separated us geographically. We had both become more interested in taking better care of ourselves and came to *Cooking Light* for nutrition advice and better-for-us recipes. It was a given that the recipes would be healthy, but what blew us away was how good they were. One of the first recipes I remember making was the Hearty Lasagna featured on the January/February 1995 cover. I cooked it for a dinner party, and at least three guests hounded me for the recipe. I called Becky to report my success, and she countered with her own recipe triumphs. And thus, a pattern emerged: We'd get our issues in the mail, read them cover to cover, then hop on the phone to discuss which recipes to try. When we had plans to see each other, we would jump giddily into elaborate menu planning, choosing recipes from the magazine to anchor our feasts. This ritual became a concrete way for me to stay connected to my best friend over the miles—sharing a love of good food as a way to nurture and care for ourselves and those we love. When I joined *Cooking Light* as an editorial assistant in 1998—a dream job for

> **"I share these stories with you because I suspect many of you have similar ones—that *Cooking Light* has held a special place for you and your best friend, or your mother, or your supper club group."**

this fangirl—I would call Becky with sneak-peek intel on the stories and recipes that were planned for future issues. We cooked many of them together, from the global "Cooking Class" series of 2001, when neither of us had children, to the family-friendly "Let's Cook!" recipes from 2015 that established some new traditions once we did.

I share these stories with you because I suspect many of you have similar ones—that *Cooking Light* has held a special place for you and your best friend, or your mother, or your supper club group. I know this magazine means something to many of you, and I have always felt that, at its core, it does some good in the world. That's one of many reasons why I've loved working here for the past 20 years, with the last 8 of them as executive editor. I still believe in what the magazine has done all along: help people live a healthier life by sharing recipes they can feel proud to serve to the people they love—as an act of love.

Over the years, I have learned from and been inspired by incredibly talented colleagues who all work in service of you, our beloved readers. I will boldly speak for them in saying thank you. We worked together to create something that you could use in your everyday life, and you have kindly let us know when we hit the

mark and when we have gone off course. We understand that you have done so because you care, because you feel just as invested in *Cooking Light* as we have always been. If you have picked us up at the newsstand, we appreciate your interest and your time. If you are a subscriber, we are deeply grateful for your loyalty. Next month, your subscription will roll over to our sister magazine *EatingWell*. You may notice some of *Cooking Light*'s DNA there, with some of your favorite columns, including "Dinner Tonight," transferring to its pages.

Some of *Cooking Light*'s footprint will live on, too. Cookinglight.com will still deliver great recipes and ideas, as will all of our social media platforms. The *Cooking Light* Diet also will continue to serve folks in need of healthy meal-planning tools and advice. And several times a year, you'll find *Cooking Light* special interest publications—those glossy, thick-papered recipe collections—on newsstands. While the monthly edition will no longer appear in your mailbox, perhaps you can still cuddle up with the SIPs, have your kids go through them and mark the recipes they'd like to try, and feed your soul a little happiness.

It's been a great run for a great magazine, and we owe our success over the years to you.

—Ann Taylor Pittman

CookingLight

THE FAREWELL ISSUE

▲
Chocolate-and-Cream Layer Cake
RECIPE P. 108

APPENDICES

HANDY SUBSTITUTIONS

INGREDIENT	SUBSTITUTION
BAKING PRODUCTS	
Baking powder, 1 teaspoon	• ½ teaspoon cream of tartar plus ¼ teaspoon baking soda
Chocolate	
semisweet, 1 ounce	• 1 ounce unsweetened chocolate plus 1 tablespoon sugar
unsweetened, 1 ounce or square	• 3 tablespoons cocoa plus 1 tablespoon fat
chips, semisweet, 6-ounce package, melted	• 2 ounces unsweetened chocolate, 2 tablespoons shortening plus ½ cup sugar
Cocoa, ¼ cup	• 1 ounce unsweetened chocolate (decrease fat in recipe by ½ tablespoon)
Corn syrup, light, 1 cup	• 1 cup sugar plus ¼ cup water • 1 cup honey
Cornstarch, 1 tablespoon	• 2 tablespoons all-purpose flour or granular tapioca
Flour	
all-purpose, 1 tablespoon	• 1½ teaspoons cornstarch, potato starch, or rice starch • 1 tablespoon rice flour or corn flour • 1½ tablespoons whole-wheat flour
all-purpose, 1 cup sifted	• 1 cup plus 2 tablespoons sifted cake flour
cake, 1 cup sifted	• 1 cup minus 2 tablespoons all-purpose flour
self-rising, 1 cup	• 1 cup all-purpose flour, 1 teaspoon baking powder plus ½ teaspoon salt
Shortening	
melted, 1 cup	• 1 cup cooking oil (don't use cooking oil unless recipe calls for melted shortening)
solid, 1 cup (used in baking)	• 1⅛ cups butter (decrease salt called for in recipe by ½ teaspoon)
Sugar	
brown, 1 cup firmly packed	• 1 cup granulated white sugar
powdered, 1 cup	• 1 cup sugar plus 1 tablespoon cornstarch (processed in food processor)
granulated white, 1 teaspoon	• ⅛ teaspoon noncaloric sweetener solution or follow manufacturer's directions
granulated white, 1 cup	• 1 cup corn syrup (decrease liquid called for in recipe by ¼ cup) • 1 cup honey (decrease liquid called for in recipe by ¼ cup)
Tapioca, granular, 1 tablespoon	• 1½ teaspoons cornstarch or 1 tablespoon all-purpose flour
DAIRY PRODUCTS	
Butter, 1 cup	• ⅞ to 1 cup shortening or lard plus ½ teaspoon salt • 1 cup margarine (2 sticks; do not substitute whipped or low-fat margarine)
Cream	
heavy (30% to 40% fat), 1 cup	• ¾ cup milk plus ⅓ cup butter (for cooking and baking; will not whip)
light (15% to 20% fat), 1 cup	• ¾ cup milk plus 3 tablespoons butter or margarine (for cooking and baking) • 1 cup evaporated milk, undiluted
half-and-half, 1 cup	• ⅞ cup milk plus ½ tablespoon butter or margarine (for cooking and baking) • 1 cup evaporated milk, undiluted
whipped, 1 cup	• 1 cup frozen whipped topping, thawed
Egg	
1 large	• ¼ cup egg substitute
2 large	• 3 small eggs or ½ cup egg substitute • 1 large egg plus 2 egg whites
1 egg white (2 tablespoons)	• 2 tablespoons egg substitute
Milk	
buttermilk, 1 cup	• 1 tablespoon vinegar or lemon juice plus whole milk to make 1 cup (let stand 10 minutes) • 1 cup plain yogurt • 1 cup whole milk plus 1¾ teaspoons cream of tartar
fat-free, 1 cup	• 4 to 5 tablespoons nonfat dry milk powder plus enough water to make 1 cup • ½ cup evaporated skim milk plus ½ cup water
whole, 1 cup	• 4 to 5 tablespoons nonfat dry milk powder plus enough water to make 1 cup • ½ cup evaporated milk plus ½ cup water

HANDY SUBSTITUTIONS

INGREDIENT	SUBSTITUTION

Milk (continued)
    sweetened condensed,
    1 (14-ounce) can (about 1¼ cups)
	• Heat the following ingredients until sugar and butter dissolve: ⅓ cup plus
	        2 tablespoons evaporated milk, 1 cup sugar, 3 tablespoons butter.
	• Add 1 cup plus 2 tablespoons nonfat dry milk powder to ½ cup warm water.
	        Mix well. Add ¾ cup sugar, and stir until smooth.

Sour cream, 1 cup	• 1 cup plain yogurt plus 3 tablespoons melted butter or 1 tablespoon cornstarch • 1 tablespoon lemon juice plus evaporated milk to equal 1 cup
Yogurt, 1 cup (plain)	• 1 cup buttermilk

MISCELLANEOUS

INGREDIENT	SUBSTITUTION
Broth, beef or chicken canned broth, 1 cup	• 1 bouillon cube or 1 teaspoon bouillon granules dissolved in 1 cup boiling water

Garlic
    1 small clove
    garlic salt, 1 teaspoon
	
	• ⅛ teaspoon garlic powder or minced dried garlic
	• ⅛ teaspoon garlic powder plus ⅞ teaspoon salt

Gelatin, flavored, 3-ounce package	• 1 tablespoon unflavored gelatin plus 2 cups fruit juice
Herbs, fresh, chopped, 1 tablespoon	• 1 teaspoon dried herbs or ¼ teaspoon ground herbs
Honey, 1 cup	• 1¼ cups sugar plus ¼ cup water
Mustard, dried, 1 teaspoon	• 1 tablespoon prepared mustard
Tomatoes, fresh, chopped, 2 cups	• 1 (16-ounce) can (may need to drain)
Tomato sauce, 2 cups	• ¾ cup tomato paste plus 1 cup water

ALCOHOL SUBSTITUTIONS

ALCOHOL	SUBSTITUTION
Amaretto, 2 tablespoons	• ¼ to ½ teaspoon almond extract*
Bourbon or sherry, 2 tablespoons	• 1 to 2 teaspoons vanilla extract*
Brandy, fruit-flavored liqueur, port wine, rum, or sweet sherry, ¼ cup or more	• Equal amount of unsweetened orange or apple juice plus 1 teaspoon vanilla extract or corresponding flavor
Brandy or rum, 2 tablespoons	• ½ to 1 teaspoon brandy or rum extract*

Grand Marnier or other orange liqueur,
    2 tablespoons
	• 2 tablespoons unsweetened orange juice concentrate or 2 tablespoons orange
	        juice and ½ teaspoon orange extract

Kahlúa or other coffee or chocolate liqueur,
    2 tablespoons
	• ½ to 1 teaspoon chocolate extract plus ½ to 1 teaspoon instant coffee dissolved
	        in 2 tablespoons water

Marsala, ¼ cup	• ¼ cup white grape juice or ¼ cup dry white wine plus 1 teaspoon brandy

Wine
    red, ¼ cup or more
 	
    white, ¼ cup or more
	
	• Equal measure of red grape juice or cranberry juice
	
	• Equal measure of white grape juice or nonalcoholic white wine

*Add water, white grape juice, or apple juice to get the specified amount of liquid (when the liquid amount is crucial).

EQUIVALENT MEASURES

3 teaspoons	= 1 tablespoon	2 tablespoons (liquid)	= 1 ounce	⅛ cup	= 2 tablespoons
4 tablespoons	= ¼ cup	1 cup	= 8 fluid ounces	⅓ cup	= 5 tablespoons plus 1 teaspoon

5⅓ tablespoons	= ⅓ cup	2 cups	= 1 pint (16 fluid
			        ounces)
				⅔ cup	= 10 tablespoons
					        plus 2 teaspoons

8 tablespoons	= ½ cup	4 cups	= 1 quart	¾ cup	= 12 tablespoons
16 tablespoons	= 1 cup	4 quarts	= 1 gallon		

NUTRITIONAL ANALYSIS

At *Cooking Light,* our team of food editors, experienced cooks, and dietitians builds recipes with whole foods, whole grains, and bigger portions of plants and seafood than meat. We emphasize oil-based fats more than saturated, and we promote a balanced diet low in processed foods and added sugars.

We use ingredients that are high in saturated fat (butter), sodium (soy sauce), or both (bacon) in small amounts as flavor-boosting solutions, rather than making them the focal point or cutting them out entirely. We don't cook with any products containing artificial sweeteners or trans fats (partially hydrogenated oils).

HOW TO PORTION

COOKING LIGHT ENSURES THAT EVERY SERVING IS A SATISFYING, REALISTIC PORTION THAT FULFILLS ITS ROLE AS PART OF A BALANCED PLATE. THIS INCLUDES THE FOLLOWING IN EACH CATEGORY:

SEAFOOD
5 ounces cooked

BEEF AND PORK
3 ounces cooked

CHICKEN
4½ ounces cooked breast or 3 ounces cooked thigh

GRAINS
About ½ cup, preferably whole

FRUITS AND VEGETABLES
At least ½ cup

ALCOHOL
1.5 ounces liquor, 5 ounces wine, or 12 ounces beer

METRIC EQUIVALENTS

The information in the following charts is provided to help cooks outside the United States successfully use the recipes in this book. All equivalents are approximate.

COOKING/OVEN TEMPERATURES

	Fahrenheit	Celsius	Gas Mark
Freeze Water	32° F	0° C	
Room Temp.	68° F	20° C	
Boil Water	212° F	100° C	
Bake	325° F	160° C	3
	350° F	180° C	4
	375° F	190° C	5
	400° F	200° C	6
	425° F	220° C	7
	450° F	230° C	8
Broil			Grill

LIQUID INGREDIENTS BY VOLUME

¼ tsp	=					1 ml
½ tsp	=					2 ml
1 tsp	=					5 ml
3 tsps	=	1 tbl	=	½ floz	=	15 ml
2 tbls	=	⅛ cup	=	1 floz	=	30 ml
4 tbls	=	¼ cup	=	2 floz	=	60 ml
5⅓ tbls	=	⅓ cup	=	3 floz	=	80 ml
8 tbls	=	½ cup	=	4 floz	=	120 ml
10⅔ tbls	=	⅔ cup	=	5 floz	=	160 ml
12 tbls	=	¾ cup	=	6 floz	=	180 ml
16 tbls	=	1 cup	=	8 floz	=	240 ml
1 pt	=	2 cups	=	16 floz	=	480 ml
1 qt	=	4 cups	=	32 floz	=	960 ml
				33 floz	=	1000 ml = 1 l

DRY INGREDIENTS BY WEIGHT

(To convert ounces to grams, multiply the number of ounces by 30.)

1 oz	=	¹⁄₁₆ lb	=	30g
4 oz	=	¼ lb	=	120g
8 oz	=	½ lb	=	240g
12 oz	=	¾ lb	=	360g
16 oz	=	1 lb	=	480g

LENGTH

(To convert inches to centimeters, multiply the number of inches by 2.5.)

1 in	=		2.5 cm
6 in	=	½ ft	15 cm
12 in	=	1 ft	30 cm
36 in	=	3 ft = 1 yd	90 cm
40 in	=		100 cm = 1m

EQUIVALENTS FOR DIFFERENT TYPES OF INGREDIENTS

Standard Cup	Fine Powder (ex. flour)	Grain (ex. rice)	Granular (ex. sugar)	Liquid Solids (ex. butter)	Liquid (ex. milk)
1	140g	150g	190g	200g	240 ml
¾	105g	113g	143g	150g	180 ml
⅔	93g	100g	125g	133g	160 ml
½	70g	75g	95g	100g	120 ml
⅓	47g	50g	63g	67g	80 ml
¼	35g	38g	48g	50g	60 ml
⅛	18g	19g	24g	25g	30 ml

BREAKING DOWN THE NUMBERS

Cooking Light recipes adhere to rigorous nutrition guidelines that govern calories, saturated fat, sodium, and sugar based on various categories (main dish, side, dessert). These standards enable you to easily incorporate our recipes into a diet that follows the most recent USDA and ADA Dietary Guidelines (see below).

CALORIES PER DAY

1,600 – 2,000

This equates to three meals that range from 350 to 550 calories and two 100- to 150-calorie snacks.

SODIUM PER DAY

2,300MG OR LESS

SATURATED FAT PER DAY

20G OR LESS

MENU INDEX

A topical guide to all the menus that appear in *Cooking Light Annual Recipes 2019*.

DINNER TONIGHT

20-Minute Dinners

BEEF

Flank Steak and Vegetables with Green Goddess Sauce (page 93) serves 4

Grilled Beef-Mushroom Burgers (page 141) serves 4

FISH & SHELLFISH

Grilled Salmon with Avocado Salsa (page 142) serves 4

PORK

Chorizo and Bell Pepper Tostadas (page 66) serves 4

POULTRY

Chicken Schnitzel with Grapefruit-Celery Slaw (page 332) serves 4

25-Minute Dinners

BEEF

Beef Kebabs with Cucumber-Mint Salad (page 171) serves 4

FISH & SHELLFISH

Blackened Shrimp with Citrus and Roasted Fennel (page 66) serves 4

Pesto Shrimp and Broccoli Fettuccine (page 255) serves 4

PORK

Kale, Tomato, and Pancetta Pasta (page 38) serves 4

POULTRY

Chicken Curry Stir-Fry (page 142) serves 4

Chicken and Honeydew Salad (page 170) serves 4

Chicken and Peach Flatbreads (page 202) serves 4

Crispy Chicken Cutlets with Lemon-Butter Carrots (page 364) serves 4

VEGETARIAN

Thai Curried Squash Soup (page 65) serves 4

Mushroom and Asparagus Grain Bowl (page 94) serves 4

Greek Eggplant Skillet Dinner (page 255) serves 4

Winter Greens Pesto Pizza (page 362) serves 4

Potato Pancakes with Apple Butter (page 362) serves 4

30-Minute Dinners

BEEF

Loaded Steakhouse Baked Potatoes (page 275) serves 4

FISH & SHELLFISH

Thai Poached Cod (page 94) serves 4

Maple-Miso Salmon with Acorn Squash (page 275) serves 4

PORK

Taco Truck Lettuce Wraps (page 119) serves 8

Sausage and Mushroom Pasta with Butternut Squash (page 334) serves 4

Rosemary-Crusted Pork with Mushrooms (page 363) serves 4

POULTRY

Korean Barbecue Pizza (page 39) serves 4

Extra-Crispy Chicken Thighs with Potatoes and Chard (page 333) serves 4

Chicken Tetrazzini (page 363) serves 6

VEGETARIAN

Herb and Leek "Orzotto" with Fried Eggs (page 64) serves 4

Creamy Artichoke Soup (page 118) serves 4

Smoked Tempeh BLT (page 141) serves 4

Creamy Corn-Mushroom Risotto (page 253) serves 4

Southwestern-Style Stuffed Sweet Potatoes (page 256) serves 4

Smoky Mushroom and Barley Salad with Poblano (page 332) serves 4

Roasted Carrot and Coconut Soup (page 333) serves 6

35-Minute Dinners

BEEF

Spice-Crusted Flank Steak with Crispy Potatoes (page 118) serves 4

Peppery Beef and Broccoli (page 254) serves 4

PORK

Pork Tenderloin and Collards Skillet (page 39) serves 4

POULTRY

Chicken Stir-Fry with Bok Choy (page 254) serves 4

40-Minute Dinners

FISH & SHELLFISH

Snapper with Corn-Okra Relish (page 170) serves 4

Poached Sea Bass with Gingery Veggies (page 277) serves 4

PORK

Pork Tenderloin with Bourbon-Peach Sauce (page 170) serves 4

Roasted Pork Tenderloin with Cabbage (page 254) serves 4

POULTRY

Glazed Chicken with Couscous and Green Beans (page 93) serves 4

Mediterranean Chicken and Couscous Bowls (page 66) serves 4

Sausage Baguette Pizzas (page 364) serves 4

VEGETARIAN

Chilled Avocado Soup (page 202) serves 4

Mushroom Quiche with Sweet Potato Crust (page 365) serves 4

RECIPE TITLE INDEX

An alphabetical listing of every recipe title that appeared in the magazine in 2018. See page 398 for the General Recipe Index.

MONTH-BY-MONTH INDEX

A month-by-month listing of every food story with recipe titles that appeared in the magazine in 2018. See page 398 for the General Recipe Index.

GENERAL RECIPE INDEX

A listing by major ingredient and food category for every recipe that appeared in the magazine in 2018

B

Bacon
  Bowl with Buttermilk-Chive Drizzle, Bacon and Avocado Quinoa, 252
  Carbonara, Spring, 100
  Carbonara, Whole-Wheat Pasta, 266
  Dressing, Job's Tears Salad with Bacon, 25
  Frittata, Sweet Potato and Bacon, 367
  Gravy, Bacon-Shallot, 365
  Jam, Kimchi-Bacon, 121
  Mashed Potatoes, Bacon-Leek, 256
  Pancetta, Kale, and Raisin Stuffing, 293
  Pancetta Pasta, Kale, Tomato, and, 38
  Pasta, Garden Greens, 78
  Slaw, Grilled Wedge-Salad, 163
  Soup, Loaded Cauliflower, 269
  Vinaigrette, Shaved Vegetable Salad with Warm Bacon, 292
  Wraps, Bacon, Arugula, and Egg, 116
Bagels, Hot-Smoked Trout on Sesame, 195
Banana
  Bread, Banana-Walnut, 62
  Leaves, Flounder Grilled on Banana, 192
  Smoothie, Citrus Sunrise, 31
Barbecue. *See also* Grilled
  Chicken, Cauliflower Puree with Barbecue Rotisserie, 98
  Korean Barbecue Pizza, 39
  Sauce, Quick Barbecue, 72
  Sauce White BBQ, 261
Barley Bowl with Cilantro Pesto, Broccoli Rabe and, 272
Barley Salad with Poblano, Smoky Mushroom and, 332
Beans. *See also* Lentils
  Baked Beans, Indian Dal, 164
  Black
    Chicken and Carrot Rice, Fiesta, 285
    Chili, Cinnamon-Laced, 22
    Hash, Southwestern Sweet Potato and Egg, 33
    Soup, Tex-Mex Chicken and Black Bean, 317
    Stuffed Sweet Potatoes, Southwestern-Style, 256
    Tostadas, Black Bean, 178
    Tostadas with Cabbage Slaw, Black Bean, 116
  Cassoulet, Chicken, 271
  Chili, Hearty Bulgur, 70
  Chili, Steak Fajita, 269
  Fava-and-Ricotta Toasts, 108
  Green
    Amandine, Green Beans, 298
    Bowls, Tuna Niçoise Whole-Grain, 161

Bundles with Crispy Mushrooms, Prosciutto-Green Bean, 298
    Casserole, Green Bean, 369
    Charred Sesame Green Beans, 256
    Chicken Stir-Fry, Garlic-Soy, 59
    Chicken with Couscous and Green Beans, Glazed, 93
    Lemon-Feta Green Beans, 369
    Meatloaf Dinner, Petite, 286
    Mustard-Tarragon Sauce, Green Beans with, 369
    Salmon with Green Beans and Smashed Potatoes, 340
    Skillet-Charred Green Beans with Salsa, 178
    Steak with Mixed Olive Tapenade, Butternut Squash, and Green Beans, 46
    Succotash, Early Summer, 148
    Trout Niçoise, Smoked, 84
  Nachos, Chili-Chorizo, 265
  Salad, Four Bean (and One Pea), 158
  White
    Moussaka, Baked Chicken, 72
    Salad, Radish, White Bean, and Olive, 71
    Salad, Salmon with Kale, Walnut, and White Bean, 27
    Soup, Roasted Carrot and Coconut, 333
    Soup, Tuscan White Bean, 72
    Soup, Tuscan White Bean and Lentil, 318
    Tartines, Mushroom and Marsala-Onion, 310
Beef. *See also* Beef, Ground
  Brisket
    Loaded Steakhouse Baked Potatoes, 275
    Smoky Brisket with Peppers and Onions, 151
  Pasta with Italian Sunday Sauce, 368
  Roasts
    Chile Colorado, Beef-and-Butternut, 324
    Hash, Roast Beef, 246
    Peppercorn-and-Coriander-Crusted Roast, 310
    Pot Roast, Oven-Braised, 245
    Pot Roast Tacos with Chimichurri, 246
    Soup, Spicy Beef Noodle, 26
    Stew, French-Style Beef, 376
    Stew with Root Vegetables, Peppery Beef, 270
  Short Ribs, Asian, 282
  Soup, Vietnamese Beef and Noodle, 342
  Steaks
    Chili, Steak Fajita, 269
    Coffee-Rubbed Steak with Brussels Sprouts Salad, 334

Filet Mignon with Apple-Fennel Slaw, 366
    Flank Steak and Vegetables with Green Goddess Sauce, 93
    Flank Steak with Crispy Potatoes, Spice-Crusted, 118
    Flank Steak with Salsa Verde, Sheet Pan, 51
    Hanger Steak with Zucchini Salsa, Grilled, 202
    Mixed Olive Tapenade, Butternut Squash, and Green Beans, Steak with, 46
    Parsley Pesto, Steak and Carrots with, 81
    Peppery Beef and Broccoli, 254
    Salad, Fajita Panzanella, 61
    Skirt Steak Salad, Korean, 160
    Stir-Fry, Beef and Cabbage, 278
    Tartine, Steak, Goat Cheese, and Onion Jam, 62
  Tenderloin with Horseradish Cream and Glazed Carrots, Beef, 44
  Tenderloin with Madeira-Dijon Sauce, Beef, 351
Beef, Ground
  Burgers
    Banh Mi Burgers, 162
    Grilled Beef-Mushroom Burgers, 141
    Smashed Chili Cheeseburgers, 208
  Chili, Cinnamon-Laced, 22
  Kebabs with Cucumber-Mint Salad, Beef, 171
  Meatballs
    Glazed Meatballs with Soba Noodles, 248
    Mini Meatballs, Saucy, 354
    Salad, Aleppo-Spiced Meatball, 286
    Salad, Meatball and Tomato, 200
  Meat Loaf, Mushroom, 267
  Sandwiches, Grilled Lamb and Feta Pita, 176
  Soup, Lazy Lasagna, 318
  Zucchini Stuffed with Lamb and Lentils, 177
Beets
  Dressing, Early Summer Salad with Tempeh Croutons and Beet, 134
  Golden Beet Bloody Mary, 88
  Meatballs, Lamb and Beet, 69
  Salads
    Carrot, and Pistachio Salad, Beet, 19
    Citrus Salad with Almond Gremolata, Beet and, 313
    Farro-Beet Salad, Chicken with Broccolini and, 38
    Golden Beet and Roasted Strawberry Salad, 112